AMERICAN ATTACK
AIRCRAFT SINCE 1926

ALSO BY E. R. JOHNSON
AND FROM McFARLAND

*United States Naval Aviation, 1919–1941:
Aircraft, Airships and Ships Between the Wars* (2011)

*American Flying Boats and Amphibious Aircraft:
An Illustrated History* (2010)

American Attack Aircraft Since 1926

E. R. Johnson

McFarland & Company, Inc., Publishers
Jefferson, North Carolina, and London

The present work is a reprint of the illustrated case bound edition of American Attack Aircraft Since 1926, *first published in 2008 by McFarland.*

**All three-view illustrations are by Lloyd S. Jones.
All photographs are courtesy David W. Ostrowski,
unless otherwise noted.**

LIBRARY OF CONGRESS CATALOGUING-IN-PUBLICATION DATA

Johnson, E.R., 1948–
American attack aircraft since 1926 / E.R. Johnson.
p.   cm.
Includes bibliographical references and index.

ISBN 978-0-7864-7162-1
softcover : acid free paper ∞

1. Attack planes—United States—History.
I. Title
UG1242.A28J64   2012   623.74'63—dc22   2008014537

BRITISH LIBRARY CATALOGUING DATA ARE AVAILABLE

© 2008 E.R. Johnson. All rights reserved

*No part of this book may be reproduced or transmitted in any form
or by any means, electronic or mechanical, including photocopying
or recording, or by any information storage and retrieval system,
without permission in writing from the publisher.*

On the cover: An A-10 Thunderbolt II flying over Afghanistan during Operation Enduring Freedom (U.S. Air Force/Capt. Justin T. Watson)

Manufactured in the United States of America

*McFarland & Company, Inc., Publishers
Box 611, Jefferson, North Carolina 28640
www.mcfarlandpub.com*

Contents

Preface   1

PART I — USAAC, USAAF, AND USAF ATTACK AIRCRAFT

Historical Note
   The Emergence of Tactical Air Power   3
   Attack Aircraft Procurement   6
First Series • 1926–1944   11
Second Series • 1946–1961   109
Third Series • 1962–present   161
Fourth Series (Adapted Attack Aircraft) • 1950–Present   205

PART II — USN AND USMC ATTACK AIRCRAFT

Historical Note
   The Role of the Aircraft Carrier   227
   The Emergence of Marine Corps Aviation   228
   Attack Aircraft Procurement   229
First Series • 1926–1946   234
Second Series • 1946–1962   332
Third Series • 1962–present   367

Appendix 1: Aircraft Designations and Nomenclature   413
Appendix 2: Attack Aircraft Unit Organization   416
Appendix 3: Attack Aircraft Designs That Never Flew   418
Appendix 4: Evolution of Weapons and Tactics   433
Bibliography   441
Index   443

To the memory of my father,
Colonel Ector R. Johnson, Jr., USMCR (Ret.),
who, through the course of a 23-year military flying career
encompassing combat duty in two wars, flew thirteen
different types of the attack aircraft listed in this book.

Preface

American Attack Aircraft Since 1926 was written to provide a concise historical survey, including technical specifications, drawings, and photographs, of the various types of fixed-wing aircraft used over an 81-year period by the U.S. armed forces to carry out air attack missions. In standard military terminology, these missions typically fall into two broad categories and are described by acronyms as follows.

DIRECT AIR ATTACK

CAS—Close Air Support: attacks on enemy personnel and weapons near the forward edge of the battle area (FEBA). Integration of air strikes with the fire and maneuver of friendly ground forces is mandatory.

BAI—Battlefield Air Interdiction: attacks on enemy objectives in rear areas that are likely to have an immediate or near-term effect on friendly forces. As with CAS, coordination of air strikes with friendly ground forces is generally required.

FAC—Forward Air Control: a controller, either airborne or ground-based, who coordinates and directs air strikes against enemy positions.

INDIRECT AIR ATTACK

AI—Air Interdiction: attacks on enemy objectives in rear areas, out of range of artillery and other concentrated air defenses. Coordination with ground forces is optional, and in modern battlefield terminology, a prescribed area in which unrestricted AI may be carried out is defined as a "kill box."

OCA—Offensive Counter-Air: attacks on enemy air bases to destroy aircraft on the ground as well as support facilities such as runways, maintenance areas, and ammunition and fuel dumps.

SEAD—Suppression of Enemy Air Defenses: air attacks on enemy antiaircraft guns and surface to air missiles (SAMs) plus the radar and control systems associated with their operation.

EW—Electronic Warfare: in the context of air attack, a non-lethal airborne system using electromagnetic energy to disrupt enemy electronic signals, especially those of radar-controlled weapons systems.

The Historical Notes appearing at the beginning of both parts of the book endeavor to show how each service has evolved its attack mission and explain the methods used to procure aircraft to perform that mission. Although a few types conceived for strategic attack are reported, the predominant focus is upon aircraft routinely used to deliver ordnance in a battlefield support role on land or at sea. For organizational purposes, the book is divided between U.S. Army Air Corps, U.S. Army Air Forces, and U.S. Air Force types in Part I and U.S. Navy and U.S. Marine Corps types in Part II. Each part is further sub-divided into chronological series, and within each series, aircraft types are reported in alpha-numeric sequence by their military designations, or in a few cases, by factory model numbers. Supplementing Parts I and II are four appendices: 1—Attack Aircraft Designations and Nomenclature, 2—Attack Aircraft Unit Organization, 3—Attack Aircraft Designs That Never Flew, and 4—Evolution of Weapons and Tactics.

PART I

USAAC, USAAF, and USAF Attack Aircraft

HISTORICAL NOTE

"Offense is the essence of air power."—General Henry H. "Hap" Arnold, Chief of the U.S. Army Air Corps 1937–1941, and U.S. Army Air Forces, 1941–1945

The Emergence of Tactical Air Power

The earliest attack doctrines evolved by the U.S. Army Air Service, which became the U.S. Army Air Corps (USAAC) on July 2, 1926, were heavily influenced by the lessons of World War I. Significantly, early theorists concluded that aircraft operating in close proximity to the battle lines were simply too vulnerable to justify the risk of providing close air support (CAS) by direct air attack. On the other hand, air interdiction (AI)—indirect air attack on less heavily defended objectives in the rear areas—was seen as practical. Theorists reasoned that AI missions flown against targets like forces in reserve and vital supplies would not only slow down or stop the enemy's ability to continue battle, but would reduce his morale as well. Accepted tactics, low-level attacks with machine guns and fragmentation bombs, were based on World War I experience. As the influence of the Air Corps Tactical School (ACTS)[1] increased during the 1930s, attack doctrine extended to offensive counter-air (OCA), consisting of attacks on enemy air bases to destroy aircraft on the ground and impair support facilities such as runways, maintenance areas, and fuel dumps. ACTS theorists believed that the application of OCA would help achieve air superiority for what was perceived as the main focus of air power: long-range strategic bombardment of the enemy's military-industrial infrastructure.[2]

After attack units had reequipped with modern monoplanes during the early and mid-1930s, combat reports from the Spanish Civil War (1936–1939) and the emergence of a powerful German *Luftwaffe* caused the USAAC hierarchy to doubt the effectiveness of using

---

[1]*After being organized in 1920 as the Air Service Field Officer's School, it was renamed the Air Corps Tactical School in 1926 and went on to become the U.S. Army Air Corps' most important "think tank" with regard to the military role of air power. By the time the school suspended operations in mid-1940, it had produced 1,091 officer graduates, of which 261 became general officers in the U.S. Army Air Forces during World War II.*

[2]*Euphemistically referred to by latter-day historians as the ACTS "Bomber Mafia." Spurred by developments like the Norden bombsight and the Boeing B-17, advocates believed that any potential enemy could ultimately be subdued by a sustained campaign of long-range strategic bombardment.*

lightly-armed, single-engine airplanes in the attack role. This led, in 1938 and 1939, to new requirements for twin-engine light and medium bombers having greater payloads and range. Then in early 1940, following the conspicuous success of German *Stukas* in Poland, the USAAC developed a sudden interest in dive-bombing tactics[3] and made plans to acquire aircraft and train units to perform direct attack roles like CAS and battlefield air interdiction (BAI). BAI,[4] while similar to AI, contemplates destruction of targets nearer the locus of battle that are likely to have a more near-term effect on friendly ground forces. When America declared war on the Axis in December 1941, USAAF (U.S. Army Air Forces as of June 20, 1941) attack doctrine centered on using light and medium bombers in AI/OCA roles and specialized dive-bombers for CAS/BAI; however, combat experience soon revealed the slow dive-bombers to be highly vulnerable to fighter attack, with the result that most dive-bomber units were reequipped with fighter-bombers before deploying overseas.[5] The Army's need for better direct air support during the early campaigns of World War II led to significant increases in fighter-bomber units dedicated to the CAS/BAI role along with development of fighter-bomber aircraft armed with greater payloads of bombs and rockets. Tactics differed according to the nature of enemy air defenses in various combat theaters, for example, in the Pacific air attacks were routinely carried out at low altitudes that would have been suicidal against the more concentrated air defenses of the European and Mediterranean theaters.

The post-war demobilization and reorganization of the USAAF witnessed the creation of Tactical Air Command (TAC) in March 1946, which assumed control over fighter-interceptor, fighter-bomber, and light bombardment units (all medium groups had been deactivated by that time), as well as troop carrier operations, and in July 1947, TAC was absorbed into the newly-created, independent U.S. Air Force (USAF). TAC's role was refined even further by the inter-service Key West Agreement of 1948, which placed all responsibility on the USAF to provide the Army's ground support, and in the years that followed, opened the door to occasional Army intervention[6] and criticism of various USAF aircraft procurement programs. During the Korean War (June 1950 to July 1953) CAS/BAI and AI/OCA missions completed by TAC accounted for nearly half of all USAF combat sorties flown. In 1952, in response to the need to improve coordination between aircraft flying CAS/BAI missions and ground forces, TAC began using North American T-6 trainers manned by forward air controllers (FAC) to direct fire into enemy positions and also assigned pilots to serve with ground forces as air liaison officers (ALO). When the North Koreans were forced to move significant amounts of their war material at night, due in large part to successful daytime AI operations, TAC responded with new night intruder tactics[7] that enabled Douglas B-26s to locate and destroy targets in darkness.

The USAF added tactical nuclear weapons to its attack doctrine in 1950 and became operational in 1952 using nuclear-armed North American B-45s. The mission, code-named "Backbreaker," was designed to launch from bases in England and stop or at least slow down an all-out invasion of Europe by Soviet and Warsaw Pact armies. As lighter nuclear weapons became available,[8] single-seat jet fighters such as F-84s, F-86s, F-100s, F-101s, and F-104s were con-

---

[3]*The USAAC borrowed several SBD-1s from the Marine Corps in mid–1940 and assigned them to the 24th Bombardment Squadron for evaluation.*

[4]*Before and during World War II, the term battlefield air interdiction (BAI) was not used, and any type of direct air attack would have been classified as close air support (CAS).*

[5]*Two USAAF units equipped with Douglas A-24s saw action in 1942 and 1943; single-seat North American A-36As remained in combat well into 1944.*

[6]*The intervention of the joint Army–USAF Wright Board in 1951 resulted in the selection of the British Canberra (produced as the B-57) instead of the Martin XB-51.*

[7]*Though initially using flares to find targets, B-26s were later fitted with radar altimeters and SHORAN (short-range navigation), a system that allowed the aircraft to home-in on intersecting radar beacons.*

[8]*The 1,700-lb. Mk. 7 nuclear bomb was developed in 1952 and initially carried by F-84Gs.*

World War II. Events of the late 1930s conspired to have a long-lasting impact on all future USAAC/USAAF aircraft procurement programs. First, the military rise of Nazi Germany and its belligerent expansionist policy was moving the nations of Europe toward the brink of a new world war. In the midst of this, in early 1938, the USAAC solicited proposals for a twin-engine "light bomber" design that would hopefully produce an attack aircraft equal to those seen in the new German *Luftwaffe*. Selection of an aircraft for production was to be decided by a competitive fly-off, the standard procurement practice of requiring manufacturers to build prototypes at their own expense then deliver them for evaluation (i.e., "fly before you buy"). Later the same year, President Franklin Delano Roosevelt, alarmed by European developments, informed USAAC chief, Maj. Gen. H. H. Arnold, that he wanted (1) the USAAC built up to a force of 20,000 planes (current strength at the time stood at 1,600 aircraft, many of which were obsolete biplanes) and (2) military aircraft production increased to an unheard-of 2,000 planes per month! Although Congress, in 1939, subsequently reduced the projected force level to 5,500 aircraft, the USAAC, to achieve anything near those numbers within a three to four year period, would be forced to abandon the old fashioned fly-off method and begin ordering new aircraft types directly into production *before* they were tested (i.e., "buy before you fly").

In the intervening time, four light bomber prototypes had been completed, three of which had arrived at Wright Field during the spring of 1939.[15] Douglas's DB-7 prototype, considered to be the most promising of the four, was destroyed before it could undergo competitive trials. Ignoring precedent, USAAC officials summarily announced that the fly-off had been cancelled; that a selection would be made according to detailed design submissions, then a month later, declared the DB-7 as the winner and immediately ordered it into production as the A-20. The DB-7/A-20, when it had flown in late 1938, was probably the most modern twin-engine military aircraft in the world and had surpassed its German contemporary, the Junkers Ju 88, in virtually every aspect of performance. After that, the medium bomber competition announced in early 1939 was based entirely upon detailed design submissions from the outset, and the first and second place entries, the Martin B-26 and the North American B-25, respectively, were both ordered into production in August 1939. The Douglas A-26 appeared as a stand-alone project in late 1940 and was ordered into mass production in October 1941 nine months before the first example flew. Another source of many new USAAC attack aircraft were those which had been originally developed for foreign users: Lockheed A-28/A-29, Vultee A-31/A-35, and North American P-51/A-36. And the USAAC's newfound interest in dive-bombing also generated orders for existing Navy types, the Douglas SBD as the A-24 and the Curtiss SB2C as the A-25, both in late 1940; Brewster's yet to fly SB2A was assigned the designation A-34 but none were ordered.

Equally important as the change in procurement methods was the USAAC/USAAF policy, implemented during 1939 and 1940, which generally froze research and development of new aircraft designs so that manufacturers could concentrate on mass-producing the thousands upon thousands of aircraft needed for the expected war effort.[16] With some notable exceptions in the attack and fighter categories,[17] most USAAF aircraft procured during the wartime era had been derived from designs laid down before 1941. Since the freeze did not apply to improvement of existing designs, most USAAF aircraft underwent numerous changes during production, not only to enhance performance, but also in response to new combat requirements and

---

[15] *The Steaman (Boeing) X-100, Martin 167, and North American NA-40.*
[16] *Over 300,000 aircraft were delivered by American companies from 1939 to the end of 1945.*
[17] *A-32 and A-41 began in 1941-1942 as improved dive-bombers, the A-38 as a "bomber destroyer"; both the B-42 and P-82 arose in 1943 out of effort to create very long-range aircraft for Pacific operations; and the P-59, started in late 1941, and P-80, in mid–1943, were both derived from jet-propulsion technology received from Britain.*

tactics. Increases in armor protection and defensive firepower became universal. From mid–1943 onwards, fighter-bombers became standard equipment in the CAS/BAI role rather than specialized attack types, with the result that existing fighters were progressively optimized for ground attack.[18] In Pacific operations, to increase suppressive fire during low-level skip-bombing runs, light and medium bombers were field-modified to a gunship configuration (see, A-20 and B-25, below), and these changes were quickly incorporated to new production aircraft.

Post-war Changes. In 1944, with aircraft production quotas firmly established, the USAAF removed the research and development freeze and instead began encouraging manufacturers to develop new aircraft, jets in particular, that were expected to achieve unprecedented levels of performance. Highly ambitious requirements for new aircraft were to a great extent prompted by the USAAF's new Research and Development Board,[19] which had been established to foster cutting-edge aeronautical concepts. This led, ultimately, to a "speed at all costs" mindset that served to dominate all tactical aircraft programs for nearly two decades (1945–1965). Moreover, the wartime "buy before you fly" policy became more or less institutionalized during the late 1940s as the Cook-Craigie[20] production plan. The plan was founded upon the assumption that major design flaws could be identified and eliminated during the detailed design and mockup stages, while other minor changes indicated by initial testing could be incorporated after the aircraft had been placed in production.

Korea and Vietnam. Post-war procurement programs left the USAF poorly prepared to carry out its battlefield support role when the Korean War started in June 1950. TAC's new jet fighter-bombers like the F-80C and F-84D/E were seriously restricted in range, payload, and on-call mission availability because they were forced to operate from large base facilities in Japan, and the F-86A/E lacked hardpoints for air-to-ground weapons. To close the gap, mothballed F-51s and B-26s were pulled from storage and rushed into service. Although operations dramatically improved after USAF jets moved onto new Korean bases in 1951, propeller-driven Navy and Marine attack planes (e.g., ADs and F4Us) continued to provide most of the CAS for UN forces, leaving AI targets to the jets. Once the war was over, USAF planners essentially pigeonholed Korea as a one-time "diversion" and continued unabated with their speed-at-all-costs procurement policy: the real threat, according to the USAF hierarchy, was an all-out nuclear attack by the Soviets—World War III. This view was largely responsible for the procurement of 5,525 Century Series fighters between 1953 and 1964, some as pure interceptors[21] and others as nuclear-armed tactical fighters.[22] Army concerns over the aging fleet of Douglas B-26s forced the USAF to order the Martin B-57 as a compromise choice in 1951, but an immediate return to an emphasis on speed characterized the tactical bomber program which oversaw development of the B-66 and B-68 (see Appendix 3). The Lockheed F-104, ordered into full-scale production in 1956 without having a well-defined mission, serves as one of the most conspicuous examples of this system.

The USAF's nearly autonomous aircraft procurement methods effectively came to an abrupt halt in 1961 when the Department of Defense (DOD) ordered it to collaborate with the Navy on the TFX (tactical fighter experimental) program—the General Dynamics F-111. Sim-

---

[18]*P-38J/L, P-39Q, P-40N, P-47D (Block 25), and P-51D (Block 25).*

[19]*Created by Gen. H. H. Arnold and headed by Doctor Theodore von Karmen, the Board foresaw a post-war USAAF (USAF) equipped with supersonic aircraft and nuclear weapons.*

[20]*Maj. Gen. Orval R. Cook, Deputy Chief of Staff for Material, and Maj. Gen. Laurence C. Craigie, Deputy Chief of Staff for Development.*

[21]*The Convair F-102A and F-106A came from the two phase "1954 Interceptor" program; the Republic F-103 was cancelled in 1957 while still in the mockup stages. Both the McDonnell F-101B and Lockheed F-104A were unplanned additions due to chronic delays in the F-106 program.*

[22]*North American F-100C/D, McDonnell F-101A/C, Lockheed F-104C, and Republic F-105B/D.*

ilarly, in 1962, DOD directed the USAF to adopt the Navy's McDonnell F-4 as its new air superiority and tactical fighter, and then in 1965, this time as a result of Army pressure, the USAF made plans to acquire the Navy's subsonic LTV A-7 for the CAS/BAI role. These changes in procurement, however, did not take effect soon enough to prepare the USAF for the Vietnam War (1962–1972). Because TAC lacked any aircraft suited to CAS, BAI, and COIN (counterinsurgency) missions over the dense jungles of Southeast Asia, it was compelled pull propeller-driven Douglas B-26s from storage and acquire surplus Douglas A-1Es from the Navy. Reconfigured trainers like the North American AT-28 and Cessna A-37 were also used to make up for the deficit in CAS and COIN aircraft. TAC's large fleet of F-100s was employed primarily to fly conventional interdiction strikes against Viet Cong positions in South Vietnam, while its faster F-105s assumed a strategic bombardment role against the better defended targets of the North. A system of FAC coordination between strike aircraft and ground forces was in effect created from scratch. FAC operations commenced with Cessna O-1 lightplanes, developed originally for the Army as artillery spotters, until they could be replaced with twin-engine (tractor/pusher) Cessna O-2s starting in 1966; however, the extreme vulnerability of lightplanes types to ground fire led, ultimately, to joint service development of the first purpose-built FAC platform, the North American OV-10. An interesting innovation appeared in late 1964 as side-firing AC-47 gunships began operating in response to a specialized CAS need to protect isolated outposts, and as better-equipped AC-19s and AC-130s reached operational service, gunships were able add night interdiction to their mission. The first deployment of "smart" weapons with modified B-57s flying night interdiction sorties simultaneously increased destruction of targets and reduced aircraft losses. Finally, after a premature start in 1968, the long-awaited F-111 demonstrated itself to be a highly effective all-weather attack platform in the final months of the war.

Developments since 1970. Unlike Korea 20 years earlier, the Vietnam experience proved to have a profound effect on USAF aircraft procurement. DOD and U.S. Congress oversight have become established elements of the process; with some exceptions,[23] aircraft selection has returned to a variation of the pre–1940 "fly before you buy" system in which a final decision rests upon competitive trials between flying prototypes. The AX (attack experimental) program of 1970–1972, which produced the Fairchild-Republic A-10 as a specialized CAS platform, serves as case in point. The General Dynamics F-16 emerged from the ACF (air combat fighter) program of 1971–1975 as the most versatile USAF tactical fighter since the F-86, and the second-place YF-17 eventually metamorphosed into the F/A-18. Since the 1970s DARPA (Defense Advanced Research Projects Agency[24]) has become increasingly involved in military aircraft procurement programs. The *Have Blue* project, organized in the mid–1970s to test low observable (i.e., stealth) technology, was spearheaded by DARPA and ultimately resulted in the ultra-secret production of the Lockheed F-117A. To find a replacement for the USAF's aging fleet of F-111s, the ETF (enhanced tactical fighter) program, conducted from 1980 to 1984, applied state-of-the-art radar and targeting systems to well-proven airframes, the F-15 and F-16, to ultimately arrive at the selection of the F-15E. And continued development of existing airframes has also produced precision attack and SEAD versions of the F-16 (i.e., F-16C/D and F-16CJ/DJ).

Despite improvements in EW and SEAD after Vietnam, early experience with the F-117A

---

[23]*Although the YF-15A did not fly until mid–1974, the project had originated in 1965 under a "buy before you fly" procurement scheme; the development of the Navy's Grumman F-14A was similar. To maintain secrecy, the Lockheed F-117A was derived from the stand-alone* Have Blue *project.*

[24]*Organized in 1958 as Advanced Research Projects Agency, its name was changed to DARPA in 1972. Acting as an independent agency of DOD, DARPA does not exercise general oversight of military programs but focuses on specific projects that utilize advanced technology.*

clearly demonstrated that low-RCS (stealth) is the ultimate form of defensive countermeasure. It is no surprise, therefore, that one of the USAF's principal goals since the early 1980s has been to procure new aircraft which combine the F-117's stealthiness with the performance and capabilities of fighters like the F-15 and F-16.[25] The ATF (advanced tactical fighter) and DARPA-sponsored JAFE (joint advanced fighter engine) programs, both commenced in 1983, represented a dual effort to develop a fast and maneuverable stealth airframe powered by new engines that would enable the aircraft to "supercuise" (i.e., maintain supersonic speed without afterburning). Although both of the resulting ATF prototypes, the Lockheed YF-22 and Northrop YF-23, and both JAFE engines, the Pratt & Whitney F-19 and General electric F-120, met or exceeded official expectations, the F-22/F-19 combination was declared winner of the competition in April 1991. However, in the 15-year interval between the F-22's first flight (1990) and operational deployment (2005), spiraling development and production costs, together with projected USAF force reductions, have slashed planned procurement from 750 aircraft to just 183 as of late 2005.

The USAF initiated the MRF (multi-role fighter) in 1991 with the aim of finding a low-cost replacement for the F-16 and the A-10, but because of official uncertainties over fighter procurement due to the ending of the Cold War, the program was placed on hold in mid-1992, then cancelled altogether in early 1993. Within almost the same timeframe, the Navy had been engaged in A/F-X (attack/fighter-experimental), a project intended to develop a stealth attack aircraft that would augment the F/A-18, while the Marines and the British Royal Navy, since 1989, had been working together on a wholly separate DARPA-sponsored venture to find a next generation V/STOL aircraft to succeed the *Harrier*. In early 1994, all of these efforts were rolled into JAST (joint advance strike technologies) with the goal of generating a common stealth airframe that would satisfy multi-service needs. A request for design proposals was issued to aircraft manufacturers by the JAST group in March 1996, after which the project was renamed JSF (joint strike fighter). Later the same year, following a review of preliminary design proposals submitted by three manufacturers, the competition was narrowed to Boeing's X-32 and Lockheed-Martin's X-35. Prototypes of both aircraft were flown in late 2000, and in October 2001, DOD declared Lockheed-Martin's X-35 (re-designated F-35) to be the winner of the JSF competition.

In terms of sheer cost, JSF is probably the single largest contract in the history of military aircraft procurement, with the possibility of producing up to 3,000 airplanes at a total outlay of $200 Billion. Evaluation aircraft are projected for delivery to all services between 2008 and 2010, with the first operational examples expected to follow in 2012. The USAF version, the F-35A, is slated to replace both the F-16 and the A-10; the Marine version, the V/STOL F-35B, will replace both F/A-18C/Ds and AV-8Bs; and the Navy version, the F-35C, will replace F/A-18C/Ds. F-35A JSFs, together with F-22As, will likely form the cutting edge of USAF tactical air power through the first half of the 21st Century. Beyond stealth, the next step may be an unmanned system, better known as the UCAV (unmanned combat air vehicle). To this end, under DARPA supervision, the USAF started a UCAV project in 1999 and flew the first of two X-45A concept demonstrators in May 2002. The USAF project was merged with similar Navy efforts (i.e., the X-47 UCAV-N) under the heading J-UCAS (Joint Unmanned Combat Air Systems) in 2003, and it looked as if the program were assuming a pattern similar to JSF. However, the USAF withdrew its support from J-UCAS on March 2006 and terminated the X-45A test program. At the date of this writing, the USAF has announced no plans to pursue the UCAV concept.

---

[25]*The Northrop B-2 obviously extends the same principle to long-range strategic bombardment.*

First Series • 1926–1944

Designation	Manufacturer	Dates
A-2	Douglas Aircraft Co.	1926–1927
A-3, -4	Curtiss Aeroplane Co.	1927–1937
A-7	Fokker Aircraft Co.	1930–1931
A-8, -10, -12	Curtiss-Wright Corp.	1931–1938
A-9	Lockheed-Detroit Corp.	1931
A-11	Consolidated Aircraft Co.	1933–1935
A-13, -16	Northrop Corp.	1933–1936
A-14, -18	Curtiss-Wright Corp.	1935–1940
A-17, -33	Northrop Corp./Douglas Aircraft Co.	1935–1942
A-19	Vultee Aircraft Co.	1935–1939
A-20	Douglas Aircraft Co.	1939–1945
A-21	Boeing Airplane Co., Stearman Div.	1939–1940
A-22, -23	Glenn L. Martin Co.	1939–1940
NA-40	North American Aviation, Inc.	1939–1940
A-24	(See, SBD in Part II)	
A-25	(See, SB2C in Part II)	
A-26	Douglas Aircraft Co.	1942–1970
A-27	North American Aviation, Inc.	1940
A-28, -29	Lockheed Aircraft Corp.	1942–1944
A-30	Glenn L. Martin Co.	1942
A-31, -35	Consolidated-Vultee Aircraft Corp.	1941–1944
A-32	Brewster Aeronautical Corp.	1943–1944
A-34	(See, SB2A in Part II)	
A-36	North American Aviation, Inc.	1942–1944
A-37	Hughes Aircraft Co.	1943–1944
A-38	Beech Aircraft Co.	1942–1944
A-41	Consolidated-Vultee Aircraft Corp.	1942–1944
B-23	Douglas Aircraft Co.	1939–1945
B-25	North American Aviation, Inc.	1940–1959
B-26	Glenn L. Martin Co.	1940–1945
B-28	North American Aviation, Inc.	1942–1944
B-34	Lockheed Aircraft Corp.	1941–1945
B-42 (A-42)	Douglas Aircraft Co.	1944–1948
P-38	Lockheed Aircraft Corp.	1939–1946
P-39	Bell Aircraft Corp.	1939–1945
P-40	Curtiss-Wright Corp.	1938–1945
P(F)-47	Republic Aviation Corp.	1941–1955
P(F)-51	North American Aviation, Inc.	1940–1957
P-63	Bell Aircraft Corp.	1942–1945

Douglas A-2 (1926–1927)

TECHNICAL SPECIFICATIONS (XA-2)

Type: Two-place ground attack
Manufacturer: Douglas Aircraft Co., Santa Monica, California
Total produced: 1
Power plant: One 433-hp Liberty V-1410 (inverted) 12-cylinder air-cooled engine driving a two-bladed Hamilton Standard fixed-pitch propeller.

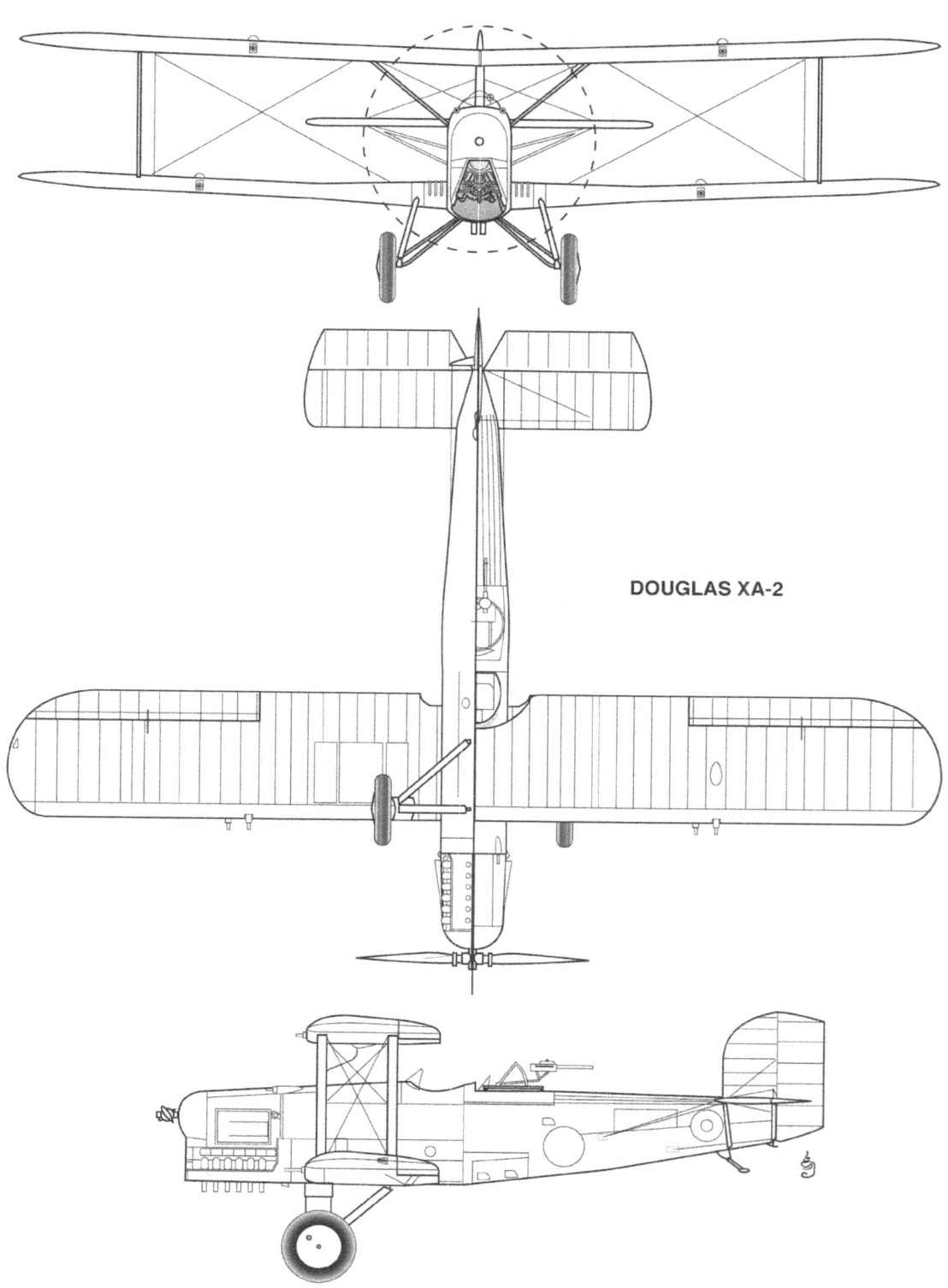

DOUGLAS XA-2

Armament: Six fixed forward-firing .30-cal. machine guns and two flexible .30-cal. rear machine guns (no bomb load specified but 200-lbs. estimated).
Performance: Max. speed 130-mph at s.l.; ceiling 17,000 ft.; range 400 mi.
Weights: 3,179-lbs. empty, 4,985-lbs. loaded.
Dimensions: Span 39 ft. 8 in., length 29 ft. 7 in., wing area 414 sq. ft.

Though never selected for production, the Douglas A-2 holds the distinction of having been the first Army aircraft to receive the "A" for attack designation (XA-1 had already been assigned to the Cox-Klemin ambulance plane) and was a direct development of the Douglas O-2. In 1924, when the War Department staged a competitive fly-off at McCook Field, Ohio with the purpose of acquiring a new type of observation plane to eventually replace the Army's aging fleet of World War I–era DH-4Bs and DH-4Ms, the Douglas XO-2, a single-bay, Liberty-powered biplane, had been selected for production over the Curtiss XO-1. Liberty engines had been the specified for both aircraft in order to utilize surplus government stocks and because it was one of the most reliable powerplants available at the time. Douglas received an initial contract in 1924 to manufacture 45 O-2s, followed in 1925 by an order for 30 more. Production O-2s were lightly armed, having one fixed .30 caliber Browning machine gun synchronized to fire through the nose plus one flexible .30 caliber Lewis machine gun in the rear cockpit.

In March 1926, the Army directed that the 46th O-2 airframe be converted to an experimental ground attack version armed with six fixed, forward-firing .30-caliber machine guns, two in the nose and four in the wings outside the propeller arc, plus two .30-caliber Lewis guns in the flexible mount. The prototype, designated the XA-2, was also modified to accept installation of an inverted, air-cooled variant of the Liberty engine, which was thought to be less vulnerable to ground fire than a liquid-cooled engine with a radiator. The XA-2 was delivered

The sole prototype XA-2 as it appeared at McCook Field in 1927. It was the first aircraft to be built to an attack specification following the Army's unsuccessful venture with six different types between 1920 and 1923.

to McCook Field for flight trials sometime in 1926 and was pitted in a competitive fly-off against the Curtiss XA-3 in late 1927. However, Curtiss was subsequently selected as the winner and development of the XA-2 was discontinued.

Curtiss A-3, -4 Falcon (1927–1937)

TECHNICAL SPECIFICATIONS (A-3B)

Type: Two-place ground attack
Manufacturer: Curtiss Aeroplane Co., Garden City, New York.
Total produced: 146 (all versions)
Power plant: One 435-hp Curtiss V-150-5 (D-12) 12-cylinder liquid-cooled engine driving a two-bladed Hamilton Standard fixed-pitch propeller.
Armament: Four fixed forward-firing .30-cal. machine guns, two flexible .30-cal. rear machine guns, and 200 lbs. of bombs carried on external racks.
Performance: Max. speed 139-mph at s.l.; ceiling 16,100 ft.; range 628 mi.
Weights: 2,875-lbs. empty, 4,476-lbs. loaded.
Dimensions: Span 38 ft., length 27 ft. 2 in., wing area 353 sq. ft.

The A-3, the Air Corps first operational attack aircraft, was a derivative of the two-seat *Falcon* series produced by Curtiss in numerous variants—observation, attack, and two-seat fighter—and sold to the Army and the Navy and exported abroad. The design was character-

A-3B prototype as delivered to McCook Field for official acceptance in 1929. The "P-595" on the rudder refers to the McCook Field project number. The A-3B incorporated the improvements of the corresponding O-1E observation type.

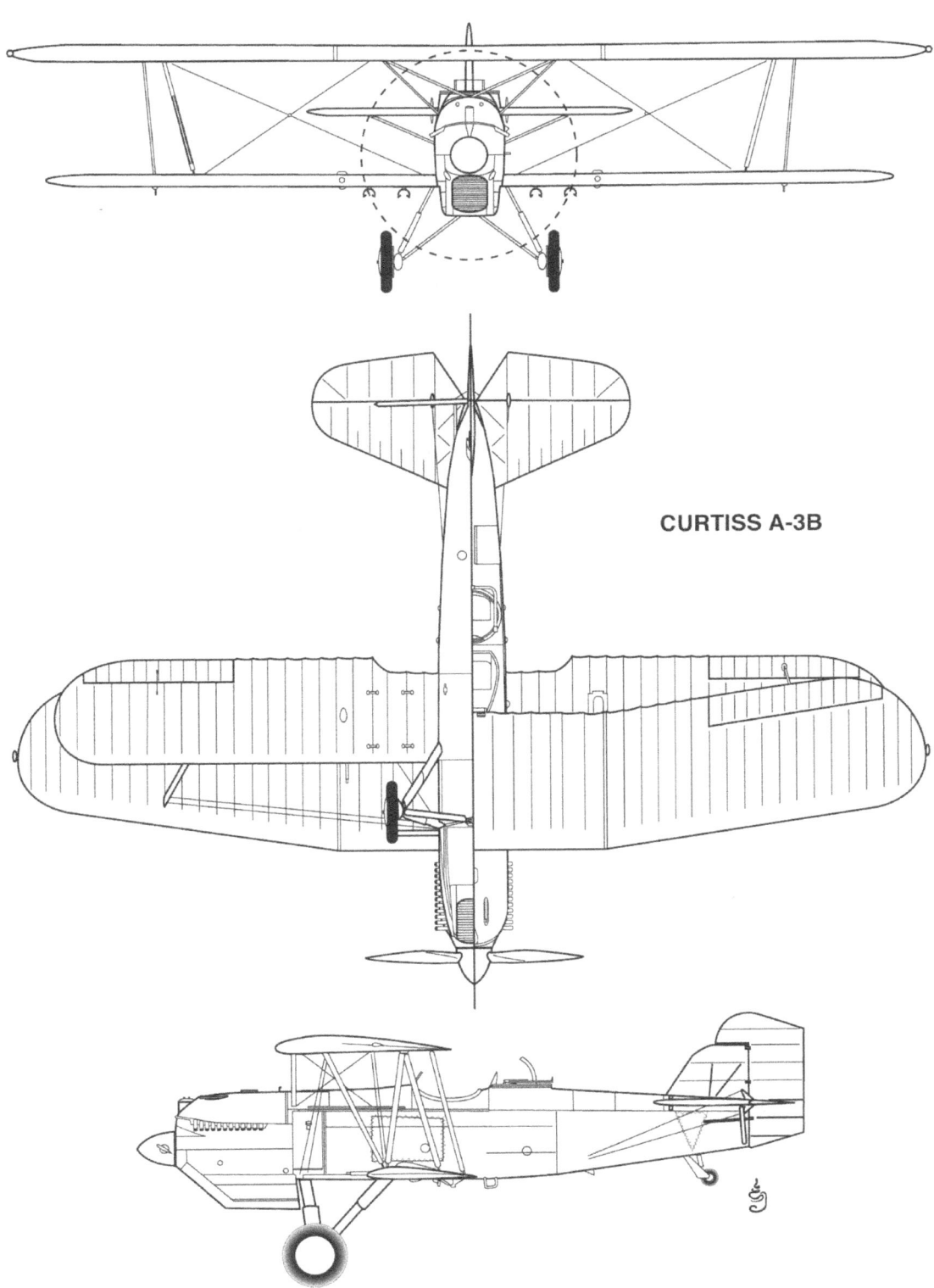

CURTISS A-3B

ized by a large, swept upper mainplane, staggered lower wings braced by a single bay of N-type struts, and an innovative fuselage structure consisting of riveted, wire-braced duraluminum tubing covered by fabric. Designed by Rex Biesel, the original *Falcon* flew in 1924 with a Liberty engine and participated in the Army's first observation contest as the XO-1. While not winning the competition, improved *Falcon* observation variants were still placed in production: ten service test O-1s with Curtiss D-12 engines delivered in 1926; 25 D-12-powered O-1Bs with brakes and jettisonable auxiliary tanks in 1927; and 66 Liberty-powered O-1s in 1927–1928. In 1926 Army officials directed Curtiss to modify an O-1B airframe to ground attack requirements, which involved adding two fixed forward firing .30 caliber machine guns in the lower wing plus underwing racks to carry up to 200-lbs.of bombs. The prototype, designated the XA-3, was delivered to McCook Field in 1927 for competitive trials against the Douglas XA-2. Curtiss also delivered a second attack prototype, the XA-4, which was essentially an O-1B airframe powered by an air-cooled 450-hp Pratt & Whitney R-1340 *Wasp* engine.

Following official evaluations conducted in late 1927, the XA-3 was selected as the winning design and Curtiss received an order under three separate contracts to manufacture 66 aircraft as the A-3. The XA-4 was not placed in production but was later evaluated and accepted by the Navy as the XF8C-1 two-seat fighter. All production A-3s had been delivered by the end of 1929 and six were later re-designated A-3A after being fitted with dual controls for training purposes. The A-3B (based on the improved O-1E), which appeared in 1929, incorporated additional streamlining, balanced controls, pneumatic oleos, two more fixed .30-caliber guns synchronized to fire from the upper engine cowling, plus a 36-gallon belly tank. The Army ordered 77 A-3Bs under two contracts and all had been delivered by the end of 1930.

Upon entering service during 1928–1930, A-3s and A-3Bs equipped three squadrons of the 3rd Attack Group at Fort Crockett, Texas as well as the 26th Attack Squadron based in Hawaii. A-3Bs were retired from frontline duties during 1936 and the last examples were stricken from the active Air Corps inventory in late 1937. The designations A-5 and A-6 were reserved for *Falcon* attack derivatives that were planned but never built.

General Aviation (Fokker) A-7 (1931)

TECHNICAL SPECIFICATIONS (XA-7)

Type: Two-place ground attack
Manufacturer: General Aviation Corp., Teterboro, New Jersey (formerly a subsidiary of Fokker).
Total produced: 1
Power plant: One 600-hp Curtiss V-1570-27 *Conqueror* 12-cylinder liquid-cooled engine driving a two-bladed Hamilton Standard fixed-pitch propeller.
Armament: Four fixed forward-firing .30-cal. machine guns, one flexible .30-cal. rear machine gun, and up to 400-lbs. of bombs carried on external racks.
Performance: Max. speed 184-mph at s.l.; ceiling 19,000 ft.; range 500 mi.
Weights: 3,866-lbs. empty, 5,650-lbs. loaded.
Dimensions: Span 46 ft. 9 in., length 31 ft., wing area 333 sq. ft.

Attack units were the first elements of the Air Corps to begin replacing their biplanes with monoplanes. The process was instigated in early 1930 when the Army circulated proposals to manufacturers for a new monoplane attack aircraft of all-metal construction, to be powered by a Curtiss *Conqueror* engine. A contract to build one prototype, under the designation XA-7, was given to General Aviation Corp., formerly a subsidiary of the Dutch-owned Fokker company. Reminiscent of earlier Fokker designs, the XA-7 emerged with thick, cantilevered wings and fixed landing gear encased in large wheel pants, with the pilot and observer/gunner being placed in open cockpits arranged in tandem.

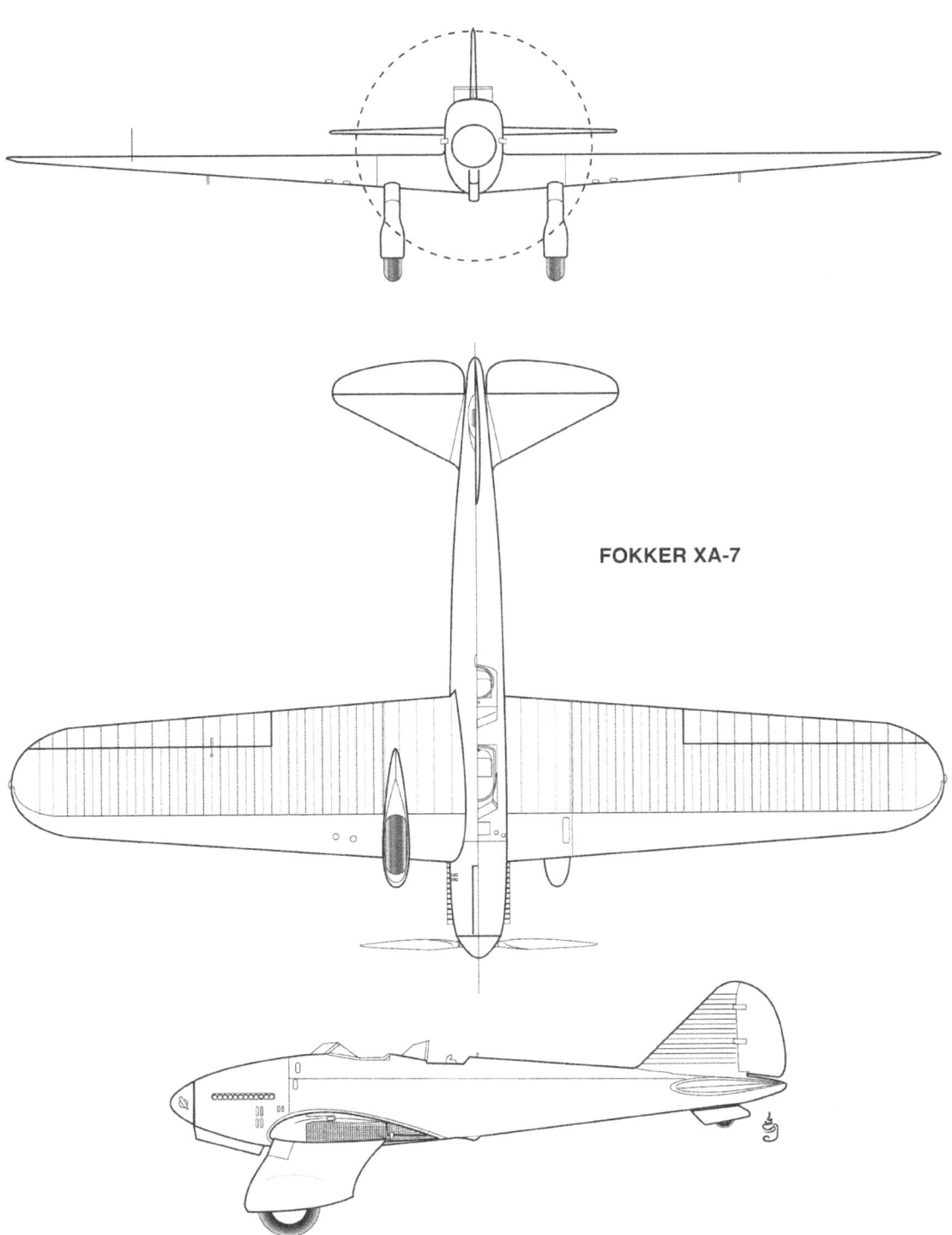

FOKKER XA-7

The single XA-7 prototype at Wright Field in 1931. Although losing out to the rival Curtiss A-8, the XA-7 nevertheless represented swift progress in the aerodynamic state-of-the-art over previous biplane designs.

The completed prototype was delivered to Wright (formerly McCook) Field in June 1931 to be evaluated against the competing Curtiss XA-8. When trials were concluded in September 1931, however, Curtiss was declared the winner and development of the XA-7 was discontinued, the sole prototype being eventually dismantled.

Curtiss A-8, -10, -12 Shrike 1931–1941

TECHNICAL SPECIFICATIONS (A-12)

Type: Two-place ground attack
Manufacturer: Curtiss Aeroplane Co., Garden City, New York.
Total produced: 59 (all versions)
Power plant: One 670-hp Wright R-1820–21 *Cyclone* 9-cylinder air-cooled engine driving a three-bladed Hamilton Standard fixed-pitch propeller.
Armament: Four fixed forward-firing .30-cal. machine guns, one flexible .30-cal. rear machine gun, and up to 464-lbs. of bombs carried on external racks.
Performance: Max. speed 177-mph at s.l.; ceiling 15,150 ft.; range 510 mi.
Weights: 3,898-lbs. empty, 5,756-lbs. loaded.
Dimensions: Span 44 ft., length 32 ft. 3 in., wing area 285 sq. ft.

The Curtiss A-8 was the second of two monoplane attack prototypes to be considered by the Army during mid–1931. Powered by the same 600-hp Curtiss V-1570 Conqueror liquid-cooled V12 engine as the rival XA-7, the XA-8 appeared with thinner-section, externally wire-braced wings, large spats fully enclosing the wheels, and widely spaced enclosed cockpits for the pilot and observer/gunner, a first for a U.S. combat aircraft. Other innovations introduced on the prototype were leading-edge wing slots and split flaps to enhance low-speed handling and landing characteristics. The radiator was positioned on the belly aft of the engine to permit better nose streamlining. The XA-8 was delivered in June 1931 and following trials, thirteen service test examples were ordered, five as the YA-8 and seven as the Y1A-8. The company

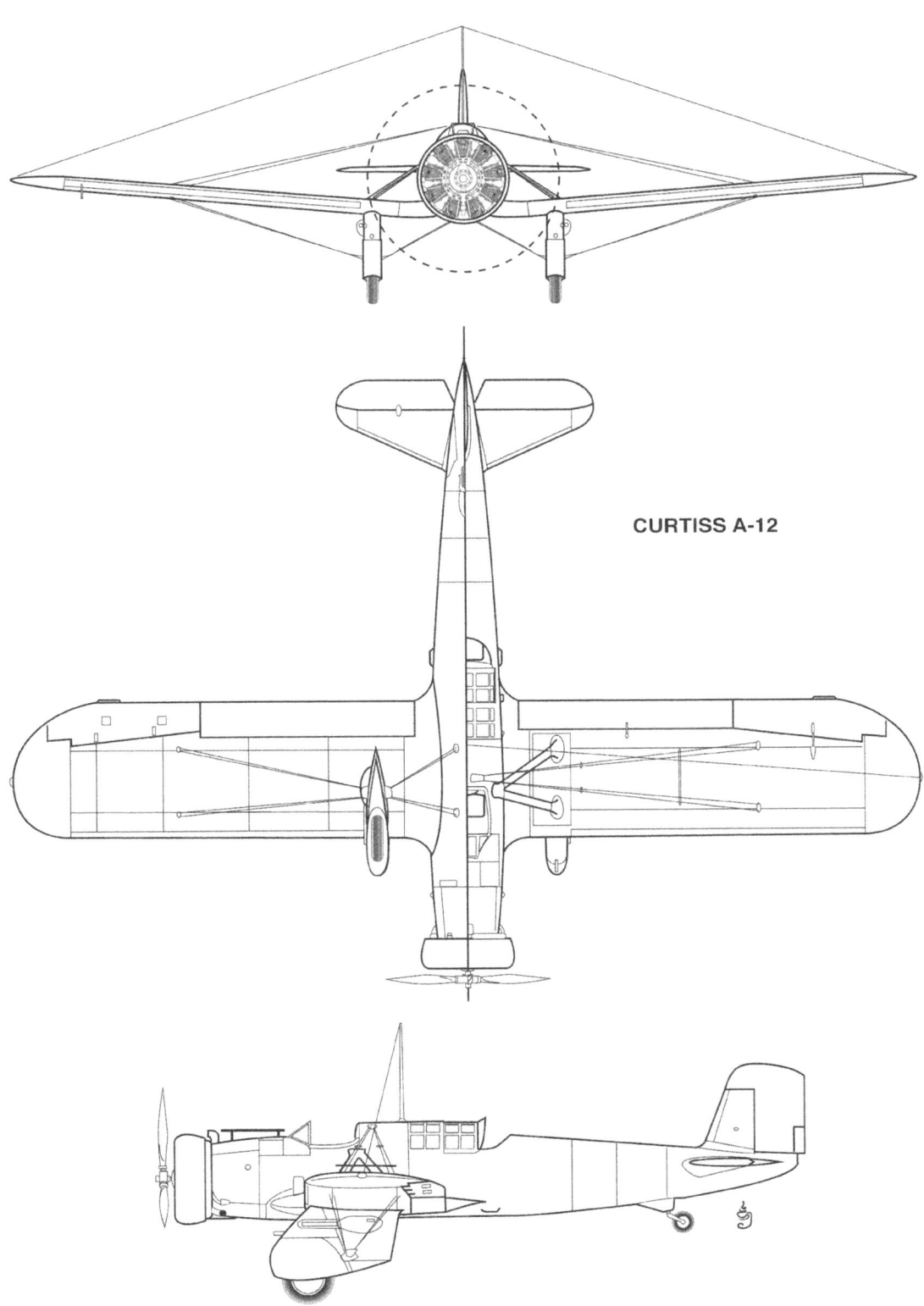

CURTISS A-12

Top: **A-8 belonging to the 3rd Attack Group in 1932. The leading edge slots, one of the design's most innovative features, are clearly visible.** *Bottom:* **A-12, based with the 3rd Attack Group at Ft. Crockett, dropping a stick of 30-lb. bombs. At the altitude shown, aiming the bombs would have been a matter of guesswork. A radial engine was thought to be less vulnerable to ground fire than a water-cooled type.**

name *Shrike* was assigned but never used officially by the Air Corps. All service test aircraft were later re-designated A-8 and eleven went into active service with the 3rd Attack Group during 1932. The last Y1A-8 became the Y1A-8A when it was fitted with a 657-hp, geared *Conqueror* engine for test purposes. In February 1933 the Army awarded Curtiss a contract to manufacture 46 aircraft as the A-8B, virtually the same as the A-8 but with open cockpits.

The first YA-8 was modified in mid-1932 to receive installation of a 625-hp Pratt & Whitney R-1690 *Hornet* air-cooled radial engine and was re-designated YA-10. Although the radial engine afforded no actual improvement in general performance, it was easier to maintain and much less vulnerable to battle damage, as a result of which the Army directed that the existing A-8B order be completed with the air-cooled engines under the new designation A-12. All production A-12s, delivered from late 1933 to early 1934, came with 690-hp Wright R-1820 *Cyclone* engines. Other than the radial engine, the most noticeable change to the A-12 was relocating the observer/gunner's position forward to a faired enclosure behind the pilot's cockpit. A-12s initially served alongside A-8s in the 3rd Attack Group at Fort Crockett and both types went to the new 37th Attack Squadron at Langley Field, Virginia. As they were replaced by newer aircraft, 15 A-12s were assigned to Kelly Field, Texas as trainers and 20 went to the 26th Attack Squadron in Hawaii, where they served until 1941.

Consolidated A-11 1933–1936

TECHNICAL SPECIFICATIONS (Y1A-11)

Type: Two-place ground attack
Manufacturer: Consolidated Aircraft, Co., Buffalo, New York.
Total produced: 5
Power plant: One 675-hp Curtiss V-1570-59 *Conqueror* 12-cylinder liquid-cooled engine driving a two-bladed Hamilton Standard variable-pitch propeller.
Armament: Four fixed forward-firing .30-cal. machine guns, one flexible .30-cal. rear machine gun, and up to 400-lbs. of bombs carried on external racks.
Performance: Max. speed 227-mph at s.l.; ceiling 23,300 ft.; range 470 mi.
Weights: 3,805-lbs. empty, 5,490-lbs. loaded.
Dimensions: Span 43 ft. 11 in., length 29 ft. 3 in., wing area 297 sq. ft.

After testing the highly innovative Lockheed-Detroit YP-24 two-seat fighter in 1931, the Army placed an order for four more as the Y1P-24 plus five service test attack versions as the Y1A-9, which was basically identical except for added armament. The YP-24 featured an all-metal fuselage, a fully enclosed canopy for the pilot and gunner, plus the cantilever wooden wing and retractable landing gear derived from the Lockheed *Sirius* transport, and with a top speed of 215-mph, it was faster than any other aircraft in the Air Corps inventory. But when delivery of the Y1P-24s and Y1A-9s failed to materialize due to the financial collapse of Lockheed-Detroit, the Army authorized Consolidated, who had obtained Lockheed-Detroit's production rights along with its project engineer, Robert Woods, to continue development of fighter and attack variants under the respective designations Y1P-25 and Y1A-11. As the designs progressed, they differed from the YP-24 in having all-metal wings, a more streamlined nose contour, and enlarged vertical tail surfaces. The attack version came with two more fixed .30-caliber machine guns and external bomb racks, and because it would operate at lower altitudes, lacked a turbo-supercharger.

Arriving at Wright Field in January 1933, the Y1A-11 posted an impressive top speed of 227-mph during testing but was destroyed in a crash before trials could be completed. By the time the remaining four Y1A-11s were delivered during 1934, the Army had shifted to a preference for air-cooled engines in attack aircraft, and no production resulted. The parallel fighter version was more successful, 50 examples being ordered in 1934 as the P-30 (re-designated

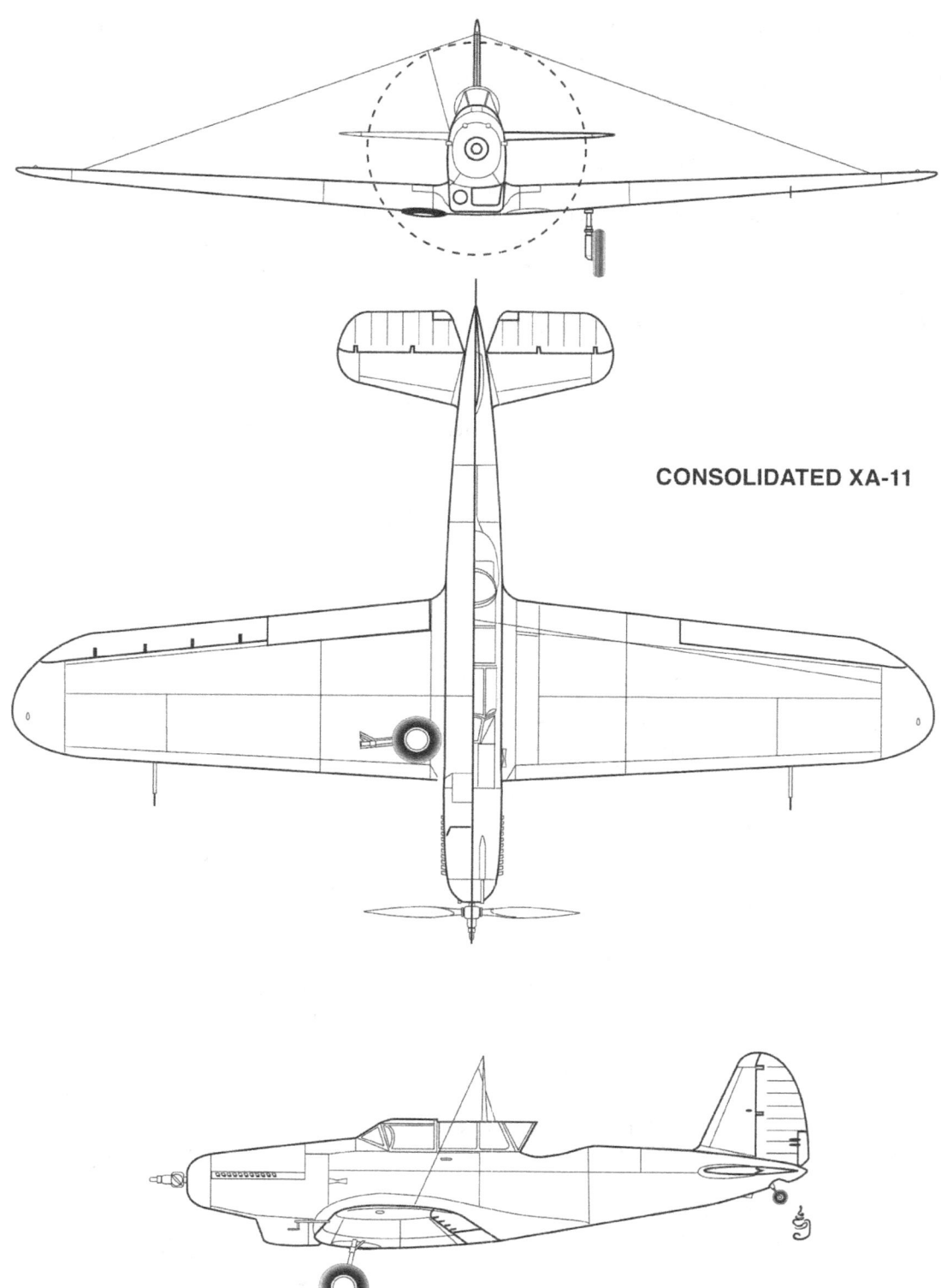

CONSOLIDATED XA-11

Y1A-11 in Wright Field markings, probably in 1934 or 1935. By the time the service test aircraft were delivered, the Army had shifted to a preference for air-cooled engines in attack types. The PB-2A fighter version was more successful.

PB-2A in 1936). One Y1A-11 was re-designated XA-11A when it was modified for use by Bell Aircraft Co. as a flying testbed for the Allison V-1710 V12 liquid-cooled engine.

Northrop A-13, -16 1933–1936

TECHNICAL SPECIFICATIONS (XA-13)

Type: Two-place ground attack
Manufacturer: Northrop Corp., El Segundo, California.
Total produced: 1 (50 exported)
Power plant: One 690-hp Wright SR-1820-37 *Cyclone* 9-cylinder air-cooled engine driving a two-bladed Hamilton Standard fixed-pitch propeller.
Armament: Four fixed forward-firing .30-cal. machine guns, one flexible .30-cal. rear machine gun, and up to 600-lbs. of bombs carried on external racks.
Performance: Max. speed 207-mph at 3,300 feet; ceiling 21,750 ft.; range 550 mi.
Weights: 3,600-lbs. empty, 6,463-lbs. loaded.
Dimensions: Span 48 ft., length 29 ft. 2 in., wing area 362 sq. ft.

As a private venture in 1933, Northrop undertook development of an Army attack aircraft based upon the design of its single-engine, fixed-gear Gamma transport. The resulting Gamma 2C or "Gamma Attack," powered by a Wright *Cyclone*, retained the wings and tail surfaces of the transport but featured a redesigned fuselage in which the cockpit had been moved forward to accommodate the pilot and gunner under a greenhouse canopy enclosure. After being flown in early 1933 under a civilian registration (NX12291), the 2C prototype was leased to the Army for evaluation at Wright Field. While awaiting an Army decision, Northrop sold 49 similar aircraft to the Chinese Nationalist Air Force as the Gamma 2E, the last of which was delivered in 1936; and at least one more 2E was sold to Great Britain for evaluation. Meanwhile, in early 1934, NX12291 was returned to Northrop for modifications, most noticeably a reshaped fin and

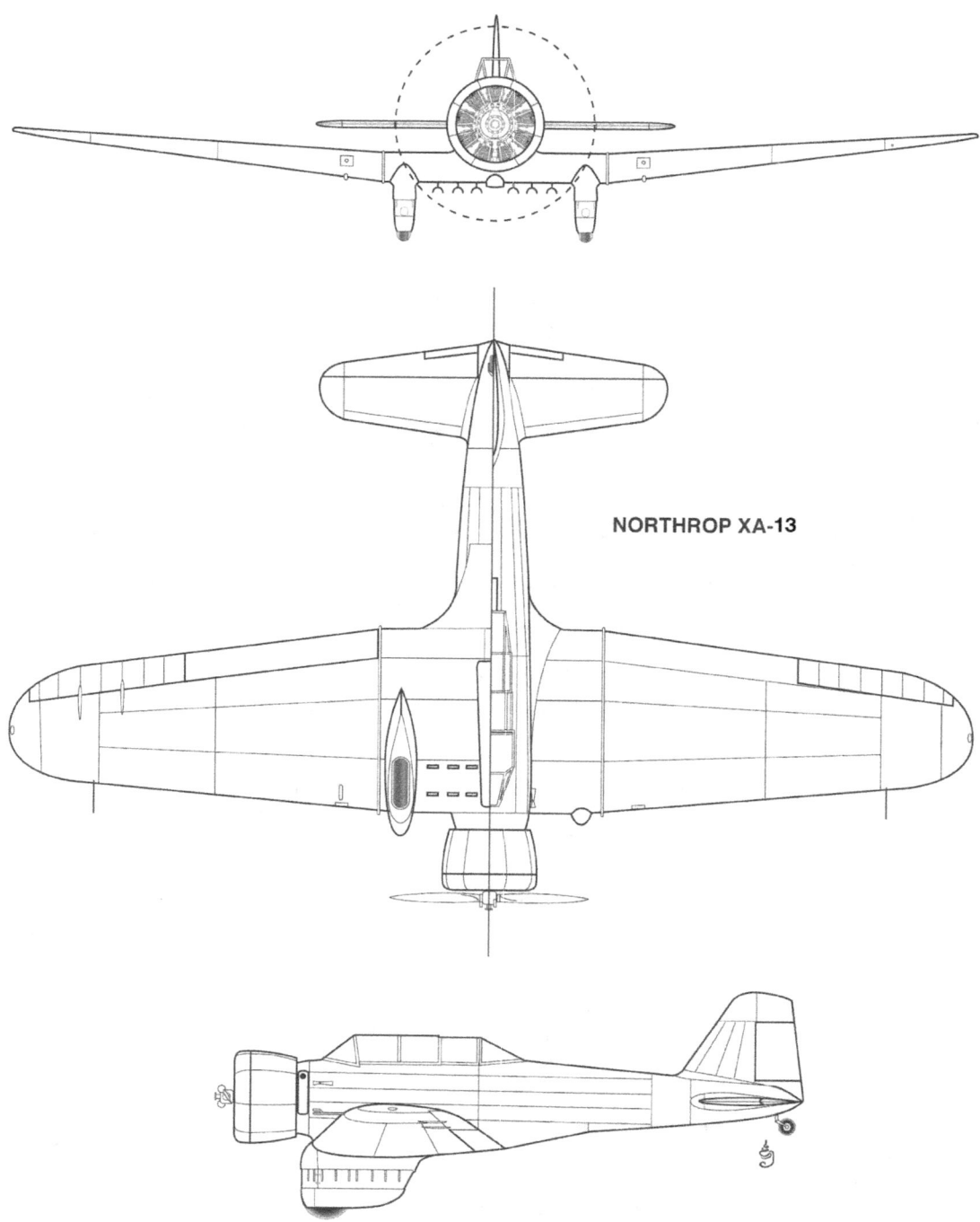

NORTHROP XA-13

rudder, and after being redelivered to Wright Field in June 1934, the Army finally accepted it under the designation XA-13.

While the XA-13 was still under official consideration, Northrop delivered yet another private venture demonstrator, the extensively modified Gamma 2F, to Wright Field in October 1934. The Gamma 2F was ultimately placed in production and is reported in detail under a sep-

The YA-13 in 1934 following modification of fin and rudder. After a change to an R-1830 engine in 1935, the same aircraft was re-designated YA-16.

arate heading as the A-17. After the A-17 contract had been concluded, the XA-13 was returned again to Northrop to be refitted with a smaller diameter Pratt & Whitney R-1830 *Twin Wasp* engine and, under the new designation XA-16, was redelivered to the Army in early 1935, however, no production was undertaken and the aircraft reportedly finished its days at an aircraft mechanic's school at Roosevelt Field, Long Island.

Curtiss A-14, -18 Shrike II 1935–1943

TECHNICAL SPECIFICATIONS (Y1A-18)

Type: Two-place ground attack
Manufacturer: Curtiss-Wright Corp., Buffalo, New York, California.
Total produced: 14
Power plant: Two 930-hp Wright R-1820-47 *Cyclone* 9-cylinder air-cooled engines driving three-bladed Hamilton Standard variable-pitch propellers.
Armament: Four fixed forward-firing .30-cal. machine guns, one flexible .30-cal. rear machine gun, and a 400-lb. bomb load in wing bays plus 200-lbs. on external racks.
Performance: Max. speed 239-mph at 2,500 feet; ceiling 28,650 ft.; range 654 mi.
Weights: 9,410-lbs. empty, 12,679-lbs. loaded.
Dimensions: Span 59 ft. 6 in, length 42 ft. 4 in., wing area 526 sq. ft.

The A-18 was a forerunner of the well-known twin-engine attack and bomber aircraft (e.g., A-20, A-26, B-25, B-26) that would see such widespread use throughout World War II. Despite the better performance of the single-engine attack monoplanes introduced in the early 1930s, the Army began to realize that, to achieve significant improvements in load-carrying ability, speed, and range, a larger, twin-engine aircraft would be needed. And during 1934 the Army went so far as to articulate a new twin-engine attack requirement, but due to Depression era budgetary restraints, was unwilling to fund development of entirely new airplanes. Since it

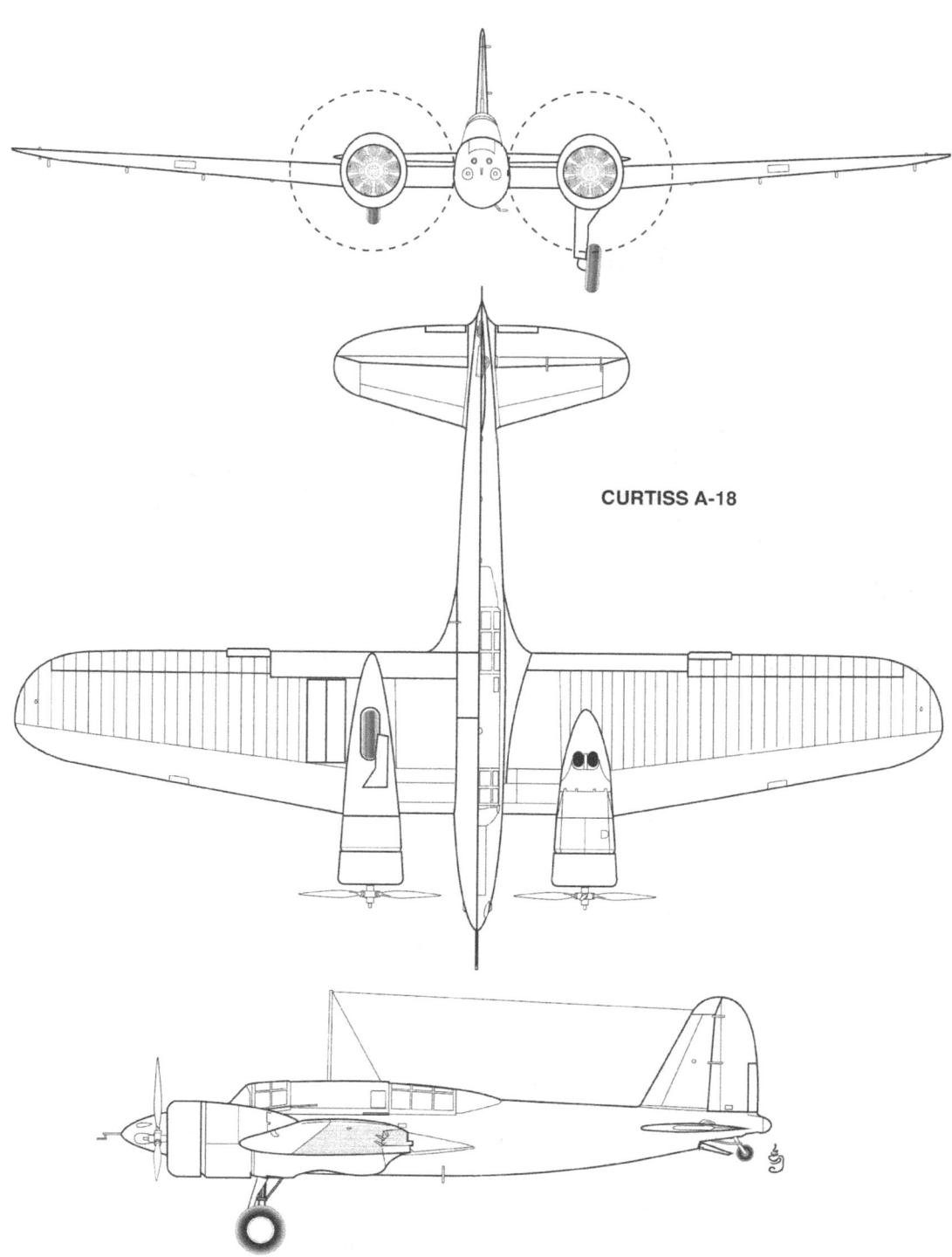

CURTISS A-18

would cost much less to modify an aircraft already in production, Army officials initiated a feasibility study (under the assigned designation XA-15) to determine whether a Martin B-10 bomber could be adapted to attack requirements; almost simultaneously, Curtiss-Wright embarked upon a company-funded effort to create an original twin-engine design with the hope that the Army would later buy it. Smaller and lighter than the proposed XA-15, the Curtiss

First Series • 1926–1944　　　27

First USAAC twin-engine attack type, this A-18 was one of thirteen that served with the 8th Attack Squadron at Barkesdale Field from 1937 to 1941. Reports from the Spanish Civil War indicated that the type would be outclassed in combat by similar German aircraft.

Model 76 emerged with a slim, oval-section fuselage ending in a pointed nose, broad-chord wings swept from the leading edges, and landing gear that retracted rearward into the engine nacelles leaving the wheels partially exposed. The fuselage was of all-metal, semi-monocoque construction and the wings were metal structures with fabric covering aft of the main spar. The fully enclosed pilot and gunner positions were widely spaced to permit visibility over the wings. The civilian prototype (NX15315), powered by experimental 765-hp Wright R-1510 engines, flew in July 1935 but was refitted with 735-hp Wright R-1670 engines before being delivered to Wright Field later in the fall. In November 1935, following brief trials, the Army purchased the prototype as the XA-14.

Though faster than any attack aircraft then in service (faster than the projected XA-15 by 40-mph), the XA-14's high unit cost ($90,000 per airplane) caused Army officials to decide against full-scale production; instead, Curtiss was given a contract to produce thirteen service test examples, which, after a change to 930-hp Wright R-1820-47 *Cyclone* engines, were given the new designation YlA-18. Deliveries were completed between July and October 1937 and all thirteen examples were assigned to the 8th Attack Squadron at Barkesdale Field, Louisiana. In service, they were re-designated A-18. During 1941, the A-18s were transferred to the 15th Attack Squadron at Lawson Field, Georgia, where they served until being withdrawn in 1943.

Northrop A-17, -33 1934–1942

TECHNICAL SPECIFICATIONS (A-17A)

Type: Two-place ground attack
Manufacturer: Northrop Corp., El Segundo, California.
Total produced: 242 (A-17, A-17A, and A-33)
Power plant: One 825-hp Pratt & Whitney R-1535-13 *Twin-Wasp Junior* 14-cylinder air-cooled engine driving a three-bladed Hamilton Standard variable-pitch propeller.

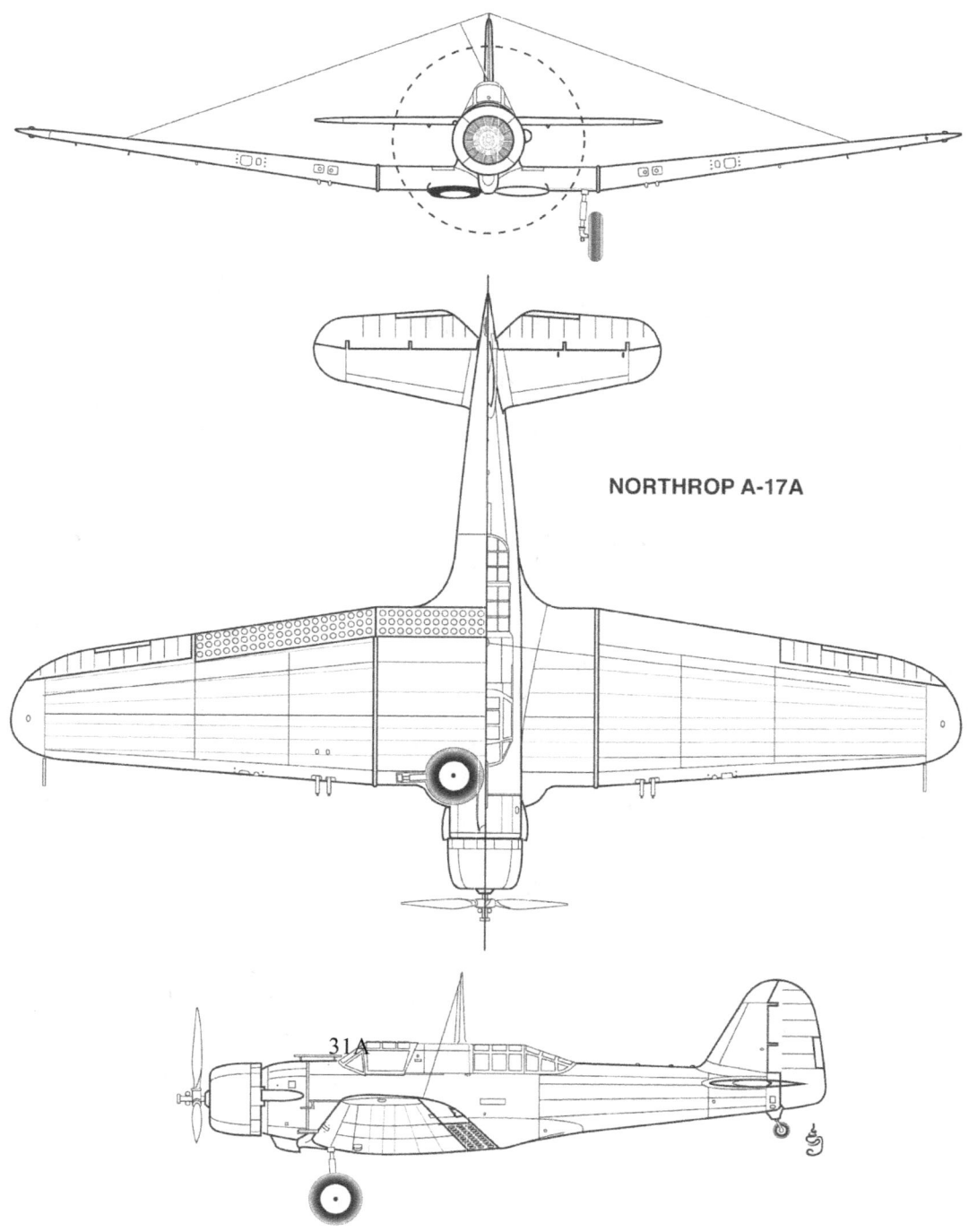

NORTHROP A-17A

Armament: Four fixed forward-firing .30-cal. machine guns, one flexible .30-cal. rear machine gun, and up to 900-lbs. of bombs carried on external racks.
Performance: Max. speed 220-mph at 2,500 feet; ceiling 19,400 ft.; range 732 mi. Weights: 5,106-lbs. empty, 7,550-lbs. loaded.
Dimensions: Span 47 ft. 9 in., length 31 ft. 8 in., wing area 362 sq. ft.

Top: Nearly new A-17 serving with the 3rd Attack Group at Barkesdale Field in 1936 or 1937. Its colors were a blue fuselage with yellow wings and tail group. *Bottom:* Natural metal A-17A with the new 7th Attack Group at March Field. By the time A-17As began reaching service in 1937, the Army was having second thoughts about the effectiveness of single-engine attack aircraft.

The Northrop A-17 series was the most numerous type of attack aircraft in the Army inventory from 1936 to 1940 and a direct development of the XA-13 reported above. With no orders on XA-13 forthcoming, Northrop delivered a second private venture demonstrator, the extensively modified Gamma 2F, to Wright Field in October 1934. The 2F was powered by a 750-hp Pratt & Whitney R-1535-11 engine and featured semi-retractable landing gear that folded backwards into fairings on the bottom of the wings, a revised canopy, and enlarged tail surfaces. Following evaluations, the 2F demonstrator was returned to the factory to replace the semi-retractable gear with a fixed type (the bulky mechanisms had been judged to offer an insignificant increase in performance) and for other smaller changes. Working posthaste, Northrop not only modified the prototype to incorporate a fixed gear having faired struts with open-sided wheel pants, but made additional streamlining improvements to the cowling and fuselage, revised the canopy configuration, and further enlarged the tail fin. Soon after redelivery, in December 1934, the Army awarded Northrop a contract to manufacture 110 aircraft as the A-17 (notably, the largest pre–World War II contract for an attack aircraft). The first production A-17s were sent to Wright Field for further evaluation and in early 1936, began re-equipping the 3rd Attack Group based at Barkesdale Field, Louisiana, the last example being delivered in January 1937.

While production of the A-17 was still underway, Northrop proposed development of another retractable gear version, which, unlike the 2F, introduced main gear struts that folded inward, fully flush with the bottom of the wing center-section. Other then the addition of wing root extensions to house the retracted wheels, the airframe was essentially unchanged and gained only a nominal increase in empty weight. In January 1936, the Army responded with an order for 100 aircraft under the new designation A-17A. The initial production A-17A made its first flight in July 1936, however, malfunctions in the gear retraction mechanism delayed delivery to Wright Field until February 1937. Despite a further delay in service entry due to persistent problems with the gear, all 100 production aircraft had been delivered by the end of 1937. A-17As equipped the 3rd Attack Group and also the 7th Attack Group based at March Field, California, where they supplemented and eventually replaced fixed-gear A-17s.

Even though the A-17 was arguably the most advanced single-engine attack aircraft in the world when it entered service in 1936, military developments abroad, combined with an official shift in Army policy toward procurement of twin-engine attack types, dictated a brief service career, with all A-17s and A-17As having been withdrawn from frontline units before the end of 1940. A number of fixed-gear A-17s continued in Army service as trainers and utility hacks, but most of the A-17As were sold to the French *Armée de l'Air*, only to be re-sold to Great Britain after the fall of France. None were used in combat and reportedly ended their days as trainers serving in the South African Air Force. When Northrop's El Segundo plant was absorbed by Douglas in 1938, a further 141 A-17 variants were exported as the Douglas 8A (31 fixed-gear 8A-1s and 110 retractable-gear 8A-3s, -4s, and -5s). Thirty-one *Cyclone*-powered 8A-5s intended for Peru were commandeered by the Army in early 1942 and received into service as the A-33, but were used only as utility aircraft. The factory name *Nomad* was applied to the exports but rarely used.

Vultee A-19 1938–1942

TECHNICAL SPECIFICATIONS (YA-19)

Type: Two-place ground attack
Manufacturer: Vultee Aircraft Corp., Los Angeles, California.
Total produced: 6

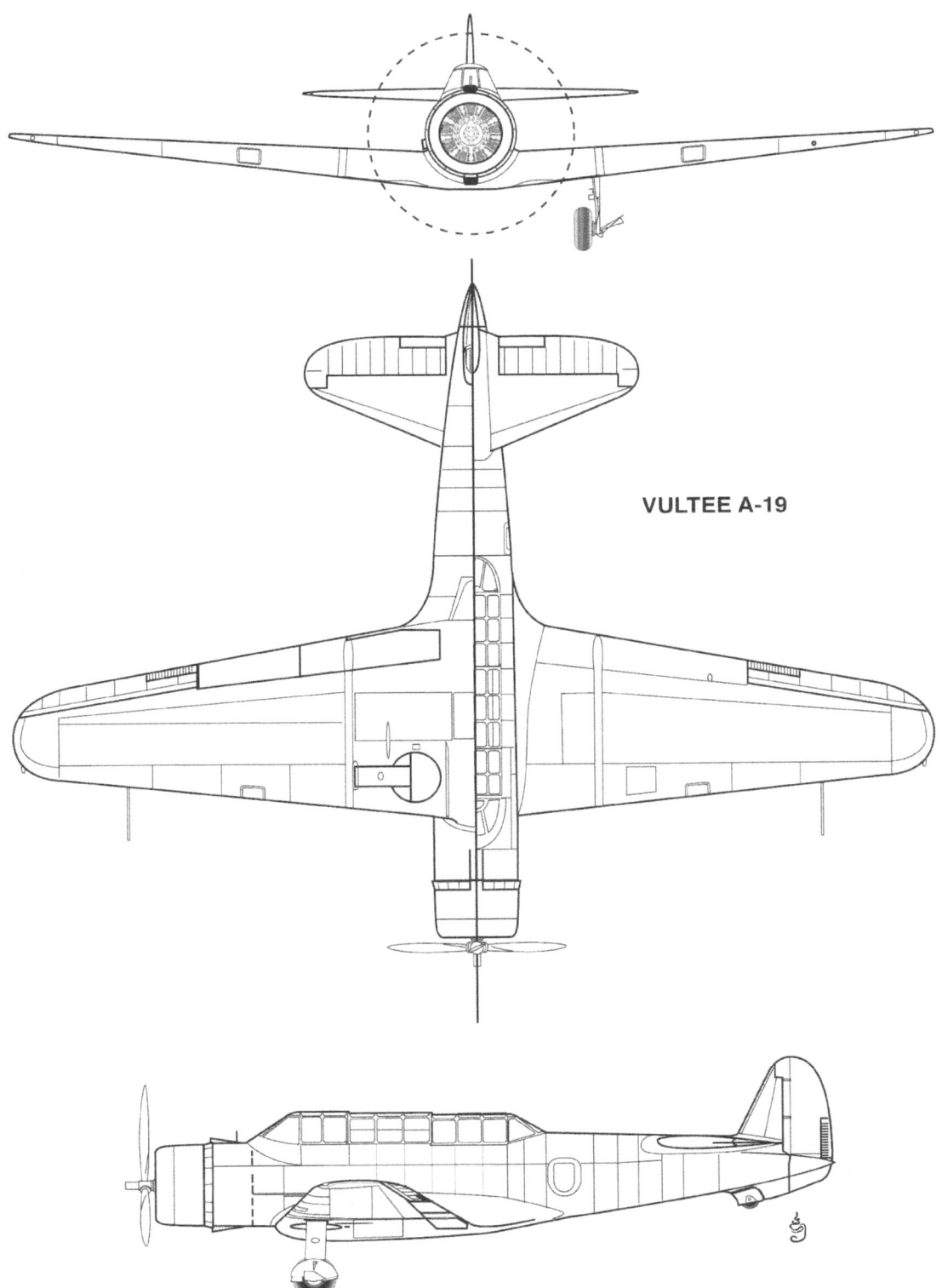

The YA-19 as delivered in original configuration in mid–1939. By the time the seven service test examples arrived for testing, the Army had already made a decision not to acquire any further single-engine attack types.

Power plant: One 1,200-hp Pratt & Whitney R-1830-17 *Twin-Wasp* 14-cylinder air-cooled engine driving a three-bladed Hamilton Standard variable-pitch propeller.
Armament: Four fixed forward-firing .30-cal. machine guns, two flexible .30-cal. machine guns, one in the rear cockpit and one in the ventral bay, and up to 1,080-lbs. of bombs carried on external racks.
Performance: Max. speed 230-mph at 6,500 feet; ceiling 28,000 ft.; range 1,100 mi. Weights: 6,452-lbs. empty, 10,421-lbs. loaded.
Dimensions: Span 50 ft. 9 in., length 37 ft. 10 in., wing area 384 sq. ft.

A military derivative of Gerald Vultee's V-1 transport design of 1934, the *Cyclone*-powered V-11 flew for the first time in September 1935. Even though this sleekly modern all-metal, retractable-gear plane was intended to compete with Northrop's A-17 series, over 100 examples had been sold abroad to foreign air forces before the Army indicated sufficient interest to place an order for seven service test aircraft in June 1938. The service test models were assigned the designation YA-19 and ordered with supercharged *Twin-Wasp* engines in place of the *Cyclones*. All seven YA-19s were delivered by the middle of 1939, but by that time the Army's emphasis had shifted to twin-engine attack aircraft and the type, despite acceptable performance, was not placed in full-scale production.

Two of the YA-19s were subsequently employed as engine testbeds: the XA-19A fitted with a 1,200-hp Lycoming O-2130 inline engine and the XA-19B tested with a 1,800-hp Pratt & Whitney R-2800. The other five YA-19s were initially assigned to March Field but were later transferred to the Canal Zone where they were used by military attaches at neighboring American embassies.

Douglas A-20 Havoc 1939–1945

TECHNICAL SPECIFICATIONS (A-20G)

Type: Two or three-place light bomber
Manufacturer: Douglas Aircraft Co., El Segundo Division, El Segundo, California.
Total produced: 7,478 (all versions, including exports)
Power plant: Two 1,600-hp Wright R-2600-23 *Twin-Cyclone* 14-cylinder air-cooled engine driving three-bladed Hamilton Standard constant-speed propellers.
Armament: Four fixed 20-mm cannon and two .50-cal. machine guns in nose or six .50-cal. machine guns in nose, two .50-caliber machine guns in a powered dorsal turret, one flexible .50-cal. machine gun in the ventral bay, and up to 4,000-lbs. of bombs carried in an internal bomb bay.
Performance: Max. speed 333-mph at 12,300 feet; ceiling 23,700 ft.; combat range 1,000 mi.
Weights: 16,993-lbs. empty, 24,127-lbs. loaded.
Dimensions: Span 61 ft. 4 in., length 48 ft., wing area 464 sq. ft.

After discussing requirements with Army officials in 1936, John Northrop and his project engineer, Edward Heinemann, began the preliminary work on a light (9,500-lbs.) twin-engine attack design, listed as the Model 7, however, before the detailed design phase could be completed, military reports from the Spanish Civil War strongly suggested that the aircraft would probably be obsolete before it flew. With more up-to-date combat requirements in mind, the Army solicited bids (i.e., Circular Proposal 38–385) in March 1938 calling for a twin-engine 'light-bomber' capable of carrying a 1,200-lb. bomb load over a range of 1,200 miles at a cruising speed not less than 200-mph. The deadline for completion of prototypes was one year. Northrop by that time had sold his company to Douglas Aircraft, but Heinemann had remained behind as its new chief of military projects. Using the shelved Model 7 project as a starting point, Heinemann began laying down a new design for a heavier, more powerful aircraft that would fulfill the Army specifications. The new Douglas Model 7B emerged as a strikingly modern aircraft with sharply tapered, shoulder-mounted wings that joined to a deep, oval-section fuselage, all-resting upon a tricycle landing gear. Power came from a pair of 1,100-hp Pratt & Whitney R-1830 14-cylinder radial engines driving three-bladed, fully-controllable propellers. Integral to the design was the novel innovation of interchangeable noses: a glass-paneled nose with a bombardier's station or a solid attack nose containing eight fixed machine guns. The Model 7B made its first flight in October 1938 and factory testing soon revealed a top speed of 304-mph and a cruise of 270-mph combined with superb handling qualities; however, in January 1939, disaster struck when the prototype was destroyed in a crash before it could be delivered for Army evaluations.

By the spring of 1939, three other prototypes—the Stearman X-100, the Martin 167, and the North American NA-40—had all been flown to Wright Field to compete for the contract, but none of them rivaled the known performance of the Douglas 7B. In a conspicuous departure from standard procurement procedures, the Army extended the deadline and announced that the winner would be selected on the basis of detailed design submissions rather than a fly-off between prototypes. Predictably, in late June 1939, the Army declared Douglas the winner and awarded a contract to manufacture 123 aircraft as the A-20. Because of a production priority placed on foreign contracts (64 to France as DB-7s; 206 to Great Britain, 36 as *Boston Is* and 170 as *Boston IIs*), no A-20s were delivered to the Air Corps until November 1940. And the Army versions were completed to a different specification than export models: a strengthened airframe, armor and self-sealing fuel tanks, a revised nose enclosure with more Plexiglas glazing, increased fin area, and more powerful Wright R-2600 engines of 1,600-hp each. Armament was heavier, too: four forward-firing .30-caliber guns in external blisters, twin flexible .30-caliber guns in the dorsal position, one flexible .30-caliber gun the belly, plus one fixed .30-caliber gun firing rearward out of each engine nacelle. In the initial order, 63 were to be

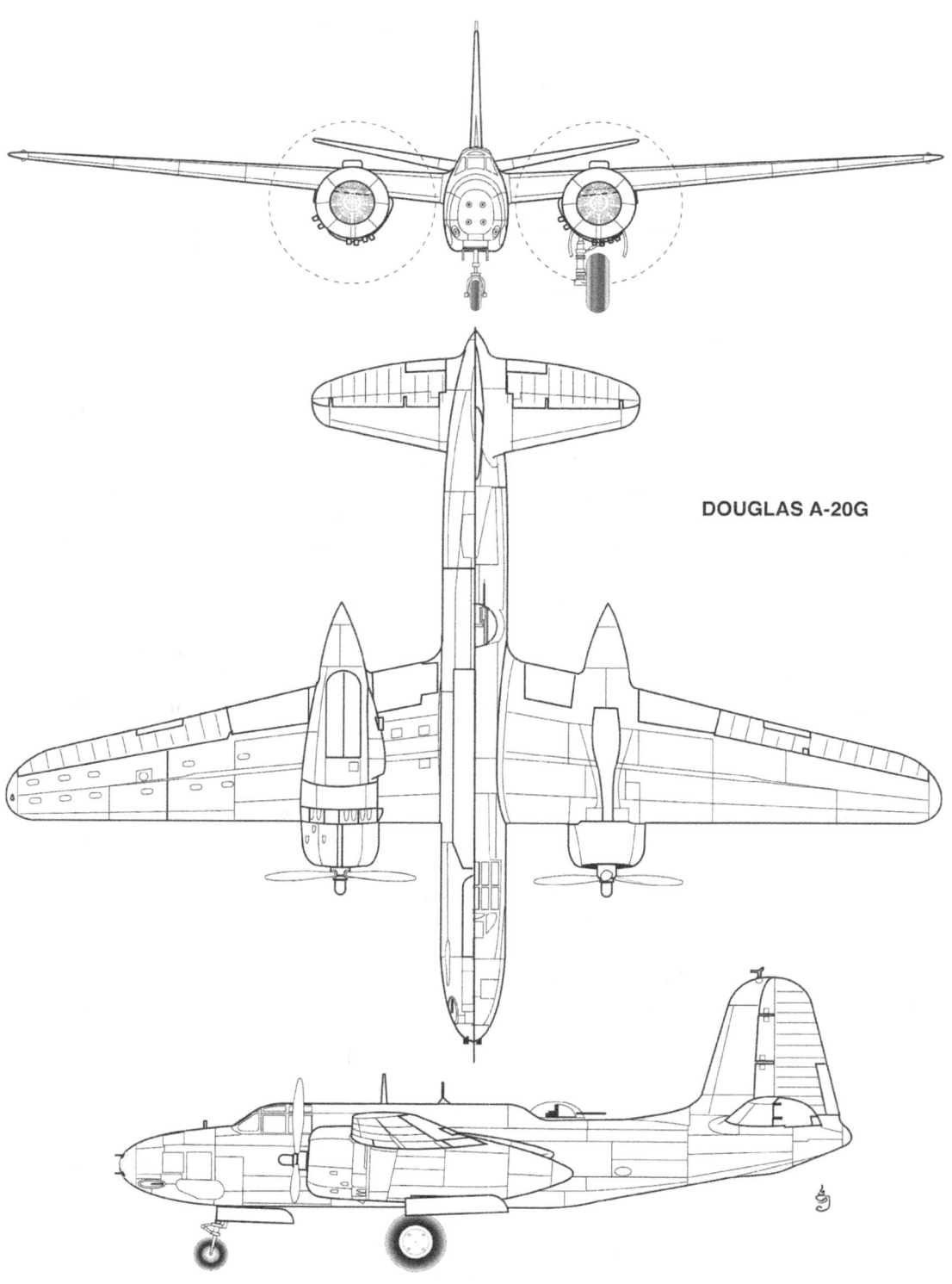

DOUGLAS A-20G

Top: A-20A of 3rd Bombardment Group (Light) over Hawaii in mid–1941. Export versions serving with France and Britain had already seen extensive combat. *Bottom:* Later block A-20G with power dorsal turret and four .50-caliber guns in the nose. The A-20G was the most numerous of the series, a total of 2,850 being completed by 1944.

completed as A-20 high-altitude versions with turbo-superchargers (R-2600-7) and 60 as A-20A low/medium altitude versions (R-2600-3); however, cooling problems related to the turbo-superchargers together with an official decision that the type would not be employed in high-altitude operations, led to 64 aircraft being completed as A-20As and the remaining 59 as P-70 night-fighter versions with solid noses and fixed-antenna British radar. Transition to

A-20J over the U.S., probably in 1944. Glazed nose A-20Js, carrying bombardiers and equipped with Norden bombsights, led solid-nosed A-20Gs on strike missions, primarily in the ETO.

A-20As by Army Air Corps operational units began in the spring of 1941 with the 3rd Bombardment Group (Light); the P-70s were delivered in early 1942 to the 481st Night Fighter Operational Training Group in Orlando, Florida, the first radar-equipped aircraft in American service.

The first sizeable Army contract came in October 1940 for 999 aircraft as the A-20B. Interestingly, this production run was built to an earlier specification, lacking the revised nose glazing, armor, and self-sealing tanks of the A-20A. Three hundred thirty-four were delivered to the U.S. Army Air Forces (AAF) during 1942, serving primarily with the 12th AF in North Africa, but the remaining 665 were exported to the Soviet Union under Lend-Lease. Following U.S. entry into World War II, all A-20/P-70 aircraft were assigned the popular name *Havoc*. The next AAF version, the A-20C, was similar to the A-20A but represented an effort by Douglas to standardize differences between AAF models and export versions. The rearward firing guns were deleted and 500-lbs. of armor was added for crew protection. Although some were taken over by the AAF, many of the 808 A-20Cs went to foreign users under Lend-Lease—the RAF, Soviet Air Force, and RAAF (Australia)—as *Boston IIIs*. The A-20D never proceeded beyond the design stage, 17 A-20As were later re-designated A-20E when they were used in experimental projects, and the sole A-20F served as a test bed for the remote-control turret system developed for the Douglas A-26. The A-20G was the most widely produced version of the series, a total of 2,850 being built at Douglas's Santa Monica plant in 1943 and 1944. Influenced largely by Pacific-based A-20As and Cs, the G model introduced a solid nose equipped initially with four fixed 20-mm and two .50-caliber machine guns, along with R-2600-23 engines uprated to 1,675-hp. The flexible guns in the dorsal and belly position were retained in early production Gs but later production blocks featured an electrically-powered Martin dorsal turret armed with two .50-caliber guns. Early problems with the 20-mm cannons led to replacement with four .50-caliber guns, six total, that were less prone to jamming. All but 278

A-20Gs served with AAF units (250 early production models went to the Soviet Union and 28 to the RAAF). The 412 A-20Hs delivered to the AAF were identical to the late G except for R-2600-29 engines rated at 1,700-hp. The A-20J was essentially an A-20G with nose glazing for a bombardier, built to serve alongside solid-nosed Gs as formation leaders during bombing runs. The Js were easily distinguishable by their blown plexiglas, one-piece noses. A total of 450 were built at Santa Monica, of which 169 were delivered to the RAF as the *Boston IV*. The last variant built, the A-20K, was identical to the J except for more powerful R-2600-29 engines, and 413 had been delivered when A-20 production terminated in September 1944. Altogether, 7,098 DB-7s, *Bostons, Havocs,* and A-20s were produced by Douglas and another 380 by Boeing under license.

When Germany invaded France during the spring of 1940, French DB-7s became the first examples of the type to take part in combat, and these same aircraft, as part of the Vichy Air Force, were used to carry out retaliatory strikes against Gibraltar after the British attacked the French fleet in Morocco in July 1940, making it one of the few type of planes that fought on both sides in World War II. Britain used its initial batch of 20 *Boston Is* for RAF crew training, and all of the second group of 181 *Boston IIs* were converted to a night fighters and intruders under the new name *Havoc I,* the converted aircraft first being introduced to combat operations in early 1941. Under Lend-Lease, between 1941 and 1944, Britain received a further 1,100 *Boston III, IIIA, IV, V,* and *Havoc II* aircraft, operating them in daylight attack strikes and night intruder and night fighter operations. The largest single user of the type was the Soviet Union, receiving some 3,125 A-20s from 1942 onwards. The Soviet A-20s were reportedly used in every conceivable tactical role, including close air support and attacking ships with torpedoes. Sixty-nine *Boston IIIs* and miscellaneous A-20 variants, 48 of which had been DB-7Cs ordered by the Dutch government before the East Indies fell to the Japanese, served with the RAAF in the southwest Pacific from late 1942 to early 1945.

The first AAF use of the type in combat occurred in July 1942, staging out England to attack targets on the occupied Dutch coast with *Boston IIIs* 'borrowed' from the RAF. A-20As operating with the 5th AF began combat operations in the southwest Pacific in August 1942. Many Pacific-based A-20s were subsequently field modified as "strafers" under the supervision of AAF Maj. Paul I. "Pappy" Gunn in Australia. The modification entailed replacing the bombardier's position with fixed, .50-caliber forward-firing machine guns and was ultimately incorporated into the production A-20G. By early 1944, the 5th AF possessed three A-20 bombardment groups and used them in the invasions of the Philippines and Formosa right up through the cessation of hostilities in 1945. In late 1942, A-20Bs of the 47th Bombardment Group of the 12th AF commenced combat operations out of Algeria in support of the advancing Allied armies during Operation Torch. Upgrading to A-20Gs and Js over time, 12th AF units continued to operate A-20s from Mediterranean bases in Malta, Sicily, Italy, Corsica, and France until finally reequipping with the Douglas A-26 in early 1945. Commencing in early 1944, A-20s began to equip three bombardment groups attached to the 9th AF in England. In the European Theatre, experience had shown that any type of low-level attack resulted in prohibitive losses due to the concentration of radar-directed German antiaircraft defenses, with the result that A-20s were used primarily to precision bomb military targets from medium altitudes (9,000 to 14,000 feet). As invading Allied armies moved onto the European continent in June 1944, the A-20 groups moved with them to operate from forward bases in France and Belgium. By the time of V-E Day, all A-20s in the ETO had been replaced by A-26s. After World War II, remaining A-20s were rapidly withdrawn from the active AAF inventory and most were scrapped; however, in 1944–1945, 30 ex-AAF A-20Gs and Ks were transferred to the Brazilian Air Force where they served well into the 1950s.

Stearman A-21 1939–1940

TECHNICAL SPECIFICATIONS (XA-21)

Type: Three-place light bomber
Manufacturer: Stearman Division of Boeing Airplane Co., Wichita, Kansas.
Total produced: 1

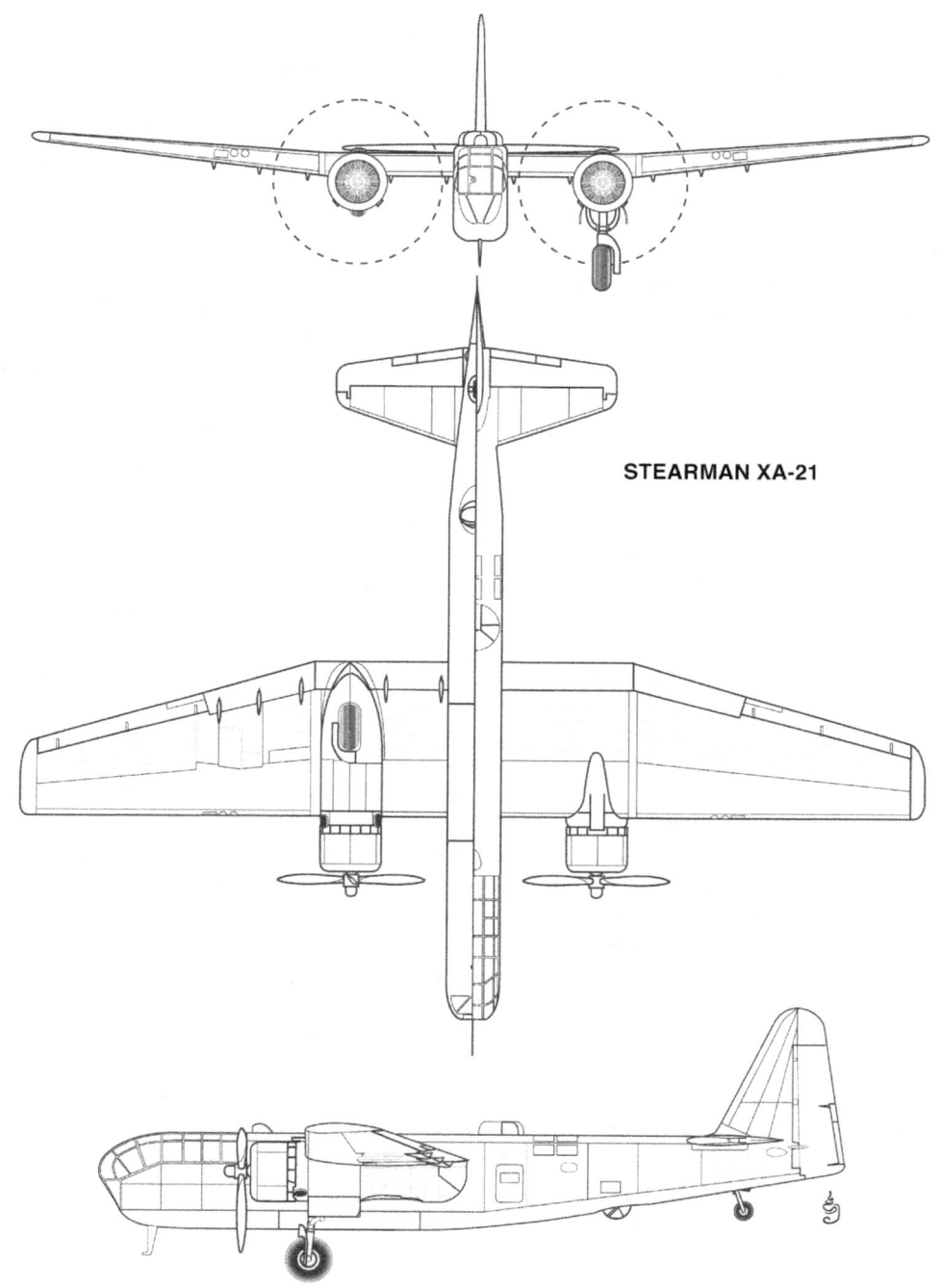

STEARMAN XA-21

The sole XA-21 prototype at Wright Field after being rebuilt with a conventional stepped cockpit configuration. It was the first all-metal monoplane to be designed and built by the company's Stearman Division in Wichita.

Power plant: Two 1,400-hp Pratt & Whitney R-2180-7 14-cylinder air-cooled engine driving three-bladed Hamilton Standard constant-speed propellers.
Armament: Four fixed .30-cal. machine guns in the wings, two flexible .30-caliber machine guns in the waist position, one flexible .30-caliber machine gun in the nose, one flexible .30-caliber machine gun in a dorsal turret, one flexible .30-caliber machine gun in a belly position, and up to 2,700-lbs. of bombs carried in an internal bomb bay.
Performance: Max. speed 257-mph at 5,000 feet; ceiling 20,000 ft.; range 1,500 mi. max.
Weights: 12,760-lbs. empty, 18,257-lbs. loaded.
Dimensions: Span 65 ft., length 53 ft. 1 in, wing area 607 sq. ft.

    One of the four prototypes built for the Army light bomber competition according to Circular Proposal 38-385 of March 1938, the Model X-100 was still in the design stages when Stearman was merged into Boeing. For the Wichita-based group, it was their very first attempt to conceive an airplane of all-metal, monoplane design. The aircraft emerged with a relatively conventional layout, having moderately tapered wings that were shoulder-mounted to a very deep, slab-sided fuselage. The landing gear was of conventional tail wheel arrangement, with the main struts folding rearward into the engine nacelles to leave the wheels partially exposed. The design's most prominent characteristic was a fully streamlined, plexiglas-paneled nose seating the bombardier ahead of the pilot in tandem fashion. A third crewmember functioning as a gunner/radio operator was stationed in a waist position just aft of the wing. The X-100 featured such modern innovations as electrically actuated landing gear, integral fuel tanks, sealed fuselage and wing compartments for flotation, plus Fowler-type trailing-edge flaps both inboard and outboard the engine nacelles. The plane was powered by a pair of experimental Pratt & Whitney R-2180-7 twin-row, 14-cylinder engines, which were enlarged versions of the R-1830 *Twin Wasp* originally developed for the Douglas DC-4E. Boasting five flexible machine guns, Stearman's entry carried the heaviest defensive armament of any of the four competing prototypes.

    The X-100 was delivered to Wright Field in April 1939 and was purchased by the

Army under the designation XA-21. Air Corps test pilots found the cockpit arrangement to be unsatisfactory, so the prototype was returned to Boeing-Stearman where the nose was rebuilt with a conventional stepped cockpit configuration. It was the slowest of the prototypes tested, and in any event, the Army cancelled the fly-off and announced a decision to order the A-20 in quantity, with the result that further development of the XA-21 was soon discontinued. None were exported.

Martin A-22 Maryland 1939–1940

TECHNICAL SPECIFICATIONS (XA-22)
Type: Three-place light bomber
Manufacturer: Glenn L. Martin Co., Baltimore, Maryland.
Total produced: 1 (340 exported)
Power plant: Two 1,200-hp Pratt & Whitney R-1830-37 *Twin Wasp* 14-cylinder air-cooled engine driving three-bladed Hamilton Standard constant-speed propellers.
Armament: Four fixed .30-cal. machine guns in the wings, one flexible .30-caliber machine gun in a retractable dorsal turret, one flexible .30-caliber machine gun in the belly position, nose, and up to 1,800-lbs. of bombs carried in an internal bomb bay.
Performance: Max. speed 280-mph at 5,000 feet; ceiling 20,000 ft.; combat range 600 mi.
Weights: 11,170-lbs. empty, 16,000-lbs. loaded.
Dimensions: Span 61 ft. 4 in., length 46 ft. 8 in, wing area 538.5 sq. ft.

Of the military contractors participating in the light bomber competition announced by the Army in 1938, the Glenn L. Martin Co. was the most experienced, having sold airplanes to both the Army and the Navy for nearly 20 years. The company's light bomber entry under Circular Proposal 38-385 had been assigned to James S. McDonnell as project engineer, who, a year later, would leave Martin to form his own company in St. Louis, Missouri. With little apparent reference to Martin's earlier attack effort (e.g., XA-15 of 1934), McDonnell and his staff evolved the Model 167 as a low-wing aircraft with a very slim-bodied, oval-section fuselage and a noticeably humped empennage where the horizontal stabilizer carried through over the fuselage itself. In order to create space for the bombardier's compartment and the bomb

A-22 as delivered to the USAAC during the spring of 1939. Martin's anger at the cancellation of the fly-off was offset by large orders from France and Britain.

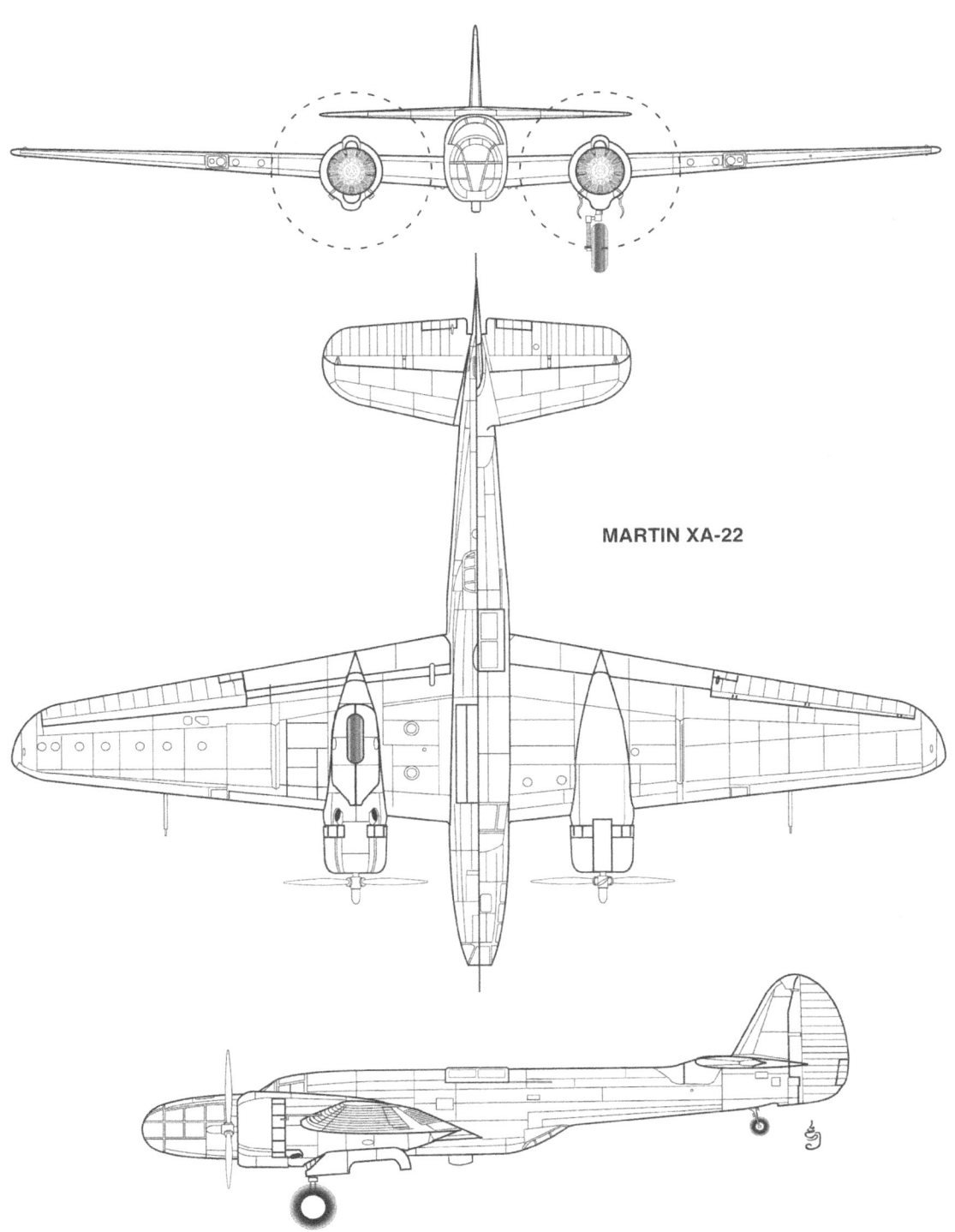

bay, the fuselage possessed a deeper profile between the nose and the trailing edge of the wing, producing a shape that resembled a trout. Landing gear was a conventional layout with main gear struts that retracted backward into the engine nacelles and a fixed tail wheel. Normal crew was three, pilot, bombardier, and gunner, and the comparatively light defensive armament of three flexible .30-caliber machine guns was typical of the era.

The Model 167 made its first flight in February 1939 and was delivered to Wright Field ahead of schedule, where it was subsequently purchased by the Army as the XA-22. Representatives of the French *Armée de l'Air*, with Europe by that time on the verge of war, took an interest in this plane as well as the Douglas 7B. When the Army cancelled the fly-off and announced its decision to order the A-20, Martin officials protested the abrupt change in procurement procedures; however, the company's complaint became superfluous when France ordered 115 aircraft as the Model 167F. When France fell to Germany, Great Britain took over the last 50 167Fs and purchased 225 more under two contracts 1940 and 1941. The Model 187, a project for an improved Army version to be designated the XA-23, was cancelled but later re-emerged as the A-30, which is reported in detail under a separate heading.

North American NA-40 1939

TECHNICAL SPECIFICATIONS (NA-40B)

Type: Five or four-place light bomber
Manufacturer: North American Aviation, Inc., Inglewood, California.
Total produced: 1
Power plant: Two 1,500-hp Wright R-2600-A71 *Twin Cyclone* 14-cylinder air-cooled engine driving three-bladed Curtiss Electric constant-speed propellers.
Armament: Four fixed .30-cal. machine guns in the wings (not installed), one ball-mounted .30-caliber machine gun in the nose, one flexible .30-caliber machine gun in a retractable dorsal turret, one flexible .30-caliber machine gun in the waist position, and up to 1,200-lbs. of bombs carried in an internal bomb bay.
Performance: Max. speed 309-mph at 14000 feet; 282-mph cruise; ceiling 25,000 ft.; combat range 600 mi.
Weights: 13,961-lbs. empty, 19,741-lbs. loaded.
Dimensions: Span 66 ft., length 48 ft. 3 in, wing area 598.5 sq. ft.

Though never receiving a military designation, the North American NA-40 still deserves mention here because of its role in the eventual development of the B-25 medium bomber. After an unsuccessful effort with its XB-21 bomber design of 1937, North American viewed the light bomber competition under Circular Proposal 38-385 as an opportunity to not only obtain a major Army contract, but as something that could also potentially result in significant international orders. Led by the design team of Lee Atwood and J. S. Smithson, the NA-40 emerged as the largest of the four competing designs. The aircraft's aerodynamic configuration was very advanced: a relatively thin wing utilizing several different NACA airfoil sections which was high shoulder-mounted to a very narrow, slab-sided fuselage. The NA-40's most prominent characteristics were its extensive nose glazing, low-riding tricycle landing gear stance, and twin-finned empennage. Provision was made for up to five crewmembers: a pilot and co-pilot under along greenhouse canopy, a bombardier-navigator in the nose position, plus a radio operator/gunner and another gunner in the waist. The flexible waist gun could be moved to the right or left sides or the belly to fire downward.

The NA-40 prototype, originally powered by 1,100-hp Pratt & Whitney R-1830 engines, made its flight in January 1939, but initial trials indicated that aircraft was underpowered (a top speed of 268-mph), and serious tail buffeting had been encountered at higher airspeeds. With a mere two months remaining on the Army deadline, North American's staff decided to remove the engines and replace them with Wright R-2600s of considerably more power. When the revised NA-40B arrived at Wright Field in mid–March, top speed had risen to 309-mph, which was marginally faster than the as yet undelivered Douglas 7B. Moreover, during early flight trials, Air Corps test pilots gave the type very favorable reviews. Then in early-April, before an Army serial number or designation could be applied, the NA-40B was utterly

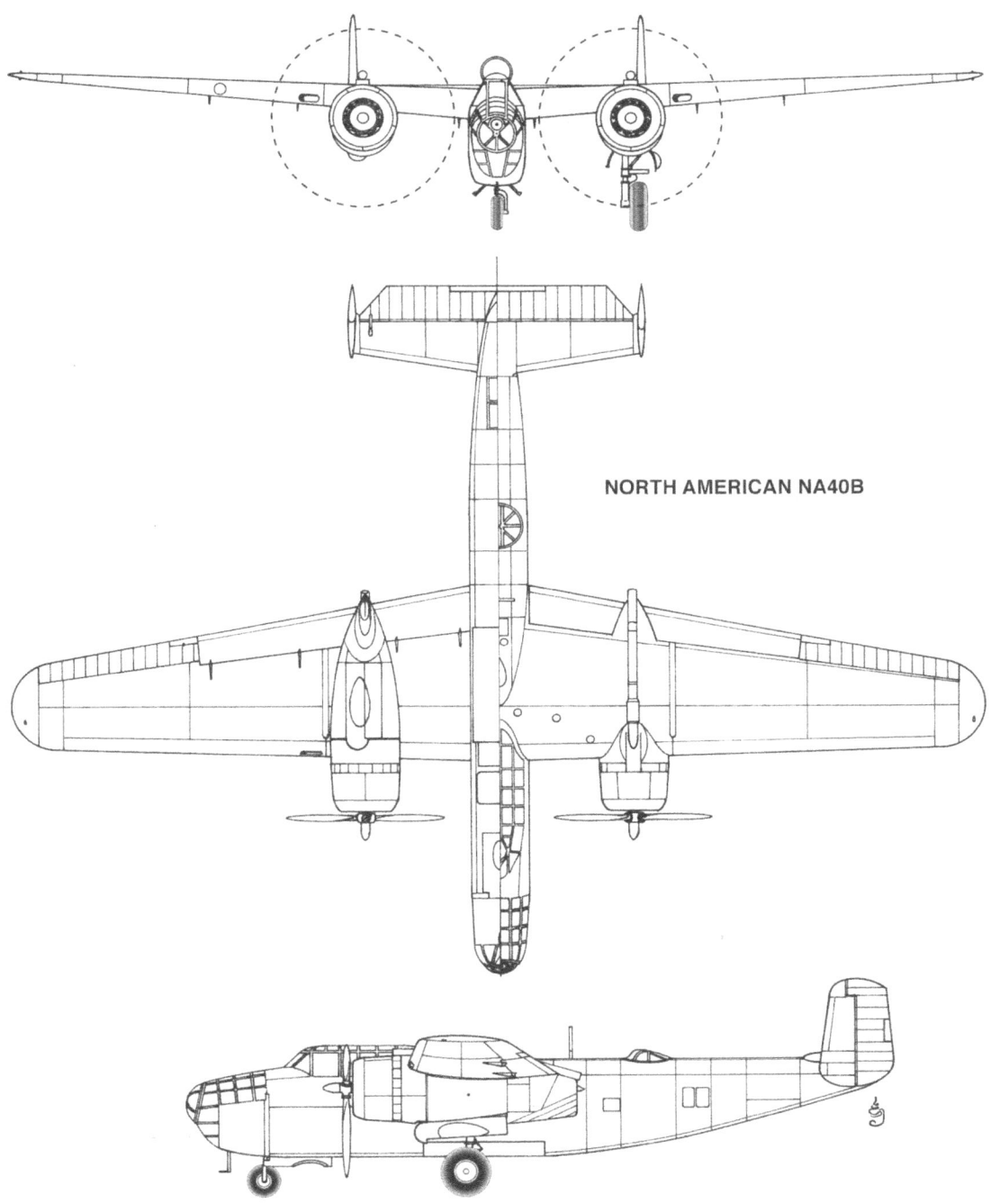

NORTH AMERICAN NA40B

destroyed in a simulated single engine landing that was attributed to pilot error. Although North American emerged from the competition with nothing—no airplane and no contract—Army officials encouraged the company to continue development for the recently announced medium bomber requirement under Circular Proposal 39-640; and in just a matter of months, Atwood and Smithson came up with the completely revised and enlarged NA-62, an aircraft that within a few years would immortalize itself as the B-25 *Mitchell*.

NA-40B with more powerful engines in spring of 1939. Although this aircraft was destroyed in 1939 before being assigned a military designation, North American was encouraged to continue development and it reemerged soon afterward as the B-25.

Douglas A-26 Invader 1942–1972

TECHNICAL SPECIFICATIONS (A-26B-60)
Type: Two or three-place light bomber
Manufacturer: Douglas Aircraft Co., El Segundo and Long Beach, California and Tulsa, Oklahoma.
Total produced: 2,451 (all versions)
Power plant: Two 2,350-hp Pratt & Whitney R-2800-79 18-cylinder air-cooled engines with water injection driving three-bladed Hamilton Standard constant-speed propellers.
Armament: Eight fixed forward-firing .50-cal. machine guns in the nose, six fixed forward-firing .50-cal. machine guns in the outer wing panels, four .50-cal. machine guns, two each in powered, remotely-controlled dorsal and ventral turrets, and up to 6,000-lbs. of ordnance bombs, 4,000-lbs. of bombs carried in an internal bomb bay and 2,000-lbs of bombs or rockets on underwing pylons.
Performance: Max. speed 355-mph at 15,000 feet, 284-mph cruise; ceiling 22,100 ft.; combat range 1,400 mi., maximum 3,200 mi.
Weights: 22,362-lbs. empty, 35,000-lbs. loaded.
Dimensions: Span 70 feet, length 50 ft. 8 in, wing area 540 sq. ft.

Regarded by many as the best propeller-driven light bomber ever produced, the Douglas A-26 began life in late 1940 as joint venture between Douglas Aircraft at El Segundo under the leadership of Edward Heinemann and the Air Corps' Experimental Engineering Section at Wright Field, Ohio. The objective of the study was far-reaching: to find a successor not only for the A-20, but one that would eventually replace the North American B-25 and the Martin B-26 as well, although none of these aircraft had actually entered service at the time. Using the A-20 as a starting point, Air Corps officials laid down a requirement for a design that, though still categorized as an attack/light-bomber, would nevertheless be larger, structurally stronger, faster, and more heavily armed. The requirement also specified a need for better crew interchangeability between the forward and waist sections plus the ability to takeoff and land within shorter distances to permit operations from forward bases. By early 1941 Heinemann and his chief engineer, Robert Donovan, had come up with a design that resembled the A-20 in general layout but introduced an entirely new mid-mounted wing featuring laminar-flow airfoil sections and electrically-powered double-slotted flaps. A twenty-five percent increase in power would come from a pair of 2,000-hp Pratt & Whitney

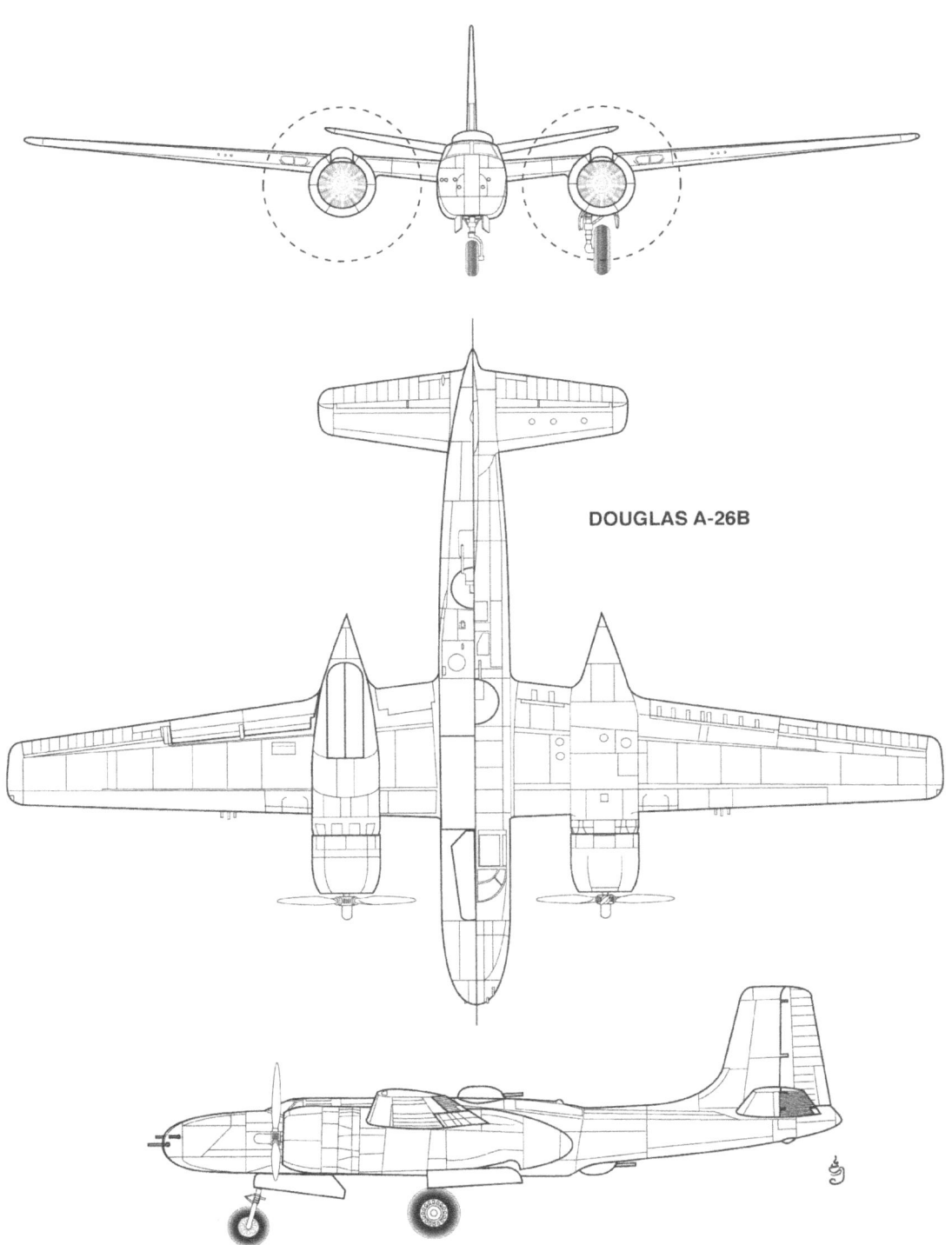

DOUGLAS A-26B

R-2800-27 engines. The internal bomb bay was larger and provision was made for an additional 2,000-lbs. of external ordnance to be carried on wing racks. Proposed defensive armament consisted of a highly innovative system of remote-controlled dorsal and ventral turrets, each containing two .50-caliber machine guns, operated via periscopic sights by a single gunner in the waist position. The XA-26, as proposed, would be built in two basic versions:

Top: Overhead of Block 10 A-26B, probably in mid–1944. This aircraft features the early "all-purpose" nose with one 37-mm cannon and four .50-caliber machine guns. *Bottom:* B-26C in all-black night intruder livery for Korean War. Note three antennas, two under the wings and one on the nose, for the SHORAN system. At night, bombs could be targeted on the intersecting radar signals.

One of 40 B-26Ks rebuilt by On-Mark Engineering between 1964 and 1965 for counterinsurgency missions in Vietnam. Note enlarged rudder and addition of tip tanks.

a three-place attack bomber with a glazed nose and a two-place night fighter with a solid nose.

Mockup inspections were completed in April 1941 and the following June the Army's Material Division awarded Douglas a contract to build two prototypes, one as the XA-26 attack bomber and the other as the XA-26A night fighter. Soon afterward, a change order added a third prototype, an XA-26B ground attack version with a solid nose that incorporated a 75-mm cannon. In late-October 1941, while the prototypes were still under construction, the government decided to initiate full-scale production, awarding Douglas a contract to manufacture 500 aircraft as the A-26. The three-place XA-26 made its first flight on July 10, 1942 followed shortly thereafter by the XA-26A night fighter. The radar-equipped XA-26A, despite achieving performance expectations, was not placed in production because the Army had in the intervening time selected the Northrop P-61 as its principal type of night fighter. Combat developments during 1942 prompted the Material Division to direct that the first 500 production aircraft be patterned on the solid-nosed XA-26B ground attack version, armed with a 75-mm cannon, to be accompanied by 200 interchangeable noses armed with six .50-caliber guns. Continued military testing of the XA-26 revealed that production models would require very few changes. General performance and handling qualities were rated as outstanding, and cooling problems encountered early on were soon remedied by modification of the engine cowlings and deletion of the spinners.

Production of the A-26B was seriously delayed, however, by shortages of tooling and personnel at Douglas' new Long Beach, California plant where the aircraft was to be manufactured, to the extent that the assembly line did not actually commence operations until July 1943. Despite delays, Douglas received a contract in March 1943 for a second batch of 500 A-26s to be manufactured concurrently at its new plant in Tulsa, Oklahoma. The first Long Beach production models, five A-26B-1s armed with a 75-mm cannon and two .50-caliber machine guns in the nose, were delivered in September 1943, followed shortly by 15 nearly identical A-25B-5s which arrived in natural metal finishes. Starting with the introduction of the all-purpose nose on the A-26B-10 in March 1944, differing variations in nose armament were evaluated, i.e., one 75-mm and one 37-mm cannon, two 37-mm cannons, one 37-mm cannon and two .50-caliber guns, and one 37-mm cannon and four .50-caliber guns. On the A-26B-15 nose armament could be augmented by eight .50-caliber guns mounted on wing racks in two-gun packages. As the pace of production gathered speed, nose armament on early B-models was standardized with six .50-caliber guns. Five of the early Long Beach aircraft were completed as A-26Cs with a glazed bombardier's position and two fixed .50-caliber guns in the nose. In late 1944 all A-26B production was allocated to the Long Beach plant and A-26Cs to Tulsa. A number of refinements were incorporated during production: a tail buffeting problem was eliminated by altering the shape of the upper turret; the oil cooler inlets on the wings were redesigned to improve air flow; and starting with the A-26B-30 production block, the flat-topped canopy was replaced with a raised, clamshell type that greatly improved cockpit visibility over the engines and to the rear. The A-26B-45 block brought a change to Ford-built R-2800-79 engines with water injection, raising available power to 2,350-hp, and in the A-26B-50, armament was increased to eight .50-caliber guns in the nose plus three .50-caliber guns permanently installed in each outer wing panel to keep the underwing racks accessible for bombs and rockets. Improvements seen on the -30, -45, and -50 blocks were later retrofitted to many earlier production models.

A third contract for 5,000 A-26s was awarded to Douglas in March 1944, however, approximately 1,000 had been completed by the time World War II ended, and the balance of the order was cancelled. Altogether, when A-26 production terminated in September 1945, 1,150 A-26Bs had been manufactured at Long Beach and a further 205 A-26Bs and 1,091 A-26Cs at Tulsa. The cancellation included the solid-nose A-26D and glazed nose A-26E, powered by Chevrolet-built R-2800-83 engines, both of which were scheduled to succeed the A-26B and C on the production lines. The sole XA-26F high-speed version was tested with R-2800-83 engines driving four-bladed propellers together with a 1,600-lbs.s/t J31 turbojet installed in the rear fuselage, however, even with a top speed of 435-mph, this variant was deemed to offer an insufficient improvement in performance over the A-26D to justify production. Improved variants were proposed in late 1945—a solid-nose A-26G and a glazed-nose A-26H having more powerful versions of the R-2800 engine, a new canopy and revised crew arrangement, plus droppable tip tanks—but never ordered. In June 1948, the recently established U.S. Air Force (USAF) dropped the 'A' for attack category and all A-26s remaining on hand were re-designated B-26. Some 30 B-26Cs modified to a reconnaissance configuration with the installation of electronic and photographic equipment received the designation RB-26C.

Following the outbreak of the Korean War in June 1950, many B-26Bs and Cs were drawn from storage and recalled from Air National Guard and reserve units to be made ready for active combat duties. B-26s intended for the night interdiction role were fitted with SHORAN (short range navigation) sets that homed-in on two radar signals set to intersect over the target. Later, from 1961 to 1963, 16 B-26s were pulled from storage, four configured as RB-26Bs and ten as B-26Bs, and returned to service for counter-insurgency operations in Vietnam; however, all were grounded in 1964 after two aircraft experienced wing failures attributed to structural fatigue. Even before this time, concerns over the age of the aircraft prompted the USAF to contract with On-Mark Engineering for the rebuilding and modification of the airframe as the B-26K *Counter-Invader*. On-Mark, a firm with extensive experience converting B-26s to executive configuration, completed the first YB-26K COIN (counter-insurgency) prototype in October 1962, followed in November 1963, by a contract to modify a further 40 aircraft, which were delivered to the USAF between June 1964 and April 1965. The rebuild involved not only a change to 2,500-hp R-2800-103W water-injected engines driving new fully-reversible propellers, but also the installation of steel straps on the tops and bottom of the wing spars, an enlargement of rudder area, new instrumentation and dual controls, a new avionics package, and de-icing equipment. Permanent 165-gallon tanks were added to the wing tips and the dorsal and ventral turrets were removed and faired over. Maximum bomb load rose to 12,000-lbs., including eight new wing pylons capable of carrying carry up to 8,000-lbs. of external stores. B-26Ks could be operated with an eight-gun solid nose for attack missions or, within a matter of hours, be converted to a glazed nose for reconnaissance tasks.

AAF service entry of the A-26 began in May 1944 when four early production A-26Bs joined the 13th Bombardment Squadron in the Southwest Pacific Theatre for combat trials. Early evaluations were not favorable: visibility from the cockpit was restricted and forward-firing armament was insufficient for low-level strafing. Deliveries to units of the 9th AF in Europe commenced in June 1944 and the type was first introduced to combat in September, participating in medium altitude bombing strikes with A-20Ks carrying bombardiers. During this interval AAF planners reached a decision to start reequipping European and Mediterranean Theatre units with the A-26 before sending more to the Pacific. As A-26Bs and Cs arrived, the 416th Bombardment Group, 9th AF was the first to fully convert, and by early 1945, the 409th, 386th, and 391st Bombardment Groups were reequipped with the type, and when the war ended in Europe, the 410th Bombardment Group was also in the process of conversion. In the Mediterranean, starting in early 1945, A-26Bs and Cs joined the 47th Bombardment Group, 12th AF and flew combat sorties alongside its A-20s during the last four months of the war. As block 30 A-26B/Cs with improved canopies became available, A-26s began reequipping the 3rd Bombardment Group, 5th AF in the Southwest Pacific during the summer of 1945 and commenced combat operations in July. The 319th Bombardment Group, 7th AF in the Central pacific was in the process of conversion when hostilities ended in August 1945.

In the immediate post-war period, as a result of massive military downsizing, the AAF (becoming the independent USAF in September 1947) determined that the A-26B/C would replace A-20s, B-25s, and Martin B-26s in all light and medium bombardment units, and from March 1946, remaining units of the 9th and 12th AF were absorbed into the new Tactical Air Command (TAC). However, as overall force size continued to diminish, most A-26s (later B-26s) were transferred in to USAF reserve and ANG units or placed in storage. B-26s served briefly with the 38th Bomb Wing (Light) in Europe during the early Cold War era, but after 1948, the 3rd Bombardment Wing (Light) based in Japan, maintaining a force of 26 B-26Bs and Cs, was the only frontline USAF unit still equipped with the type; another 46 RB-26Cs remained in service with various Tactical Reconnaissance Wings. One hundred forty-two B-26Cs were transferred to the Navy in 1948 where, under the designation JD-1, they were used as target tugs, and later, as the JD-1D, as drone controllers. When the Tri-Service Designation system was adopted in 1962, remaining Navy JD-1s and JD-1Ds became UB-26Js and DB-26Js, respectively.

When the Korean War began in 1950, 1,054 B-26s remained on the USAF inventory, though most were serving with reserve or ANG units or in storage. B-26B/Cs of the Japan-based 3rd BW were the first to see combat in late-June 1950, flying air strikes against North Korean targets. In October, they were joined by B-26s of the 452nd BW, a called-up USAF reserve unit from California. During the same timeframe, the 731st Bomb Squadron, 3rd BW, commenced the first B-26 night intruder operations over Korea. In the Korean combat theater most B-26B/C units were initially employed in conventional daylight strike and interdiction sorties, however, losses due to enemy antiaircraft fire caused a shift to night intruder tactics. Unarmed RB-26Cs of the 162nd (later 12th) Tactical Reconnaissance Squadron also flew night missions over Korea as airborne target directors. In mid–1952 the reactivated 17th BW replaced the 452nd BW, and with the 3rd BW, the two B-26 wings continued combat operations in Korea right up to the armistice in July 1953. Altogether, B-26s flew 60,096 combat sorties over Korea, mostly at night, being credited with the destruction of 38,500 enemy vehicles, 3,700 railways cars, 406 locomotives, and seven aircraft.

Following the Korean War, TAC continued to operate B-26B/Cs and RB-26Cs, but all had been withdrawn from active service by the end of 1956 except for a small number retained as liaison and staff transports. The remainder were transferred to reserve and ANG units or placed in storage. In 1961, as U.S. involvement in Southeast Asia began to escalate, four reactivated RB-26Bs were sent to Vietnam as part of Operation Farm Gate. Although these were ostensibly reconnaissance planes attached to the south Vietnamese Air Force, they were combat capable and flown by USAF aircrews. Organized as 1st Air Commando Squadron, ten B-26Bs and two more RB-26Bs arrived in Vietnam in early 1963 and were employed in counter-insurgency attack missions until withdrawn in early 1964. Totally remanufactured B-26Ks began to equip Air Commando units between June 1964 and April 1965 but none were sent overseas until the spring of 1966, when they deployed to Nakhon Phanom Air Base in Thailand. Because the Thai government did not technically permit "bombers" to be based in their country, the B-26K was re-designated A-26A. Most A-26A combat missions were flown at night along the Loation panhandle and border of North Vietnam in an area known as the Ho Chi Minh Trail, primarily to interdict trucks carrying enemy supplies into South Vietnam. They continued combat operations until November 1969, when they were replaced by AC-130A and AC-130E gunships. Remaining A-26As were returned to storage except for ten examples retained on operational status until 1973. The final VB-26B staff transport operated by the National Guard Bureau was retired in 1972.

From 1951 until the mid–1960s a number of ex-USAF B-26s were transferred to foreign air forces: 111 to France, where they were employed in combat operations in both Vietnam (1953–1954) and Algeria (1960–1962); 38 to Chile; 30 to Brazil, 19 to Columbia, 18 to Cuba (pre–Castro); nine to Saudi Arabia, eight to Peru; and six to Nicaragua. A few were supplied to Cuban Air Force pilots in exile during the Bay of Pigs incident in 1962 and B-26Ks were supplied to the Congolese/Zaire Air Force during the mid–1960s. An unspecified number of B-26Ks were operated covertly by the CIA, and one B-26B, possibly ex-French, is reported to have operated with the Biafran Air Force in 1967 and another served with the Indonesian Air Force until mid–1977.

North American A-27 1940–1942

TECHNICAL SPECIFICATIONS (A-27)

Type: Two-place ground attack
Manufacturer: North American Aviation, Inc., Inglewood, California.
Total produced: 10
Power plant: One 785-hp Wright R-1820-75 *Cyclone* 9-cylinder air-cooled engine driving a three-bladed Hamilton Standard constant-speed propeller.
Armament: Two synchronized, fixed forward-firing .30-cal. machine guns in the nose, one flexible .30-cal. machine gun in the rear cockpit, and up to 400-lbs. of bombs carried on external racks.
Performance: Max. speed 250-mph at 11,500 feet, cruise 220-mph; ceiling 28,000 ft.; range 575 mi. loaded, 800 mi. max.
Weights: 4,250-lbs. empty, 6,006-lbs. loaded.
Dimensions: Span 42 ft., length 29 ft., wing area 258 sq. ft.

North American, organized in 1934, made its start as a military contractor with basic and advanced trainer designs that ultimately produced the ubiquitous AT-6/SNJ series. Wright R-1820-powered attack derivatives of the NA-26 retractable-gear basic combat trainer (i.e., BC-1) were developed for the export market between 1937 and 1940 as the NA-44, -69, and -72. Ten Model NA-69s (which featured the improvements seen on the early AT-6) ordered by Thai-

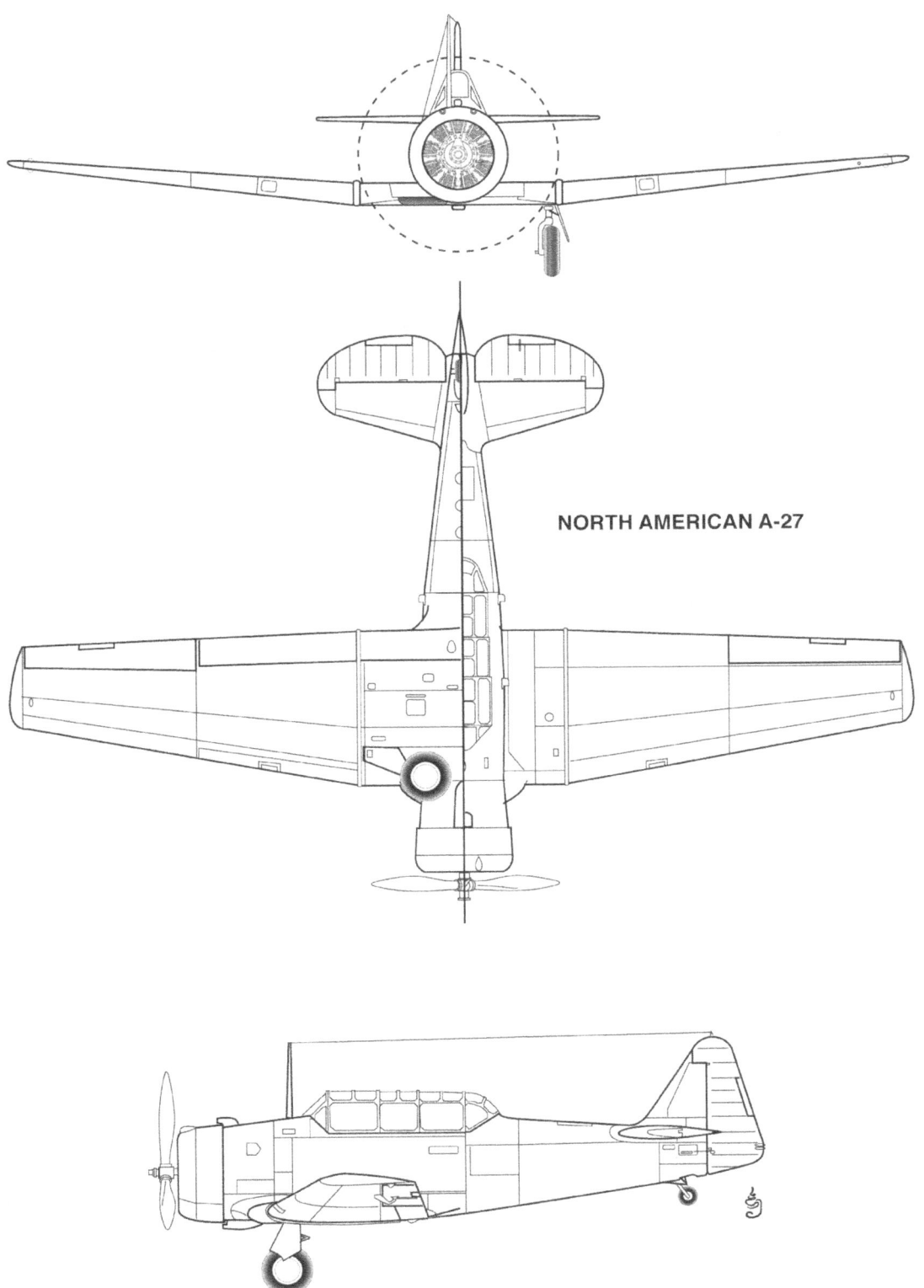

NORTH AMERICAN A-27

One of ten NA-69s originally sold to Thailand. These aircraft were intercepted in late 1940 while en route and subsequently placed in USAAC service in the Philippines as A-27s. Thirty similar aircraft were sold to Brazil.

land in 1939 and shipped in late 1940 were intercepted by the Army to prevent them from falling into Japanese hands. Eventually, in late 1941, they were taken into Army service in the Philippines under the designation A-27. Thirty very similar NA-72s were sold to Brazil in 1940.

Lockheed A-28, -29 1942–1945

TECHNICAL SPECIFICATIONS (A-29)

Type: Four-place light bomber
Manufacturer: Lockheed Aircraft Corp., Burbank, California.
Total produced: 2,942 (all versions, including exports)
Power plant: Two 1,200-hp Wright R-1820–87 *Cyclone* 9-cylinder air-cooled engines driving three-bladed Hamilton Standard constant-speed propellers.
Armament: Two fixed .30-cal. machine guns in nose, one flexible .50-caliber machine gun in a dorsal position, up to 1,400-lbs. of bombs (or depth charges) carried in an internal bomb bay.
Performance: Max. speed 253-mph at 15,000 feet, cruise 205-mph; ceiling 26,500 ft.; range 1,550 mi. loaded, 2,800 mi. max.
Weights: 12,825-lbs. empty, 20,500-lbs. loaded.
Dimensions: Span 65 ft. 6 in., length 44 ft. 4 in., wing area 551 sq. ft.

Lockheed originally developed a militarized version of the Model 14 transport in 1938, of which over 2,000 examples were either sold or Lend-Leased to Great Britain and British Commonwealth nations between 1938 and 1943 as the *Hudson I, II, II, IV, V,* and *VI*. When the Lend-Lease program was established in March 1941, the aircraft being supplied to Allied nations technically remained the property of the U.S. government under AAF assigned designations and serial numbers. Thus, the 1,302 *Hudsons* manufactured after that date became the A-28 and A-28A (*Hudson IVA, V,* and *VI*; R-1830 engines) and the A-29 and A-29A/B (*Hudson III*

First Series • 1926–1944

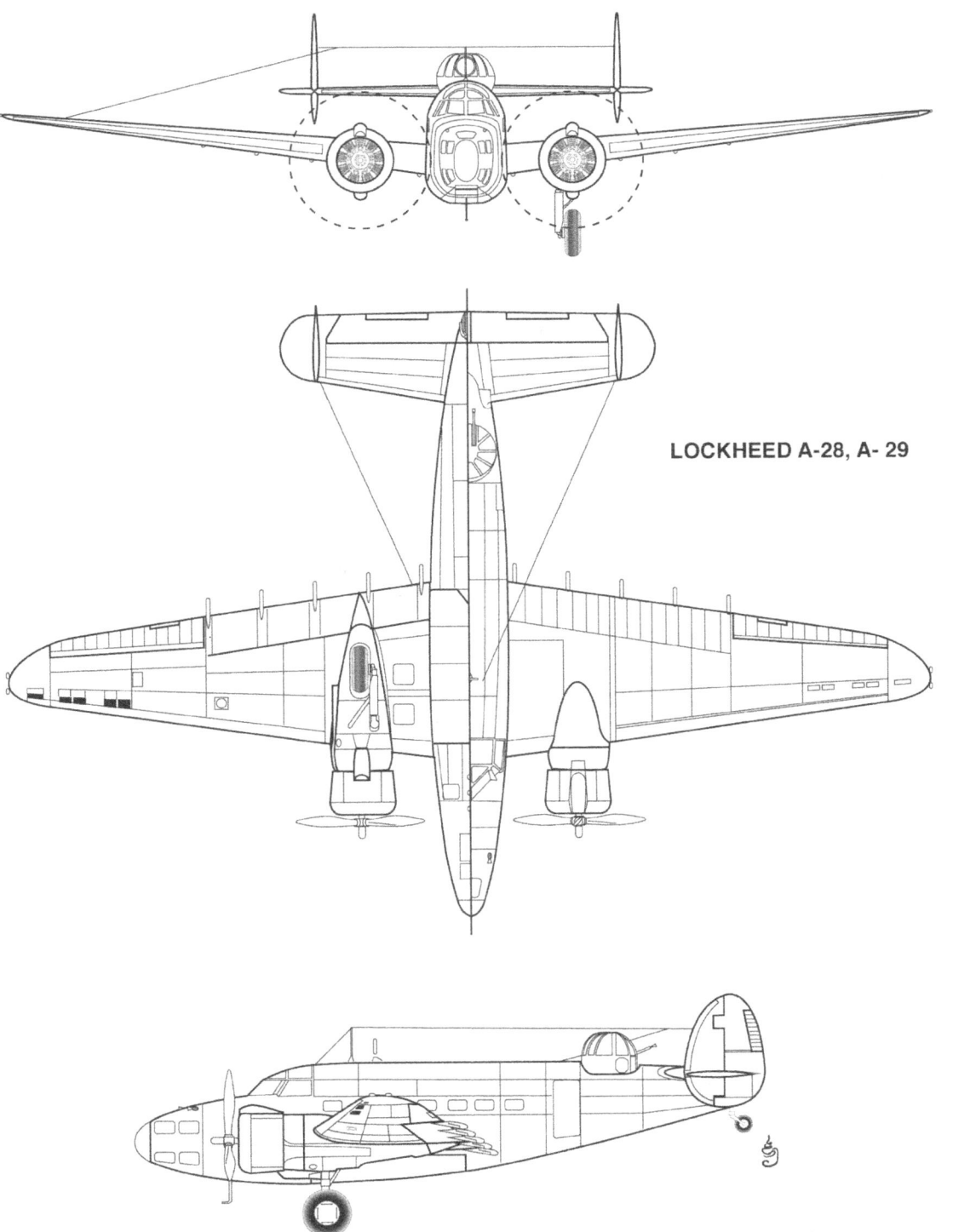

LOCKHEED A-28, A-29

One of 152 *Hudson IIIAs* commandeered by the USAAF in early 1942 and taken into service as the A-29. The example shown retains the RAF camouflage scheme and features a windscreen in front the opening normally occupied by the British-made turret.

and *IIIA*; R-1820 engines). The type finally entered service with U.S. forces in early 1942 when 20 A-29s were diverted to the Navy under the designation PBO-1. While assigned to VP-82 operating out of Argentia, Newfoundland in March 1942, PBO-1s attacked and sank the first two German U-Boats credited to the Navy. Soon afterward, three A-28As and 152 A-29s were redirected to the Army Air Force and subsequently assigned to the 13th, 30th, and 41st Bomb Groups to perform antisubmarine patrols off the American coast. Twenty-four A-29s later became A-29Bs when they were reequipped for photographic survey work.

In May 1942 Lockheed was given a direct Army contract for 300 A-29s that, with small modifications, were to be delivered as the AT-18 and AT-18A. The 217 AT-18s subsequently accepted by the AAF served as gunnery trainers equipped with Martin powered dorsal turrets having two .50-caliber machine guns and the 83 AT-18As were used as unarmed navigational trainers.

Martin A-30 1941–1944

TECHNICAL SPECIFICATIONS (A-30)

Type: Three-place light bomber
Manufacturer: Glenn L. Martin Co., Baltimore, Maryland.
Total produced: 1,575 (all versions, including exports)
Power plant: Two 1,600-hp Wright R-2600-19 *Twin-Cyclone* 14-cylinder air-cooled engines driving three-bladed Curtiss Electric fully-controllable propellers.
Armament: Four fixed .50-cal. machine guns in the nose, four fixed .30-caliber machine guns in the belly (at 9(down angle and 1.5(to the side), two .50-caliber machine guns in a powered dorsal turret, and up to 2,000-lbs. of bombs carried in an internal bomb bay.
Performance: Max. speed 305-mph at 11,500 feet, cruise 225-mph; ceiling 23,300 ft.; range 1,100 mi. loaded, 2,800 mi. max.
Weights: 15,460-lbs. empty, 22,600-lbs. loaded.
Dimensions: Span 61 ft. 4 in., length 48 ft. 6 in., wing area 538.5 sq. ft.

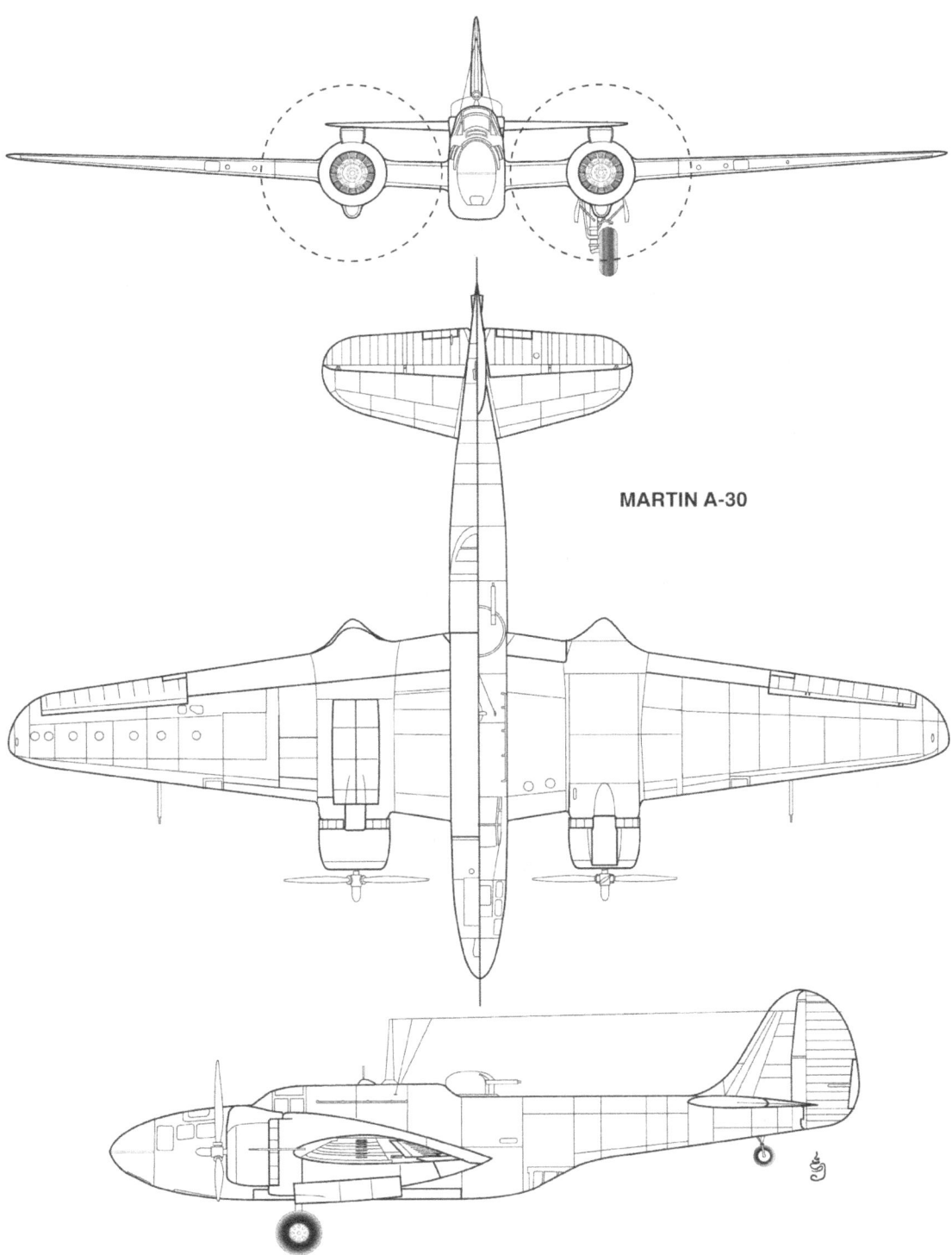

MARTIN A-30

Although the A-30 was the second most numerous aircraft type produced by Martin during the wartime era, only a few were obtained by the USAAF via reverse Lend-Lease and none were used in combat.

Following a pattern similar to the A-28 and A-29 reported above, the A-30 Army designation and corresponding serial numbers arose as a result of Lend-Lease requirements. When the Army cancelled Martin's proposed XA-23 project in early 1940, the analogous Model 187 was developed as a replacement for the Model 167 then in production for the French *Armée de l'Air*; however, after France fell to the Germans in June 1940, Great Britain indicated interest in the design and followed with an order for 400 aircraft that would be built to a somewhat revised specification as the Model 187B, with the first prototype flying in June 1941. One hundred forty-seven 187Bs were completed for the RAF by the end of 1941 as the *Baltimore I, II, and III*; and after the Lend-Lease requirements went into effect, the remaining 1,428 examples were delivered as the A-30 and A-30A. Although the aircraft has the distinction of having been the second most numerous aircraft produced by the Martin company during the war (the B-26 *Marauder* was first and the PBM *Mariner* was third), none were ever employed operationally by U.S. forces, and the few examples actually received by the AAF from the RAF under a reverse Lend-Lease arrangement were used only for transportation and utility duties.

Vultee A-31, -35 Vengeance 1941–1945

TECHNICAL SPECIFICATIONS (A-35B)

Type: Two-place dive-bomber
Manufacturer: Vultee Division of Consolidated-Vultee Aircraft Corp., Nashville, Tennessee; and Northrop Aircraft, Hawthorne, California.
Total produced: 1,931 (all versions, including exports)
Power plant: One 1,700-hp Wright R-2600-13 *Twin-Cyclone* 14-cylinder air-cooled engine driving a three-bladed Hamilton Standard constant-speed propeller.
Armament: Six fixed .50-cal. machine guns in the wing, one flexible .50-caliber machine gun in the rear cockpit, and up to 1,000-lbs. of bombs carried in an internal bomb bay plus 500-lbs. carried on wing racks.

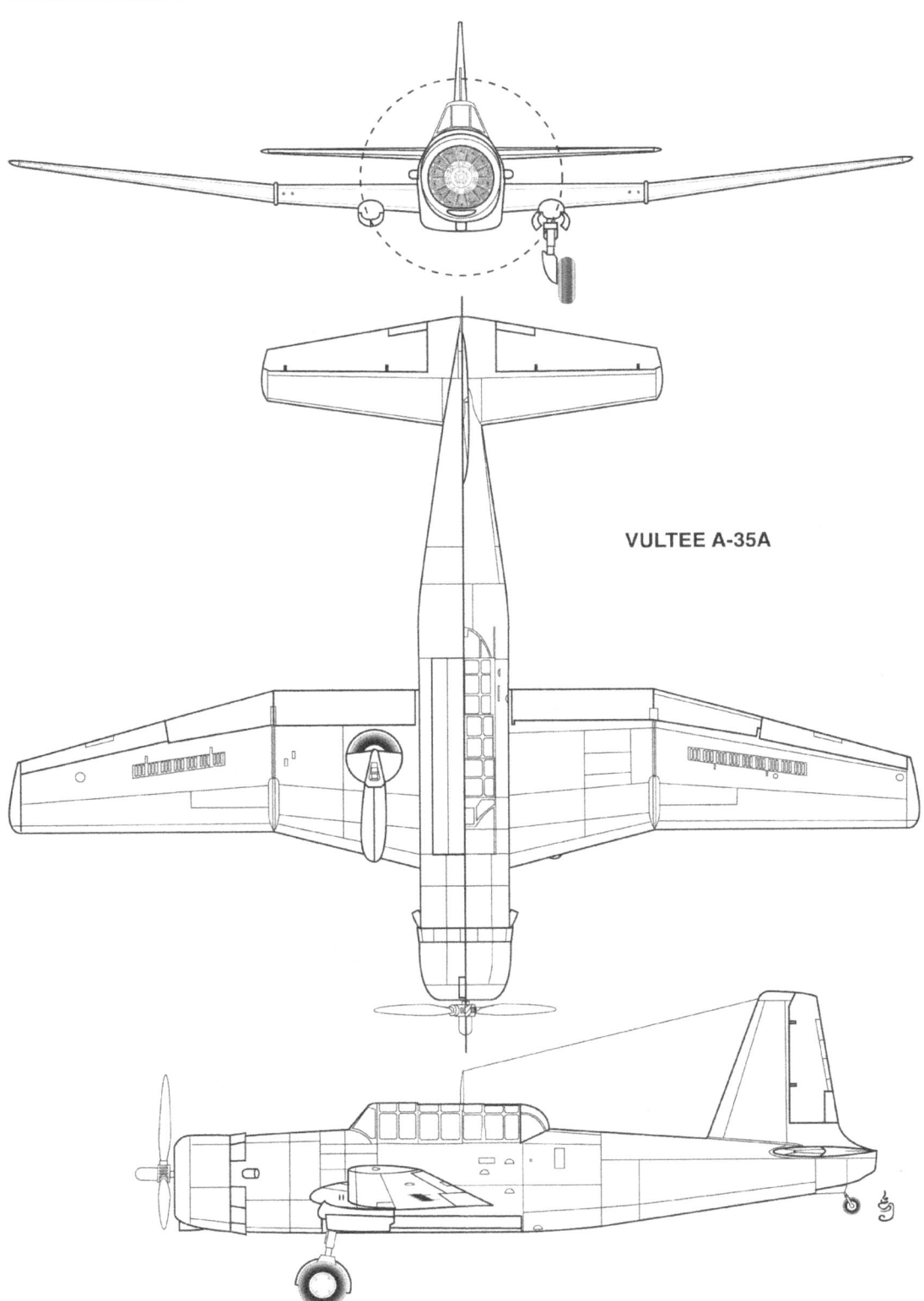

VULTEE A-35A

Top: One of the earliest USAAF A-31s intercepted from the British Lend-Lease order. As the *Vengeance I* and *II,* the type saw combat with the RAF on the Burma Front. *Bottom:* The A-35A, probably in early 1943. Although the type equipped operational USAAF dive-bombing groups in 1942 and 1943, they were replaced by A-36s and P-47s before deploying overseas for combat.

Performance: Max. speed 279-mph at 13,500 feet, cruise 230-mph; ceiling 22,300 ft.; range 550 mi. loaded, 2,300 mi. max.
Weights: 10,300-lbs. empty, 16,400-lbs. loaded.
Dimensions: Span 48 ft., length 39 ft. 9 in., wing area 332 sq. ft.

While dive-bombing had been an accepted tactic of the Navy and Marine Corps since the late 1920s, the Army did not adopt it until 1940. Army officials by that time had had the opportunity to observe the German *Luftwaffe's* skillful use, as part of its *Blitzkrieg* tactics in Spain and later in Poland and France, of specially configured dive-bombing aircraft such as the Junkers Ju 87 *Stuka*. At nearly the same time, in mid–1940, the British Purchasing Commission had ordered 700 American-designed, two-place dive-bombers listed as the Vultee Model V-72, of 500 were to be built by Vultee and another 200 under license by Northrop. The British specification called for an armament of four fixed .303 guns in the wing, two more flexibly mounted in the rear cockpit, and a bomb load of 1,500-lbs. Designed by Vultee's Richard Palmer, the V-72's most prominent feature was a wing center-section with substantial leading edge sweepback which merged into outer panels having sharply tapered trailing edges, producing a swept forward effect. Other noticeable characteristics were landing gear struts that retracted rearward into large clamshell-type fairings and the lattice-type dive brakes that extended from the outer wing panels. The first pre-production prototype flew in March 1941 under the factory name *Vengeance,* which was subsequently adopted by the RAF. In June 1941, 600 more *Vengeances* were added to the British order, which, due to the intervention of Lend-Lease, received the Army designation A-31.

During 1942, while delivery to the RAF was in progress, 122 of the British A-31s were commandeered by the Army and thereafter transferred to AAF service. The sole XA-31A was accepted by the AAF in June 1942 as an engine testbed and five more A-31s were modified as testbeds under the designation YA-31C. Following evaluations conducted in mid–1942, AAF test pilots recommended that the incidence angle of the wing be increased and future aircraft equipped according to AAF armament standards. Once these changes were incorporated, which included a shift to .50-caliber armament, the aircraft was re-designated A-35A. The A-35A was soon followed by the A-35B with increased horsepower and bomb load. Between September 1942 and June 1944, the AAF accepted delivery of 99 A-35As and 224 A-35Bs.

During 1942, the A-31s initially equipped three new AAF light bombardment groups that had been organized for dive-bombing operations, and in 1943, four more groups began receiving A-35As and Bs. By the end of 1943, however, while the operational training of dive-bombing groups was still underway, the Army decided that A-31s and A-35s would not be used in combat and instead the units would convert to single-seat aircraft, i.e., P-47 fighter-bombers or A-36 dive-bombers. Afterward, remaining A-31s and A-35s were withdrawn from frontline service and used for utility duties.

Of the 1,205 examples delivered to the RAF as the *Vengeance I, IA , II* (A-31), *III* (A-35A), and *IV* (A-35B), four squadrons were used on combat on the Burma front of the China-Burma-India theatre between March 1943 and June 1944. Three hundred forty-two *Vengeances* were transferred to the RAAF where they flew dive-bombing sorties against Japanese-held positions in the Southwest Pacific from June 1943 to March 1944. Once withdrawn from combat operations, RAF and RAAF *Vengeances* were used for target towing and utility duties. Twenty-nine ex-AAF A-35Bs were transferred to Brazil and an estimated 50 were given to the Free French in late 1943.

Brewster A-32 1943–1944

TECHNICAL SPECIFICATIONS (XA-32)

Type: Single-place dive-bomber
Manufacturer: Brewster Aeronautical Corp, Johnsville Division, Johnsville ,Pennsylvania.
Total produced: 2
Power plant: One 2,100-hp Pratt & Whitney R-2800-37 *Double-Wasp* 18-cylinder air-cooled engine driving Curtiss Electric four-bladed fully-reversible, constant-speed propeller.

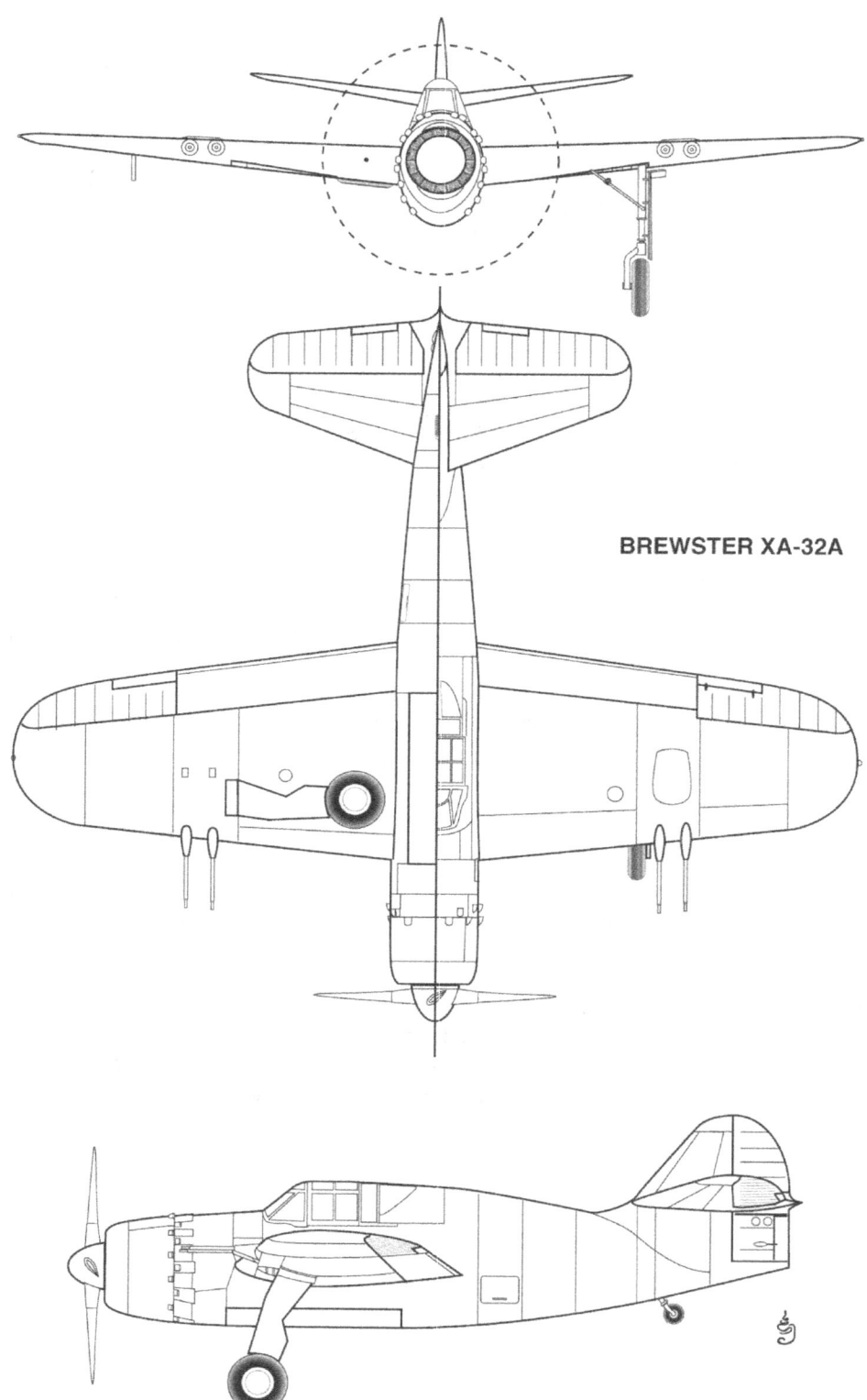

BREWSTER XA-32A

The XA-32 as it appeared in 1944, shortly before the project was terminated. The aircraft was originally envisioned as a single-seat dive-bomber that would eventually replace A-24s, A-25s, and A-31/35s in USAAF dive-bombing units.

Armament: Eight fixed .50-cal. machine guns in the wing and up to 1,000-lbs. of bombs carried in an internal bomb bay and 2,000-lbs on underwing racks.
Performance: Max. speed 311-mph at 13,200 feet, cruise 236-mph; ceiling 26,000 ft.; range 500 mi. loaded, 1,600 mi. max.
Weights: 11,820-lbs. empty, 15,512-lbs. loaded.
Dimensions: Span 45 ft. 1 in., length 40 ft. 7 in., wing area 425 sq. ft.

The XA-32 was the final offspring of the chronically mismanaged Brewster Aeronautical Corporation. Originating in response to a 1941 Army requirement for a single-seat dive-bomber, Brewster's initial XA-32 proposal was accepted in April 1941 and two prototypes were ordered the following October. One of the premises behind the single-seat dive-bomber concept was that a gunner would be unnecessary if the type were fast enough to evade fighter attacks. When the mockup was inspected in May 1942, Army officials viewed the XA-32 as a potential replacement for the two-seat types (i.e., A-24, A-25, and A-31/-35) that would initially equip the AAF's planned dive-bombing groups. The mid-wing planform and general aerodynamic characteristics of Brewster's design were similar to its SB2A two-seat Navy dive-bomber. The XA-32 prototype was originally scheduled to fly within a year of the order date, but slippages at Brewster delayed the first flight until May 22, 1943, by which time the North American A-36 was already entering service with the dive-bomber groups.

The XA-32's suitability trials conducted during 1943 revealed satisfactory handling qualities but performance, particularly in terms of speed and range, fell substantially below official expectations. Moreover, Brewster's difficulties in other areas rendered any production plans impractical. While being evaluated, the XA-32 was refitted and tested with four 20-mm cannons in place of four of the machine guns, and when the second prototype appeared, the XA-32A, it was armed with four 37-mm cannons. After completion of trials with the prototypes, development of the project was terminated.

North American A-36 (Apache, Invader) 1942–1944

TECHNICAL SPECIFICATIONS (A-36A)

Type: Single-place dive-bomber
Manufacturer: North American Aviation, Inc., Inglewood, California.
Total produced: 500
Power plant: One 1,323-hp Allison V-1710-87 12-cylinder V12 liquid-cooled engine driving a Hamilton Standard three-bladed constant-speed propeller.
Armament: Six fixed .50-cal. machine guns, two synchronized to fire through the nose and four in the wings, and up to 1,000-lbs. of bombs carried on wing racks.
Performance: Max. speed 366-mph (clean) at 5,000 feet, cruise 250-mph; ceiling 25,100 ft.; range 550 mi. loaded, 2,300 mi. max.
Weights: 6,610-lbs. empty, 8,370-lbs. loaded.
Dimensions: Span 37 ft., length 32 ft. 3 in., wing area 233 sq. ft.

The A-36, an Allison-powered attack derivative of the famed P-51, was not only the Army's last dive-bomber, but also the only AAF attack aircraft to be equipped with a liquid-cooled engine. Its origins can be traced to April 1940, when the British Purchasing Commission approached North American to license-build Curtiss H87As (P-40Es) for the RAF, and the company's President, J. H. "Dutch" Kindelberger, counter-offered with a proposal to build an entirely new design around the same Allison V-1710 powerplant. The NA-73, which made its first flight on October 26, 1940, was destined to become what many authorities consider to have been the best all-around piston-engine fighter of World War II. In May 1940 the British placed an order for 320 aircraft (later increased to 620) as the *Mustang I*, specifying armament of two .50-calibre machine guns in the nose plus two .50-caliber guns and four .30-caliber guns in the wings. When the U.S. government approved the sale to Britain, it specified that two of the aircraft be allocated to the Army as the XP-51, and the first example was flown to Wright Field in August 1941. In early 1942, to essentially the same requirement issued for the XA-32, the

A-36A is easily distinguishable from Allison-powered P-51s by its cheek guns and dive brakes. The type saw action in the Mediterranean and CBI theaters during 1943 and 1944. Last dive-bomber used by the USAAF.

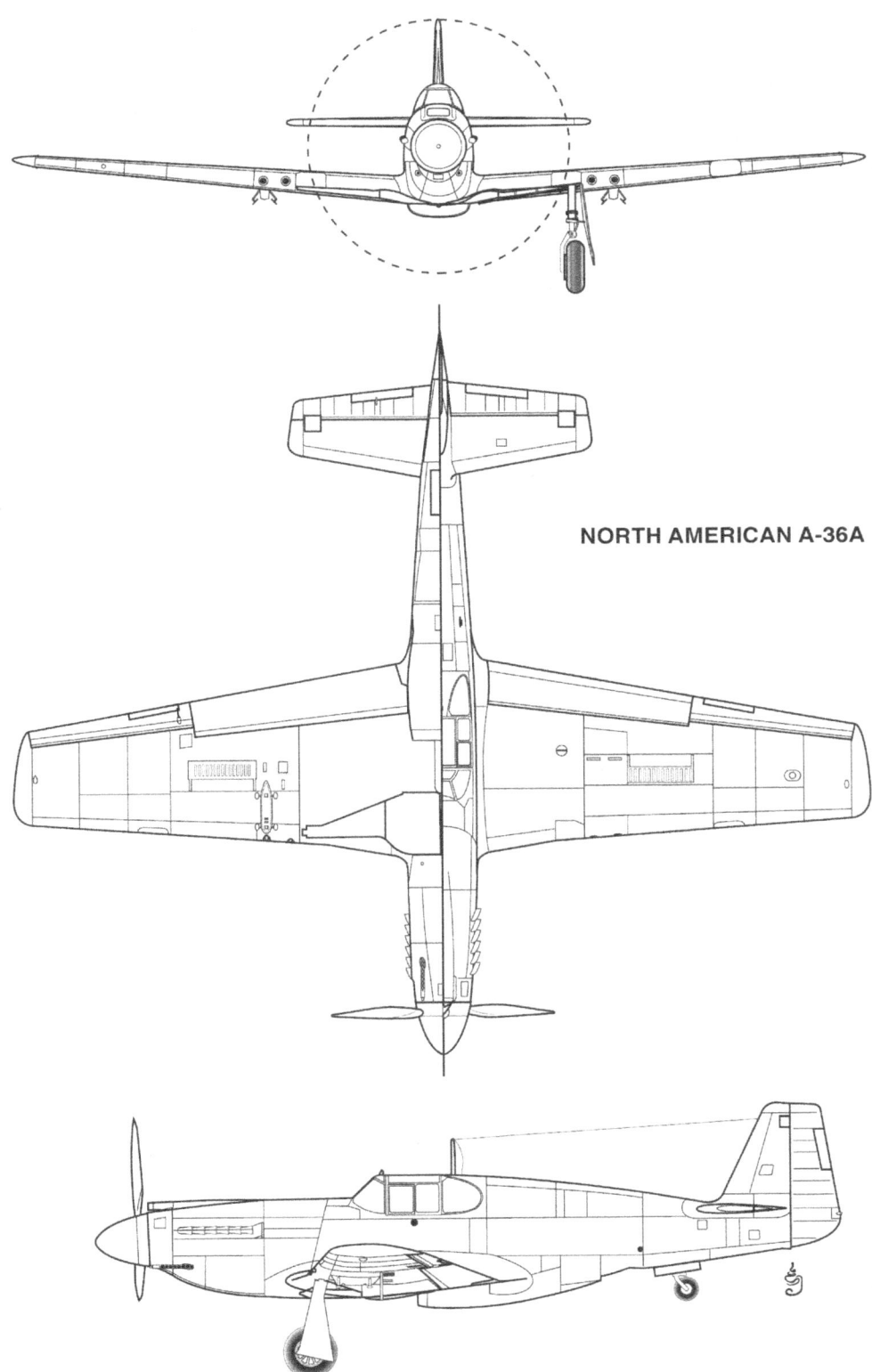

NORTH AMERICAN A-36A

Army directed North American to develop a dive-bombing variant of the P-51, and followed in April 1942 with an order to manufacture 500 aircraft as the A-36A. AAF service entry actually occurred in mid–1942 when 55 RAF *Mustang IAs*—armed with two 20-mm Hispano cannons mounted in each wing and powered by V-1710-81 engines—were diverted from a Lend-Lease contract and accepted under the designation P-51. The A-36A differed from the P-51/*Mustang 1A* in having machine gun armament rather than cannons, bomb shackles under the wings, the -87 engine, a revised radiator scoop, and most importantly, lattice-type dive brakes that extended from the upper and lower wings.

All of the 500 A-36As produced were delivered from October 1942 to March 1943. Because of its 390-mph dive speed even with the brakes deployed, there has been some debate over the A-36A's effectiveness as a dive-bombing platform. The type entered operational service with the 27th Fighter Bomber Group, 12th AF in April 1943 and flew its first combat sorties from Rasel Ma, French Morocco two months later as part of an aerial assault against the island of Pantelleria. As deliveries proceeded, A-36As also equipped the 86th FBG, 12th AF and the India-based 311th FBG, 10th AF. Before being replaced by P-47s during 1944, A-36As flew a total of 23,373 combat sorties in two theatres, delivering 8,014 tons of bombs on enemy targets and destroying 101 enemy aircraft (air and ground), against 177 aircraft lost to enemy action. When the A-36A went into service, attempts were made to name it *Apache* and later *Invader*, but reporters always called them *Mustangs*, and the names never stuck.

Hughes A-37 1943–1944

TECHNICAL SPECIFICATIONS (XA-37)
Type: Two or three-place light bomber
Manufacturer: Hughes Aircraft Co., Culver City, California.
Total produced: 1
Power plant: Two 2,000-hp Pratt & Whitney R-2800-49 *Double-Wasp* 18-cylinder air-cooled engines driving three-bladed Hamilton Standard constant-speed propellers.
Armament (proposed): None other than 2,200-lbs. of bombs carried in an internal bomb bay.
Performance: Max. speed 433-mph at 25,000 feet, cruise 274-mph; ceiling 36,000 ft.; range 1,000 mi. loaded, max. (unknown).
Weights: Empty (unknown), 31,670-lbs. loaded.
Dimensions: Span 60 ft., length (unknown), wing area 616 sq. ft.

Shrouded in mystery, the groundwork leading to development of the A-37 began in late 1939 when Howard Hughes made an unsolicited proposal to interest the Army in the development of twin-engine "pursuit type airplane." Hughes agreed to sell the engineering data for $50.00, provided that he be permitted build a prototype—at his own expense—with which he intended to establish a new around-the-world record. The Army's Material Division sent Hughes a $50.00 check in May 1940 with a request for more information on the proposed design and the approximate date the data would be delivered. With such government sanction, Hughes hoped to obtain experimental Pratt & Whitney XH-2400 24-cylinder engines to power the prototype, however, development of these powerplants was discontinued in late 1940. Known variously as the D-2, DX-2, XD-2, D-2A, and D-3 on Army records, the design was evolved as a twin boom planform with a central fuselage nacelle, to be constructed of "Duramold," a plastic bonded plywood molded under heat and pressure. Even after protracted contract negotiations over the prototype fell through in late 1941, the Material Division nevertheless made arrangements to supply Hughes with three R-2800 engines (two for installation plus one spare) in May 1942. Although negotiations between Hughes and the Army continued, including at one point, in mid–1942, the direct intervention of AAF chief Lt. Gen. H. H. Arnold, no firm contract was ever consummated, and the D-2 remained classified as a "hold project." Since the

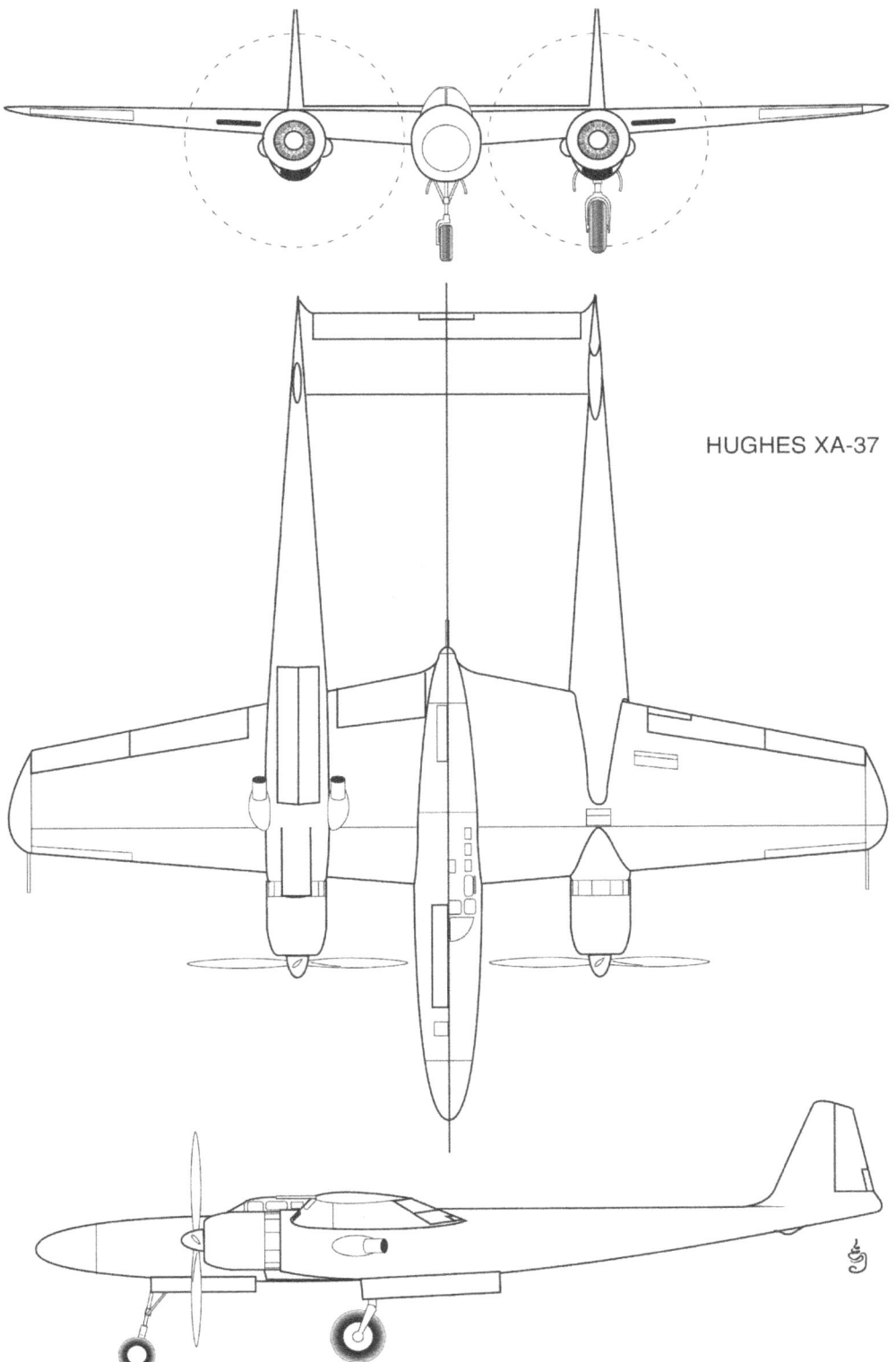

HUGHES XA-37

Only known photograph of XA-37 while under construction in Culver City. Howard Hughes is in the foreground on the right inspecting the accessory section of one of the plane's R-2800 engines. This aircraft was lost in a mysterious hangar fire.

aircraft was not being developed to any defined set of military specifications, it was initially carried on Army records as the XP-73 but had been changed to XA-37 by the time Hughes had the prototype under construction at his Culver City plant on the outskirts of Los Angeles.

The D-2/XA-37 prototype was completed during the spring of 1943 and made its first flight, with Howard Hughes at the controls, on June 20, 1943. The nine hours of flight-testing that followed revealed lateral (roll) instability problems serious enough to suggest a complete redesign of the prototype's laminar-flow wing. Besides the new wing, Hughes planned to enlarge the bomb bay area of the central nacelle, and once the changes had been incorporated, re-offer the prototype to the Army as the D-5. At this point Army officials perceived the XA-37 as the AAF's answer, potentially, to the RAF's de Havilland *Mosquito*, and asked Hughes to fly the D-2 prototype to Bolling Field (Washington, D.C.) for inspection. Hughes declined the request, inasmuch as the aircraft would be unsafe to fly until modifications were completed, then over a year later, in November 1944, before the D-5 modifications had been accomplished, the aircraft was mysteriously destroyed in a hangar fire attributed to a lightning strike. Hughes, by this time, had lost interest in the XA-37 and was hard at work on the larger, all-metal XF-11 high-speed reconnaissance aircraft, which shared its predecessor's twin-boom planform but little else. There are no photographs available of the completed D-2/XA-37 at the date of this writing.

Beech A-38 Grizzly 1944–1945

TECHNICAL SPECIFICATIONS (XA-38)

Type: Two or three-place ground attack
Manufacturer: Beech Aircraft Corp., Wichita, Kansas.
Total produced: 2
Power plant: Two 2,700-hp Wright R-3350-53 18-cylinder air-cooled engines driving three-bladed Aeroproducts constant-speed propellers.
Armament: One fixed 75-mm cannon in the nose, two fixed .50-caliber machine guns in the nose, two .50-caliber machine guns each in remote-controlled dorsal and ventral turrets, and up to 2,000-lbs. of bombs carried on underwing racks.
Performance: Max. speed 376-mph at 4,800 feet, cruise 344-mph; ceiling 27,800 ft.; range 1,070 mi. loaded, 1,960 mi. max.
Weights: 22,480-lbs. empty, 29,900-lbs. loaded.
Dimensions: Span 67 ft. 4 in., length 51 ft. 9 in., wing area 626 sq. ft.

Originating from a 1942 Army request to develop a twin-engine "bomber destroyer," the A-38 was the first combat aircraft to be designed and built by Beech Aircraft Corporation. While work was still in the preliminary stages, the Army changed the aircraft's mission to ground attack, specifically, one that was heavily armed enough to attack tanks, bunkers, and other hardened targets. In December 1942, after The Army accepted Beech's Model 28 proposal, the company received a contract to build two prototypes under the designation XA-38. Beech had originally selected the name *Destroyer* for the Model 38, but changed it to *Grizzly* after construction began. As it emerged, the low-wing, twinned-fin design of the XA-38 bore an outward resemblance to Beech's well-known Model 18 light transport and trainer series (i.e., C-45,

XA-38 prototype in 1944. Production plans were placed on hold because the B-29 program had priority on all R-3350 engines, and by the time engines were available, the war effort had wound down to the extent that no production was ordered.

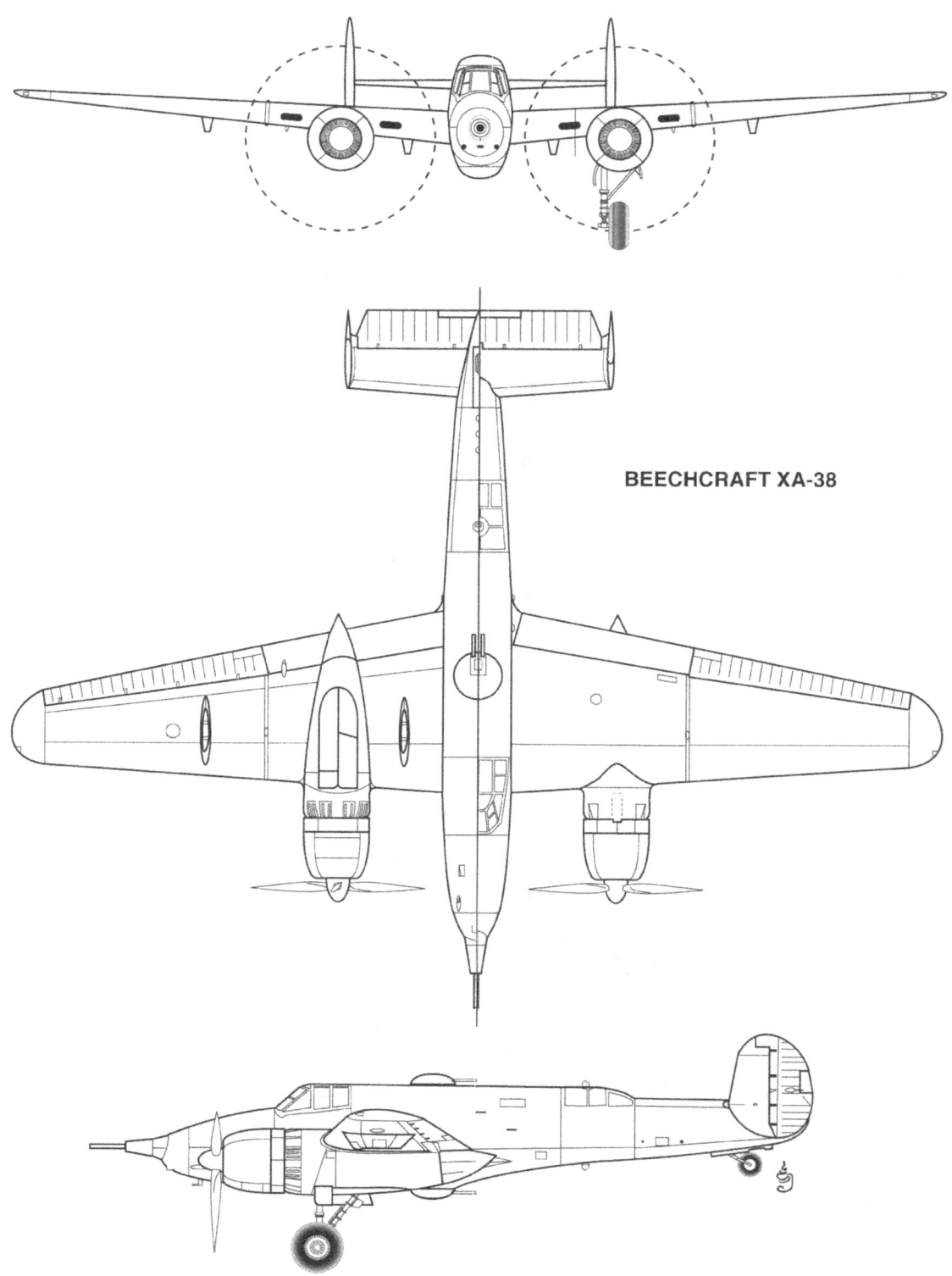

BEECHCRAFT XA-38

AT-7, AT-11, JRB, and SNB) but was in reality a completely original airframe. The defensive system of remote-controlled turrets operated by one gunner in the waist compartment was similar to that developed for the Douglas A-26. In order to keep the nose free for the planned armament, the XA-38 was designed with the tail wheel landing gear configuration of the Model 18. The long-barreled, high-velocity 75-mm cannon, which gave the aircraft its characteristic snout, possessed an automatic loader with a capacity of 20 rounds.

Completion of the prototypes was seriously delayed because of the unavailability of Wright R-3350 engines. When the first flight of the XA-38 prototype did finally take place on May 7, 1944, testing soon revealed very good overall performance combined with satisfactory handling qualities; and in gunnery trials, conducted during 1944 and 1945, the aircraft showed itself to be a very stable gun platform. Unfortunately, production plans were placed on hold due to the priority of supplying R-3350 engines to the B-29 program, and by the time engines did become available, in mid–1945, the war effort was winding down to the extent that production was never ordered.

Consolidated-Vultee A-41 1944–1945

TECHNICAL SPECIFICATIONS (XA-41)
Type: Single-place ground attack
Manufacturer: Consolidated-Vultee Corp., Nashville Division, Nashville, Tennessee.
Total produced: 1
Power plant: One 3,000-hp Pratt & Whitney R-4360-9 Wasp Major 28-cylinder air-cooled engine driving a Hamilton Standard four-bladed constant-speed propeller.
Armament: Four 37-mm M-9 cannons plus four fixed .50-cal. machine guns in the wings and up to 3,000-lbs. of bombs in an internal bomb bay plus 4,400-lbs. of ordnance on wing racks.
Performance: Max. speed 353-mph at 15,500 feet, cruise 270-mph; ceiling 27,000 ft.; range 950 mi. loaded, 2,000 mi. max. (est.).
Weights: 13,400-lbs. empty, 23,260-lbs. loaded.
Dimensions: Span 54 ft., length 44 ft. 8 in., wing area 540 sq. ft.

Starting life in late 1942 as the Vultee Model 90, the A-41 was originally conceived for the same dive-bombing requirement issued for the A-32 and A-36. Early on, Vultee chose to plan the design around the massive R-4360 engine, which itself was still in the development stages. The Army ordered two prototypes in November 1942 under the designation XA-41; however, in the spring of 1943, while construction was still in progress, the specification was revised to require an aircraft specifically designed to perform the low-level ground attack role. Other than a mid-wing planform and an internal bomb bay, the design of the XA-41, as it emerged, bore little likeness to its A-31/-35 *Vengeance* predecessor. The cockpit was located well forward to provide good visibility over the nose and the inward retracting landing gear was housed in wells flush with the bottom of the wing.

The XA-41 prototype flew for the first time on February 11, 1944, and in the service trials that followed, revealed very good performance for a single-engine aircraft of that size and mass. But by that time, the AAF had firmly settled into a routine of utilizing twin-engine types (e.g., A-20, A-26, B-25, B-26) in conjunction with single-engine fighter-bombers (e.g., mostly P-47s) to accomplish its tactical mission. Moreover, for low-level close air support, the .50-caliber machine gun armament of the fighter-bombers, due to its reliability and superior rate-of-fire, was favored over the heavier cannon armament seen on the XA-32 and XA-41. In any event, the XA-41 was not ordered and the second prototype cancelled prior to delivery. After the war, the XA-41 was sold to Pratt & Whitney where it was used as an R-4360 engine testbed until 1950. It was the last flying aircraft to receive the 'A' for attack designation until the classification was revived in the 1960s.

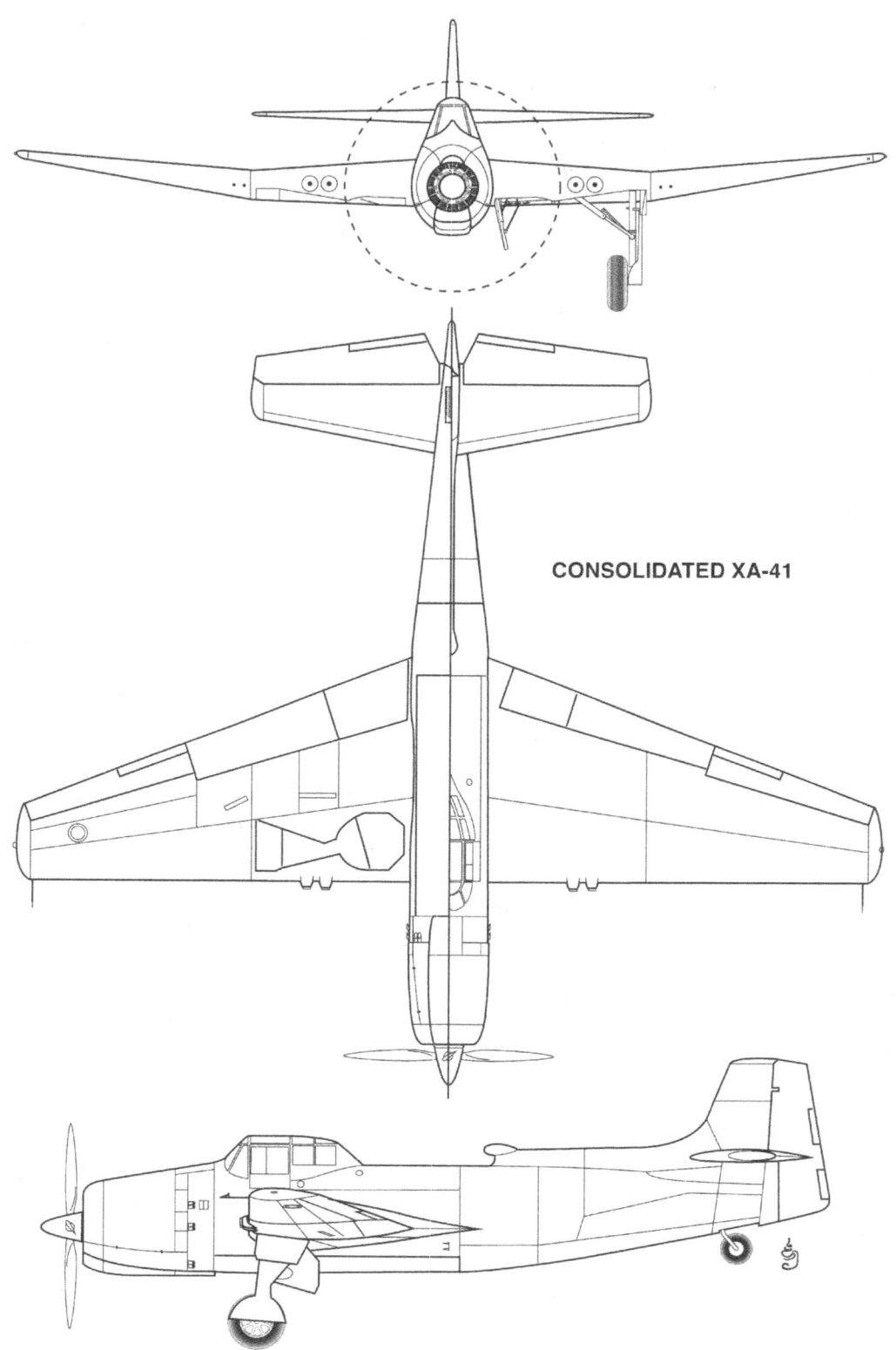

CONSOLIDATED XA-41

First Series • 1926–1944 71

Massive XA-41 conducting engine run-up during testing in 1944. Despite the good performance of the prototype, the USAAF had established a policy of using single-engine fighter-bombers and twin-engine bombers to perform the attack role.

Douglas B-23 Dragon 1939–1945

TECHNICAL SPECIFICATIONS (B-23)

Type: Six-place medium bomber
Manufacturer: Douglas Aircraft Co., Santa Monica, California.
Total produced: 38
Power plant: Two 1,600-hp Wright R-2600-3 *Twin-Cyclone* 14-cylinder air-cooled engines driving three-bladed Hamilton Standard constant-speed propellers.
Armament: One flexible .30-caliber machine gun in the nose, one flexible .30-caliber machine gun on a swing mount in the waist that could be positioned to fire right, left or upward, one flexible .30-caliber machine gun in a ventral hatch, one flexible .50-caliber machine gun in a in the tail, and up to 4,000-lbs. of bombs carried in an internal bomb bay.
Performance: Max. speed 282-mph at 12,000 feet, cruise 210-mph; ceiling 31,600 ft.; range 1,400 mi. loaded, 2,750 mi. max.
Weights: 19,059-lbs. empty, 26,500-lbs. loaded.
Dimensions: Span 92 ft., length 58 ft. 4 in., wing area 993 sq. ft.

    The B-23 was originally designed according to a long-range bomber requirement issued by the Army in 1938 with the objective of replacing the Douglas B-18. After the Douglas's XB-22 proposal was rejected (basically a B-18 refitted with *Twin-Cyclone* engines), the follow-on XB-23 represented an attempt to offer a redesigned and more streamlined fuselage which incorporated the newest ideas in defensive armament. Due to a projected top speed in excess of 280-mph, nose armament was deemed unnecessary, but to ward off stern attacks, the design introduced a glazed gunner's position in the extreme tail, the first American bomber to do so. One of the B-23's most noticeable features was an extremely tall vertical fin and rudder, which looked like it belonged to a much larger aircraft. After reviewing the proposal, the Army was sufficiently impressed to direct Douglas to complete the last 38 B-18As on the contract as B-23s. In mid–1939, when it became apparent the Army intended to acquire the Boeing B-17 as

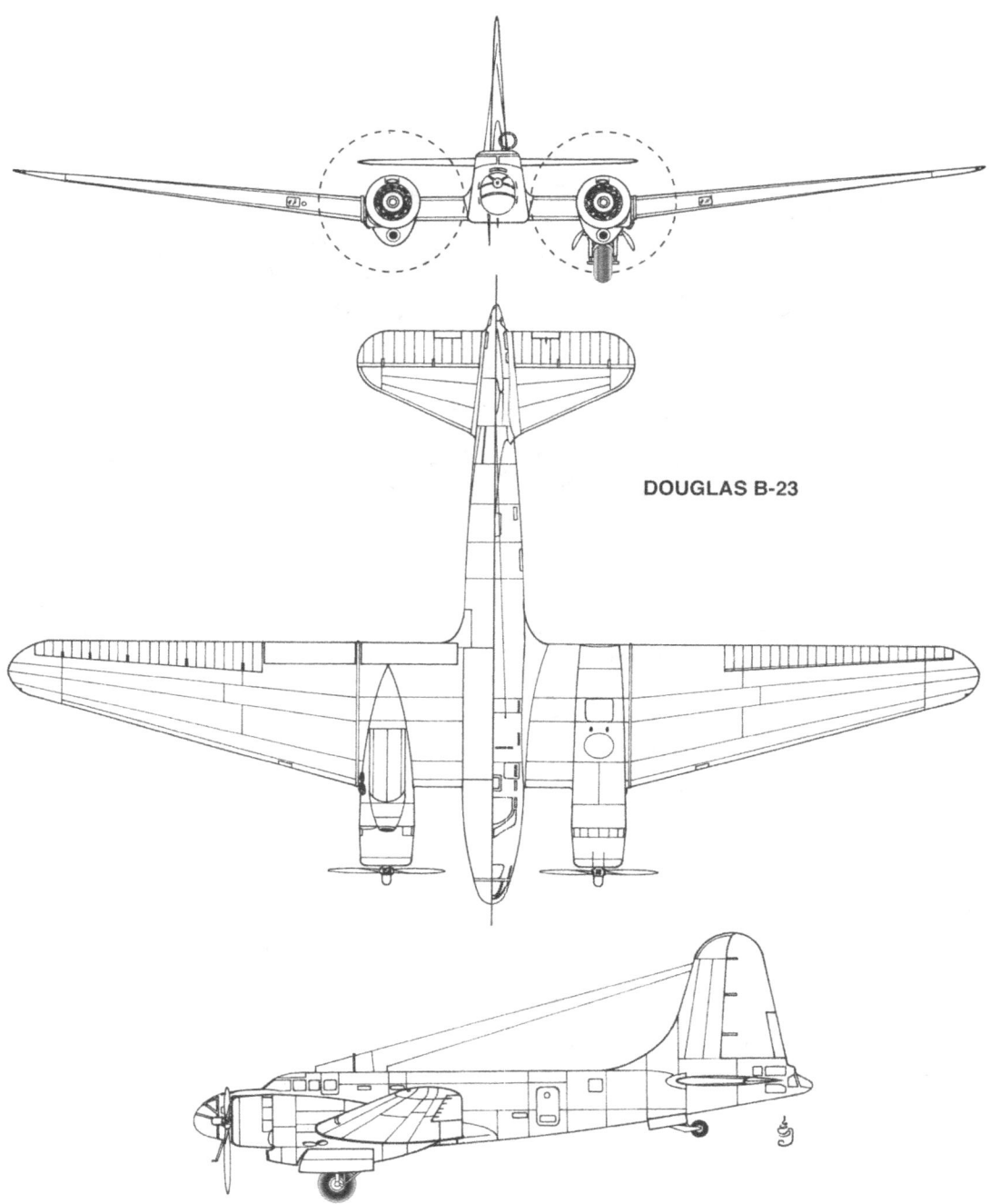

DOUGLAS B-23

its primary long-range bomber, Douglas re-submitted the B-23 as a contender in the medium bomber competition announced in March 1939 under Circular Proposal 39-640. The first B-23 (no experimental prototype) flew on July 27, 1939, while the other five medium bomber entries were still in the design phase. But the early arrival was of no advantage since the competition was to be based solely upon detailed design submissions that would be graded on a quality point system. In August 1939, after considering six proposals, the Material Division announced

Although a heavy bomber derivative of the B-18, the B-23 scored third in the USAAC's medium bomber competition. The example show is in pre-war markings, probably belonging to the 17th Bombardment Group at March Field.

the top three scores: Martin XB-26, 813.6 points; North American B-25, 673.6 points; and Douglas B-23, 610.3 points; the B-26 and B-25 were thereafter placed in production, the B-23 was not.

Following brief trials conducted at Wright Field, the first B-23 entered service with the 89th Reconnaissance Squadron based at March Field, California; the remaining 37, delivered between February and September of 1940, replaced the A-17As of the 17th Bomb Group, also at March Field. But the B-23's frontline service career was decidedly brief, being replaced by new B-25s delivered during the spring of 1941. None were ever used in combat and 19, stripped of armament, were converted to transports under the designation UC-67. A number of B-23s were subsequently used as engine testbeds and for other experimental purposes. After the war, many surplus UC-67s became civilian transports, a few of which were still said to be flying in the 1970s.

North American B-25 Mitchell 1940–1959

TECHNICAL SPECIFICATIONS (B-25J)

Type: Four to six-place medium bomber
Manufacturer: North American Aviation, Inc., Inglewood, California and Kansas City, Missouri.
Total produced: 9,816 (all versions)
Power plant: Two 1,700-hp Wright R-2600-29 *Twin-Cyclone* 14-cylinder air-cooled engines driving three-bladed Hamilton Standard constant-speed propellers.
Armament: One fixed and one flexible .50-caliber machine gun in the nose, two fixed .50-caliber machine guns on each side of the fuselage in blister packs, two .50-caliber machine guns in a dorsal powered turret, one flexible .50-caliber machine gun in right and left waist positions, two .50-caliber machine guns in a powered tail turret, and up to 4,000-lbs of bombs carried in an internal bomb bay.
Performance: Max. speed 293-mph at 13,850 feet, cruise 242-mph; ceiling 24,500 ft.; range 1,520 mi. loaded, 3,240 mi. max.
Weights: 19,490-lbs. empty, 27,560-lbs. loaded.
Dimensions: Span 67 ft. 7 in., length 53 ft. 6 in., wing area 610 sq. ft.

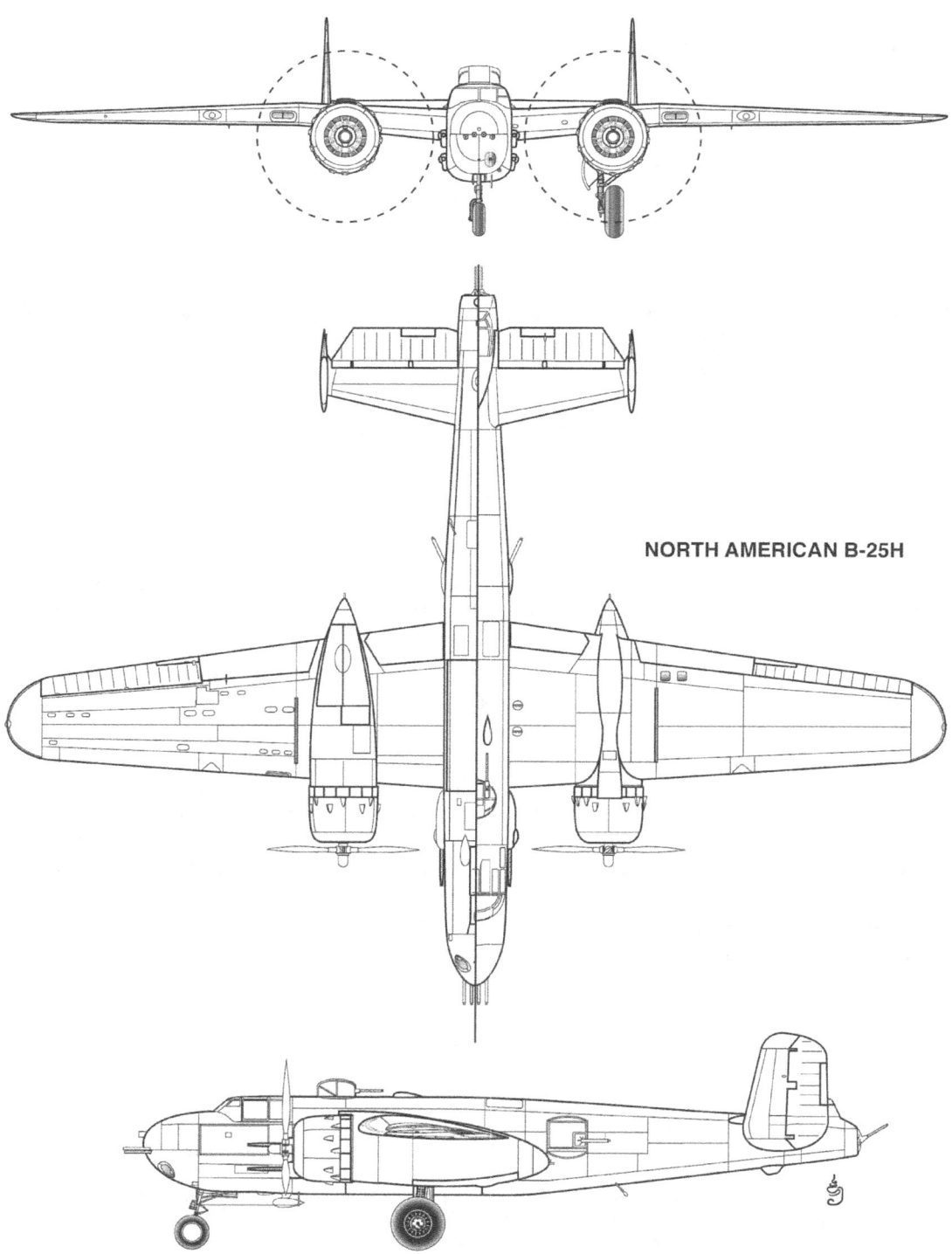

NORTH AMERICAN B-25H

The most produced and arguably the best American medium bomber of World War II, the origins of the B-25 *Mitchell* can be traced to the ill-fated NA-40 of 1939. Even before the light bomber competition concluded in June 1939 (see, A-20, above), the Army had reached the conclusion that, in order to build up to the planned Air Corps force levels authorized in late 1938 (5,500 aircraft vs. 1,600 on hand), it would be necessary to abandon the fly-off system and

First Series • 1926–1944

Top: **One of 120 B-25Bs, most of which equipped the 17th Bombardment Group at McChord Field. On April 18, 1942, sixteen B-25Bs from this unit launched from the deck of the U.S.S.** *Hornet* **and made the first U.S. attack on the Japanese home islands.** *Bottom:* **Late production B-25H in natural metal finish. B-25Hs primarily served with the 5th AF in the Pacific and the 10th AF and 14th AF in the CBI. Two hundred forty-eight were assigned to the USMC as the PBJ-1H.**

order new aircraft while they were still in the design stage, i.e., "off the drawing board." Circular Proposal 39-640, announced in March 1939, called for a 'medium bomber' with a top speed of 300-mph, capable of carrying a 3,000-lb. bomb load over a 1,500-mile combat radius. The proposal further specified a twin-engine aircraft to be powered by either Wright R-2600, Pratt & Whitney R-2800, or Wright R-3350 engines, the latter two of which were still under

Early production glazed-nose B-25J over the U.S., probably in early 1944. A total of 4,318 Js were completed before production was terminated. With armament removed, the type remained in service after World War II as the USAF's standard multi-engine trainer.

development. The winning entry (or entries) would be selected according to detailed design submissions due within 6 months, and deliveries of production models were expected to commence within 24 months of the contract date. Proceeding from the aerodynamic concept of the NA-40, the North American team led by Lee Atwood evolved a larger and heavier design under the company designation NA-62. The fuselage was significantly widened to accommodate a larger bomb bay, resulting in a side-by-side cockpit enclosure flush with the top of the fuselage. While the tricycle landing gear and twin fin arrangement of the NA-40 was retained, the high shoulder aspect of the wings was lowered to the mid-fuselage level and the engine nacelle fairings were extended past the trailing edges of the wings to fully house the wheels. To power the NA-62, Atwood's team selected the readily available Wright R-2600 powerplants.

In August 1939, after all six submissions had been graded by the Material Division, the NA-62 was awarded second place; however, when Martin, the winner, informed the military authorities that it could only fulfill 201 of the 385-plane requirement within the expected timeframe, the Army gave North American a contract to produce 184 NA-62s under the designation B-25. The first B-25 (technically a production model) was rolled out for its maiden flight on August 19, 1940 and delivered to Wright Field in February 1941 for acceptance trials. At the suggestion of Lee Atwood, the plane received the company name *Mitchell*, in honor of the late Brig. Gen. Billy Mitchell. Early testing revealed some directional instability and a dynamic resistance to flat, rudder turns, which were essential to making small course corrections during a bomb run. Both problems were cured by removing all dihedral from the outer wing panels—which gave the B-25 its characteristic gull-like appearance from the front—and increasing fin area to a more squared-off shape. Trials were highly successful: a top speed of 315-mph and a range of 1,400-miles with a 3,000-lb. payload, plus very docile handling qualities. The first B-25 production models were lightly armed, carrying only four flexible machine guns, one .30-caliber in the nose, waist, and dorsal positions and one .50-caliber fired from a prone position in the tail; the next 40, produced as the B-25A, introduced armor plating for the crew and self-sealing tanks; and the remaining 120, produced as the B-25B, deleted the tail gun and featured powered Bendix dorsal and ventral turrets, each armed with two .50-caliber guns. The dorsal turret was manned while the ventral guns were aimed remotely via a periscope; however, the periscopic sighting system was deemed ineffective, frequently causing the gunner to suffer nausea and vertigo, so that the ventral turrets were removed from existing B-25Bs and eventually deleted on future production models.

The first large order came soon after the first flight, a contract for 1,025 B-25Cs (including 162 allocated to the Dutch East Indies) in September 1940, which were identical to the later Bs except for R-2600-13 engines and small internal improvements. In June 1941 the Army ordered 1,200 identical B-25Ds, the majority of which were to be manufactured at North American's new plant in Kansas City. During production, B-25Cs and Ds were given increased fuel capacity and external wing racks that could carry an additional 2,000-lbs of bombs; defensive armament was brought up to five flexible .50-caliber guns plus a fixed .50 caliber gun in the nose glazing. The B-25C production run was subsequently increased by 1,000 aircraft, the last of 1,619 examples being completed in May 1943. Similarly, B-25D production was increased by 1,090 and continued until March 1944. Later block Ds differed from Cs in having improved winterization, individual exhaust stacks in place of a collector ring, more armor protection, and one additional fixed .50-caliber gun in the nose. The XB-25E and XB-25F were both B-25Cs modified in early 1944 to conduct experiments with anti-icing equipment. Starting in early 1943, many B-25Cs and Ds were field modified as "strafers" under the supervision of Maj. Paul I. "Pappy" Gunn with the 5th AF in Australia, and with some variations, similar modifications were later accomplished on B-25C/Ds serving with the 12th AF in the Mediterranean and the 10th AF in India. The modification generally involved the installation of four fixed .50-caliber guns in the bombardier's compartment plus four more .50-caliber guns in two-gun blister packs on either side of the fuselage. Eleven B-25Ds stripped of armament and fitted with photographic equipment went into AAF service as the F-10. Development of the solid-nose B-25G began in mid–1942 specifically for low-level anti-shipping strikes in the Pacific theatre. It was essentially a B-25C airframe having a nose shorted by two feet that housed a 75-mm M4 cannon and two fixed .50-caliber machine guns. After modifying five aircraft to G standard, Material Division instructed North American to complete the last 400 B-25Cs as B-25Gs, and all had been delivered by August 1943. B-25Gs were likewise field modified by the 5th AF to include two more .50-caliber guns in the nose plus four in blister packs on the fuselage.

With initial development beginning during 1942, the solid-nose B-25H represented major changes to the type's airframe, armament, and equipment. Significantly, the co-pilot's position was deleted and replaced by a new navigator's crew station; staggered, bay-window type waist positions, each having a flexible 50-caliber gun, were added behind the wing; the rear fuselage was deepened and the tailplane raised seven inches to accommodate a powered, twin. 50-caliber tail turret which housed the gunner under a clear canopy; and to maintain c.g. limits, the powered dorsal turret was moved up to a new location even with the leading edge of the wing. Standard forward-firing armament on the H was a lighter T13E 75-mm cannon and four .50 caliber machine guns in the nose, augmented by two .50-caliber guns in fuselage blister packs (increased to four starting with Block-5). One thousand B-25Hs were ordered in August 1942, initial deliveries commencing in July 1943, and all production had been completed by July 1944. The B-25J was the final and most numerous version of the *Mitchell*, 4,318 examples having been completed at the Kansas City plant when production ceased in August 1945. The Js reverted back to the glazed nose of the B-25C/D, and restored the co-pilot's position, while retaining the other improvements of the H. Standard crew was six: pilot, co-pilot, navigator-bombardier/gunner, engineer/turret gunner, radio operator/waist gunner, and tail gunner. Deliveries commenced in mid–1944, and starting with Block 11, the glazed nosed could be replaced with a sold nose housing eight .50-caliber machine guns, which, when combined with the blister guns and upper turret, brought forward firing armament to fourteen guns total, the most carried by any Allied attack aircraft. Many changes were introduced during the production run to improve the braking system, internal heating, armor protection, fire-control and gun-sighting equipment, and external weapons capability, such as HVAR rockets, glide bombs, and aerial mines. The company-funded NA-98X, a modified B-25H airframe, never received a military designation. In early 1944 North American attempted to create an alternative to the Douglas A-26 by offering a more streamlined B-25 fitted with R-2800 engines. The first flight occurred in March 1944, and although testing revealed a 50-mph increase in top speed and twice the rate-of-climb of the B-25H, there were immediate concerns about the excessive aerodynamic loads being placed on the aircraft. When the sole prototype was destroyed only a month later in a crash caused by catastrophic failure of the outer wing panels, the project was abandoned.

The first B-25s entered Air Corps service with the 17th BG based at McChord Field, Washington in the spring of 1941. This unit would more than any other bring the B-25 to combat-ready status and later made up the crews of the sixteen B-25Bs which launched from the deck of the U.S.S. *Hornet* on April 18, 1942 in the famous Tokyo raid led by Lt. Col. James H. Doolittle. Twenty-three B-25Bs received by the RAF as the *Mitchell I* were used only for crew training. As production stepped-up in 1942, new B-25C/D groups were formed in the Australia-based 5th AF, the India and China-based 10th AF, the North Africa-based 12th AF, and the Aleutian-based 11th AF. A further 538 B-25C/Ds were assigned to Britain under Lend-Lease and taken into RAF service as the *Mitchell II*, and 26 more were transferred to Brazil. Most production B-25Gs served with 5th AF groups in the Pacific, and as B-25H deliveries proceeded, they were primarily allotted to the 5th AF, the 10th AF, and the China-based 14th AF, and during 1944, B-25Js, many of which were subsequently converted to solid gun noses, replaced older B-25s in all theaters. By the end of 1944, the AAF was operating to total of eleven B-25 groups overseas. Under Lend-Lease, 314 B-25Js were received by Britain as the *Mitchell III* and saw combat as part of the RAF's 2nd Tactical Air Force in Europe. From 1943 to 1945, a total of 706 B-25s were either transferred or delivered new to the Navy under the designation PBJ: 50 B-25Cs (PBJ-1C), 152 B-25Ds (PBJ-1D), one B-25G (PBJ-1G), 248 B-25Hs (PBJ-1H), and 255 B-25Js (PBJ-1J). Most PBJs were assigned to the Marine Corps, where, starting with VMB-413, they were used as land-based bombers in the southwest and central Pacific areas. Altogether, seven Marine PBJ squadrons saw action in the Pacific combat theater and five more became operational too late to deploy overseas. Arresting gear was experimentally installed on one PBJ-1H and carrier trials were successfully completed aboard the U.S.S. *Shangri-La* in late-1944, however, continued development of the carried-based PBJ program was deemed unnecessary after the U.S. captured bases close to the Japanese home islands.

Although the B-25's active combat career ended shortly after World War II, with virtually all B-25Cs, Ds, and Hs being sold for scrap, many B-25Js survived to become active in the post-war AAF/USAF. A large number, stripped of their combat equipment, were re-designated TB-25Js and widely used in the training role; others became staff transports as the VB-25J. Many B-25Js received specialized trainer modifications: 117 became TB-25Ks when they were converted to train crews for the E-1 fire-control system, which involved fitting a radome to the front of the glazed nose; 75 were re-designated TB-25Ls after being completely rebuilt as advanced multi-engine trainers; 25 became TB-25Ms when modified for the E-5 fire-control system; and 380 were rebuilt as TB-25N advanced trainers. Between 1952 and 1954 virtually all active service USAF TB/VB-25s underwent a refurbishment program where they received R-2600-29 or -35 engines and were equipped with new avionics, autopilots, bomb bay fuel tanks, and demand oxygen systems. Many TB-25s were transferred to ANG units during the 1950s and the final example was stricken from the USAF inventory in 1959.

Martin B-26 Marauder 1940–1945

TECHNICAL SPECIFICATIONS (B-26B [BLOCKS10–55])
Type: Five or six-place medium bomber
Manufacturer: Glenn L. Martin Co., Baltimore, Maryland and Omaha, Nebraska.
Total produced: 5,157 (all versions)
Power plant: Two 1,920-hp Pratt & Whitney R-2800-43 *Double-Wasp* 18-cylinder air-cooled engines driving four-bladed Curtiss electric fully-controllable propellers.
Armament: One fixed and one flexible .50-caliber machine gun in the nose, two fixed .50-caliber machine guns on each side of the fuselage in blister packs, two .50-caliber machine guns in a powered dorsal turret, one flexible .50-caliber machine gun in right and left waist positions, two .50-caliber machine guns in a powered tail turret, and up to 4,000-lbs of bombs carried in an internal bomb bay.
Performance: Max. speed 282-mph at 15,000 feet, cruise 214-mph; ceiling 21,700 ft.; range 1,150 mi. loaded, 2,600 mi. max.
Weights: 24,000-lbs. empty, 37,000-lbs. loaded.
Dimensions: Span 71 ft. 7 in., length 58 ft. 3 in., wing area 658 sq. ft.

Though not as well regarded as its B-25 stablemate, the Martin B-26 nonetheless flew more missions, destroyed more targets, with fewer losses, than any other type of bomber in the European Theater of Operations (ETO) during World War II. Designed by Peyton Magruder to meet the medium bomber requirements of Circular Proposal 39-640 issued by the Army in March 1939, it, along with the B-25, was the first type of aircraft to be ordered into mass production before it actually flew. Listed as the company Model 179, the design bore no likeness to the Model 167 (XA-22) that had preceded it in the light bomber competition. Magruder and his team came up with a low-drag, completely circular fuselage section that gave the plane a decidedly cigar-shaped appearance from the side. A twin-fin layout had been adopted initially but was abandoned in favor of a single fin to afford the tail gunner a better field of view. A tricycle landing gear configuration was selected and the wing was high shoulder mounted to the fuselage. Power came from the still experimental 1,850-hp Pratt & Whitney R-2800-5 engines. Since no minimum landing speed had been specified, Magruder calculated a wing loading of 51-lbs. per square foot—the highest of any American military aircraft yet designed—which would yield a touchdown speed well over 100-mph. When the Material Division tallied the points of the design competition in August 1939, Martin's entry, having received the designation B-26, was the hands-down winner, but due to the unprecedented numbers of aircraft needed by the Air Corps from 1939 onwards, the second-place B-25 was placed in production as well.

The maiden flight of the B-26 took place on November 25, 1940, and after 133 hours of factory testing, the first four production models were delivered to the Air Corps in February 1941. Other than the expected high landing speeds, few problems were revealed during initial acceptance trials. While the airplane was "hot" by the standards of the day, general handling qualities, including single-engine operations, were acceptable, thought certainly not docile. Trials demonstrated a top speed of 315-mph and a range of 1,000-miles with a 3,000-lb. bomb load. The B-26 was the first American aircraft designed from the start to incorporate a power-operated turret. The Martin-designed dorsal turret, located just ahead of the tail fin, was armed with two .50-caliber machine guns. Other armament included a flexible .30-caliber mount in the nose, another firing downward in the belly aft of the bomb bay, and a .50-caliber gun in

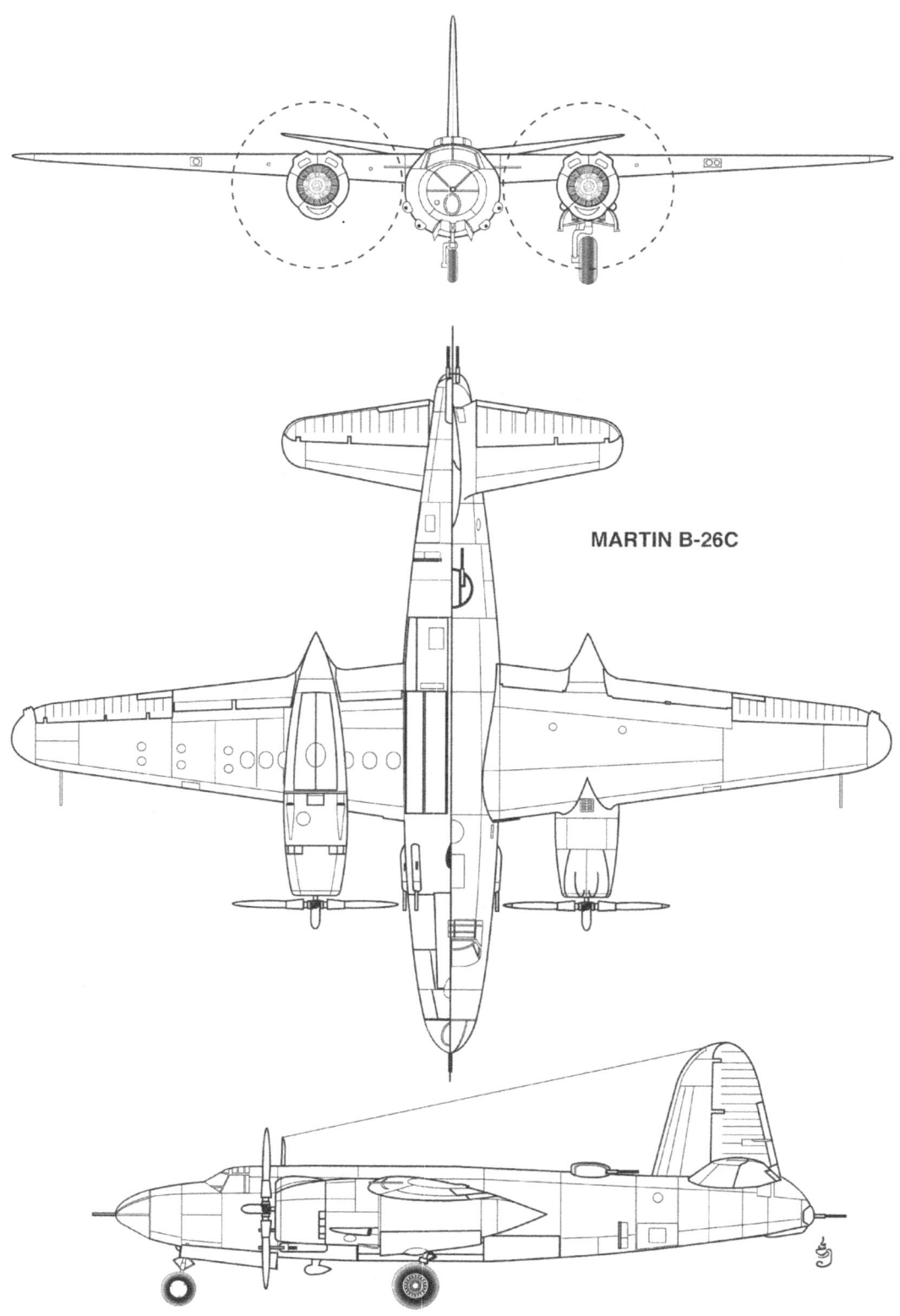

MARTIN B-26C

Top: Well-used B-26B serving with the 9th AF. This is a later block B equipped with the Bell M-6 powered tail turret. By late 1944, all B-26 combat operations were limited to the ETO, where tactical bombardment was carried out at medium altitudes. *Bottom:* B-26G featured a 3.5-degree increase in wing incidence. Most went to 9th AF to replace combat attrition of B and Cs, though some, with armament removed, ended up at U.S. bases as TB-26G advanced trainers.

the tail fired by a gunner in an upright position. The original 1939 contract for 201 B-26s was augmented in September 1940 by an order for 139 B-26As, which differed in having a 165-gallon ferry tank in the bomb bay, and then only two weeks later, the Army ordered 791 B-26Bs with a revised tail armament of two .50-caliber guns, self-sealing tanks, and improved armor protection for the crew. All B-26s and B-26As were delivered between February and October of 1941, including 54 B-26As Lend-Leased to Britain and thereafter taken into RAF service as the *Marauder I*, later adopted as the type's official name (rather than "Martian," as recommended by Martin).

In early 1941 the B-26B contract was increased to 1,883 aircraft (the most numerous of the series), followed in June by another contract for 1,210 essentially identical B-26Cs, to be built in parallel at Martin's new Omaha, Nebraska plant. Initial deliveries of B-26Bs to the AAF commenced in May 1942 and B-26Cs began arriving in August. Operational experience with earlier B-26 versions led to many improvements and modifications being incorporated to the B-26B/C assembly lines during the course of production (Blocks correspond to B-26B): spinners deleted, one flexible and one fixed .50-caliber machine gun added to nose, fuel capacity increased by 500-gallons, and air intakes on top of engine cowlings enlarged (first production batch); 1,920-hp R-2800-41 engines installed, nose gear strut lengthened (Block 2); four fixed .50-caliber guns in blister packs added to sides of fuselage, belly gun deleted and replaced by two .50-caliber waist guns mounted to fire abeam and downward (Block 4); wingspan increased from 65 to 71 feet, adding 57 square feet of wing area, fin and rudder height increased one foot, eight inches (Block 10); Martin-Bell M-6 powered twin .50-caliber tail turret installed, changing the rear fuselage contour and affording an enlarged field of fire, rear bomb bay racks and doors deleted (Block 25); and finally, more cockpit armor plating, shark-nosed ailerons, and improved sighting and bombing equipment added (Blocks 30–55). During Block 55, painting was discontinued and the aircraft were delivered in bare metal finish. The last B-26B was delivered to the AAF in February 1944 and the last B-26C in April. Nineteen B-26Bs went to the RAF as the *Marauder IA* and 100 B-26Cs as the *Marauder II,* the latter being transferred to the SAAF. The removal and fairing over of the dorsal turret plus deletion of all armament and bombing equipment from 208 B-26Bs and 350 B-26Cs resulted in a change to advanced trainer designations AT-23A and AT-23B, respectively, then later to TB-26B and TB-26C. In AAF service the trainer versions were used primarily for high altitude target towing; 225 were later transferred to the Navy as the JM-1 where they were used for the same purpose.

The sole XB-26D was an early B-26 modified in 1943 to test deicing equipment, and though the system proved to be satisfactory, the feature was never incorporated to the production line. A B-26C became the XB-26E in early 1943 when it was extensively modified by removing 2,600-lbs of equipment, deleting the co-pilot's position, and moving the dorsal turret forward to a position right behind the cockpit. While the testing program revealed a general improvement in combat capability, no action was ever taken to place the new version into production. After one B-26B fitted with two nose-mounted 37-mm cannons was tested as a strafer, AAF officials concluded that other types currently in service (e.g., A-20, B-25, and later, the A-26) were better suited to this role. The 300 B-26Fs built during early 1944 came with a 3.5-degree increase in wing incidence, giving the engine nacelles noticeable upward slant. The F also dispensed with the fixed nose gun and featured a revised fuel system, new bombing and radio equipment, and the improved M-6A powered tail turret. One hundred B-26Fs were delivered to the AAF and the remaining 200 went into service with the RAF as the *Marauder III*. The final production version, the B-26G, differed from the F in minor mechanical details, and all B-26 production ended when the last G was completed at Baltimore in April 1945. Of the 950 B-26Gs built, 150 were supplied to Britain as *Marauder IIIs* and a 57 were completed as TB-26G trainers lacking armament and bombing equipment. Forty-six TB-26Gs were transferred to the Navy as JM-2s where they were used as target tugs and utility aircraft. The sole XB-26H was a B-26G modified in 1945 to test the tandem bogie wheel and outrigger arrangement that would be used on proposed jet bombers such as the Boeing B-47 and Martin B-48.

Four of the earliest unarmed B-26 production models entered service in February 1941 with the 22nd BG (Medium), a B-18 unit based at Langley Field, Virginia. Initial conversion was plagued by a series of nose gear failures later shown to have been caused by loading too much weight forward of the aircraft's c.g. The 22nd was the only fully operational AAF B-26 unit when the U.S. entered World War II in December 1941 and was the first to deploy overseas. After arriving in Australia in March 1942 as part of the recently organized 5th AF, the 22nd commenced combat operations in early April when nine B-26s flying shuttle missions from Port Moresby, New Guinea attacked Japanese targets in Rabaul, New Britain. By mid–1942, two more B-26 squadrons attached to the 38th BG had joined the 5th AF in the combat theater. In the early days of June 1942, four B-26As configured to carry torpedoes took off from Midway Island to attack the oncoming Japanese fleet; however, during the low-level torpedo runs, two of the bombers were shot down and the other two heavily damaged, while no hits were scored against the enemy ships. The AAF subsequently determined that B-26s (and other medium bombers) were too vulnerable to be employed in torpedo attacks. By early 1943, for a variety of reasons, the AAF had decided to withdraw B-26s from Pacific combat operations and replace them with B-25s. As Allied forces pushed northward in the southwest Pacific, B-25s were more capable of operating from the shorter runways on newly established island bases and far more amenable to the strafer modifications needed for low-level skip-bombing tactics. The B-26's final combat sortie in 5th AF was flown in early-January 1944.

As deliveries proceeded in 1942, nine new AAF units were activated as B-26 Groups. One of them, the 21st BG, was organized as a stateside B-26 operational training unit (OTU), based first at Jackson Army Air Base in Mississippi, then at MacDill Field in Florida. During 1942, B-26 training accidents reached such scandalous proportions (i.e., 34 crashes involving 56 fatalities) that the U.S. Senate pressed the AAF to terminate all B-26 production. It was during this period that the plane acquired epithets such as the "Martin Murderer, the "Widow Maker," and the "Flying Prostitute" (i.e., no visible means of support). Many of the accidents were produced by loss of an engine on takeoff. Part of the problem was ascribed to an electrical fault that shorted the circuits on the Curtiss propellers and caused them to overspeed, most commonly occurring when the aircraft was at takeoff power. An investigation conducted at the behest of AAF chief Lt. Gen. H. H. Arnold by Maj. Gen. Carl Spaatz led, among other things, to the increased wing and tail area seen on the B-26B, Block 10; and in the fall of 1942, a related inquiry headed by Brig. Gen James H. Doolittle revealed that most of the accidents could have been avoided with proper training. Ironically, after the training program was totally revamped, B-26 accident rates dropped to levels comparable to those of units training with similar types of aircraft (e.g., B-25s and A-20s).

After joining the Alaska Air Force (later 11th AF) in January 1942, one squadron of B-26s participated in combat operations during the Japanese invasion of the Aleutian Islands in June but reequipped with B-25s during early 1943. The 319th BG flew their B-26B/Cs to England in September 1942 and moved to Algeria in November, where they joined the 12th AF and flew their first combat sortie over Tunis in late December. Two more B-26 groups (17th and 320th) became operational with the 12th AF in early 1943, and with the 319th, conducted bombardment missions, primarily from medium altitudes (9,000–12,000 feet), until the conclusion of the North African campaign. Afterward, the 12th AF B-26 groups moved their offensive operations to Italy, and the 17th and 319th converted to B-25s in late 1944 while the 320th continued to fly its B-26s until the end of the war. After making an inauspicious start, the B-26 enjoyed its greatest successes in the ETO. B-26Bs of the 322nd BG, 8th AF arrived in England in February of 1943 and flew their first combat sortie, a low-level, unescorted strike against a power plant on the Dutch coast in mid–May; however, because of delayed fuses, the bombs were disarmed before they could explode. When eleven B-26s tried to duplicate the mission only three days later, the Germans were prepared: all, except one plane that had returned to base early with mechanical difficulties, were completely destroyed over the target. As a result, the 322nd was placed on indefinite stand down from further combat operations amid a high-level debate as to whether the B-26 should be withdrawn from combat altogether. Then in mid–July, after three months of intensive retraining, the B-26s returned to combat, this time with a fighter escort and in tight group formation boxes at medium altitudes against targets in occupied France and Belgium. Five B-26 groups were operating from English bases at the time they transferred to the 9th Tactical AF in November 1943, and by April 1944, there were eight groups in the ETO. After the Normandy invasion in June 1944, the B-26 units started moving to forward bases in France and Belgium in support of the advancing Allied armies. They typically attacked targets like bridges, rail marshalling yards, artillery parks, airfields, supply depots, and ammunition and oil storage dumps. When the war in Europe ended in May 1945, the B-26 groups were rapidly demobilized. Since the AAF had made the decision not to use the B-26 in post-war units, most were simply scrapped in Europe; those placed in U.S.-based storage facilities suffered a similar fate, nearly all having been disposed of by the end of 1949. A small number survived as civilian transports and the last Navy JM-2 was retired in 1955.

The B-26 was actually introduced to combat by the RAF in August 1942 after *Marauder Is* (B-26As) began operating with the Desert Air Force in North Africa. The 398 *Marauder IIs* (B-26Cs) and *IIIs* (B-25F/Gs) received by Britain also operated with RAF and SAAF units based in North Africa, Sicily, Italy, and southern France. Ex-AAF *Marauders* (number unknown) were likewise supplied to Free French Forces in late 1943, where they were operated out of Italy initially and later participated in the invasion of southern France in August 1944. French B-26 units were disbanded in June 1945.

North American B-28 Dragon 1942–1944

TECHNICAL SPECIFICATIONS (XB-28)
Type: Four or five-place medium bomber
Manufacturer: North American Aviation, Inc., Inglewood, California.
Total produced: 2
Power plant: Two 2,000-hp Pratt & Whitney R-2800-11 *Double-Wasp* 18-cylinder air-cooled engines driving four-bladed Curtiss electric fully-controllable propellers.
Armament: Six remotely-controlled .50-caliber machine guns, two each in dorsal and ventral turrets and two in a tail turret, and 4,000-lbs. bombs of bombs carried in an internal bomb bay.
Performance: Max. speed 372-mph at 25,000 feet, cruise 255-mph; ceiling 34,600 ft.; range 2,040 mi. loaded, max. (unknown).
Weights: 25,575-lbs. empty, 35,740-lbs. loaded.
Dimensions: Span 72 ft. 7 in., length 56 ft. 5 in., wing area 676 sq. ft.

Shortly after issuing the CP 39-640 medium bomber requirement in 1939 (see, B-23, B-25, and B-26, above) the Army circulated a similar specification for a 'high-altitude' variant to be equipped with turbo-supercharged engines and pressurized crew accommodations. Two proposals were received: the Martin Model 182 and the North American Model NA-63, to which were assigned the respective designations XB-27 and XB-28. In February 1940, after considering both proposals, the Martin project was cancelled while North American received a contract to proceed with construction of two prototypes. The final design of the XB-28, char-

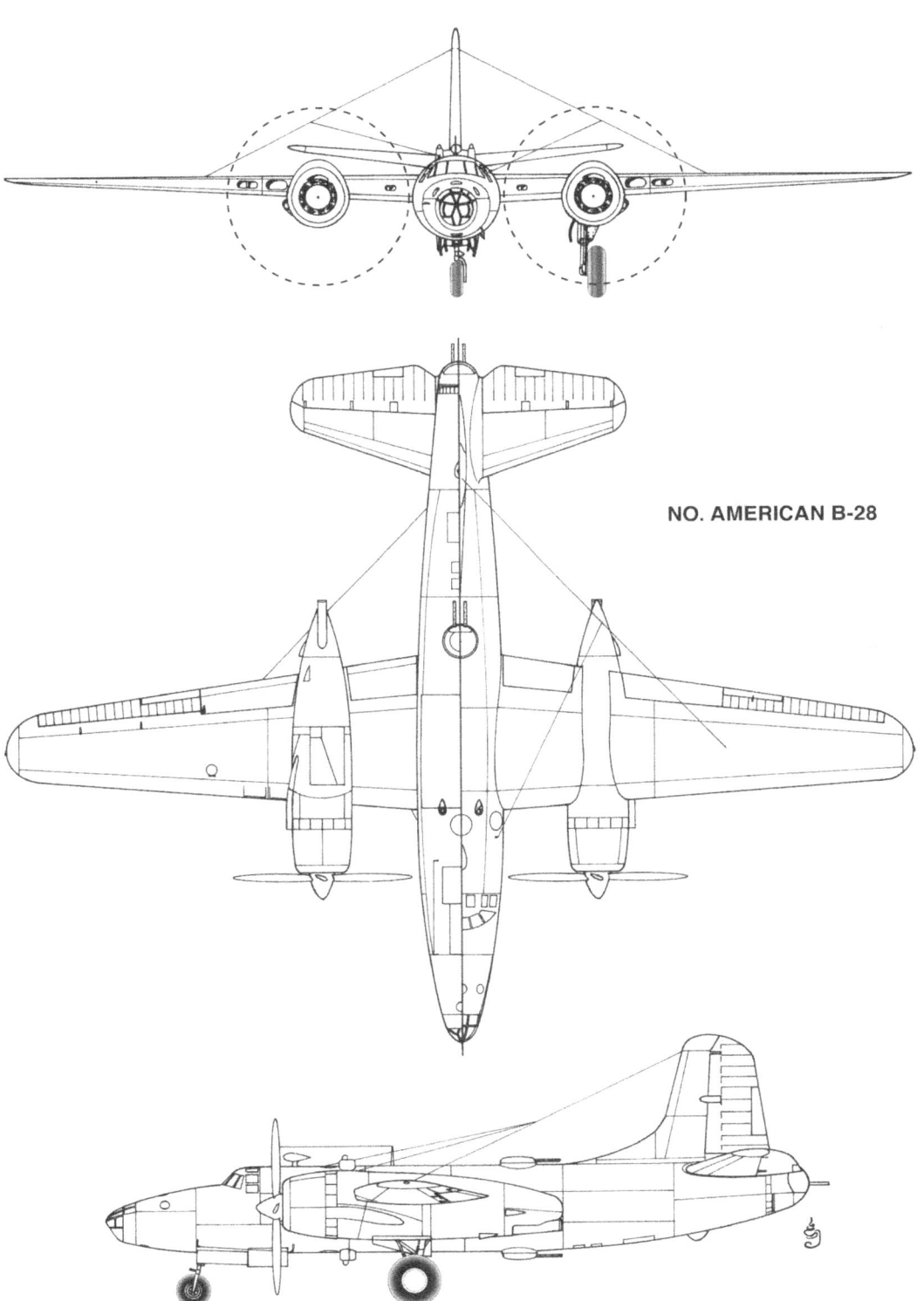

NO. AMERICAN B-28

The first XB-28 prototype in 1943. By the time the test program was underway, the USAAF had entirely discarded the notion of operating medium bombers from the high altitudes and saw no reason to disrupt B-25 production.

acterized by a perfectly circular fuselage and large single fin flanked by horizontal stabilizers of moderate dihedral, had very little in common with the B-25.

After making its first flight on April 26, 1942, the XB-28 prototype was delivered the AAF for trials. Performance, in terms of speed, ceiling, and range, exceeded both the B-25 and B-26 by a considerable margin, but by the time testing was complete, the AAF had reached the decision not to place the type into production. Combat experience had shown that unpredictable conditions like wind and cloud cover rendered tactical bombing from high altitudes impractical. And at low and medium altitudes, the XB-28 did offer a sufficient performance advantage over the proven design of the B-25 to justify a major disruption of North American's production schedule. The second prototype, the XB-28A, was completed as a high altitude reconnaissance aircraft but likewise was not placed in production.

Lockheed B-34, -37 Ventura 1941–1945

TECHNICAL SPECIFICATIONS (B-34A)

Type: Four or five place medium bomber.
Manufacturer: Vega Division of Lockheed Aircraft Corp., Burbank, California.
Total produced: 893
Power plant: Two 2,000-hp Pratt & Whitney R-2800-31 *Double-Wasp* 18-cylinder air-cooled engines driving three-bladed Hamilton Standard constant-speed propellers.
Armament: Two fixed .50-caliber machine guns in the nose, two flexible .30-caliber machine guns in the nose, two .50-caliber machine guns in a powered dorsal, two flexible .30-caliber machine guns in ventral bay, and up to 3,000-lbs. bombs of bombs carried in an internal bomb bay.
Performance: Max. speed 315-mph at 15,500 feet, cruise 230-mph; ceiling 24,000 ft.; range 950 mi. loaded, 2,600 mi. max.
Weights: 17,275-lbs. empty, 25,600-lbs. loaded.
Dimensions: Span 65 ft. 6 in., length 51 ft. 5 in., wing area 551 sq. ft.

First Series • 1926–1944

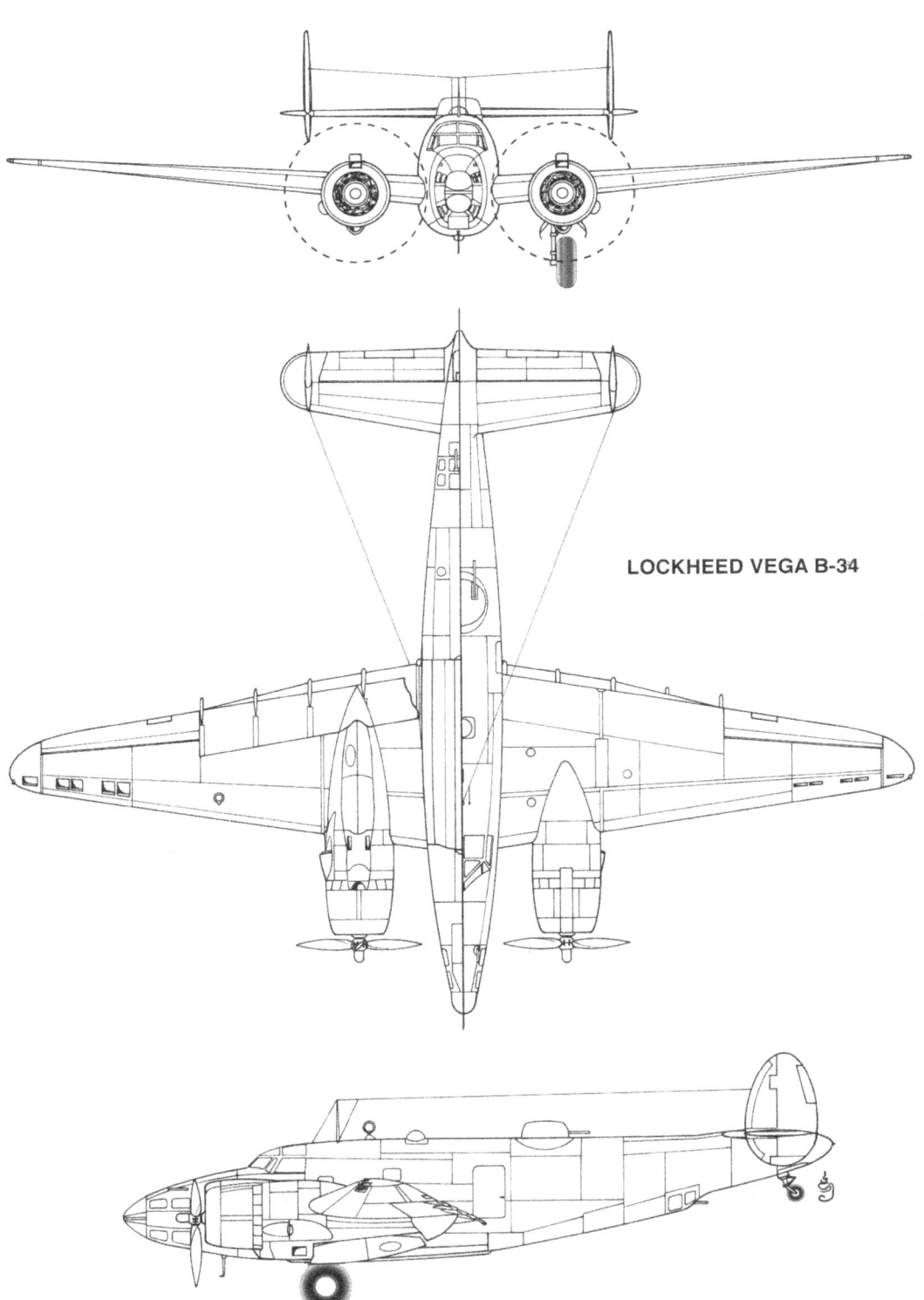

LOCKHEED VEGA B-34

One of 139 *Ventura IIA*s intercepted from the British Lend-Lease order during 1942 and taken into USAAF service as the B-34A. Used briefly for coastal patrol, most saw service as bombing and gunnery trainers or target tugs.

The Lockheed Model 37, a military adaptation of Lockheed's Model 18 *Lodestar* transport, was originally ordered by Great Britain in 1940 as a replacement for the *Hudson* (see, A-28, -29, above). From late 1941 to early 1944, over 1,200 aircraft were delivered to the RAF and British Commonwealth air forces (RCAF, RAAF, RNZAF, and SAAF) and taken into service as the *Ventura I, II, IIA,* and *V,* which differed from each other mainly in armament and versions of the R-2800 engine. And when Lend-Lease took effect, the following U.S. designations were applied: B-34 and B-34A (*Ventura IIA*) and PV-1 (*Ventura V*). During 1942, 264 pre–Lend-Lease *Ventura IIs* were commandeered into AAF service as the R-37 ('R' denoted restricted status) and a further 27 to the Navy as the PV-3 (PV-1 and PV-2 had been reserved for future Navy versions), where they were used for coastal patrol and training. Another 139 Lend-Lease *IIA*s were redirected into AAF as B-34s, B-34As, and B-34Bs. The 25 B-34s became RB-34s and like the R-37s, were used only for coastal patrol and training. Of the 101 B-34As accepted by the AAF, 57 were subsequently equipped as bombing trainers, 27 as gunnery trainers, and 16 as target tugs. The 13 B-34Bs were delivered as navigation trainers.

The first direct Army contract for the type came in August 1941 with an order for 550 aircraft under the reconnaissance/observation designation O-56, however, before the first example could be completed, the designation was changed initially to RB-34B, then to B-37. The B-37 differed from the *Ventura*/B-34 series mainly in having 1,700-hp Wright R-2600 engines in place of the R-2800s. But even before the first B-37 flew in September 1942, the decision had already been reached to devote all future production to the Navy PV-1, with the

First Series • 1926–1944   89

Navy PV-1 shown in late war markings. Note drop tanks for increased patrol range. PV-1s were the most numerous *Ventura* variant produced and also served in small numbers with Marine squadrons in the southwest Pacific.

result that only 18 B-37s were completed. A solid gun-nose, strafer version of the B-37 was studied but never built. The PV-1, which saw widespread use in the Navy, was basically a B-34 with increased fuel capacity, revised armament, and special equipment for the maritime role. Between December 1942 and May 1944, a total of 1,600 were built, of which 888 were delivered to the Navy as the PV-1 and 712 to the RAF and Commonwealth air forces as the *Ventura V.*

Douglas B-42 Mixmaster 1944–1948

TECHNICAL SPECIFICATIONS (XB-42)

Type: Three-place medium bomber.
Manufacturer: Douglas Aircraft Co., Santa Monica, California.
Total produced: 2
Power plant: Two 1,800-hp Allison V-1710-125 12-cylinder liquid-cooled engines driving a six-bladed Curtiss Electric contra-rotating, fully-controllable propeller.
Armament: Two fixed, forward-firing .50-caliber machine guns, two moveable, remotely-controlled .50-caliber machine guns in the trailing edge of each wing, and up to 3,000-lbs. bombs of bombs carried in an internal bomb bay.
Performance: Max. speed 410-mph at 23,440 feet, cruise (unknown); ceiling 29,400 ft.; range 1,840 mi. loaded, 5,400 mi. max.
Weights: 20,888-lbs. empty, 33,208-lbs. loaded.
Dimensions: Span 70 ft. 6 in., length 53 ft. 7 in., wing area 555 sq. ft.

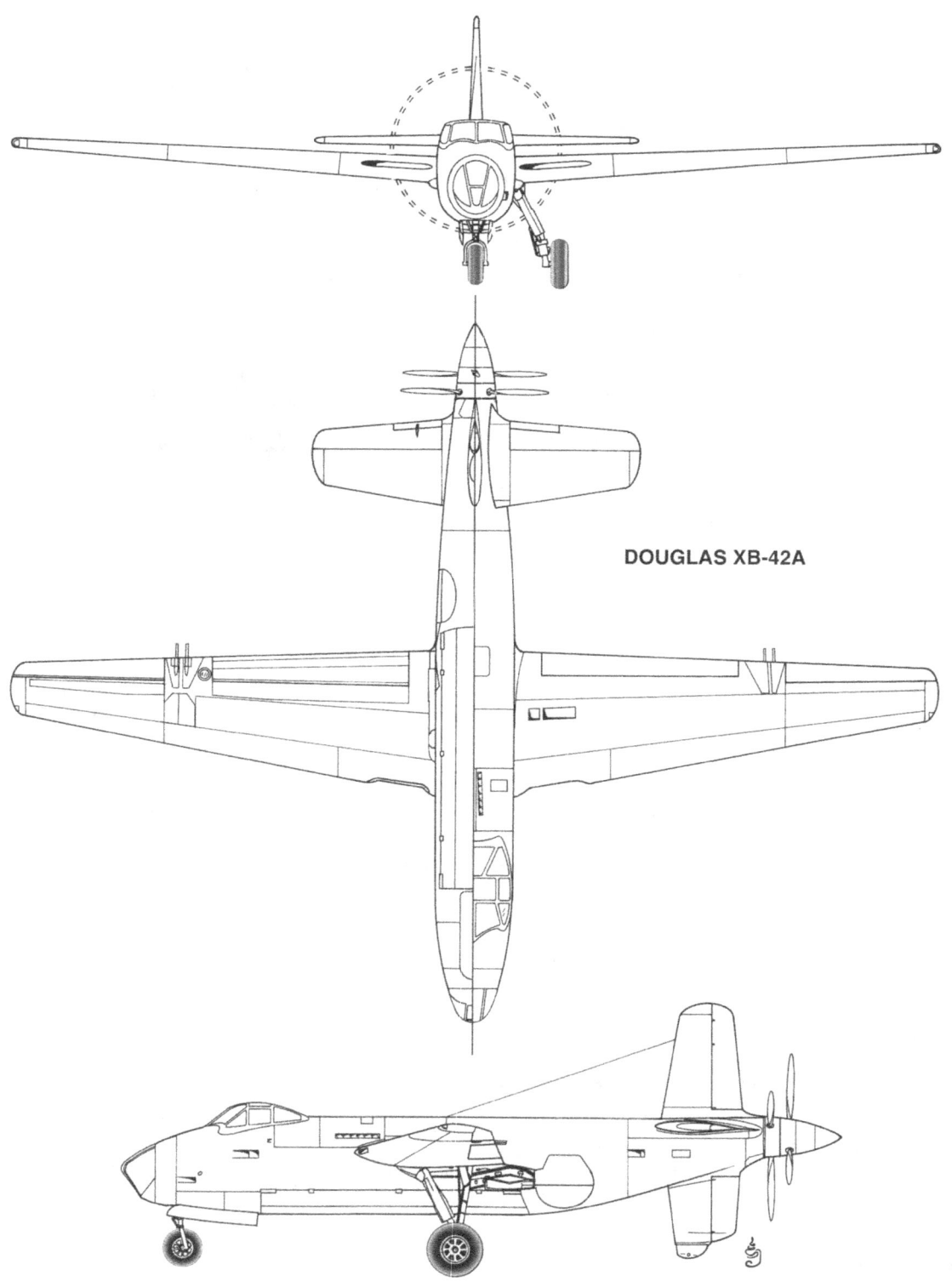

DOUGLAS XB-42A

The first XB-42 prototype after the twin bubble canopies had been replaced by a more conventional cockpit enclosure. It was severely underpowered with piston engines, but the two J-30 jet engines added later caused a drastic reduction in range.

Eclipsed by the advent of jet propulsion, Douglas's XB-42 was nevertheless one of the most advanced propeller-driven bombers ever conceived. When proposed in June 1943 as the XA-42, the design was envisaged as a tactical bomber having twice the combat radius of current types (e.g., A-20, A-26, B-25, B-26) and sufficient speed (400-mph+) to outrun attacking fighters. Due to its unorthodox configuration, the project was classified as experimental from the start with no plans to place the type into production. In late 1943, while the project was still in the design phase, the designation was changed to XB-42 (the matching numbers were sheer coincidence). The Douglas engineering team led by Ed Burton proceeded from the notion that the design would need to be very clean aerodynamically in order to achieve the desired performance. By choosing a pusher layout that placed the two engines and landing gear within the fuselage, the laminar flow wings were freed of drag-producing protrusions. The engines were mounted side-by-side at the c.g. and connected to the 13-foot diameter contra-rotating propeller via five sets of P-39 drive shafts. The pilot and co-pilot were seated side-by-side under individual bubble canopies, giving the aircraft a decidedly bug-eyed appearance, while the bombardier was stationed in the glazed nose. To fire the remote-controlled wing guns, the co-pilot would swing his seat 180-degrees aft and operate a sighting system. Mockup inspection was completed in the fall of 1943, following which Douglas was given the go-ahead to build two prototypes.

The first XB-42 made its maiden flight on May 4, 1944, becoming the first bomber of American design to utilize all-pusher propulsion. The second XB-42 flew three months later but was completely destroyed in December 1945 in an accident related to a landing gear malfunction. In any case, the XB-42 test program yielded generally disappointing results. Despite its sleekness, the design turned out to be seriously underpowered, degrading not only speed and range but causing a very long takeoff run of 6,415 feet. Testing also revealed yaw stability problems, excessive vibration in the contra-rotating propellers and shafting, inefficient engine cooling, and poor control harmony in general. The XB-42 prototype was returned to Douglas in late 1946 to add two Westinghouse J30 turbojet engines in nacelles mounted under each wing. The two bubble canopies, which the test pilots disliked, were replaced with a more standard glazed cockpit enclosure. The revised XB-42A flew in May 1947, but testing soon revealed that, despite a 78-mph increase in speed and 10,000-foot gain in ceiling, range had been reduced to a mere 650 miles as a result of increased fuel consumption. The project was finally cancelled in August 1948.

Lockheed P-38 Lightning 1939–1946

TECHNICAL SPECIFICATIONS (P-38L)
Type: One or two-place fighter-bomber
Manufacturer: Lockheed Aircraft Corp., Burbank, California.
Total produced: 9,942 (all versions)
Power plant: Two 1,425-hp Allison V-1710-89/91 12-cylinder liquid-cooled engines driving three-bladed Curtiss Electric fully-controllable propellers.
Armament: One 20-mm cannon and four .50-caliber machine guns in the nose and up to 3,200-lbs. bombs or 10 HVAR rockets carried on external racks.
Performance: Max. speed 414-mph at 25,500 feet, cruise 290-mph; ceiling 44,000 ft.; range 450 mi. loaded (external ordnance), 2,600 mi. max.
Weights: 12,800-lbs. empty, 17,500-lbs. loaded.
Dimensions: Span 52 ft., length 37 ft. 10 in., wing area 327.5 sq. ft.

The well-known Lockheed P-38 saw only limited operational use as a fighter-bomber during World War II, primarily with the 9th Tactical AF in the European Theater of Operations after 1943. Moreover, only the later production versions, namely the P-38J and L, possessed

One of the 3,810 P-38Ls built during the last two years of the war. A late-comer in the ground support role, the addition of dive brakes and wing hardpoints turned the P-38 into an effective attack platform.

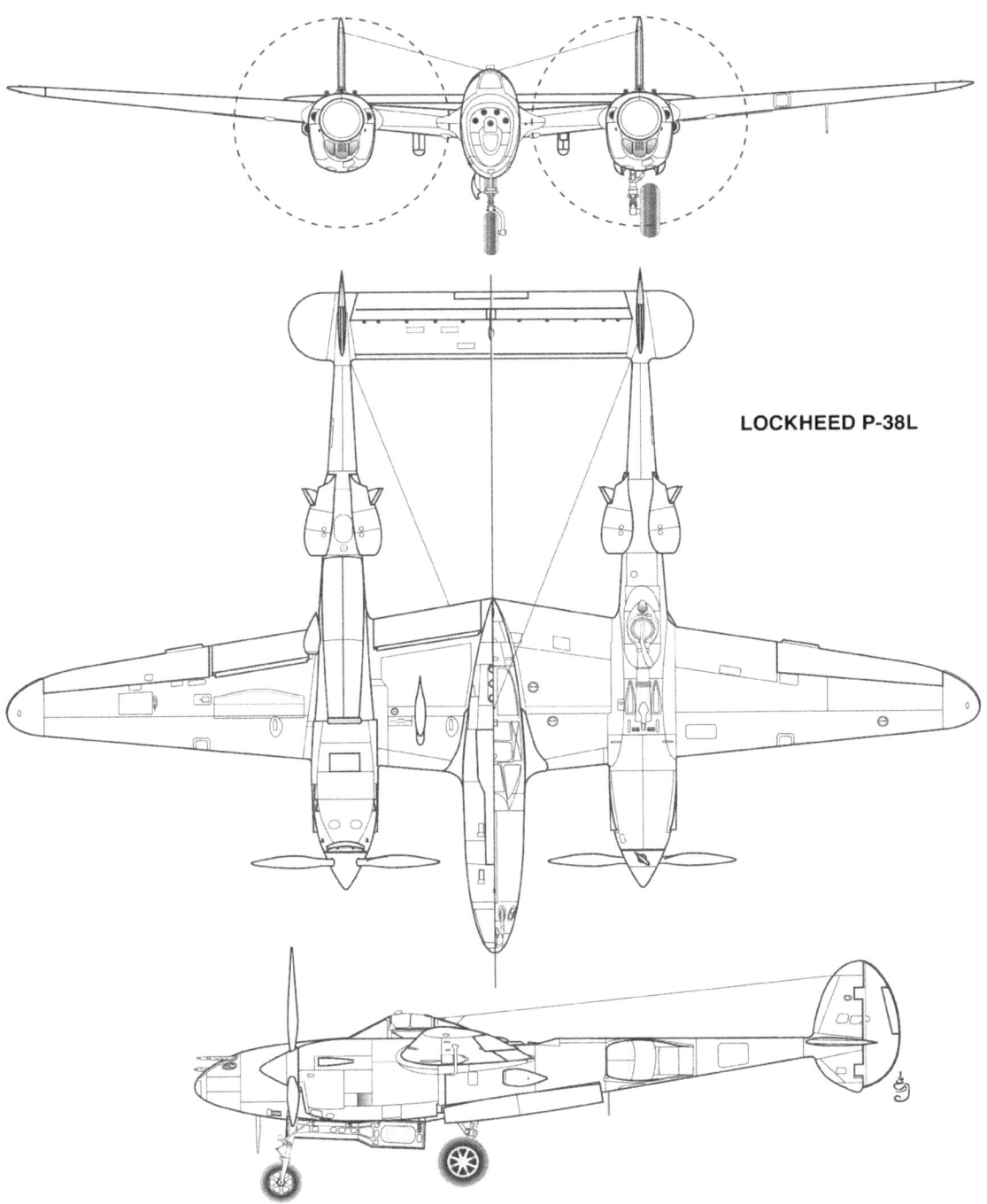

LOCKHEED P-38L

any significant air-to-ground capability. The P-38J, flown in August 1943, was distinguishable from earlier models by a chin-type scoop under each engine cowling that housed the oil cooler and inter-cooler intakes and was the first to feature electrically operated dive brakes under each wing. The P-38L, which began appearing in mid–1944, introduced underwing trees for 10 HVAR 5-inch rockets. A number of P-38Js and Ls underwent a "droop snoot" retrofit, in which the entire nose section was removed to be replaced by a new glazed unit containing a bombardier's station and a Norden bomb sight.

As more North American P-51s reached Europe to take over fighter escort duties, P-38s of the 474th, 367th, and 370th Fighter Groups were detached from the 8th AF and transferred to the 9th TAF, where they began flying fighter-bomber sorties in April 1944. External ordnance was carried on wing pylons normally occupied by drop tanks and typically consisted of either two 500-lb., 1,000-lb., or 1,600-lb. bombs; HVAR rockets were carried on trees under the outboard wing panels. The droop snoot P-38s, functioning as lead aircraft, enabled the other bomb-laden P-38s to make precision drops on targets from medium altitudes. The 367th FG converted to P-47s and the 370th to P-51s, both in March 1945, so that 474th was the only 9th TAF unit still flying P-38s at the time of VE Day. Once World War II ended, P-38s were rapidly withdrawn from AAF service and most were scrapped. A few P-38Ls were transferred to the Honduran Air Forces where they served into the 1950s.

Bell P-39 Airacobra 1939–1945

TECHNICAL SPECIFICATIONS (P-39Q)

Type: One-place fighter-bomber
Manufacturer: Bell Aircraft Corp., Buffalo, New York.
Total produced: 9,588 (all versions)
Power plant: One 1,325-hp Allison V-1710-85 12-cylinder liquid-cooled engines driving a three-bladed Curtiss Electric fully-controllable propeller.
Armament: One 37-mm cannon firing through the propeller hub and two synchronized .50-caliber machine guns in the nose, two .50-caliber machine guns in the wings, and one 250-lb., 325-lb. or 500-lb. bomb carried on the centerline.
Performance: Max. speed 376-mph at 15,000 feet, cruise 250-mph; ceiling 32,100 ft.; range 525 mi. loaded, 1,075 mi. max.
Weights: 5,645-lbs. empty, 7,650-lbs. loaded.
Dimensions: Span 34 ft., length 30 ft. 2 in., wing area 213 sq. ft.

The Bell P-39 deserves mention as a fighter-bomber due to its broad use as ground attack machine by the Soviet Air Force during World War II, a role in which it excelled. Designed by Robert Woods (see, A-11, above) in response to a 1937 Army fighter requirement, the P-39 was unusual in having its engine located behind the pilot on the c.g., so that space in the nose could be devoted to its heavy cannon armament. Because the Army decided to omit turbo-superchargers on production P-39s, performance above medium altitudes was seriously hampered. In AAF service, P-39s were removed from frontline service as quickly as P-38s, P-47s, and P-51s became available to replace them, and were thereafter relegated to fighter training duties. The P-39Q was the most numerous version, 4,905 examples having been completed when *Airacobra* production terminated in August 1944. Over one-half—4,925 aircraft—of all P-39 production was Lend-Leased to the Soviet Union.

From late 1942 onwards, P-39s of the 81st and 350th Fighter Groups and 68th Observation Group, attached to the North-Africa-based 12th AF, did see some use as a low-level strafers, initially in the Middle East campaign and later in the Allied landings in Tunisia, Sicily, and Italy. The RAF's 601 Squadron flew its *Airacobra Is* on one cross-channel strike mission before the type was withdrawn from combat. P-39s (diverted from the original British order) began entering service with the Soviet Air Force during the late spring of 1942 where they were used both for low-altitude escort and ground attack. In Soviet service, the wing guns were frequently removed to reduce weight, and as the American-made armament became unserviceable, it was replaced by a Russian-made 20-mm B-20 cannon and 12.7-mm UBS machine guns. Soviet P-39s remained in service throughout World War II and a small num-

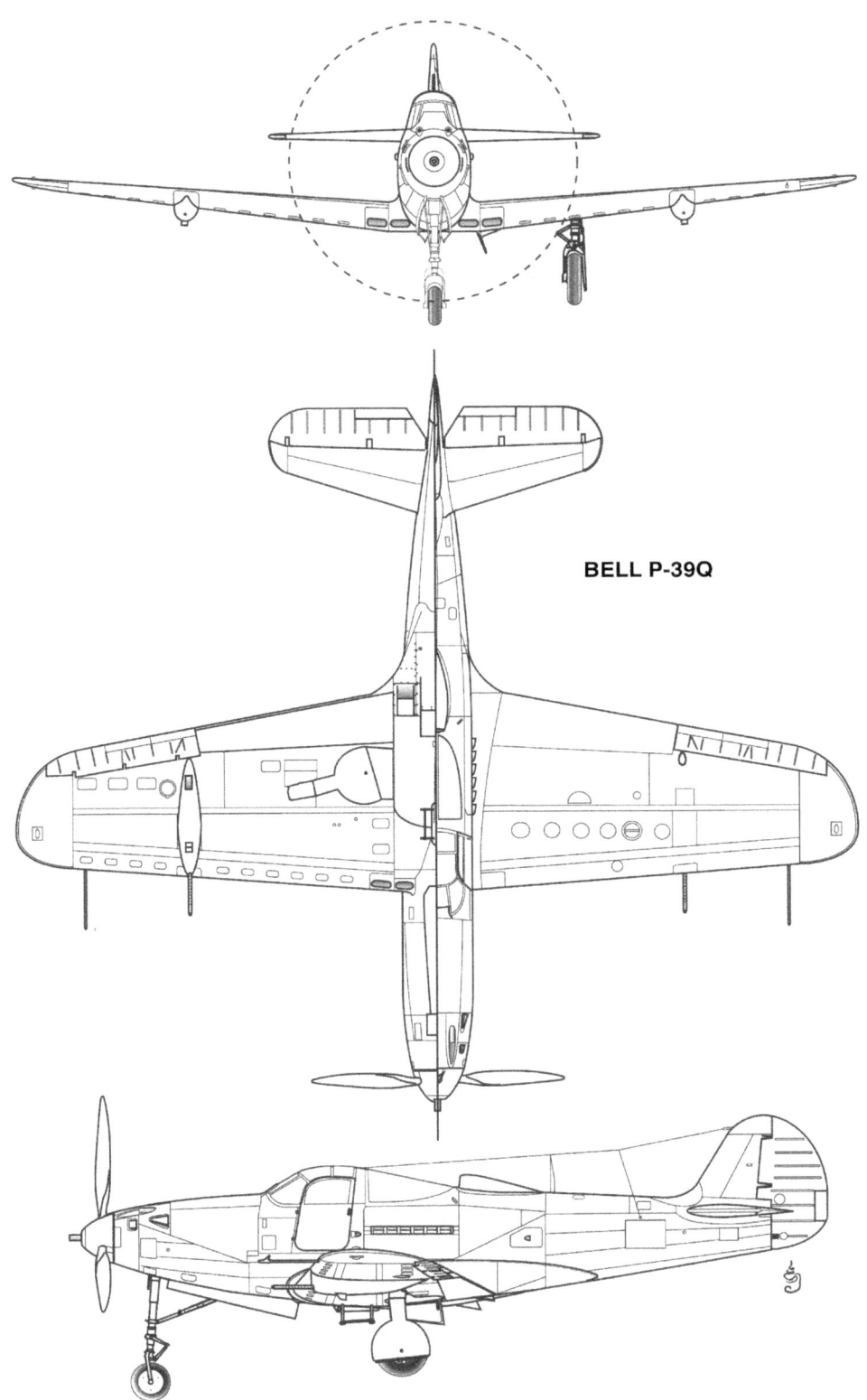

BELL P-39Q

P-39Q, the most capable ground attack variant, showing .50-caliber guns in underwing bays. Thousands were Lend-Leased to the Soviet Union, where they saw extensive use in the attack role.

ber actually wound up with the (North) Korean Peoples' Air Force during the early months of the Korean War.

Curtiss P-40 Warhawk 1938–1945

TECHNICAL SPECIFICATIONS (P-40N)

Type: One-place fighter-bomber
Manufacturer: Curtiss-Wright Corp., Buffalo, New York.
Total produced: 13,738 (all versions)
Power plant: One 1,200-hp Allison V-1710-81 12-cylinder liquid-cooled engine driving a three-bladed Curtiss Electric fully-controllable propeller.
Armament: Six .50-caliber machine guns in the wings and up 1,500-lbs of bombs carried on centerline and wing racks.
Performance: Max. speed 343-mph at 15,000 feet, cruise 288-mph; ceiling 31,000 ft.; range 340 mi. loaded, 1,080 mi. max.
Weights: 6,200-lbs. empty, 8,350-lbs. loaded.
Dimensions: Span 37 ft. 4 in., length 33 ft. 4 in., wing area 236 sq. ft.

The Curtiss P-40 was the AAF's most numerous frontline fighter at the time the U.S. entered World War II and was exported and Lend-Leased in significant numbers to Britain and its Commonwealth Nations (4,309 aircraft) as well as the Soviet Union (2,430 aircraft). In AAF service, P-40s were never employed in the European Theater and had largely been withdrawn from combat by late 1944. As more capable aircraft (i.e., P-38s, P-47s, and P-51s) arrived to assume the fighter role during 1943 and 1944, remaining P-40 units of the 12th (Mediterranean) and 14th (China) Air Forces were routinely called upon to perform fighter-bomber missions. The P-40N, the final and most numerous version produced (5,244 delivered by November

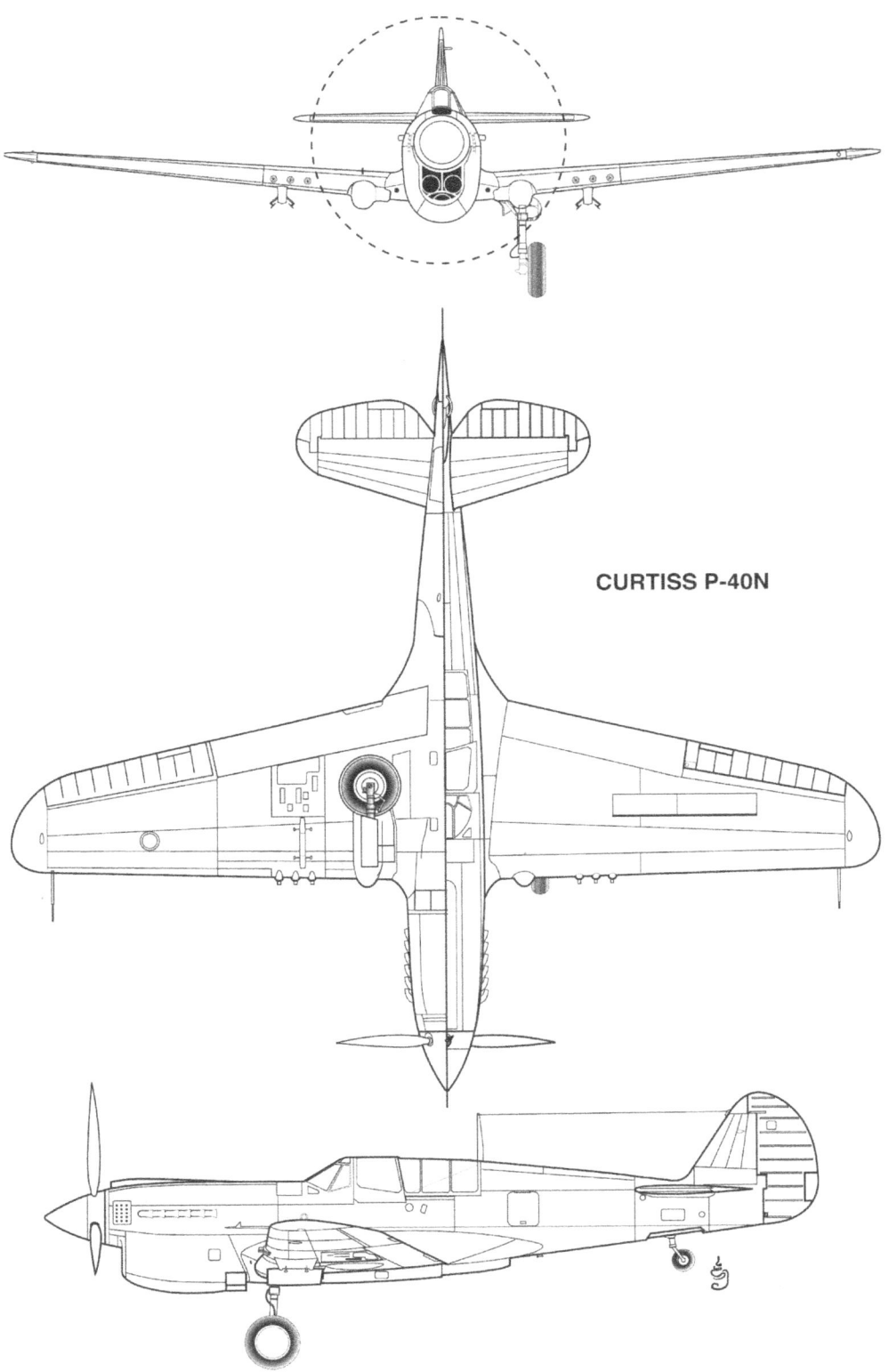

Late-production P-40N over the U.S., probably in late 1944. Although P-40Ns were better suited to ground attack than previous variants, most of the 5,244 built were Lend-Leased or sent directly to fighter training schools in the U.S.

1944), was the best fighter-bomber of the series, featuring a strengthened wing with outboard pylons for bombs; however, most were either Lend-leased or sent directly to stateside AAF fighter training schools.

In RAF and Commonwealth (RCAF, RAAF, RNZAF, and SAAF) service, as the *Tomahawk I* (P-40), *II-IIA* (P-40B), and *IIB* (P-40C) and *Kittyhawk I* (P-40D), *IA* (P-40E), *II* (P-40F/L), *III* (P-40K/M) and *IV* (P-40N), the type was widely used for ground attack in every Allied combat theater except Europe, and remained active as a fighter-bomber with Mediterranean-based RAF units and southwest Pacific-based RAAF and RNZAF units until cessation of hostilities. The first 240 Lend-Leased P-40s (which included 170 re-routed British *Tomahawks*) reached the Soviet Union by sea in late 1941, however, the vast majority, consisting of P-40Es, Ks, Ms. And Ns, were delivered via the Alaska-Siberia route between 1942 and 1944. After seeing early service as a fighter in defense of Moscow, Leningrad, and Stalingrad, Soviet P-40s were primarily used for ground attack in support of offensive operations by Frontal Army units. In the attack role, Soviet pilots preferred the P-39 over the P-40, which they claimed was underarmed and more vulnerable to battle damage. Besides Britain and the USSR, 74 ex-AAF P-40Fs and Ls were supplied to Free French forces, 393 P-40Ks, Ms, and Ns to the Chinese-American Composite Wing (in addition to the 100 P-40Cs and 30 P-40Es previously received by the American Volunteer Group), 83 P-40Ks, Ms, and Ns to Brazil, and 59 P-40Ns to the Dutch East Indies, which, after the war, were reportedly used against Indonesian nationalists.

Republic P/F-47 Thunderbolt 1941–1955

TECHNICAL SPECIFICATIONS (P-47D [BLOCKS 25–30])
Type: One-place fighter-bomber
Manufacturer: Republic Aviation Corp., Farmingdale, New York and Evansville, Indiana, and Curtiss-Wright Corp., Buffalo, New York.
Total produced: 15,683 (all versions)
Power plant: One 2, 300-hp Pratt & Whitney R-2800-59 Double-Wasp 18-cylinder air-cooled engine driving a four-bladed Curtiss Electric fully-controllable or Hamilton Standard constant-speed propeller.
Armament: Eight .50-caliber machine guns in the wings and up 2,500-lbs of bombs or HVAR rockets carried on external racks.
Performance: Max. speed 428-mph at 30,000 feet, cruise 300-mph; ceiling 42,000 ft.; range 475 mi. loaded, 1,700 mi. max.
Weights: 10,700-lbs. empty, 19,400-lbs. loaded.
Dimensions: Span 40 ft. 9 in., length 34 ft. 10 in., wing area 300 sq. ft.

Republic's famed P-47 was not only produced in greater numbers than any other American fighter type, but also became the AAF's most important single-seat attack aircraft of World War II. Starting with the 15th production block, P-47Ds gained substantial air-to-ground capability with the incorporation of underwing pylons and stronger wings enabling them to carry either two 1,000-lb. bombs or three 500-lb. bombs. A larger diameter, paddle-bladed propeller was introduced on the P-47D-22, and the D-25 came with 20 percent greater internal fuel capacity and was the first to be built with a bubble canopy. A dorsal fillet to improve directional stability was added to the P-47D-27 and underwing launch stubs for 10 HVAR rockets became a standard feature on the P-47D-30. In order to assist recovery from the high diving speeds encountered during ground attack maneuvers, P-47Ds were retrofitted with blunt-nosed ailerons and electrically-operated dive flaps under the wings. The P-47M, equipped with a 2,800-hp R-2800-57(C) engine having water injection and a larger turbo-supercharger, began appearing in late 1944, which, boasting a top speed of 470-mph at 32,000 feet, made it the fastest production *Thunderbolt* of the series. The need for increased range in Pacific operations resulted in the development of the P-47N, which featured an eleven-inch spanwise addition to each wing panel at the root to accommodate a 93-gallon fuel tank on each side. P-47Ns, easily identified by their squared-off wingtips and larger dorsal fillets, began reaching operational service in late 1944, and 1,816 had been completed when *Thunderbolt* production ended in December 1945.

The 354 P-47Gs completed by Curtiss were identical to the P-47D-1 through D-15. A number of P-47 experimental versions were evaluated during the war but never placed in production. The XP-47E, a P-47B airframe modified for installation of a pressurized cockpit, was successfully tested during 1943, but because the type's operational emphasis was shifting to low-level fighter-bomber missions, the feature was never incorporated to any production models. Another P-47B airframe became the XP-47F when it served as a testbed for new laminar-flow wings. In 1943 two P-47D-15 razorback airframes were mated to experimental to 2,300-hp Chrysler XIV-2220 16-cylinder liquid-cooled engines under the designation XP-47H. Although the XP-47H attained 490-mph during flight trials, the experimental Chrysler powerplant was never put into production. The XP-47J was a lightened P-47D razorback airframe having a tighter cowling which fan-cooled its more powerful R-2800-57(C) engine, and in August 1944, achieved a level speed of 504-mph, the first propeller-driven fighter to exceed 500-mph mark.

As more P-51Bs and Cs arrived in the European Theater during 1944 to undertake the fighter escort role, all but one (56thFG) of the thirteen P-47 groups in the 8th AF were transferred to the 9th TAF, where they joined two pre-existing P-47 groups. After the Normandy invasion in June 1944, 9th TAF P-47s provided close air support to the advancing Allied armies until hos-

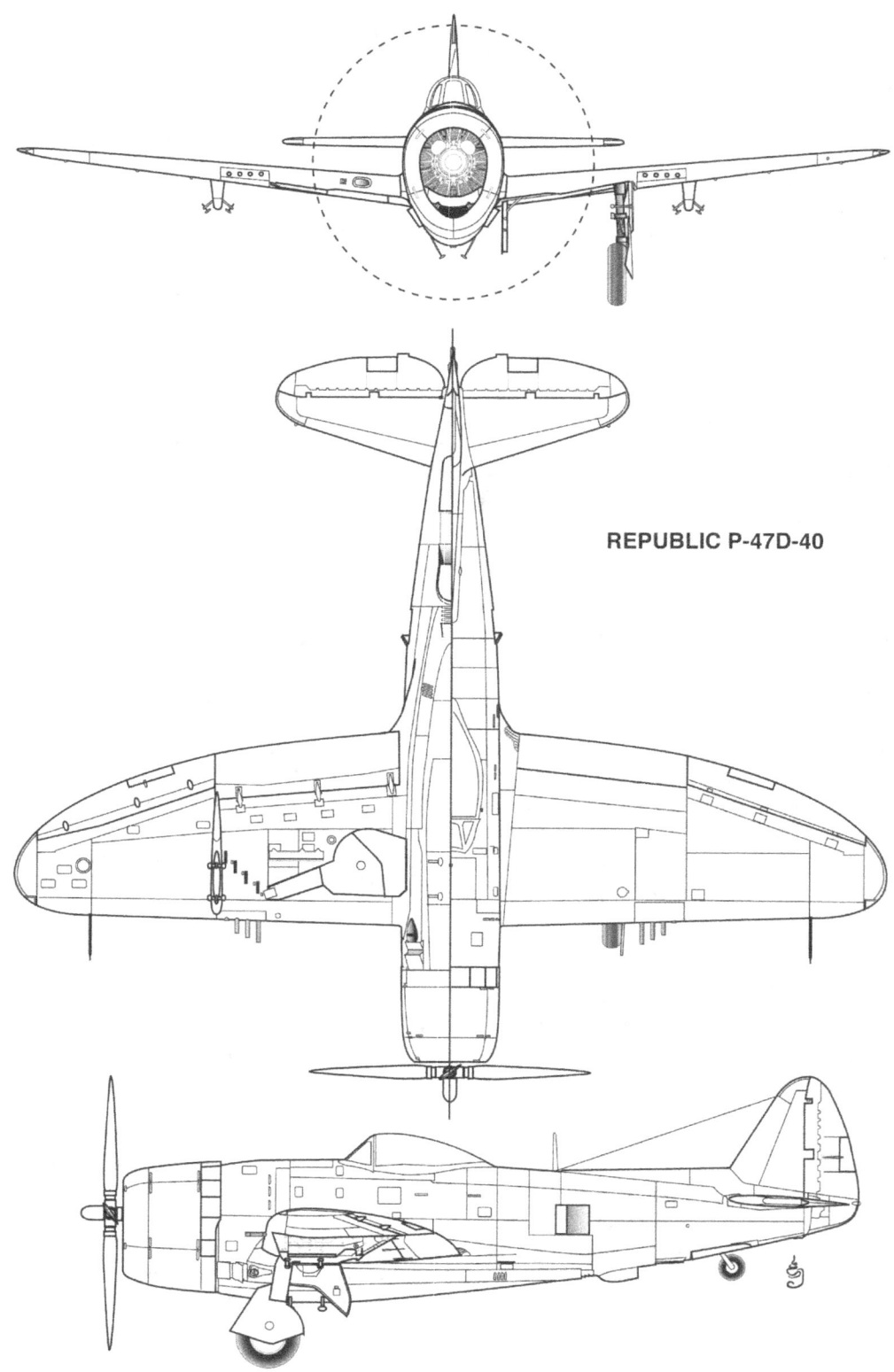

REPUBLIC P-47D-40

Top: A block 25 P-47D, the first bubble canopy version. A strengthening of the wings plus the addition of pylons for weapons stores turned the P-47 into the USAAF's premier fighter-bomber of World War II. *Bottom:* Post-war USAF F-47N shown in Europe over the Alps. The aircraft was better suited to the ground attack role than its F-51 contemporary, but none were used in Korea. Many served with ANG units until mid–1950s.

tilities ceased in May 1945. The 8-gun P-47s proved themselves to be outstanding bombing and strafing platforms which were more resistant to battle damage from ground fire than the RAF's liquid-cooled Hawker *Typhoons*. Six fighter-bomber groups of the 12th AF, after trading-in their A-36s and P-40s for P-47s during 1944, supported the progress of Allied armies up the Italian peninsula and in the invasion of southern France. In the Pacific, P-47Ds began equipping the 5th AF in Australia in mid–1943 and had grown to a strength of three complete groups plus one squadron by the middle of 1944. Two P-47D groups of the 7th AF that had been formed in Hawaii commenced combat operations from Saipan in the fall of 1944, then after moving to bases on Iwo Jima and Le Shima in the spring 1945, were the first units to re-equip with the new P-47Ns; and by the middle of the summer, P-47Ns were also operational with three new groups of the 20th AF based in Okinawa. The Ns were used principally as long-range escorts for the B-29s attacking Japan from bases in the Mariannas.

A significant number of P-47s were also provided to foreign air forces before World War II ended. During 1944 a total of 830 P-47Ds entered RAF service as the *Thunderbolt I* (razor-back) and *II* (bubble canopy), where they commenced combat operations, primarily as fighter-bombers, on the Burma Front from late 1944 to the war's end. And from late 1943 to late 1944, 196 P-47Ds were flown to the Soviet Union via the Alaska-Siberia route. France also received 446 P-47Ds which served in seven Free French fighter squadrons, initially out of Corsica and later in southern France. Eighty-eight P-47Ds eventually equipped the 1st Group of the Brazilian Air Force, and from late 1944 onwards, fought alongside the 12th AF in the Mediterranean; and in June 1945, 25 P-47Ds were transferred from the 5th AF to Mexico's 201st Fighter Squadron, which thereafter initiated offensive operations against Japanese forces from the Philippines.

In the immediate post-war period, most P-47 units were disbanded, while some P-47D and Ns remained in the active AAF/USAF inventory until replaced by newer jet aircraft (F-80s and F-84s) during the mid and late 1940s. In 1948, when the USAF changed its designation system, the P-47 became the F-47. F-47s continued to serve in many Air National Guard Units, and because of the vast numbers of both F-47s and P/F-51s available following demobilization, a decision was made to equip ANG units on the east coast, south, Puerto Rico, and Hawaii with F-47s and those in the southeast, southwest, and far west regions with F-51s. This regional dichotomy would have significant operational and logistical consequences later when, despite being better suited to fighter-bomber role than F-51s, no F-47s were utilized for combat operations during the Korean War. Some ANG F-47 units were in fact federalized during Korea but used mainly for fighter-bomber training in the U.S. F-47s ultimately served in 24 different ANG units, the last F-47N being retired from the Puerto Rico ANG in 1955. The French F-47Ds remained in service with the post-war *Armée de l'Air* until 1950. Surplus USAF F-47s were also transferred or sold second-hand to the air forces of Iran, Turkey, Italy, Portugal, Yugoslavia, Bolivia, Brazil, Chile, Columbia, Dominican Republic, Ecuador, Honduras, Nicaragua, Peru, and Venezuela, some of which are said to have served well into the 1960s.

North American P/F-51 Mustang 1940–1957

TECHNICAL SPECIFICATIONS (P-51D [BLOCKS 25–30])

Type: One-place fighter-bomber
Manufacturer: North American Aviation, Inc., Inglewood, California and Dallas, Texas.
Total produced: 15,586 (all versions, including the A-36)
Power plant: One 1,695-hp Packard-built Rolls-Royce V-1650-7 *Merlin* 12-cylinder liquid-cooled engine driving a four-bladed Hamilton Standard constant-speed propeller.

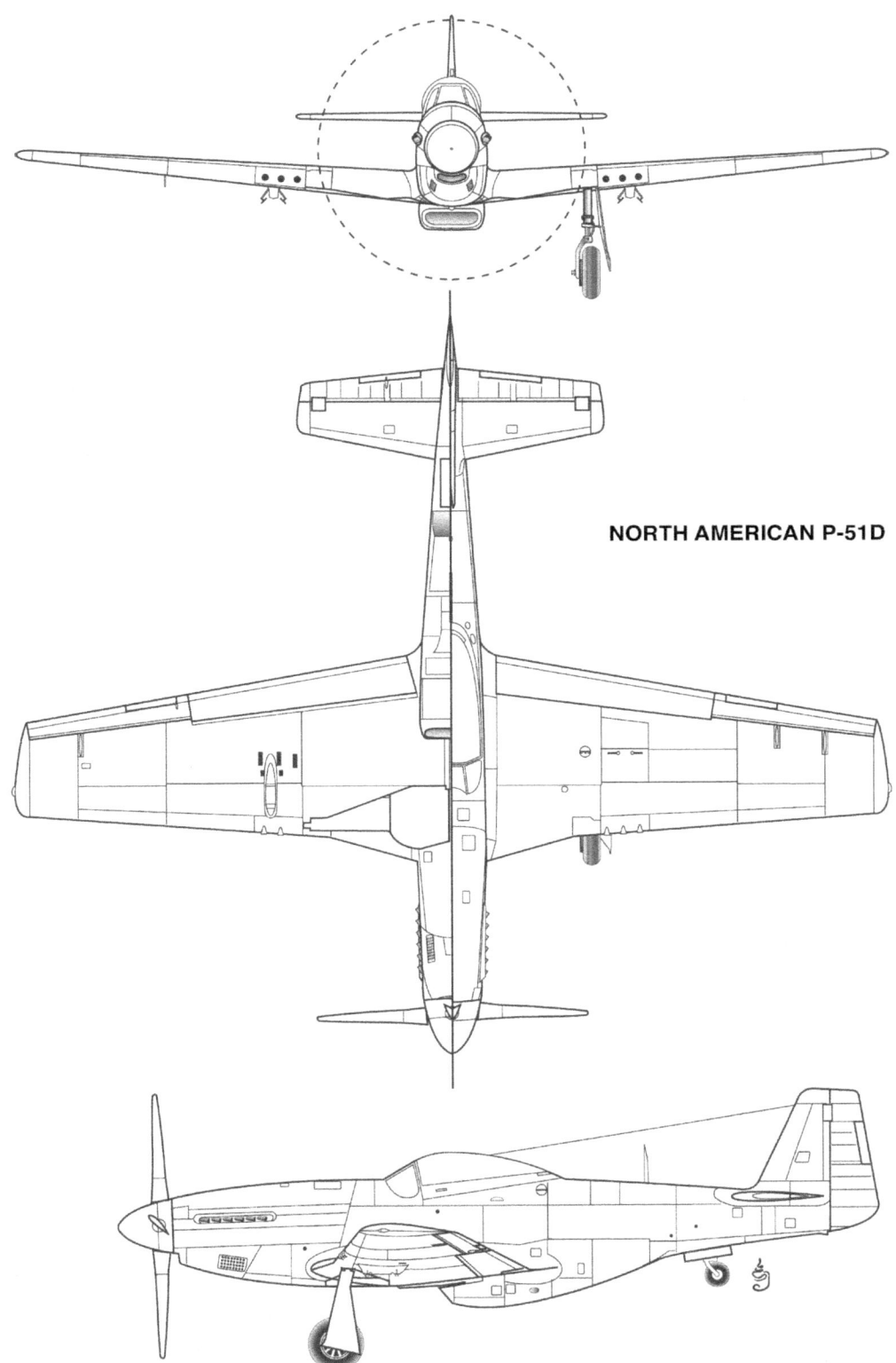

Top: Pair of F-51Ds in Korea being prepared for a ground attack sortie. F-51s pulled from storage and acquired from ANG units were rushed into combat because jets were incapable of operating from primitive airstrips on the Korean mainland. *Bottom:* NamP-51H. F-51H shown in post–1947 livery. Although the aircraft was fully capable in the ground attack role, none were used in Korea due to the greater availability of F-51Ds and Ks. Many saw service with ANG units during the 1950s.

Armament: Six .50-caliber machine guns in the wings and 1,000-lbs of bombs or 10 HVAR rockets carried on wing racks.
Performance: Max. speed 437-mph at 25,000 feet, cruise 362-mph; ceiling 41,900 ft.; range 650 mi. loaded, 2,300 mi. max.
Weights: 7,125-lbs. empty, 11,600-lbs. loaded.
Dimensions: Span 37 ft. 1/2 in., length 32 ft. 3 in., wing area 233 sq. ft.

After establishing itself as the AAF's primary air superiority fighter during World War II, the celebrated North American P-51 saw extensive use as a fighter-bomber in the post-war era. For more detail on the early development of the Allison-powered NA-73/P-51, see A-36, above. The *Merlin*-powered P-51s possessed limited air-to-ground capability until the appearance of the P-51D, Block 25, in 1945, which featured multiple wing hardpoints allowing a variety of external ordnance loads. Combat loads could include a combination of bombs, 5-inch HVAR rockets, Bazooka tubes in triple clusters, or drop tanks, depending on the mission. The P-51D series also introduced the bubble canopy, an increase in wing root chord to accommodate stronger landing gear, six-gun wing armament, K-14 gyro-computing gunsight, and with Block-10, a fin fillet to improve directional stability. The P-51Ks produced on North American's parallel production line at Dallas were identical to the P-51D except for the substitution of an Aeroproducts propeller, and included wing hardpoints from the P-51K-10 onwards. By the time the war ended in August 1945, the Inglewood and Dallas plants had produced a total of 8,100 P-51Ds and 1,500 P-51Ks.

Three lightweight *Mustang* versions, the XP-51F, XP-51G, and XP-51J (powered by a 1,720-hp Allison V-1710-119), tested between early 1944 and early 1945, not only featured a 1,425-lb reduction in empty weight but a new low-drag wing without the root extensions, an elongated bubble canopy, and other aerodynamic refinements. A level top speed of 472-mph was ultimately attained by the XP-51G. In mid–1944, AAF officials decided to incorporate the aerodynamic and structural improvements of the lightweight *Mustangs* into a P-51H production version, which would be powered by a *Merlin* V-1650-6 engine with water injection that could produce 2,218-hp for brief periods and have the air-to-ground capabilities of the P-51D-25. Two thousand P-51Hs had been ordered by the time the first one flew in February 1945; however, the contract was cancelled after V-J Day, limiting production to the 555 examples completed by early 1946. The H was the fastest *Mustang* to be placed in production, delivering a top speed of 487-mph at 25,000 feet, and beginning with the twenty-first production model, featured a taller tail fin that eliminated previous directional stability problems. The end of the war also brought the cancellation of 1,700 P-51Ls, essentially a P-51H airframe powered by a 2,270-hp Merlin V-1650-11 engine. The sole P-51M was a P-51D-30 airframe fitted with a *Merlin* V-1650-9A engine capable of producing 2,220-hp at emergency power.

By the time the war ended in Europe, several groups of the 9th TAF had converted to P-51Ds, but too late, apparently, to see any action as fighter-bombers. In the Pacific area, however, as Japanese fighter opposition dwindled during mid–1945, P-51Ds operating out of the Philippines were used to bomb and strafe Japanese positions on Formosa, and similarly, Iwo Jima-based P-51Ds armed with rockets attacked airfields on the Japanese mainland. During World War II, Great Britain and its Commonwealth Nations received 875 P-51Ds and Ks via Lend-Lease as the *Mustang IV*. While most were used in air defense, at least one RAAF squadron based in northern Italy is known to have used its *Mustang IVs* for ground attack operations against the retreating German armies. In the immediate post-war period, the AAF/USAF retained P-51D/Ks and Hs as its standard day fighter until they were replaced over time by newer jet aircraft, and in 1948, the type's designation was changed to F-51. Starting in 1946, both P/F-51D/Ks and Hs became operational with many Air National Guard units, eventually equipping no fewer than 75 of 98 flying squadrons within the organization.

At the time the Korean War began in June 1950, there were 1,804 F-51s listed on the USAF inventory, either serving with ANG units or in storage. Following activation, the USAF had ten F-51 Fighter-Bomber Wings (FBW) in frontline service by the middle of 1951. Since they were more plentiful and thus easier to replace, only F-51D/K variants were selected for deployment in the combat theater. In their close air support role, as compared to USAF jets of that period, F-51s were capable of operating from the shorter, forward airfields of Korea and possessed significantly more loiter time over targets. On the negative side, their unarmored, belly-mounted cooling systems rendered them highly vulnerable to enemy ground fire. During the Korean conflict, the USAF typically maintained three F-51 Wings in the combat theater on a rotation basis, augmented by other F-51squadrons serving with South Korean, Australian, and South African forces within the United Nations group. Interestingly, among the RAAF F-51s were some of the 200 CA-18 *Mustang* copies that had been license-built in Australia. When they were withdrawn from combat operations in early 1953, F-51s had flown 62,607 fighter-bomber sorties for a loss of 184 aircraft to enemy action. Although devoted entirely to ground attack operations, F-51s were nevertheless credited with shooting down several North Korean propeller-driven Yaks during the early part of the war. Following Korea, many of the activated F-51s were returned to ANG service, the very last P-51D being retired from the West Virginia ANG in 1957.

Following World War II large numbers of surplus P-51s were supplied to foreign nations, serving in no less than fifty-five different air forces worldwide, probably a record for a military fighter, and some served into the 1970s. The venerable *Mustang* briefly reappeared in the USAF inventory in 1967, not as an active aircraft but this time through a military assistance program providing airplanes to the Bolivian Air Force to counter Communist insurgents. Twenty-four P-51Ds were remanufactured to specific ground attack requirements by Cavalier Aircraft of Florida, receiving in the process new *Merlin* engines, strengthened wings, new avionics, a raised tailfin, and tip tanks. Cavalier, who had acquired production rights to the P-51, also rebuilt two unarmed *Mustangs* for the U.S. Army in 1968, to be used as chase planes in the *Cheyenne* helicopter program, and is also known to have privately supplied a number of other P-51s to South and Central American nations. Again, in 1972, the USAF directed Cavalier to remanufacture six more P-51Ds for the Indonesian Air Force. In a private venture aimed at extending the combat usefulness of the P-51, Cavalier mated a P-51D airframe during 1968 to a 1,740-shp Roll-Royce *Dart* turboprop engine, however, no military sales resulted. After Cavalier sold its rights to Piper Aircraft, the project resurfaced in 1971 as the PA-48 *Enforcer*, which had been modified even further with the installation of a 2,455-shp Lycoming T-55 turboprop. Piper tried to interest the USAF in purchasing *Enforcers* as part of the a program known as *Pave Coin*, which was designed to supply military aircraft to friendly foreign nations, but as with Cavalier, no sales were forthcoming. The final episode materialized in 1981, when Congressional pressure led the USAF to award Piper a contract to build two more PA-48s for yet another evaluation. Both aircraft flew in mid–1983 under civilian registrations and underwent military testing during 1983 and 1984; however, no additional PA-48s were ordered, and the USAF placed both in storage in late 1986.

Bell P-63 Kingcobra 1942–1950

TECHNICAL SPECIFICATIONS (P-63C)

Type: One-place fighter-bomber
Manufacturer: Bell Aircraft Corp., Buffalo, New York
Total produced: 3,303 (all versions)
Power plant: One 1,800-hp Allison V-1710-117 12-cylinder liquid-cooled engine with water injection driving a four-bladed Aeroproducts constant-speed propeller.

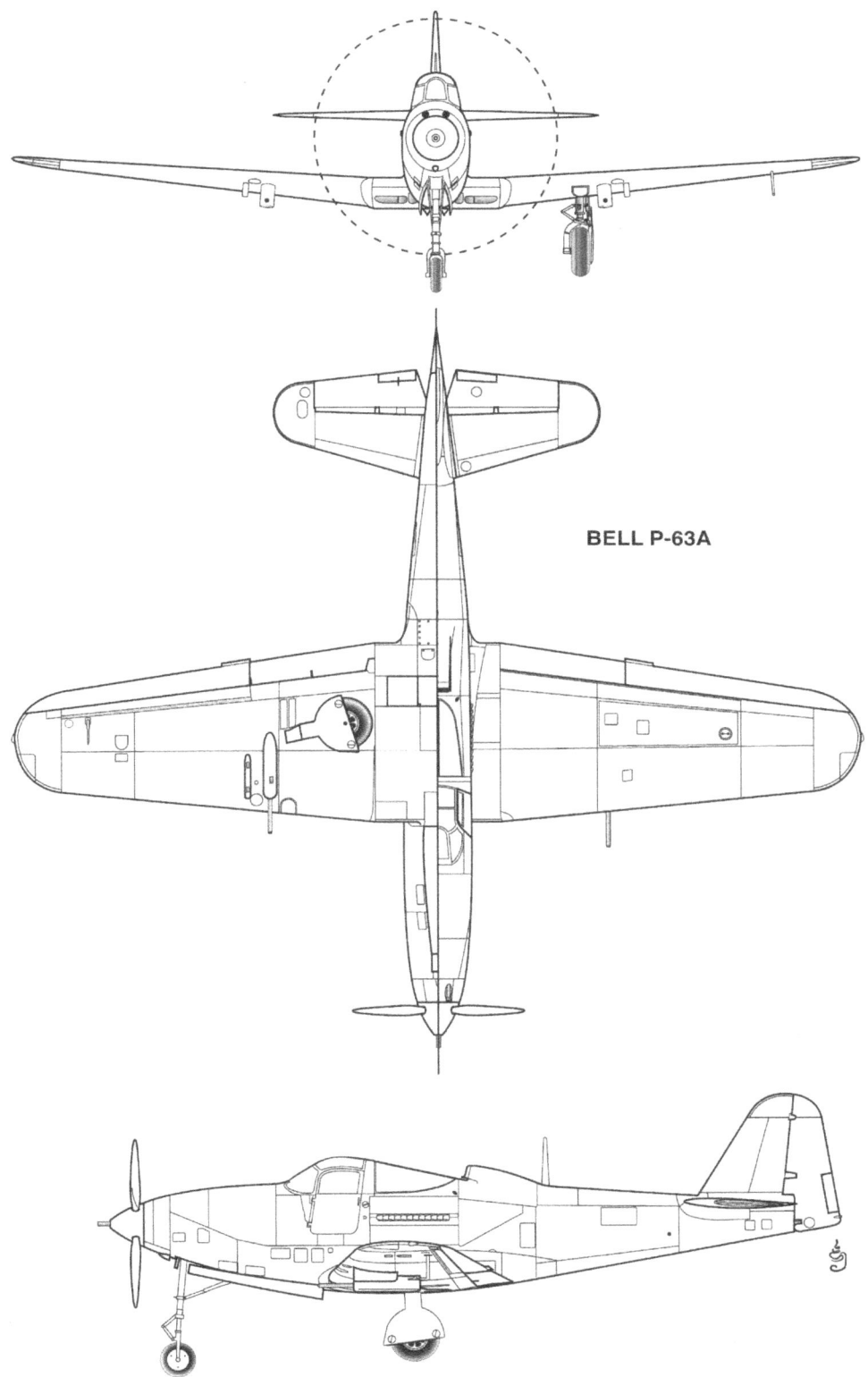

BELL P-63A

108   I—USAAC, USAAF, and USAF Attack Aircraft

A P-63C in service with the French *Armée de l'Air* following World War II. The French P-63s were used to fly ground attack sorties against Viet Minh insurgents in Vietnam from 1949 to 1951.

Armament: One 37-mm cannon firing through the propeller hub, two synchronized .50-caliber machine guns in the nose, two .50-caliber machine guns mounted in pods under the wings, and 1,500-lbs of bombs carried on the centerline and wing racks.
Performance: Max. speed 410-mph at 25,000 feet, cruise 356-mph; ceiling 38,600 ft.; range 320 mi. loaded, 2,100 mi. max.
Weights: 6,800-lbs. empty, 8,800-lbs. loaded.
Dimensions: Span 38 ft. 4 in., length 32 ft. 8 in., wing area 248 sq. ft.

Like its P-39 forebear, the P-63 is worthy of mention because of its service as an American-made attack aircraft with foreign air forces both during and after World War II. The P-63 arose in early 1941 as an effort by Bell to develop a fighter without the low-altitude shortcomings of the P-39, which was just entering service. A laminar-flow wing of increased span, an uprated V-1710-47 of 1,325-hp, plus many other aerodynamic refinements were integrated into the final design of the XP-63, which made its first flight in December 1942. It had already been ordered into full-scale production the previous September as the P-63A, and the first of 1,725 production models began arriving in October 1943, by which time the AAF was already planning to standardize on P-38s and P-51s in the air superiority role and P-47s for ground attack. As a consequence, all but 339 P-63As were allocated to the Soviet Union and subsequently delivered via the Alaska-Siberia route. The P-63B was a proposed *Merlin*-powered version that was never built. The AAF also ordered 1,227 improved P-63Cs, which differed in having a more powerful V-1710-177 engines and a 10-inch reduction in wingspan, and starting with the P-63C-5, a ventral fin beneath the aft fuselage. Although deliveries began in December 1944, nearly all P-63C production was Lend-Leased, most to the Soviet Union, plus 114 transferred to the French *Armée de l'Air* right at the war's end. The P-63D, appearing in early 1945, featured a bubble canopy, cleaner aerodynamics, and the larger P-63A wing, and with a 437-mph top speed, was the fastest of the *Kingcobra* series, but never reached production. The 2,943 P-63Es ordered specifically for Lend-lease to the Soviet Union incorporated the improvements of the P-63D but retained the standard car-door cockpit arrangement of the P-63A/C; however, the contract was cancelled after delivery of 13 examples in May 1945.

In AAF service, P-63s were used initially for operational training and never saw combat. One hundred P-63As became RP-63As when they were stripped of armament and re-skinned with thicker aluminum so they could be used as target aircraft. Attacking aircraft were armed with lead-graphite "frangible" bullets designed to shatter on impact, and when a bullet struck the skin of a RP-63A, pressure-sensitive plates caused a light to flash on front of the spinner, which earned it the knick-name "pinball." Two hundred P-63Cs were similarly modified while still on the assembly line and thereafter entered service as the PR-63C. RP-63As and Cs remained active until the late 1940s. A total of 2,376 P-63s reached the Soviet Union from early 1944 and to mid–1945 and saw action on the Eastern Front during the last year of the war, predominantly in the ground attack role. *Kingcobras* remained in service with the Soviet Air Force during the early Cold War era, ultimately receiving the NATO code name "Fred." The French *Armée de l'Air* received its P-63Cs too late to see action during World War II, but later, in 1949, five *Kingcobra* squadrons were deployed to Indo-China (Vietnam), where they flew ground attack sorties against insurgent Viet Minh forces. The P-63s were withdrawn from combat in 1951 after being replaced by ex-Navy Grumman F8F-1 *Bearcats*.

SECOND SERIES • 1945–1961

Designation	*Manufacturer*	*Dates*
B-43	Douglas Aircraft Co.	1946–1953
B-45	North American Aviation, Inc.	1947–1958
B-46	Convair (Consolidated-Vultee) Corp.	1947–1950
B-51 (A-45)	Glenn L. Martin Co.	1949–1956
B-57	Glenn L. Martin Co.	1953–1982
B-66	Douglas Aircraft Co.	1954–1976
F-80	Lockheed Aircraft Corp.	1944–1958
F-82	North American Aviation, Inc.	1945–1953
F-84 (straight-wing)	Republic Aviation Corp.	1946–1958
F-84 (swept-wing)	Republic Aviation Corp.	1950–1972
F-86	North American Aviation, Inc.	1947–1970
F-100	North American Aviation, Inc.	1953–1979
F-101	McDonnell Aircraft Corp.	1954–1982
F-104	Lockheed Aircraft Corp.	1954–1975
F-105	Republic Aviation Corp.	1955–1983
F-107	North American Aviation, Inc.	1956–1959

Douglas B-43 1946–1953

TECHNICAL SPECIFICATIONS (XB-43)

Type: Three-place tactical bomber.
Manufacturer: Douglas Aircraft Co., Santa Monica, California.
Total produced: 2
Power plant: Two General Electric J-35-3 turbojet engines, each rated at 4,000-lbs./s.t. Armament: Planned gun armament not installed; up to 6,000-lbs. bombs of bombs carried in an internal bomb bay.

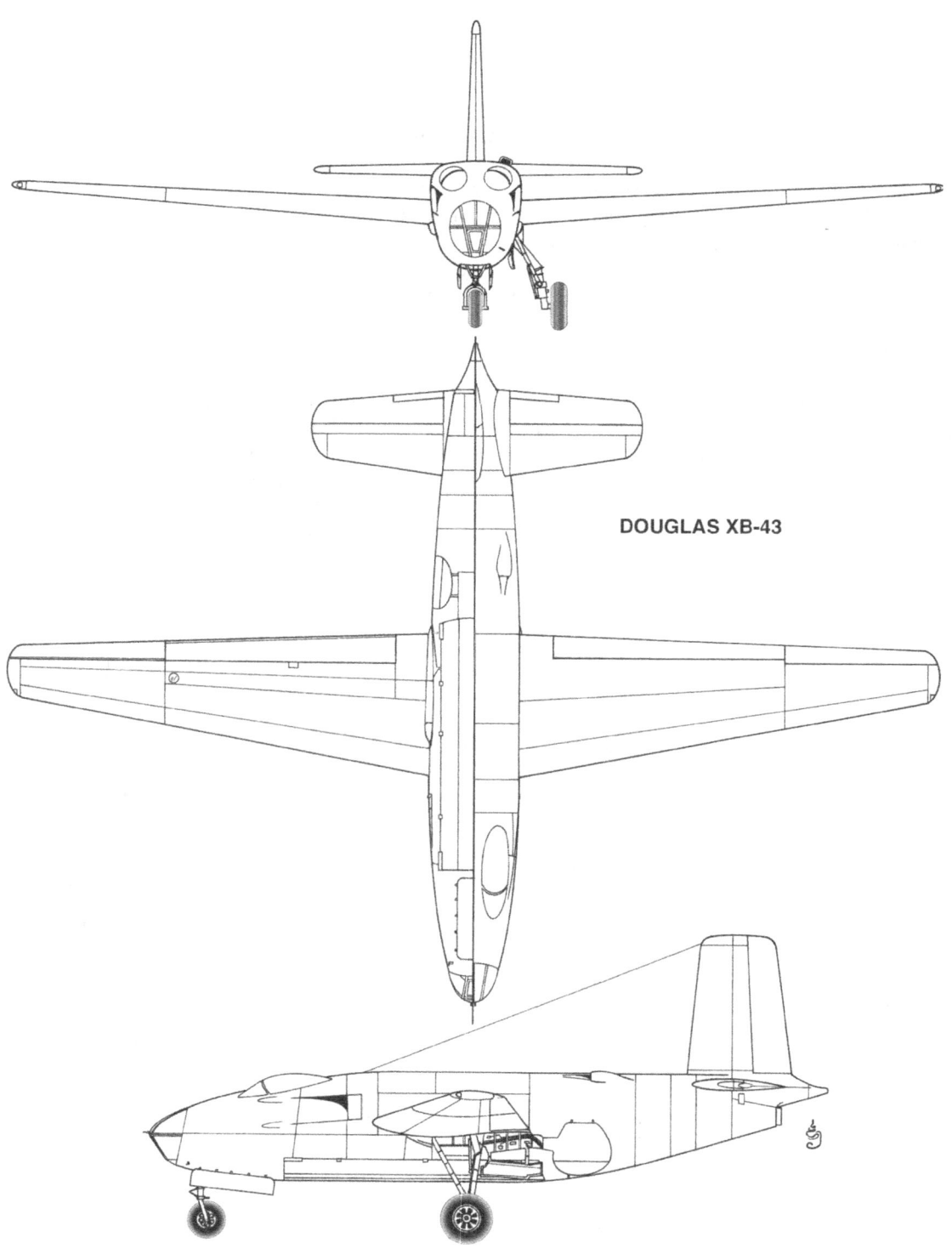

DOUGLAS XB-43

The second prototype, the YB-43. This aircraft was kept flying until 1953 with parts taken from the XB-43. Though underpowered as a bomber, it provided valuable information on high-altitude jet operations.

Performance: Max. speed 515-mph at s.l., cruise 420-mph; ceiling 38,200 ft.; range 1,100 mi. loaded, 2,840 mi. max.
Weights: 21,755-lbs. empty, 37,000-lbs. loaded.
Dimensions: Span 71 ft. 2 in., length 51 ft. 2 in., wing area 563 sq. ft.

Originally authorized by the AAF in September 1943, the Douglas B-43 holds the distinction of having been the first jet-propelled bomber of American design to fly. While sharing a common aerodynamic configuration with the piston-engine XB-42, early progress on the XB-43 project proceeded much slower due to protracted development of the General Electric TG-180 (later J-35) axial-flow turbojet engines that would power it. Douglas received the go-ahead to built two prototypes in January 1944, and by the end of the year, the detailed design data was sufficiently promising that Air Technical Service Command requested Douglas to tender a tentative proposal for production of 50 B-43s. Two versions were contemplated: a glazed-nose tactical bomber carrying up to 6,000-lbs. of bombs and a solid-nose ground attack type armed with sixteen fixed .50-caliber machine guns and 35 HVAR 5-inch rockets. Both would feature a remote-controlled, radar-directed tail turret armed with two .50-caliber guns. However, the project was repeatedly delayed by problems associated with availability and testing of the jet engines, including at one point, structural damage to the XB-43 prototype when an engine's compressor blades separated from the spool during a ground run-up in October 1945. As a consequence, the first flight did not take place until May 17, 1946, by which time any AAF plans to acquire more B-43s had been overtaken by the newer XB-45 and XB-46 programs.

The XB-43 emerged with the side-by-side bubble canopies of the XB-42, giving it the same bug-eyed appearance. Flight-testing of the XB-43 at Muroc Army Airfield revealed acceptable handling characteristics, but the aircraft, in terms of overall performance, was deemed to be underpowered for its size and weight. When cracks developed in the blown nose glazing due to temperature and pressure changes, it was replaced by a solid unit made of plywood. The second prototype, designated YB-43, featured a conventional cockpit enclosure and made its first flight in May 1947. The official evaluation and acceptance program on both aircraft was concluded in mid–1948. Thereafter, Air Research Development Command used the XB-43 for a variety of tests until the aircraft was damaged beyond repair in 1951; the YB-43 served with Air Material Command's Power Plant Laboratory as an engine and high-altitude systems testbed until being retired in 1953.

North American B-45 Tornado 1947–1958

TECHNICAL SPECIFICATIONS (B-45A[AFTER TACTICAL NUCLEAR MODIFICATIONS])
Type: Four-place tactical bomber.
Manufacturer: North American Aviation, Inc., Inglewood, California.
Total produced: 142 (including RB-45C)
Power plant: Two General Electric J-47-7 or -13 turbojet engines, each rated at 5,500-lbs./s.t. and two General Electric J-47-9 or -15 turbojet engines, each rated at 5,000-lbs./s.t.
Armament: Two .50-caliber machine guns in a powered tail turret and up to 22,000-lbs. bombs of bombs carried in an internal bomb bay, including a Mk. V atomic bomb.
Performance: Max. speed 566-mph at s.l., cruise 461-mph; ceiling 41,250 ft.; range 1,757 mi. loaded, 2,530 mi. max.
Weights: 47,022-lbs. empty, 92,745-lbs. max. takeoff.
Dimensions: Span 89 ft. (96 ft. over tanks), length 75 ft. 4 in., wing area 1,175 sq. ft.

The North American B-45 was the first type of USAF jet bomber to become operational and the first to possess tactical nuclear capability. Its origins can be traced back to the middle of World War II, when U.S. military officials became increasingly concerned about German advances in jet propulsion. During 1944, while the earliest American-made turbojet engines were still being tested, the War Department circulated an incredibly ambitious requirement among aircraft manufacturers asking for a multi-engine jet bomber that would have a top speed of 550-mph, a range of 3,000-miles, and a ceiling of 45,000 feet, with projected takeoff weights varying from 80,000 to 200,000-lbs. Only four manufacturers responded: the North American Model 130 (XB-45), the Convair Model 109 (XB-46), the Boeing Model 432 (XB-47), and the Martin Model 223 (XB-48). Although the AAF originally intended the four proposals to compete for a single production contract, it was evident by 1946 that the smaller designs of the XB-45 and XB-46 were both likely to become operational much sooner than the larger and considerably more complex projects submitted by Boeing and Martin. For that reason, the AAF decided to evaluate the XB-45 and XB-46 separately and reserve the XB-47 and XB-48 for future consideration. In August 1946, based on mockup inspections, AAF officials determined that the XB-45 would surpass the XB-46 in terms of general performance and operational versatility; therefore, Convair's contract was limited to one prototype while North American received approval to build 96 production models as the B-45A. Other than the four J-35 turbojet engines paired in underwing nacelles, the straight-wing aerodynamic layout of North American's prototype was fairly straightforward.

The XB-45 lifted off on its maiden flight on March 17, 1947, and early trials revealed impressive performance for a bomber of that period: a top speed of 516-mph, a ceiling of 37,600 feet, and a range of 2,240 miles with a combat load. Further evaluation by USAF test pilots indicated a number of changes needed to bring the plane to operational standards: ejection seats for the pilot and co-pilot together with better escape hatches for the bombardier-navigator and tail gunner; an increase in stab/elevator area; and a redesign and strengthening of

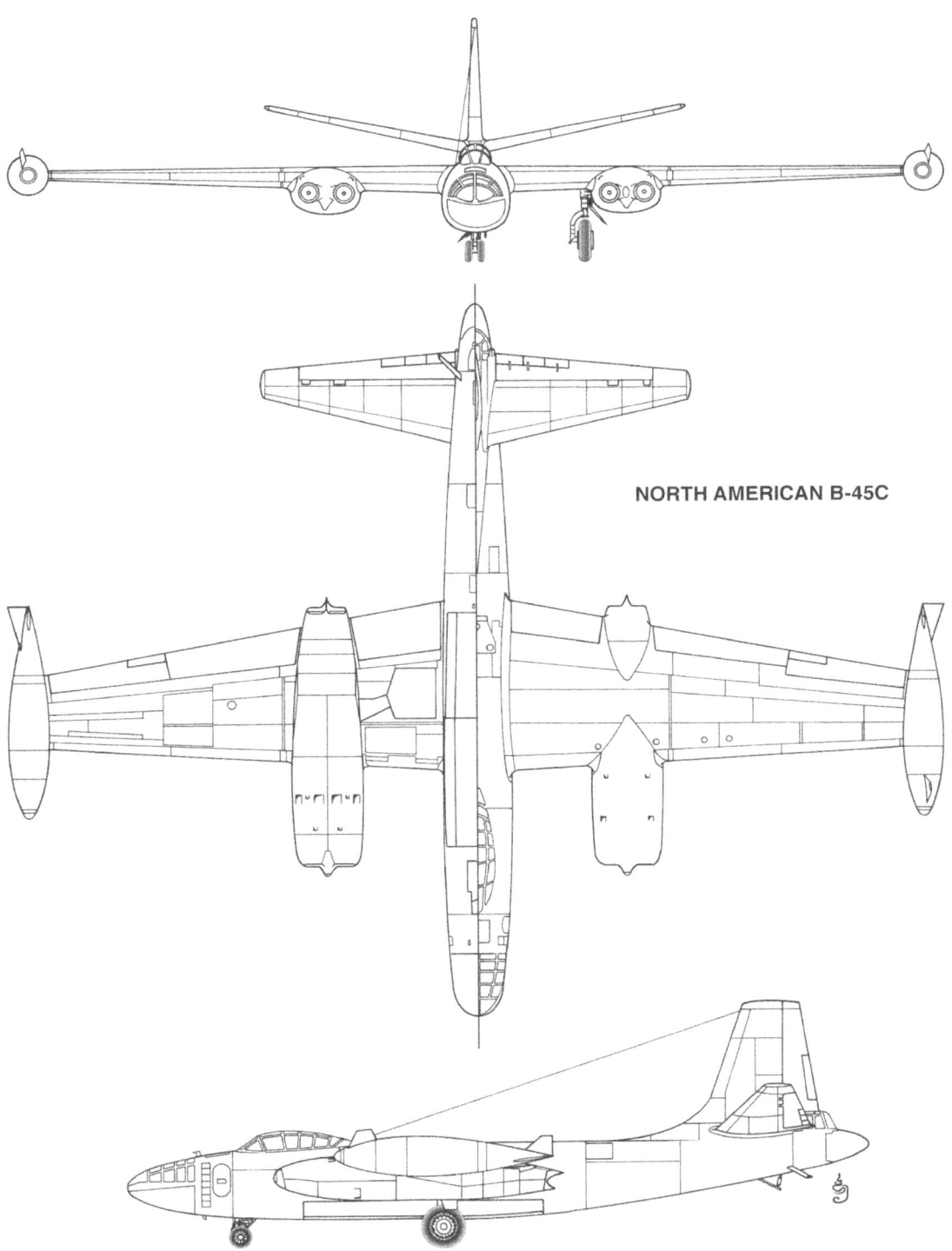

NORTH AMERICAN B-45C

the nose compartment. The first 22 production aircraft, B-45A-1s powered by J-35 engines, were considered too underpowered to be rated for combat, and after being re-designated TB-45As, would serve initially as transition trainers. Performance was significantly enhanced in the second production block of 74 B-45A-5s, powered by the higher thrust J-47s, which boosted top speed to 570-mph and service ceiling to 46,600 feet. Deliveries of first production B-45A-

B-45A of the 47th Bomb Wing (Light) based at RAF Alconbury, England, in the mid–1950s. Operating under the code-name "Backbreaker," the mission of the 47th was designed to stall an attack by Soviet ground forces with the earliest tactical nuclear bombs.

5s commenced in November 1948. Tactical Air Command (TAC) originally requested two wings—192 aircraft—of B-45s, but drastic reductions in the 1949 defense budget caused TAC's allocation to be limited to one light bomb wing (74 B-45A-5s), one tactical reconnaissance squadron (33 RB-45s projected in 1950), and one high-speed target towing squadron (derived from converted TB-45A-1s). The improved B-45C, which flew in May 1949, featured a redesigned canopy with additional framing, 1,200-gallon tip tanks, airframe strengthening, and was the first USAF aircraft built with a mid-air, boom-type refueling system. For the budgetary reasons cited above, B-45C production was terminated after completion of only ten examples, but the improvements of the C were later incorporated to most operational B-45As. Deliveries of the first of 33 camera-equipped RB-45Cs began mid–1950, and they were initially attached to SAC. From late 1950 to early 1952, 41 of the B-45A-5s underwent extensive modifications to add nuclear weapons capability, which involved not only structural changes to the bomb bay and strengthening of the wing spars, but installation of radar and SHORAN navigation and bombing systems plus Norden M9C optical bombsights. Later, in 1953 and 1954, 15 of the TB-45A-1s, after being refitted with J-47 engines and brought up to B-45C standards, also received the tactical nuclear modifications.

The first B-45A-5s entered operational service with the 47th Bomb Wing (Light) at Langley AFB in Virginia in late 1948, yet within a year, the unit was forced to deactivate and place its aircraft in storage due to the unavailability of bombing and fire-control systems, and more seriously, a lack of spare J-47 engines. All supplies of engines, which typically ran only 15 hours between overhauls, had been earmarked for the F-86 fighter program. The B-45s received a reprieve in mid–1950, however, when TAC was directed to reactivate the 47th BW(L) to prepare for eventual deployment overseas in anticipation of a tactical nuclear mission code-named "Backbreaker." In May 1952, modifications and aircrew training having been accomplished, the 47th BW(L) and its 41 B-45s debarked to a new base in Sculthorpe, England, where they commenced operations for the new Backbreaker mission. Similarly, in March 1954, when 15 additional B-45s were deemed combat-ready, they were deployed to a neighboring base at Alconbury, England. The B-45s thereafter functioned as a tactical nuclear tripwire: in the event of invasion by the enormous number of Soviet Army divisions stationed in central and eastern Europe, Backbreaker was intended to stop them before they rolled over the seriously outnumbered NATO Allies. The Backbreaker B-45s of the 47th BW(L) were phased out of service during early 1958 as the unit transitioned to the swept-wing Douglas B-66B; the RB-45Cs, having been transferred to TAC in 1953, remained in service only a year longer. After the B-45s were withdrawn, the USAF had no further use for them and none were allocated to reserve or ANG units, with the result that most were broken up for scrap. TAC had previously studied the feasibility of converting B-45s to high-speed tankers for F-84F fighter-bombers, but the idea was abandoned before any aircraft could be converted.

Convair B-46 1947–1950

TECHNICAL SPECIFICATIONS (XB-46)

Type: Three-place tactical bomber.
Manufacturer: Convair (Consolidated-Vultee Aircraft) Corp., Ft. Worth, Texas
Total produced: 1
Powerplant: Four General Electric J-35-C3 turbojet engines, each rated at 3,820-lbs./s.t. Armament: Two .50-caliber machine guns in a powered tail turret and up to 22,000-lbs. bombs of bombs carried in an internal bomb bay.
Performance: Max. speed 545-mph at 15,000 ft., cruise 438-mph; ceiling 40,000 ft.; range 1,387 mi. loaded, 2,870 mi. max.
Weights: 48,000-lbs. empty, 94,400-lbs. max. takeoff.
Dimensions: Span 113 ft., length 105 ft. 9 in., wing area 1,285 sq. ft.

The sole XB-46 over southern California, probably in 1948. The aircraft's exceptionally slender fuselage section, ultimately deemed to be a limiting factor in terms of equipment and weapons storage, shows to very good advantage.

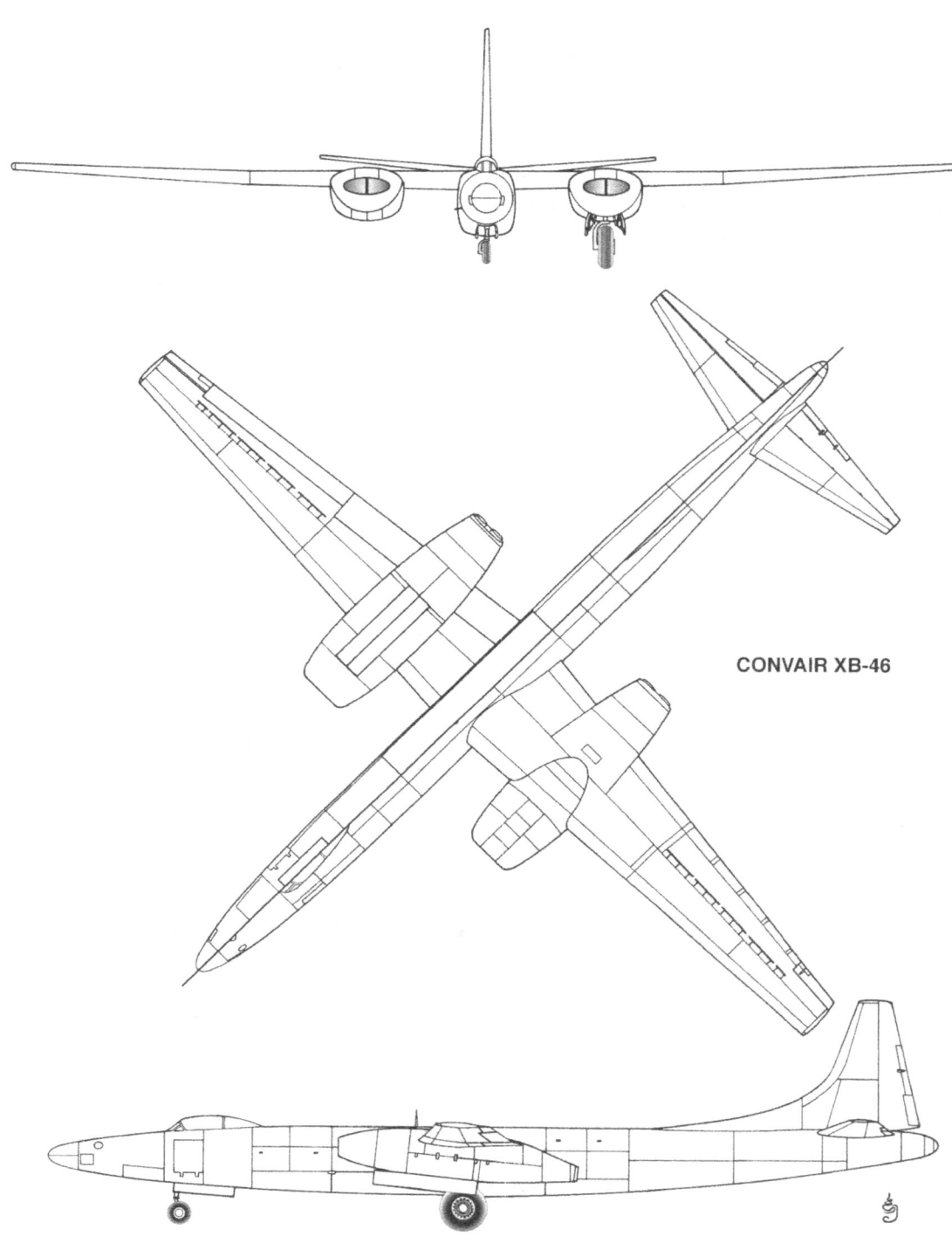

CONVAIR XB-46

Arising from the same 1944 AAF jet bomber requirement as the B-45, Convair's slightly larger B-46 appeared with an exceptionally sleek aerodynamic design. The AAF approved Convair's Model 109 development proposal in January 1945, assigning the designation XB-46, followed within a month by a contract to build three experimental prototypes. When mockup inspections were completed in August 1946, however, the XB-45 was selected for production and the XB-46 program reduced to only one prototype. In general, inspectors felt that the XB-

46 had less development potential as a combat aircraft. The long, pencil-thin fuselage that gave the type its characteristic look was viewed as also limiting the interior space needed to house crew, radar, navigation and bombing equipment, and weapons.

The XB-46 made its first flight on April 2, 1947, 16 days behind the XB-45, and the official acceptance program was completed in November after 101 hours of USAF testing. General flying characteristics were rated as satisfactory, but the aircraft exhibited lateral control problems at high speeds that were attributed to the spoiler system. Because the aircraft's fowler-type flaps ran nearly full span, roll control was achieved through a combination of small ailerons augmented by 20-foot spoilers. Another novel feature was the use of a pneumatic system (as opposed to hydraulic or electric) to operate the landing gear, bomb bay doors, and brakes. From late 1947 to mid–1949, the USAF used the XB-46 to conduct a variety of air testing that included noise measurements, vibration analysis, and stability and control experiments. The aircraft was flown to Eglin AFB in Florida in mid–1950, where climatic ground testing was performed on the pneumatic system. In early 1952, the nose section was removed and sent to Wright-Patterson AFB in Ohio for storage and the remainder of the airframe was scrapped.

Martin B-51 1949–1956

TECHNICAL SPECIFICATIONS (XB-51)
Type: Two-place tactical bomber.
Manufacturer: Glenn L. Martin Co., Baltimore, Maryland
Total produced: 2
Power plant: Three General Electric J-47-13 turbojet engines, each rated at 5,200-lbs./s.t. Armament: Eight fixed 20-mm cannons and up to 6,400-lbs. bombs of bombs carried in an internal bomb bay, or 4,000-lbs. of bombs on external racks, and eight HVAR 6-inch rockets.
Performance: Max. speed 645-mph at s.l., cruise 532-mph; ceiling 40,500 ft.; range 870 mi. loaded, 1,600 mi. max.
Weights: 29,584-lbs. empty, 55,923-lbs. max. takeoff.
Dimensions: Span 53 ft. 1 in., length 85 ft. 1 in., wing area 548 sq. ft.

Although never achieving production, the Martin B-51 nonetheless deserves to be recognized as one of the most advanced aircraft designs of its time. Design work on the Martin Model 234 began in early 1946 in response to an AAF design competition for a multi-engine attack/light bomber type having a top speed not less than 505-mph. Martin's entry, assigned the designation XA-45, won the competition with a very conventional straight-wing design to be powered by two turboprop and two turbojet engines, similar in layout to its Navy P4M *Mercator*. Before any prototypes were ordered, however, Air Material Command reclassified the project as a "ground support bomber" and issued brand new speed requirements that effectively dictated pure turbojet power. The re-design effort that followed at Martin was undoubtedly influenced by the fact its recent straight-wing heavy bomber entry, the XB-48, using the same six powerplants, had turned out to be 100-mph slower than Boeing's swept-wing XB-47. Thus, when the Model 234 reemerged as the XB-51, it proved to be stunning departure from the earlier XA-45 proposal, featuring a very thin-section wing of 35-degrees sweepback, mid-mounted to a long fuselage. The wing was freed of any drag-producing extremities by locating the landing gear wholly within the fuselage on two tandem, double-wheel bogies, laterally balanced by retractable outrigger wheels located below the wingtips. The engine layout was unorthodox, two J-47s in nacelles on the lower fuselage and a third buried in the tail. Relying primarily on speed for protection, the two-man crew consisted of a pilot seated under a bubble canopy and a bombardier-navigator located in a compartment just aft of the pilot. The thin wing was of very advanced design, incorporating spoilers for roll control and leading-edge slats and full-span flaps to lower takeoff and landing speeds. The design also pio-

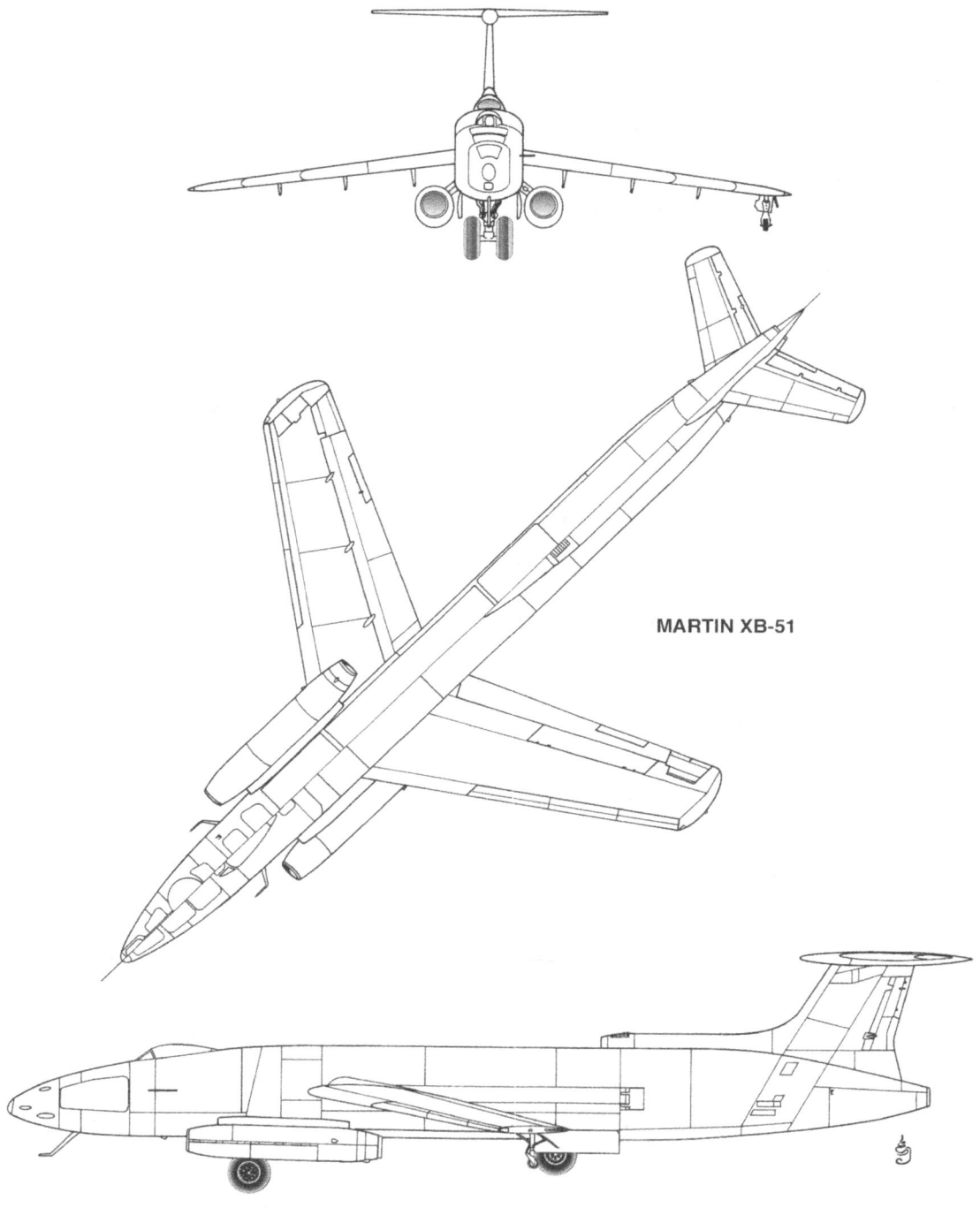

MARTIN XB-51

neered a variable-incidence control system that allowed the entire wing to be moved from three to seven degrees positive incidence, thereby providing the higher angles-of-attack needed by swept-wing aircraft during takeoff and landing. The unique "T-tail" arrangement of the XB-51's empennage was among the earliest seen on a jet aircraft. And to reduce high-speed drag, Martin developed a rotary bomb bay system that spun the weapons out like a horizon-

Factory photograph of the first XB-51 prototype over Maryland countryside in early 1950. Although it exceeded design requirements, the aircraft became the victim of a procurement controversy between the Army and the USAF.

tal revolving door. After reviewing the new proposal in May 1946, the AAF gave Martin the go-ahead to build two prototypes.

The first XB-51 flew on October 18, 1949, followed by the second prototype in April 1950. Early trials demonstrated levels of performance nearly equal to North American's F-86 fighter, combined with exceptional maneuverability. But while the test program was still in progress, the USAF was directed to convene a board of senior USAF and Army officers (i.e., the Wright Board) to hear recent Army concerns over the selection of a new tactical bomber. Army officials were chiefly interested in finding an aircraft to replace the USAF's aging fleet of Douglas B-26s, with particular emphasis on the interdiction and night intruder roles. Although the XB-51 was the USAF's obvious choice, the Army insisted that the board consider four other aircraft: the North American AJ-1, the North American B-45, the Avro Canada CF-100, and the English Electric *Canberra*. The selection process ultimately came down to a fly-off between the XB-51 and the British-made *Canberra,* which took place during mid–1951. In this contest, the highly innovative design of the XB-51 became a major drawback: the 3.7 G-load limit imposed on the thin wing restricted tight tactical maneuvering around targets, whereas the low loading of the broad-winged *Canberra* posed no similar problems, and perhaps most important, its range with comparable bomb load was less than half that of its British competitor, placing serious limits on its loiter time in the target area. The USAF's suggestion that both aircraft be procured was rejected with the result that the XB-51 program was cancelled in November 1951 and arrangements made with the British government to license-produce the *Canberra* in the U.S. Afterward, the two XB-51 prototypes continued to be flown from Edwards AFB in various USAF tests until both met their demise in crashes attributed to pilot error, the last occurring in 1956.

Martin B-57 Canberra 1953–1982

TECHNICAL SPECIFICATIONS (B-57B)

Type: Two-place tactical bomber.
Manufacturer: Glenn L. Martin Co., Baltimore, Maryland
Total produced: 403 (all versions, including RB-57A/F)
Power plant: Two Wright (Buick) J-65-5 turbojet engines, each rated at 7,220-lbs./s.t.
Armament: Four fixed 20-mm cannons and up to 4,500-lbs. bombs of bombs carried in a rotary bomb bay, plus 2,800-lbs. of bombs or eight HVAR 5-inch rockets on wing racks.
Performance: Max. speed 598-mph at 2,500 ft., cruise 476-mph; ceiling 45,100 ft.; range 1,895 mi. loaded, 2,722 mi. max.
Weights: 28,793-lbs. empty, 56,965-lbs. max. takeoff.
Dimensions: Span 64 ft., length 65 ft. 6 in., wing area 960 sq. ft.

When the USAF selected a license-built version of the English Electric *Canberra* for production in 1951, it was the first military aircraft of foreign design to be manufactured in the U.S. since the World War I-era De Havilland DH.4. Equally, the process leading to its selection—a fly-off against the Martin XB-51 at the behest of the Army—was a conspicuous departure from normal post-war USAF procurement methods. Even before the fly-off had been concluded, the Glenn L. Martin Co. was approached with the suggestion of license-building *Canberras* in the event B-51 production was not ordered. In March 1951, once the B-51 project had been officially cancelled, Martin was awarded a contract to build 250 *Canberras* under the USAF designation B-57. Due to production priorities on the Roll-Royce *Avon* engines that powered the British version, Martin-built B-57s would instead use Armstrong-Siddeley *Sapphire* turbojets manufactured under license by Curtiss-Wright as the J-65. Two British *Canberra* B.2 aircraft were flown to the Martin factory at Baltimore to be used as patterns. The first American production model, the B-57A, was aerodynamically identical to the B.2 but differed in certain details: it incorporated the rotary bomb bay system developed for the XB-51, added wingtip tanks for additional fuel storage, and reduced crew from three to two by combining bombardier-navigator functions. Like the British version, no defensive armament was carried.

The first B-57A flew on July 20, 1953, and by the end of the year, seven more had been delivered. Since Air Material Command had determined beforehand that the *Canberra* did not meet USAF tactical standards, the B-57As were to be used solely for testing and evaluation. The first operational model was the RB-57A reconnaissance version, 67 examples of which were accepted in 1954 and 1955. In order to bring the bomber version up to USAF requirements, development of the B-57B was begun in 1952. And with the recent introduction of lightweight nuclear weapons, (i.e., 1,700-lb. Mk. 7 bomb), the tactical role of the aircraft would be expanded. The most noticeable change was a complete redesign of the cockpit area, which placed the pilot and bombardier-navigator in a tandem arrangement under a long bubble canopy. Tactical equipment included a SHORAN navigation and bombing system, an M-1 bomb-toss computer, and an APW-1 guidance radar to locate targets. Because the B's flat-paneled windscreen permitted use of an optical gunsight, a fixed armament of eight .50-caliber guns was fitted in the wings, and in later production blocks, four 20-mm cannons. Other improvements included the addition of board-type speed brakes, power-boosted controls, and four pylons on the outer wing panels for external weapons stores. USAF plans to acquire 293 B-57Bs were

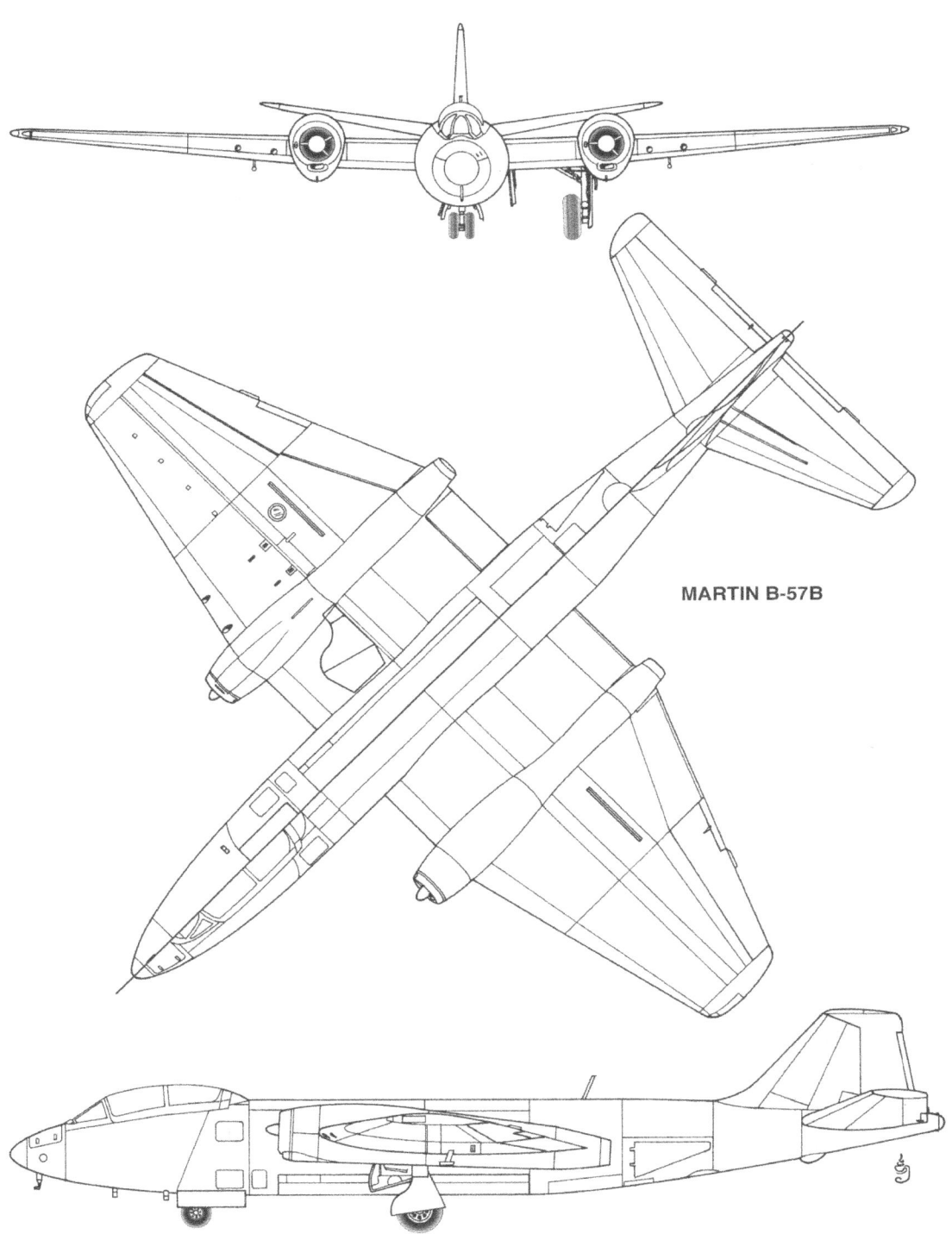

MARTIN B-57B

subsequently reduced to the 202 examples delivered from June 1954 to May 1956. Also produced in 1955 and 1956 were 38 B-57C dual-control trainers that would serve in tactical bombing units equipped with the B-57B. The RB-57D, 20 of which were built in 1955, was a high-altitude reconnaissance version featuring a 60 percent increase in wing area and two Pratt & Whitney J-57 engines. From 1955 to 1957, all B-57Bs went through an improvement pro-

Top: Publicity photograph of black-painted B-57B with full external weapons load. During 1957 and 1958, most were displaced in the tactical nuclear role by single-seat fighter bombers. *Bottom:* One of sixteen B-57Bs modified as a B-57G. New nose configuration featured larger APQ-39 radar and chin-mounted forward-looking infrared system. In 1967 and 1968, these aircraft combat tested the first operational "smart" bombs over Vietnam.

gram to receive LABS (low-altitude bombing system) toss-bomb computers, new search radars, and chaff dispensers. Sixty-Eight B-57Es equipped with towing equipment in the bomb bay space were delivered in 1956 and 1957 to serve as high-altitude target tugs. During the mid–1960s, 19 B-57Es refitted with camera equipment were re-designated RB-57Es and another 23 that received ECM gear became EB-57Es. The 21 W/RB-57Fs high-altitude reconnaissance and weather versions completed between 1963 and 1967 were B-57 airframes remanufactured by General Dynamics with entirely new wings and tail surfaces of 100 percent greater area and Pratt & Whitney TF-33 turbofan engines.

The RB-57A became operational in 1954 with the 363rd Tactical Reconnaissance Wing (TRW) at Shaw AFB in South Carolina. B-57Bs and Cs began entering service during 1955, and by mid–1957 equipped four Tactical Bomb Groups (TBG), the 345th and 463rd in the U.S., the 3rd in Japan, and the 38th in France. The chief mission of the B-57 groups was to deliver tactical nuclear weapons using a loft-bombing technique assisted by a LABS computer. However, with one exception, the B-57Bs service life was decidedly brief, being displaced in the tactical nuclear role during 1957 and 1958 by supersonic North American F-100 fighter-bombers. The Yokota Japan-based 3rd TBG remained on nuclear alert status until mid–1964, at which time two of its squadrons, the 8th and 13th, were ordered to Clark AFB in the Philippines to prepare for conventional combat operations in Southeast Asia. In August 1964, elements of both B-57 squadrons deployed to Ben Hoa Air Base in South Vietnam and commenced combat operations in February 1965, becoming the first USAF jets to bomb Viet Cong targets in the South. The two squadrons primarily flew night interdiction strikes against the heavily defended North Vietnamese supply lines moving along the Ho Chi Min Trail into North Vietnam. To make up for combat losses, 12 B-57Es were reconfigured as B-57Bs and sent to units in Vietnam, but by early 1968, combat attrition had reduced the number of serviceable aircraft to just one squadron, and all were withdrawn from combat in July 1969. Of the 94 B-57Bs operated from Ben Hoa during this period, 36 were lost in combat or accidents, 15 were destroyed on the ground, and 11 were withdrawn for other projects. During 1967 and 1968, as a result of a project known as "Tropic Moon," 16 B-57Bs were re-designated B-57Gs following modifications that included installation of an APQ-139 radar set, a forward-looking infrared system (FLIR), and a low-light television camera. The camera and FLIR were linked to a laser guidance system operated by a weapons specialist in the rear cockpit, who, while moving servo-controlled fins on the bombs, could actually steer the weapons to the target (i.e., the first 'smart' bombs). Re-equipped with 11 B-57Gs, the 13th Bomb Squadron deployed to Ubon, Thailand in September 1970, where they began flying bombing missions over the Ho Chi Min Trail at night. The 13th flew numerous combat sorties with the loss of only one aircraft until being deactivated in April 1972. The last active USAF *Canberras* were EB-57Es operated by Defense Systems Evaluation Squadrons in support of various USAF training missions, the final examples being phased-out in mid–1979

Following retirement from the USAF, a significant number of B-57s continued in service with Air National Guard units: RB-57As operated with Arkansas, Kentucky, Michigan, and New York ANG units until 1965; RB-57Es with the Kansas ANG until 1972; B-57Gs (formerly of the 13th BS) with the Kansas ANG until 1974; and EB-57Es with the Kansas ANG until 1978 and, finally, with the Vermont ANG until 1982. At the date of this writing, two of the three W/RB-57Fs acquired by NASA are still flying, providing service to the Department of Energy as upper atmosphere air samplers.

Douglas B-66 Destroyer 1954–1976

TECHNICAL SPECIFICATIONS (B-66B)

Type: Three-place tactical bomber.
Manufacturer: Douglas Aircraft Co., Long Beach, California and Tulsa, Oklahoma.
Total produced: 294 (all versions, including E/RB-66A/E)
Power plant: Two Allison J-71-11 or -13 turbojet engines, each rated at 10,200-lbs./s.t. Armament: Two 20-mm cannons in a radar-directed, remote-=controlled tail turret and up to 15,000-lbs. of bombs carried in an internal bomb bay.
Performance: Max. speed 630-mph at 6,000 ft., cruise 573-mph; ceiling 41,500 ft.; range 1,826 mi. loaded, 2,470 mi. max.
Weights: 42,549-lbs. empty, 83,000-lbs. max. takeoff.
Dimensions: Span 72 ft. 6 in., length 75 ft. 2 in., wing area 780 sq. ft.

Intended originally to supplement the B-57 and replace the B-45 in the tactical bomber role, the Douglas B-66 was nonetheless viewed by USAF planners as a temporary stopgap until the supersonic Martin B-68 (see Appendix 3) could be brought into service. Its origins can be traced to mid–1951, when the USAF solicited proposals for a new jet tactical bomber and reconnaissance aircraft that would offer improved performance and greater payload than that of the recently selected B-57. Boeing offered an adaptation of its six-engine B-47, but a more promising proposal came from Douglas for a land-based derivative of its yet-to-be-flown XA3D-1 carrier-based bomber (see Part II, Third Series). The USAF approved the Douglas proposal in January 1952, assigning the designation B-66 to the bomber version and RB-66 to the reconnaissance version. Originally, USAF officials believed the B/RB-66 would essentially be an off-the-shelf copy of the Navy A3D, in which case an experimental prototype would be unnecessary. Because early acquisition of the reconnaissance version was deemed most important, Douglas received a preliminary contract in February 1952 to manufacture five RB-66As that would be used only for testing and evaluation. In August, after mockup inspections had been completed and a decision made to substitute Allison J-71 engines (instead of the problematic Westinghouse J-40s used on the XA3D), the USAF issued a definitive contract for 73 RB-66Bs and 26 B-66Bs, with the expectation that a total of 202 RB-66s and 141 B-66s would ultimately be acquired under future contracts.

Development of the B/RB-66, however, proved to be very protracted. USAF tactical requirements led to so many systemic, structural, and aerodynamic changes, that the production aircraft actually bore little in common with the Navy A3D other than general layout. The first production RB-66A flew on June 28, 1954, six months behind schedule, followed between August and December by delivery of four more. The test program revealed a host of problems—poor handling, restricted visibility, malfunction of landing gear doors, wing vibration, flight control system failures, plus a dangerous pitch-up tendency in certain flight regimes. Air Material Command came seriously close to canceling the entire program in early 1955, but subsequently determined that resolving the plane's problems would be less costly than developing an interim replacement; instead, the tactical bomber program was reduced to 72 B-66Bs (one operational bomb wing) with a planned phase-out in 1961. The B-66B made its first flight on January 4, 1955, and the last of 72 production models was delivered in October 1957. Despite development delays, it was a highly advanced aircraft for its day: acceptance trials revealed that the B-66B was very well adapted to low-level flight, could handle a variety of weapons, and could be aerially refueled up to 96,000-lbs.; its Western Electric K-5 bombing system, developed specifically for the program, gave the ability to locate and attack targets in all weather conditions; and during production, radar warning receivers and chaff dispensers were added to help defeat enemy radars. During 1964 and 1965 thirteen B-66Bs were re-designated EB-66Bs following a modification program in which the bombing equipment and tail turret were

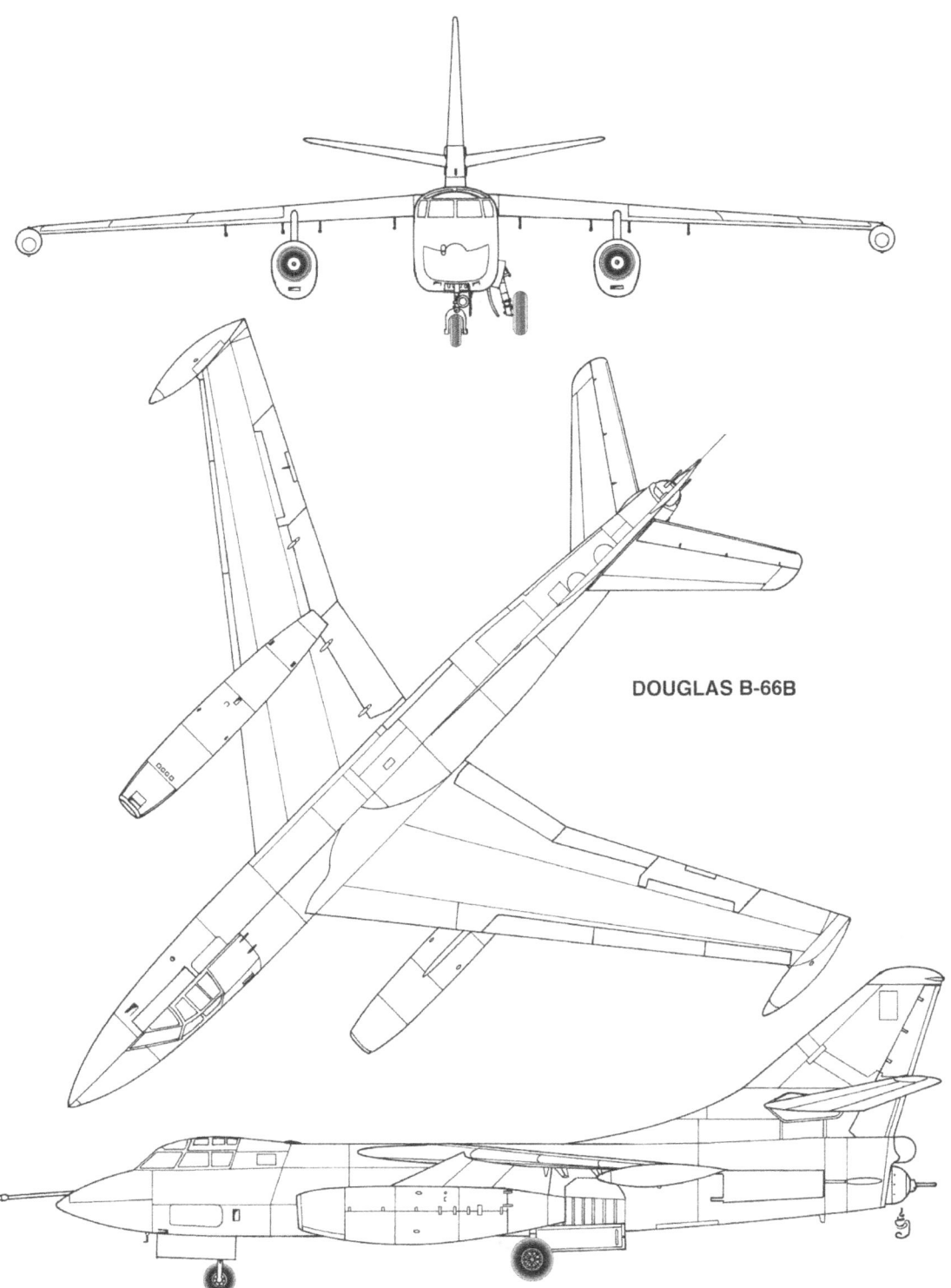

DOUGLAS B-66B

Top: One of 72 B-66Bs delivered in 1956 and 1957. The introduction of this aircraft gave the USAF all-weather tactical nuclear capability in Europe. After being withdrawn from frontline service in 1963, many were converted as electronic warfare platforms. *Bottom:* An EB-66B in formation with KC-135 tanker over Laos or Thailand during the Vietnam War. Note antennae array along bottom of fuselage. These aircraft ventured far enough into North Vietnam to be within range of antiaircraft gun and missile batteries.

removed to be replaced with an a special ECM package located in the bomb bay (known as the Brown Cradle) and a new tail cone equipped with sensors and antennae. In early 1967, eleven more B-66Bs, which had been deactivated, were withdrawn from storage and became EB-66Bs after receiving the ECM modifications described above.

Despite major cutbacks in the tactical bomber program, a further 217 photo-reconnaissance, electronic warfare, and weather reconnaissance types were completed before all production ended in 1958. The USAF accepted delivery of 145 RB-66Bs between October 1955 and October 1957, and during the mid-1960s, 47 of these were re-designated EB-66Es after receiving Brown cradles and other ECM modifications similar to those of the EB-66Bs. The 36 RB-66Cs completed from October 1955 to June 1957 were seven-seat electronic reconnaissance and countermeasures variants, especially equipped to locate and classify enemy antiaircraft and missile radars; and in 1966, when the USAF assigned all electronic warfare aircraft an "E" prefix, they became EB-66Cs. The final version was the five-seat weather reconnaissance WB-66D, thirty-six examples of which were delivered in January 1958.

B-66Bs began entering operational service with the 17th Bomb Wing (Light) at Hurlbert Field, Florida in March 1956. In early 1958, all squadrons of the 17th were transferred to the England-based 47th BW (Tactical) to replace its obsolescent B-45s; however, due to problems related to installation of bomb shackles for the tactical nuclear weapons and required engine retrofits, full operational readiness was not achieved until the middle of the year. Thereafter, the B-66Bs performed a tactical nuclear role similar in scope to the Backbreaker mission of the B-45s. Since the Martin B-68 was no longer forthcoming, the original phase-out deadline was extended two years, so that the process of withdrawing the B-66Bs from alert status was not completed until mid-1963. The EB-66Bs with the ECM modifications were initially attached to the 42nd Tactical Reconnaissance Squadron in Europe but deployed to southeast Asia for combat operations from late 1965 onwards. From 1965 to 1973, EB-66Bs, EB-66Cs, and EB-66Es based in Thailand conducted electronic surveillance and jamming missions over North Vietnam in what became known as the "invisible war." In this role, they typically preceded the aircraft of the strike force for the purpose of detecting and then jamming enemy search and fire-control radars. At least four EB-66s were lost to enemy action and another twelve were damaged or destroyed in operational accidents. After being withdrawn from the combat theater in 1973, all EB-66s were deactivated. The last active B-66, a WB-66D being used for electronic testing by Westinghouse at Baltimore, was retired in 1976. In the early 1960s, one B-66 airframe was re-designated X-21A upon receiving new wings and J-79 engines mounted on the aft fuselage and was used until 1964 to perform a variety of tests pertaining to an experimental boundary-layer control system.

Lockheed F-80 Shooting Star 1944–1958

TECHNICAL SPECIFICATIONS (F-80C)

Type: One-place fighter-bomber.
Manufacturer: Lockheed Aircraft Corp., Burbank, California.
Total produced: 1,609 (all single-seat versions, including RF-80)
Power plant: One Allison J-33-35 turbojet engine, rated at 5,400-lbs./s.t.
Armament: Six .50-caliber machine guns and up to 2,000-lbs. of bombs or 16 HVAR 5-inch rockets carried on wing racks.
Performance: Max. speed 580-mph at s.l., cruise 439-mph; ceiling 42,750 ft.; range 825 mi. loaded, 1,380 mi. max.
Weights: 8,240-lbs. empty, 16,856-lbs. max. takeoff.
Dimensions: Span 38 ft. 9 in. (39 ft. 11 in. over tanks), length 34 ft. 6 in., wing area 237.6 sq. ft.

Though remembered primarily as America's first truly combat-capable jet fighter, the

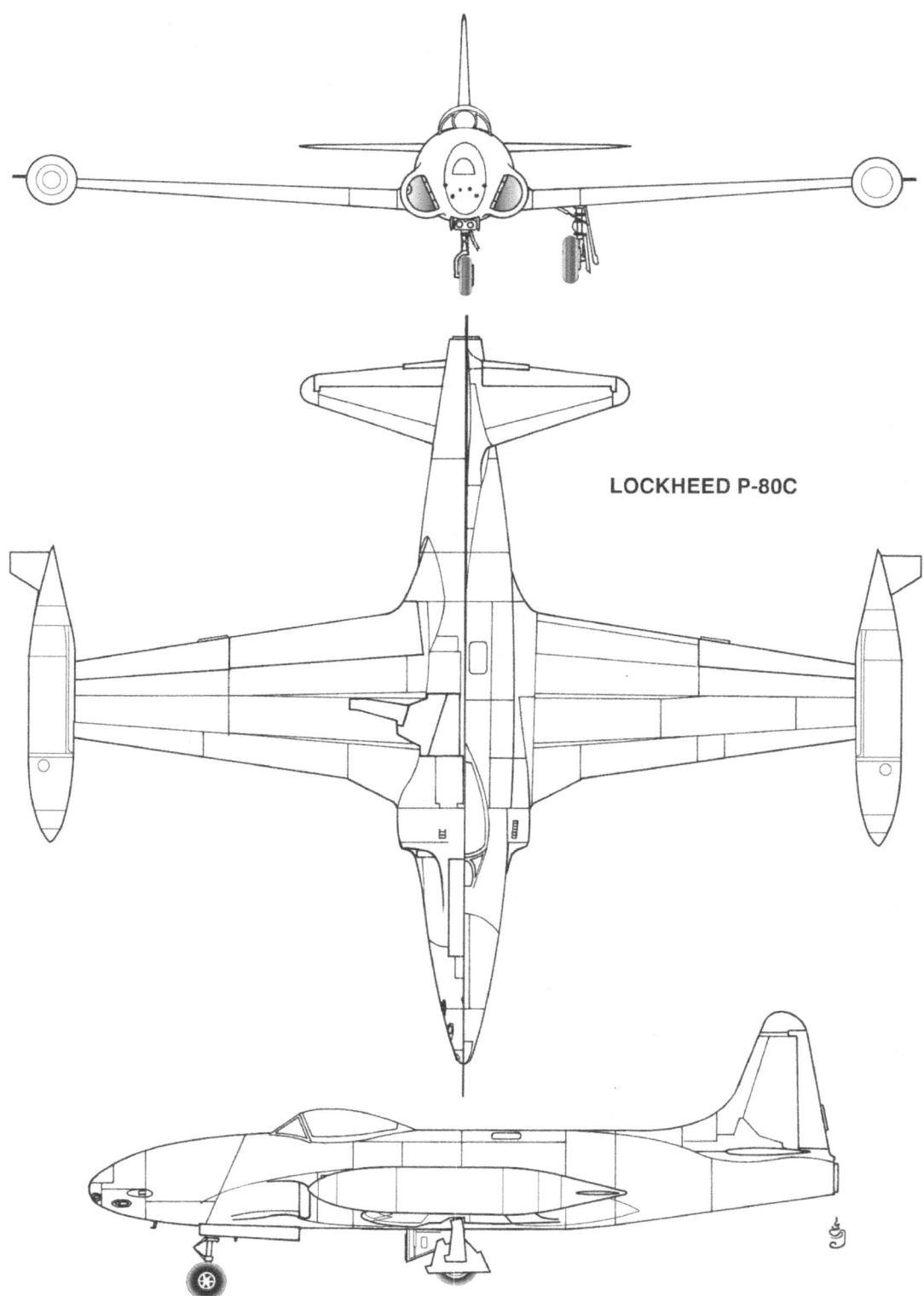

LOCKHEED P-80C

F-80C with long-range Misawa tanks in post–Korea markings as shown by large U.S. Air Force lettering on nose. Many F-80s served with reserve and ANG units after being phased out in frontline service.

Lockheed F-80 saw considerable use as an attack aircraft after being overtaken by the swept-wing F-86 in the air superiority role. The origins of the F-80 date back to 1939, when Clarence (Kelly) Johnson and Hall Hibbard of Lockheed began engineering studies on a jet-propelled aircraft, but the XP-80 itself did not come into existence as a definite AAF project until June 1943. As with other wartime jet schemes, the chief difficulty lay with the lack of American-made turbojet engines, so that the XP-80, which flew in early 1944, was in reality a 75 percent scale testbed powered by a British Halford H.1 engine. The larger XP-80A, powered by a General Electric I-40 centrifugal-flow (later produced as the GE and Allison J-33), made its first flight in June 1944, and was followed by delivery of thirteen YP-80A service test aircraft. By January 1945, the government had placed orders for 5,000 P-80As, half of which were to be built at North American's Dallas plant, and deliveries of the first production models commenced in February; however, cutbacks following V-J Day caused the contract to be reduced to 677 aircraft, which included 152 RP-80A recon versions. When the USAF changed its designation system in 1948, P-80s became F-80s. In post-war contracts, a further 240 F-80Bs were delivered from March 1947 to March 1948, along with 670 F-80Cs from March 1948 to June 1950. While both F-80As and Bs possessed air-to-ground capability, the added power of the -35 engine (from block ten onwards) and the strengthened wing of the F-80C permitted take-off weights to be upped by 2,300-lbs. And the ground-attack potential of most Cs was further enhanced in the field by retrofitting two additional wing pylons for external ordnance and 265-gallon tip tanks to increase loiter range.

At the time the Korean War began, in late June 1950, two fighter-bomber wings, the 8th FBW and 49th FBW, and two fighter-interceptor wings, the 35th FIS and 51st FIS, were operating F-80Cs from bases in Japan. In the early part of the war, the F-80 wings performed double-duty, providing both air cover and ground support to UN forces, however, the appearance of Soviet-built MiG-15s starting in late 1950 caused the type to be withdrawn from the fighter role by the spring of 1951. Early combat operations were hampered in terms of range and payload due to the necessity of flying missions from Japan but became much more effective once the F-80 wings moved to bases on the Korean mainland during early 1951. Even so, the USAF began phasing the F-80s out of combat units in mid–1951, replacing them over time with either F-84s or F-86s, so that by the time of the Armistice in July 1953 the RF-80As of the 67th TRW were the only examples of the type remaining in the combat zone. Over the course of the conflict, F-80s dropped 41,593 tons of bombs and napalm and fired over 81,000 rockets for a loss of 127 aircraft to enemy action. Outside Korea, USAF units in the U.S. and Europe initiated the process retiring their F-80B/Cs from frontline service in 1951, reequipping with F-84s in fighter-bomber wings and F-86s or F-94s in fighter-interceptor units. The last RF-80s were withdrawn from active service in late 1957. After retirement from frontline USAF units, F-80s remained in service with USAF Reserve and Air National Guard units until 1958.

Soon after World War II ended, the Navy acquired three P-80As from the AAF for service evaluations, one of which was fitted with arrestor gear and used to perform deck trials aboard the *Roosevelt* (CV-42). During 1948 the Navy acquired a further 50 F-80Cs under the naval designation TO-1 (later TV-1) for use as advanced jet trainers, 16 of which actually went into operational service with Marine squadron VMF-311 until the unit received its Grumman F9F-2s. Ex-USAF F-80s were also supplied to a number of South American air forces under the U.S. military assistance program: 33 to Brazil, 16 to Peru, 16 to Columbia, 16 to Ecuador, and 14 to Uruguay. The last South American F-80s were reportedly retired in the mid–1970s.

North American F-82 Twin Mustang 1945–1953

TECHNICAL SPECIFICATIONS (F-82E)

Type: Two-place fighter-bomber.
Manufacturer: North American Aviation, Inc., Inglewood, California.
Total produced: 272 (all versions)
Power plant: Two 1,600-hp Allison V-1710-143 or -145 V12 liquid-cooled engines driving four-bladed Aeroproducts constant-speed propellers
Armament: Six fixed .50-caliber machine guns in the wing center-section and up to 4,000-lbs. of bombs or 25 HVAR 5-in. rockets carried on wing racks.
Performance: Max. speed 465-mph at 21,000 ft., cruise 300-mph; ceiling 38,400 ft.; range 2,245 mi. loaded, 2708 mi. max.
Weights: 14,914-lbs. empty, 24,864-lbs. max. takeoff.
Dimensions: Span 51 ft. 3 in., length 39 ft. 1 in., wing area 408 sq. ft.

Although billed as a "long-range escort," the P/F-82B and E variants were nonetheless designed with substantial air-to-ground capability, being rated to carry a weapons load comparable to that of the Douglas A-26. They were also the very last type of piston-engine fighter to be ordered by the AAF. The twin-fuselage, two-pilot concept arose in late 1943 from an attempt to provide a multi-role aircraft capable of operating over the very long distances required for the Pacific campaign. The XP-82, ordered in January 1944, though utilizing components similar to those of the lightweight P-51H, was in effect a completely new airframe in which the fuselages had been lengthened 57 inches and the outer wing panels strengthened to carry much higher loads. The XP-82 made its first flight in July 1945, but like so many other late war programs, the contract for 500 Merlin-powered P-82Bs, the main production version, was reduced to only 19 aircraft after V-J Day. The program received a partial reprieve in October 1946 when the AAF awarded a contract for 250 Allison-powered P-82Es (re-designated F-82E in 1948), 96 of which were ultimately delivered as F-82Es, the remainder being night fighter/all-weather

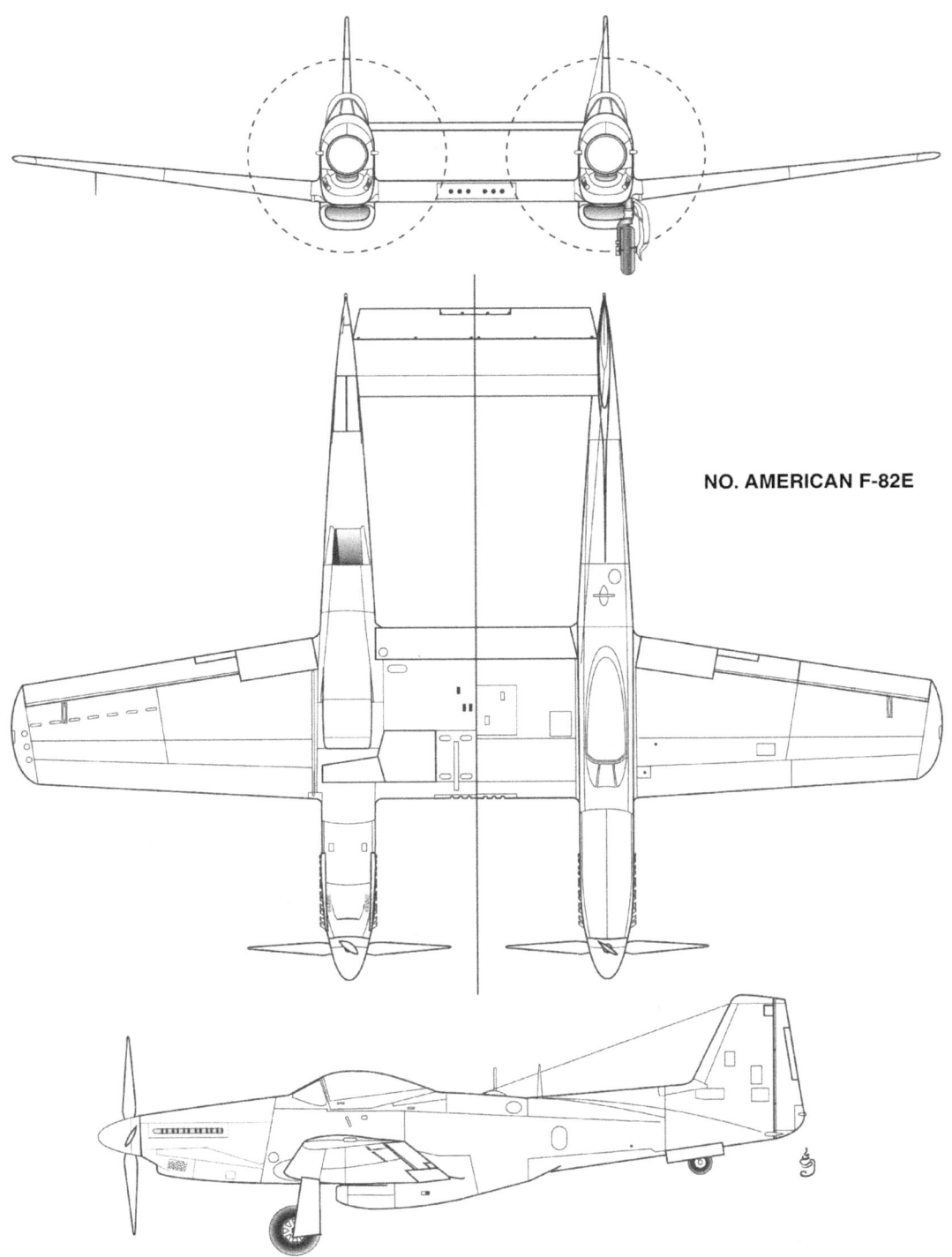

NO. AMERICAN F-82E

interceptor variants—91 F-82Fs, 45 F-82Gs, and 14 F-82Hs. The F and G differed only in radar equipment and the F-82Hs were F and G models specially winterized for cold-weather operations.

The air-to-ground capabilities of the F-82E were never realized. Because of their superior range, as soon as F-82Es began entering operational service in May 1948, they were imme-

NamF-82E. F-82E in early 1948 before buzz letter were changed from PQ to FQ. Though having significant air-to-ground capabilities, most were assigned to SAC as bomber escorts because of their excellent range.

diately attached to Strategic Air Command (SAC) to provide escort duties for B-50 bombers, but their service life was very brief, being replaced in frontline service by F-84Es during early 1950. Forty F-82F/G night fighters were attached to the 347th Fighter Group in Japan at the time the Korean War began in June 1950, and one of its F-82Gs scored the first air-to-air kill of the war when it shot down a Yak-7 on June 25, 1950. As they were superceded in the all-weather fighter role by F-94s, bomb and rocket-laden F-82s were employed to fly night intruder sorties, but all had been withdrawn from combat operations by November 1951, and the final example was retired from active USAF service in mid–1953. None were used by reserve or ANG units.

Republic F-84 Thunderjet (straight-wing) 1946–1958

TECHNICAL SPECIFICATIONS (F-84G)

Type: One-place fighter-bomber.
Manufacturer: Republic Aviation Corp., Farmingdale, New York.
Total produced: 4,354 (all versions, including exports)
Power plant: One Allison J-35-29 turbojet engine, rated at 5,600-lbs./s.t.
Armament: Six .50-caliber machine guns and up to 4,000-lbs. of bombs or two 11.75-in. or 16 HVAR 5-in. rockets carried on wing racks.
Performance: Max. speed 621-mph at s.l., cruise 481-mph; ceiling 40,500 ft.; range 1,700 mi. loaded, 2,000 mi. max.
Weights: 11,095-lbs. empty, 25,525-lbs. max. takeoff.
Dimensions: Span 36 ft. 5 in., length 38 ft. 1 in., wing area 260 sq. ft.

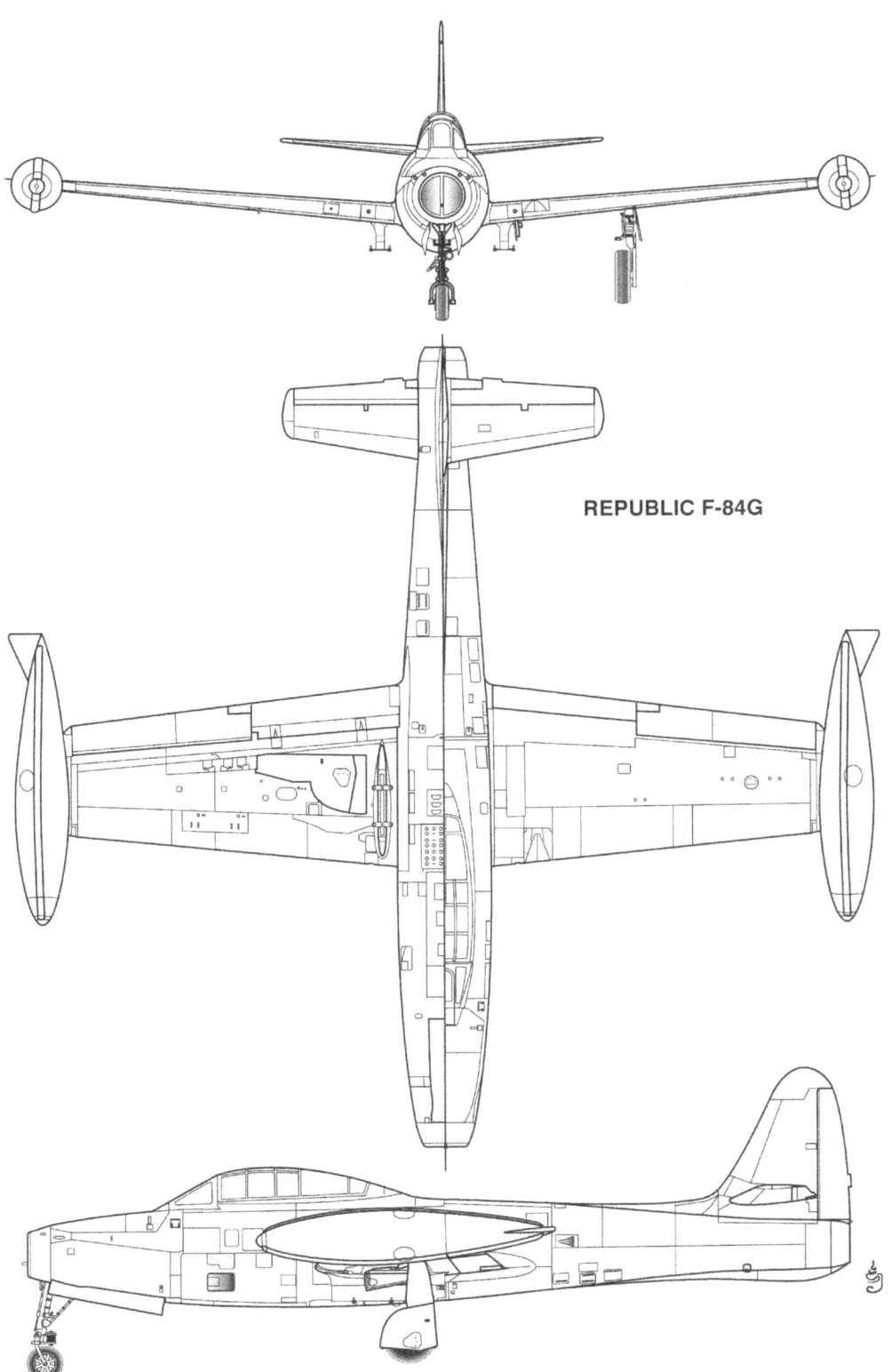
REPUBLIC F-84G

Top: F-84D showing two 500-lb. bombs mounted under the wings. Ds of the 27th Fighter Escort Group were the first variants to fly combat missions over Korea in June 1950. Surviving F-84Ds remained in ANG service until 1957. *Bottom:* A flight of F-84Gs from the 20th Fighter Bomber Group over the English countryside. The G was the first single-seat USAF aircraft capable of carrying a tactical nuclear weapon.

The Republic F-84 became the USAF's most important fighter-bomber during the Korean War and was the first single-seat jet capable of carrying a tactical nuclear weapon. The original AAF requirement issued in September 1944 specified a day fighter having a top speed of 600-mph and a combat radius of 850 miles, to be powered by a General Electric TG-180 (later J-35) axial-flow turbojet engine. From the beginning, the Republic design team led by Alexander Kartveli perceived this project to be the jet-propelled successor to their illustrious P-47 *Thunderbolt*. Because of the need for internal fuel storage dictated by range requirements, a much thicker airfoil section was adopted than that seen on the F-80, but drag of the wing was considerably offset by the low-drag fuselage cross-section allowed by the smaller-diameter axial-flow engine. The proposed Model AP-23F was approved in November 1944, and a contract for 100 aircraft—25 service test examples as the YP-84A and 75 production models as the P-84B—was awarded in January 1945. This was later amended to include three XP-84As and add ten more P-84Bs to the contract. The maiden flight of the first XP-84A took place on February 28, 1946, and the next October, the second XP-84A prototype established a U.S. national speed record of 611-mph. Delivery of the 15 YP-84As, the first to be equipped with tip tanks and armament, was completed in February 1947, and the first of 226 P-84B production models started reaching operational units the following December. All P-84 variants were re-designated F-84 in June 1948.

The 191 F-84Cs accepted by the USAF from May to November 1948 featured improved -13C engines and refinements to the fuel and electrical systems. The 154 F-84Ds, delivered from November 1948 to April 1949, introduced thicker wing skins to increase allowable G-loads, winterized fuel systems, and improved hydraulics. The 743 F-84Es completed from mid–1949 to mid–1951 came with -17D engines of 5,000-lbs./s.t., strengthened wings, radar gunsights, improved tip tanks, and fuselages lengthened one foot to provide more cockpit space. The final and most numerous version was the out-of-sequence F-84G, ordered in 1951 because of unexpected delays in bringing the swept-wing F-84F (YF-96A) into production. Powered by a -29 engine of 600-lbs. greater thrust, the F-84G was the first USAF fighter built with a boom and receptacle in-flight refueling system and also the first single-seat jet configured to carry a Mk. 7 tactical nuclear weapon. Other improvements included an autopilot, new A-4 gunsight, and an instrument landing system (ILS), and with a useful load upped by 1,500-lbs, Gs could carry more weapons than previous versions. F-84Gs were initially distinguishable by their ribbed, reinforced canopies, but this feature was later retrofitted to many D and E models. The USAF accepted a total of 3,025 F-84Gs from July 1951 to July 1953, of which 2,236 went directly to NATO allies or other nations participating in the Mutual Defense Assistance Program (MDAP). Starting in mid–1953, as part of their nuclear mission, many USAF F-84Gs were equipped with LABs bomb-toss computers.

P/F-84Bs entered initial operational service in December 1947 with the with 14th Fighter Group based at Dow Field in Maine, and by the end of 1948, three more groups, the 20th at Shaw AFB, North Carolina, the 33rd at Otis AFB, Massachusetts, and the 78th at Hamilton AFB, California, were equipped with F-84Bs and Cs. F-84Ds started equipping the 27th Fighter Escort Group in 1949, and it became the first *Thunderjet* unit to deploy to the Far East after the Korean War started in June 1950. Because of the short overhaul periods of their earlier J-35 engines, F-84Bs and Cs were not utilized in combat operations; however, as F-84Es became available from late 1949 onwards, they replaced F-51s and F-80s in many Korea-based units, including activated ANG squadrons, and by early 1953 were equipping four fighter-bomber wings (49th, 58th, 116th, and 474th) in the combat theater. F-84Gs began arriving in late 1951 to replenish the number of F-84Ds and Es lost to combat attrition. By the time of the Armistice in July 1953, *Thunderjets* had flown a total of 86,400 sorties and dropped 55,897 tons of bombs for a loss of 122 aircraft to enemy action, most to ground fire. Following Korea, F-84Es and

Gs continued to serve with active USAF units until the final examples were retired from SAC in 1955 and from TAC in 1956.

F-84Bs and Cs entered service with the District of Columbia ANG in 1949, and during the 1950s, the F-84D/E/G became the most numerous type of jet in ANG service, equipping 14 different units at its peak. The last F-84Es and Gs were retired from Ohio and Iowa ANG units in 1958. From 1953, F-84Gs served with 21 fighter-bomber wings in the following NATO countries: Belgium, Denmark, France, Greece, Italy, Netherlands, Norway, Portugal, and Turkey; under MDAP, they were also supplied to the air forces of Iran, Taiwan, Thailand, and Yugoslavia.

Republic F-84 Thunderstreak (swept-wing) 1950–1972

TECHNICAL SPECIFICATIONS (F-84F [BLOCK 50])

Type: One-place fighter-bomber.
Manufacturer: Republic Aviation Corp., Farmingdale, New York and General Motors Corp., Kansas City, Missouri
Total produced: 3,426 (all versions, including RF-84F)
Power plant: One Wright J-65-7 turbojet engine, rated at 7,800-lbs./s.t.
Armament: Six .50-caliber machine guns and up to 6,000-lbs. of bombs or 4,000-lbs. of bombs and 8 HVAR 5-in. rockets carried on wing racks.
Performance: Max. speed 690-mph at s.l., cruise 539-mph; ceiling 44,300 ft.; range 863 mi. loaded, 2,343 mi. max.
Weights: 14,014-lbs. empty, 28,000-lbs. max. takeoff.
Dimensions: Span 33 ft. 7 in., length 43 ft. 5 in., wing area 325 sq. ft.

When the 613-mph top speed of the F-84E (Mach 81.1 at sea level) brought the straight-wing planform almost to its Mach .82 limit, Republic began work in 1949 on a swept-wing successor that would utilize 55 percent of the F-84E's tooling. Initially designated the YF-96A, the J-35-powered YF-84F prototype, first flown on June 3, 1950, was essentially an F-84E airframe fitted with new wings and tail surfaces swept to 40-degrees. After trials conducted at Edwards AFB from June to November established that the aircraft was too underpowered to perform its expected missions, USAF officials recommended that future prototypes be re-engined with the more powerful Wright YJ-65 (a license-built Armstrong-Siddeley *Sapphire* rated at 7,200-lbs./s.t.). But to accommodate the larger powerplant, the fuselage had to be completely redesigned to a deeper, oval-section, and the first flight of the revised YF-84F prototype did not occur until February 1951. Republic received an initial contract in April 1951 to produce 274 F-84Fs, with the expectation that the first aircraft would be delivered in the fall; however, the program was seriously delayed by unavailability of J-65 engines plus certain industrial equipment needed to fabricate the wings (i.e., forging equipment that had been earmarked for B-47 production). Although the latter problem was ultimately resolved by redesigning the wing structures so that they could be completed with available tooling, the first F-84F production models did not fly until November 1952. Production F-84Fs differed from the prototype in having a stronger, hinged canopy that abutted a raised fuselage spine, two perforated speed brakes on the fuselage sides (in place of the single belly brake of the F-84E), leading edge slats to improve airflow characteristics, and an irreversible boosted control system to replace aileron trim tabs. During their production run, F-84Fs received a number of improvements, including: 7,330-lb./s.t. J-65-3 engines (block 5), all-flying horizontal stabilizers (block 25), 7,800-lb./s.t. J-65-7 engines (block 50), and ventral fairings for drogue chutes (block 75). When production ended in August 1957, a total of 2,112 F-84Fs had been completed by Republic in Farmingdale plus another 599 by General Motors in Kansas City. Developed in parallel with the F, the RF-84F *Thunderflash* was a reconnaissance variant which differed in having wing root air intakes and a solid nose occupied by cameras. The prototype flew in February

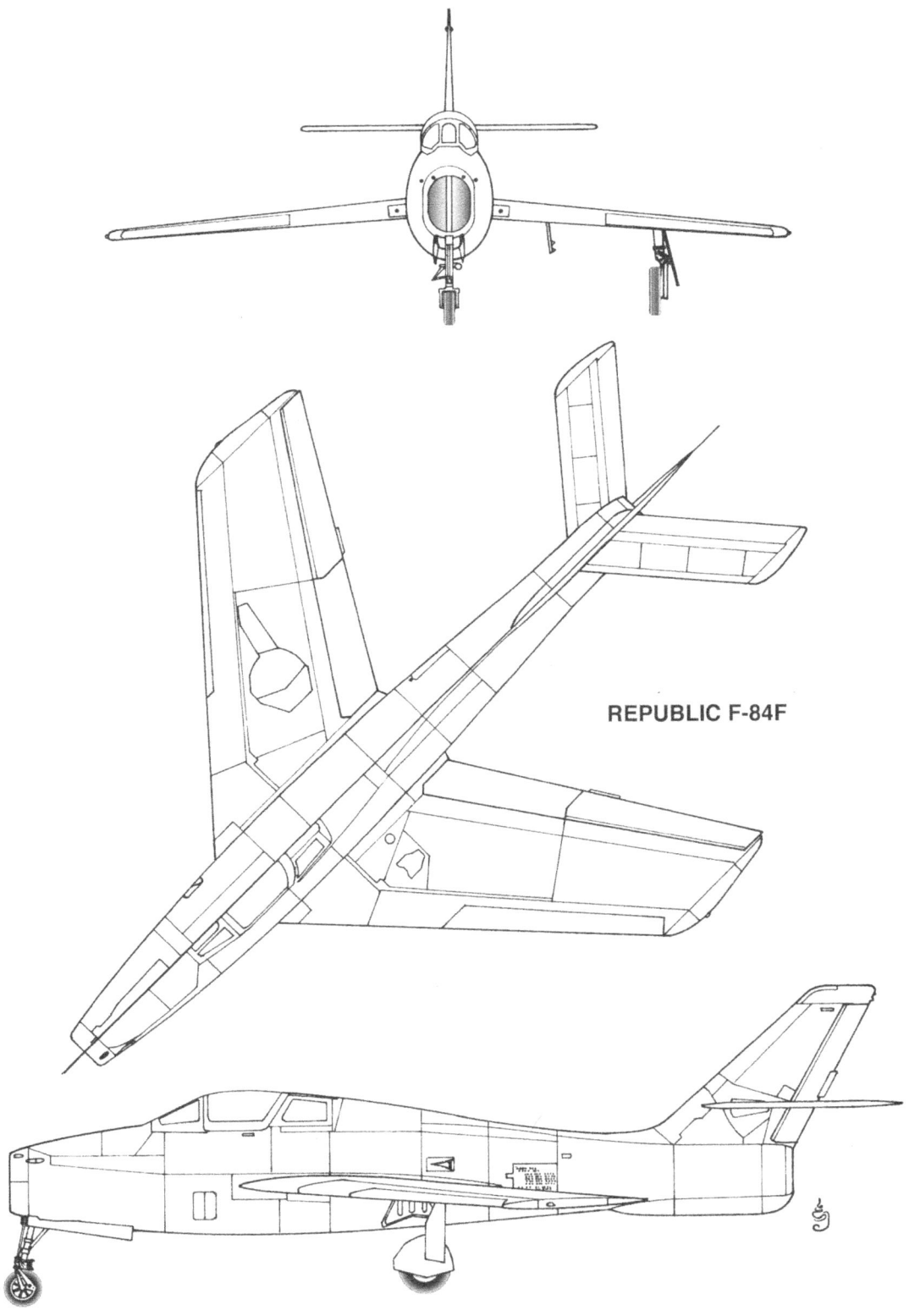

REPUBLIC F-84F

F-84F showing external stores that could be carried in various tactical configurations. The primary role of TAC F-84Fs while in active serve was low-level delivery of tactical nuclear weapons. Most were replaced in 1957-1958 by F-100Ds.

1952, and 715 RF-84F production models were completed between September 1953 and December 1957.

F-84Fs entered operational service in January 1954 with SAC's 506th Strategic Fighter Wing based at Dow AFB in Maine, and by mid–1955 were equipping five more SFWs. While attached to SAC, F-84Fs served as long-range escorts for B-29s, B-50s, and B-36s. F-84Fs began joining TAC units in mid–1954, serving initially with the 405th Fighter Bomber Wing at Langley AFB, Virginia, with the primary mission of delivering tactical nuclear weapons at low levels. Five TAC wings were operating the type by the middle of 1955 and operational strength grew to eight wings after SAC relinquished its F-84Fs in mid–1957. But the process of phasing-out the F-84F actually began in late 1956 when supersonic F-100Ds first started

RF-84Fs saw active service only from 1954 to 1958, when they were replaced by supersonic RF-101s but continued to operate with ANG units until 1972. RFs served with some of the NATO air forces even longer.

reaching TAC units, and all had been withdrawn from frontline fighter-bomber units (renamed tactical fighter wings) by January 1958. During the Berlin crisis in 1961, four ANG F-84F wings were called-up for active USAF service but were returned to ANG duty in 1962. A number of F-84Fs remained in service with Air Training Command at Luke AFB, Arizona until mid–1964, where they had been used to train foreign pilots under various military assistance programs. The active career of the RF-84F was similarly brief, equipping SAC and TAC reconnaissance units from March 1954 to May 1958, until being replaced by RF-101s.

F-84Fs served with the ANG for eighteen years. The first examples, fourteen block ones with J-65-1 engines, were transferred from SAC to the Pennsylvania ANG in early 1954, but the majority were received between 1956 and 1964 as they were released from USAF service, and eventually equipped 24 different ANG squadrons. The last F-84Fs were retired from Illinois and Ohio ANG units in 1972. RF-84Fs also enjoyed a long ANG career, serving with 11 tactical reconnaissance squadrons until the final examples were retired in from the Nebraska ANG in 1972. A total of 1,301 F-84Fs were supplied to NATO air forces in Belgium, France, Greece, Italy, Netherlands, West Germany, and Turkey. French F-84Fs were the only examples to actually see combat when they were used to attack Egyptian airfields in 1956 during the Suez War. While many of these nations began to reequip with F-104Gs during the early 1960s, the Greek and Turkish F-84Fs remained operational into the late 1970s. Three hundred eighty-six RF-84Fs were also supplied to tactical recon squadrons in the same NATO countries.

North American F-86 Sabre 1947–1970

TECHNICAL SPECIFICATIONS (F-86F [BLOCKS 25/35])
Type: One-place fighter-bomber.
Manufacturer: North American Aviation, Inc., Inglewood, California and Columbus, Ohio.
Total produced: 2,196 (includes F-86F blocks 25/35 and F-86H)
Power plant: One General Electric J-47-27 turbojet engine, rated at 5,910-lbs./s.t.
Armament: Six .50-caliber machine guns and up to 4,000-lbs. of bombs or 8 HVAR 5-in. rockets carried on wing racks.
Performance: Max. speed 695-mph at s.l., cruise 486-mph; ceiling 48,000 ft.; range 916 mi. loaded, 1,615 mi. max.
Weights: 10,890-lbs. empty, 20,357-lbs. max. takeoff.
Dimensions: Span 37 ft. 1 in., length 37 ft. 6 in., wing area 302 sq. ft.

In late 1951, while the F-86 was enjoying a resounding success as an air superiority fighter, the USAF asked North American to initiate development of a fighter-bomber adaptation. Although F-86As and Es had been tried in the ground attack role, they suffered from inadequate range when loaded with bombs and had only a single hardpoint beneath each wing. In August 1952, the USAF approved a contract for 859 Block 30 F-86Fs, which would feature two additional hardpoints plus the stronger, unslatted "6–3" wing (i.e., leading edge extended by six inches at the root and three inches at the tip, increasing area from 287.9 to 302.3 square feet) and directed North American to incorporate the same specification to the 600 F-86F Block 25 aircraft to be built at the Columbus plant. These were followed by 264 similar F-86F, Block 35s, that were additionally fitted to carry a 1,200-lb. Mk. 12 tactical nuclear weapon and came with LABs bomb-toss computers. In fighter-bomber configuration, F-86F-25/35s typically carried a 200 or 120-gallon drop tank on each outer pylon and 2,000-lbs. of bombs or 1,500-lbs. of napalm on the inner pylons. The final F-86F variant, 280 Block 40s completed in December 1955 for the export market, incorporated the slatted wing of the early F together with the two-foot tip extension of the F-86H.

Development work on the first true ground attack version, the F-86H, began in March 1951 while the first F-86Fs were entering production. Since the specification called for the slightly larger General Electric J-73 engine of 9,000-lbs./s.t., the fuselage was deepened six inches and lengthened one foot four inches, which enabled internal fuel capacity to be increased by 127 gallons. Aerodynamic changes included an increase in vertical fin area and removal of all dihedral from the horizontal tail surfaces; the hinged canopy and enlarged cockpit arrangement of the F-86D all-weather interceptor were also incorporated into the design. Armament was the same as that of the F-86F-25/35 and tactical equipment included an A-4 radar-ranging gun/bombsight and LABS computer. While the first of two YF-86Hs flew on May 9, 1953, production was delayed due to priorities in the F-86F program, so that no production models actually projected for operational use were delivered until the fall of 1954. The wing loading limitations encountered on early H models was rectified on the 15th aircraft with the introduction of the 6–3 wing plus tip extensions that increased span by two feet; and with the 5th production block, gun armament was upgraded to four 20-mm M-39 cannons. The last of 473 F-86Hs was delivered in October 1955.

The first F-86F-30s arrived in Korea in January 1953 to replace F-51Ds of the 18th Fighter-Bomber Wing based at Osan, and a month later, more arrived to replace F-80Cs of the 8th FBW at Suwon. These FBWs operated their new F-86Fs in both roles, flying either fighter sweeps or ground attack sorties as the tactical situation dictated.

F-86Hs began joining the 312th FBW based at Clovis AFB, New Mexico during the fall of 1954, and by the end of 1955, were equipping four more wings (50th, 83rd, 413th, and 474th). Like the F-84F, the F-86H was rapidly overtaken in the tactical fighter role by the supersonic

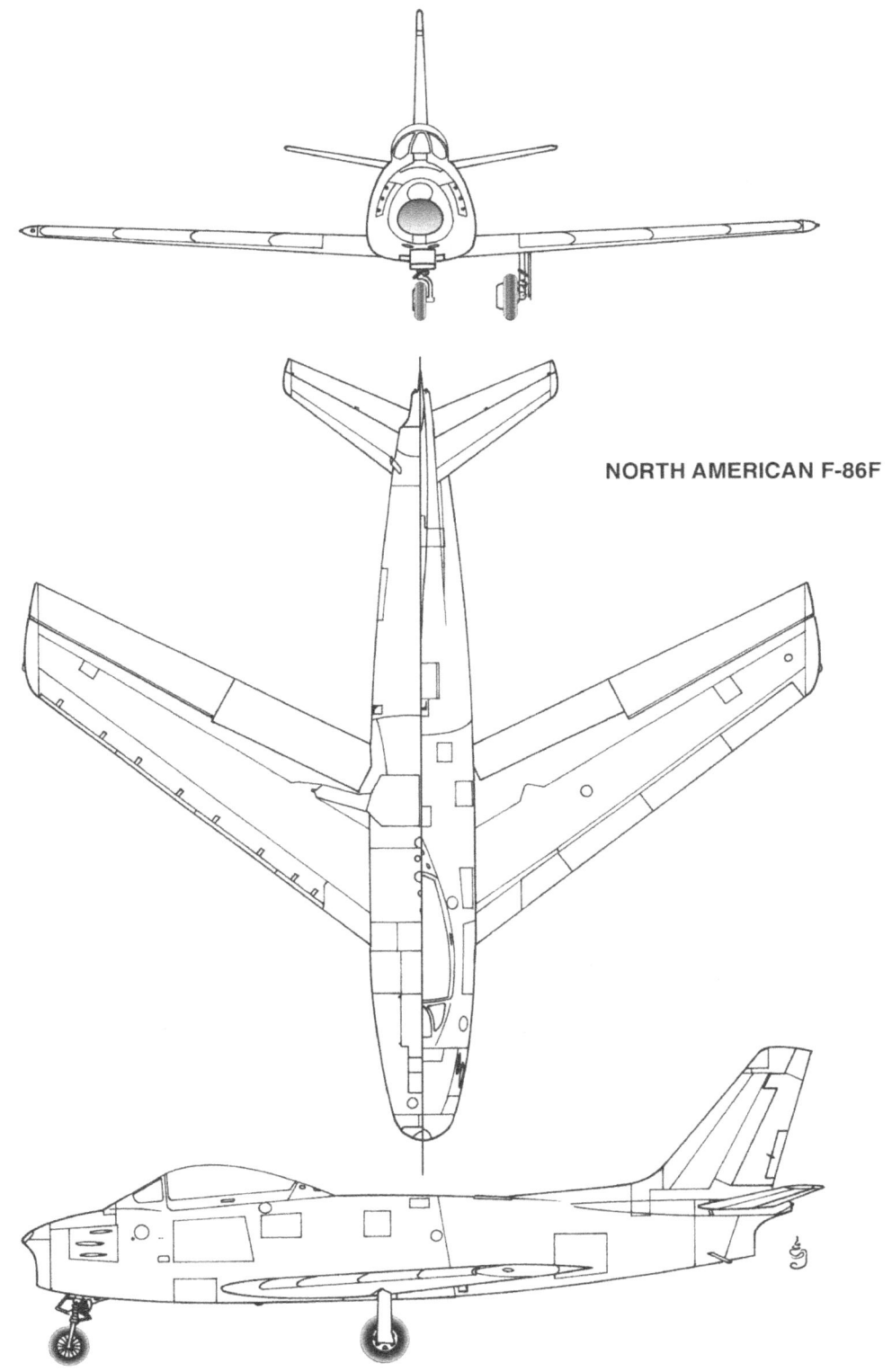

NORTH AMERICAN F-86F

Top: Block 30 F-86F showing ten MiG kills. Yellow identification bands on the tail and fuselage became standard for F-86s operating in Korea. Block 25s and 30s were truly swing-role aircraft, their missions dictated by the external load carried. *Bottom:* Almost new production F-86H shown in 1955, the first dedicated fighter-bomber version of the *Sabre*. The type eventually equipped five tactical fighter wings but had been completely replaced by supersonic F-100Ds by the end of 1958.

F-100D, and the final examples had been withdrawn from active service by June 1958. Two F-86H squadrons of the Massachusetts ANG were activated during the Berlin crisis in 1961 and remained in USAF service until August 1962.

F-86A/E/Fs served with 31 different ANG units from 1953 to 1958, mainly in fighter-interceptor squadrons. F-86Hs began entering service with ANG tactical fighter squadrons in 1957, eventually equipping 14 units, and remained in service until the last examples were retired from Maryland and New York ANG squadrons during 1970. From 1954 to 1969, many F-86Fs, including Blocks 25–35s, were transferred to foreign air forces under MDAP and other military assistance programs: 320 to Taiwan, 244 to Spain, 115 to Norway, 5 to Belgium, 50 to Portugal, 14 to Peru, 22 to Venezuela, 28 to Argentina, 112 to South Korea, 36 to Philippines, 40 to Thailand, 18 to Saudi Arabia, 5 to Iraq, 12 to Tunisia, and 14 to Ethiopia. Japan received 28 ex-USAF F-86Fs in 1955 then took delivery of 180 factory new F-86F-40s in 1957, together with parts for 300 more which were subsequently license-built by Mitsubishi from 1956 to 1961. Another 120 F-86F-40s (including 45 that had been returned by Japan) were supplied directly to Pakistan from 1956 to 1957 and were later used in combat during that nation's war with India in 1965. Some of the foreign F-86Fs remained in service until the mid–1980s.

North American F-100 Super Sabre 1953–1979

TECHNICAL SPECIFICATIONS (F-100D)

Type: One-place tactical fighter.
Manufacturer: North American Aviation, Inc., Inglewood, California and Columbus, Ohio.
Total produced: 2,249 (all versions)
Power plant: One Pratt & Whitney J-57-21A turbojet engine, rated at 10,200-lbs./s.t. dry, 16,000-lbs./s.t. with afterburning.
Armament: Four 20-mm cannons and up to 7,040-lbs. of bombs on six underwing pylons or 38 FFAR 2.75-in. rockets or 4 AIM-9 *Sidewinder* missiles carried on wing racks.
Performance: Max. speed 909-mph at 35,000 feet., cruise 590-mph; ceiling 47,700 ft.; range 1,058 mi. loaded, 1,995 mi. max.
Weights: 20,638-lbs. empty, 39,750-lbs. max. takeoff.
Dimensions: Span 38 ft. 9 in., length 49 ft. 4 in., wing area 400 sq. ft.

The F-100 was not only the USAF's first operational supersonic fighter but was also the first supersonic aircraft of any type to be placed in mass-production. When first proposed in 1951, the design of the F-100 was molded by recent combat experience with the F-86 in Korea, and like many other USAF aircraft procured during the early Cold War era, was ordered into mass-production on the strength of mockup inspections before any prototypes had flown. The first YF-100A flew on May 25, 1953 and F-100As began equipping operational units in September 1954, in spite of continuing stability and control problems; within two months, however, all were grounded due to a series of major crashes attributed to "roll-coupling" (i.e., an uncontrollable yawing and rolling motion encountered during dive pullouts). The fault was ultimately resolved by increasing vertical tail area, extending the wing tips, and introducing pitch and yaw dampening to the control system. Most of the 203 F-100As produced from September 1954 to July 1955, because of their limited range and load-carrying ability, were unsuited for the ground attack role and placed in service as air superiority day fighters. The F-100B, a project started in late 1954 to compete with the Republic F-105, was such a broad departure from the F-100's basic design that it was subsequently re-designated YF-107A.

When it appeared in early 1955, the F-100C was the first production version to possess true fighter-bomber capability. With its more powerful J-57-21 engine, increased fuel storage, and eight wing pylons, the C could deliver 5,000-lbs. of bombs or rockets over a 575-mile combat radius while doubling as an air superiority day fighter, and was the first configured to carry

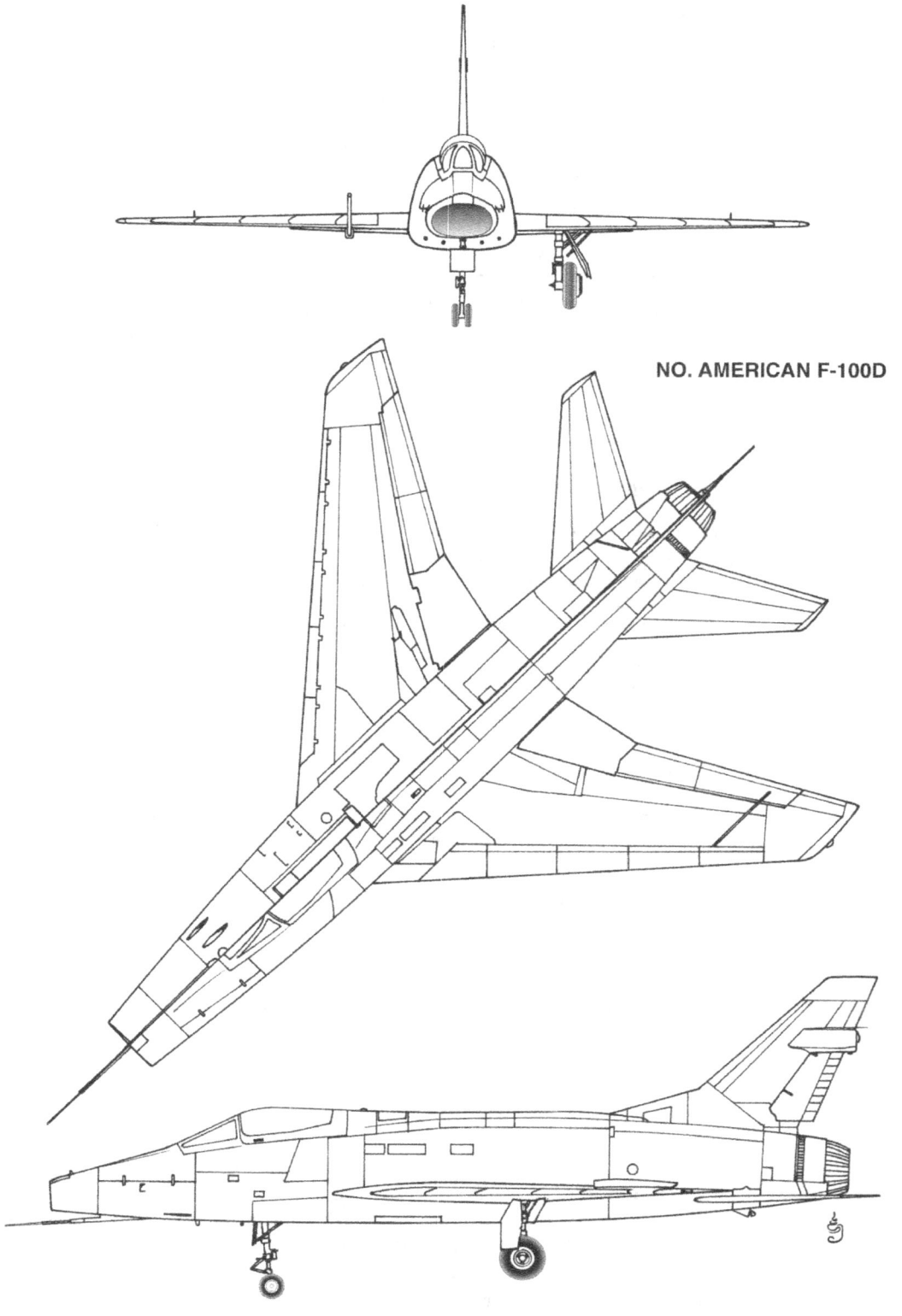

NO. AMERICAN F-100D

Top: F-100C during a live firing exercise. F-100Cs experienced a relatively short service life with TAC, as they were overtaken by F-100Ds during 1958 and 1959, but they did eventually see combat with four different activated ANG units in Vietnam. *Bottom:* Bombed-up F-100Ds en route to target over South Vietnam. F-100Ds were the mainstay of TAC air-to-ground operations in South Vietnam from mid–1964 to mid–1971. Last examples were retired from ANG in late 1979.

a Mk. 7 tactical nuclear weapon and have in-flight refueling capability. The USAF accepted a total of 476 F-100Cs between September 1955 and April 1956. In mid–1954, before the first F-100C had flown, the USAF asked North American to develop yet another version that would be dedicated solely to the ground-attack mission. The F-100D, when it flew in January 1956, featured a kinked wing of increased area at the root chord, enlarged vertical fin and rudder, and a 2,000-lb. gain in useful load over the C. The D also introduced a programmable autopilot tied to the LABS system and had the capability to carry six different tactical nuclear weapons with yields ranging from one kiloton to almost ten megatons. The last of 1,274 F-100Ds was delivered in August 1959. Starting with the 184th production model, F-100Ds were equipped to carry up to four AIM-9 *Sidewinder* heat-seeking air-to-air missiles as defensive armament, and in late 1959, some received modifications enabling them to carry the AGM-12 *Bullpup* optically-guided air-to-ground missile. The F-100E was a proposed improvement of the D that was never built. The final production version, the F-100F, was a fully mission-capable, two-seat adaptation intended for use as a refresher and conversion trainer in units equipped with the F-100D. All F-100 production ended in August 1959 with the 339th F-100F, 45 of which were delivered directly to foreign air forces under the MDAP program.

After resolution of the problems mentioned earlier, F-100As achieved full operational status in the fall of 1955 with the 479th Day Fighter Wing based at George AFB in California, but their service was brief, all being withdrawn from frontline TAC units by the end of 1958. The USAF retained some F-100As for aircrew training, but 70 were transferred directly to the ANG and 118 were eventually supplied to the Nationalist Chinese Air Force (Taiwan). F-100Cs began entering operational service with the 450th TFW at Foster AFB in Texas in mid–1955, and by the end of 1956, were equipping two more fighter-bomber wings based in Europe and Asia. But as F-100Ds became available, TAC began the process of phasing-out F-100Cs in 1958 and had replaced them completely by the end of 1959, a majority of which ended up in ANG tactical fighter units. F-100Cs remained with the Thunderbirds flight demonstration team until 1964 and some continued in USAF service as combat crew trainers until 1970. TAC units began receiving their first F-100Ds in September 1956, replacing F-84Fs, F-86Hs, and F-100Cs, and the type eventually equipped ten tactical fighter wings. F-100Ds of the 3rd TFW arrived in South Vietnam during February 1964 and flew their first combat sortie on June 9. Throughout most of the war, four TAC F-100 wings worked in rotation from bases at Tan Son Nhut, Da Nang, and Bien Hoa until the 35th TFW was finally withdrawn from combat in July 1971. The wings typically flew daylight ground support missions in South Vietnam and Laos, armed variously with napalm, conventional iron bombs, high-drag bombs, cluster bomb units (CBUs), and/or 2.75-inch FFARs. In early 1965, F-100Ds armed only with their 20-mm cannons also escorted (i.e., MiG-CAP) F-105s en route to targets in North Vietnam until sufficient numbers of F-4Cs became available to undertake the role. TAC utilized two-seat F-100Fs until mid–1970 on "Misty" FAC (forward air control) missions which identified and marked targets for incoming air strikes. Equipped with special radar-homing equipment and AGM-45 anti-radiation missiles (ARM), F-100Fs flying over North Vietnam in 1966 and 1967 pioneered the "Wild Weasel" concept of detecting and attacking enemy surface-to-air missile (SAM) sites. The last F-100Ds and Fs were retired from the USAF active inventory in June 1972.

F-100s equipped ANG units for over 20 years, serving in 26 different squadrons. The New Mexico ANG converted to F-100As in mid–1958 and eight other units received F-100Cs from 1959 to 1962. Activated ANG squadrons from Colorado, New York, Iowa, and New Mexico, while assigned to tactical fighter wings in Viet Nam, were the only units that flew the F-100C in combat. As F-100Ds and Fs were taken out of active USAF service, many were transferred to ANG units between 1970 and 1973. Ten ANG squadrons operated their F-100Ds and Fs through 1978 and the last examples were not retired until November 1979. The French *Armée de l'Air* received 85 F-100Ds and 15 F-100Fs starting in 1959 and kept them in service until 1978. French F-100s were the first of the type to actually be used in combat when they participated in air strikes against targets in Algeria in the early 1960s. Another 48 F-100Ds and 10 Fs were supplied to the Danish Air Force during 1959 and 1960 and remained active until replaced by F-16s in the early 1980s. Coming mostly from ex-USAF stocks, Turkey received 206 F-100Ds and Fs, which later saw action during the Greek-Cypriot War in 1974. The last Turkish F-100s were retired in 1982.

McDonnell F-101 Voodoo 1954–1982

TECHNICAL SPECIFICATIONS (F-101C)
Type: One-place tactical fighter.
Manufacturer: McDonnell Aircraft Corp., St. Louis, Missouri.
Total produced: 805 (all versions, including RF-101A/C and F-101B/F)
Power plant: Two Pratt & Whitney J-57-13 turbojet engines, each rated at 10,200-lbs./s.t. dry, 15,000-lbs./s.t. with afterburning.
Armament: Four 20-mm cannons and one Mk. 7 (1,700-lb.), 28 (2,320-lb.), or 43 (2,060-lb.) tactical nuclear weapon carried on a centerline station.
Performance: Max. speed 1,012-mph at 35,000 feet., cruise 550-mph; ceiling 55,100 ft.; range 1,208 mi. loaded, 2,100 mi. max.
Weights: 26,277-lbs. empty, 48,908-lbs. max. takeoff.
Dimensions: Span 39 ft. 8 in., length 67 ft. 6 in., wing area 368 sq. ft.

But for the intervention of Tactical Air Command, the USAF career of the single-seat F-101A/C might have ended in 1957 when Strategic Air Command decided to abandon the long-range fighter concept. After McDonnell's original *Voodoo*, the XF-88A "Strategic Penetration Fighter," was cancelled in 1950 due to budgetary cuts, the project reemerged a year later as the considerably larger and more powerful F-101. Its primary mission—long-range fighter escort for SAC's B-36 fleet—was not changed, but the USAF expanded the F-101's potential mission uses by specifying the capability to carry a nuclear weapon on an external rack. In July 1952, after mockup inspection, McDonnell received a contract for small production run of 39 aircraft as the F-101A. While production had almost been assured under applicable procurement policies, some USAF officials were dubious about the aircraft's strategic bomber escort mission and had no definite agenda for alternative roles in which it might be used.

The first F-101A was flown from Edwards AFB on September 24, 1954, and early testing demonstrated very impressive performance—a top speed of Mach 1.54 (1,009-mph), an initial climb rate of 44,100 feet per minute, a ceiling of 55,800 feet, and a maximum range of almost 3,000 miles—but also revealed aerodynamic flaws that were serious enough for the USAF to place a hold on production in May 1956. The chief concern was a dangerous "pitch-up" tendency at certain G-levels and angles-of-attack during which the aircraft would enter an uncontrolled flat spin oscillating between 20 and 70-degrees nose up, and this condition was frequently accompanied by engine flame-outs due to compressor stalls. The problem was improved (though never fully corrected) by installing a pitch inhibitor that restricted stick movements at certain speeds and redesigning intake and engine ducting to allow better air flow at various angles-of-attack. The production hold was lifted in November 1956 and the first F-101As started entering operational service in May 1957. Of the 77 F-101As ultimately completed by October 1957 (including 38 added to the original contract), 50 were allocated to operational units while the others were retained as experimental and test inventory. Development and testing of the unarmed RF-101A reconnaissance version, featuring a camera-equipped nose lengthened by one foot ten inches, paralleled the fighter project and the first of 35 production models began reaching operational units in May 1957. Forty-seven improved F-101Cs, delivered between August 1957 and

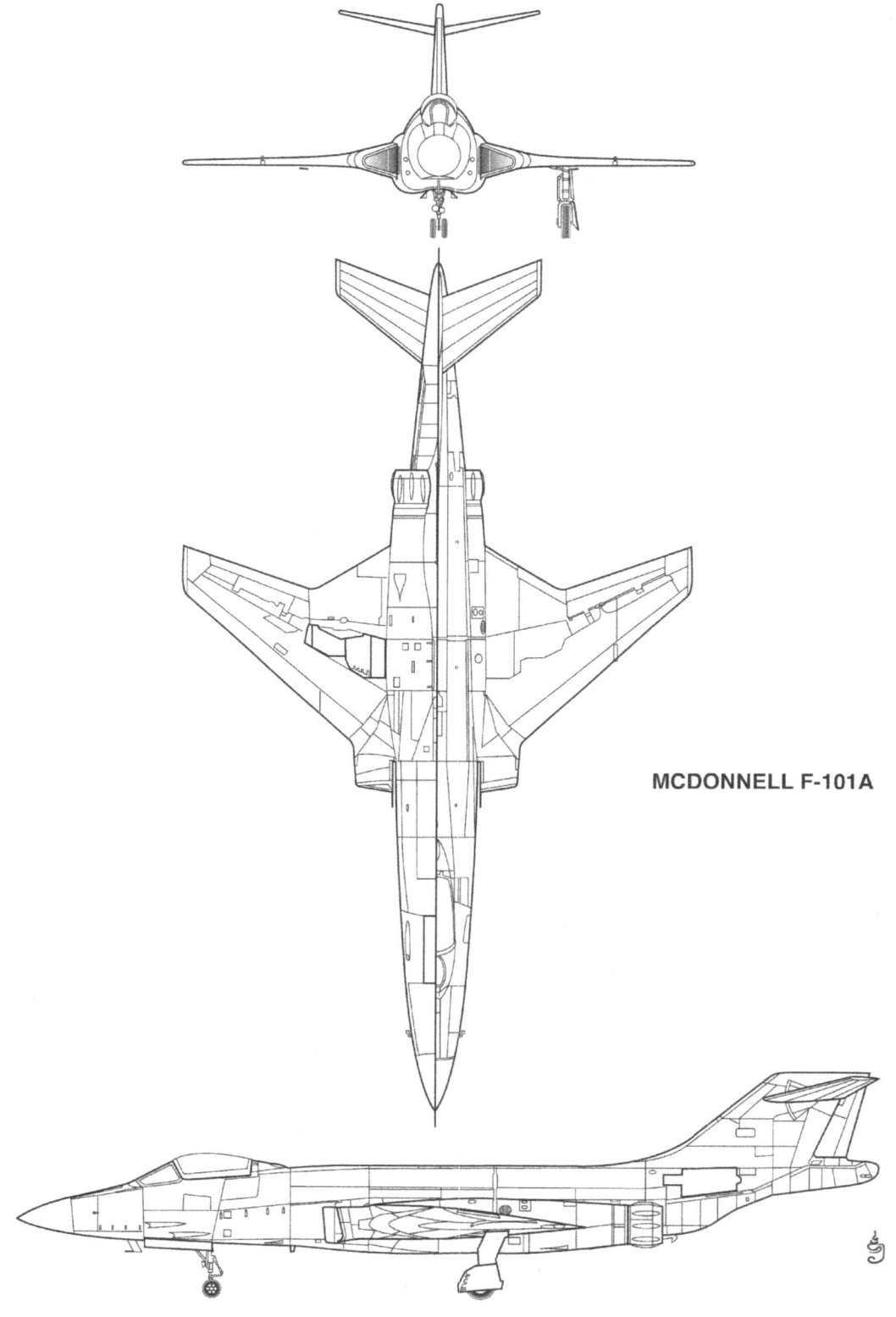

MCDONNELL F-101A

Top: The very large size of F-101A—67 feet, 6 inches long—is evident in this photograph. Only 50 of these aircraft were actually assigned to operational units, while the remaining 27 were retained as experimental and test inventory. *Bottom:* RF-101As and Cs began making surveillance flights over Southeast Asia in 1961. From 1964 onwards, they had to fly into the most lethal air defenses of North Vietnam to obtain pre- and post-strike target data. Last examples were retired from ANG in 1979.

May 1958, were externally identical to the A models but, due to the shift from strategic escort to a fighter-bomber role, had strengthened airframes to permit higher load limits. These were followed by 166 RF-101Cs having the same structural improvements, and the last example was accepted in August 1959. The most numerous and by far longest serving of the series was the two-seat, all-weather fighter-interceptor version, the F-101B. Unexpected setbacks in Convair's F-106 program combined with an urgent need for supersonic interceptors in Air Defense Command (ADC) led to production of 480 two-seat *Voodoos* between January 1959 and March 1961, 401 as F-101Bs and 79 as mission-capable F-101Fs with dual controls.

F-101As became operational in May 1957 with the 27th Strategic Fighter Wing in their original bomber escort role, yet even with external tanks, the type's 2,100-mile range was inadequate to accompany SAC's B-36s, B-47s, and B-52s to targets deep within the Soviet Union; as a consequence, the entire unit was transferred within a matter of months to TAC, becoming the 27th Fighter-Bomber Wing based at Bergstrom AFB in Texas. After joining TAC, F-101As were retrofitted with LABS and their original MA-7 fire-control/radar systems adapted to mapping of ground targets. The 27th was still taking delivery of new F-101Cs when its aircraft were transferred en masse to the 81st Tactical Fighter Wing based at RAF Bentwaters in England in mid–1958, where they replaced the unit's F-84Fs. During their term of service with the 81st, both F-101As and Cs were equipped with Low-Angle Drogue Delivery (LADD) systems that enabled them to drop a parachute-retarded tactical nuclear weapon from a low-altitude release. F-101As and Cs remained in service with the 81st until replaced by F-4Cs during 1965 and 1966. In 1965, 29 F-101As and 31 F-101Cs were re-designated RF-101G and RF-101H, respectively, after undergoing modifications in which the nose radar and gun armament were removed to be replaced by a new nose housing cameras and electronic equipment, and were thereafter assigned to three ANG Tactical Reconnaissance Squadrons. RF-101As initially entered service with the 363rd TRW at Shaw AFB in North Carolina, becoming the first USAF photo-recon unit to operate a supersonic aircraft. As RF-101Cs became available during 1958 and 1959, they augmented the RF-101As of the 363rd and also equipped the 66th TRW in Europe and the 67th TRW in the Far East. During the Cuban Missile Crisis of October 1962, RF-101s of the 363rd were tasked to fly low-level reconnaissance missions over Cuba. Starting in early 1961, RF-101Cs of the 67th operating out of Okinawa made the earliest surveillance flights over Vietnam and Laos, then in 1965, commenced tactical reconnaissance operations over North Vietnam from bases in Thailand and South Vietnam. As they started being replaced by RF-4Cs in late 1967, RF-101Cs were restricted from flying missions over the North and withdrawn from combat altogether by late 1970. Two-seat F-101Bs and Fs began reaching ADC units during early 1959 and equipped 17 fighter-interceptor squadrons by the end of 1961. ADC began the process of phasing-out its B and Fs from USAF service in mid–1968 and all had been withdrawn by mid–1971.

F/RF-101s served with various ANG units over an 18-year career. RF-101Gs and Hs of the 154th (Arkansas), 165th (Kentucky) and 192nd (Nevada) Tactical Reconnaissance Squadrons were activated in early 1968 during the Pueblo Crisis, during which time they served in rotational tours from Itazuke AFB in Japan until 1969. Two other ANG squadrons received RF-101As and Cs as they were released from active USAF service. All RF-101Gs and Hs were withdrawn by 1976 and the Mississippi ANG retired its last RF-101C in 1979. F-101Bs and Fs eventually equipped seven different ANG fighter-interceptor squadrons until being replaced in 1980 and 1981 by F-4Cs, RF-4Cs, and KC-135s. Eight RF-101As were transferred to Taiwan in 1959 and reportedly remained in service until the late 1970s. In 1962, 46 F-101Bs and 10 F-101Fs were transferred to Canada and subsequently served with four squadrons until replaced by F/A-18s in 1984; two Canadian F-101Bs fitted with special electronic equipment for ECM aggressor exercises remained active until mid–1987.

Lockheed F-104 Starfighter 1954–1975

TECHNICAL SPECIFICATIONS (F-104C)

Type: One-place tactical fighter.
Manufacturer: Lockheed Aircraft Corp., Burbank, California.
Total produced: 663 (all versions, including exports built by Lockheed)
Power plant: One General Electric J-79-7 turbojet engine, rated at 10,000-lbs./s.t. dry, 15,800-lbs./s.t. with afterburning.
Armament: One M61 20-mm Gatling gun, four AIM-9 *Sidewinder* missiles carried on wingtips and underwing racks, and up to 2,000-lbs. of bombs or tactical nuclear weapons on wing and centerline racks.
Performance: Max. speed 1,328-mph (Mach 2.0) at 35,000 feet., cruise 584-mph; ceiling 58,000 ft.; range 703 mi. loaded, 1,727 mi. max.
Weights: 12,760-lbs. empty, 27,853-lbs. max. takeoff.
Dimensions: Span 21 ft. 11 in. (without tanks), length 54 ft. 9 in., wing area 196 sq. ft.

The F-104 was the USAF's first operational Mach 2 fighter and served longer in foreign air forces than any other type of American combat aircraft. After interviewing fighter pilots in Korea during 1951, Clarence L. "Kelly" Johnson returned to Burbank and assembled his Lockheed engineering team to begin formulating a proposal for a lightweight fighter design that would reverse the contemporary trend toward increasingly larger and more complex aircraft. When submitted in late 1952 as the Lockheed Model 83, its aerodynamic concept—short trapezoidal wings of extreme thinness mated to a rocket-like fuselage—had been completely optimized for maximum flight performance. In March 1953, after reviewing the proposal, the USAF awarded Lockheed a contract for two experimental prototypes under the designation XF-104. The first XF-104, powered by a non-afterburning Wright J-65 engine, made its first flight on February 28, 1954, and the second prototype, with an afterburner installed, flew in October, then five months later achieved a level top speed of Mach 1.79 at 60,000 feet (1,181-mph). In October 1954, while the XF-104 test program was in progress, the USAF ordered 17 YF-104As to be powered the new General Electric J-79, with the expectation that the engine (which was still being tested) would be available sometime in 1955. The maiden flight of the first service test YF-104A took place on February 17, 1956 from Edwards AFB. The YF-104A differed from the XF-104s in having a fuselage lengthened five feet six inches to accommodate the larger J-79 engine, a slightly taller vertical fin, a forward-retracting nose gear, a dorsal spine, and fixed shock cones in the intakes to reduce air inlet speeds. Two months after it flew, the YF-104A achieved Mach 2 in level flight, the first USAF fighter to do so.

In March 1956 the USAF granted the first full-scale production contract for 153 F-104As with the intention that they would eventually replace F-100s in TAC units; however, by the time production models were scheduled for delivery in early 1958, a decision had been made to allocate them to Air Defense Command (ADC) fighter-interceptor squadrons as a stop-gap until the long-awaited F-106 arrived. The USAF accepted its last F-104A in December 1958. Twenty-six F-104B unarmed two-seat trainers were also delivered before the end of 1958. The first dedicated fighter-bomber version, the F-104C, appeared in mid–1958 with a more powerful -7 engine, a better fire-control system, and provisions to carry 2,000-lbs. of bombs or rocket pods or a Mk. 28 or Mk. 43 tactical nuclear weapon, and when armed for the air superiority role, four AIM-9 *Sidewinder* missiles. The first of 71 F-104Cs entered operational service in September 1958 and the final example was delivered in June 1959. The USAF also purchased 26 F-104D unarmed two-seat trainer variants between October 1958 and September 1959. The last Lockheed built versions, 30 two-seat F-104Fs, 116 two-seat TF-104Gs, and 221 F-104G fighter-bombers, completed between July 1962 and June 1964, were manufactured entirely for export under military assistance programs. From 1961 to 1979, significant numbers of *Starfighters* were built under license in foreign countries: Canada, 238 CF-104s and CF-104Ds; Japan, 198 F-104Js and F-104DJs; and Europe (Germany, Belgium, and Italy) 1,300 F-104Gs, TF-105Gs, and F-104Ss.

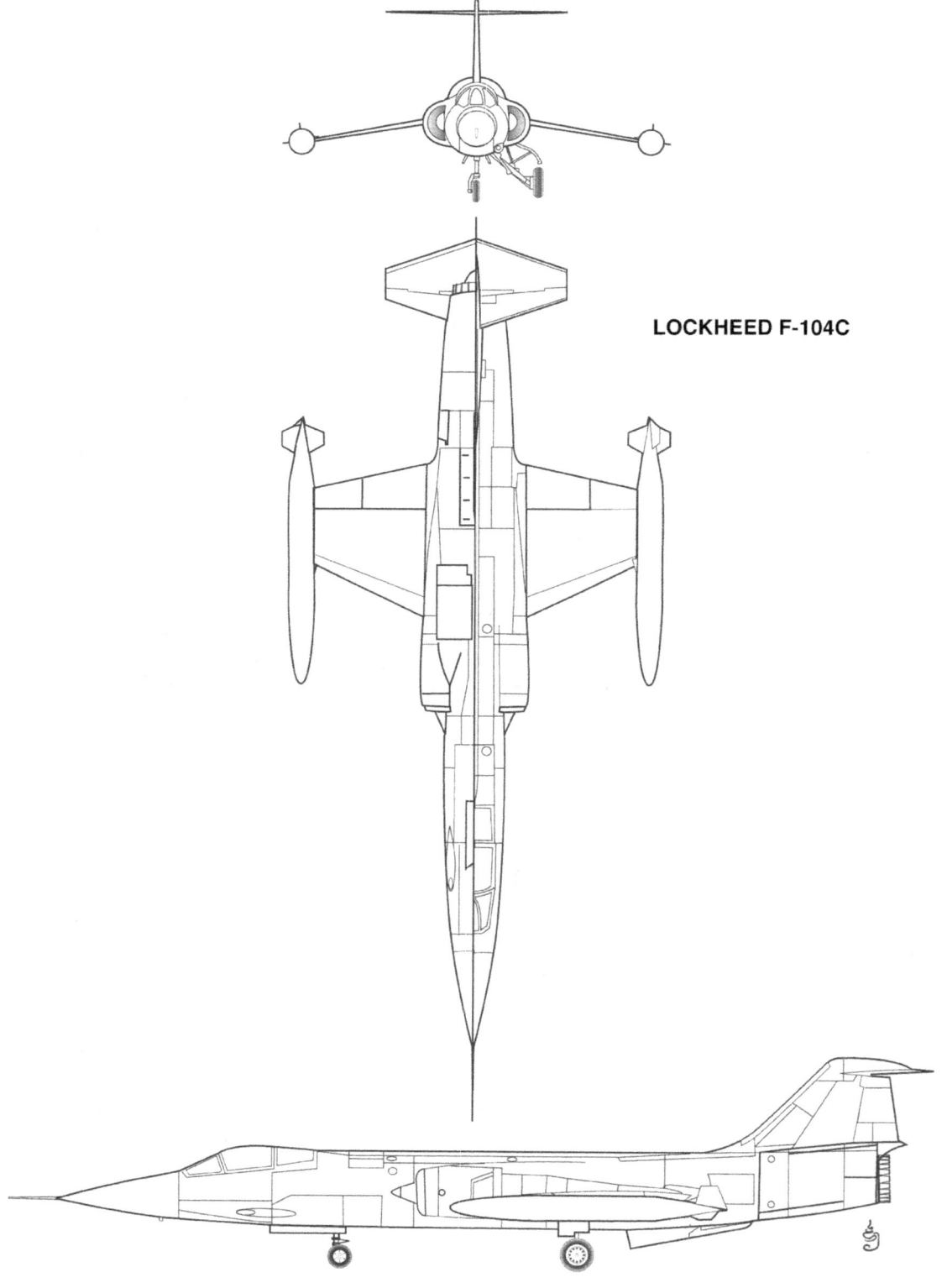

LOCKHEED F-104C

F-104C seen in Vietnam-era camouflage. All had been withdrawn from Southeast Asia by early 1967. F-104Cs served a while longer with ANG units; the last was retired in 1975. F-104Ss were finally phased out by the Italian air force in 2004.

In February 1958 the 83rd Fighter Interceptor Squadron based at Hamilton AFB in California was the first unit to become operational with F-104As, and before the end of the year, the type was equipping three more squadrons of ADC. However, because the F-104As were range limited and lacked the radar needed for all-weather interceptions, all of them were replaced by F-101Bs and F-106s during 1960 and were thereafter transferred to three ANG squadrons. All three ANG squadrons were activated during the Berlin crisis in 1962, but, interestingly, after being returned to state control, the USAF retained the F-104s and subsequently reassigned them to two active ADC squadrons. One of these, the 319th FIS based at Homestead AFB in Florida, operated its F-104As until December 1969, becoming the last active duty examples of the type. F-104Cs began reaching TAC units in the fall of 1958 and by mid–1959 were equipping four squadrons of the 479th Tactical Fighter Wing based at George AFB in California. During the Cuban Missile Crisis of October 1962, the F-104Cs of the 479th were deployed to NAS Key West in Florida where they remained on standby for possible air strikes against Cuba. F-104Cs saw action during the early Vietnam War in both air superiority and ground attack roles. Two squadrons of the 479th deployed to Taiwan in November 1965 and began combat tours in rotation from Da Nang Air Base in South Vietnam. At first, the F-104s flew escort missions (i.e., MiGCAP) for EC-121s (AWACS) operating over the Gulf of Tonkin and for strike aircraft, mainly F-105s, flying missions into North Vietnam; later, they were employed for close air support against Viet Cong targets in the South. In June 1966, while the 479th was in the process of converting to F-4Cs, one of its F-104C squadrons (435th TFS) was reassigned to the 8th TFW for combat duty and moved to Udorn RTAFB in Thailand. From Udorn, the 435th provided a MiG screen for strike aircraft returning from targets over North

Vietnam and was also used to bomb ground targets in South Vietnam and Laos. When withdrawn from combat in early 1967, two F-104s had been lost to SAM missiles, six to ground fire, and six in operational accidents. All remaining F-104Cs and Ds were phased-out of the active USAF inventory during 1967.

F-104A/Bs served with three ANG fighter-interceptors squadrons from 1960 to 1963. The 198th TFS of the Puerto Rico ANG began equipping with F-104C/Ds in mid–1967 and operated them until July 1975, when the unit converted to LTV A-7Ds. F-104s served with eleven different foreign air forces over a 44-year span, beginning with the first 29 ex-USAF F-104A/Bs transferred to Taiwan in 1960 and 1961. Most of the European F/TF-104Gs (Germany, Belgium, Netherlands, Norway, Denmark, Greece, and Spain) were withdrawn during the 1980s. Japan phased-out its F-104s in 1986. Turkey operated F-104G/Ss until 1996 and Taiwan F-104Gs until 1998. But the active military career of the *Starfighter* did not finally end until the Italian Air Force retired it last F-104S in 2004. Three civilian F-104Gs are reported to still be flying with NASA.

Republic F-105 Thunderchief 1955–1983

TECHNICAL SPECIFICATIONS (F-105D)

Type: One or two-place tactical fighter.
Manufacturer: Republic Aviation Corp., Farmingdale, New York.
Total produced: 833 (all versions)
Power plant: One Pratt & Whitney J-75-19W turbojet engine, rated at 17,200-lbs./s.t. dry, 26,500-lbs./s.t. with afterburning.
Armament: One M61A1 20-mm rotary cannon, 8,000-lbs. of bombs (nuclear or conventional) carried in an internal bomb bay, and up to 6,000-lbs or bombs or rockets carried on five external racks (one centerline and four underwing).
Performance: Max. speed 1,381-mph (Mach 2.1) at 36,000 feet., 836-mph (Mach1.1) at s.l., cruise 778-mph; ceiling 49,000 ft.; range 778 mi. loaded, 2,208 mi. max.
Weights: 26,855-lbs. empty, 52,546-lbs. max. takeoff.
Dimensions: Span 34 ft. 11 in., length 64 ft. 3 in., wing area 385 sq. ft.

The Republic F-105 was the first supersonic USAF aircraft designed from the ground up as a dedicated fighter-bomber, and when it became operational, was the fastest military aircraft in the world at sea level. Its origins can be traced to 1951 when Alexander Kartveli and his Republic design team instigated a project to find a supersonic successor to their swept-wing F-84F. In May 1952 the USAF gave Republic approval to complete the detailed design work on its proposed Model AP-63 under the designation F-105, with the expectation that an operational aircraft would be available sometime in 1955. From the beginning, the airframe of the F-105 was optimized for high-speed, low-level penetration in the nuclear strike role. To carry its nuclear payload, the design incorporated an internal bay large enough to contain a fifteen-foot-long weapon, which effectively dictated an aircraft significantly larger and heavier than the F-84F. Likewise, its planned nose section would be of sufficient size to house the radar array needed for the aircraft's navigation and bombing system. In late 1953, when mockup inspections revealed that the F-105 would be seriously underpowered with its original Allison J-71 powerplant, the USAF and Republic elected to substitute the available Pratt & Whitney J-57 on pre-production aircraft and use the forthcoming J-75 on production models, with the hope that the new engine would be available in time. The first formal procurement contract, issued in June 1954, originally specified fifteen J-57 powered YF-105As but was later changed to two YF-105As plus ten service test F-105Bs and two RF-105B recon versions to be powered by J-75 engines.

The maiden flight of the first YF-105A took place on October 22, 1955, followed by the

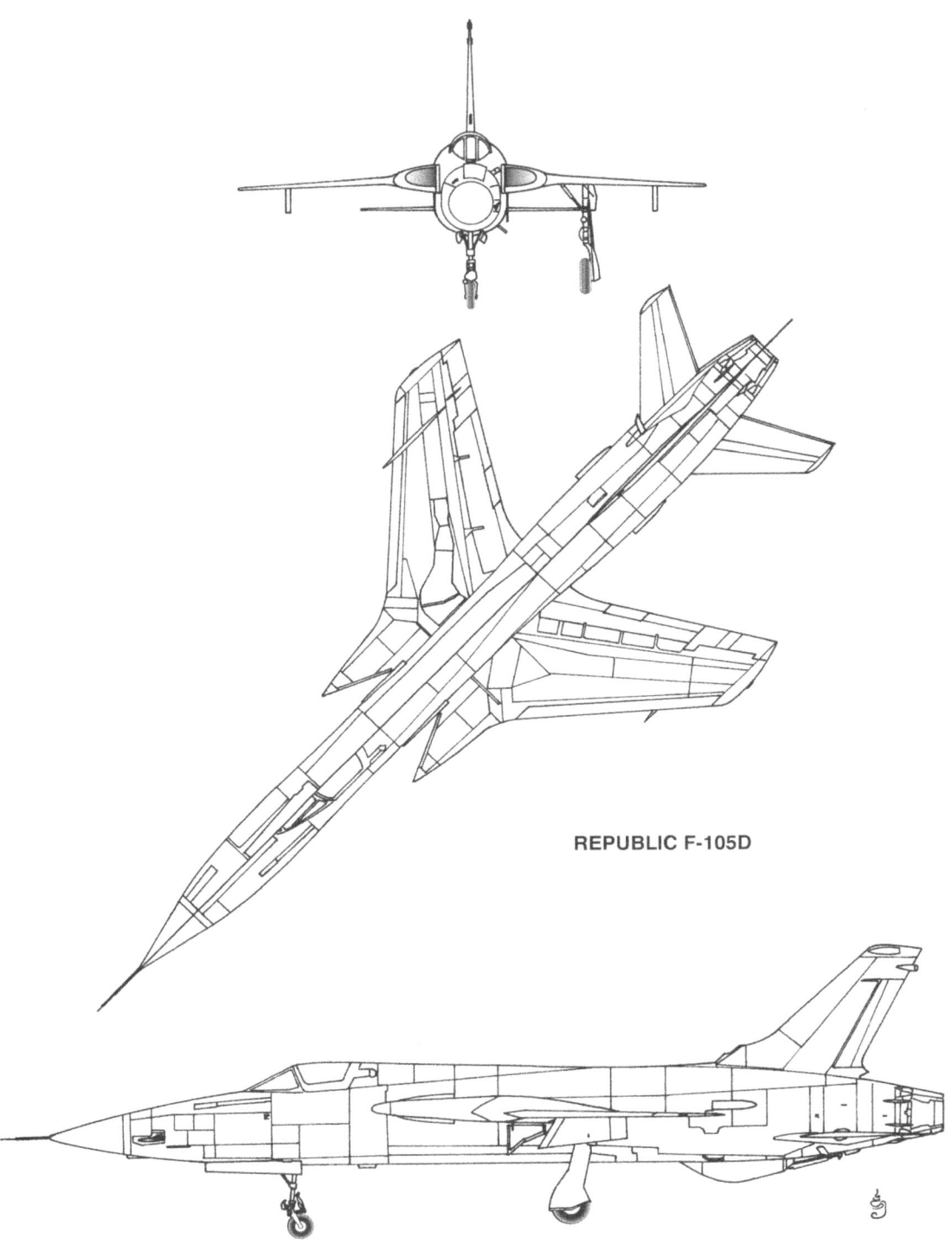

REPUBLIC F-105D

second prototype three months later. Testing demonstrated a top speed of 857-mph (Mach 1.27) at 33,000 feet and 778-mph (Mach 1.02) at sea level. The "area rule" principle discovered by NACA's Richard Whitcomb (i.e., that excessive drag build-up at the wing/fuselage junction could be avoided by a reducing the fuselage cross-section at the waist, thereby producing a coke bottle shape) came too late to be of help to the YF-105As but was incorporated into the

Top: A bombed-up F-105D of 355th Tactical Fighter Wing based at Takhli RTAFB in Thailand en route to target in North Vietnam. Intended for deep penetration nuclear strike, "Thuds" carried the brunt of conventional bombing missions over North Vietnam. *Bottom:* Korat RTAFB-based F-105G showing distinctive "wild weasel" tail code of the 561st Wild Weasel Squadron of the 388th Tactical Fighter Wing. The last F-105G was retired from ANG service in 1983.

fuselage design of the F-105B. The B also introduced forward-swept, variable geometry intakes to improve efficiency at the anticipated higher Mach numbers plus petal-types speed brakes at the very end of the fuselage which formed an annular exhaust cone. But by the time the first YF-105B flew in May 1956, cost overruns and production delays had reached the point where the USAF was on the verge on canceling the entire program in favor of the North American F-107A. Then in mid–1956, after reaching the conclusion that it would take even longer to get the F-107A to operational status, the USAF awarded Republic a contract for 65 F-105Bs, 17 RF-105Bs, and five two-seat F-105Cs. The RF-105B and F-105C were later cancelled. Deliveries of production models commenced in May 1958, three years behind schedule, and the last of 75 F-105Bs built (including 13 pre-production models) was accepted in December 1959.

Development of the chief production version, the F-105D, started during late 1957 in response to a new USAF all-weather requirement that included capability to carry the new Mk. 43 nuclear weapons on external pylons. This entailed installation of new radar and flight control systems that that permitted the aircraft to perform either low-level or high-level missions under any weather conditions. The system also incorporated a terrain-following feature that allowed to pilot to operate at nap-of-the-earth levels over an unfamiliar landscape. A modernized cockpit arrangement replaced the conventional analog instruments with vertical tape readouts that were easier to scan. D models were externally distinguishable from Bs by their lengthened and deepened nose radomes. Although the USAF had originally planned acquire both F-105Ds and two-seat F-105Es on the same production run, the Es were subsequently cancelled in order to free up funds to procure more F-105Ds. The first F-105D flew in June 1959 and production models started entering operational service during the fall of 1960, with a total of 610 being delivered to the USAF by January 1964. Because there was still a pressing need for advanced bombing and navigation training in F-105D units, the two-seat F-105F, featuring a five foot four inch fuselage plug for a second cockpit, was approved in May 1962 and began reaching operational units in December 1963. The USAF took delivery of the last of 143 F-105Fs in December 1964, at which point all F-105 production ended. In early 1966, the first of 86 F-105Fs began undergoing modifications to enhance their capability to perform Wild Weasel missions against the Soviet-supplied SAM missiles that were appearing in increasing numbers in North Vietnam. The improvements included installation of electronic equipment to detect and track enemy fire-control radars, combined with the ability to attack the sites with AGM-45 *Shrike* antiradar missiles. Under The Weasel III program in late 1968, Fs were further retrofitted to carry AGM-78 *Standard* antiradiation missiles which could 'remember' the location of a SAM site after its radar had been switched off. Beginning in late 1969, approximately 60 F-105Fs were re-designated F-105Gs when they received enhanced avionics consisting not only of advanced radar homing and warning systems but new side blisters that housed powerful ECM jamming transmitters.

The 335th Tactical Fighter Squadron of the 4th TFW at Eglin AFB in Florida received its first F-105Bs in May 1958, but due to production slippages, lack of spare parts, and a delays in the test program, did not achieve full operational readiness until mid–1960. Because it was considered an interim model until the all-weather F-105Ds became available, only three squadrons of the 4th equipped with the F-105B, and all had been withdrawn from active service by early 1964. F-105Bs were used by the Thunderbirds flight demonstration team briefly during 1964, but after a fatal crash, they were replaced with F-100Ds. The 4th TFW began taking delivery of its first F-105Ds in June 1960, and by early 1964, a total of seven tactical fighter and fighter-bomber wings were operating the type. Two of the wings were based in Europe and two in Japan, where they were placed on nuclear alert status. As F-105Fs were delivered, they were divided among units equipped with Ds. Starting with the 20th production block in 1962, the nuclear role was de-emphasized, so that F-105Ds were built with expanded conventional weapons capabilities and also received systems and related fire-control equipment for AGM-12 *Bullpup* missiles; and most earlier block aircraft were eventually upgraded to this standard. In conventional configuration, all weapons were carried externally, on centerline and wing racks, and the internal bay was normally used to house a 390-gallon fuel tank. As a result of combat experience in Southeast Asia, F-105s received numerous field modifications, including extra armor protection, backup flight control systems, radar altimeters, improved bombsights, new weapons release systems, RHAW equipment, and ECM pods.

F-105Ds were introduced to combat in late 1964 when the Japan-based 18th TFW deployed squadrons to Korat RTAFB in Thailand, where they commenced flying strike missions against Communist targets in northern Laos. Although not designed for the role, F-105Ds were used as the USAF's primary military instrument to bomb strategic targets in North Vietnam from early 1965 to mid–1969, during which time a strength of two wings was maintained from bases in Thailand, the 355th TFW at Tahkli RTAFB and the 388th at RTAFB Korat. On normal missions, involving a 1,250-mile flight to Hanoi plus in-flight refueling both during ingress and egress, *Thunderchiefs* (or "Thuds," as they were called by aircrews) typically carried six 750-lb. bombs or five 1,000-lb. bombs, together with two 450-gallon drop tanks. Once in Hanoi airspace, F-105s were required to make dive and glide-bombing attacks against their targets, where they were confronted by the most dangerous antiaircraft defenses in the history of air warfare, consisting of radar and optically-guided AAA guns from .51-caliber up to 100-mm, SA-2 SAMs, plus MiG-17s and -21s operating in concert with a sophisticated GCI (ground controlled intercept) system. Combat attrition became so serious in 1965 and 1966 that consideration was given to re-opening the F-105 production line but was rejected in favor of buying newer aircraft like the F-4 and F-111. Responsibility for bombing the North was taken over by F-4s during 1969, and F-105s were thereafter restricted to lower-threat targets in Laos, then finally removed from combat altogether in late 1970. At the time they were withdrawn, 350 F-105s (Ds and Fs) had been lost due to enemy action, most to ground fire, but between 17 and 27 losses were attributed to enemy MiGs. Though not very well suited for the air-to-air role, F-105s were nevertheless credited with shooting down 27 MiGs, primarily with their 20-mm rotary cannons. Two-seat F-105Fs entered combat in the bomber role alongside the Ds but from 1966 onwards were progressively dedicated to Wild Weasel missions. Modified Fs began operating over North Vietnam from bases in Thailand in June 1966, and with their F-105G counterparts, supported USAF air operations throughout the entire conflict, flying their final missions to escort B-52s over North Vietnam in December 1972.

After Vietnam, F-105s were rapidly retired from the active USAF inventory and transferred to USAFR and ANG units. One USAFR squadron and two New Jersey ANG units operated F-105Bs at various intervals between 1964 and 1981. F-105Ds equipped four USAFR units from 1971 to 1984 and they also served with four ANG units from 1971 to 1983. Two USAFR squadrons flew F-105Fs and Gs until late 1982 and two ANG units until 1983. F-105s never served with foreign air forces.

North American F-107 1956–1959

TECHNICAL SPECIFICATIONS (YF-107A)

Type: One-place tactical fighter.
Manufacturer: North American Aviation, Inc., Inglewood, California.
Total produced: 3
Power plant: One Pratt & Whitney J-75-9 turbojet engine, rated at 17,200-lbs./s.t. dry, 24,500-lbs./s.t. with afterburning.
Armament: Four 20-mm M39 cannons and up to 10,000-lbs. of bombs (nuclear or conventional) carried on centerline (recessed) and six underwing racks.

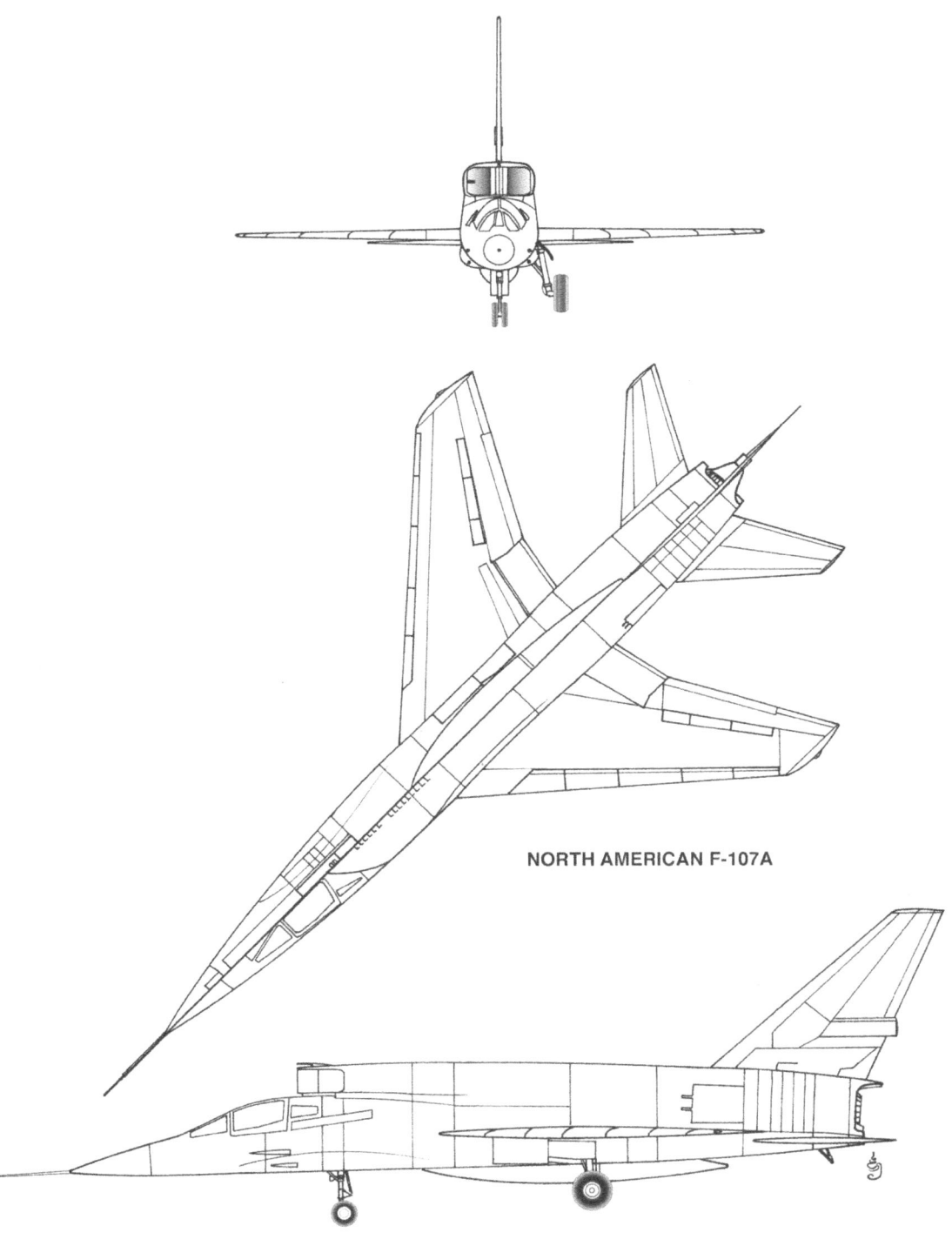

NORTH AMERICAN F-107A

Performance: Max. speed 1,295-mph (Mach 1.95) at 36,000 feet., 890-mph (Mach1.1) at s.l., cruise 598-mph; ceiling 53,200 ft.; range 788 mi. loaded, 2,428 mi. max.
Weights: 22,696-lbs. empty, 41,537-lbs. max. takeoff.
Dimensions: Span 36 ft. 7 in., length 61 ft. 10 in., wing area 376 sq. ft.

The last fighter design produced by North American, the F-107 went through an interest-

The F-107A was one of the first aircraft to be equipped with a fly-by-wire control system. USAF plans to proceed with full-scale production of the F-105 effectively spelled the end of the F-107 program.

ing series of permutations before achieving its final form in 1956. As the F-100B, it was essentially to have been an improved F-100A with a more powerful J-57 engine, a somewhat thinner wing, and an area-ruled fuselage. A top speed of Mach 1.8 was projected. After that, the F-100BI was a proposed all-weather interceptor version having, in addition to the aerodynamic improvements of the B, a chin intake under a nose radome like the F-86D. However, the USAF never indicated adequate interest in either project to justify progressing to an advanced stage of development. Then in April 1954, during the time the USAF was facing significant delays in the F-105 program, North American re-worked the F-100BI design and resubmitted it as a radar-equipped fighter-bomber. In June 1954, the USAF gave North American a provisional contract for 33 aircraft under the new designation F-107A, but two months later, cut it back to nine service test examples as the YF-107A.

As the design progressed, it proved to be a major departure from the basic configuration of the F-100BI. To boost overall flight performance, North American selected the more powerful J-75 engine in place of the J-57. The wing was redesigned to depend on a system of spoilers and slot-deflectors for lateral control rather than ailerons, and for low-speed handling, the entire trailing edge was made up of slotted flaps, with the inboard pair utilizing a 'blown' boundary-layer control system. The vertical tail surface emerged as a single, all-moving piece. In order to avoid pitch-up problems, the YF-107A introduced a control system known as ALCS (augmented longitudinal control system), one of the earliest applications of the "fly-by-wire" principle. Wind tunnel testing subsequently revealed a major airflow disturbance between the chin intake and the nuclear weapon carried in the centerline recess on the bottom of the fuselage, which led the designers move the intake to an unusual location on the top of the fuselage immediately behind the cockpit. To adjust inlet air at higher Mach numbers, the intake was fitted with a system of variable inlet ramps that would work automatically. Another departure from the F-100BI design was moving the main landing gear from the wings to bays in the sides of the fuselage similar to the arrangement seen on the F-104. In the event production was ordered, North American's Autonetics Division was developing an advanced fire-control system (MA-12) that would enable the F-107A to duplicate the tactical capabilities of the F-105.

The first YF-107A took off from Edwards AFB on September 10, 1956 and went supersonic on its first flight, and less than two months later, achieved Mach 2.0 in level flight. The second prototype, the only example to be equipped with cannons and a weapons delivery system, was delivered in November, and the third, the first with fully-automatic variable inlet ramps, appeared in early 1957; yet, by this time, the USAF had already reached a decision to proceed with full-scale production of the F-105 and limit the YF-107A program to the three prototypes. The USAF retained the second YF-107A to carry out control system testing, but it was apparently not flown again after 1958.

The first prototype was transferred to NACA (later NASA) in 1957 but was grounded after only four flights due to serious mechanical problems. The third YF-107A was similarly transferred to NACA for test purposes but was destroyed in September 1959 during an aborted take-off run after experiencing severe control problems.

THIRD SERIES • 1962–PRESENT

Designation	*Manufacturer*	*Dates*
A-1	(See, AD in Part II)	
A-7	(See, A-7 in Part II)	
A-9	Northrop Aerospace Corp.	1972–1973
A-10	Fairchild-Republic Co.	1972–Present
F-4	(See, F-4 in Part II)	
F-5, -20	Northrop Corp.	1959–Present
F-111	General Dynamics Corp.	1965–1998
F-15	McDonnell-Douglas Corp.	1972–Present
F-16	General Dynamics Corp.	1974–Present
F-117	Lockheed Aircraft Corp.	1981–Present
F/A-22	Lockheed-Martin Corp.	1990–Present
F-23	Northrop Aerospace Corp.	1990–1992
(X)F-32	Boeing Aerospace Co.	2000–2001
F-35	Lockheed-Martin Corp.	2000–Present
X-45	Boeing Aerospace Co.	2002–Present

Northrop A-9 1972–1973

TECHNICAL SPECIFICATIONS (YA-9A)

Type: One-place ground attack.
Manufacturer: Northrop Corp., Hawthorne, California.
Total produced: 2
Power plant: Two Lycoming F-102-LD-100 turbofan engines, each rated at 7,500-lbs./s.t.
Armament: One M61A1 20-mm rotary cannon and up to 16,000-lbs. of bombs or rockets carried on ten external stations.
Performance: Max. speed 449 at s.l., cruise 322-mph; ceiling 40,000 ft.; range 576 mi. loaded, 3,622 mi. max.
Weights: 20,754-lbs. empty, 41,795-lbs. max. takeoff.
Dimensions: Span 57 ft., length 53 ft. 6 in., wing area 580 sq. ft.

A combination of combat experience in Vietnam and pressure from the U.S. Army led the USAF to establish the AX (attack experimental) Office in the spring of 1970 with the express aim of developing a modern, jet-propelled aircraft that would be specialized for the close air support (CAS) role. A request for proposals was issued in May 1970 to twelve aircraft compa-

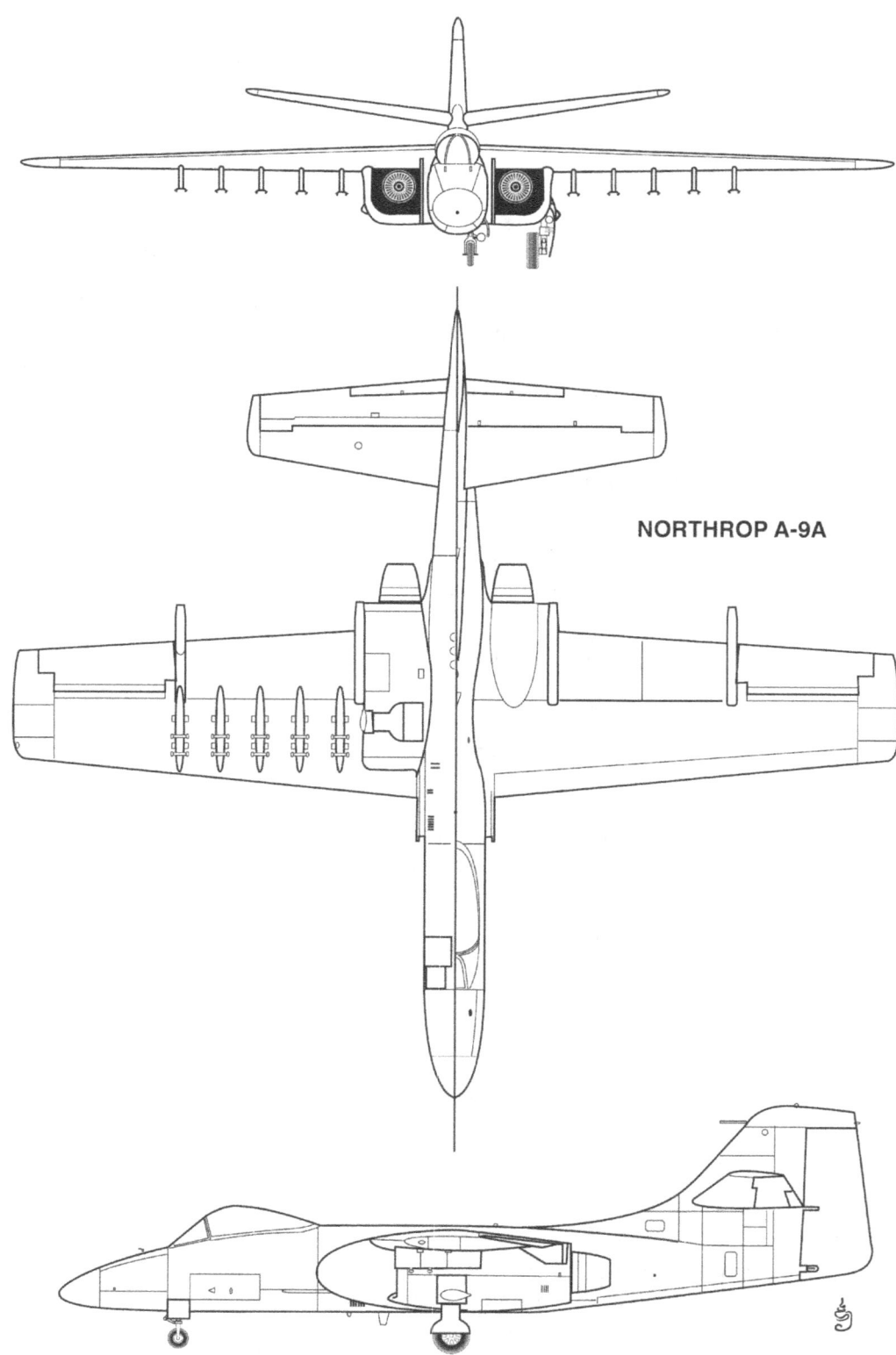

One of two YA-9A prototypes during tests in 1972. Light wing loading combined with generous tail surface area provided tight battlefield maneuvering at lower airspeeds. The Russian-made Su-25 appeared with a very similar aerodynamic arrangement.

nies listing three broad tactical requirements: (1) short takeoff and landing characteristics (i.e., at a minimum, the ability to takeoff from 2,000 foot runways while loaded) in conjunction with a landing gear sufficiently rugged to permit continuous operations from unimproved airfields; (2) adequate range for extended loiter time in the vicinity of the battlefield; (3) cruise speed high enough to allow rapid deployment from one battle zone to another; and (4) future provision to carry the General Electric GAU-8 30-mm rotary cannon, which was still under development (prototypes would use the available M61A1 20-mm unit for evaluation purposes). Six of the twelve companies responded with design proposals, Boeing, Cessna, Fairchild (Republic Aircraft Division), General Dynamics, Lockheed, and Northrop, and in December 1970, the USAF announced that the competition had been narrowed to Fairchild-Republic and Northrop. Shortly thereafter, Northrop and Fairchild-Republic received the go-ahead to proceed with the design and construction of AX prototypes under the designations YA-9A and YA-10A, respectively. The winner of the competition would be selected according to a fly-off scheduled to take place sometime in 1972.

The AX concept, with its total focus on the CAS combat environment, dictated an aircraft that possessed a high degree of survivability while operating low and slow over the battlefield in range of virtually every enemy weapon. In contrast to the preceding generation of USAF tactical aircraft, speed, sophisticated all-weather avionics, and nuclear weapons capability were not factors. Instead, emphasis was placed on the ability to deliver a variety of conventional munitions—gunfire, bombs, rockets, and missiles—against identified ground targets like tanks, armored vehicles, and hardened bunkers. Northrop's YA-9A, resembling a throwback from 1940s, emerged with broad, unswept wings shoulder-mounted to the fuselage, in company with two large-diameter turbofan engines slung in bays beneath the wings. The side view of the aircraft was dominated by a very large fin and rudder flanked by high-mounted horizontal stabilizers set at about ten-degrees dihedral. Generous wing area combined with high-lift airfoil sections produced load factors (i.e., 50-60-lbs. per sq. ft.) that permitted very tight maneuvering at low altitudes. And to protect itself, the YA-9A depended on a triple-redundant hydraulic control system, foam filled self-sealing fuel tanks, and a "bathtub" surrounding the cockpit with 2.5-inches of aluminum alloy armor plating; other vital components were likewise protected by 1.25-inches of the same alloy.

During 1971 the aerodynamic design of the YA-9A was subjected to extensive wind tunnel testing. The flight of the first prototype took place on May 30, 1972, and it was delivered to Edwards AFB for the AX fly-off in early October. Official evaluations commenced on October 10 and concluded on December 9, after the YA-9A had made 123 flights totaling 146 hours flying time. On January 18, 1973 the USAF announced the Fairchild-Republic YA-10A as winner of the competition. While both aircraft had demonstrated themselves to be very well adapted to the CAS role, military officials nonetheless judged the YA-10A to be superior in terms weapons loading, underwing space for large ordnance loads, ground handling, overall operational simplicity, and projected unit cost. After the competition, both A-9A prototypes were transferred to NASA for further flight-testing before finally being retired. If imitation is the sincerest form of flattery, it can be said to have happened to the A-9A when the very similar appearing Russian-made Sukhoi Su-25 "Frogfoot" made its public debut in 1979.

Fairchild (Republic) A-10 Thunderbolt II 1972–Present

TECHNICAL SPECIFICATIONS (A-10A)
Type: One-place ground attack.
Manufacturer: Fairchild Industries, Inc. (Republic Aircraft Div.), Farmingdale, New York.
Total produced: 715
Power plant: Two General Electric TF34-100 turbofan engines, each rated at 9,000-lbs./s.t.
Armament: One GAU-8/A 30-mm rotary cannon and up to 16,000-lbs. of bombs, rockets, or guided missiles carried on eleven external stations.
Performance: Max. speed 448 at s.l., cruise 345-mph; ceiling 44,200 ft.; range 576 mi. loaded (with 1.8 hour loiter), 2,542 mi. max.
Weights: 21,519-lbs. empty, 47,000-lbs. max. takeoff.
Dimensions: Span 57 ft. 6 in., length 53 ft. 4 in., wing area 506 sq. ft.

Known widely as the "Warthog" or simply the "Hog," the USAF's A-10 is probably the most capable close air support (CAS) aircraft in the world today. The AX (attack experimental) concept originated during the late 1960s when combat experience in Vietnam pointed to the need for a modern close air support (CAS) aircraft that could maneuver low over the battlefield and survive an intense amount of small-arms fire. By the time the USAF issued a clear-cut requirement to aircraft manufacturers in May 1970 (see, A-9 above), the AX specification had been expanded to include sufficient firepower to deal with the tanks and armored vehicles that were likely to be encountered in a confrontation with the Soviet Army. Simultaneously, the USAF issued a related requirement for development of a 30-mm rapid-fire cannon to be used in the eventual AX aircraft. In January 1973, the USAF declared the Fairchild-Republic YA-10A as the winner of the AX fly-off against Northrop's rival A-9A. Both aircraft had satisfactorily met the overall CAS mission requirements, however, evaluating officials concluded the YA-10A had demonstrated a number of qualities that made it a better aircraft from an operational standpoint. Locating the twin turbofans in nacelles high on the aft fuselage made them

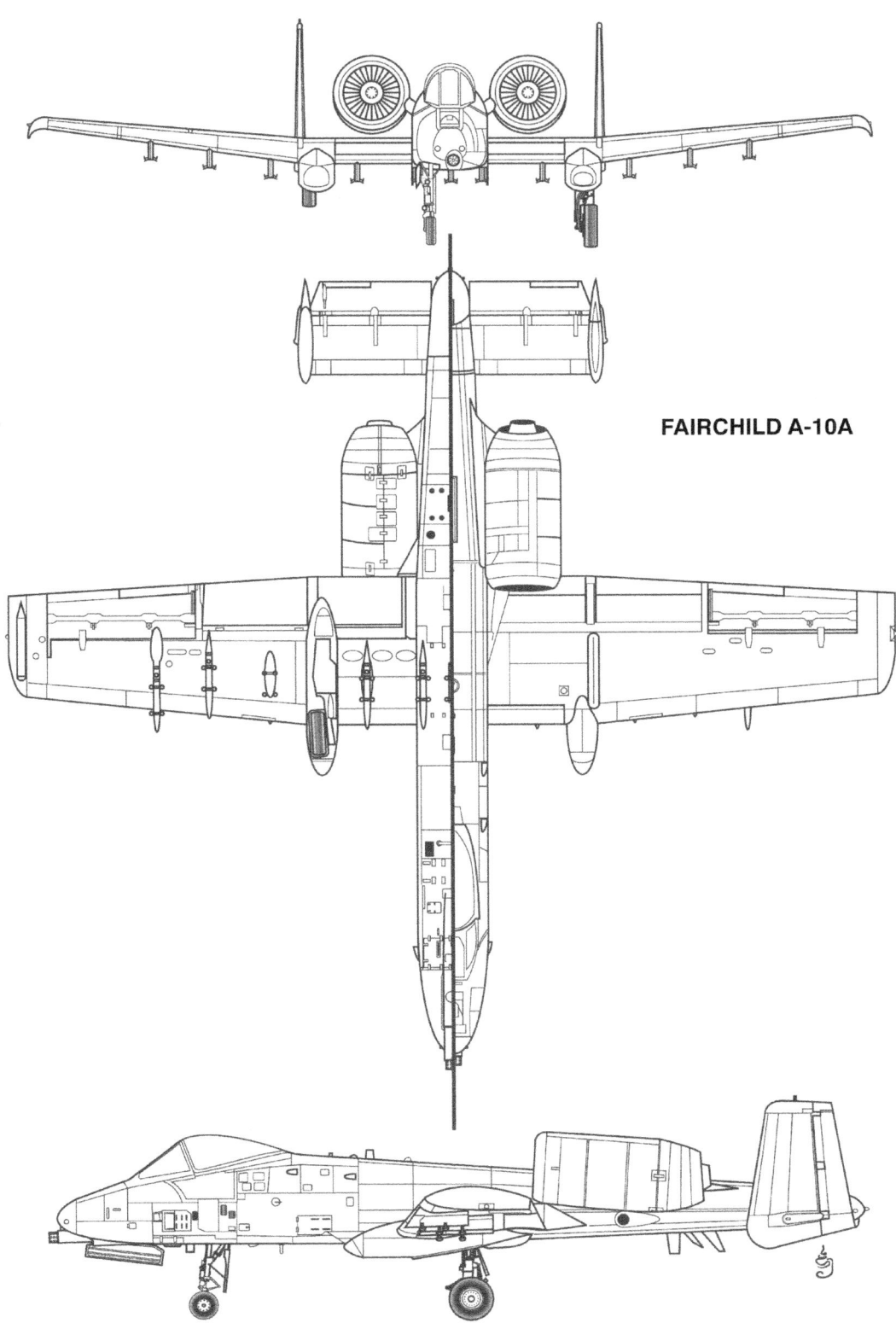

FAIRCHILD A-10A

Top: A-10A of the 602nd Tactical Air Control Wing based at Davis-Monthan AFB in Arizona. In the original Cold War scenario, A-10s would have been employed to stop or delay the massed armored divisions of the Soviet and Warsaw Pact armies. *Bottom:* The A-10A's superb combat record during the first Gulf War removed official doubts about its effectiveness as an attack platform. With the planned A-10C upgrades, the type is expected to remain in service until 2028.

less vulnerable to foreign object ingestion while operating from unimproved airfields and freed the entire bottom of the wing for weapons stores. The low position of the wing also provided better access for weapons loading. As important, since the overall design of the YA-10A was less complex, it would be easier to maintain and somewhat cheaper to mass-produce. Yet before the USAF was authorized to place the A-10A in full-scale production, members of the U.S. Congress insisted that the aircraft be subjected to a second fly-off against the LTV A-7D (see, A-7 in Part II), and flight evaluations subsequently took place between the two aircraft at Fort Riley, Kansas during the spring of 1974. After the YA-10A showed itself to be superior in every aspect of CAS operations (i.e., survivability, firepower, payload, and maneuverability), the USAF received approval to proceed with production plans.

The six A-10A development aircraft delivered during 1975 were all armed with the new General Electric GAU-8 30-mm rotary cannon. Firing up to 1,350 depleted uranium armor-piercing shells at a rate of 3,900 rounds per minute (65 per second), the cannon was capable of penetrating heavy tank armor and destroying hardened targets like bunkers and equipment within revetments. Eleven weapons pylons, eight under the wings plus three under the fuselage, could be loaded with a variety of air-to-ground munitions including optically guided AGM-65 *Maverick* missiles. The cockpit area was protected by a titanium "bathtub" that would defect projectiles up to 23-mm. A-10As also came with Pave Penny laser tracking systems which enabled them to guide GBUs (i.e., "smart" bombs). By the end of 1975 the test program was complete, and production A-10As began entering operational service with TAC during the spring of 1976. In early 1979 one A-10A was re-designated the A-10N/AW (night/all-weather) when it received a second cockpit to accommodate an electronics warfare officer plus components for a laser ranging system, terrain-following radar, inertial navigation, a radar altimeter, and an electronic moving map display. External pods also housed a forward-looking infra-red (FLIR) system and low-light television camera (LLLTV). Although the test program proved to be successful, no production of the A-10N/AW was ordered. All A-10A production ended in 1983 with the delivery of the 715th example (including prototypes and pre-production aircraft) and in 1987, Northrop-Grumman replaced Fairchild-Republic as the type's primary support contractor.

Starting in 1990, A-10s were upgraded with a system known as low-altitude safety and targeting enhancement (LASTE), which included computerized weapon aiming equipment, an autopilot, and a ground collision warning system. At the same time, a number of A-10s were shifted to the forward air control (FAC) role and re-designated OA-10A, while otherwise retaining full CAS weapons capability. In the FAC mission, the aircraft is typically armed with up to six pods of five-inch *Zuni* rockets that are used to mark targets. Commencing in 1999, the navigational capabilities of A/OA-10A fleet were greatly enhanced with the installation of the embedded global positioning/inertial navigation system (EGI). In 2005 the USAF commenced the A-10C Precision Engagement Upgrade Program under which 125 aircraft are scheduled to undergo a wide range of improvements that will include a hands-on stick and throttle control (HOTAS), two Raytheon multi-function displays (i.e., a glass cockpit), an integrated flight and fire-control computer (IFFCC), a Sniper XR targeting pod, and a helmet-mounted sighting system. This upgrade will enable A-10Cs to utilize newer precision weapons like the joint direct attack munition (JDAM) and wind-corrected munitions dispenser (WCMD). The first A-10C was delivered in August 2006 and the program should be complete by the end of 2009. The phase-out of the A-10 fleet was originally scheduled to start in 2005 as aircraft reached 8,000 airframe hours; however, in view of current upgrade and refurbishment plans, the type's service life has been extended to 2028, with projected airframe times up to 20,000 hours.

Production A-10As began entering service in March 1976 with the 333rd Tactical Training Squadron at Davis-Monthan AFB in Arizona. After achieving initial operational readiness in mid-1978 with the 354th Tactical Fighter Wing, A-10s deployed overseas to join the 81st TFW in the United Kingdom, where they eventually grew to a strength of six squadrons. While serving there, their primary mission was to support NATO ground forces against any attack by Soviet or Warsaw Pact armored divisions. During the 1980s the USAF advocated a plan to transfer its entire A-10 fleet to the Army and Marine Corps with the object of replacing them with a CAS version of the F-16; however, the idea was evidently discarded after A-10s overwhelmingly established their value as a CAS platform during Operation Desert Storm. By the time the Gulf War ended in early 1991, A-10s had flown a total of 8,100 combat sorties in which they were credited with the destruction of 1,000 enemy tanks, 2,000 military vehicles, and 1,200 artillery pieces, for a loss of only five aircraft; and they accomplished their mission while maintaining an above-average in-service rate of 95.7 percent. A-10s again saw action in the Kosovo War in 1999 and participated in the invasion of Afghanistan in 2001, and more recently, 60 A-10s derived from one USAF Reserve squadron and five Air National Guard units were deployed to Iraq in the spring of 2003 where they provided support to U.S. troops on the ground. According to current USAF statistics, over 350 OA/A-10As and A-10Cs remain operational with seventeen different squadrons, which include eight active USAF, three USAFR, and five ANG.

Northrop F-5/F-20 Tiger/Tigershark 1959–Present

TECHNICAL SPECIFICATIONS (F-5E)

Type: One-place fighter-bomber
Manufacturer: Northrop Corp., Hawthorne, California.
Total produced: 1,869 all versions (not including license-built)
Power plant: Two General Electric J-85-21A turbojet engines, each rated at 3,280-lbs./s.t. dry, 10,000-lbs. with afterburning.
Armament: Two M39A2 20-mm cannons, two AIM-9 Sidewinder air-to-air missiles on wingtips, and up to 1,700-lbs. of ordnance carried on one centerline and four wing stations.
Performance: Max. speed 1,083-mph (Mach 1.63) at 36,000 ft., cruise 678-mph, ceiling 51,800 ft.; range 390 mi. loaded, 1,543 mi. max.
Weights: 9,683-lbs. empty, 24,676-lbs. max. takeoff.
Dimensions: Span 27 ft. 12 in., length 46 ft. 6 in., wing area 186 sq. ft.

The F-5 was conceived during the mid–1950s to offer a simple and inexpensive supersonic fighter for nations participating in the Department of Defense (DOD) Military Assistance Program (MAP). Even though the USAF had no interest in procuring a lightweight fighter for itself, it did announce plans to acquire a two-seat advanced trainer version as the T-38, and took delivery of 1,187 examples between 1961 and 1972, of which 562 are reported to still be active. The first flight of the company Model N-156, subsequently designated F-5, took place on July 30, 1959, and DOD announced that the type had been selected for MAP in August 1962. The definitive F-5A production model was flown in July 1963, followed in seven months by the F-5B two-seat variant. The F-5A/B, with limited air-to-air capabilities and lacking a fire-control radar, was intended primarily for the ground attack role under clear, daylight conditions. Deliveries of 636 F-5As and 200 F-5Bs commenced in January 1965, initially to Iran, followed over a seven year period by deliveries to South Vietnam, Korea, Philippines, Taiwan, Thailand, Norway, Greece, Turkey, Morocco, Libya, Jordan, Yemen, Ethiopia, and Pakistan. The camera-equipped RF-5A made its first flight in May 1968 and 89 were subsequently sold to Iran, Greece, Norway, Morocco, South Vietnam, South Korea, Thailand, and Turkey. In 1965, under a program known as "Skoshi Tiger," the USAF 'borrowed' 12 F-5As from MAP distributions which were placed into service with the 4503rd Tactical Fighter Squadron and deployed to Ben Hoa Air Base, South Vietnam where they were used to fly ground attack missions in the South. After completing approximately 3,500 air-to-ground combat sorties for a

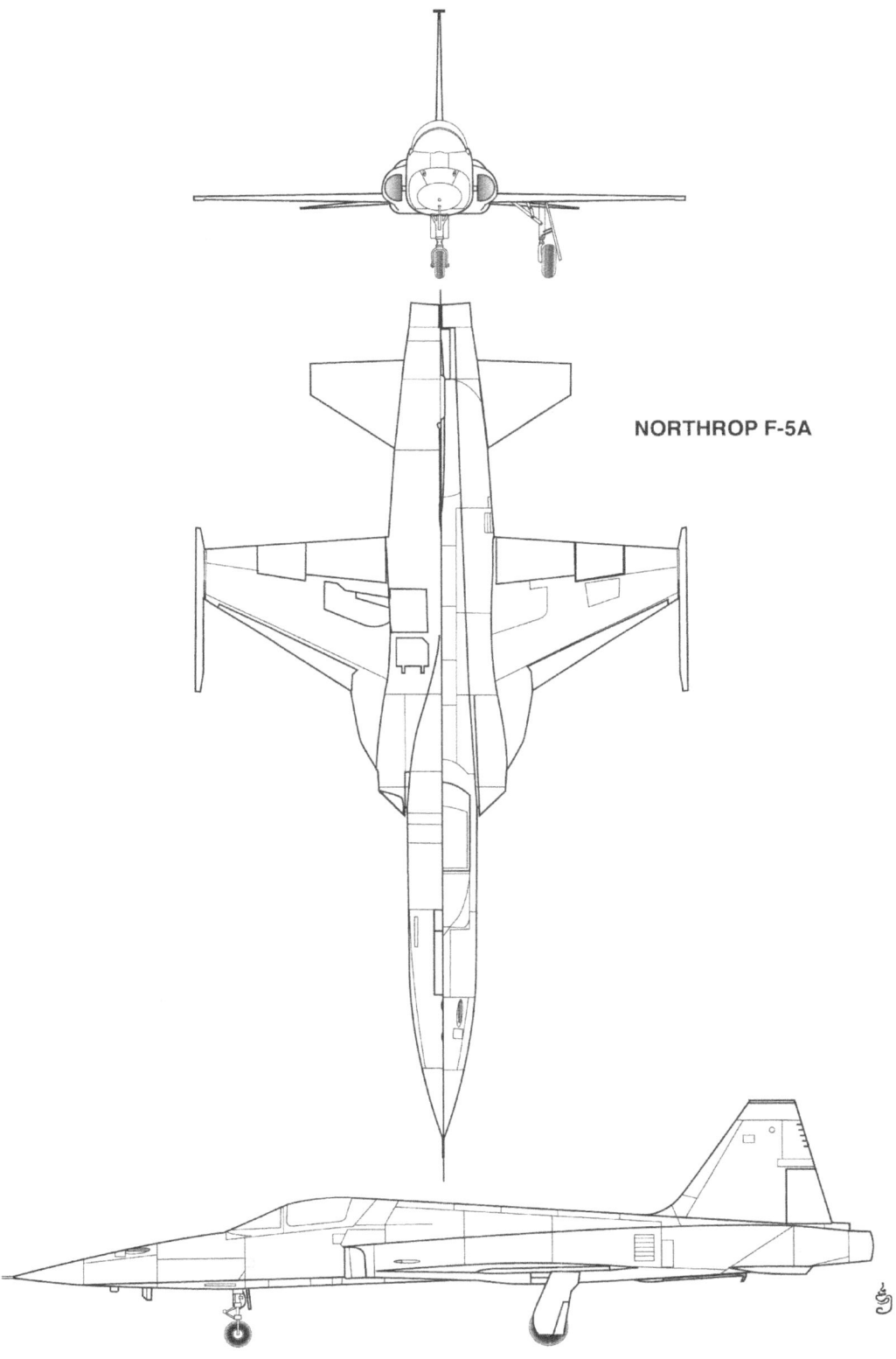

NORTHROP F-5A

Top: F-5A "Skoshi Tigers" which operated with the 4503rd Tactical Fighter Squadron out of Ben Hoa Air Base in South Vietnam during 1965. After completing their USAF combat tour, these aircraft were transferred to the South Vietnamese air force. *Bottom:* USAF F-5Es of the 57th Tactical Fighter Wing in markings of aggressor aircraft used for dissimilar air combat training. Over 800 F-5E/Fs had been sold to foreign air forces by early 1989, in addition to the 117 originally delivered to the USAF.

loss of two aircraft, they were transferred to the South Vietnamese Air Force. The F-5C and D were proposed USAF versions that were never produced.

In early 1969, in response to a follow-on MAP fighter competition, Northrop commenced testing of an improved F-5 fitted with more powerful -21 engines. In order to enhance air-to-air capability, the new type, later designated F-5E (single-seat) and F-5F (two-seat), came with a fire-control radar augmented by a lead-computing optical sighting system. Northrop was named winner of the MAP competition in November 1970, and deliveries of production aircraft commenced in 1972. When all production ceased in early 1989, a total of 692 F-5Es, 130 F-5Fs, and 12 RF-5Es had been sold to air forces in the nations of Taiwan, Switzerland, Saudi Arabia, Jordan, South Korea, Indonesia, Malaysia, Singapore, Thailand, South Vietnam, Tunisia, Sudan, Morocco, Kenya, Brazil, Chile, Mexico, Bahrain, Iran, and Honduras. In addition to foreign sales 112 F-5Es and Fs were delivered to the USAF starting in March 1973 and were initially used by the 425th Tactical Fighter Training Squadron at Williams AFB, Arizona to train foreign aircrews who would fly the type under MAP. In 1975, 70 F-5Es were turned over to the 57th Tactical Fighter Wing at Nellis AFB in Nevada to be used as aggressor aircraft in dissimilar air combat training (DACT) and later equipped two other aggressor squadrons, one in the United Kingdom and another in the Philippines. The USAF started the process of retiring its F-5E/F fleet during the late 1980s, the final example being withdrawn in 1990. From 1976 to 1996 the Navy operated ten F-5Es and three F-5Fs obtained from USAF stocks as DACT aircraft at its fighter weapons school (i.e., "Top Gun") at NAS Miramar, California. Also derived from ex-USAF stocks, the Marine Corps acquired eleven F-5Es and one F-5F in 1989, which, at the date of this writing, are still serving as DACT aircraft with VMFT-401 based at MCAS Yuma, Arizona.

In early 1980 Northrop initiated yet another development effort, the F-5G, which eventually became known as the F-20A *Tigershark*. With hopes of competing for both international and USAF sales, the significantly altered F-20A appeared in August 1982 with a General Electric F404 turbofan engine that produced 17,000-lbs./s.t. in afterburner and boosted top speed to 1,395-mph (Mach 2.1). Although the USAF gave some consideration to purchasing F-20As as an alternative to the more expensive F-16C, no contact was ultimately forthcoming, and when no foreign orders materialized, Northrop officially abandoned the project in 1986.

General Dynamics F-111 Aardvark 1965–1996

TECHNICAL SPECIFICATIONS (F-111A)
Type: Two-place multipurpose tactical fighter-bomber
Manufacturer: General Dynamics Corp., Ft. Worth, Texas.
Total produced: 563 (all versions)
Power plant: Two Pratt & Whitney TF30-3 turbofan engines, each rated at 12,000-lbs./s.t. dry, 18,500-lbs. with afterburning.
Armament: One 20-millimeter M61A1 rotary cannon and up to 30,000-lbs. of bombs or guided missiles carried in an internal bay and on six underwing pylons, including six AIM-9 *Sidewinders*.
Performance: Max. speed 1,453-mph (Mach 2.2) at 53,450 ft., 914-mph at s.l. (Mach 1.2); ceiling 56,650 ft.; range 2,380 mi. loaded, 3,165 mi. max.
Weights: 46,172-lbs. empty, 98,850-lbs. max. takeoff.
Dimensions: Span 63 ft. (extended), 31 ft. 11 in. (fully swept), length 73 ft. 6 in., wing area 525 sq. ft.

After starting life as the most criticized aircraft project in the history of U.S. military procurement, the F-111 became, once its problems were identified and corrected, the best all-weather strike aircraft of its day. The project originated in mid–1961 when the Secretary of Defense, Robert S. McNamara, ordered the USAF and the Navy to collaborate in the development of a new aircraft to be known as the TFX (tactical fighter experimental). In Novem-

172 I—USAAC, USAAF, and USAF Attack Aircraft

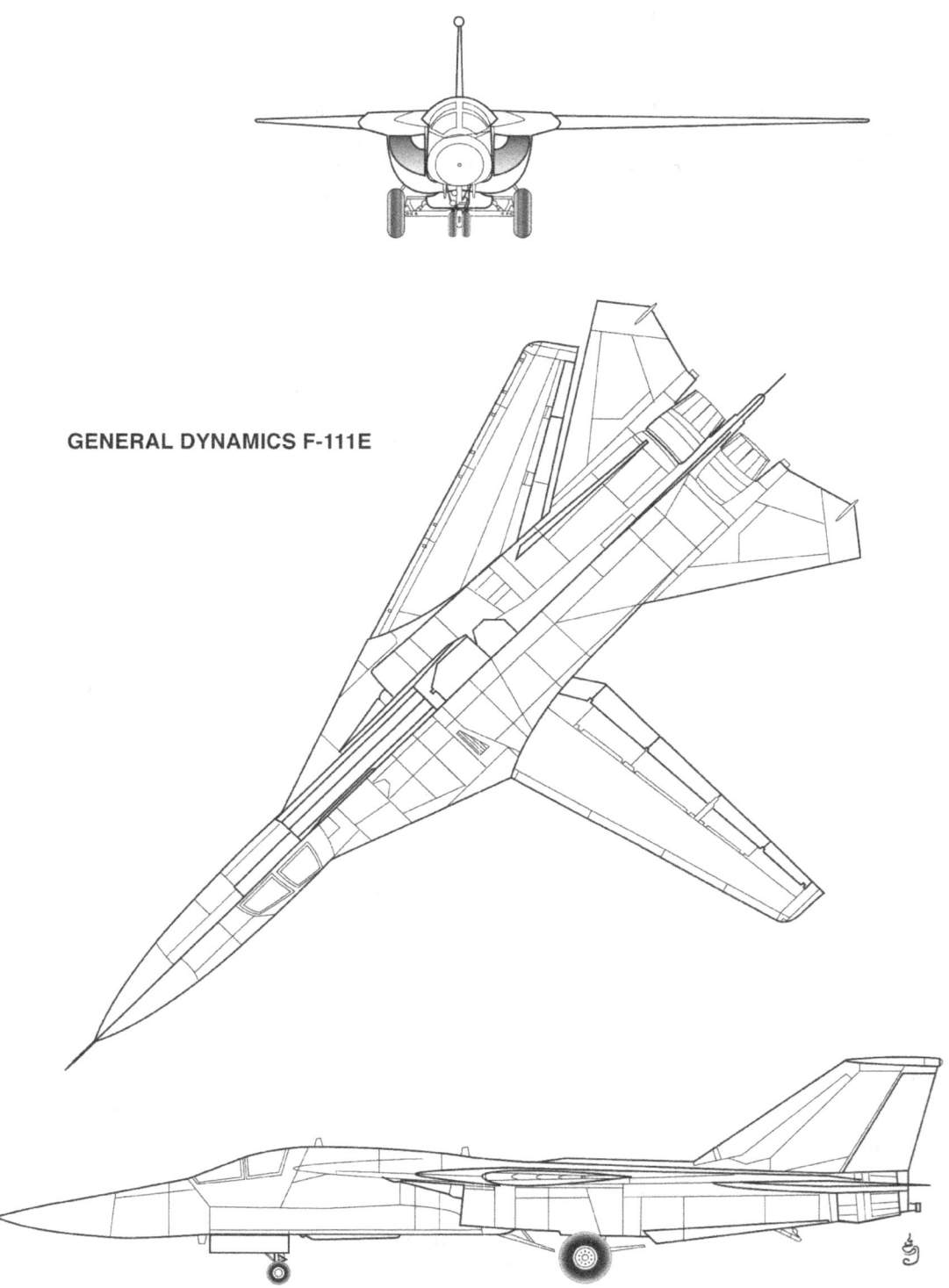

GENERAL DYNAMICS F-111E

Top: One of the 17 pre-production F-111As. Although production models began reaching operational units in mid–1967, it took four more years to solve its problems. F-111As showed their worth as an all-weather bombing platform in the final months of the Vietnam War. *Bottom:* The aircraft shown here, an F-111F of the England-based 48th Tactical Fighter Wing, was destroyed in a midair collision with another F-111 in April 1979. The crews of both aircraft ejected and survived.

ber 1962, after considering nine proposals, the Department of Defense (DOD) announced that General Dynamics had been selected as general contractor under the designations F-111A (USAF) and F-111B (USN). Though sharing the same general fuselage and variable-geometry wing structure, fuel system, engines, and side-by-side cockpit arrangement, the forward fuselage of the F-111A would be eight and half feet longer in order to accommodate its bulkier attack and terrain-following radar system while the F-111B would possess five percent more wing area to reduce landing speeds and improve range. The initial contract covering 23 development aircraft, issued by DOD in December 1962, specified that the 17 USAF versions (F-111As) would be completed and tested by General Dynamics and the seven Navy versions (F-111Bs) by Grumman as co-contractor. Grumman, a long time Navy contractor having wide experience with carrier-based aircraft, also received a sub-contract to manufacture the aft fuselage and landing gear assemblies on all F-111 models.

The maiden flight of the first pre-production F-111A was made on December 21, 1964, followed almost five months later by the first F-111B. DOD had originally contemplated procurement of approximately 1,000 F-111s in all versions; however, by mid–1965, after unit cost had risen from $4.5 to $6 million per airplane, the program was scaled back to 445 aircraft, including 24 F-111Bs for the Navy. In December 1965, despite public controversy over rising costs, DOD expanded the program by directing General Dynamics to develop a long-range bomber version, the FB-111A, as a hedge against prolonged delays in the Advanced Manned Strategic Aircraft program (AMSA, designated B-1A in 1969). Meanwhile, the F-111 test program was being delayed by problems attributable to engine malfunctions, engine compressor stalls, and the general overweight condition of the aircraft. Subsequent efforts to reduce weight were largely offset by installation of the encapsulated escape system, however, a switch to more reliable P-3 engines and a redesign of the variable-inlet intakes greatly improved other problems. But the overweight condition impacted performance of the carrier-based F-111B so severely that the Navy asked to be released from the contract in late 1967. Although F-111B development was officially cancelled in July 1968, the last of seven examples built was accepted in early 1969 and Navy testing continued until 1971.

USAF plans for the F-111A moved ahead and production models began reaching operational units during the fall of 1967 and all 158 (including 17 development aircraft) had been accepted by August 1969. While operational testing generally confirmed the effectiveness of aircraft's tactical systems, a series of crashes traced to control problems and flaws in the wing-pivot forgings caused the entire F-111 fleet to be grounded from December 1969 to July 1970 until structural modifications could be completed. The FB-111A prototype, converted from a service test F-111A, made its first flight in July 1967. FBs differed from Fs in having a fuselage lengthened two feet to increase internal fuel storage, the larger wing of the F-111B, and strengthened landing gear to permit a 21,000-lb. increase in takeoff weight. The FB-111A's primary weapons consisted of six AGM-69 short-range attack missiles (SRAM), each armed with a nuclear warhead yielding an explosive force of 200 kilotons. The last of 76 FB-111As built was delivered to SAC in June 1971. Because of the protracted development of the F-111A, delivery of 24 F-111Cs ordered by Australia in 1963 was not accomplished until December 1973. Though very similar to the F-111A, the F-111C incorporated the larger wing of the B and the strengthened landing gear of the FB. The first of 94 F-111Es, featuring revised intakes and a simplified avionics suite, appeared in August 1969 and the final example was delivered in May 1971. Though ordered before the E, development of the F-111D was seriously hindered by major difficulties with its complex Mark II avionics package, the first to use computer-driven screens rather than conventional instrument displays (i.e., a "glass cockpit"). All of the 96 F-111Ds built were accepted between June 1970 and February 1973, but due to ongoing problems with the avionics, the type did not become fully combat-ready until early 1974. Ordered in July 1970, the F-111F featured more powerful P-9 engines of 25,100-lbs./s.t. in afterburner and an avionics suite adapted from the Mark II system of the F-111D together with digital navigational and attack components from the FB-111A. Top speed was boosted to 1,653-mph (Mach 2.5) at 43,000 feet. One hundred and six Fs were delivered to the USAF between January 1972 and September 1976, after which all F-111 production ended. With the aim of finding a low-cost replacement for the EB-66B/E (see B-66, above), the USAF entered into a contractual arrangement with Grumman in 1975 whereby some F-111As would be converted to electronic warfare platforms and returned to service as the EF-111A *Raven,* and 42 conversions were ultimately completed by the end of 1985. Carrying electronics in place of weapons, *Ravens* were easily identified by their 16-foot long ventral 'canoe' radomes and fin-tip pods.

Production F-111As began equipping the 474th Tactical Fighter Wing at Cannon AFB, New Mexico in July 1967. Under a program known as "Combat Lancer," a small detachment of F-111As from the 474th deployed to Takhli RTAFB in Thailand in March 1968 for combat operations in Vietnam; however, they were withdrawn after the loss of three aircraft over a five-week period. An investigation later revealed that the crashes were not due to enemy action, but to malfunctions in the aircraft, and in one case, pilot error. In September 1972, after four years of extensive testing and modifications, two squadrons of F-111As returned to Thailand where they participated in the bombing offensive against North Vietnam known as "Linebacker II." A single F-111A carried a bomb load equivalent to that of five F-4s and could still attack targets when all other aircraft were grounded due to adverse weather conditions. At the time they were withdrawn from combat in early 1973, F-111As had completed 4,000 sorties for a loss of only five aircraft (by comparison, 17 B-52s were lost in the same operation). Four F-111As were modified to F-111C standards before being transferred to Australia in 1982 and the remainder (those not converted to EF-111As) were retired from active USAF service during the early 1990s and placed in storage.

The first FB-111As entered service with SAC's 340th Bomb Group at Carswell AFB, Texas in October 1969 but were transferred in 1971 to the 380th Strategic Aerospace Wing at Plattsburg AFB in New York. The last SAC FB-111A was retired from alert status in 1990. As they were replaced by B-1Bs during the mid–1980s, a number of FB-111As were re-designated F-111G when they were converted to a tactical configuration and used as trainers. The last G was withdrawn from service in 1993 and 15 were subsequently sold to Australia to augment its F-111Cs. After achieving operational status with the 27th TFW in the U.S. during 1969, all F-111Es were transferred to the 20th TFW based in the England in late 1970. During Operation Desert Storm in early 1991, the 20th's F-111Es moved to Incirlik, Turkey, where they completed numerous bombing strikes against targets in northern Iraq without losing a single aircraft. All F-111Es were retired from active service during 1993. Though getting a late start because of their troublesome avionics package, F-111Ds eventually equipped three squadrons of the U.S.-based 27th TFW from 1971 until the last example was retired in late 1992. F-111Fs began entering service with the 374th TFW at Mountain Home AFB, Idaho during early 1972 but were later assigned to the both the 48th TFW in England and the 57th Fighter Weapons Wing at McClellan AFB in California. Twenty-four F-111Fs of the 48th carried out retaliatory strikes against targets in Libya in April 1986, during which one was lost to ground fire. In 1991 the 48th deployed 67 F-111Fs to air bases in Saudi Arabia to participate in Operation Desert Storm, where they completed 2,500 combat sorties in which 2,203 targets were destroyed, including 920 tanks, 252 artillery pieces, 245 aircraft revetments, 13 runways, 113 bunkers, and 12 bridges, for a loss of no aircraft. Nearly 85 percent of 5,500 bombs dropped consisted of precision-guided munitions. USAF service of the F-111 fighter-bomber series finally ended in October 1996 when the last F-111F was placed in storage. As conversions were completed from 1981 onwards, EF-111As ultimately equipped two electronic combat squadrons. They saw their first combat action in 1986 while providing EW support to USAF aircraft involved in attacks on Libya, then in 1991, flew 900 EW sorties during the Gulf War. The last EF-111A was withdrawn from active USAF service in May 1998. At the date of this writing, Australia is still operating its F-111C/Gs, although reports differ on how long they may remain in service.

McDonnell-Douglas F-15 Strike Eagle 1986–Present

TECHNICAL SPECIFICATIONS (F-15E)
Type: Two-place multipurpose tactical fighter-bomber
Manufacturer: McDonnell-Douglas Corp. (later Boeing Aerospace Corp.), St. Louis, Missouri.
Total produced: 353 (including export variants)
Power plant: Two Pratt & Whitney F-100-229 turbofan engines, each rated at 17,800-lbs./s.t. dry, 29,100-lbs. with afterburning.
Armament: One 20-millimeter M61A1 rotary cannon, up to 24,500-lbs. of external ordnance carried on the centerline, two underwing stations, and racks on conformal tanks, and four AIM-7 *Sparrow* and four AIM-9 *Sidewinder* or eight AIM-120 AMRAAM air-to-air missiles.
Performance: Max. speed 1,676-mph (Mach 2.54) at 40,000 ft., ceiling 50,000 ft.; range 1,580 mi. loaded, 2,765 mi. max.
Weights: 31,700-lbs. empty, 81,000-lbs. max. takeoff.
Dimensions: Span 42 ft. 10 in., length 63 ft. 9 in., wing area 608 sq. ft.

Although originally conceived in the late 1960s as a multi-role aircraft, all of the 832 F-15A/D *Eagles* manufactured for the USAF from 1972 to 1986 were dedicated air superiority fighters. During the late 1970s, USAF officials began investigating a concept for an enhanced tactical fighter (ETF) that could not only duplicate the mission of the F-111, but also be capable of operating without need of fighter escort or support from other EW and AWACs aircraft. With the ETF concept in mind, McDonnell-Douglas and Hughes Aircraft joined forces to study the feasibility of adapting the proven F-15 airframe and engine combination to the air-to-ground role. In July 1980, McDonnell-Douglas unveiled its "Strike Eagle" demonstrator, a two-seat F-15B fitted with a state-of-the-art synthetic aperture radar (i.e., a high resolution ground mapping technique which uses of the forward motion of the aircraft together with pulsed radar signals to synthesize the effect of a much larger antenna aperture) plus a rear cockpit that had been reconfigured for a weapons system officer (WSO). At the time the USAF formally announced the ETF requirement in 1981, General Dynamics was at an advanced stage of development with its own strike fighter candidate, a highly modified F-16 billed as the F-16XL. Featuring a strengthened airframe and a cranked delta wing, the F-16XL flew in mid–1982 and was subsequently delivered to Edwards AFB for competitive trials against the *Strike Eagle* and several other specially configured F-15s. In February 1984, after trials had been completed, the USAF declared McDonnell-Douglas winner of the competition and placed the *Strike Eagle* into production as the F-15E. The maiden flight of the first F-15E took place on December 11, 1986 and deliveries of production models began in the spring of 1988.

Though externally similar to the D, the F-15E has been strengthened to permit a 15,000-lb. increase in takeoff weight and given other structural improvements that will extend airframe life to 16,000 hours, twice that of earlier F-15s. Its APG-70 radar system, which can identify large targets at a distance of 100 miles, is much harder to detect because it can be switched on and off while tracking a target. Tied to the radar is a low-altitude navigation and targeting infra-red for night (LANTIRN) system carried in two separate pods. The navigation pod under the starboard intake contains a forward-looking infra-red (FLIR) system and a terrain-following radar which may also be used to depict video images of oncoming terrain on the pilot's heads up display (HUD). The targeting pod under the port intake contains a high-resolution tracking FLIR, a missile bore sight correlator, and a laser designator. The front cockpit has three multifunction screens plus an eye-level HUD that displays vital flight and tactical information to the pilot, while the rear cockpit has four screens that enable the WSO to simultaneously use data from radar, infra-red, navigation, ECM, weapons, and targeting systems. F-15Es can carry most of the air-to-ground weapons in the current USAF inventory, including AGM-65 *Maverick* missiles and precision munitions like the GBU-10/-15, JDAM (GBU-29/32), and

Third Series • 1962–Present

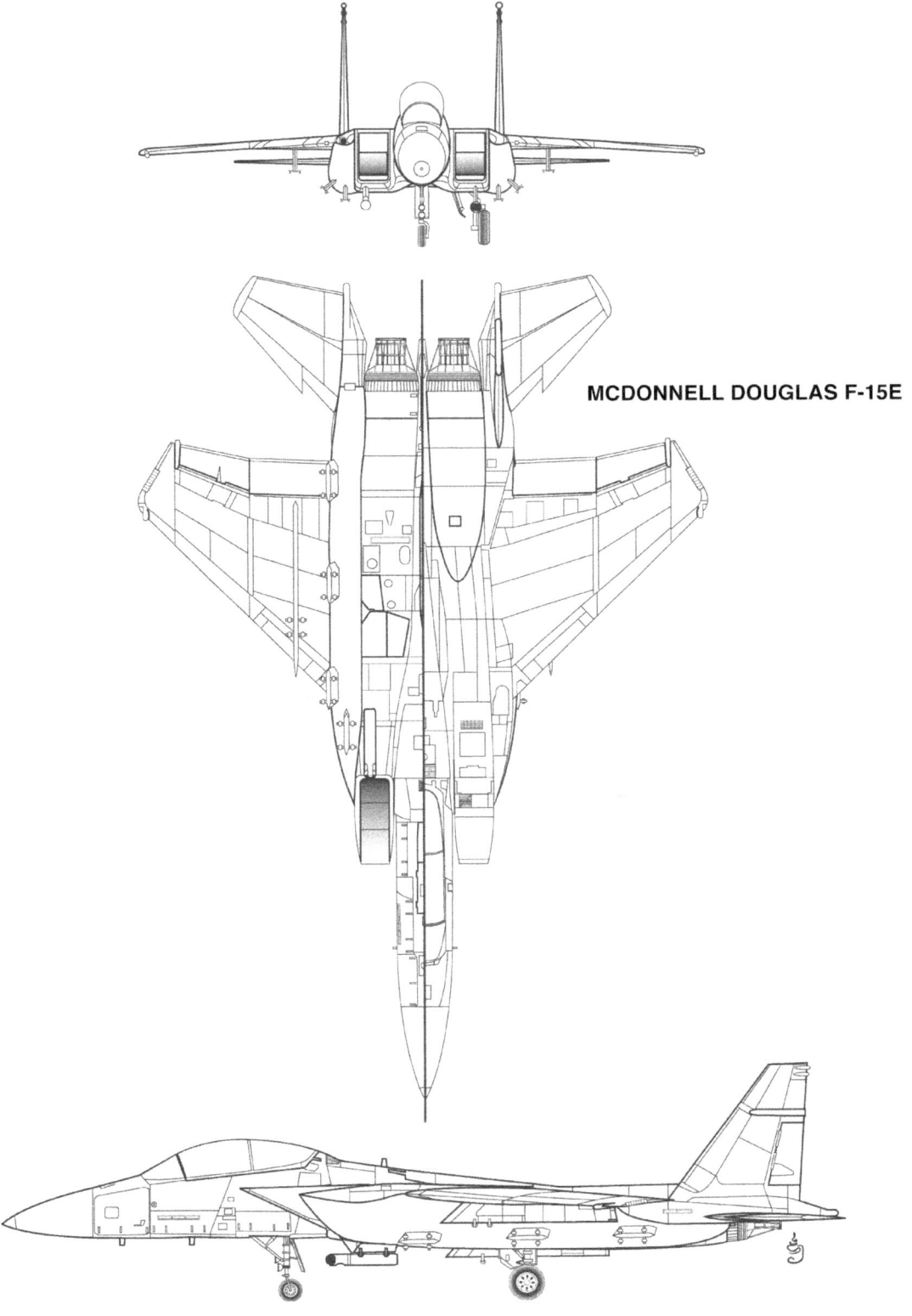

MCDONNELL DOUGLAS F-15E

Two F-15Es of the 4th Fighter Wing based at Seymour Johnson AFB in North Carolina. Called the "cosmic jet" by aircrews, the F-15E can perform on both the low-altitude strike mission of the F-111 and the air-to-air mission of the F-15D.

WCMD, but when loaded with AIM-7, -9, or -120 missiles, can duplicate the air-to-air capabilities of the F-15D. Since the 135th production model, F-15Es have been powered by P-229 engines, which raise afterburning thrust by 5,670-lbs. per engine. The 200th and what was originally to have been the last F-15E was delivered to the USAF in June 1994, however, 17 more examples have since been completed and delivered to replace losses. Boeing Aerospace, after acquiring McDonnell-Douglas in 1996, has taken over all F-15 production and support.

Between 1995 and 1999, 72 F-15E export derivatives, designated the F-15S, were manufactured and delivered to Saudi Arabia. While having the same airframe and engine as the F-15E, its radar, electronics and weapons systems are much less sophisticated. Similarly, 24 F-15Is with limited avionics were delivered to Israel in 1998 and 1999, with the understanding that they would be supplemented with other electronic and weapons systems supplied by Israel. In April 2002, the government of South Korea announced plans to purchase the F-15K, and the first of 40 aircraft on order was delivered in 2005. Unlike preceding *Strike Eagle* exports, the F-15K features systems as advanced as those of the USAF's F-15E and has been given expanded capabilities with AGM-84D *Harpoon* and AGM-84E SLAM missiles. In their complementary air-to-air role, Ks will be equipped to handle two of the world's most advanced missiles, the AIM-9X and AIM-120C. Deliveries of F-15Ks are scheduled to continue until 2008.

The first F-15E production models entered service with the 405th Tactical Training Wing at Luke AFB, Arizona in April 1988 and the type achieved operational status in mid–1990 with the 4th Tactical Fighter Wing at Seymour Johnson AFB in North Carolina. When the Gulf War commenced in early 1991, 48 F-15Es of the 4th TFW were rushed overseas for combat duty in Operation Desert Storm despite the fact that they lacked the targeting pods needed for smart bombs. As a consequence, they were tasked to attack targets from medium altitudes with "dumb" bombs, and two were subsequently lost to Iraqi SAMs. Later, when fitted with LANTIRN targeting pods and armed with GBUs, F-15Es destroyed 80 percent of the targets assigned to them with no loss of aircraft. After the war, F-15Es were used on numerous occasions to deliver precision-guided weapons in retaliatory strikes related to violations of the "no-fly" zone. In late 1993, F-15Es deployed to Aviano AFB in Italy where they flew over 2,500 non-combat sorties in support of NATO operations in Boznia-Herzegovina, and in August 1995, were used to carry out bombing strikes against Serbian ground targets. One month after September 11, 2001, F-15Es operating out of Kuwait began attacking Taliban targets in Afghanistan. During their three-month tour, *Strike Eagles* performed a variety of both close air support and interdiction missions, becoming the first type of aircraft to launch a BLU-118/B in combat, a thermobaric (fuel-air) bomb designed to create tremendous overpressure in confined areas like tunnels and caves. F-15Es deployed again to the Persian Gulf in early 2003 in support of Operation Iraqi Freedom where they commenced bombing sorties to take out key Iraqi targets such as air defenses, radar sites, communication facilities, as well as centers of command, control, and government. Before returning home, F-15Es were credited with having destroyed 60 percent of the Republican Guard as well as 65 MiG aircraft on the ground. According to current USAF estimates, its F-15Es will remain in service through 2030.

General Dynamics F-16 Fighting Falcon 1974–Present

TECHNICAL SPECIFICATIONS (F-16C [BLOCKS 40/42])
Type: One or two-place tactical fighter
Manufacturer: General Dynamics Corp. (Lockheed-Martin after 1993), Ft. Worth, Texas.
Total produced: 4,000 (estimated, including export variants)
Power plant: One Pratt & Whitney F-100-220 turbofan engine, rated at 23,770-lbs. with afterburning or one General Electric F-110-100 turbofan engine, rated at 28,984-lbs./s.t. with afterburning.
Armament: One 20-millimeter M61A1 rotary cannon, up to 12,430-lbs. of external ordnance carried on one centerline and six wing pylons, plus two AIM-9 *Sidewinder* air-to-air missiles on wingtips.
Performance: Max. speed 1,333-mph (Mach 2.02) at 40,000 ft., ceiling 50,000 ft.; range 680 mi. loaded, 2,100 mi. max.
Weights: 18, 238-lbs. empty, 37,500-lbs. max. takeoff.
Dimensions: Span 32 ft. 8 in., length 49 ft. 5 in., wing area 300 sq. ft.

After a humble beginning as a technology demonstrator, the F-16 has become the most-produced USAF fighter design since the F-86 and presently serves with 22 nations all over the world. Like all post–1970 American fighters, the F-16 is a byproduct of the lessons learned from the Vietnam War. The light weight fighter (LWF) requirement issued by the Department of Defense (DOD) in January 1971 placed emphasis on an aircraft having a high thrust-to-weight ratio, a gross weight not exceeding 20,000-lbs., superior maneuverability, and low unit cost. And though not specifically intended by DOD, contractors could not fail to recognize that the LWF contract was likely to generate additional sales to NATO, MAP, and other foreign users. Competing proposals were afterward received from Boeing, General Dynamics, Ling-Temco–Vought, Lockheed, and Northrop, and by April of 1972, DOD had narrowed the competition to General Dynamics and Northrop under the respective designations YF-16 and YF-17. For the sake of simplicity and weight savings, the General Dynamics engineering team led by Harry Hillaker evolved the YF-16 around a single Pratt & Whitney F-100 turbofan engine. A variety of wing planforms were considered, but the team settled on a low-sweep, straight wing that seemed to offer the best combination of maneuverability, acceleration, and lift. The ventral and noticeably aft location of the intake was selected over more conventional side intakes because it offered better airflow at higher angles-of-attack. The aerodynamic blending of the wing and fuselage junction produced a lifting body effect that enhanced lift and maneuverabil-

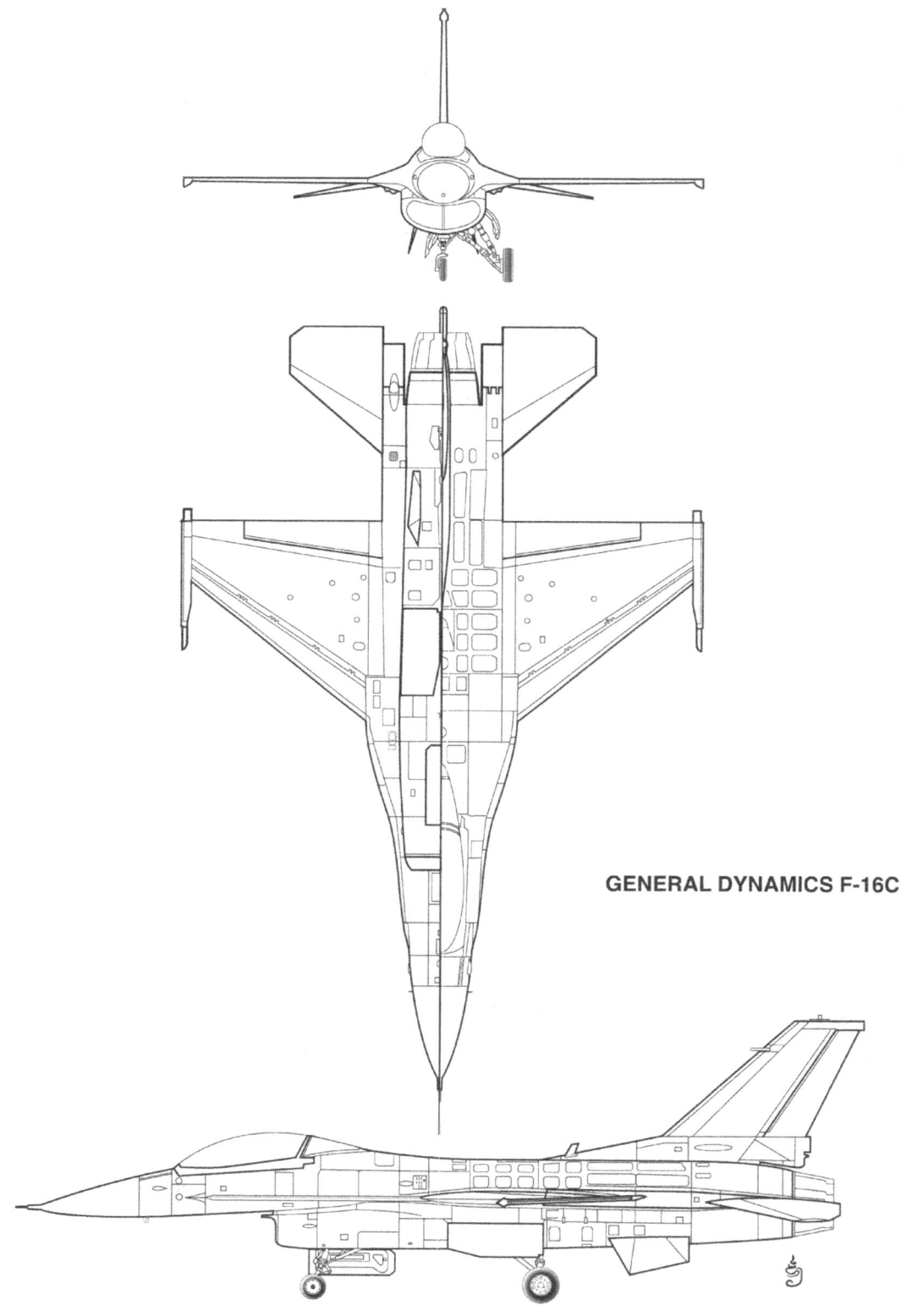

GENERAL DYNAMICS F-16C

Third Series • 1962–Present

Top: F-16A shown in the marking of the 388th Tactical Fighter Wing based at Hill AFB in Utah, the first USAF unit to become operational with the type. F-16A/Bs went on to equip twelve more TAC wings by 1985. *Bottom:* F-16C serving with the 20th Fighter Wing based out of Shaw AFB in South Carolina. The F-16, in all variants, has become the most widely produced USAF fighter design since the F-86. Derivatives are expected to remain in production until 2010.

Second F-16XL shown in its demonstrator paint scheme. After the F-15E won the ETF competition, both F-16XLs were turned over to NASA, where they are still listed on flying status.

ity. One of the YF-16's most technologically advanced features was a fly-by-wire (FBW) control system in which there was no direct connection between the pilot and the aircraft's control surfaces; instead, cockpit control inputs sent signals to quadruple-redundant computers that actually moved the ailerons, elevators, and rudder. A novel cockpit arrangement featuring a side-stick control (originally unmovable) and a seat tilted to a 30-degree angle enabled the pilot to function up to the airframe's 9-G maneuvering limit.

The first flight of the prototype YF-16 was made from Edwards AFB on January 21, 1974, and the fly-off between it and the YF-17 commenced several months later. While trials were underway, the project was renamed ACF (air combat fighter) in order to distinguish it from the USAF's ADF (air defense fighter) program which involved production plans for the F-15. In January 1975, DOD announced that the YF-16 had been selected as the winner of the ACF contest and General Dynamics received a contract to produce fifteen development aircraft as the single-seat F-16A and two-seat F-16B. Although both ACF entries had excelled in trials, the F-16 had shown itself to be superior in terms of overall performance, range, maneuverability, and operating costs. The USAF announced plans to procure 650 F-16s with the possibility of increasing the order to 1,400 or more. In early 1975, to bolster overseas sales, the U.S. government allowed General Dynamics to sub-contract major F-16 sub-assemblies and engines to foreign manufacturers; a few months later the YF-16 was flown to Europe for a NATO sales tour.

The first production F-16A, flown in December 1976, differed from the prototype in having a 13-inch fuselage extension to accommodate more fuel and the APG-66 radar system, slightly enlarged vertical and horizontal tail surfaces, larger ventral fins, and a 20-square-foot increase in wing area. The production F-16B, identical to the A except for a second cockpit and less internal fuel capacity, flew in August 1977. F-16s started entering operational service during early 1979, and by March 1985, the USAF had accepted a total of 674 F-16As and 121 F-16Bs. From 1979 to 1991, 519 F-16As and Bs completed under European sub-contracts were delivered to Belgium, Denmark, Netherlands, and Norway, and further 75 U.S.-built F-16As and Bs were sold to Israel. A J-79-powered F-16A (i.e., F-16/79), intended as a low-cost export derivative, was flown in October 1980, but the project was cancelled after no sales materialized. In response to the USAF's ETF (enhanced tactical fighter) requirement for an all-weather strike fighter, one F-16A and one F-16B became F-16XLs when they were lengthened five feet, fitted with cranked delta wings, and received additional tactical equipment. The first F-16XL flew in July 1982 and the second in October, and both subsequently participated in the ETF trials conducted at Edwards AFB during 1983. After the F-15E won the competition, both F-16XL prototypes were turned over to NASA where, according to recent reports, they are still being operated for various test purposes. In 1982 one F-16A fitted with twin canards and a digital flight control system was tested as the F-16AFTI (advanced fighter technology integration) and has since been assigned to NASA.

The F-16C and D (two-seat), which superceded the F-16A/B on the production line in late 1984, represented a major expansion of the F-16's tactical role. Cs and Ds have since been manufactured for the USAF in five major production block variants: Block 25 introduced an APG-68 multi-mode radar system with new cockpit displays that added night/all-weather attack capability and systems to carry AGM-65 *Maverick* missiles, and, in air-to-air mode, beyond-visual-range (BVR) interception capability with AIM-7 *Sparrow* or AIM-120 AMRAAM missiles; Block 30/32 added two different engine upgrades, the General Electric F-110-100 on Block 30 and the Pratt & Whitney F-100-220 on block 32, and on both, provision to carry AGM-45 *Shrike* and AGM-88 HARM anti-radiation missiles; Block 40/42 acquired broader precision attack capabilities with low-altitude navigation and targeting for night (LANTIRN) pods and the ability to handle smart weapons such as the GBU-10, -12, -15, and -24; Block 50/52 featured two more engine upgrades, the F-100-239 on Block 50 and the F-110-129 on 52, and also included systems enabling it to handle newer smart weapons like the wind-corrected munitions dispenser (WCMD), AGM-154 JSOW and GBU-31/32 JDAM; and Block 50D/52D (known as the F-16CJ/F-16DJ *Wild Weasel*), specialized for the suppression of enemy air defense (SEAD) mission, came with an ASQ-213 HARM targeting system (HTS) and ALQ-119 electronic jamming pod for self-protection. Deliveries of F-16Cs and Ds to USAF operational units commenced in late 1985 and did not end until March 2005, at which point a total of 1,216 F-16Cs and 205 F-16Ds had been accepted. Between 1987 and 1988, the Navy took delivery of 22 F-16Cs and four F-16Ds, re-designated F-16N, to be used as adversary aircraft in dissimilar air combat training (DACT). Starting in the mid–1980s the USAF lobbied for a dedicated close air support (CAS) version of the F-16 (i.e., the A-16) as a replacement for the A-10, however, DOD effectively vetoed the idea in 1990. Since 1989 F-16Cs and Ds have been one of America's most successful military exports, approximately 1,000 having been delivered to foreign users by the end of 2006 with orders for about 250 more still outstanding. In the late 1980s the Japanese government initiated development of the Mitsubishi F-2, a license-built F-16, and flight-tested the first prototype in early 1995. While similar to the F-16C/D, the F-2 incorporates a larger wing of 25-percent greater area and is equipped with avionics systems developed in Japan. Original plans suggested production of up to 140 aircraft by 2010, however, unanticipated development problems and cost overruns have reduced current projections to 81.

Production F-16As and Bs entered initial operational service with the 388th Tactical fighter Wing at Hill AFB in Utah in January 1979, and as deliveries multiplied, the type went on to equip 12 more wings within TAC by 1985. The Thunderbirds flight demonstration team transitioned to F-16s in November 1982. As production F-16Cs and Ds became available in late 1985, they initially replaced F-4s in overseas units but from mid–1986 onwards, started replacing F-16A/Bs in TAC wings based in U.S. When Operation Desert Storm began in January 1991, F-16s were the most numerous type of USAF fighter in the combat theater. As the Iraqi air threat diminished, F-16s were primarily devoted to air-to-ground operations, typically being armed with a mix of Mk. 84 (2,000-lb.) and Mark 82 (500-lb.) dumb bombs, CBU cluster munitions, plus AGM-65 *Maverick* missiles, while still retaining two AIM-9 *Sidewinders* on the wingtips for self-protection. When the conflict ended, F-16s had flown over 13,000 combat sorties, the most completed by any type of aircraft in the war, for a loss of only three aircraft to enemy action. The first aerial victory scored by an F-16 came after the Gulf War, in December 1992, when an F-16D of the 363rd TFW shot down an Iraqi MiG-25 that had illegally entered the no-fly zone. In a similar incident a year later, an F-16 shot down an Iraqi MiG-23 with the first AIM-120 AMRAAM missile to be used in combat. During Bosnian peacekeeping operations from mid-1993 to late 1995, F-16s of the 86th TFW operating from Aviano AFB, Italy completed over 400 missions and were credited with shooting down three Serbian attack aircraft. One F-16 lost to a Serbian SAM during the campaign led to the much-publicized escape and ultimate recovery of USAF Capt. Scott O'Grady. F-16CJs of the 52nd TFW commenced SEAD missions in the Iraqi no-fly zone during early 1995 and were subsequently used to launch HARM missiles against several Iraqi SAM sites that were illegally tracking friendly aircraft on their missile radars. In 1999, USAF F-16s conducted operations over Yugoslavia in support of the UN Kosovo campaign, during which time one F-16 was lost to ground fire. In October 2001 three USAF Reserve F-16 units initiated precision air strikes against Taliban and Al Qaeda forces in Afghanistan and were later augmented by a tri-national detachment of 18 F-16A/Bs from Denmark, Netherlands, and Norway. When Operation Iraqi Freedom began in March 2003, F-16C/Ds derived from active USAF, USAFR, and ANG units completed approximately 4,000 combat sorties during the initial phase of the air campaign, providing forward air control, close air support, precision attack with smart munitions, and SEAD.

According to recent figures (end of 2006), there are presently 1,273 F-16s carried on the USAF inventory, of which 738 are in the active force, 69 in USAFR, and 473 in ANG. While F-16s are likely to remain in frontline service for the foreseeable future, recent reports suggest that active USAF units will soon be flying only Block 40/42 and Block 50/52 F-16C/Ds while the older C/D variants will be transferred to USAFR and ANG units or placed in storage. Over the long-term, the USAF has announced plans to start replacing both its F-16 and A-10 fleets with the F-35A *Lightning II* Joint Strike Fighter. Due to defense cuts after the Gulf War, the Navy retired its 26 F-16Ns in early 1995 and placed them in storage. Air forces of the following nations currently are or will be operators of the F-16: Belgium, 72 upgraded F-16A/Bs; Denmark, 61 upgraded, F-16A/Bs; Netherlands, 136 upgraded F-16A/Bs; Norway, 56 upgraded F-16A/Bs; Greece, 140 F-16C/Ds, plus 30 more on order; Poland, purchased 48 F-16C/Ds with deliveries scheduled from 2006 to 2009; Italy, 30 ex-USAF F-16A/Bs on lease; Portugal, 39 F-16A/Bs; Turkey, 156 F-15C/Ds, plus 80 more on order; Bahrain, 12 F-16C/Ds; Egypt, 42 F-16A/Bs and 178 F-16C/Ds; Israel (second largest F-16 user after USAF), 125 F-16A/Bs, 135 F-16C/Ds, plus orders for 102 F-16Is (F-16D, Block 52) with deliveries scheduled from 2004 to 2009; Jordan, 33 F-16A/Bs; United Arab Emirates, 80 F-16C/Ds (Block 60); Indonesia, 12 F-16A/Bs; Pakistan, 40 F-16A/Bs (follow-up order for 71 more was embargoed in 1990); Singapore, 28 F-16C/Ds, plus 20 more on order; South Korea, 156 F-16C/Ds (72 assembled in Korea), plus 20 more on order; Thailand, 43 F-15A/Bs (7 ex-Singapore); Taiwan, 150 F-16A/Bs; Chile, 10 F-16C/Ds, plus plans to buy 20 ex-USAF; and Venezuela, 22 F-16A/Bs.

Northrop F-17 Cobra 1974–1977

TECHNICAL SPECIFICATIONS (YF-17A)

Type: One-place tactical fighter
Manufacturer: Northrop Corp., Hawthorne, California.

Third Series • 1962–Present

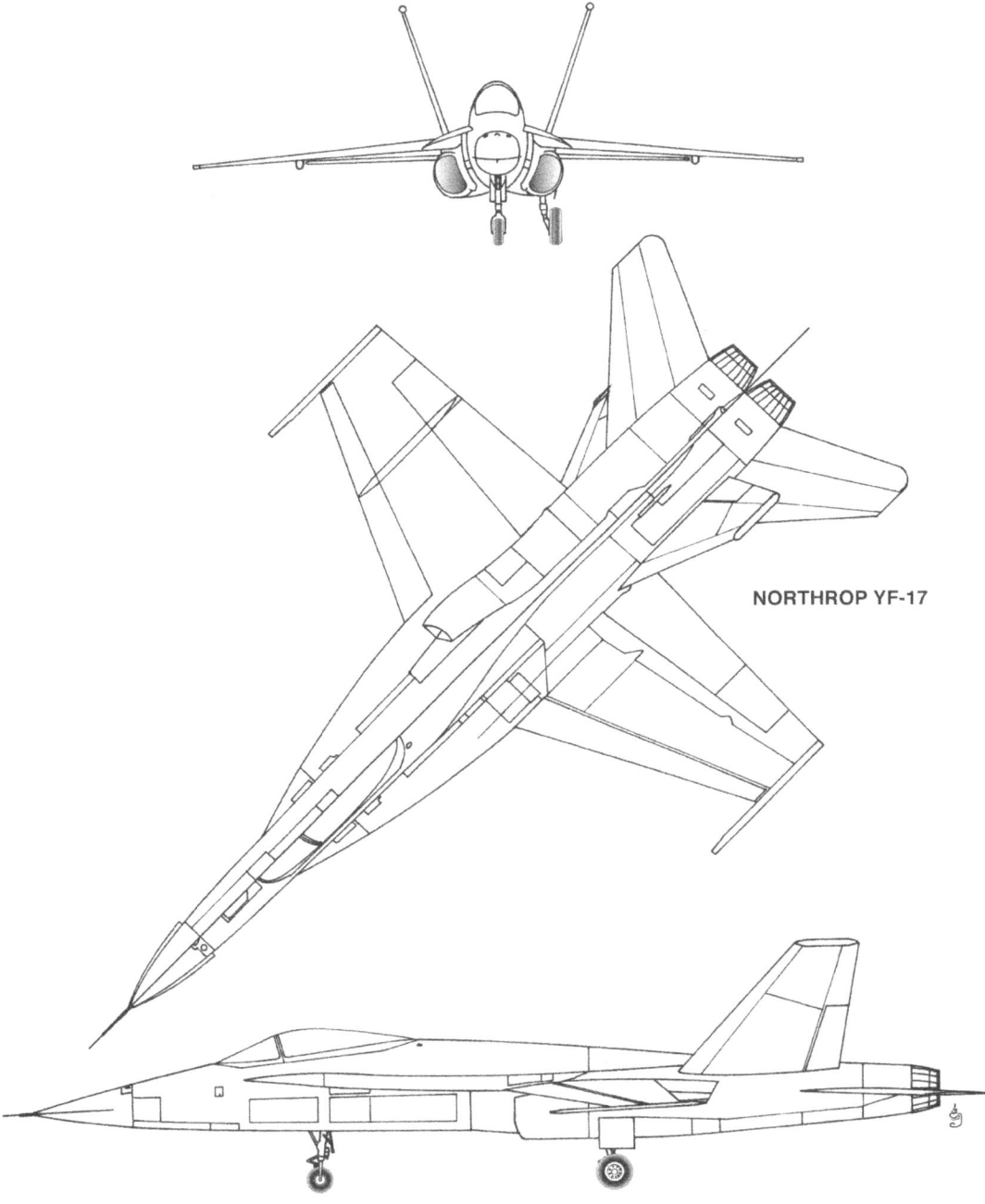

NORTHROP YF-17

Total produced: 2
Power plant: Two General Electric J101-100 turbojet engines, each rated at 15,000-lbs./s.t. with afterburning.
Armament: One 20-millimeter M61A1 rotary cannon, up to 20,450-lbs. of external ordnance carried on one centerline and four wing pylons, plus two AIM-9 *Sidewinder* air-to-air missiles on wingtips.
Performance: Max. speed 1,390-mph (Mach 2.13) at 44,000 ft., ceiling 55,000 ft.; range (not listed).
Weights: 15, 000-lbs. (approx.) empty, 30,630-lbs. max. takeoff.
Dimensions: Span 35 ft., length 55 ft. 6 in., wing area 350 sq. ft.

One of two YF-17A demonstrators evaluated for the ACF competition during 1974 and 1975. Even though it lost the USAF competition to the YF-16, the design was selected by the Navy and the Marines and re-emerged as the McDonnell-Douglas F-18.

The highly innovative design concept behind the YF-17 was originally conceived by Northrop in the late 1960s as the likely successor to its series of F-5 export fighters. The twin-engine Model P-530 emerged with a trapezoidal wing planform featuring distinctive leading-edge root extensions (LREX) that tapered into the fuselage from the intakes up to the front of the cockpit. The LREX, according to wind tunnel studies, would significantly enhance maneuvering at high angles-of-attack while adding to overall lift. Early concerns over adequate yaw control at extreme angles-of-attack were resolved by utilizing twin fins and rudders canted at an 18-degree angle. Much to Northrop's disappointment, no foreign orders materialized after the P-530 was unveiled in early 1971; however, at virtually the same time, the Department of Defense (DOD) circulated the lightweight fighter (LWF) fighter requirement to five aircraft manufacturers, including Northrop. Using the same aerodynamic layout and J-101 powerplants of the P-530, Northrop revised the design and submitted it for consideration in the LWF competition as the Model P-600. Unlike the P-530, the P-600 incorporated new technologies like a fly-by-wire (FBW) control system and a high proportion of lightweight composite materials in its airframe components. In April 1972, DOD limited the LWF (later renamed ACF) entries to the proposals received from General Dynamics and Northrop and subsequently awarded each company a contract to build two "technology demonstrators" under the respective designations YF-16 and YF-17.

The first YF-17A was trucked to Edwards AFB where it completed its first flight on June 9, 1974. Two days later it achieved the distinction of becoming the first American fighter to exceed the speed of sound in level flight without use of an afterburner. During the ACF flight trials which followed, the YF-16 and YF-17 were never pitted against each other but were flown against contemporary USAF fighters as well as MiG-17s and MiG-21s that had been 'acquired' by the USAF. In January 1975, after both aircraft had logged over 300 hours of trials, USAF officials announced that General Dynamics had been selected as winner of the ACF competition. Although the YF-17A had demonstrated superb handling qualities and acceptable performance, the less expensive YF-16 was seen as more practical choice for mass-production. But this was not the end of Northrop's airplane: In late 1974, while the ACF trials were still underway, the U.S. Congress directed the Navy to consider either the YF-16 or YF-17 as a potential candidate to replace it aging fleet of A-4s and F-4s. After considering both ACF contestants, Navy officials concluded that the airframe design and twin-engine layout of the YF-17 came closer to meeting naval requirements. Because Northrop had no recent experience with carrier-based aircraft, McDonnell-Douglas was brought in to collaborate on a navalised development of the YF-17. The reworked design emerged in mid–1975 as the McDonnell-Douglas F-18A (see, F/A-18 in Part II).

Lockheed F-117 Nighthawk 1981–Present

TECHNICAL SPECIFICATIONS (F-117A)

Type: One-place tactical fighter
Manufacturer: Lockheed Aircraft Corp., Burbank, California.
Total produced: 89
Power plant: Two General Electric F404-F1D2 turbofan engines, each rated at 10,800-lbs./s.t.
Armament: Up to 5,000-lbs. of bombs, missiles, or air-to-ground munitions carried in two internal bays.
Performance: Max. speed 700-mph (Mach 0.92) at s.l., 648-mph (mach 0.87) at 5,000 ft., ceiling (not listed); range 1,800 mi. loaded (est.).
Weights: 30,000-lbs. (approx.) empty, 52,500-lbs. max. takeoff.
Dimensions: Span 43 ft. 4 in., length 65 ft. 11 in., wing area 1,140 sq. ft.

Certainly one of the best-kept military secrets of recent times, the existence of the F-117 was not made public until November 1988—over seven years after the first example flew. Its origins can be traced to a computer program developed by the famous Lockheed "Skunk Works" in 1975 which indicated that very low radar observability or "stealth" could be achieved by building an aircraft from radar absorbing materials and arranging its external configuration into facets that scattered the radar returns away at odd angles; the resulting radar cross-section (RCS) would be reduced to that of a tiny object. The chief disadvantage of the concept was that an aircraft optimized for stealth characteristics would be inherently instable about all three axes (pitch, roll, and yaw) of flight. In early 1977, under a highly classified project known as *Have Blue*, the Defense Advanced Research Projects Agency (DARPA) awarded Lockheed a contract to construct two 60-percent scale flying testbeds for the purpose of evaluating both RCS and flying characteristics. To compensate for the predicted instability, both were to be equipped with fly-by-wire (FBW) control systems adapted from the F-16. The first *Have Blue* prototype was taken in secrecy to Groom Lake near Nellis AFB in Nevada and flown for the first time in February 1978. Testing proceeded routinely until May, when the aircraft was destroyed after Lockheed's test pilot was forced to eject due to a landing gear malfunction; then only two months later, because of an in-flight engine fire, the second prototype was lost after its pilot safely ejected. But despite the abbreviated test program, the stealth concept had been decisively verified: while not totally invisible, the *Have Blue* aircraft nonetheless produced radar returns that were virtually indistinguishable from background clutter until they were at extremely close range, i.e., inside minimum launch parameters of missile tracking radars.

The first full-scale F-117A was flown in June of 1981. The "117" was not derived from the pre–1962 numbering system that ended with the F-111 but apparently came from a project number randomly assigned to technical manuals pertaining to the aircraft before any official designation had been applied. In the logical sequence, it should have been the F-19, and this designation did in fact appear in some unclassified publications before the official designation had been announced. According to some, USAF officials eventually determined that it would be cheaper and easier to simply designate the airplane F-117 rather than reprint all the manu-

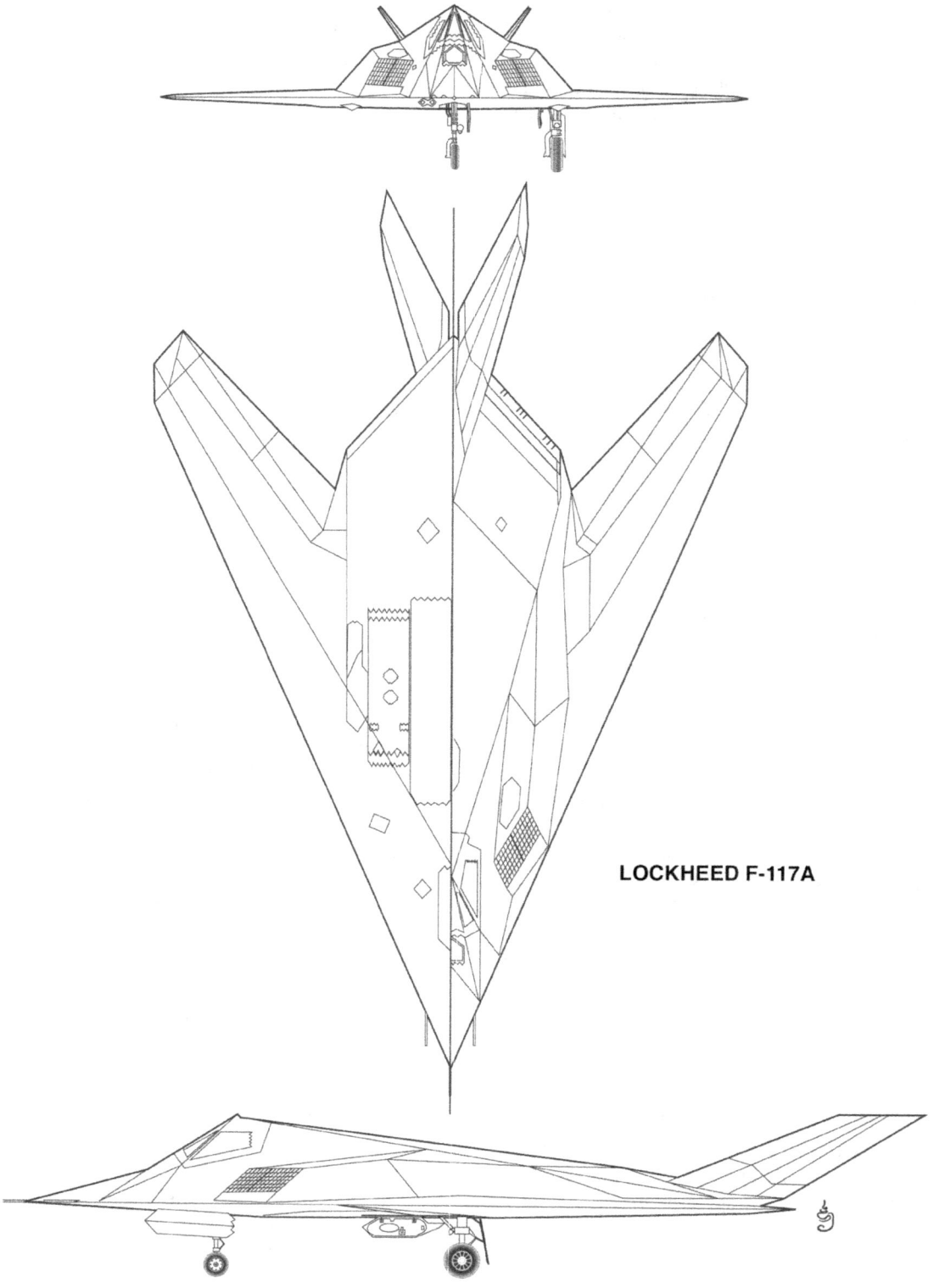

LOCKHEED F-117A

F-117A shown dropping a smart bomb from a level flight attitude. F-117As of the 49th Tactical Fighter Wing flew the first wave of precision air strikes in the opening hours of the Operation Desert Storm in January 1991.

als. While retaining the same general planform and faceting arrangement of the *Have Blue* prototypes, the final design of the F-117A differed in a number of respects: the airframe was larger by a factor of 74-percent and four times heavier; for structural reasons, the twin vertical tail surfaces were relocated forward of the exhaust ejectors and angled outward rather than inward: an enlarged canopy consisting of five faceted panels replaced the V-type windscreen, with the nose being sloped downward to match the new canopy angle; wing sweep was reduced from 72.5 to 67.5-degrees in order to improve payload and range; and finally, two weapons bays, each capable of holding up to 2,500-lbs. of munitions, were added to the belly of the plane. A quadruple-redundant FBW control system that worked off four pitot-static probes in the nose enabled the pilot to keep the F-117 within controlled flight; in the event of a complete FBW system failure, the pilot would be forced to eject. The aircraft's aluminum and titanium airframe was completely covered by a radar absorption material (RAM), which, though its composition is still classified, was thought to consist of magnetic iron particles bonded in some type of polymer. The RAM was initially applied in sheets but later was reportedly sprayed-on using a process in which the entire aircraft was rotated like a chicken on a rotisserie. Power was derived from two non-afterburning F-404 turbofans similar to those used by the F/A-18 *Hornet*. Each turbofan was located in a faceted nacelle behind two rectangular intake gratings that prevented radar waves from reaching the engine. Radar detection from the rear was substantially diminished by ducting the engine exhaust through a series of flattened slots that scattered the returns; infrared signature was reduced with a combination of engine bypass air and heat-reflecting ceramic tiles located behind the exhaust ducts.

Since the F-117A was intended solely for the precision strike role and possessed no air-to-air capability, its "fighter" designation was a misnomer. For tactical navigation and weapons delivery, the aircraft depended solely upon forward-looking infrared (FLIR) and downward-looking infrared (DLIR) systems rather than radar. Together, these components formed the infrared acquisition and designation system (IRADS), which used a bore-sighted laser to illuminate targets for laser-guided smart weapons. The cockpit came with a heads up display (HUD) and three separate cockpit screens that reported flight data plus navigational and tactical information from FLIR/DLIR systems. For en route navigation, the pilot relied upon a highly accurate inertial navigation system (INS) that guided the aircraft into the target area, then pointed the FLIR towards the target. Once acquired, the pilot utilized IRADS to designate and track the target up to the point of weapons release. The weapons bays of the F-117A accommodated most of the USAF's inventory of smart munitions (e.g., GBU-10, -12, -24, and -27; BLU-109: and AGM-130) and could be configured to carry two Mk. 61 tactical nuclear weapons, although the aircraft had no assigned nuclear mission. The USAF made a rapid decision to place the F-117A into low-rate production and accepted delivery of 89 examples from 1982 to 1990. During and after production, F-117As underwent a number of retrofits: starting in 1987, the all-metal vertical tail surfaces were replaced with units made of composite materials; in 1991, continuing problems with the exhaust system led to installation of new rear assemblies behind the exhaust ducting; more recently, the cockpit was upgraded with new color multi-function displays as well as an INS having a laser-ring gyro and global positioning system (GPS) receiver.

The 4450th Tactical Group based at Tonapah Airfield near Nellis AFB in Nevada began receiving the first production F-117As during 1982 and achieved full operational status with the type in October 1983. The 4450th TG was deactivated in October 1989 and simultaneously reactivated as the 49th Tactical Fighter Wing, and in 1992, moved to its present location at Holloman AFB in New Mexico. F-117s saw combat for the first time in 1989 when six were flown from Tonapah to attack targets in Panama during Operation Just Cause. On the night of January 17, 1991, *Nighthawks* of the 49th TFW led the first wave of precision attacks against Iraqi targets in the Gulf War. During Operation Desert Storm, F-117's flew 1,300 combat sorties and destroyed 1,600 key targets in Iraq, and was the only type of U.S. aircraft tasked to strike targets in downtown Baghdad. After the war, F-117s of the 49th returned to the Persian Gulf to fly retaliatory strikes, and on their first sortie completed an 18.5-hour non-stop flight from Holloman AFB to Kuwait, a record for single-seat fighters that stands today. In March 1999, 24 F-117s operating from Aviano AFB in Italy led the air strikes against Yugoslavia in support of NATO's Operation Allied Force. *Nighthawks* returned to the skies over Iraq on March 20, 2003, when 12 aircraft of the 49th initiated Operation Iraqi Freedom with precision attacks on key Iraqi command and control targets. The USAF has recently announced that it will start retiring its F-117As in 2008 as new F-22As *Raptors* enter active service to replace them.

Lockheed-Martin F-22 Raptor 1990–Present

TECHNICAL SPECIFICATIONS (F/A-22A)

Type: One-place tactical fighter
Manufacturer: Lockheed-Martin Corp., Marietta, Georgia and Palmdale, California.
Total produced: 183 (projected)
Power plant: Two Pratt & Whitney F119-100 turbofan engines, each rated at 23,500-lbs./s.t. dry, 35,000-lbs./s.t. in afterburning.
Armament: On M61A2 20-mm rotary cannon, two 1,000-lb. GBU-32 JDAMs and two AIM-120 AMRAAM missiles in a ventral weapons bay (attack configuration), one AIM-9 *Sidewinder* missile in each side bay, plus four AIM-120 AMRAAM missiles carried on underwing racks.
Performance: Max. speed 1,450-mph (Mach 2.2) at 40,000 ft., 990-mph (Mach 1.5) supercruise at 40,000 ft., ceiling 65,000 ft., range 1,500 mi. loaded (est.).
Weights: 33,000-lbs. (approx.) empty, 62,000-lbs. max. takeoff.
Dimensions: Span 44 ft. 6 inches, length 62 ft. 2 in., wing area 840 sq. ft.

The F-22 represents the sum of American aeronautical technology combined into a single tactical weapons system that can equally perform air superiority or precision attack missions while being fully cloaked with stealth characteristics. It also probably holds the record—15

Third Series • 1962–Present

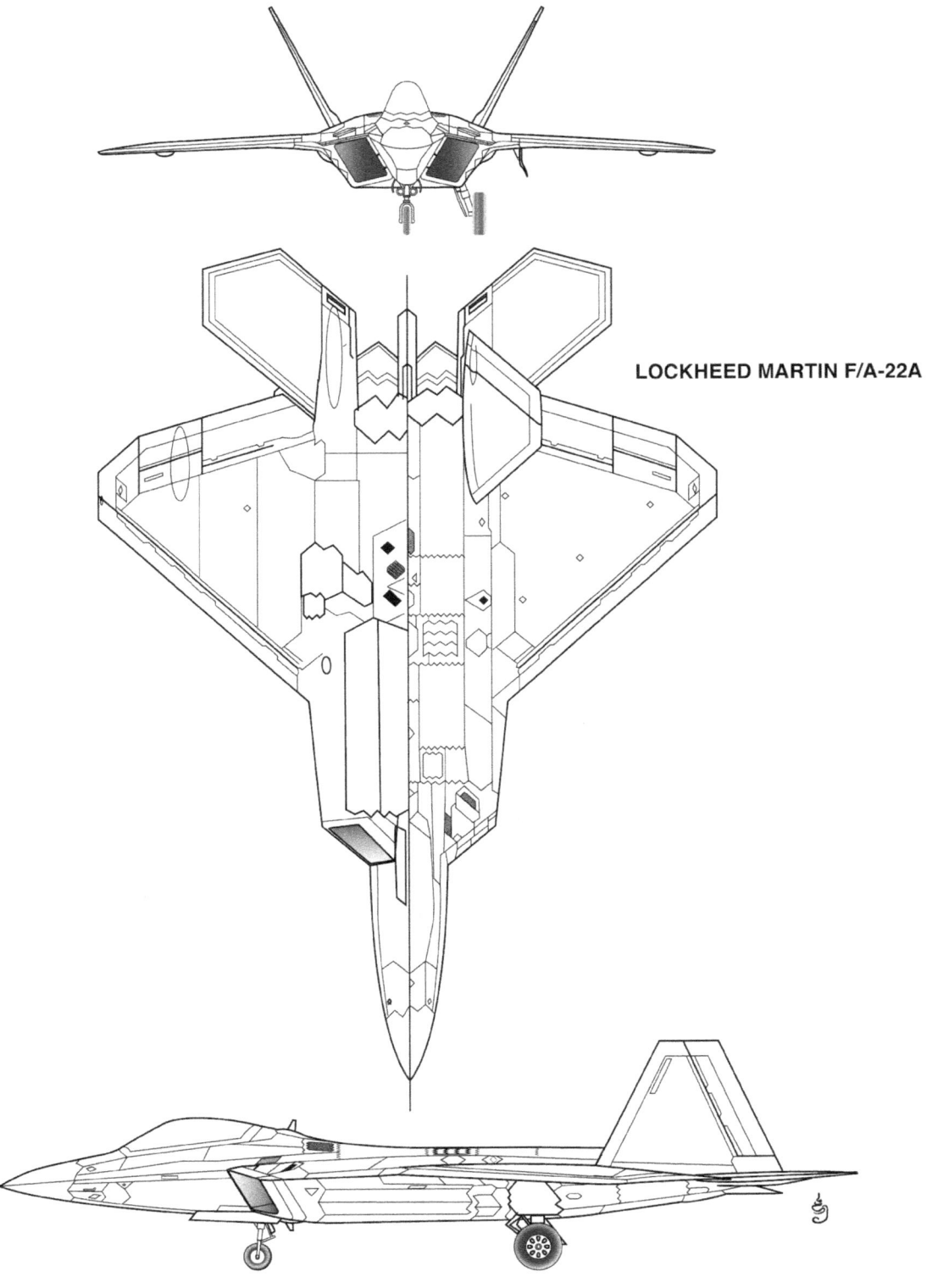

LOCKHEED MARTIN F/A-22A

Top: One of two externally identical YF-22 demonstrators flown for the first time in 1990. The engines, developed in parallel by General Electric and Pratt & Whitney, enabled the aircraft to "supercruise"—maintain supersonic speed without afterburning. *Bottom:* F-22A as seen from the boomer's window on a tanker. The type became operational with the 43rd Fighter Squadron in 2005, and the USAF plans to build up to a strength of five more squadrons in the near future.

years—for the time elapsed between making a first flight and entering full-rate production. The advanced tactical fighter (ATF) concept emerged in the early 1980s out of a USAF desire to acquire an aircraft that combined the stealth capability of the F-117 with the air-to-air potency of the F-15. In May 1983 the USAF invited Boeing, General Dynamics, Grumman, Lockheed, McDonnell-Douglas, Northrop, and Rockwell to submit proposals for what was termed a concept definition investigation (CDI) of the ATF design and simultaneously asked Pratt & Whitney and General Electric to develop the engines. Under a separate program known as the joint advanced fighter engine (JAFE), the new turbofans were expected produce continuous power that would enable the aircraft to 'supercruise' (i.e., maintain supersonic speed without afterburning). By the middle of 1985, when the USAF was finally in a position to issue a definitive request for ATF design proposals, the project had grown to be so complex and costly that Grumman and Rockwell withdrew while the remaining manufacturers agreed to pool their efforts—Lockheed, Boeing and, General Dynamics forming one ATF design team and Northrop and McDonnell-Douglas the other. Another complexity was added in April 1986 when the Navy joined the ATF project to find a replacement for the F-14. In October 1986, as prime contractors, Lockheed and Northrop both received contracts to each built two flyable ATF prototypes, Lockheed's entry as the YF-22A and Northrop's as the YF-23A. Huge advances in computer technology since the appearance of first stealth designs in the mid–1970s had made it possible to develop models and simulations of low-observable aircraft with supersonic performance and excellent maneuverability. At the same time, better types of radar absorbing materials (RAM) were in the process of being developed. The USAF originally contemplated procuring 750 of the new stealth fighters with the hope that they would achieve operational status sometime in 1996.

Lockheed's YF-22A design, which at first looked a lot like the F-117A, underwent sweeping changes before reaching final form. Using computer-aided techniques called planform shaping and alignment, designers ultimately produced a configuration having a very low radar cross-section (RCS) without compromising aerodynamic performance. Other stealth measures included reducing infrared signature, muffling noise, lessening radio transmissions, and making the aircraft less visible to the eye. The curves designed into the YF-22A's crucial surfaces and edges made it unnecessary to cover the entire airframe in RAM, so that it was used only on the edges of the wings and around the exhaust nozzles. Unparalleled agility in maneuvering was made possible by utilizing engine nozzles that could be vectored 20-degrees up or down at any power setting. To take full advantage of its superior maneuverability, the YF-22A incorporated a fly-by-wire (FBW) control system in which control inputs from the pilot were fed into a central processor coordinating the operation of the leading-edge flaps, ailerons, stabilizers, rudders, and speed brake, as well as the thrust-vectoring nozzles. Other advanced systems included an integrated avionics suite built around a powerful flight computer having three times the memory and sixteen times the speed of that used on the F-15. Pilot workload was lessened by navigational and tactical systems that used artificial intelligence to control and prioritize the flow of information. In order to evaluate the new powerplants, the first YF-22A demonstrator was to be powered by General Electric F-120s while the second would come with Pratt & Whitney F-119s.

The first YF-22A completed its maiden flight from Lockheed's Palmdale plant on September 29, 1990, followed within a month by the second demonstrator. Neither aircraft carried full armament or radar. YF-22A number one achieved a critical milestone in early November when it attained a speed of Mach 1.58 without afterburners, and with afterburning, demonstrated it could easily exceed Mach 2 at altitude. Further flight-testing revealed that the vectoring thrust nozzles not only increased turning rate by a factor of 35-percent but enabled the F-22A to achieve rates of roll and pitch at supersonic velocities that had been attainable formerly only at subsonic speeds. Competitive trials against the two YF-23A demonstrators delivered by Northrop commenced in the fall of 1990 from Edwards AFB. Although the actual comparative data between the two aircraft is still classified, the general consensus seems to be that the YF-23A was somewhat stealthier and faster while the YF-22A was more maneuverable, especially at lower airspeeds. In any event, on April 23, 1991, the USAF declared Lockheed (Lockheed-Martin after 1993) as winner of the ATF competition and selected the Pratt & Whitney F-119 as the winning powerplant. Official factors cited in favor the F-22 by the USAF included better maintainability, greater future development potential, and somewhat lower cost. As to powerplant selection, the F-120, though slightly more powerful, was apparently viewed as having more development risks. In August 1991, Lockheed received a contract to build eleven engineering, manufacture, and development (EMD) aircraft, to include nine F-22As plus two two-seat F-22Bs, with the expectation that the first aircraft would fly in 1995. The Navy by that time had withdrawn from the ATF program in order to pursue development of the less complex F/A-18E/F *Super Hornet* (see, F/A-18 in Part II). Besides being fully armed and equipped with avionics, the EMD F-22As differed from the demonstrators in the following respects: fuselage shortened two feet and cockpit moved forward; nose and radome profile changed to blunter shape; engine inlets moved aft one foot six inches; wingspan increased one foot six inches with sweep angle reduced to 42-degrees; and tail planform modified to diamond shape. The first of nine EMD F-22As (the two F-22Bs were cancelled) flew on September 7, 1997, at which time the name *Raptor* became official.

In the interval, as a result of delays, rising production costs, and projected force reductions, planned F-22 production levels were progressively dropped, first from 750 aircraft to 438, then to 339 by late 1997. The last F-22A EMD aircraft was delivered in April 2002 and initial low-rate production (36 aircraft per year) was approved the following August. The *Raptor's* designation was changed to F/A-22A in 2002, but was changed back to F-22A when the type began entering frontline service in 2005. Production F-22As were initially delivered to the 43rd Fighter Squadron, 325th Fighter Wing, at Tyndall AFB, Florida in September 2003, which presently serves as the operational training unit for the type. The 27th FS, 1st FW, based at Langley AFB in Virginia, received its first F-22As in May 2005 and became fully operational the following December. Although full-rate production was ordered in December 2005, the USAF has since announced that F-22A procurement will be limited to 183 aircraft with deliveries continuing through 2012. A second squadron of F-22As attached to the 1st FW, the 94th FS, became operational in early 2007, and according to most recent plans, the USAF expects to build-up to a strength of at least five more squadrons of 18 aircraft each as deliveries proceed.

Northrop F-23 1990–1992

TECHNICAL SPECIFICATIONS (YF-23A)

Type: One-place tactical fighter
Manufacturer: Northrop Corp., Hawthorne, California.
Total produced: 2
Power plant: Two Pratt & Whitney F119–100 or two General Electric F-120–100 turbofan engines, each rated at 23,500-lbs./s.t. dry, 35,000-lbs./s.t. in afterburning.
Armament: None.
Performance (est.): Max. speed 1,450-mph (Mach 2.2) at 36,000+ ft., 1,059-mph (Mach 1.6) supercruise at 36,000+ ft., ceiling 65,000 ft., range 1,500 mi. loaded (est.).
Weights: 29,000-lbs. (approx.) empty, 62,000-lbs. max. takeoff.
Dimensions: Span 43 ft. 7 inches, length 67 ft. 5 in., wing area 900 sq. ft.

The Northrop/McDonnell-Douglas design team, when it came together for the USAF's

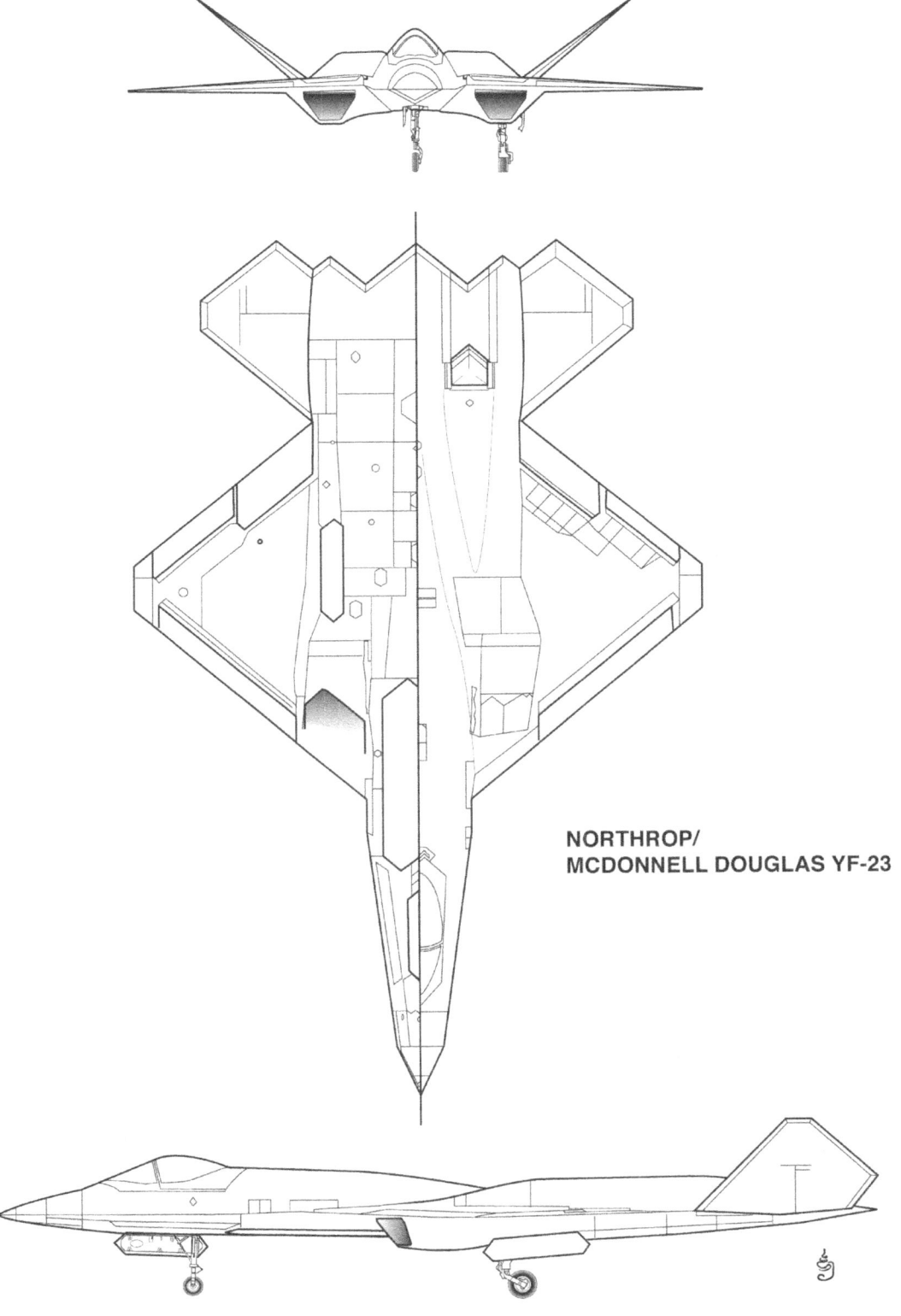

**NORTHROP/
MCDONNELL DOUGLAS YF-23**

Both YF-23 ATF demonstrators in flight over southern California. In terms of aerodynamic layout, these airplanes were more unorthodox than the competing YF-22s and reportedly possessed slightly better stealth characteristics.

advanced tactical fighter (ATF) competition in 1985, possessed more experience with modern fighter development (i.e., the F-4, F-5/-20, YF-17, F/A-18, and F-15) than any other combination of American defense contractors. In October 1986, Northrop was selected, as prime contractor, to build two flyable ATF demonstrators under the designation YF-23A, to be pitted in a future fly-off against Lockheed's rival YF-22A. In order to evaluate the two new engines being developed for the ATF project, one YF-23 would be powered by GE F-120s and the other by Pratt & Whitney F-119s.

Like the YF-22, the stealth characteristics of the YF-23's design were generated via sophisticated computer programs pertaining to aerodynamic planform shaping and alignment. These programs enabled designers to keep radar cross-section (RCS) at a minimum, while producing an airframe that would otherwise meet the expected criteria for performance and air-to-air agility. Driven by the desire to optimize both stealth and supercruise characteristics, Northrop's design of the YF-23 emerged as the more unorthodox of the two ATF concepts. To avoid the aerodynamic drag penalty created by a faceted geometry, the design of the fuselage employed extensive planform blending, very similar to that seen on the B-2 stealth bomber. The blending of the fuselage into the wing formed large chines that functioned like the leading-edge root extensions (LREX) seen on the YF-17, improving maneuvering at high angles-of-attack and increasing rates of turn. The wings and tail surfaces were all aligned to 40-degree sweep angles on the leading and trailing edges, producing a noticeably clipped diamond shape. The empennage was an all-flying V-tail configuration set at the very rear of the fuselage, with each surface being canted to a 50-degree angle. The V-tail surfaces were programmed, through a fly-by-wire (FBW) control system, to simultaneously effect pitch, roll, and yaw, while also serving to shield the aircraft from an engine exhaust heat signature at all angles except above and behind. Thrust vectoring was not used; instead, to minimize RCS, infra-red emission, and drag, Northrop employed a "beaver tail" arrangement (again, similar to the B-2) in which engine exhaust was ported through ventral troughs.

In order to speed development and lower costs, the two YF-23 demonstrators did not come with radar or the state-of-the-art avionics required for future models but utilized many off-the-shelf components derived from F-15s and F/A-18s. The first YF-23A demonstrator was shipped to Edwards AFB during the summer of 1990 and made its first flight on August 27; the second YF-23A arrived in late-October. On its fifth flight, the first YF-23A (powered by F-119s) achieved supercruise, and in subsequent testing, ultimately sustained Mach 1.6 without afterburning. Details on the performance of the second YF-23A (powered by F-120s) have never been released. On April 23, 1991, following six months of comparative testing between the YF-23s and YF-22s, the USAF announced that Lockheed had won the demonstration phase of the competition and would be authorized to continue the engineering, manufacture, and development (EMD) phase. Why Lockheed was chosen over Northrop has been the source of much speculation. Official factors cited in favor the F-22 by the USAF included better maintainability, greater future development potential, and somewhat lower cost. Some commenters claim that the Northrop/McDonnell-Douglas/General Dynamics team was out of favor with the government because of problems relating to the B-2 and A-12 programs. The two YF-23As demonstrators, after their engines were removed, were placed in storage at NASA's Dryden facility at Edwards AFB until 1996, after which time they were transferred to air museums.

Boeing X(F)-32 JSF 2000–2001

TECHNICAL SPECIFICATIONS (X-32A [X-32B VSTOL])

Manufacturer: Boeing Aerospace Corp., St. Louis, Missouri.
Total produced: 2
Power plant: One Pratt & Whitney F119-PW-614C turbofan rated at 34,000-lbs. /s.t. dry, 40,000-lbs. in afterburning. [Pratt & Whitney F119-PW-614S with thrust vectoring].
Armament: (No internal guns); provision for six AIM-120 *AMRAAM* missiles or two AIM-120 plus 2,000-lbs. of bombs carried in two internal bays; and up to 11,000-lbs. of mixed munitions on wing and fuselage stations.
Performance (estimated): Max. speed 996-mph (Mach 1.5) at 35,000 ft.; ceiling, 50,000 ft.; range 700 mi. [both versions] with combat load.
Weights: 22,046-lbs. empty, 50,000-lbs. max. loaded
Dimensions: Span 36 ft. [30 ft.], length 45 ft. [43 ft. 9 in.], wing area 590 sq. ft. [443 sq. ft.]

The X-32 represents the first serious venture by Boeing to obtain a fighter contract since the XF8B-1 of 1944–1945. Boeing's involvement began in the early 1990s as part of a Defense Advanced Research Projects Agency (DARPA) study being conducted under the heading Common Affordable Lightweight Fighter (CALF), with the goal of producing a stealth tactical aircraft, in conventional and VSTOL versions, that would utilize the powerful new engines developed for the YF-22 and YF-23. In 1995, CALF was absorbed into the multi-service Joint Advance Strike Technology (JAST) program, then a year later renamed the Joint Strike Fighter (JSF) program. In late 1996, the Department of Defense (DOD) announced that future JSF competition would be restricted to Boeing (X-32) and Lockheed-Martin (X-35) and thereafter awarded both companies four-year contracts to complete the concept demonstration phase of the program.

Compared to the fairly conventional layout of Lockheed-Martin's X-35, Boeing's X-32 aerodynamic concept was more novel, emerging as a true-delta planform with a V-tail and a cavernous air intake positioned under the nose. While Lockheed's VSTOL scheme was planned around a separate shaft-driven lift fan operating in conjunction with a vectored exhaust, the VSTOL version of the X-32 was designed to achieve all of its lift thrust via a pair of vectoring nozzles sited under the aircraft's center-of-gravity (similar to the AV-8). The VSTOL X-32B differed from the conventional X-32A in having a moveable intake to allow more engine

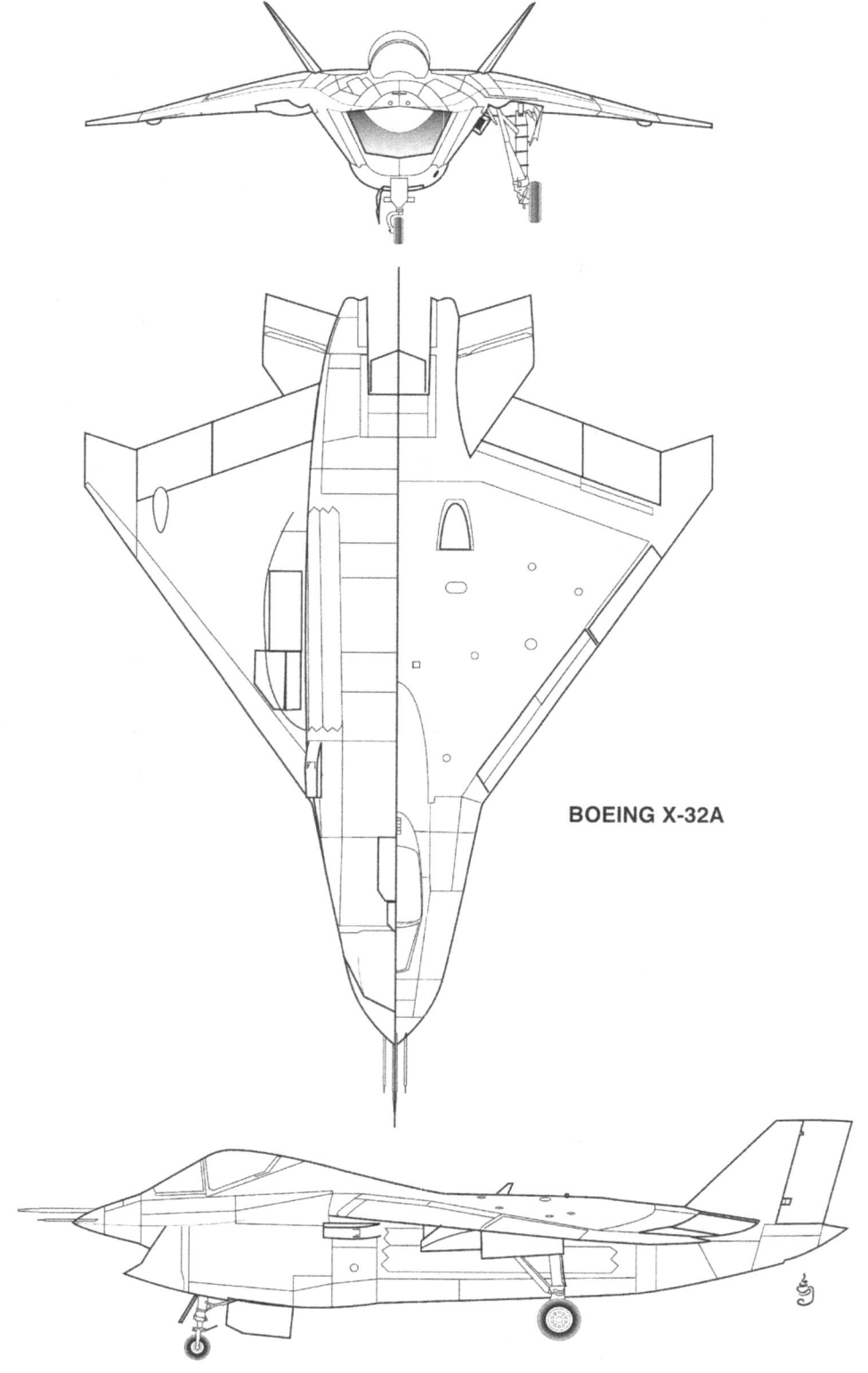

BOEING X-32A

Side view of one of two X-32 demonstrators flown in 2000. The EMD versions, had they been built, would have featured horizontal stabilizers on the aft fuselage.

air volume during hover, shorter wings without leading edge lift devices, and a slightly shorter fuselage. In 1998 Boeing initiated a major JSF redesign aimed at reducing cost and weight, during which the basic aerodynamic configuration was altered to include horizontal stabilizers mounted on the aft fuselage. However, the two demonstrators (X-32A and X-32B), then in advanced stages of construction, were not changed.

The X-32A demonstrator was rolled out of the former Rockwell assembly facility at Palmdale, California and flown for the first time on September 18, 2000. The aircraft was taken to Edwards AFB, where testing was continued until early February 2001. On March 29, 2001, the X-32B VSTOL demonstrator completed its first flight and began hovering tests the following June. On October 24, 2001, in what the aviation media described as a "winner take all" contest, DOD declared Lockheed-Martin's X-35 to be the winner of the JSF competition. DOD officials maintained that, despite similar unit acquisition costs, Lockheed-Martin's entry had generally demonstrated lower long-term development risks and life-cycle costs. And as to specific engineering features, DOD cited Lockheed-Martin's lift fan STVOL approach, stealth methods (e.g., better engine masking and fewer external protrusions), sensor systems, and the fact that there would be more aerodynamic commonality between X-35 demonstrators and follow-on system design and development models.

Although the loss of the JSF contact was seen as a serious financial blow to Boeing, the company is expected to use much of the technology derived from JSF in the DARPA and USAF-sponsored program for the X-45 Unmanned Combat Air Vehicle (UCAV).

Lockheed-Martin F-35 Lightning II 2000–Present

TECHNICAL SPECIFICATIONS (F-35A [F-35B VSTOL])
Manufacturer: Lockheed-Martin Corp., Fort Worth, Texas.
Total produced (planned): 1,763 F-35A; 500 F-35B; 480 F-35C.
Power plant: One Pratt & Whitney F-135 augmented turbofan (derivative of F-119-PW-100 used on F-22) rated at 30,000-lbs. /s.t. dry, 40,000-lbs. in afterburning. [Roll-Royce shaft-driven, vertical lift fan rated at 18,500-lbs./s.t.] A General Electric/Roll-Royce F-136 alternate engine is under development.
Armament: Internal 25-mm GAU-12 rotary cannon [external 25-mm GAU-12 pod F-35B/C]; two AIM-120 AMRAAM missiles carried in two internal bays and/or two AIM-9 *Sidewinder* missiles on wingtip rails (air-to-air load); and up to 15,000-lbs. [13,000-lbs.] of mixed munitions carried in two internal bays and on seven [five] wing and fuselage stations (air-to-ground load).
Performance (estimated): Max. speed 1,200-mph (Mach 1.8) at 36,000 ft.; ceiling, not published; range 1,357 mi. [1,035 mi.] with combat load.
Weights: 22,500-lbs. [23,500-lbs.] empty, 60,000-lbs. max. loaded.
Dimensions: Span 35 ft., length 50 ft. 5 in., wing area 460 sq. ft.

The F-35, when it becomes operational (projected during 2011–2012), will be USAF's primary strike fighter and the first tactical aircraft operated by the Navy and Marine Corps to possess true stealth capability. Current production plans for the F-35 are the culmination of a ten-year effort commonly known as the Joint Strike Fighter (JSF) program. The F-35 will be built in three major variants: the USAF F-35A, which comes with a 25-mm internal cannon, will replace the F-16 and A-10; the USMC F-35B, the VSTOL version, will replace both the AV-8B and F/A-18C/D; the USN F-35C, the carrier version, with reinforced airframe and landing gear, 35 percent greater wing area, and foldable wings, will replace the F/A-18C/D. Additionally, in the United Kingdom, the VSTOL F-35B is also slated to replace the British Aerospace (BAe) *Harrier* in the Royal Air Force and Royal Navy. As of late 2006, besides the United Kingdom, Australia, Canada, and the Netherlands have thus far committed to buy production F-35s, and Norway, Denmark, Italy, Turkey, and Singapore will acquire SDD aircraft for evaluation purposes. And should additional overseas sales be made at some future point to current F-16 and F/A-18 users, it could potentially add hundreds more F-35s to existing production plans.

Much of the F-35's aerodynamic, structural, and systems design has benefited from Lockheed-Martin's accumulated experience with the F-22 *Raptor*. To minimize weight without sacrificing strength, extensive use of composites is made throughout the airframe. Stealth characteristics (i.e., reduced radar cross-section [RCS]) are achieved by a combination of radar-absorbent structural materials and external features, such as: identical sweep angles in the leading and trailing edges of the wings and tail surfaces (i.e., planform alignment); blended canopy-fuselage contours; canted vertical fins; and sawtoothed edges of intakes and seams of fuselage openings. The heart of the F-35's electronic and sensor suite is the Northrop-Grumman AN/APG-81 multi-function radar (a derivative of the F-22's AN/APG-77), a system that brings forward a state-of-the-art advanced electronically scanned array (AESA) in conjunction with a radio frequency subsystem and agile beam steering capabilities. For countermeasures, BAe is currently developing an internally housed fully integrated information and

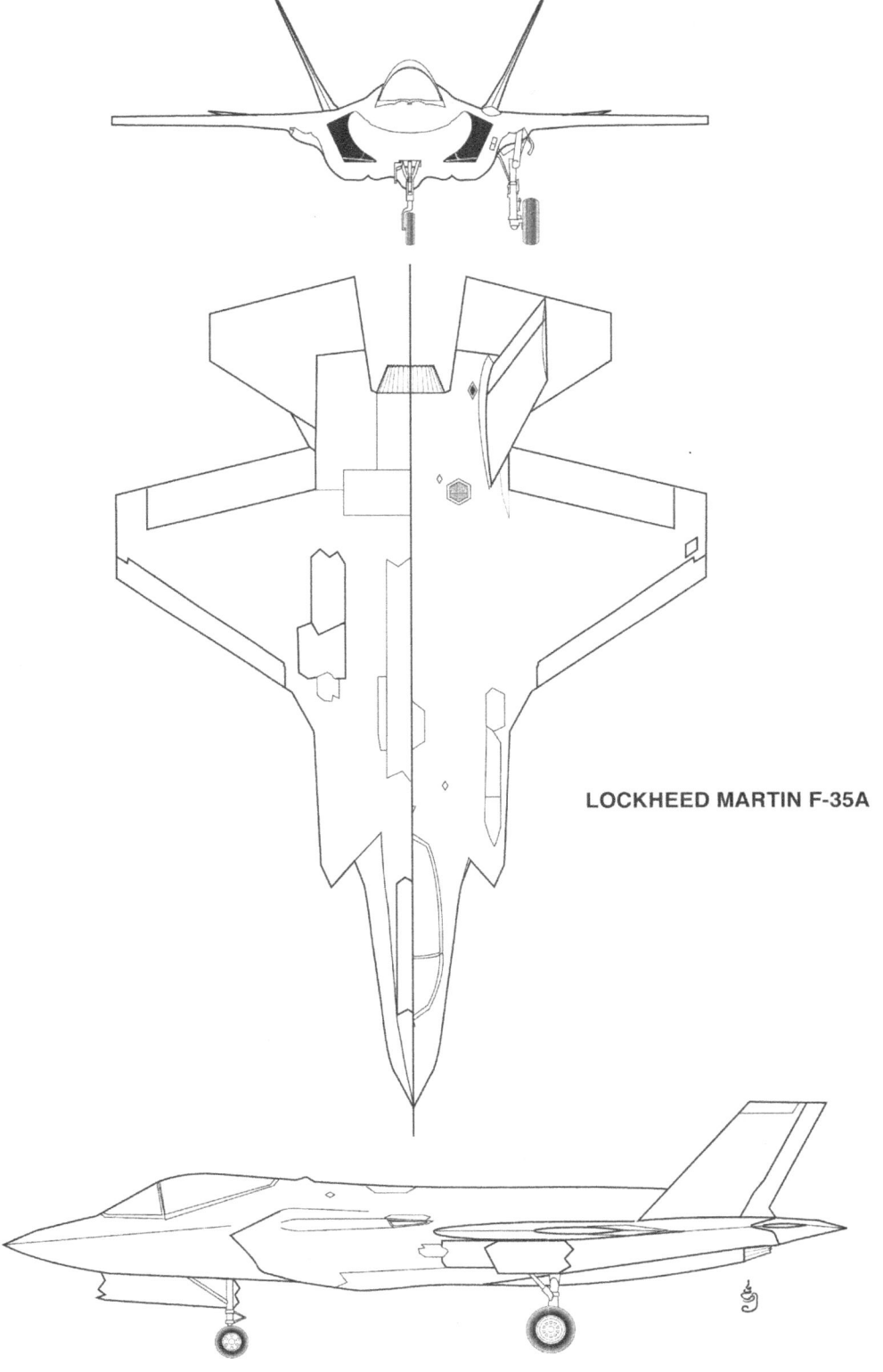

LOCKHEED MARTIN F-35A

The F-35C naval variant also known as the F-35CV. This carrier-capable version has 35 percent more wing area and is stressed for arrested landings. The Navy plans to buy at least 480 to replace its existing fleet of F/A-18C/Ds.

electronic warfare system (IEWS). The F-35's software platform will run on an integrated core processor (ICP), a central 'brain' (i.e., artificial intelligence) which simultaneously assimilates all electronic systems and coordinates the data displayed to the pilot. The pilot will receive information from the F-35's electronic systems via a cockpit layout that features a full-width panel display (8 in. x 20 in.), and like the F/A-18, all important data and control inputs are executed by means of hands-on-stick-and-throttle (HOTAS) controls. In place of a heads up display (HUD), F-35 pilots will be using a specially developed helmet-mounted display (HMD) system.

The first X(F)-35 demonstrator left the runway at Palmdale, California on October 24, 2000 and was ferried to Edwards AFB to undergo flight testing. The larger X(F)-35C concept aircraft was flown in mid–December 2000, and after initial flight trials, delivered to NAS Patuxent River in early February 2001 for naval evaluations. In the interval, the original F-35 demonstrator was returned to Lockeed-Martin for installation of the Roll-Royce lift engine; thereafter, hover testing commenced in March 2001 and the first transition to level flight was completed on June 24, 2001. In October 2001 the Department of Defense (DOD) announced that Lockheed-Martin's X(F)-35 had been selected as the winner of the JSF competition over Boeing's rival X-32. As a whole, Lockheed-Martin's design was viewed by DOD as involving lower development risks and better life-cycle costs, but more specifically, the lift fan of its VSTOL version was judged superior to Boeing's direct-lift, vectored thrust approach. The JSF program has now gone into the system design and development (SDD) phase, involving production of 22 SDD aircraft. The first USAF F-35A SDD flew in December 2006 while the F-35B SDD is scheduled to fly in 2007, and the F-35C in 2008. Low-rate initial production is expected to commence in 2007, with the USAF and Marines receiving their first evaluation aircraft during 2008 and achieving operational capability sometime in 2011. The Navy and the United Kingdom are scheduled to receive their first evaluation aircraft in 2010, leading to operational capability in 2012. In 2005 the USAF expressed an intention to also acquire the F-35B VTOL version; however, the number to be purchased, or how it may impact planned procurement of F-35A, has not been announced. Most recently (in 2006), defense media sources stated the USAF is making plans to reduce its acquisition of F-35s from 1,763 to between 1,000 and 1,200 aircraft.

According to DOD reports, development of a two-seat electronic warfare (EW) version of the JSF (i.e., an EF-35) is under consideration and could possibly lead to a shared effort between the USAF and the Marine Corps. The USAF has had no dedicated strike escort EW platform in its inventory since the retirement of F-4G *Wild Weasels* in 1996 and EF-111A *Ravens* in 1998, and under current plans, the Marine Corps will not order the Navy's EF-18G *Growler* as a replacement for its aging EA-6B *Prowler* fleet.

Boeing X-45 UCAV 2002–Present

TECHNICAL SPECIFICATIONS X-45A [X-45C]
Manufacturer: Boeing Aerospace Corp., St. Louis, Missouri.
Total produced: 2 X-45A; 3 X-45Cs ordered.
Power plant: One Honeywell F-124-100 non-afterburning turbofan rated at 6,300-lbs. /s.t. dry [two General electric F-404-102D non-afterburning turbofan, rated at 10,000-lbs./s.t. dry].
Armament: One 250-lb. small smart bomb (SSB) carried in an internal bay [2,000-lbs. of precision-guided munitions to be carried in an internal bay].
PERFORMANCE (ESTIMATED): Cruise speed Mach 0.75 [Mach 0.85], combat ceiling 35,000 ft. [40,000 ft.]; range 1,150 mi. [2,990 mi.].
Weights: 12,190-lbs. [36,500-lbs.] max. loaded.
Dimensions: Span 33 ft. 8 in. [49 ft.], length 26 ft. 6 in. [49 ft.], wing area (unknown [unknown]).

Developed under the acronym UCAV (unmanned combat air vehicle), the Boeing X-45 is first pilotless system designed primarily for the tactical role. Unmanned air vehicles (UAVs) in various forms (e.g., target drones, glide bombs, cruise missiles, etc.) have been used since World War II, but the level of technology that enables them to perform more complex, two-way missions is a fairly recent development. Just within the past twenty years, reconnaissance UAVs capable of transmitting 'real time' information have evolved from miniature aircraft powered by snowmobile or motorcycle engines (e.g., the AAI Corp./Israel Aircraft Industries *Pioneer*, operational in 1986 and deployed by the Army, Navy, and Marine Corps during the Gulf War in 1991) to larger, more versatile systems like the General Atomics Aeronautical Systems, Inc. RQ-1 *Predator*, which became fully operational in 1999 during the Kosovo campaign. The *Predator*, nominally a full-size aircraft (span 41 ft. 8 in., gross weight 2,250-lbs.) carrying an array of electro-optical, infra-red, and radar sensor equipment, can be controlled beyond line-of-sight range via a satellite downlink, then loiter on station for up to 24 hours. The even newer, jet-powered Northrop-Grumman RQ-4A *Global Hawk* is larger yet (span 116 ft., gross weight 25,600-lbs.) and can range almost 14,000 miles at speeds up to 400-mph and altitudes up to 65,000 ft. *Global Hawks* began entering service with the USAF in late 2001; a definitive naval version specially equipped for maritime operations, made its first flight in November 2004.

In the mid–1990s, the Defense Advanced Research Projects Agency (DARPA) began seriously considering the possibility of developing a UAV with offensive capabilities, i.e., an unmanned combat air vehicle (UCAV), and since that time, two major programs materialized under DARPA supervision: the USAF's Boeing X-45 land-based UCAV in 1999 and the Navy's Northrop-Grumman X-47 carrier-based UCAV-N in 2000. The X-45A demonstrator made its

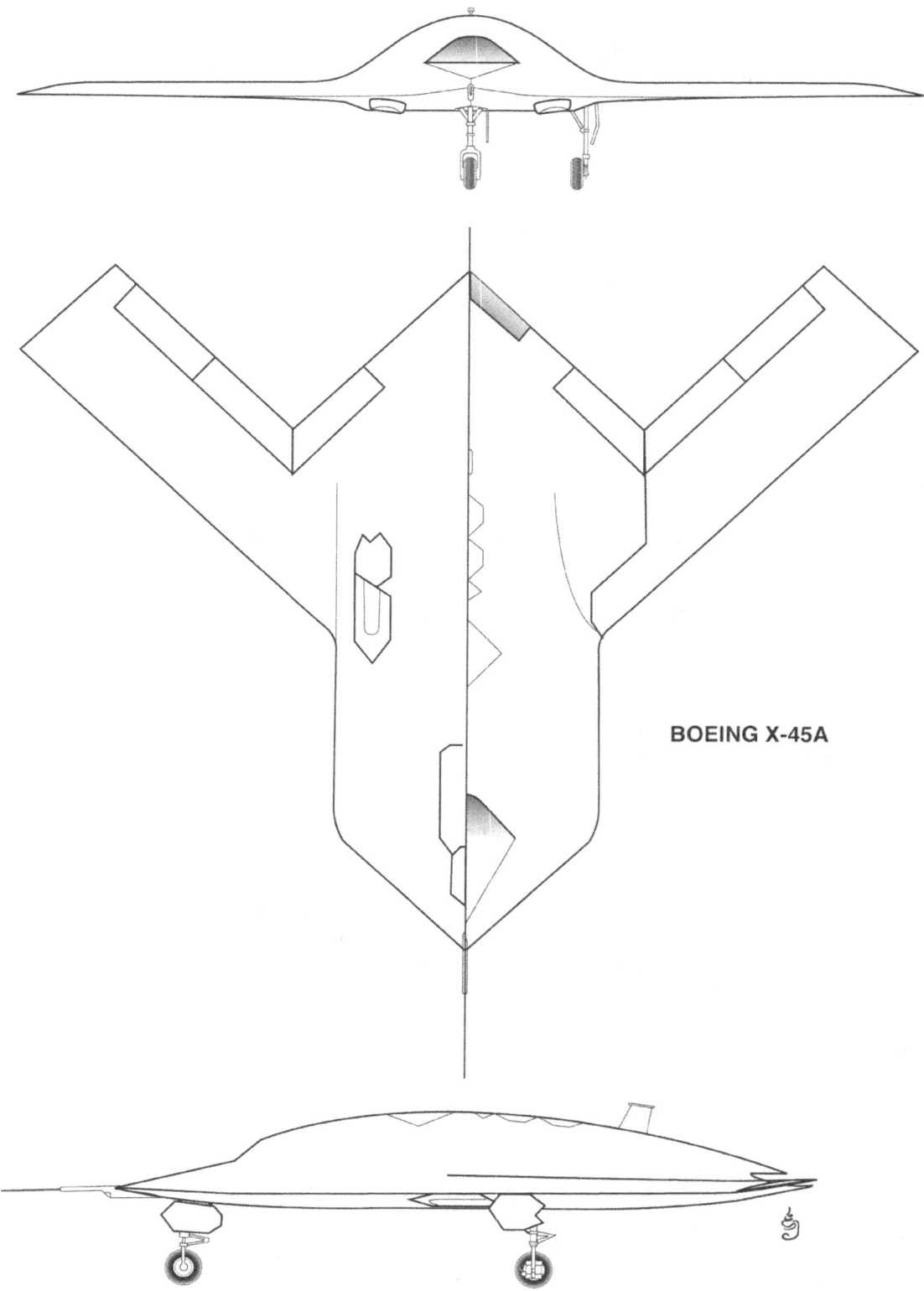

BOEING X-45A

One of two X-45A UCAV demonstrators shown at the moment of touchdown. Due to its withdrawal from the J-UCAS program in 2006, USAF plans to acquire a UCAV at a future date are uncertain.

first flight in May 2002 and subsequently entered the concept demonstration phase of flight-testing. DARPA envisaged fully operational X-45s as working cooperatively with manned systems such as F-15s, F-16s, F-22s, and F-35s, undertaking inherently dangerous missions such as suppression of enemy air defenses (SEAD); and over a longer term, X-45 derivatives were foreseen as possibly being developed to the level where they would completely supplant manned aircraft in the tactical role.

In a move that bore a strong resemblance to the earlier JSF contest, the UCAV program underwent a major shift in June 2003 when DARPA announced that the X-45 and X-47 programs were to be merged under the title Joint Unmanned Combat Air Systems (J-UCAS). Like JSF, the goal of J-UCAS was to eventually select a single prime contractor to manufacture the definitive UCAV production model. However, as of March 2006, the USAF withdrew from J-UCAS and plans were announced to continue only the UCAV-N (i.e., X-47A/B) portion of the program. The X-45C, which was scheduled to fly in 2007, is reportedly still at Boeing's St. Louis facility and plans for its ultimate disposition have not been revealed. According to a spokesman from the Navy's UAV office, the two X-45As, presently based at Edwards AFB, will be modified for carrier operations and demonstrated against the X-47 as part of what is now called Navy Unmanned Combat Air Systems (N-UCAS).

FOURTH SERIES (ADAPTED ATTACK AIRCRAFT) • 1950–PRESENT

Designation	Manufacturer	Dates
AC-47	Douglas Aircraft Co.	1964–1969
AC-119	Fairchild Aircraft Co.	1968–1971

Designation	Manufacturer	Dates
AC-123	Fairchild Aircraft Co.	1967–1970
AC-130	Lockheed Aircraft Co.	1967–Present
AT-28	North American Aviation, Inc.	1963–1970
AT-33	Lockheed Aircraft Co.	1950–1980
A-37	Cessna Aircraft Co.	1963–1992
AT-38	Northrop Corp.	1975–Present
Model 48	Convair Aircraft Corp.	1965–1966
OV-10	North American Aviation, Inc.	1965–1995

Douglas AC-47 "Spooky" 1964–1969

TECHNICAL SPECIFICATIONS (AC-47D)

Type: Side-firing gunship.
Manufacturer: Douglas Aircraft Co., Santa Monica, California.
Total produced: 53
Power plant: Two 1,200-hp Pratt & Whitney R-1830–90C 14-cylinder air-cooled radial engines driving three-bladed Hamilton Standard constant-speed, fully-feathering propellers.
Armament: Three 7.62-mm SUU-11A or MXU-470A Rotary Miniguns mounted on the port side of the fuselage and up to 54,000 rounds of ammunition.
Performance: Max. speed 230-mph., cruise 190-mph; ceiling 23,200 ft.; range 2,125 mi. max.
Weights: 16,865-lbs. empty, 25,200-lbs. max. takeoff.
Dimensions: Span 95 ft. 6 in., length 63 ft. 9 in., wing area 987 sq. ft.

The DC-3/C-47 had been in existence for almost 30 years when the USAF decided to convert one into a side-firing gunship. The idea of mounting a machine gun to fire from the side of an aircraft while flying in a banked circle had actually been explored as far back as the mid–1920s, however, the Army had never taken a serious interest. The side-firing idea resurfaced in the early 1960s when the USAF found itself in need of an effective weapon to defend what were termed "strategic hamlets" (i.e., defensive outposts) in the countryside of South Vietnam. Under a project known as Gunship I, initial testing of the concept was carried out during mid–1964 at Eglin AFB in Florida using a Convair C-131 equipped with one side-firing 7.62-mm SUU-11A rotary minigun and a Mk. 20 gunsight (same as that used by the Douglas A-1E) mounted on the left side window of the cockpit. In the fall of 1964, similar tests were performed at Eglin with a C-47 in which four standard .30-caliber machine guns had been mounted to side fire just aft of the cargo door. In October 1964, three SUU-11A gun pods and a Mk. 20 gunsight were shipped to Bein Hoa AB in South Vietnam to be installed in a C-47D that had been hauling cargo for the 1st Air Commando Squadron. Each gun was capable of firing 6,000 rounds per minute and the aircraft carried 54,000 rounds. After being converted, the aircraft (later named "Puff, the Magic Dragon") was re-designated FC-47D (F = fighter) and commenced combat testing in mid–December 1964 under the call sign "Spooky." The side-firing system subsequently proved itself to be a highly successful means of suppressing and dispersing enemy attacks around hamlets and other confined defensive positions.

In 1965 and 1966, 52 more C-47Ds were converted into side-firing gunships, most by the firm of Air International in Miami, Florida, and a gunship training program was established at Forbes AFB in Kansas. The aircraft by this time had been re-designated AC-47D, reportedly as a result of criticism from Tactical Air Command over the use of the 'fighter' designation. In August 1965 the 4th Air Commando Squadron (ACS) was created as the first AC-47 operational unit and thereafter commenced combat operations from Tan Son Nhut AB in South Vietnam. As gunship operations expanded, the AC-47s were deployed to forward locations in Bien Hoa, Pleiku, Na Trang, Dan Nang, and Can Tho. Another AC-47 unit, the 3rd ACS, was added to the combat theater in 1967 and the gunship units were re-designated Special Opera-

Fourth Series (Adapted Attack Aircraft) • 1950–Present

**GUNSHIPS
(NOT TO SCALE)**

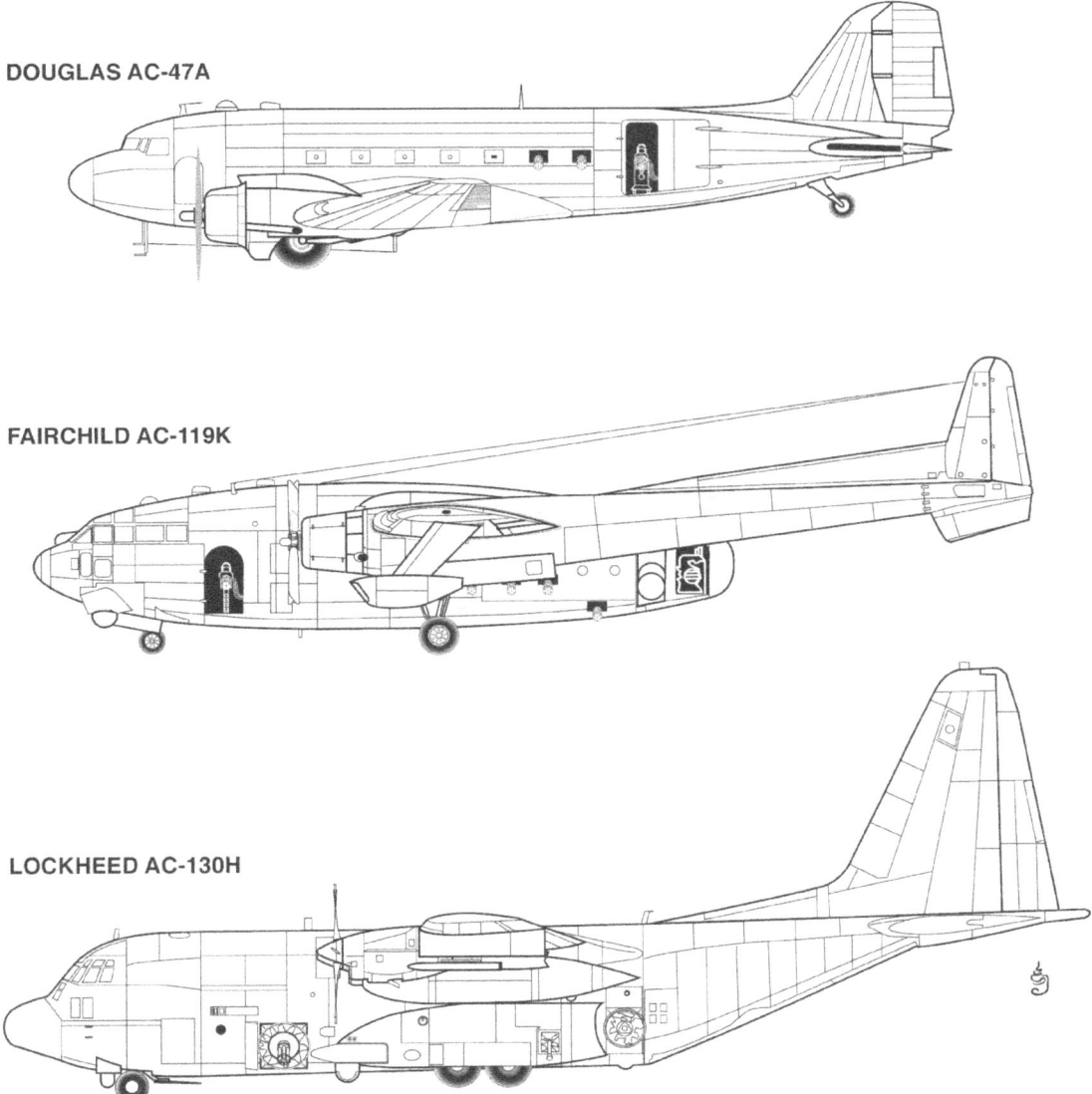

DOUGLAS AC-47A

FAIRCHILD AC-119K

LOCKHEED AC-130H

tions Squadrons (SOS) in 1968. On a typical sortie, after being directed-in by airborne or ground controllers, the AC-47 entered a constant-rate bank at about 3,000 feet over the target and was able to maintain fire within an elliptical cone that measured approximately 150 feet in diameter. To identify targets during night operations, the aircraft dropped flares that produced a light magnitude of two million candlepower. From 1965 until they were withdrawn from combat in 1969, AC-47s successfully defended 3,926 different positions, firing over 97 million rounds and killing over 5,300 enemy soldiers. No defensive position or outpost under the protection of "Spooky" was ever lost to the enemy. During their tour of combat, 15 AC-47s were lost to ground fire.

AC-47 on ramp showing detail of three SUU-11A miniguns. Side-firing system proved to be highly effective and led to development of new types of gunships that could be used not only for "hamlet" defense but for night interdiction as well.

Fairchild AC-119 "Shadow" or "Stinger" 1968–1971

TECHNICAL SPECIFICATIONS (AC-119G)
Type: Side-firing gunship.
Manufacturer: Fairchild Aircraft Co., Hagerstown, Maryland
Total produced: 52
Power plant: Two 3,350-hp Wright R-3350–85WA 18-cylinder, turbo-compound air-cooled radial engines driving four-bladed Hamilton Standard constant-speed, fully-reversible propellers (two General Electric J-85-17 turbojet engines, each rated at 2,850-lbs./s.t., added to AC-119K).
Armament: Four 7.62-mm SUU-11A or MXU-470A Rotary Miniguns mounted (two 20-mm M61A1 rotary cannons added to AC-119K) to the port side of the fuselage.
Performance: Max. speed 250-mph., cruise 200-mph; ceiling 24,000 ft.; range 1,900 mi. max.
Weights: 39,982-lbs. empty, 77,000-lbs. max. takeoff.
Dimensions: Span 109 ft. 3 in., length 86 ft. 6 in., wing area 1,447 sq. ft.

Well known as the *Flying Box Car*, the C-119 had been serving as a tactical transport for nearly 20 years when the USAF decided to convert some of them to a gunship configuration. Following the success of "Spooky" gunship operations in Vietnam, the USAF initiated Project Gunship III with the aim of replacing the AC-47s with larger, more heavily armed, and better equipped gunship platforms. In mid–1968 Fairchild-Hiller received a contract to convert 26 C-119Gs to a side-firing configuration that involved the installation of four 7.62 SUU-11A rotary miniguns on the left side of the fuselage, plus a 20-kilowatt illuminator, aluminum ceramic

AC-119K with addition of two auxiliary J-85 turbojet engines. The extra boost provided by the jets gave the gunship a higher takeoff weight and enabled it to operate over the more mountainous terrain of northern Laos and North Vietnam.

armor in the crew and cargo areas, a semi-automatic flare-launching system, foam lining in the fuel tanks, and new communications equipment. Like the AC-47D, the sighting system for the guns was installed on the aircraft commander's left side cockpit window. The first AC-119G operational sortie was flown in early January 1969 by the 17th Special Operations Squadron (SOS) from Tan Son Nhut AB in South Vietnam. Soon after entering combat, with the primary missions of airbase defense and troop support, the AC-119Gs became known by the call-sign "Shadow."

In the second phase of Gunship III, another 26 C-119Gs became AC-119Ks when they underwent a conversion that, in addition to the AC-119G modifications, included installation of two auxiliary J-85 turbojet engines mounted in pods under each wing, two side-firing 20-mm M61A1 rotary cannons, a forward-looking Doppler radar, a forward-looking infrared system (FLIR), plus a search radar. The extra power of the auxiliary jet not only allowed greater takeoff weights, but provided a higher combat ceiling for operations in the more mountainous areas of Vietnam and Laos. The primary mission of the AC-119K was to provide interdiction (i.e., a truck killer) and armed reconnaissance along the Ho Chi Minh Trail in North Vietnam and northern Laos. The first AC-119Ks deployed to Southeast Asia in late 1969 and commenced combat operations with the 18th SOS out of Nha Trang AB under the call-sign "Stinger." In combat, the AC-119G and Ks, as part of the 14th Special Operation Wing, flew an average of 175 sorties per day and had completed over 200,000 missions by the middle of 1971, and the AC-119Ks were credited with destroying 2,206 trucks. When the 14th SOW was deactivated in September 1971, a number of its aircraft were turned over to the Vietnamese Air Force while the remainder were returned to the U.S.

Fairchild AC/NC-123 "Black Spot" 1967–1970

TECHNICAL SPECIFICATIONS (AC/NC-123K)

Type: Night attack system.
Manufacturer: Fairchild Aircraft Co., Hagerstown, Maryland
Total produced: 2
Power plant: Two 2,300-hp Pratt & Whitney R-2800-99W 18-cylinder air-cooled radial engines driving three-bladed Hamilton Standard constant-speed, fully-reversible propellers and two General Electric J-85-17 turbojet engines, each rated at 2,850-lbs./s.t., in underwing pods.
Armament: Up to 6,372-lbs. (1-lb. per bomb) of Cluster Bomb Units housed in a 12-cell dispenser.
Performance: Max. speed 245-mph., cruise 190-mph; ceiling 24,000 ft.; range 1,470 mi. max.
Weights: 35,336-lbs. empty, 60,000-lbs. max. takeoff.
Dimensions: Span 110 ft., length 75 ft. 3 in., wing area 1,223 sq. ft.

    The USAF initiated "Project Black Spot" in late 1965 with the object of developing airborne systems that would give an aircraft specialized night attack capability to detect and destroy targets in areas like the Ho Chi Minh Trail where daytime operations were too dangerous and it was virtually impossible to identify targets at night. Once the concept was approved by the Department of Defense, a contract was given to LTV E-Systems in February 1966 to modify two Fairchild C-123K *Providers*. Each aircraft was equipped with a long nose radome housing an x-band radar and a chin-type turret that held a forward-looking infrared system (FLIR), low-level-light television (LLLTV), and laser range-finder/illuminator. Other new components included a low-level Doppler navigation radar and a weapons release computer. For weapons delivery, two rectangular, 12-cell cluster bomb unit (CBU) dispensers were installed in the cargo area, which could hold up to 6,372 one-pound cluster bombs released through twelve openings in the cargo floor. Release of the bombs was controlled via a weapons panel located behind the flight deck. The Black Spot AC/NC-123s were not intended to be true oper-

One of three "Blackspot" NC/AC-123Ks on ramp at Phan Rang Air Base in South Vietnam. While not true gunships, the Blackspots helped to combat test the night systems that would be incorporated into later gunships designs.

ational platforms but testbeds to develop systems that could be applied to future gunship types. Even though these modified aircraft were officially designated NC-123Ks, they were generally referred to as AC-123Ks in the field.

The first modified AC/NC-123K was delivered to Eglin AFB in Florida in August 1967 and the second in February 1968. Both aircraft were initially deployed to Osan AB in Korea to be evaluated against the high-speed boats used by the North Koreans to infiltrate agents into the South. In November 1968, upon completion of foregoing assignment, the aircraft transferred to Phan Rang AB in South Vietnam, where they began flying combat missions under the call sigh "Black Spot." From this time until May 1969, The AC/NC-123s completed 186 sorties over the Mekong Delta and Ho Chi Minh Trail, accounting for the destruction of or damage to 688 trucks and 151 rivercraft. In late 1969, both were fitted with radar warning and homing receivers (RHAW) and moved their operations to Ubon RTAFB in Thailand, where they resumed their night missions until June 1970, after which time Project Black Spot was terminated and the aircraft converted back to a standard C-123K configuration.

Lockheed AC-130 "Spectre" and "Spooky II" 1967–Present

TECHNICAL SPECIFICATIONS (AC-130H)
Type: Side-firing gunship.
Manufacturer: Lockheed Aircraft Corp. (Lockheed-Martin after 1993)., Marietta, Georgia
Total produced: 51
Power plant: Four 4,910-hp Allison T-56-15 turboprop engines driving four-bladed Aeroproducts constant-speed, fully-reversible propellers.
Armament: Two 20-mm M61A1 rotary cannons (one 25-mm GAU-12 rotary cannon on AC-130U), one (dual mount) 40-mm Bofors L60 cannon, and one 105-mm M102 howitzer.
Performance: Max. speed 300-mph. at s.l., ceiling 25,000 ft.; range 1,495 mi. max.
Weights: 155,000-lbs. max. takeoff.
Dimensions: Span 132 ft. 7 in., length 97 ft. 9 in., 1,223 sq. ft.

Considered by military experts to be the best all-around tactical transport ever built, the venerable Lockheed C-130 *Hercules* has also become the most potent side-firing firing gunship in existence. In the wake of the success the AC-47 "Spooky, " the USAF initiated Project Gunship II in early 1967 to convert a number of its older C-130As to a gunship configuration under the designation AC-130A. In addition to being more heavily armed than the AC-47, the AC-130A was equipped with a more sophisticated avionics suite that included a forward-looking infrared system (FLIR), side-looking radar, beacon tracking radar, plus a fire-control computer and a 20-kilowatt illuminator. Testing of the first modified example began in June 1967, and the aircraft deployed to Nha Trang AB in South Vietnam the following September, where it immediately commenced combat evaluations. The first truck-hunting interdiction sorties along the Ho Chi Minh Trail were flown in November. Between 1968 and 1970, 18 more C-130As received the gunship conversion, of which 14 were deployed for combat to Ubon RTAFB as part of the 16th Special Operations Squadron. The first of 11 AC-130E "Pave Spectre" aircraft (subsequently shortened to Spectre, which became the call sign for all AC-130s) was completed in December 1971, and following installation of a 105-mm howitzer, deployed to Ubon for combat testing in early 1972. After the first aircraft was damaged, the second howitzer-armed AC-130E resumed testing, and by the end of March 1972, 32 sorties had been flown over the Ho Chi Minh Trail in which 218 trucks had been destroyed, 76-percent with the 105-mm cannon. Despite their small numbers, the Ubon-based AC-130s accounted for a large majority of the 10,609 trucks destroyed during the Vietnam conflict, against a loss of five aircraft to enemy action.

In late 1972 the USAF instituted a major gunship upgrade program that resulted in the

Top: Early AC-130A shown in Vietnam-era markings. The first gunship variants were converted from USAF's oldest C-130A airframes and were actually tested in combat before the first AC-119s. *Bottom:* LocAC-130H. AC-130H with the 16th Special Operations Wings based at Hurlbert Field in Florida. The H models have been augmented by the AC-130U, which has twice the munitions capacity and can fire at two different targets simultaneously.

AC-130H. The H, in addition to more powerful T-56-15 engines, received enhanced night detection and fire-control systems such as a moving target indicator/forward-looking search radar, heads-up-display (HUD) gun sights for the pilot and fire-control officer, low-level-light television camera (LLLTV), laser target designator, side-looking tracking radar, and Black Crow Direction Finder (detected signals emitted by vehicle ignitions), plus flare pods for protection against heat-seeking missiles. The first AC-130Hs were based at Ubon during the final months of the Vietnam War. During the invasion of Granada in 1983, Spectres were used to suppress enemy air defense systems and provide close air support to American troops, and in 1989, they were called upon again to destroy the Panamanian centers of command and control in Operation Just Cause. When Operation Desert Storm commenced in January 1991, AC-130 gunships were tasked to fly missions for air base defense and close air support for coalition forces, during which time one aircraft lost to ground fire.

In mid–1987 Rockwell International received a contract to modify 13 aircraft to into the more advanced AC-130U gunship configuration, involving installation of an armor protection system, high-resolution sensors, infrared detection system, multi-mode strike radar, new electronic warfare systems, and a software-controlled fire-control system. The new strike radar provided extreme long-range target detection and worked in conjunction with a fire-control system that allowed two targets within a kilometer of each other to be simultaneously engaged by different weapons. The AC-130U possessed twice the munitions capacity of the H and included more advanced systems for defensive countermeasures. After being flown in late 1990, the AC-130U underwent testing and evaluation until 1994. The 16th Special Operations Wing at Hurlbert Field in Florida received their first AC-130Us in mid–1994, and since September 11, 2001, AC-130H/U gunships have been widely used to provide armed reconnaissance, interdiction, and close air support in Operation Enduring Freedom and Operation Iraqi Freedom. According to recent figures, there are currently eight AC-130Hs and thirteen AC-130Us in active USAF service.

Since 2001, the USAF has been pursuing a project known as gunship-transport experimental [AC(X)] with the aim of finding an eventual replacement for the AC-130 sometime in the 2015–2020 timeframe. Compared to the AC-130, the AC(X) will reportedly be smaller, more maneuverable, and possess stealth-like characteristics.

North American AT-28 Nomad 1963–1964

TECHNICAL SPECIFICATIONS (AT-28D)
Type: Two-place attack-trainer.
Manufacturer: North American Aviation, Inc., Inglewood, California.
Total produced: 393
Power plant: One 1,425-hp Wright R-1820–86 9-cylinder, air-cooled radial engine driving a three-bladed Hamilton Standard constant-speed propeller.
Armament: Two .50-caliber machine guns and up to 1,800-lbs. of bombs or rockets carried on four underwing stations.
Performance: Max. speed 352-mph. at 18,000 ft., cruising 203-mph; ceiling (not listed); range 1,355 mi. max.
Weights: 7,750-lbs. empty, 15,600-lb. max. takeoff.
Dimensions: Span 40 ft. 7 in., length 32 ft. 10 in., 271 sq. ft.

After having served for over ten years as USAF and Navy trainers, surplus T-28s were turned into combat aircraft for the counter-insurgency (COIN) role. Previous to this, in the late 1950s, France had performed a number of T-28 attack conversions, known as *Fennecs*, to be used in their conflict in Algeria. Then in 1961, when the USAF suddenly found itself in need of a light attack aircraft for the military assistance program (MAP) in Southeast Asia, North

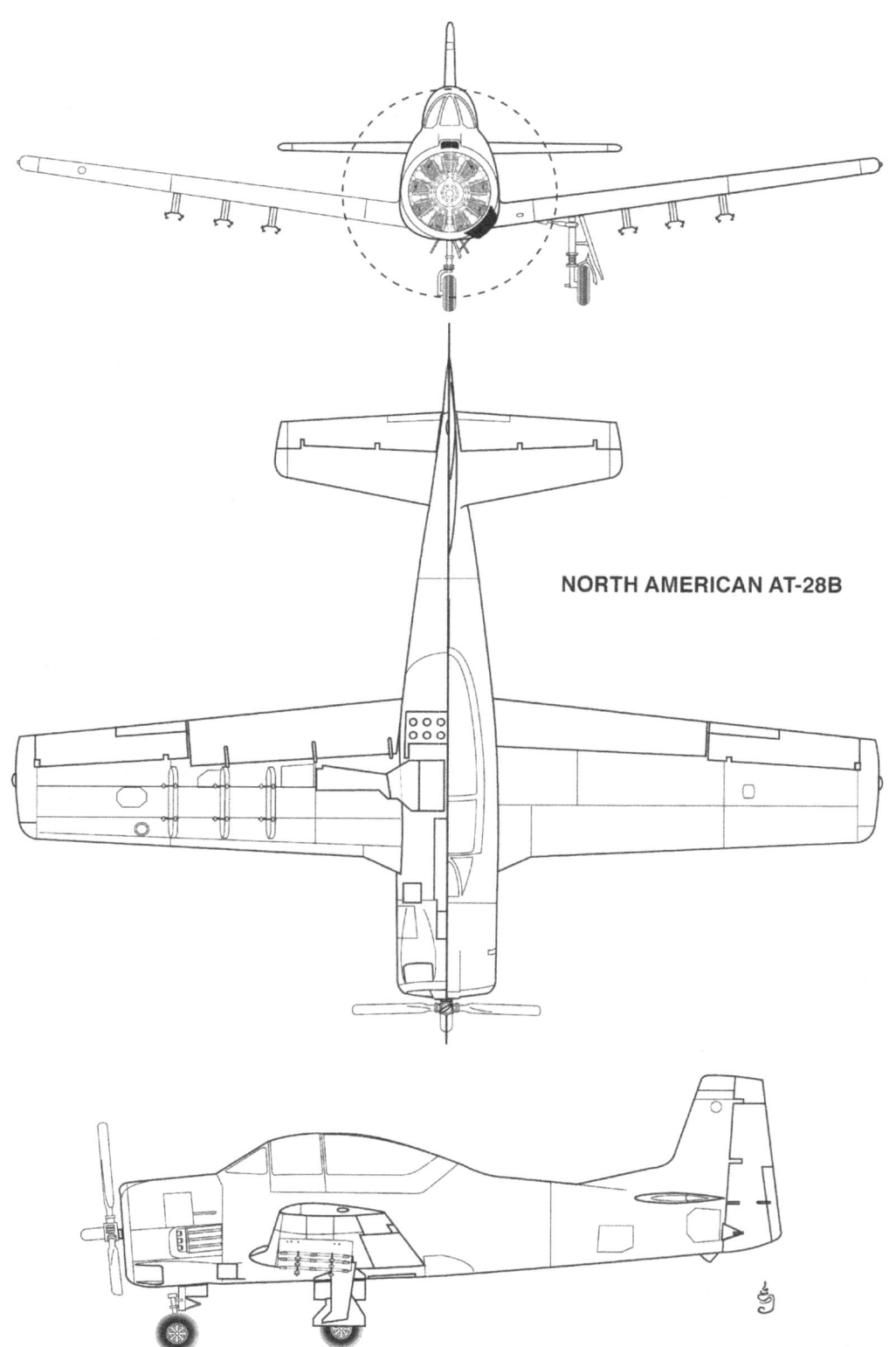

Fourth Series (Adapted Attack Aircraft) • 1950–Present

Two well-worn AT-28Ds about to depart on a mission from a South Vietnamese base, probably in 1963 or 1964. The 1st Air Commando Group stopped operating them after experiencing wing failures caused by the stress of carrying weapons.

American was asked to refurbish and add armament to T-28Ds that had previously been placed in storage. The conversion, 393 of which were completed by North American and Fairchild between 1961 and 1969, entailed mounting two .50-caliber machine guns in pods under the wings plus racks for bombs or rockets. The first 31 AT-28Ds arrived in South Vietnam in late 1962 to form the 2nd Fighter Squadron of the Vietnamese Air Force (VNAF). As part of Operation Farm Gate, the AT-28s, carrying VNAF markings and observers, were in fact flown by American pilots attached to the 1st Air Commando Squadron. After completing numerous combat sorties against Viet Cong targets, American operation of the AT-28s ceased in early 1964 when two USAF pilots were killed as a result of wing failures. Even so, AT-28Ds were supplied through MAP to air forces of Cambodia, Laos, Thailand, Argentina, Bolivia, Zaire (Congo), Ecuador, Ethiopia, Haiti, Philippines, South Korea, and Taiwan.

During early 1963, as a follow-up to the AT-28D, North American tried to market the YAT-28E, a variant powered by a 2,445-hp Lycoming YT-55 turboprop and capable of carrying 4,000-lbs. of bombs or rockets, however, when no orders were forthcoming, the project was cancelled.

Lockheed AT-33 1960–1980

TECHNICAL SPECIFICATIONS (AT-33A)

Type: Two-place attack-trainer.
Manufacturer: Lockheed Aircraft Corp., Burbank, California.
Total produced: 5,691 (U.S. production).
Power plant: One Allison J-33-35 turbojet engine, rated at 5,400-lbs./s.t.

The aircraft depicted is actually a T-33A belonging to the 103rd Tactical Fighter Group of the Connecticut ANG. AT-33s, none of which ever served in the USAF, were equipped with two .50-caliber machine guns and four underwing stations for weapons.

Armament: Two .50-caliber machine guns and up to 2,000-lbs. of bombs or rockets carried on four underwing stations.
Performance: Max. speed 525-mph. at 5,000 ft., cruising 440-mph; ceiling 45,000 feet.; range 1,100 mi. max.
Weights: 8,084-lbs. empty, 14,442-lb. max. takeoff.
Dimensions: Span 38 ft. 11 in., length 37 ft. 9 in., 238 sq. ft.

The ubiquitous T-33 "T-Bird," produced as an advanced jet trainer for the USAF and Navy from 1948 to 1959, was later supplied in large numbers to foreign nations through military assistance programs, where many were thereafter adapted to a light attack configuration as the AT-33A. While no attack variants are known to have been operated by U.S. forces, they served in tactical role with the air forces of Bolivia, Ecuador, Iran, Japan, Mexico, Paraguay, South Korea, Thailand, and Turkey, some reportedly remaining in service until the 1980s.

Cessna A(T)-37 Dragonfly 1964–1992

TECHNICAL SPECIFICATIONS (A-37B)

Type: Two-place light attack.
Manufacturer: Cessna Aircraft Co., Wichita, Kansas.
Total produced: 618 (all versions).
Power plant: Two General electric J-85-17A turbojet engines, each rated at 2,850-lbs./s.t.
Armament: One 7.62-mm GAU-2/A rotary minigun and up to 6,000-lbs. of mixed ordnance on eight underwing stations.
Performance: Max. speed 502-mph at 12,000 ft., cruising 304-mph; ceiling 41,800 feet.; range 246 mi. loaded, 1,082 mi. max.

Fourth Series (Adapted Attack Aircraft) • 1950–Present

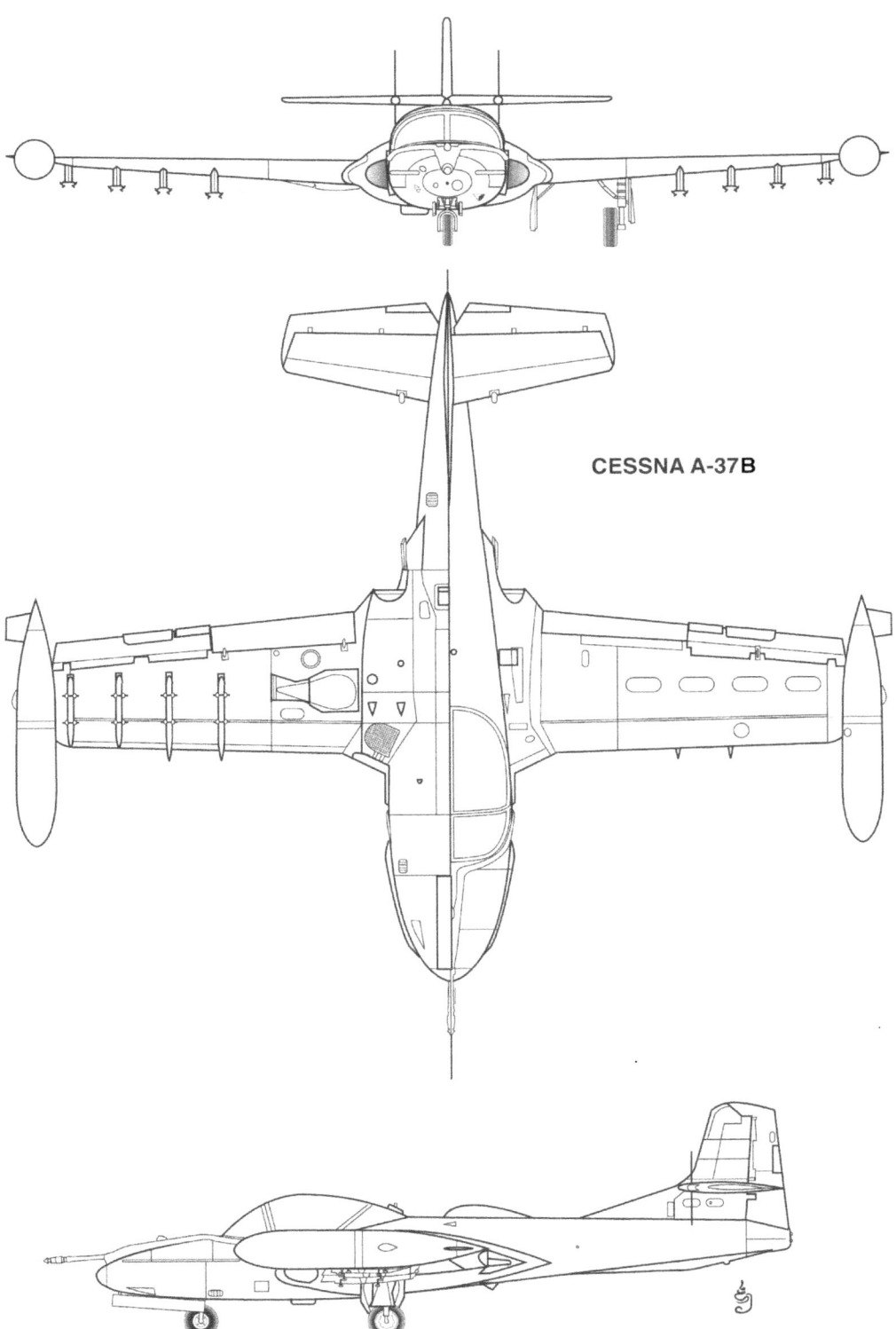

CESSNA A-37B

The first A-37B at Edwards AFB in 1968. Of the 577 A-37Bs built, 134 were delivered to the USAF and served in frontline units until 1975. The final examples were retired from USAFRES and ANG service in 1992.

Weights: 6,008-lbs. empty, 14,000-lb. max. takeoff.
Dimensions: Span 38 ft. 5 in., length 29 ft. 4 in., 184 sq. ft.

The Cessna A-37 stands out as one of the most successful adaptations of a trainer airframe to the light attack role. Increasing USAF interest in developing a low-cost aircraft for counter-insurgency (COIN) operations during the early 1960s led to a contract with Cessna in May 1963 to modify two T-37B trainers into a light attack configuration under the designation YAT-37D. The modifications entailed strengthening the wings and landing gear, plus adding 90-gallon tip tanks, a GAU-2/A minigun, six (eight on the second prototype) wing pylons for bombs or rockets, and a gun sight. To compensate for the more than doubled takeoff weight, J-85 engines replaced the Continental J-69s. The first YAT-37D made its maiden flight on October 22, 1963, and testing subsequently revealed the aircraft to be well suited to the light attack mission, but soon afterward, the COIN program became the victim of official indecision and both YAT-37Ds were consigned to the USAF Museum at Wright-Patterson AFB. Then in mid–1966, as U.S. involvement in Vietnam escalated and the need for a COIN aircraft became more apparent, the USAF issued Cessna a second contract to modify a further 39 T-37Bs as AT-37Ds, but by the time the first modified aircraft were delivered in July 1967, their designation had been changed to A-37A. In early 1967 Cessna received yet another contract for 57 new construction aircraft as the improved A-37B. The B, which made its first flight in May 1968, featured more airframe strengthening, uprated -17A engines, modified control surfaces, a mid-air refueling probe in the nose, updated instruments and avionics, plus provision for pod-mounted 20 or 30-mm underwing cannons. From 1968 to 1977 Cessna manufactured a total of 577 A-37Bs, of which 134 were delivered to the USAF and the balance to nations participating in the military assistance programs (MAP), mostly South Vietnam and Latin America.

In July 1967 new A-37As began entering service with the 604th Air Commando Squadron at England AFB in Louisiana and a month later, under a program known as "Combat Dragon," deployed to Bein Hoa AB in South Vietnam where they began 90 days of combat evaluations. When the program drew to a close, the A-37As had completed over 4,000 combat sorties without a single loss due to enemy action. The A-37B made it debut with the 4410th Combat Crew Training Wing during early 1968 to initiate training of Vietnamese Air Force (VNAF) personnel and later joined regular USAF Tactical Air Command units. A total of 254 A-37Bs were subsequently transferred to the VNAF, 95 of which fell into Communist hands when South Vietnam fell in early 1975. In 1975, all USAF A-37Bs were assigned to one USAF Reserve unit, the 434th Tactical Fight Wing at Grissom AFB, Indiana, and two Air National Guard units, the 174th Tactical Fighter Group in New York and the 175th TFG in Maryland. In USAFRES and ANG service, the aircraft were used in the forward air control role and re-designated OA-37Bs, the final examples being retired in 1992 when they were replaced by Fairchild OA-10As. Under MAP, A-37Bs were given to Peru (36), Chile (34), Columbia (26), Ecuador (12), Uruguay (8), Honduras (15), Guatemala (13), and El Salvador (18), and some of these reportedly remain in service today.

Northrop AT-38 Talon 1975–Present

TECHNICAL SPECIFICATIONS (AT-38B)
Type: Two-place light attack.
Manufacturer: Northrop Corp., Hawthorne, California.
Total produced: 30+
Power plant: Two General electric J-85-5A turbojet engines, each rated at 2,700-lbs./s.t. dry, 3,850-lbs./s.t. in afterburning.
Armament: One centerline pylon for carrying a bomb/rocket dispenser, gun pod, or bomb container.
Performance: Max. speed 812-mph (Mach 1.08) at s.l., cruising 592-mph (mach 0.9); ceiling 45,000 feet.; range 1,093 mi. max.
Weights: 7,165-lbs. empty, 12,093-lb. max. takeoff.
Dimensions: Span 25 ft. 3 in., length 46 ft. 4 in., 170 sq. ft.

Not to be confused with the two-seat F-5B/F reported earlier, the AT-38B is a minor modification of the USAF's T-38 advanced jet trainer. As part of a program initiated by the USAF in 1975 under the heading lead-in-fighter program (LIFT), a number of stock T-38Bs became AT-38Bs when they received gun sights and a centerline belly pylon that could be rigged for bombs, rockets, or gun pods. The weapons load could consist of a SUU-20 bomb/rocket dispenser, a SUU-11A 7.62-mm minigum pod, or an AF/B37K-1 bomb container. The purpose of the LIFT program was to provide recent pilot school graduates with a familiar aircraft for the transition to tactical training. The LIFT program ended in 1993 and the tactical curriculum was incorporated into undergraduate pilot training (UPT), following which the AT-38Bs, 30 of which are reported to be operating today, were transferred to the 12th Flying Training Wing at Randolph AFB in Texas. Whether these aircraft will receive the T-38C avionics and engine upgrade is not known.

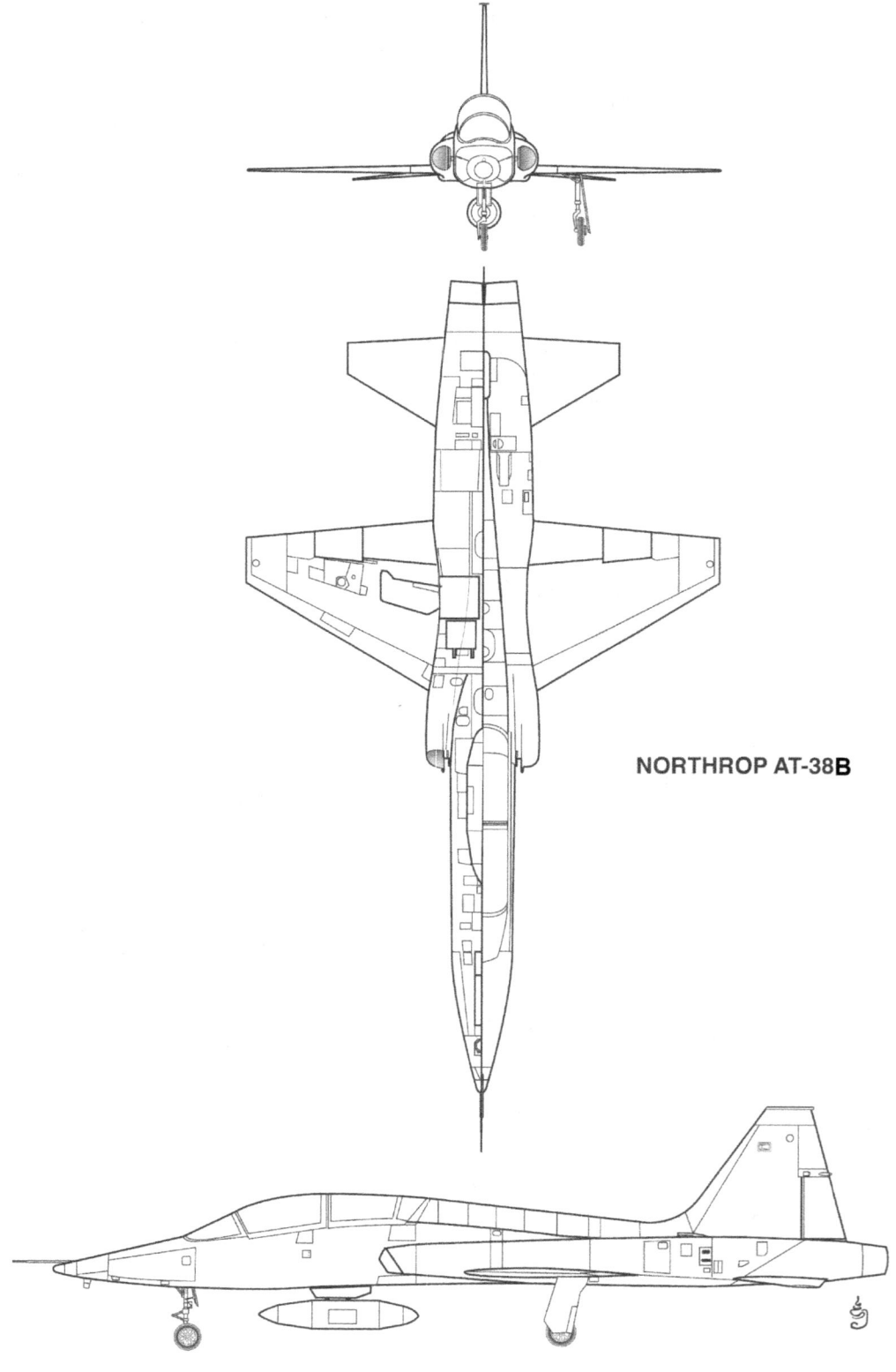

Fourth Series (Adapted Attack Aircraft) • 1950–Present

An AT-38B with the legend "AT-38 Lead-In Fighter" (LIFT) painted on the side of the fuselage. When the LIFT program was discontinued in 1993, all AT-38s were transferred to the 12th Flying Training Wing.

Convair (General Dynamics) Model 48 Charger 1964–1965

TECHNICAL SPECIFICATIONS (MODEL 48)

Type: Two-place light armed reconnaissance.
Manufacturer: Convair Division of General Dynamics Corp., San Diego, California.
Total produced: 1
Power plant: Two 650-shp Pratt & Whitney T-74-8 (PT6) turboprop engines driving three-bladed constant-speed, fully-reversible propellers.
Armament: Two 7.62-mm M60 machine guns and up 1,200-lbs. of bombs or rockets carried on one centerline and four wing stations.
Performance: Max. speed 319-mph at s.l.; ceiling 21,300 feet.; range 320mi. loaded, 1,990 mi. max.
Weights: 4,457-lbs. empty, 10,460-lb. max. takeoff.
Dimensions: Span 27 ft. 6 in., length 34 ft. 10 in., 192 sq. ft.

Going from initial design to flying prototype in a mere 25 weeks, the Model 48 became the last Convair aircraft to be completed at the San Diego plant. Its origins are traceable to a Department of Defense (DOD) requirement issued in September 1963 calling for a light, armed reconnaissance aircraft (LARA) that would be developed jointly for the USAF, Navy, and Marine Corps under a tri-service program. The requirement specified a two-place, twin-engine aircraft capable of operating from either unimproved airfields or aircraft carriers. Though the aircraft's primary mission would be armed reconnaissance, it would need to also be armed with four 7.62-mm M60 machine guns and carry up to 2,400-lbs of external munitions for close air support (CAS) operations. In March 1964, while DOD was still considering nine different proposals received on LARA designs, Convair, as a private venture, commenced construction of

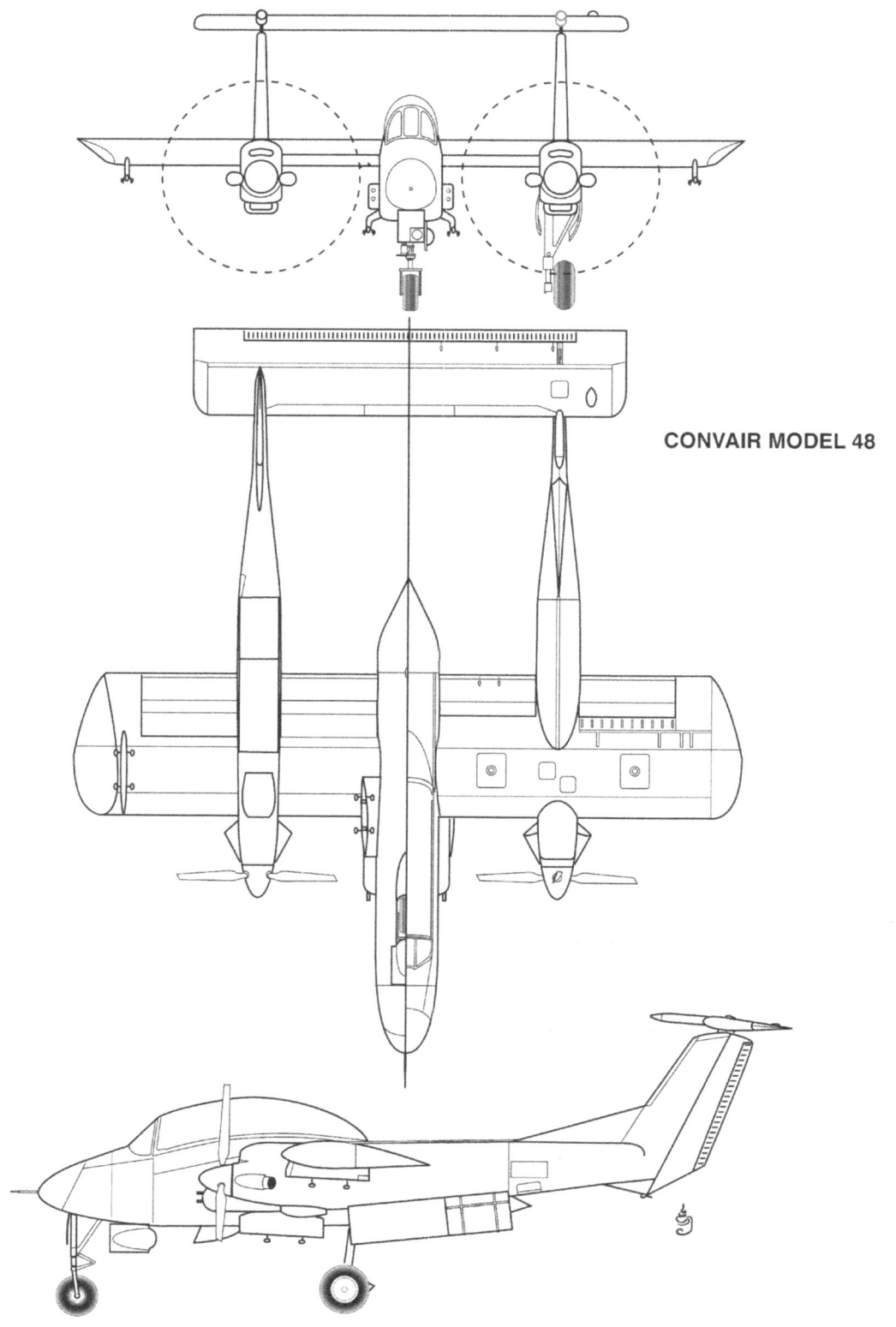

CONVAIR MODEL 48

The sole Model 48 prototype with civilian registration numbers shown in 1965. Although tested under the tri-service LARA program, the aircraft never received an official military designation.

its Model 48. Then after DOD announced North American's NA-300, designated YOV-10A, as the winning LARA design in August 1964, Convair protested the decision and continued work on its prototype, dubbed *Charger*, which flew a few months later on November 29.

The Model 48 (thought referred to sometimes as the OV-9, never received a military designation) was delivered in civilian registration (N28K) for military evaluations and thereafter flown by tri-service test pilots. When North American's rival YOV-10A appeared in mid–1965, the aerodynamic layout of the two aircraft was strikingly similar: twin booms; stubby, constant-chord wings; horizontal stabilizer high-mounted on swept fins; and aircrew seated well forward under a large canopy. During its 196th test flight on October 19, 1965, the Model 48 was completely destroyed after its Navy pilot successfully ejected from an altitude of 100 feet. After the crash, Convair elected to withdraw from the program.

North American (Rockwell) OV-10 Bronco 1965–1995

TECHNICAL SPECIFICATIONS (OV-10A)

Type: Two-place light armed reconnaissance.
Manufacturer: Rockwell Division of North American Aviation, Inc., Columbus, Ohio.
Total produced: 379 (all versions)
Power plant: Two 715-shp Garrett T-76-416/417 (opposite rotation) turboprop engines driving three-bladed constant-speed, fully-reversible propellers.
Armament: Four 7.62-mm M60 machine on sponsons, up to 4,600-lbs. of bombs or rockets carried on four sponson stations, fuselage centerline station for 20-mm gun pod, or two AIM-9 *Sidewinder* missiles on underwing stations.
Performance: Max. speed 281-mph at 5,000 ft., cruising 220-mph; ceiling 29,000 feet.; range 228 mi. loaded, 1,382 mi. max.
Weights: 7,190-lbs. empty, 14,444-lb. max. takeoff.
Dimensions: Span 40 ft., length 39 ft. 9 in., 291 sq. ft.

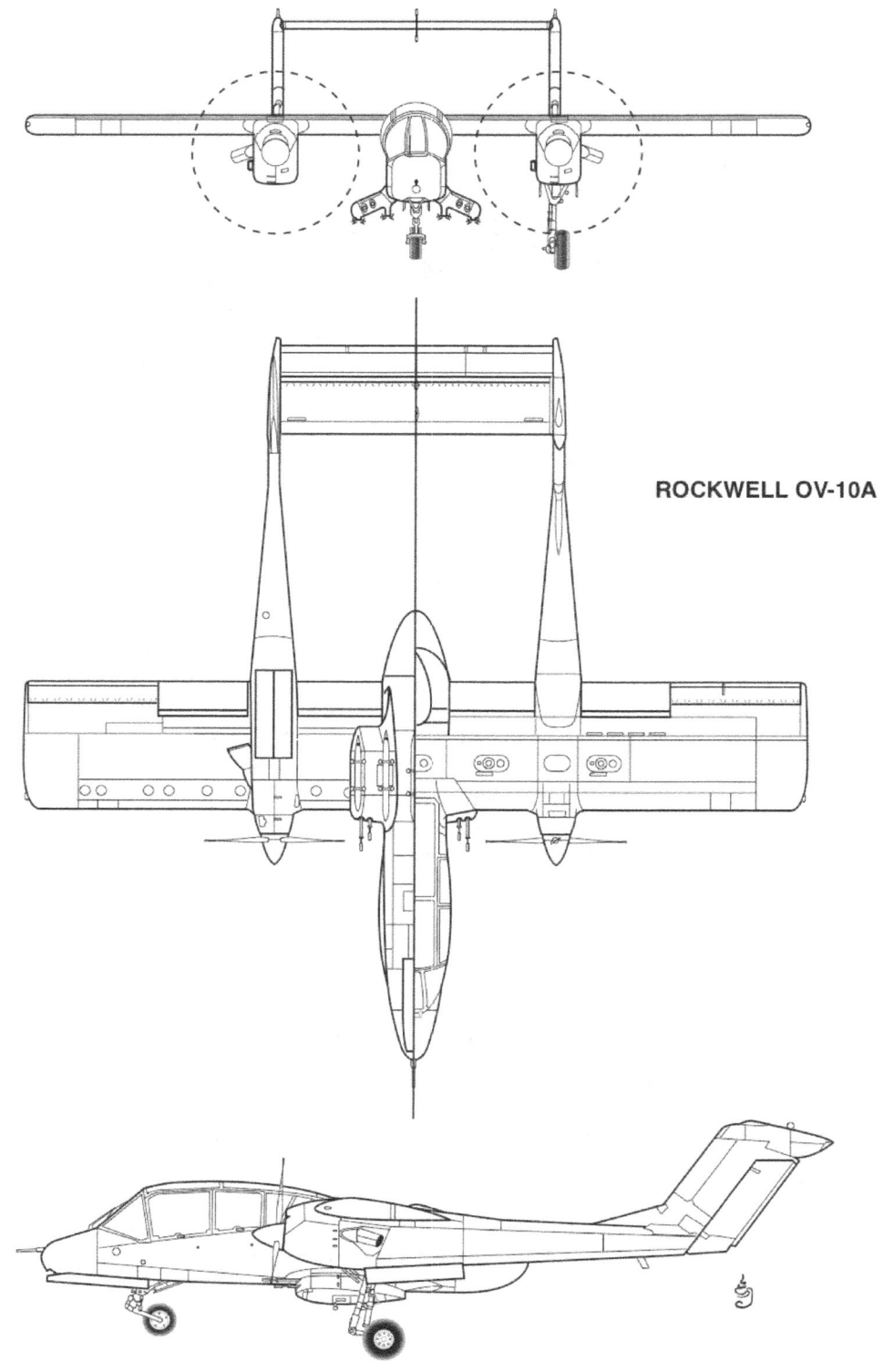

ROCKWELL OV-10A

OV-10A in overall gray USAF paint scheme. The type was phased out of USAF service during the late 1980s as OA-10As began assuming the FAC role. They remained active with the Marines until 1995.

The OV-10 was the first operational American military aircraft to be purpose-designed for the counter-insurgency (COIN) role. Department of Defense (DOD) studies that started in 1959 ultimately led, in September 1963, to the issuance of a requirement for what was termed a light, armed reconnaissance aircraft (LARA). The LARA, which would be developed under a tri-service scheme for the USAF, Navy, and Marine Corps, was perceived as an multi-role aircraft capable of operating from forward airstrips or roads or aircraft carriers. Its contemplated missions encompassed observation, forward air control (FAC), helicopter escort, armed reconnaissance, naval gunfire spotting, utility transportation, and limited close air support (CAS). Nine companies responded—Beech, Convair, Douglas, Grumman, Goodyear, Helio, Lockheed, Martin, and North American—and North American's NA-300 was selected as the winning proposal in August 1964, followed by a contract in October for seven aircraft under the designation YOV-10A.

The prototype emerged as a twin-boom planform featuring opposite rotation turboprop engines, wide constant-chord wings, horizontal stabilizer set on top of twin vertical fins, and pilot and observer seated in tandem under a bulbous canopy. The first YOV-10A flew on July 16, 1965 and was delivered for tri-service evaluations soon thereafter. North American received a production contract for 271 OV-10As, 157 for the USAF and 114 for the Marine Corps, in October 1966, and the first production model flew in August 1967. Production OV-10As differed from the prototypes in having a five-foot extension added to each wing, slightly greater span between the booms, more armor protection, additional weapons stores, and uprated (+115-hp each) engines, and all had been delivered by April 1969. In 1970, 18 unarmed OV-10Bs were delivered to the West German Air Force to be used as target tugs and 38 armed OV-10Cs were built for Thailand. From 1973 to 1976, North American completed a further 52 aircraft similar to the OV-10A, 16 to Venezuela as the OV-10E, 12 to Indonesia as the OV-10F, and finally, 24 to South Korea as the OV-10G, after which all OV-10 production ended. During 1971 two Marine OV-10As were specially modified for night operations when they received a forward-looking infrared (FLIR) sensor and a M-197 three-barrel 20-mm cannon mounted in a turret under the nose, and were re-designated OV-10D. The aiming of the cannon was slaved to the FLIR system. Starting in 1979, a further 17 OV-10D conversions were completed for the Marines, including an upgrade to 1,040-shp -420/-421 engines with heat-suppressing exhaust stacks. In 1988 the Marines instituted a program known as OV-10D+ in which the airframes were refurbished to extend service life and improvements made to instruments and avionics.

OV-10As began entering USAF service in early 1968 and had commenced FAC operations out of South Vietnam with Tactical Air Support Squadrons by mid–1968. USAF OV-10s also flew rescue combat air patrol missions to assist with the recovery of downed aircrew, and a small number based in Thailand were equipped with Pave Nail laser designation systems to guide smart bombs in attacks on the Ho Chi Minh Trail. From 1968 to 1975, 64 USAF OV-10s serving in Southeast Asia were lost due to all causes. After Vietnam, a number of USAF OV-10s were reassigned to units in Europe and last examples were replaced by OA-10As in the late 1980s; none were ever transferred to the Air Force Reserve or Air National Guard. OV-10As first entered service with the Marines in February 1968 and commenced combat operations out of Da Nang AB with VMO-2 the following July. Over the next year, OV-10s equipped four more Marine squadrons, VMO-1 and -6 in Vietnam and VMO-4 and -8 in the U.S. In January 1969, the Navy acquired 18 OV-10As from the Marines and formed VAL-4, which was tasked with the mission of supporting riverine craft operating in Vietnam's Mekong Delta. During 1971 the Marines flew its two modified OV-10Ds in Vietnam in a combat test program known as Night Observation Gunship. After 1979, the Marines maintained one reserve squadron of OV-10As and one active Squadron of OV-10Ds, the last examples being retired in 1995.

PART II
USN and USMC Attack Aircraft

HISTORICAL NOTE

> "Naval aviation cannot take the offensive from the shore;
> it must go to sea on the back of the fleet.... The fleet and naval aviation
> are one and inseparable." — Rear Admiral William A. Moffett,
> First Chief of the Naval Bureau of Aeronautics, 1921–1933.

The Role of the Aircraft Carrier

When HMS *Furious*, the world's first true aircraft carrier, made its appearance in 1917, the dominant view within the British Admiralty was that this new type of ship should be operated well behind the screening force where its aircraft would function primarily in a reconnaissance role. Over twenty years later, in late 1941 and early 1942, when confronted with war in Europe, North Africa, and Asia, Britain found herself unable to effectively counteract the might of the Japanese Imperial Navy. Japan, using invasion forces backed by aircraft carriers, swept the British from their Far East possessions in a matter of months. By that time, the only way to defeat carriers was with opposing carriers.

The American experience, fortunately, was considerably different. When the first aircraft carriers began entering service with the U. S. Navy (i.e., *Langley* in 1922, followed by *Lexington* and *Saratoga* in 1927), Rear Admiral William A. Moffett, the chief of the newly-created Naval Bureau of Aeronautics (BUAER) from 1921 to 1933, successfully advocated that the most important role of aircraft serving aboard the new carriers, in addition to scouting and observation, was to attack the enemy and thereby enlarge the fleet's striking power. At that time, there was much debate going on within the U. S. military establishment as to the emerging role of air power in the nation's future. At one extreme, Brigadier General Billy Mitchell of the Army's Air Service, insisted, to the point of a court martial, that military aviation be totally separated from *both* the Army and the Navy. Moffett, in a studied contrast, lobbied very carefully to integrate his fledgling carrier force into an overall fleet strategy then dominated by the Battle Line (i.e., battleship divisions). As a result of his efforts, plus other men like Captain Joseph M. Reeves (first commanding officer of Aircraft, Battle Fleet) and Admiral Ernest J. King (Chief of BUAER 1933–1939, Chief of Naval Operations 1942–1945), the U. S. Navy by the mid 1930s had become a leading power in the development of a carrier-borne striking force with only one serious rival, the Imperial Japanese Navy. By the eve of World War II, America's Navy numbered a force of seven fleet carriers[1] and with three more under construction, versus Japan's eight with four under construction. After the Japanese attack on December 7, 1941, with most of the Pacific Fleet's Battle Line lying on the bottom of Pearl Harbor, the U.S. Navy's aircraft carriers replaced battleships as the foremost weapon of its wartime Battle Groups/Task Forces, and their attack aircraft became the point of the spear. In the 62 years that have elapsed since the end of World War II, the essential role of the aircraft carrier—projecting strategic power at any point from the sea—has remained largely unchanged. During this timeframe, the United States has enjoyed an unchallenged superiority and, indeed, is the only nation today whose navy operates a carrier force of any significance.

The Emergence of Marine Corps Aviation

Organization. From its inception in 1912 up to the present day, Marine aviation has played a unique role in naval aviation. The earliest Marine aviation units were attached to various commands with no central scheme of organization, but commencing with the establishment of the Fleet Marine Force (FMF) in 1933, Marine aviation was divided between FMF Aircraft One on the west coast and FMF Aircraft Two on the east coast, and with variations, a similar structure of organization remains in effect today.[2] FMF was created with the prime mission of conducting offensive amphibious operations, which, since World War II, has been expanded to include specialized expeditionary campaigns. The express job of Marine aviation in the interval has been to provide FMF's tactical air support in the form of: (1) anti-air warfare; (2) offensive air support; (3) reconnaissance; (4) assault support; (5) electronic warfare [EW]; and (6) control of aircraft and missiles. EW and control of missiles are obviously post–World War II additions to the doctrine. As part of (2), which combines close air support [CAS] with deep air support [DAS[3]] to seal off the assault zone, Marines have evolved a particular type of CAS that serves as a substitute when artillery is not available.

One of the deep-rooted historical features of Marine aviation has been (and still is) its organic relationship to the FMF command structure. Experience gained during the Vietnam War led to the establishment of the Marine Air-Ground Task Force (MAGTF) organization structure in the late 1970s. Depending on the scope of the tactical objective, the aviation component of an MAGTF might comprise anything from one squadron to two complete air wings. An air wing, like the Second Marine Air Wing based at MCAS Cherry Point, North Carolina, consists today of seven fighter-attack squadrons (F/A-18s), four attack squadrons (AV-8Bs), plus four electronic warfare squadrons (EA-6Bs), two aerial refueling squadrons (KC-130s), one transport squadron (C-9s), eleven helicopter squadrons, a support group, and an air control group.

Aircraft Procurement. The types of aircraft used by the Marine Corps over the years have largely been shaped by two factors. First, the very specialized and focused nature of FMF's mission, together with the fact it has not materially changed in 70-plus years, has dictated the types and quantities of aircraft needed. From the pre–World War II era up to present day, fighters and dedicated attack aircraft (in approximately equal proportions) have formed the bulk of Marine aviation's fixed-wing combat arm. And within those proportions, Marine

---

1. Lexington, Saratoga, Ranger, Yorktown, Enterprise, Hornet, and Wasp. CV-9, -10, and -11 were under construction. Langley had been converted to a seaplane tender in 1937.
2. Presently, the First and Third Marine Air Wings are attached to Marine Forces Pacific (MARFORPAC) and the Second Marine Air Wing to Marine Forces Atlantic (MARFORLANT).
3. DAS is a Marine Corps term which combine elements of BAI and AI with armed reconnaissance.

fighters have typically flown a higher ratio of fighter-bomber sorties than their Navy counterparts. The second factor has been Marine aviation's almost symbiotic relationship to an aircraft development and procurement process dominated by the Navy (i.e., BUAER/BUWEPS). In terms of overall naval procurement, only a handful of aircraft have been built solely to Marine Corps requirements,[4] and at times, Marine aviation units have been reequipped with new types of aircraft at noticeably slower rates than Navy fleet squadrons.[5] Nevertheless, Marines have historically demonstrated admirable talent for optimizing the use of whatever aircraft they happen to have on hand and have performed the mission given them with fewer types of aircraft.[6] Interestingly, Marine Aviation made the transition to an all-jet strike force sooner than the Navy, trading-in its last propeller-driven Douglas AD-6 (A-1H) for the Douglas A4D-2 (A-4B) during the middle of 1959.

Naval Attack Aircraft Procurement

Post–World War I. In conjunction with carrier program itself, the first 20 years of carrier aviation was a period of steady, if not rapid, progress in the development of attack aircraft and their mission. When *Langley* was commissioned in March 1922, the Navy possessed no made-for-purpose carrier aircraft and had yet to develop any practical criteria upon which new aircraft requirements could be issued. Until 1927, the Navy used modified landplanes and floatplanes like Vought VE-7s and Aeromarine 39-Bs to evaluate types of arresting gear, develop procedures for handling aircraft aboard ship, and train the very first group of carrier pilots. Even after *Lexington* and *Saratoga* entered service in late 1927, budgetary constraints obliged the newly-established carrier air groups to make due with a variegated mix of aircraft, many of which were obsolescent floatplane and landplane designs adapted for carrier use. Moreover, to perform the many tasks needed from their aircraft, the early air groups often operated up to six difference types of planes—bombers, fighters, scouts, torpedo planes, observation, and utility—which was further complicated by the fact that most of these types had been constructed by different airframe manufacturers.

One of BUAER's early goals in issuing aircraft requirements was to combine as many functions possible into fewer airframes. What the air groups needed were more fighters to improve air superiority around the Battle Group and more dedicated attack aircraft to enlarge the fleet's offensive striking power. Toward this end, requirements for new carrier aircraft issued from 1927–1935 underwent an interesting series of permutations (e.g., torpedo planes, scouts, bombers, bomber-fighters, two-seat fighters, and single-seat fighters) until BUAER settled on a pattern for three basic types: (1) single-seat fighters [F] to provide air superiority around the Battle Group, escort the attack force, and, alternatively, function in a fighter-bomber role; (2) two-seat scout bombers [SB], which combined the functions of scouting (highly important in the days before radar) and dive-bombing in one airplane; and (3) three-seat torpedo bombers [TB] capable of either launching torpedoes or making level bombing runs. From about 1938 the typical air group was composed of four squadrons of 15–20 aircraft apiece, to wit: one fighter (VF), two scout-bomber (normally one VS and one VB), and

---

4. *Curtiss F8C-1 (1927), Chance Vought AU-1 (1952), McDonnell Douglas OA/A-4M (1970), McDonnell Douglas AV-8A/B (1971); the North American Rockwell OV-10 (1968) was developed as a tri-service (Army/USAF/ USMC) project. The McDonnell RF-4B was also ordered solely for Marine use.*

5. *The Marine Corps did not receive any monoplane scout bombers until late 1940 and continued to operate obsolescent biplane fighters right up to the end of 1941. A decade later during the Korean War, Navy attack squadrons received a far greater proportion of Douglas ADs, while many Marine squadrons continued to operate their old Chance Vought F4Us well into 1954.*

6. *In World War Two, the majority of Marine strike sorties were flown by Douglas SBDs, Chance Vought F4Us, and Grumman TBFs/TBMs; in Korea, by Chance Vought F4Us, Grumman F9Fs, and Douglas ADs; in Vietnam, by Douglas A-4s, McDonnell F-4s, and Grumman A-6s; and today with McDonnell Douglas F/A-18s and AV-8s.*

one torpedo-bomber (VT), and this formed the basic air group pattern for fleet carriers until the middle of World War II.

While BUAER made considerable progress in establishing the functional criteria for carrier aircraft, it was decidedly slow in taking advantage of certain advances seen in the aeronautical state-of-the-art during the 1930s. Chief among its concerns was the higher landing speeds and unforgiving stall characteristics exhibited by many of the new all-metal monoplane designs, with the result that biplanes types continued to make up most of the fleet's fighter and attack aircraft force right up to the end of 1939, and, indeed, small numbers remained in service at the beginning of World War Two.[7] BUAER's conservative approach to innovation was nowhere more apparent than in 1934–1935 when it issued simultaneous requirements for new monoplane and biplane torpedo and scout-bombers as a hedge against the possibility that the monoplane types might fail to work out. However, as events turned out, the new monoplanes[8] generally out-performed the biplanes, while still demonstrating acceptable approach speeds and wave-off characteristics. The first monoplane scout and torpedo-bombers began reaching fleet squadrons in late 1937;[9] however, the re-equipping process was lethargic and did not keep pace with the formation of new air groups necessitated by new carriers coming into commission (i.e., *Ranger* in 1934, *Yorktown* in 1937, *Enterprise* in 1938, *Wasp* in 1940, and *Hornet* in 1941).

World War II. The outbreak of war in Europe in 1939, coupled with serious concerns over Japan's intentions in the Pacific, induced U. S. policy-makers to lay plans for an unprecedented expansion of naval aviation. In 1940 the U.S. Congress authorized a massive carrier construction program, encompassing not only a new class of fleet carriers but providing for light carriers (CVLs) and escort carriers (CVEs) as well; and to equip the emergent carrier force, BUAER pressed aircraft companies hard to develop new types of combat aircraft and announced plans to order them in unheard of quantities. But the effect was far from instantaneous, so that by December of 1941, the Navy's inventory of dedicated attack aircraft stood at only 809 torpedo and scout-bombers. During the course of World War II, this figure grew exponentially, rising to 10,038 attack aircraft on hand by the middle of 1945.

The early carrier battles of World War II taught naval strategists that a higher ratio of fighter aircraft was needed in the carrier air groups to insure air superiority around the Task Force itself and provide better protection for the aircraft of the carriers' attack force. As a result, a decision was made in early 1943 to downsize the complement of torpedo and scout-bombers and replace them over time with one type of single-seat, multi-role attack aircraft under the new designation bomber-torpedo (BT). With extra fighter protection, attack aircraft would no longer need to carry gunners, and the weight normally associated with aircrew, guns, and ammunition could be exchanged for useful load and greater range. Moreover, with the more powerful engines becoming available,[10] the new BT types were likely to lift over twice the payload of existing torpedo and scout-bombers, thereby reducing the numbers of attack aircraft needed by half. To optimize overall mission flexibility, BUAER added the specification that all ordnance be carried under the aircraft on external racks. A competition between four different airframe contractors extending into the early post-war period ultimately resulted in the selection of the Douglas's celebrated AD[11] *Skyraider* as the fleet's premier aerial attack weapon.

---

7. *In December 1941, Curtiss SBC-4s were operating with VB-8, VS-8, VMO-151, and VMO-155, and Grumman F3F-2s with VMF-111 and VMF-211, though none saw any combat.*
8. *Douglas TBD-1, Chance Vought SB2U-1, and Brewster SBA-1.*
9. *The Navy's first monoplane fighter, the Brewster F2A-1, did not become operational until June 1940.*
10. *Wright R-3350 (2,500-hp.) and Pratt & Whitney R-4360 (3,000-hp.)*
11. *The bomber-torpedo (BT) designation was dropped in favor of attack (A) in 1946.*

Historical Note

Post-War Changes. Despite the rapid advances in jet propulsion that immediately followed World War II, propeller-driven aircraft with piston engines continued to form Navy and Marine aviation's principal attack component right up until the late 1950s, and the reasons were fundamentally practical. First, an across-the board reduction in naval appropriations in 1949 resulted in cancellation of the Navy's "super carrier" program and placed serious restrictions on funds available for future aircraft development and procurement. Second, the small number of fleet carriers remaining in commission,[12] while capable of handling the early generation of jet fighters (e.g., Grumman F9Fs and McDonnell F2Hs), would require extensive modifications to accommodate jet-powered attack aircraft operating at greater weights and speeds. Although budgetary restrictions were lifted after the start of the Korean War in June 1950, it took years longer to modernize the existing carrier fleet, and new carriers specifically built to handle jets did not even begin entering service until late 1955.[13] As a result, no pure-jet attack aircraft reached active naval units until 1956,[14] and the transition to jets was not fully accomplished until 1968.

After the United States successfully developed the atomic bomb in 1945, the Navy lobbied hard to gain a share of the responsibility for delivering nuclear weapons against the strategic targets of America's potential enemies. Naval advocates reasoned that carriers would provide mobile launching platforms capable of operating close to enemy waters. This policy led BUAER to issue a requirement in 1946 for a large, multi-engine attack aircraft that could operate from *Midway* class CVBs and be capable of lifting the 10,000-lb. payload required for early versions of the atomic bomb. The first aircraft developed for this mission[15] used composite powerplants (i.e., two piston engines and one turbojet) and became operational in late 1949. But in 1947, while these aircraft were still in the development stage, BUAER came out with an altogether new specification for a twin-jet nuclear attack bomber intended to operate from the Navy's hoped-for class of super carriers. The abrupt cancellation of that program in 1949 forced the Navy to place its jet bomber program on hold, so that no aircraft designed to this specification flew until 1952 (i.e., the Douglas A3D-1 [A-3A]) and none entered carrier service until 1956, by which time the carrier modernization program was well underway and the *Forrestal* and her sister ships were coming into service. An unsolicited proposal given to the Navy by North American in 1954 resulted in the development of the Mach 2 A3J-1 (A-5A), which made its maiden flight in August 1958 and its operational debut four years later. By that time, however, the Navy was in the process of phasing out its carrier-borne nuclear mission in favor of submarine-launched ballistic missiles (i.e., FBMs), with the program being formally discontinued in 1964.

During the Cold War era (1945–1991) the nuclear mission was expanded to tactical objectives. From a naval perspective, the tactical nuclear option contemplated an all-out war scenario (i.e., World War III) in which the carrier force, stationed at strategic points around the globe, would be used to unleash enormous striking power against sea and land-based forces of the Soviet Union. Atomic bombs light and compact enough to be carried externally by single-seat strike aircraft appeared in the early 1950s,[16] and the first naval attack aircraft especially configured to carry them, propeller-driven Douglas AD-4Bs, entered service in 1952, followed within a year by jet-powered McDonnell F2H-2Bs. Since that time tactical nuclear capability has become a standard feature on all naval attack aircraft, even if nuclear weapons are no longer carried aboard today's carrier force.

12. Three Midway *class and four* Essex *class carriers in 1950; most of the carrier force had been mothballed.*
13. Forrestal *(1955),* Saratoga *(1956),* Ranger *(1957), and* Independence *(1959).*
14. *Douglas A-3A (A3D-1) in March 1956 and Douglas A-4A (A4D-1) in October 1956.*
15. *The North American AJ-1. As a stopgap measure, the Navy commenced the nuclear mission with Lockheed P2V-3Cs, modified land-based patrol bombers that would be hoisted aboard the carrier, take off with the assistance of JATO rockets, then, theoretically, recover at a land bases.*
16. *The Mark 7 (1,650-lbs.) and Mark 8 (3,230-lbs.) were originally developed for the USAF.*

Korea and Vietnam. The vital tactical support role played by Navy carriers throughout the Korean War showed planners at BUAER[17] the value of combining fighter and attack functions into a single airframe. During Korea, Navy and Marine fighters primarily flew fighter-bomber sorties while most responsibility for air-to-air defense was given to the U. S. Air Force. The wisdom of a multi-role approach demonstrated itself a decade later when Navy and Marine Corps units found themselves in a far better position to conduct conventional tactical air operations in Southeast Asia than their USAF counterparts. Besides the Douglas A-4 and the newer two-place, all-weather Grumman A-6 (A2F), both leading naval fighters of that period, the Chance Vought F-8 (F8U)[18] and the McDonnell F-4 (F4H), had been designed with significant air-to-ground capabilities. Between 1961 and 1968 the "all-in-one" approach was carried to an extreme, however, when the Department of Defense (DOD) decreed that the Navy and the USAF jointly participate in the ill-fated TFX (tactical fighter experimental) project—the General Dynamics F-111. In theory, the plane would be able to perform every combat function except close air support, but following years of costly development, the naval version, the F-111B, was so overweight, complex, underpowered, and prohibitively expensive that the Navy was allowed to withdraw from the project in 1968.

Developments since 1970. In the aftermath of the F-111 debacle of the late 1960s, the Navy abandoned the all-in-one approach in favor of two separate projects—one for a dedicated fleet defense fighter and a second for a multi-mission "fighter-attack" type that would eventually replace the Douglas A-4, LTV A-7,[19] and Grumman A-6, plus retain the fighter-bomber capabilities of the McDonnell F-4. The fighter project, started earlier, resulted in the selection and development of the Grumman F-14, which shared the turbo-fan engines and variable-geometry planform of the F-111. The second program, known as VFAX (carrier fighter-attack experimental), underwent a number of variations before an airframe concept emerged. The Navy's original plan to develop a strike derivative of Grumman's F-14 (i.e., F-14X) was rejected by the House Armed Services Committee in early 1974 due to large cost overruns and development problems experienced in the fighter program. Then a few month's later, citing budgetary restrictions and reluctance to fund new and expensive aircraft programs, Congress informed naval officials that VFAX would be cancelled—the Navy and the Marines would simply have to make due with the strike aircraft on hand.[20]

Unwittingly, the Air Force came to the rescue. Its LWF/ACF (light-weight fighter/air combat fighter) contest had by that time had been narrowed down to a flyoff between two prototypes—the single-engine General Dynamics YF-16 and the twin-engine Northrop YF-17. In late 1974, under the aegis of a new program called NACF (Navy air combat fighter), Congress directed the Navy to investigate development of a navalized version of the LWF/ACF candidates as an alternative to VFAX. After considering NCAF proposals from both General Dynamics and Northrop, Navy officials subsequently determined that the airframe design and twin-engine layout of the YF-17 came closer to meeting their requirements, and because Northrop had no recent experience with carrier-based aircraft, McDonnell-Douglas was brought in to collaborate on the NCAF adaptation of the YF-17. Originally, distinct fighter versions and attack versions were to share a common airframe; however, further progress in development of the design made it practical to merge both functions into a single airplane. The fruit of this

---

17. *BUAER was absorbed into BUWEPS in 1959*
18. *The F8U-2NE (F-8E) of 1961 was the first version designed to carry out a strike role, and earlier versions were subsequently modified for air-to-ground operations as the F-8K and F-8L.*
19. *Chance Vought was merged into Ling-Temco-Vought (LTV) in 1961. The single-seat A-7, which performed essentially the same mission as the A-4, became operational in 1966.*
20. *This undoubtedly led to the remanufacture of 476 F-4Bs and F-4Js as F-4Ns and F-4Ss, the last examples of which were retired from active service in late 1980s.*

effort, the F/A-18,[21] flew in 1978 and became fully operational with Navy and Marine squadrons in 1983.

In the early and mid 1980s, the Navy became involved in two projects which, had they succeeded, would have equipped carrier aviation with an all-stealth strike and fighter force. The first project—ATA (advanced tactical aircraft)—entailed development of the McDonnell-Douglas/General Dynamics A-12, a two-place flying wing constructed largely of composite materials that was designed to assume the tactical bomber mission performed by the A-6. Originally, the Navy had planned to acquire 620 A-12s and the Marine Corps 238, with a projected service entry coinciding with the phase-out of the A-6 fleet in the mid–1990s. But as the A-12 neared the mockup stage, the project was plagued with such serious engineering problems and cost overruns the Navy announced cancellation of the entire project in early 1991. The Navy ran into similar difficulties with its plans to acquire navalized versions of the Air Force-derived ATF (advanced tactical fighter) as a stealth replacement for the F-14. As development of the ATF project unfolded, the winning design—the Lockheed YF-22[22]—had become too expensive to supply the numbers of aircraft the Navy would need after the year 2000.

Due to the cost risks associated with the navalized ATF, the Navy simultaneously investigated the feasibility of acquiring an improved derivative of the F/A-18 under a plan known as *Hornet 2000,* and this initiative eventually led to the development the F/A-18E/F *Super Hornet*, which flew in 1998 and entered active service in 1999. Replacing both the F-14 and older versions of the F/A-18, the *Super Hornet* production program is slated to continue until 2014, with up to 1,000 aircraft being procured. After the demise of the A-12 in 1991, the Navy refocused its attention on the A/F-X (attack/fighter-experimental), a less ambitious project to develop a stealth aircraft that would augment the F/A-18E/F. During the same time period, the Air Force was studying the MRF (multi-role fighter) as an F-16 and A-10 replacement, and since 1989, the Marines and the British Royal Navy had been cooperating in a project sponsored by DARPA[23] to find a next generation V/STOL aircraft to succeed the *Harrier*. In early 1994, all of these efforts were rolled into JAST (joint advance strike technologies) with the goal of generating a common stealth airframe that would satisfy multi-service needs. A request for design proposals was issued to aircraft manufacturers by the JAST group in March 1996, after which the project was renamed JSF (joint strike fighter). Later the same year, following a review of preliminary design proposals submitted by three manufacturers, the competition was narrowed to Boeing's X-32 and Lockheed-Martin's X-35. Prototypes of both aircraft were flown in late 2000, and in October 2001, DOD declared Lockheed-Martin's X-35 (re-designated F-35) to be the winner of the JSF competition. Evaluation aircraft are projected for delivery to all services between 2008 and 2010, with the first operational examples expected to follow in 2012. The Marine version, the V/STOL F-35B, will replace both F/A-18C/Ds and AV-8Bs, and the Navy version, the F-35C, will replace F/A-18C/Ds. F-35B/C JSFs, if the program proceeds as planned, together with F/A-18E/Fs, are likely to form the primary tactical component of Navy and Marine aviation through the first half of the 21st century. Beyond JSF, the next step may be unmanned tactical aircraft. Since 2000, under DARPA supervision, the Navy has been involved in a project known as UCAV-N (unmanned combat air vehicle—naval) and the first concept aircraft, the Northrop-Grumman X-47A, was flown in early 2003. Only a few months later, DARPA combined Navy and USAF efforts under a project headed J-UCAS (joint unmanned combat air system); however, in March 2006, the USAF withdrew from the proj-

---

21. *Official designation changed from F-18 to F/A-18 in 1984.*
22. *The YF-22 was selected over the Northrop/McDonnell-Douglas YF-23 in 1991.*
23. *U. S. Defense Advanced Research Projects Agency.*

ect, and its concept aircraft, two Boeing X-45As, have since been turned over to the Navy for evaluation against the X-47A.

First Series • 1926–1946

Designation	Manufacturer	Dates
BG	Great Lakes Aircraft Corp.	1933–1940
B2G	Great Lakes Aircraft Corp.	1935–1936
BM	Glenn L. Martin Co.	1931–1937
BT	Northrop Corp.	1935–1941
BY	Consolidated Aircraft Co.	1932
B2Y	Consolidated Aircraft Co.	1933–1934
BFB	Boeing Airplane Co.	1933
BFC/BF2C	Curtiss-Wright Corp.	1932–1938
BTC	Curtiss-Wright Corp.	1945–1946
BT2C	Curtiss-Wright Corp.	1946
BTK	Kaiser-Fleetwings Corp.	1945–1946
F8B	Boeing Airplane Co.	1945–1946
F8C	Curtiss Aeroplane Co.	1927–1934
FD	Douglas Aircraft Co.	1933
FF/SF	Grumman Aircraft Engr. Corp.	1931–1936
F6F	Grumman Aircraft Engr. Corp.	1942–1948
F7F	Grumman Aircraft Engr. Corp.	1943–1954
F8F	Grumman Aircraft Engr. Corp.	1945–1952
F2G	Goodyear Aircraft Corp.	1944–1947
F2J	Berliner-Joyce Co.	1933
FM	General Motors Corp.	1942–1945
F2U	Chance Vought Co.	1929
F4U(FG, F3A)/AU	Chance Vought Co.	1940–1955
SBA(SBN)	Brewster Aeronautical Corp.	1936–1941
SB2A	Brewster Aeronautical Corp.	1941–1945
S2C	Curtiss-Wright Corp.	1932
SBC	Curtiss-Wright Corp.	1933–1942
SB2C(SBF/SBW)	Curtiss-Wright Corp.	1940–1949
SBD	Douglas Aircraft Co.	1938–1945
SB2D/BTD	Douglas Aircraft Co.	1942–1945
SBF	Grumman Aircraft Engr. Co.	1936
SBU	Vought-Sikorsky Corp.	1933–1937
SB2U	Vought-Sikorsky Corp.	1936–1942
SB3U	Vought-Sikorsky Corp.	1936
T3D	Douglas Aircraft Co.	1931–1933
TBD	Douglas Aircraft Co.	1935–1942
TB2D	Douglas Aircraft Co.	1945–1946
TBF(TBM)	Grumman Aircraft Engr. Corp.	1941–1954
TB3F	Grumman Aircraft Engr. Corp.	1945–1946
TBG	Great Lakes Aircraft Corp.	1935
T3M	Glenn L. Martin Co.	1926–1928
T4M(TG)	Glenn L. Martin Co.	1927–1937
T6M	Glenn L. Martin Co.	1930–1931
TBU(TBY)	Vought-Sikorsky Corp.	1941–1945

Great Lakes BG 1933–1940

TECHNICAL SPECIFICATIONS (BG-1)

Type: Two-place dive-bomber
Manufacturer: Great Lakes Aircraft Corp., Cleveland, Ohio.

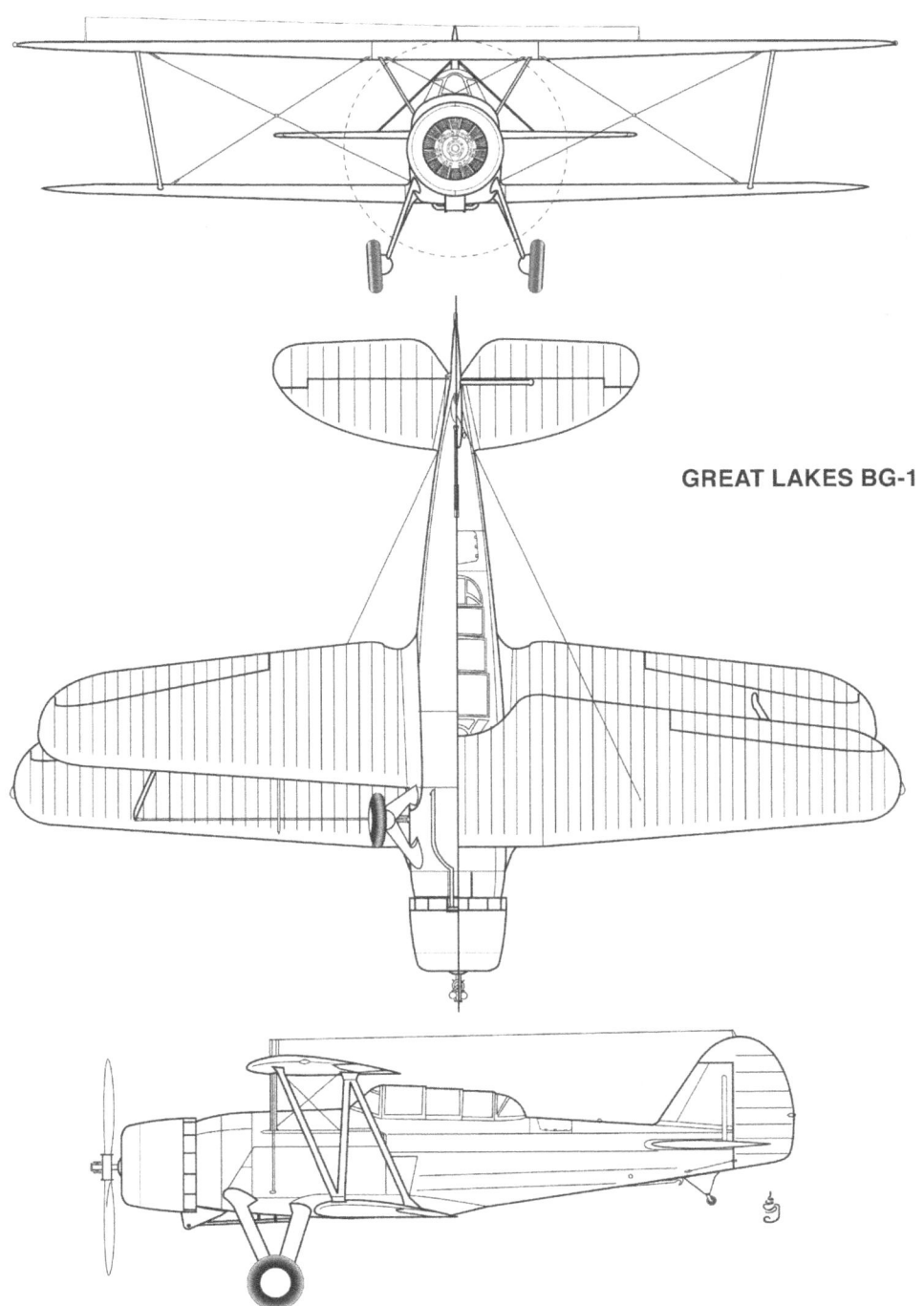

GREAT LAKES BG-1

BG-1 serving with Marine squadron VMB-2 (formerly VB-4M) while attached to FMF One in San Diego. Half of all BG production (30 aircraft) was allocated to the Marine Corps. Last examples were retired in 1940.

Total produced: 60
Power plant: One 750-hp Pratt & Whitney R-1535-82 14-cylinder radial driving a two-bladed Hamilton Standard variable-pitch propeller.
Armament: One fixed forward-firing .30-cal. machine gun, one flexible .30-cal. rear machine gun, and up to 1,000-lbs. of bombs carried externally.
Performance: Max. speed 188-mph at 8,900 ft.; ceiling 20,100 ft.; combat range 549 mi.
Weights: 3,903-lbs. empty, 6,347-lbs. loaded.
Dimensions: Span 36 ft., length 28 ft. 9 in., wing area 384 sq. ft.

The BG holds the distinction of being the only indigenous design of the short-lived Great Lakes Aircraft Corporation (1928–1936) to have been built in any quantity for the Navy and Marine Corps. Designed in response to a mid–1932 BUAER requirement for a two-place, biplane dive-bomber capable of carrying a 1,000-lb. bomb, the XBG-1 made its first flight in June 1933, and soon afterward was delivered to the Navy for service trials. A competitive fly-off conducted in late 1933 resulted in the XBG-1 being selected for production over the rival Consolidated XB2Y-1. Sixty aircraft under three contracts were manufactured by Great Lakes during 1934–1935, half of that number being assigned to the Marine Corps. Production BG-1s, which began reaching operational units in October 1934, differed from the prototype in having an enclosed canopy over the pilot and gunner/observer position.

The only frontline Navy squadron to equip with BG-1s was VB-3A. This unit initially formed part of *Ranger's* new air group but was later transferred to *Lexington*. The squadron returned to *Ranger* in 1937 as VB-4, and in 1938, began exchanging its BG-1s for monoplane SB2U-1s. Two Marine squadrons received BG-1s, VB-4M (later VMB-2) in 1935 and VB-6M (later VMB-1) in 1936, where they remained in active service until 1940. Once released from frontline squadrons, Navy and the Marine BG-1s were briefly used for utility duties at shore bases.

Great Lakes B2G 1935–1938

TECHNICAL SPECIFICATIONS (XB2G-1)

Type: Two-place dive-bomber
Manufacturer: Great Lakes Aircraft Corp., Cleveland, Ohio.

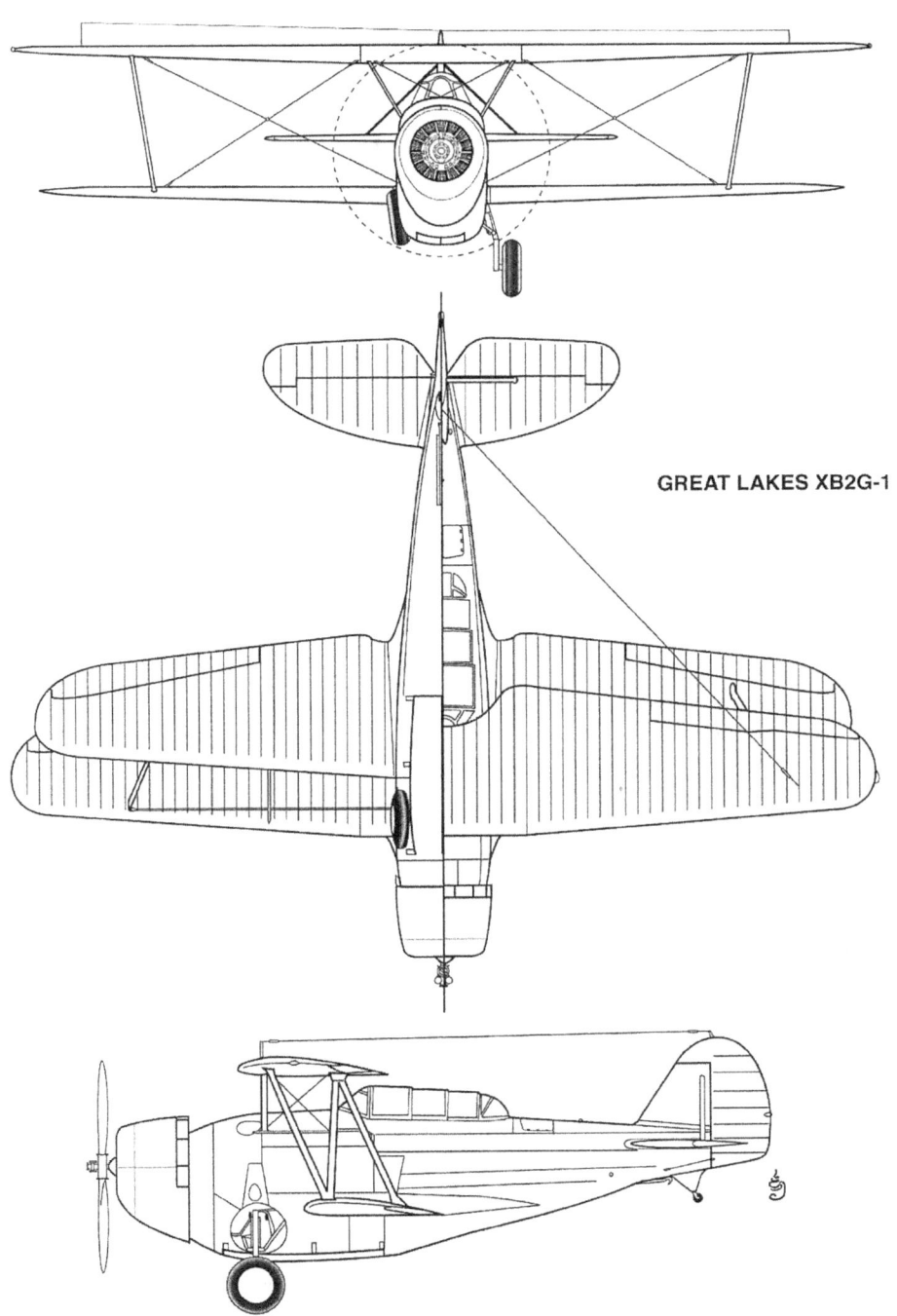

GREAT LAKES XB2G-1

Sole example of XB2G-1 in 1938 after it had been re-assigned to the Marines to be used as a command plane to tour bases. Great Lakes went out of business in 1936 after losing both the Navy dive-bomber and torpedo-bomber competitions.

Total produced: 1
Power plant: One 750-hp Pratt & Whitney R-1535-82 14-cylinder radial driving a two-bladed Hamilton Standard variable-pitch propeller.
Armament: One fixed forward-firing .50-cal. machine gun, one flexible .30-cal. rear machine gun, and up to 1,000-lbs. of bombs carried in internal bomb bay.
Performance: Max. speed 198-mph at 8,900 ft.; ceiling 19,500 ft.; combat range 582 mi.
Weights: 4,248-lbs. empty, 6,802-lbs. loaded.
Dimensions: Span 36 ft., length 28 ft. 9 in., wing area 384 sq. ft.

In 1934 BUAER issued nearly simultaneous requirements for new biplane and monoplane scout-bomber designs to be equipped with retractable landing gear. Great Lakes Aircraft, having previously achieved moderate success with its fixed-gear BG, went back and revised the basic airframe by deepening the belly to incorporate a Grumman-type, inward-retracting landing gear and adding an internal bomb bay. The single forward-firing gun was increased to .50-caliber, but other features of the previous BG design were retained. BUAER ordered one prototype in June 1934 under the designation XB2G-1. The aircraft was completed and test flown in late 1935, and then delivered to the Navy for competitive trials.

Interestingly, Great Lakes' chief competition was not the monoplanes but two other biplane designs, the Grumman XSBF-1 and the Curtiss XSBC-2. A fly-off between the three prototypes conducted from late 1935 to early 1936 ultimately resulted in the selection of the XSBC-2 for production. However, The Navy did purchase the single XB2G-1 prototype, and it was eventually transferred to the Marine Corps, where it was used as a command plane to tour reserve bases until 1938. When Great Lakes went out of business in 1936, Bell Aircraft acquired its manufacturing rights, but no effort was made to continue development of the former company's dive-bomber series.

Martin BM 1930–1937

TECHNICAL SPECIFICATIONS (BM-2)
Type: Two-place dive-bomber
Manufacturer: Glenn L. Martin Co., Baltimore, Maryland.

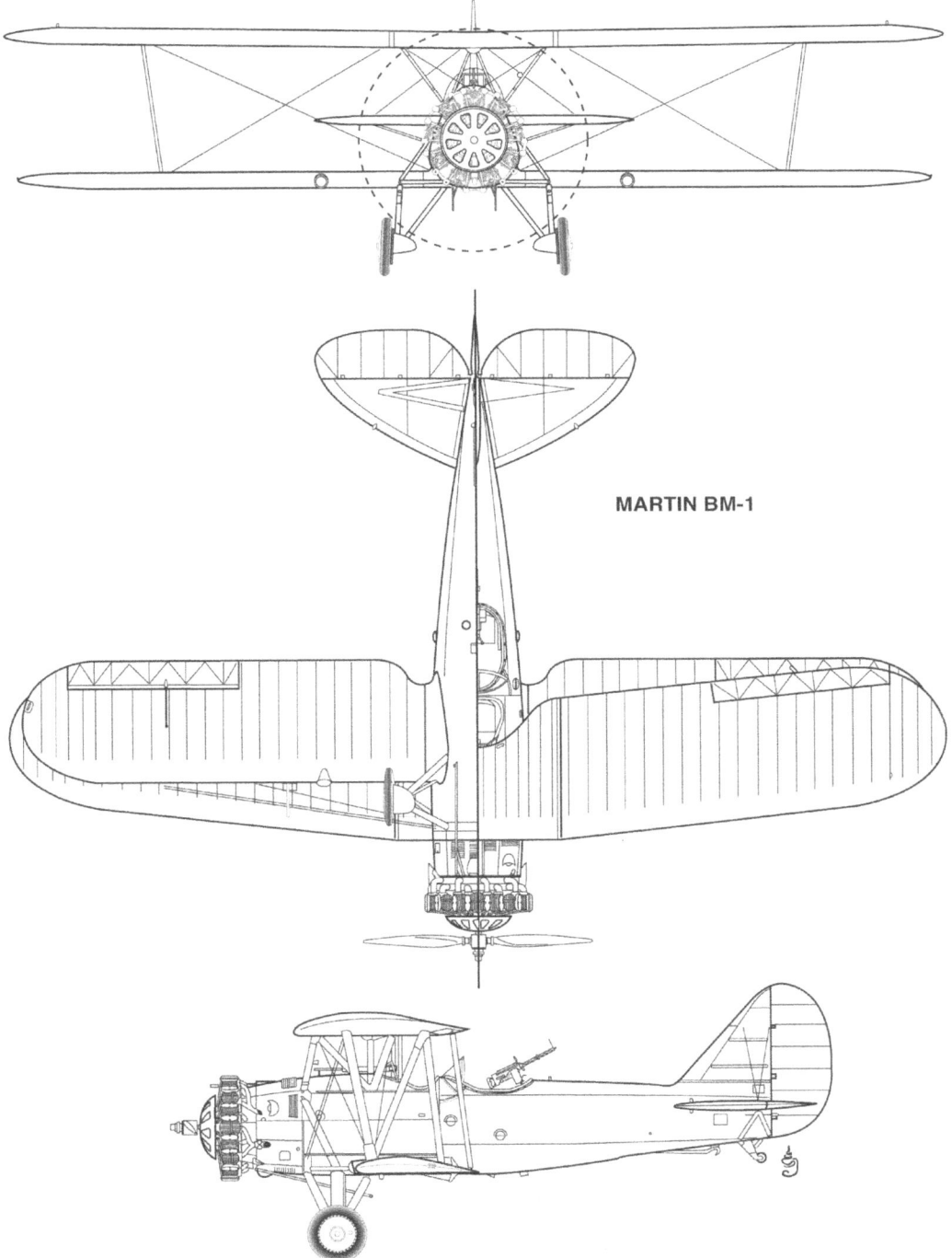

The BM was the first purpose-built dive-bomber purchased by the Navy. The example shown here is serving with a shore station after being released from fleet service in 1937.

Total produced (both models): 33
Power plant: One 625-hp. Pratt & Whitney R-1690-44 9-cylinder radial driving a two-bladed Hamilton Standard fixed-pitch propeller.
Armament: One fixed forward-firing .30-cal. machine gun and one flexible .30-cal. machine gun in rear cockpit, and up to 1,000-lbs. of bombs (or one torpedo) carried externally.
Performance: Max. speed 146-mph at 6,000 ft.; ceiling 16,800 ft.; combat range 413 mi.
Weights: 3,662-lbs. empty, 6,219-lbs. loaded.
Dimensions: Span 41 ft., length 28 ft. 9 in., wing area 436 sq. ft.

The Martin BM occupies the distinction of being the first made-for-purpose dive-bomber aircraft ordered by the Navy. Successful naval experiments with dive-bombing and recent Marine combat experience using the tactic in Nicaragua inspired BUAER in 1928 to issue a requirement for a new biplane dive-bomber type capable of lifting a bomb heavy enough (i.e., 500-lbs.+) to damage or sink an armored warship. The general aerodynamic and structural design for the new type was laid down by BUAER itself and contracts for single prototypes were issued in June 1928 to Martin for an R-1690-powered version, designated XT5M-1, and to the Naval Aircraft Factory for an R-1750-powered version, designated XT2N-1. Both aircraft featured the newly invented bomb crutch, a tubular metal device that swung the bomb past the propeller arc during steep (i.e., 70–80 deg.) dives. The XT5M-1 prototype made its first flight in March 1930 and soon thereafter was delivered to NAS Anacostia for evaluations.

In April 1931 Martin was given a contract to manufacture 12 aircraft, re-designated BM-1 under the new bomber (B) category. Later, in October 1931, the Navy ordered 16 additional examples as BM-2s, which differed only in small details, and in 1932 purchased five more from

Martin that were completed as BM-1s. The active service of BM-1s and -2s was primarily with two carrier units: VT-1S (later VB-1S) aboard *Lexington* beginning in 1932 and VB-3B aboard *Langley* in 1934. All BMs were withdrawn from fleet service during 1937 but continued to be used at shore stations for miscellaneous test and utility duties until the last example was scrapped in 1940.

Northrop BT 1935–1941

TECHNICAL SPECIFICATIONS BT-1

Type: Two-place dive-bomber
Manufacturer: Northrop Aircraft Corp. (subsidiary of Douglas Aircraft), El Segundo, California.
Total produced: 56
Power plant: One 825-hp Pratt & Whitney R-1535-94 14-cylinder radial driving a two-bladed Hamilton Standard variable-pitch propeller.
Armament: One fixed forward-firing .50-cal. machine gun, one flexible .30-cal. rear machine gun, and up to 1,000-lbs. of bombs carried externally.
Performance: Max. speed 222-mph at 9,500 ft.; cruise 192-mph; ceiling 25,300 ft.; range 550 mi. loaded, 1,150 mi. max.
Weights: 4,606-lbs. empty, 7,197-lbs. loaded.
Dimensions: Span 41 ft. 6 in., length 31 ft. 8 in., wing area 319 sq. ft.

BT-1 of VB-5 attached to *Yorktown*. Detail of split-type dive brakes shows to good advantage. A more powerful engine, flush-folding landing gear, plus other improvements turned the BT into the legendary SBD.

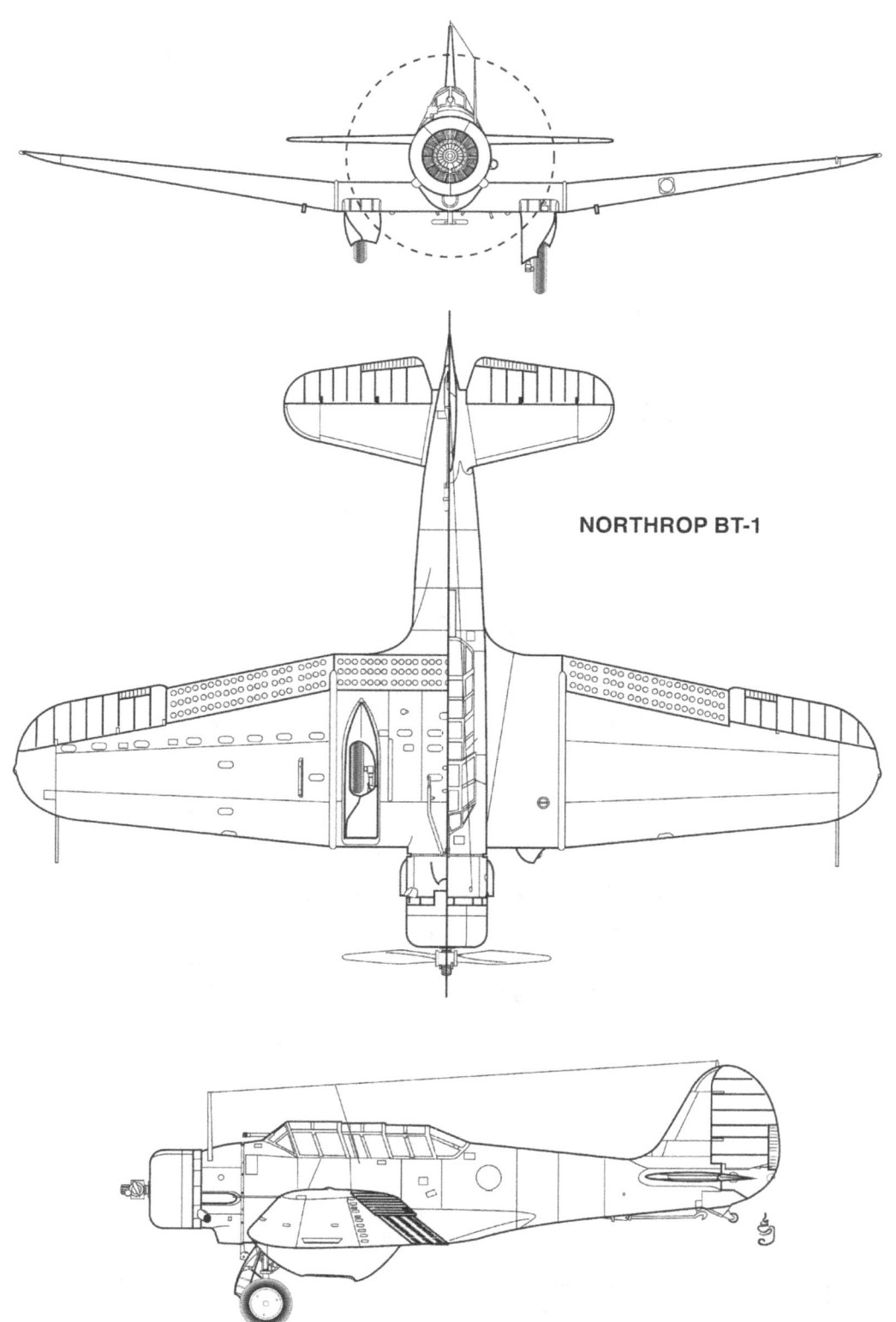

NORTHROP BT-1

The Northrop BT is recognized as being the direct precursor to the legendary SBD *Dauntless* series. When BUAER issued a 1934 requirement for a retractable-gear, monoplane scout-bomber, Northrop responded with a somewhat scaled-down version of its Army A-17 attack airplane, which had flown in 1933. Unlike the fixed, spatted landing gear of the production A-17, the Navy design retained the semi-retractable gear arrangement seen on Gamma 2F demonstrator. It also introduced a perforated, split-type dive brake that would reduce buffeting at high diving speeds. BUAER gave Northrop a contract in November 1934 for one prototype as the XBT-1, and the aircraft made its first flight on August 19, 1935. Following completion of official trials in October 1936, the Navy awarded Northrop a contract for 54 BT-1s. While production was underway, the company commenced development of an XBT-2 variant having a bigger engine and fully-flush, inward-retracting landing gear (as developed for the Army A-17A). After the company was renamed Douglas Aircraft, El Segundo Division, in 1938, the XBT-2 was ultimately placed in production as the SBD-1.

Production BT-1s first entered service in April 1938 with VB-5, becoming part of *Yorktown's* air wing, and in early 1939, began equipping VB-6 of the recently commissioned *Enterprise*. The service career of the BT was comparatively brief, however, the phase-out commencing in early 1941 as new SBD-2s and -3s began arriving to take their place.

Consolidated BY 1932–1933

TECHNICAL SPECIFICATIONS (XBY-1)
Type: Two-place dive-bomber
Manufacturer: Consolidated Aircraft Co., Buffalo, New York.
Total produced: 1
Power plant: One 600-hp Wright R-1820-78 9-cylinder radial driving a two-bladed Hamilton
Armament: One flexible .30-cal.rear machine gun fired from sliding rear dorsal hatch, and up to 1,000-lbs. of bombs (est.) carried in two internal wing bays.
Performance: Max. speed 181-mph; ceiling 22,700 ft.; range not specified.
Weights: 3,800-lbs. empty, 6,547-lbs. loaded.
Dimensions: Span 50 ft., length 33 ft. 8 in., wing area 361 sq. ft.

The monoplane XBY-1 stands out as an anomaly among the various biplane dive-bomber types considered by BUAER during the early 1930s. The airplane materialized as a direct development of Consolidated's Model 17 *Fleetster* 5-passenger monoplane transport, which first flown in 1930. BUAER ordered a naval bomber variant prototype in April 1931 as the XBY-1 and the aircraft was delivered for testing in September 1932. The design featured a high-mounted, cantilevered wing supported by a large, spatted undercarriage, and in general appearance was reminiscent of the well-known Lockheed *Vega,* though, unlike the wooden *Vega,* the XBY-1 was all-metal except for fabric-covered control surfaces. The two bomb bays, located at about 30 per cent span, were enclosed by an unorthodox system of orange-peel-type doors. Despite being faster than existing biplane types, trials completed in early 1933 revealed that the XBY-1 was not suited for dive-bombing and too large for carrier stowage, thus no production was forthcoming.

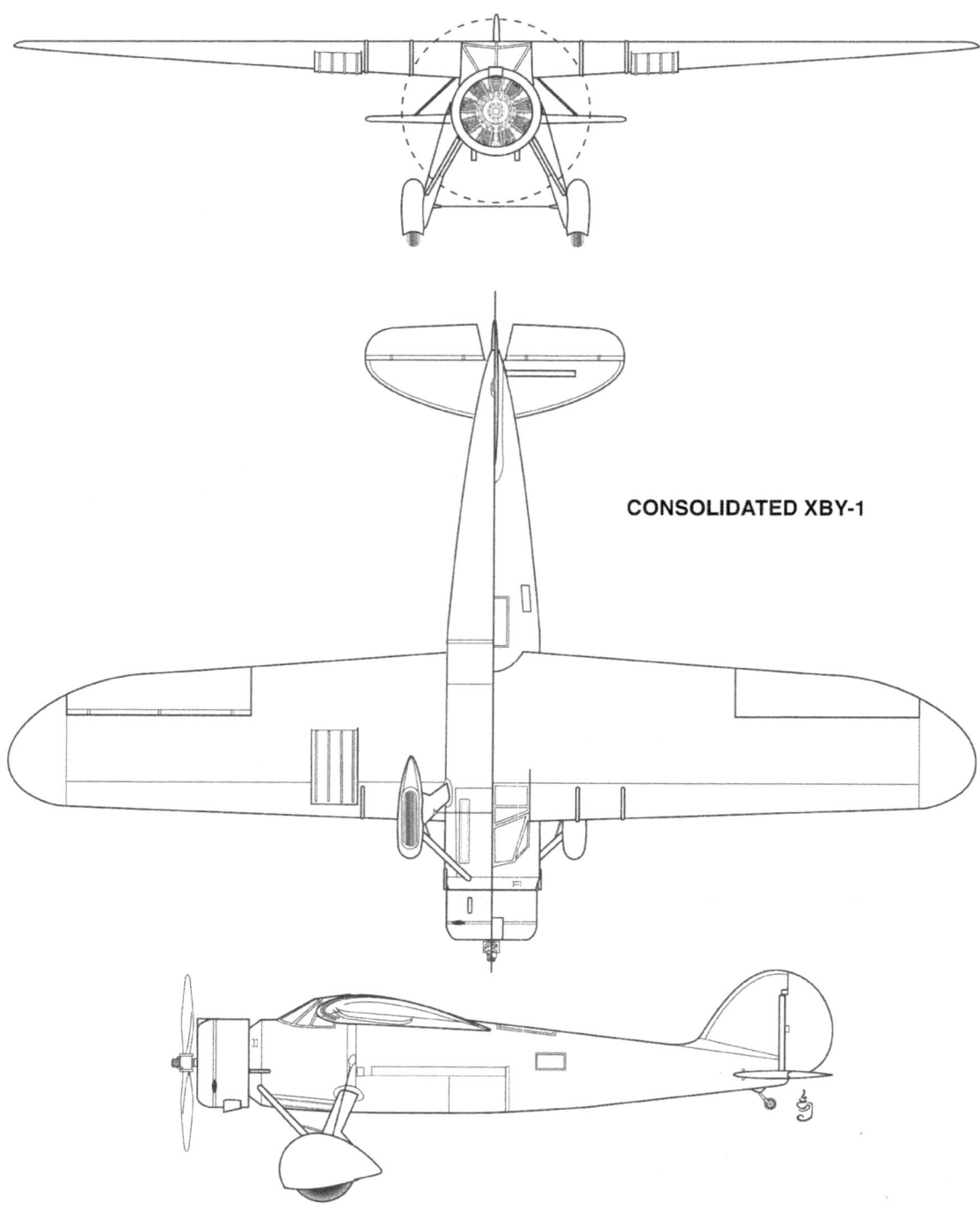

CONSOLIDATED XBY-1

A military adaptation of the *Fleetster* five-passenger transport, the one and only XBY-1 appeared for Navy trials at Anacostia in late 1932. Bombs were carried in wing bays enclosed by orange-peel doors.

Consolidated B2Y 1933

TECHNICAL SPECIFICATIONS (XB2Y-1)

Type: Two-place dive-bomer
Manufacturer: Consolidated Aircraft Co., Buffalo, New York.
Total produced: 1
Power plant: One 700-hp Pratt & Whitney R-1535-64 14-cylinder radial driving a two-bladed Hamilton Standard fixed-pitch propeller.
Armament: One fixed forward-firing .30-caliber machine gun, one flexible .30-cal. machine gun in rear cockpit, and up to 1,000-lbs. of bombs carried externally.
Performance: Max. speed 182-mph at 8,900 ft.; ceiling 21,000 ft.; combat range 487 mi.
Weights: 3,538-lbs. empty, 6,010-lbs. loaded.
Dimensions: Span 36 ft. 6 in., length 27 ft. 10 in., wing area 362 sq. ft.

After a failed effort with the BY, Consolidated's B2Y represented a more serious attempt to compete in the Navy's newest dive-bomber contest. It began in mid–1932 when Consolidated and Great Lakes were both invited to build prototypes according to BUAER plans and specifications for an R-1535-powered biplane dive-bomber capable of delivering a 1,000-lb. bomb. Great Lakes' XBG-1 was delivered to the Navy in June 1933 and Consolidated's XB2Y-1 arrived in September. Both came in an open cockpit configuration and were extremely similar in appearance, differing in small details like the cowling, shape of the fin and rudder, and landing gear struts. Instead of the more conventional belly crutch, the XB2Y-1 featured a wing-shaped bomb displacement device in front of the main gear struts. During service trials that lasted into November, the XBG-1 revealed itself to be the better bombing platform of the two, and as a consequence, was selected as winner of the competition.

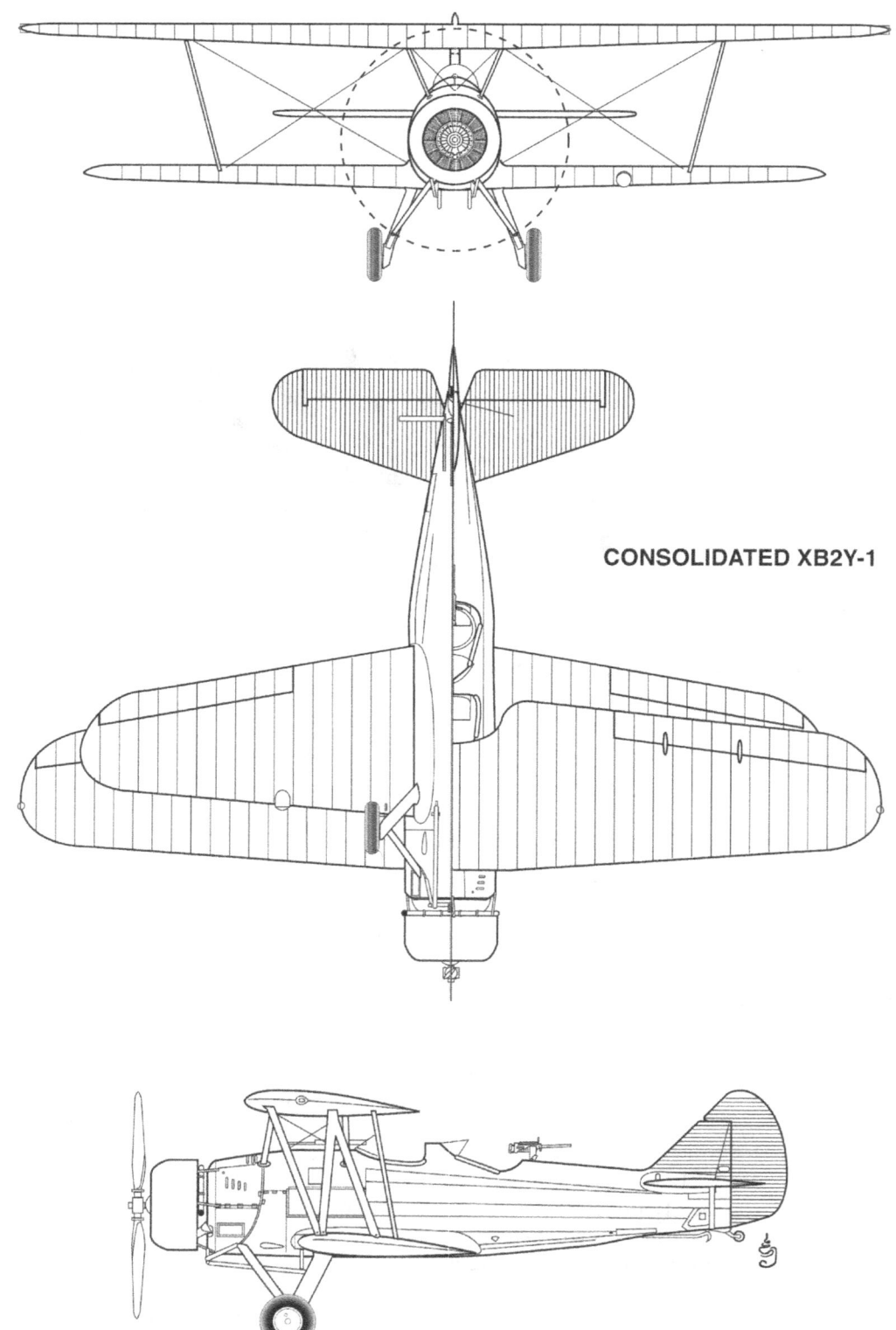

CONSOLIDATED XB2Y-1

XB2Y-1 as delivered to Anacostia for trials in September 1933. The unusual wing-shaped bomb displacement device, attached to a 1,000-lb. bomb, is clearly visible. Both the XB2Y-1 and competing XBG-1 were built according to the same BUAER plan.

Boeing BFB (F6B) 1933

TECHNICAL SPECIFICATIONS (XBFB-1)

Type: Single-place bomber-fighter
Manufacturer: Boeing Airplane Co., Seattle, Washington.
Total produced: 1
Power plant: One 625-hp Pratt & Whitney R-1535-44 14-cylinder radial driving a two-bladed Hamilton Standard variable-pitch propeller.
Armament: Two fixed forward-firing .30-caliber machine guns and up to 474-lbs. of bombs carried externally.
Performance: Max. speed 195-mph at 6,000 ft.; ceiling 20,700 ft.; combat range 437 mi.
Weights: 2,823-lbs. empty, 3,705-lbs. loaded.
Dimensions: Span 28 ft. 6 in., length 22 ft. 2 in., wing area 252 sq. ft.

The BFB was one example of the Navy's short-lived bomber-fighter concept. In 1931 Boeing was a prime contractor of the Navy's carrier-based fighters and was in the process of developing the newest of its series, the F4B-3 with a metal-clad fuselage and empennage. While this work was underway, BUAER indicated interest in a related design that would possess light dive-bombing capability, and in June of that year, authorized construction of a prototype as the XF6B-1. (Note, the XF5B-1 designation had previously been assigned to a high-wing monoplane derivative of the F4B.) However, Boeing's involvement in other Navy and Army contracts (i.e., F4B-4, P-12E, B-9, and P-26) apparently delayed completion of the XF6B-1 until February 1933, by which time Curtiss had already flown two prototypes (i.e., F11C-1 and -2) built to the same requirements. Following delivery to the Navy, the aircraft received the new designation XBFB-1. Sharing the general aerodynamic and structural characteristics of the F4B-3/-4 series, the XBFB-1 featured an enlarged lower wing plus fully cantilevered main gear legs to allow clearance for ordnance carried on the centerline. The aircraft was retained for testing but no production was ordered. It was the last biplane to be built by Boeing of Seattle.

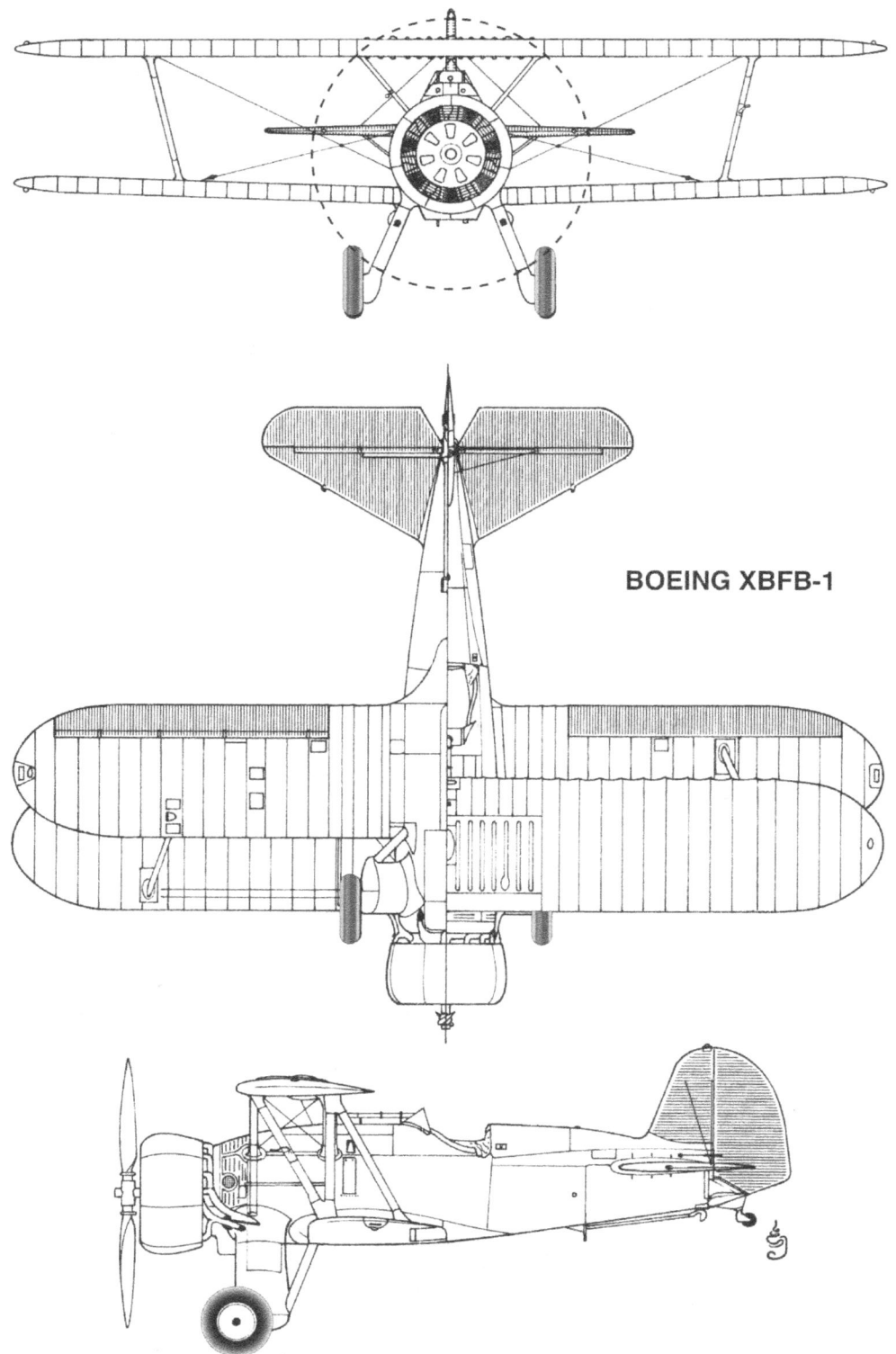

BOEING XBFB-1

Sole XBFB-1 (XF6B-1) evaluated at Anacostia during 1933. Its similarity to Boeing's successful F4B series is evident. By the time the XBFB-1 arrived, the Navy had decided to purchase the Curtiss BFC-2 (F11C-2).

Curtiss BFC/BF2C (F11C) Goshawk 1932–1938

TECHNICAL SPECIFICATIONS (BF2C-1)

Type: Single-place bomber-fighter
Manufacturer: Curtiss-Wright Corp., Curtiss Aeroplane Division, Buffalo, New York.
Total produced: 56
Power plant: One 750-hp Pratt & Whitney R-1820-53 9-cylinder radial driving a two-bladed Hamilton Standard variable-pitch propeller.
Armament: Two fixed forward-firing .30-caliber machine guns and up to 474-lbs. of bombs carried externally.
Performance: Max. speed 228-mph at 8,000 ft.; ceiling 27,000 ft.; combat range 797 mi.
Weights: 3,329-lbs. empty, 5,086-lbs. loaded.
Dimensions: Span 31 ft. 6 in., length 23 ft., wing area 262 sq. ft.

Like Boeing, Curtiss was a major supplier of carrier aircraft during the 1930s. In April 1932, BUAER ordered two biplane fighter prototypes from Curtiss based upon the company's *Hawk II* model, a radial engine design incorporating the aerodynamic and structural improvements of the Army's P-6E. The XF11C-1 was to be powered by a twin-row R-1510 and the XF11C-2 (actually the company's existing *Hawk II* demonstrator) by a single-row R-1820. Both aircraft were to have light dive-bombing capability, configured to carry either a 474-lb. bomb on the centerline or four 112-lb. bombs under the wings. The XF11C-2 was delivered for trials in June 1932 and the F11C-1 a year later. Curtiss received an order in October 1932 for 28 F11C-2s and deliveries began the following February. In 1934 these aircraft were re-designated BFC-2s and were retrofitted with half sliding canopies mounted to a raised rear turtledeck that housed a life raft. The fifth production F11C-2 was reworked to accept a Grumman-type, inward-retracting landing gear assembly and re-designated F11C-3, and the Navy ordered 27 examples in February 1934 as the BF2C-1. Deliveries of production BF2C-1s, which also featured BFC-2 retrofits, commenced in late 1934.

II—USN and USMC Attack Aircraft

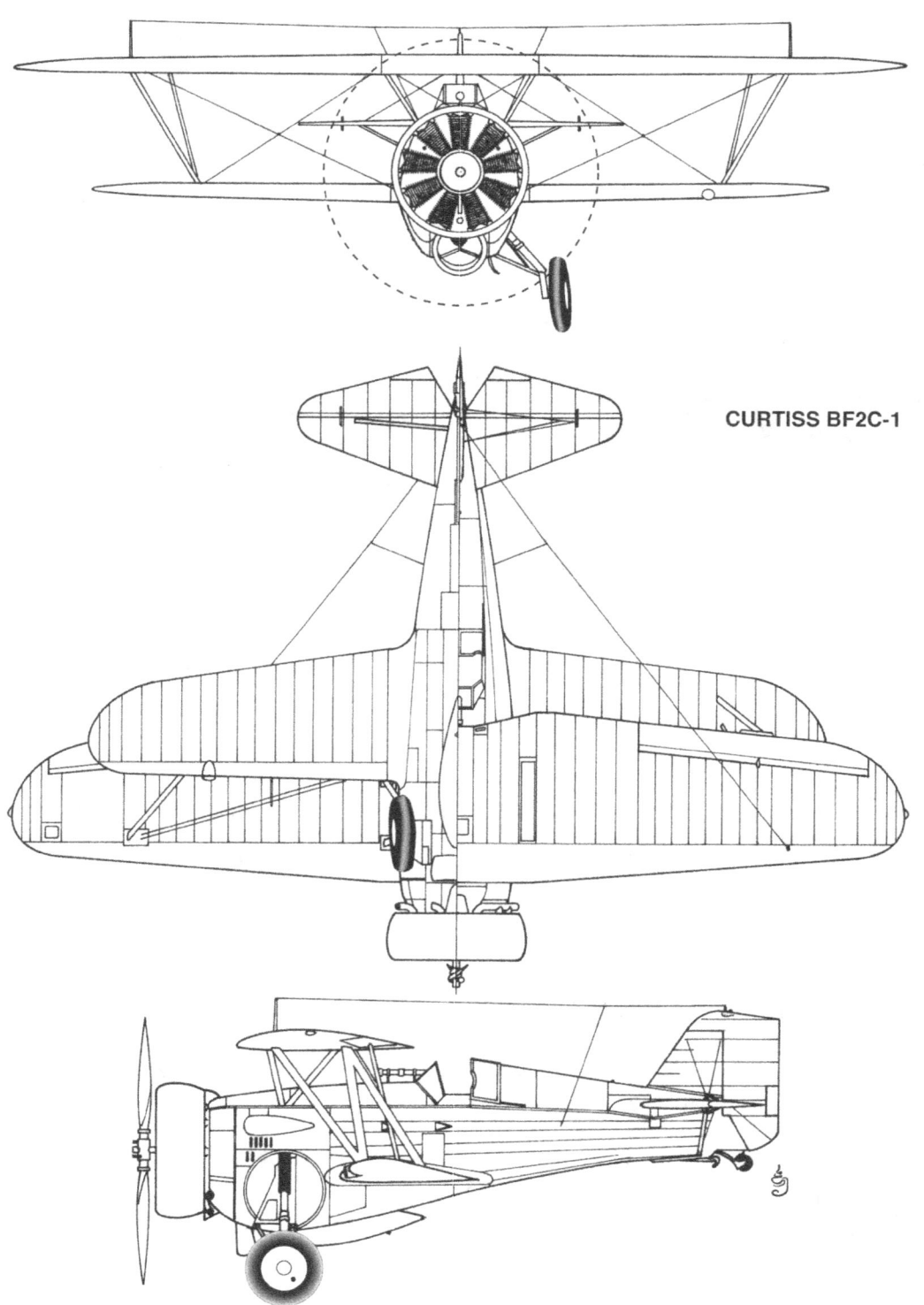

CURTISS BF2C-1

Top: BFC-2 serving with VB-2B of the *Saratoga* air group. This aircraft has been retrofitted with the half canopy and raised turtledeck behind the cockpit. Last examples were retired from fleet service in early 1938. *Bottom:* The VB-5B of the *Ranger* air group was the only unit to be equipped with BF2C-1s, starting in late 1934. Flutter problems with the metal-framed wings caused all to be withdrawn after less than three years of service.

All F11C-2s/BFC-2s served with VF-1B (later renamed VB-2B, and later still, VB-3B) aboard *Saratoga* from early 1933 until the type was withdrawn from active service in early 1938. Starting in late 1934, BF2C-1s were assigned to VB-5B of the *Ranger* air group, but after less than three years in the fleet, were withdrawn from service due to a serious wing flutter problem, which, in one case, resulted in a complete wing failure during a dive-bombing run.

Curtiss BTC 1946

TECHNICAL SPECIFICATIONS (XBTC-2)
Type: Single-place bomber-torpedo
Manufacturer: Curtiss-Wright Corp., Curtiss Airplane Division, Buffalo, New York.
Total produced: 1
Power plant: One 3,000-hp Pratt & Whitney R-4360-8A 28-cylinder radial driving an Aeroproducts six-bladed, contra-rotating constant-speed propeller.
Armament: Four fixed forward-firing 20-millimeter cannons and up to 2,000-lbs. of mixed ordnance carried externally.
Performance: Max. speed 374-mph at 16,000 ft.; cruise 188-mph; ceiling 26,200 ft.; combat range 1,245 mi.
Weights: 13,947-lbs. empty, 20,944-lbs. loaded.
Dimensions: Span 50 ft., length 38 ft. 7 in., wing area 406 sq. ft.

The BTC was one of two wholly different airframes built by Curtiss to compete under the September 1943 BUAER requirement for a single-seat bomber-torpedo (BT) aircraft to replace SBDs, SB2Cs, and TBMs. Curtiss had originally planned to follow its SB2C series with a more powerful SB3C derivative (Model 93), however, the emergence of the BT requirement effec-

XBTC-2 as it appeared in mid–1946, almost two years behind the other BT prototypes. The BTM and BT2D programs were showing such promise by this time that the second XBTC-2 prototype was cancelled before it could fly.

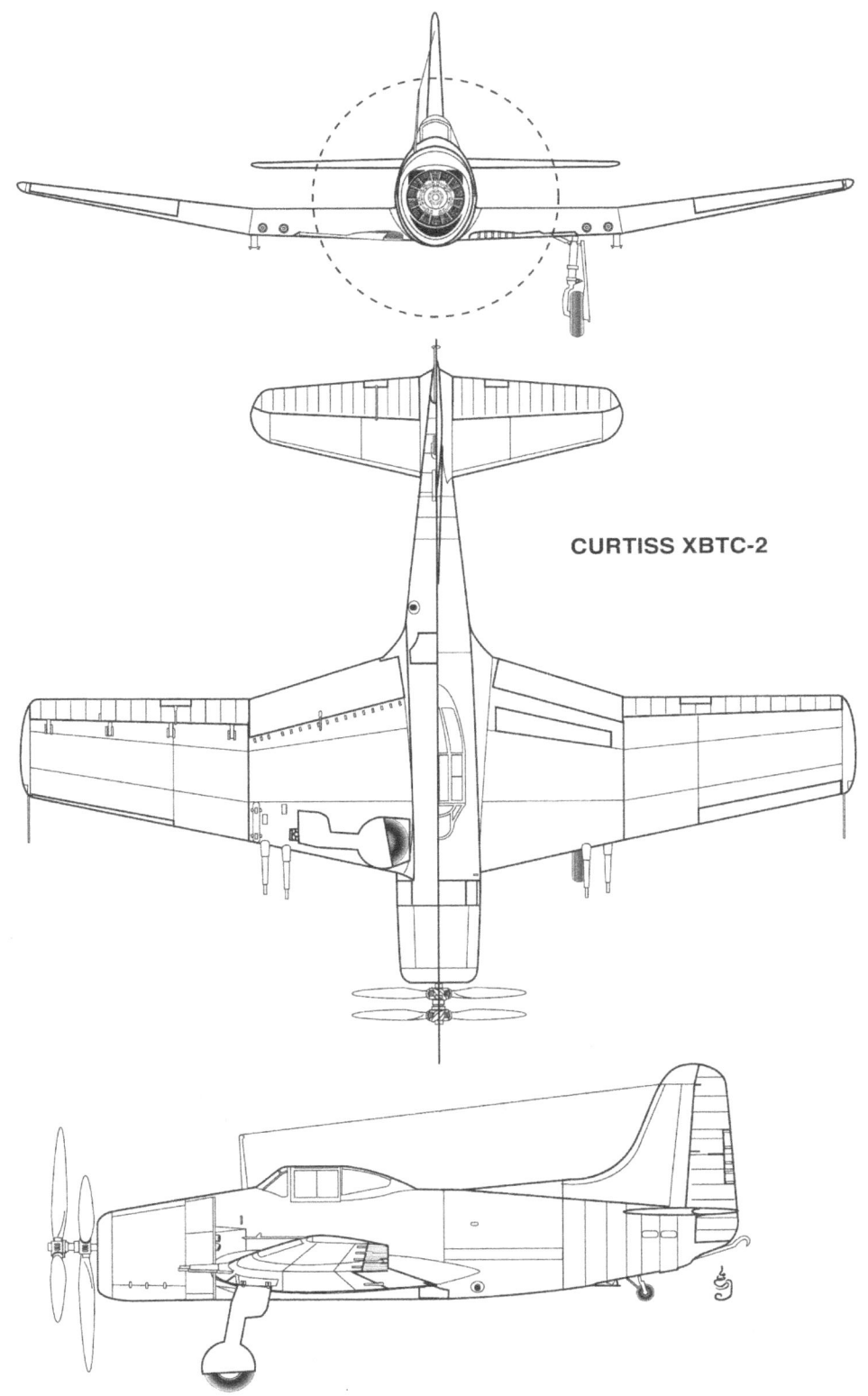

CURTISS XBTC-2

tively ruled out the need for future scout-bomber development. Curtiss next proposed an entirely new Model 96, in response to which BUAER, in December 1943, assigned the designation XBTC-1 and authorized construction of two prototypes to be powered by the then experimental R-4360 four-row radial engine. The substitution of a different version of the R-4360 engine during the design phase resulted in a designation change to XBTC-2.

Completion of the XBTC-2 prototype was prolonged to the extent that Curtiss' parallel project, the XBT2C-1, actually flew first, six months earlier. By the time the XBTC-2 did fly in July 1946, BUAER had already decided to procure the Martin (BTM-1/AM-1) and Douglas (BT2D-1/AD-1) designs, and the BTC project was cancelled before the second prototype was completed.

Curtiss BT2C 1946

TECHNICAL SPECIFICATIONS (XBT2C-1)

Type: Two-place bomber-torpedo
Manufacturer: Curtiss-Wright Corp., Curtiss Airplane Division, Buffalo, New York.
Total produced: 9
Power plant: One 2,500-hp Wright R-3350-24 18-cylinder radial driving a four-bladed Hamilton Standard fully-reversible, constant-speed propeller.
Armament: Two fixed forward-firing 20-millimeter cannons and up to 4,000-lbs. of mixed ordnance carried in an internal bay.
Performance: Max. speed 330-mph at 17,000 ft.; cruise 175-mph; ceiling 28,100 ft.; combat range 1,310 mi.
Weights: 12,268-lbs. empty, 19,022-lbs. loaded.
Dimensions: Span 47 ft. 7 in, length 39 ft. 2 in., wing area 416 sq. ft.

One of the eight XBT2C-1s with NATC in 1947. This was the only BT candidate to have an internal bomb bay and provision for a second crew member. Its similarity in layout to SB2C is apparent.

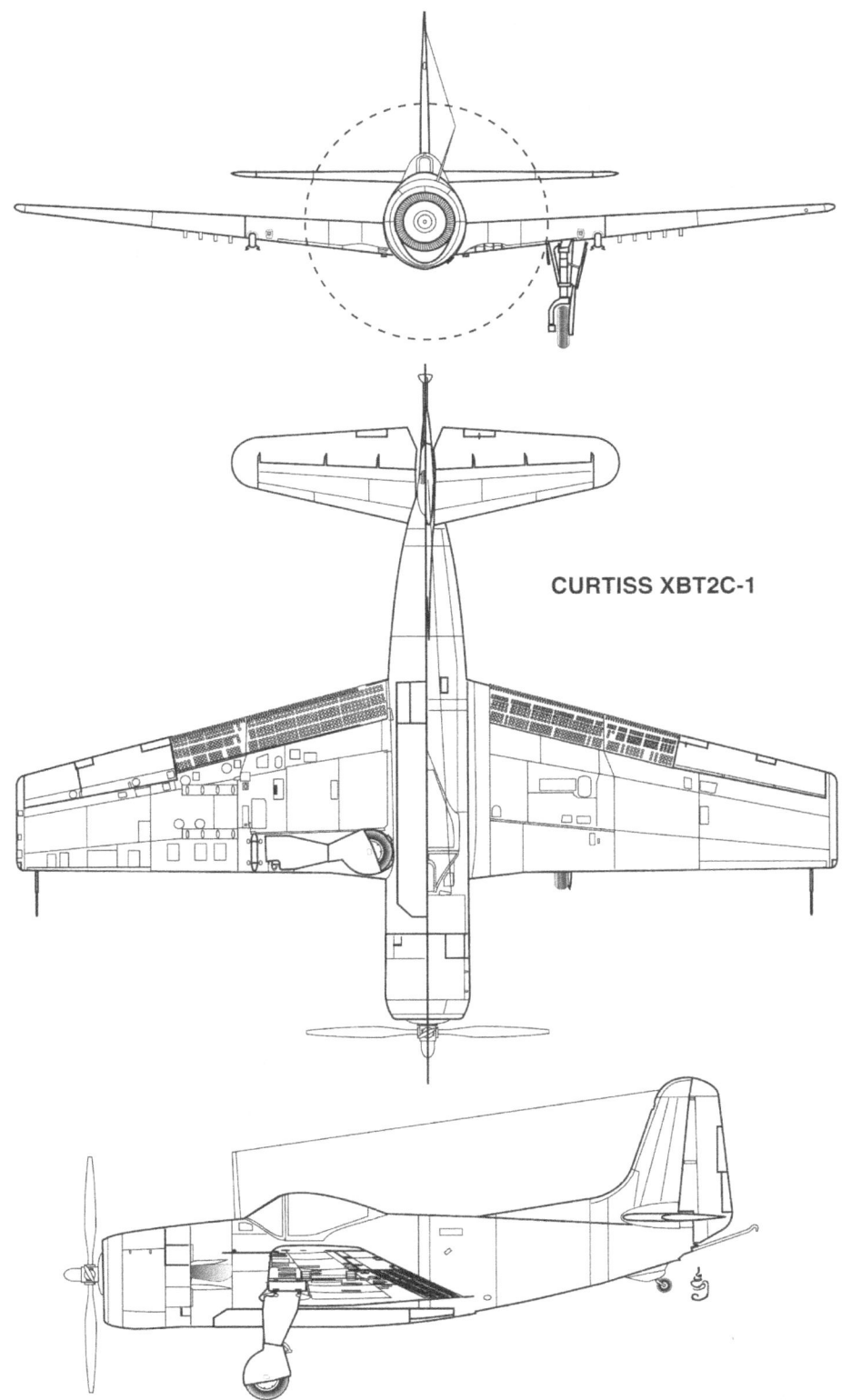

CURTISS XBT2C-1

The BT2C was the second of two Curtiss designs participating in the Navy's hotly contested bomber-torpedo (BT) competition. As XBTC development became increasingly protracted, Curtiss tendered a less complex R-3350-powered design proposed as the Model 98. In March 1945, BUAER indicated sufficient interest to place an order for ten aircraft under the designation XBT2C-1. Although sharing some aerodynamic similarities with the XBTC, the XBT2C-1 was a distinct design having a broader-chord wing, deeper fuselage accommodating an internal bomb bay, and provision for a radar operator in a compartment behind and below the cockpit. The clear similarity of the XBT2C-1's landing gear, wing-fold, and bomb bay arrangement to the SB2C suggests that much of its design concept was borrowed from the cancelled SB3C of 1943.

The timing of BUAER's March 1945 order is curious, inasmuch as Martin's XBTM-1 had flown months earlier and the Douglas and Kaiser-Fleetwings entries were scheduled to fly very soon. In any event, the first XBT2C-1 prototype flew in January 1946 and eight more aircraft were ultimately completed, the tenth cancelled. No production was ordered.

Kaiser-Fleetwings BTK 1945–1946

SPECIFICATIONS (XBTK-1)

Type: Single-place bomber-torpedo
Manufacturer: Kaiser Cargo, Inc., Fleetwings Aircraft Division, Bristol, Pennsylvania.
Total produced: 5 (includes 1 static test example)
Power plant: One 2,100-hp Pratt & Whitney R-2800-34W (water injection) 18-cylinder radial driving a four-bladed Hamilton Standard fully-reversible, constant-speed propeller.
Armament: Two fixed forward-firing 20-millimeter cannons and up to 5,000-lbs of mixed ordnance carried externally.
Performance: Max. speed 373-mph at 18,000 ft.; cruise 153-mph; ceiling 33,400 ft.; combat range 1,370 mi.
Weights: 9,959-lbs. empty, 15,782-lbs. loaded.
Dimensions: Span 48 ft. 8 in., length 38 ft. 11 in., wing area 380 sq. ft.

In September 1943, when BUAER circulated the new bomber-torpedo (BT) requirement calling for a single-seat attack aircraft, Kaiser-Fleetwings was invited to submit a proposal together with established airframe contractors like Martin, Curtiss-Wright, and Douglas. Kaiser-Fleetwings (a pseudonym for the aviation division of Henry J. Kaiser's mammoth industrial concern) had thus far been unsuccessful in its efforts to obtain a wartime production contract for an aircraft of its own design (see XA-39 in Appendix 3). After submitting its design proposal to BUAER, the company received a contract in March 1944 to build five prototypes under the designation XBTK-1, with the understanding that the first aircraft would fly before the end of the year.

Appearing as the smallest and lightest of four competing bomber-torpedo prototypes, the design of the XBTK-1 introduced a novel engine installation using exhaust gases to draw air through the cowling and exhaust it via stainless steel ducting located on either side of the cockpit. For dive-bombing, it employed finger-type dive brakes that deployed vertically above and below the trailing edge flaps. Hardpoints located beneath the wings and fuselage carried one torpedo, a radar pod, two drop tanks, or up to 5,000-lbs. of bombs and/or rockets. Completion of the first prototype, however, was delayed to the extent that its first flight did not occur until April 1945, by which time the war effort was starting to wind down. Because the XBTK-1 offered only a small advantage over existing F6F-5 and F4U-1D/-4s as fighter-bombers, BUAER made the decision to limit further consideration of new bomber-torpedo types to Martin's XBTM-1 (AM) and Douglas' XBT2D-1 (AD), thus no production order for the BTK was forthcoming. Had the war continued into 1946–1947 as originally expected, the fate of Kaiser's plane might have been different.

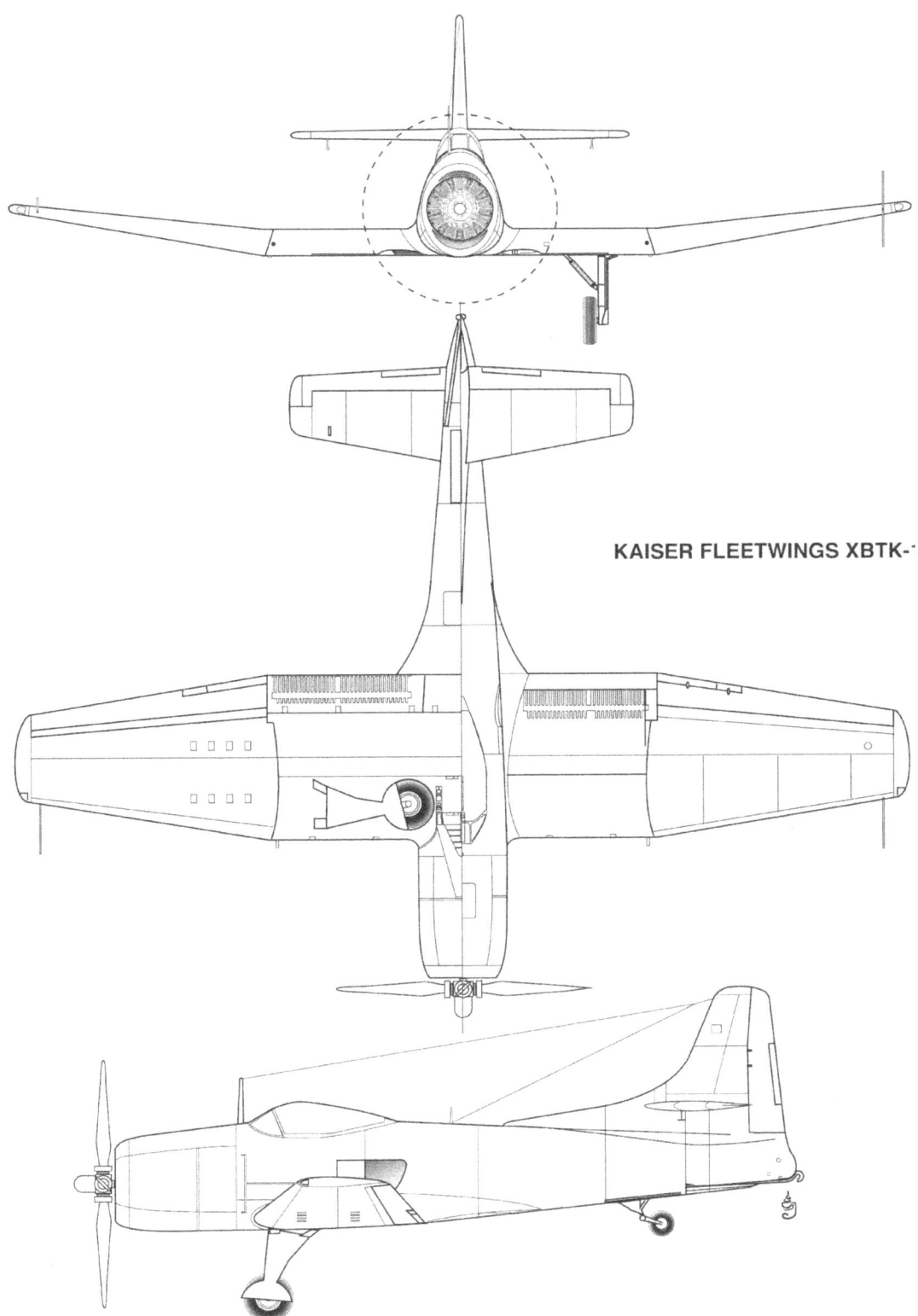

KAISER FLEETWINGS XBTK-1

The smallest of the BT candidates, the XBTK-1 is seen here in a dive-bomber configuration. It was the first and only original aircraft type built by Kaiser-Fleetwings and came too late in the war to considered for production.

Boeing F8B 1944–1945

TECHNICAL SPECIFICATIONS (XF8B-1)

Type: Single-place fighter-bomber
Manufacturer: Boeing Airplane Co., Seattle, Washington.
Total produced: 3
Power plant: One 3,000-hp Pratt & Whitney R-4360-10 28-cylinder radial driving an Aeroproducts six-bladed, contra-rotating constant-speed propeller.
Armament: Six fixed forward-firing .50-caliber machine guns or 20-millimeter cannons, up to 6,400-lbs. of ordnance: 3,200-lbs. of bombs in an internal bay and 3,200-lbs. of bombs on external racks, or two 2,000-lb. torpedoes carried externally.
Performance: Max. speed 432-mph at 26,900 ft.; ceiling 37,200 ft.; combat range 1,305 mi.
Weights: 13,519-lbs. empty, 21,691-lbs. loaded.
Dimensions: Span 54 ft. 4 in., length 43 ft. 3 in., wing area 489 sq. ft.

In early 1943, before the U. S. had acquired any island bases within striking distance of the Japanese home islands, BUAER envisaged the need for a long-range, carrier-based aircraft that could function either as a fighter escort or a torpedo and dive-bomber. Under a contract for three prototypes placed in March 1943, Boeing's proposed model 400, designated XF8B-1, subsequently evolved into the largest and heaviest single-engine fighter developed in the U. S. during the wartime period. Though technically not included in the Navy's contemporaneous bomber-torpedo (BT) competition (i.e., XBTM-1, XBT2D-1, XBTK-1, XBTC-1, and XBT2C-1), the XF8B-1 was nevertheless developed under similar tactical requirements.

The maiden flight of the first XF8B-1 prototype took place on November 27, 1944, but the other two prototypes were not completed until after the war ended. By this time, the need for

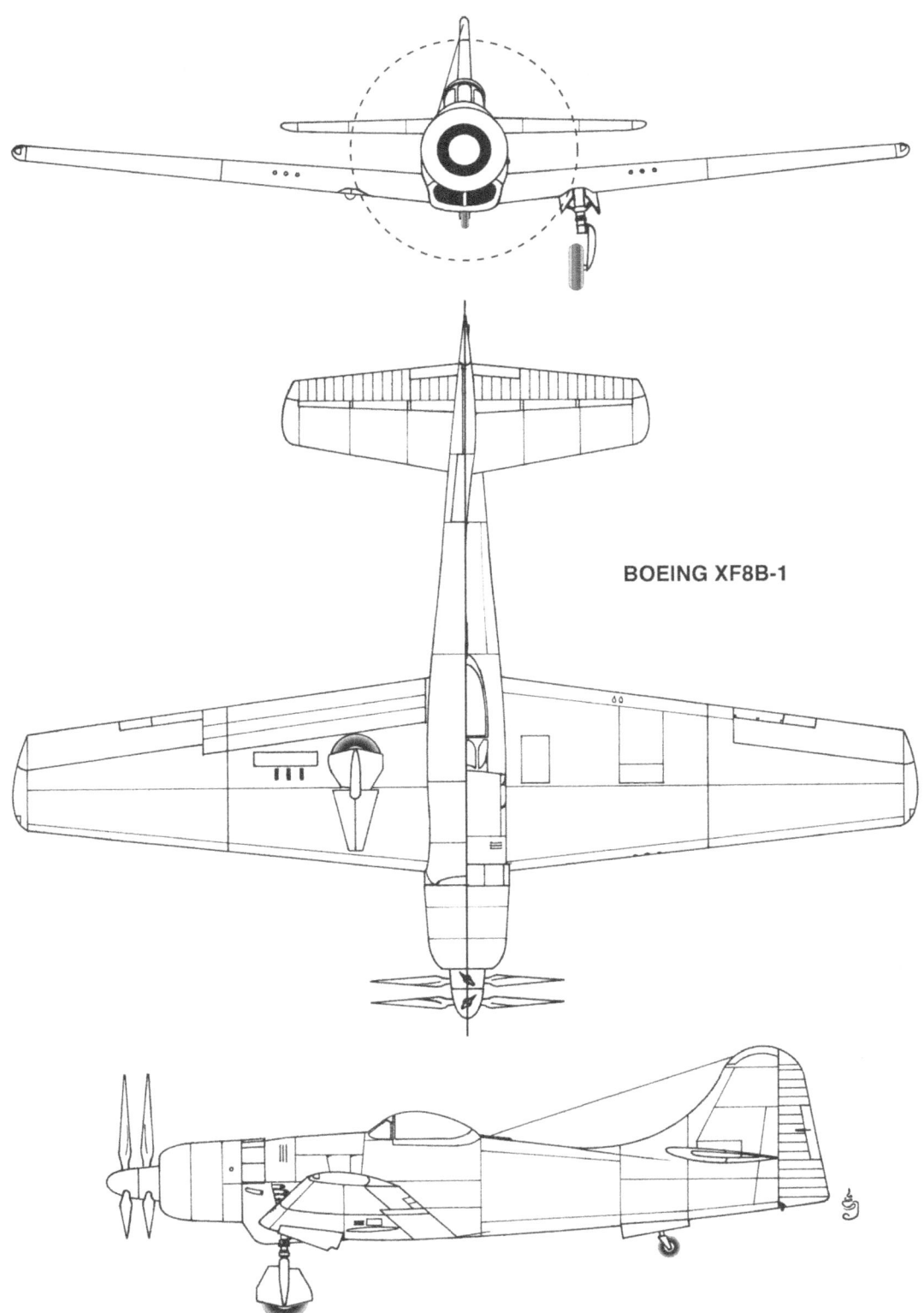

BOEING XF8B-1

The XF8B-1, the largest single-engine fighter to be built in America during the wartime period, in 1945. By the time it flew in late 1944, the Navy's need for a very long range fighter-bomber was no longer important.

a long-range, heavy fighter had disappeared and the Navy was limiting further consideration of a post-war attack types to Martin's XBTM-1 (AM) and Douglas' XBT2D-1 (AD). One of the XF8B-1 prototypes was turned over to the USAAF for evaluation at Wright Field, but development was soon discontinued.

Curtiss F8C (OC, O2C) Helldiver 1932–1938

TECHNICAL SPECIFICATIONS (F8C-5)

Type: two-place dive-bomber, ground attack
Manufacturer: Curtiss Aeroplane and Motor Co., Buffalo, New York.
Total produced (all models): 110
Power plant: One 450-hp Pratt & Whitney R-1340-4 9-cylinder radial driving a two-bladed Hamilton Standard fixed-pitch propeller.
Armament: Two fixed forward-firing .30-caliber machine guns, on flexible .30-caliber machine gun in rear cockpit, and up to 474-lbs. of bombs carried externally.
Performance: Max. speed 146-mph at s.l.; ceiling 16,050 ft.; combat range 560 mi.
Weights: 2,520-lbs. empty, 4,020-lbs. loaded.
Dimensions: Span 32 ft., length 25 ft. 8 in., wing area 308 sq. ft.

The F8C arose from a 1927 Marine Corps requirement for a multi-purpose airplane that could fulfill the roles of fighter, dive-bomber, and observation platform in one airframe. Curtiss responded by adapting its two-seat Army *Falcon* design (see, A-3, above), normally powered by a water-cooled V12, to an air-cooled radial engine approved by BUAER. In early 1928 two aircraft designated XF8C-1s were delivered to the Marine Corps and four more produc-

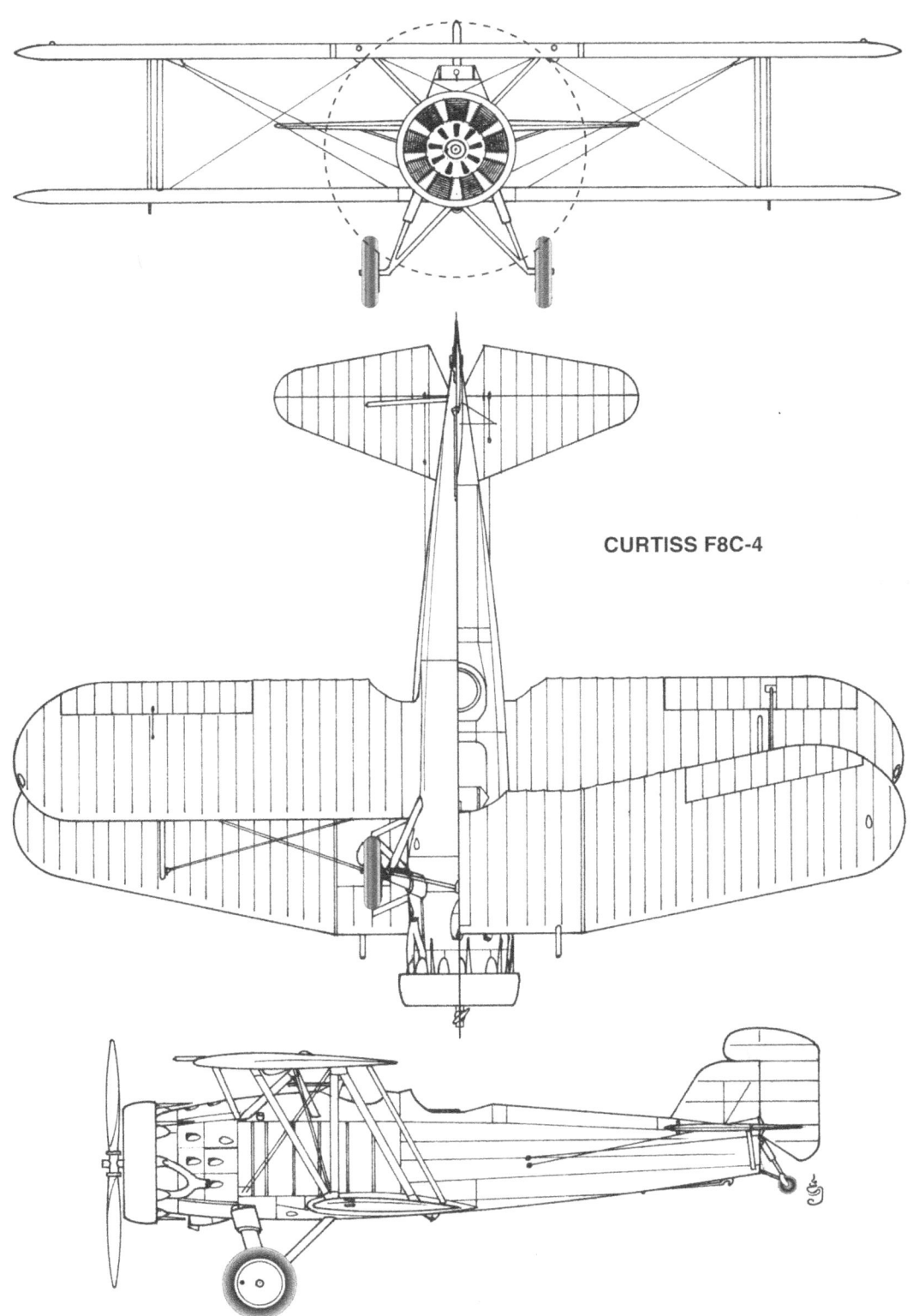

CURTISS F8C-4

One of 63 aircraft delivered to the Marine Corps in 1930 as the F8C-5 and re-designated O2C-1 in 1931. The F8C-1, a radial-engine variant of the Army A-3, was originally developed in 1928 to meet a Marine Corps requirement for a multi-role aircraft.

tion F8C-1s soon followed; and a year later, the Marines took delivery of one XF8C-3 and 21 more F8C-3 production variants. In service use, the Marines re-designated F8C-1s as the OC-1s and F8C-3s as OC-2s. They replaced World War I-era D.H.4s in many Marine units and saw combat service in Nicaragua with VO-7M.

In early 1929 BUAER authorized the improved XF8C-2 having new equal-span wings, a strengthened and redesigned fuselage, and a balanced rudder. After the flight of the first prototype in mid–1929, 25 aircraft were ordered as F8C-4s for the Navy and another 63 as F8C-5s for the Marine Corps. In 1931, two F8C-5s equipped with engine superchargers and wings slots were re-designated XF8C-6s, and one F8C airframe fitted with an R-1820 engine and an enclosed canopy was delivered to the Navy as the XF8C-7, however, neither version was ordered into production.

F8C-4s served initially with VF-1B aboard *Saratoga* but were transferred from active status to the reserves beginning in 1931. Marine F8C-5s were re-designated O2C-1s and remained active with VO-6M and VO-7M until they were replaced during 1936–1937; a few remaining examples were retained for utility duties until 1938.

Douglas FD 1933

TECHNICAL SPECIFICATIONS (XFD-1)
Type: Two-place fighter
Manufacturer: Douglas Aircraft Co., Santa Monica, California.
Total produced: 1
Power plant: One 700-hp Pratt & Whitney R-1535-64 14-cylinder radial driving a two-bladed Hamilton Standard fixed-pitch propeller.

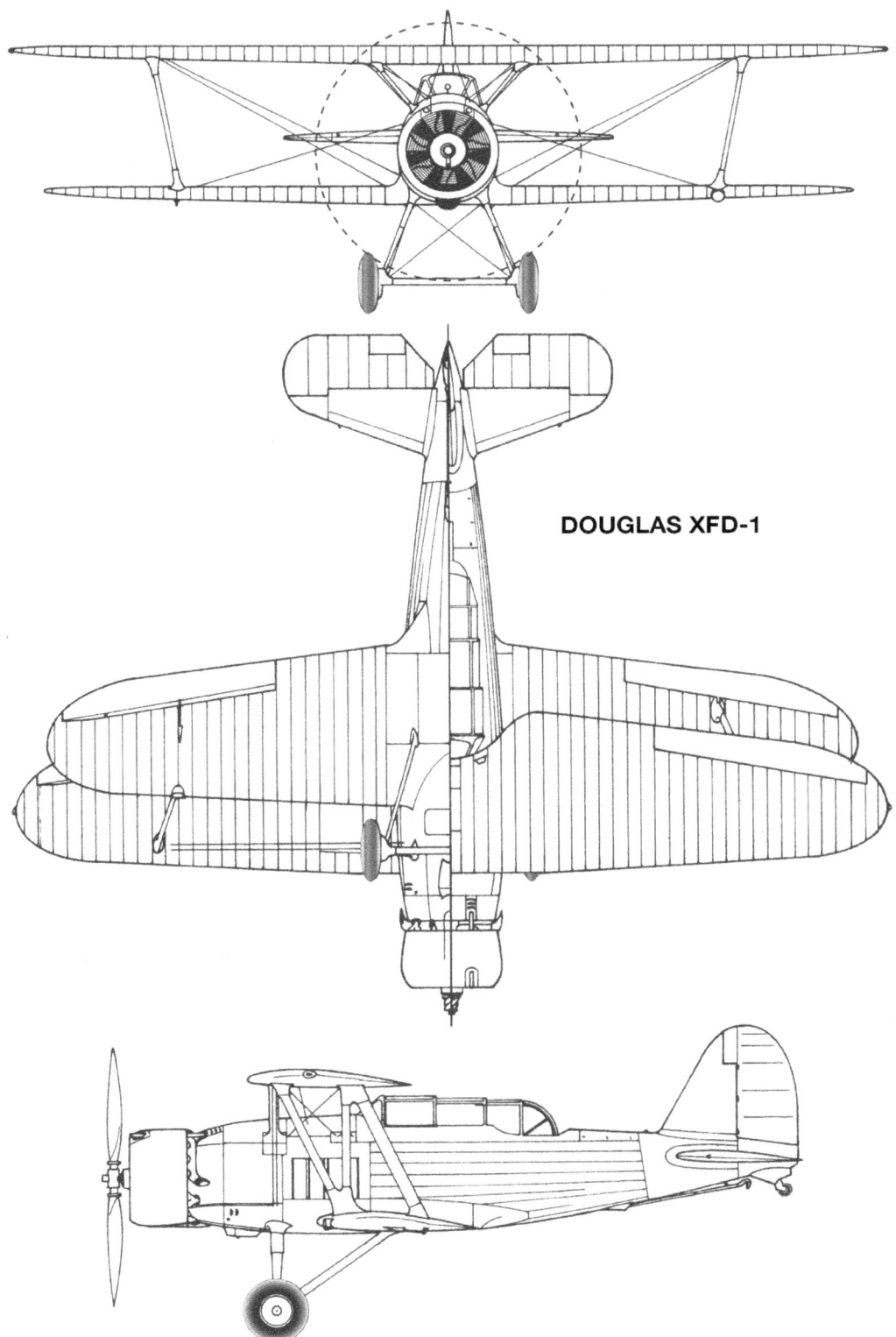

DOUGLAS XFD-1

The sole XFD-1 running up at Anacostia in 1933. The Navy was moving away from the two-seat fighter concept by the time this prototype arrived.

Armament: One fixed forward-firing .30-cal. machine gun, one flexible .30-cal. rear machine gun, and up to 500-lbs. of bombs carried externally.
Performance: Max. speed 204-mph at 8,900 ft.; ceiling 23,700 ft.; combat range 576 mi.
Weights: 3,227-lbs. empty, 5,000-lbs. loaded.
Dimensions: Span 31 ft. 6 in., length 25 ft. 4 in., wing area 295 sq. ft.

    The FD was a continuation of the two-seat fighter concept that originated with the F8C series, in which the functions of fighter, scout, and dive-bomber were combined in one airframe. A 1932 requirement listed as BUAER Design 113 called for a conventional two-seat biplane layout, fixed landing gear, 500-lb. bomb load, and an R-1535 powerplant. In June 1932 contracts for construction of single prototypes under this requirement were given to Douglas as the XFD-1 and Vought as the XF3U-1. When both prototypes arrived for testing at NAS Anacostia in June 1933 (within four days of each other), the chief differences between them was a spreader bar between the main gear struts on the XFD-1 and minor aerodynamic details.

    Ironically, by the time the XFD-1 had been delivered, the Navy had already moved away from the two-seat fighter idea in favor of scout-bomber (SB) types, which it planned to operate in conjunction with single-seat fighters. As a consequence, no further development of the XFD-1 was undertaken after 1933.

Grumman FF/SF 1931–1936

TECHNICAL SPECIFICATIONS (FF-1)

Type: Two-place fighter
Manufacturer: Grumman Aircraft Engineering Corp., Bethpage, New York.
Total produced (all USN models): 63
Power plant: One 700-hp Wright R-1820-78 9-cylinder radial driving a two-bladed Hamilton Standard variable-pitch propeller.
Armament: One fixed forward-firing .30-cal. machine gun, two flexible .30-cal. machine guns in rear cockpit, and up four 112-lb. bombs on wing racks.
Performance: Max. speed 207-mph at 4,000 ft.; ceiling 22,000 ft.; combat range 685 mi.

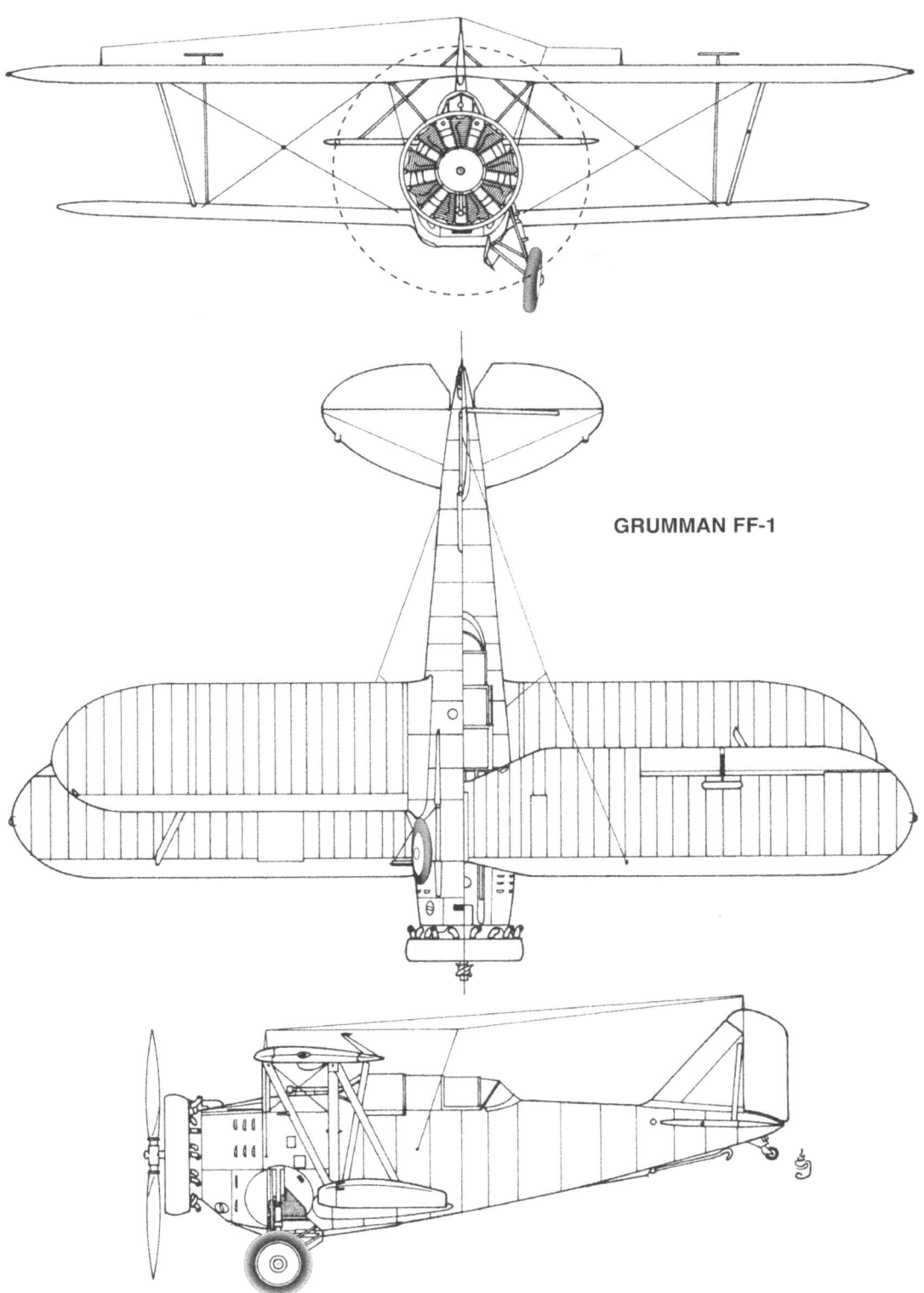

GRUMMAN FF-1

The FF-1 was the first retractable gear carrier aircraft accepted by the Navy and the first of a long line of naval aircraft to be built by Grumman. All FF-1s initially served with VF-5B in the *Lexington* air group.

Weights: 3,098-lbs. empty, 4,888-lbs. loaded.
Dimensions: Span 34 ft. 6 in., length 24 ft. 6 in., wing area 310 sq. ft.

The FF/SF was not just the Navy's first retractable-gear aircraft but was the airplane that literally got the brand new Grumman company off the ground. Soon after Grumman started an aeronautical engineering business in 1929, it obtained a Navy contract to build a new type of seaplane float that incorporated retractable landing wheels for land operations. From this beginning, the company received a contract in April 1931 to build an airplane of its own design—a two-seat-fighter designated the XFF-1—that utilized the landing gear retraction system developed for pontoons. The landing gear was manually raised and lowered by operating a hand-crank linked to a pair of long jackscrews. The XFF-1 was the first naval fighter designed around the new Wright R-1820 *Cyclone* engine and included other innovations such as an all-metal fuselage and fully enclosed canopies for the pilot and gunner/observer.

After the XFF-1 made its first flight in December 1931, testing revealed that it was faster than any single-seat Navy fighter of the day (i.e., 195-mph versus 186-mph for the F4B-2). A second prototype differing mainly in equipment carried equipment was completed as the XSF-1. In December 1932 the Navy ordered 27 production examples of the FF-1 fighter and 33 more as SF-1 scouts. Installation of R-1820-78 and -84 engines boosted top speed to over 200-mph. As deliveries commenced in 1934, FF-1s were assigned to VF-5B and SF-1s to VS-3B, both serving in *Lexington's* air group. Both types were withdrawn from active service by the end of 1936 and transferred to the reserves, where they were operated until 1940. In 1934 Canadian Car & Foundry obtained a license from Grumman to build FF-1s as the G-23, and 57 of these were subsequently manufactured between 1935–1937, fifteen examples going to the RCAF, one each to Nicaragua and Japan, and forty to the Spanish Republican forces.

Grumman F6F Hellcat 1942–1948

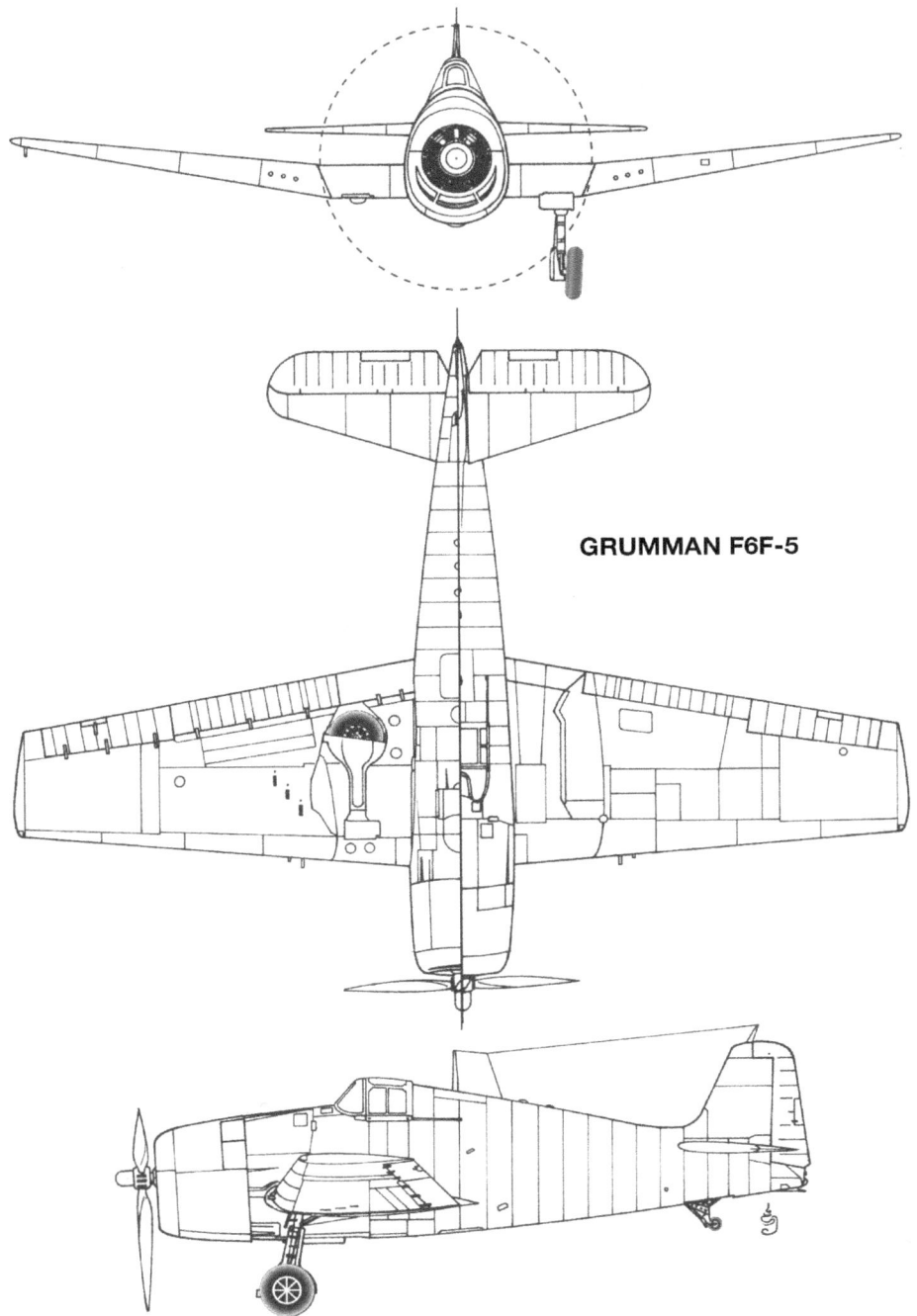

GRUMMAN F6F-5

TECHNICAL SPECIFICATIONS (F6F-5)

Type: Single-place fighter-bomber
Manufacturer: Grumman Aircraft Engineering Corp., Bethpage, New York.
Total produced (all USN/USMC models): 11,090

An F6F-5 in late war with an overall glossy sea blue paint scheme. Note stubs for HVAR rockets on wings. The -5, with strengthened wings and hardpoints for ordnance, was the first version to possess significant air-to-ground capability.

Power plant: One 2,000-hp Pratt & Whitney R-2800-10W (water injection) 18-cylinder radial driving a three-bladed Hamilton Standard fully-reversible, constant-speed propeller.
Armament: Six fixed forward-firing .50-cal. machine guns and up to 2,000-lbs. of bombs or two 11.75 in. rockets and six HVAR rockets on wing pylons.
Performance: Max. speed 386-mph at 17,300 ft.; cruise 159-mph; ceiling 37,300 ft.; range 1,530 mi. max., 1,040 mi. loaded.
Weights: 9,153-lbs. empty, 12,500-lbs. loaded.
Dimensions: Span 42 ft. 10 in., length 33 ft. 7 in., wing area 334 sq. ft.

    The F6F is best remembered as the Navy's premier carrier-based fighter of World War II, accounting for the destruction of no less than 5,156 enemy aircraft. However, with the introduction of the improved F6F-5 variant in mid–1944, the type played an increasing role as a fighter-bomber, and, indeed, during the last year of the war, many were assigned to bombing-fighter units (VFBs) as dedicated attack aircraft.

    Ordered by BUAER in June 1941 to replace the F4F and flown for the first time on June 26, 1942, the design and engineering of Grumman's XF6F-3 incorporated knowledge gained in two years of air-fighting in Europe plus the more recent combat experience of Navy and Marine pilots in the Pacific. Production F6F-3s began joining operational units in early 1943, beginning with VF-9 of *Essex,* then saw their first combat in August with VF-5 flying from *Yorktown,* and by the end of the year, had replaced F4Fs in the principal carrier units. Production of 4,423 F6F-3s included 204 F6F-3Ns equipped with APS-6 radar and 18 F6F-3Es with APS-4 radar, carried in pods under the right wing. The Royal Navy also received 252 F6F-3s as *Hellcat Is.*

    The XF6F-4 was fitted with an R-2800-27 engine but progressed no further than the prototype stage. The XF6F-5, flown in April 1944, differed in having a redesigned cowling, improved windscreen, new ailerons, stronger tail group, additional armor protection, and strengthened wings with hardpoints for bombs and rockets. Late production -5s had 20-millimeter cannons in place of the two inner .50 cal. machine guns. With these enhancements, the F6F acquired significant air-to-ground capabilities. A total of 6,940 F6F-5s, including 1,189 radar-equipped F6F-5Ns, had been delivered to Navy and Marine units by the time production ended in November 1945; a further 930 had also been delivered to the Royal Navy as *Hellcat IIs*. A number of F6F-5s were retrofitted with camera equipment and were re-designated as F6F-5Ps. Two XF6F-6s with 2,100-hp R-2800-18W engines and four-bladed propellers flew in mid–1944, but these were never placed in production.

During the massive downsizing that followed the end of World War II, many Navy and Marine F6F units were simply decommissioned. In the smaller post-war Navy, F6F-5s were rapidly replaced by newer F8F-1/-2s in fighter units and by F4U-4/-4Bs in fighter-bomber units, so that the type had almost disappeared from frontline service by 1947. Some F6F-5Ns remained in service a little longer. Many F6Fs served in the Navy and Marine reserves until the early 1950s, and Naval Training Command also used them as advanced trainers until 1953–1954. Some F6F-5s were converted to F6F-5K target drones, and in mid–1952, used as carrier-launched, remote-control missiles against targets in North Korea. The last F6F-5Ks were scrapped in 1959.

Grumman F7F Tigercat 1943–1954

TECHNICAL SPECIFICATIONS (F7F-3)
Type: Single or two-place fighter-bomber and night fighter
Manufacturer: Grumman Aircraft Engineering Corp., Bethpage, New York.
Total produced (all USN/USMC models): 363
Power plant: Two 2,100-hp Pratt & Whitney R-2800-34W (water injection) 18-cylinder radials driving three-bladed Hamilton Standard fully-feathering, constant-speed propellers.
Armament: Four fixed forward-firing 20-millimeter cannons in the wings, four forward-firing .50-cal. machine guns in the nose and up to 2,000-lbs. of bombs and six HVAR rockets on wing pylons or one torpedo on the centerline.
Performance: Max. speed 435-mph at 22,200 ft.; cruise 222-mph; ceiling 40,700 ft.; range 1,572 mi. max., 1,200 mi. loaded.
Weights: 16,270-lbs. empty, 25,720-lbs. loaded.
Dimensions: Span 51 ft. 6 in., length 45 ft. 4 in., wing area 455 sq. ft.

The F7F was the first carrier-based twin-engine, tricycle gear aircraft to be placed in production by BUAER. Conceived in early 1941, the Model G-51 owed much of its design concept to Grumman's accumulated experience with two other twin-engine fighter projects, the Navy XF5F-1 *Skyrocket* and the Army XP-50, neither of which achieved production. After reviewing Grumman's proposal in June 1941, BUAER authorized construction of two prototypes under the designation XF7F-1. Because of the aircraft's unprecedented mass (80 percent heavier than the F6F), it was slated to operate from the planned 45,000-ton *Midway* class of carriers. The XF7F-1 made its first flight on November 3, 1943 and was delivered to the Navy for testing in April 1944. Before service evaluations were completed, Grumman received the go-ahead to produce 500 F7F-1s. Unsatisfactory carrier trials, plus the Marine's urgent need for tactical aircraft, brought about a decision to allocate F7F production to shore-based Marine Corps units. However, further operational difficulties and engineering changes delayed production so that no F7Fs reached operational units in time to see combat.

Only 34 F7F-1s had been delivered when a re-evaluation of the program caused production to be shifted to the F7F-2N night fighter version. The -2N added an APS-6 radar to the nose plus a second cockpit behind the pilot for a radar operator, and 65 were ultimately delivered to the Marine Corps between January and March 1945. From March 1945 to June 1946,

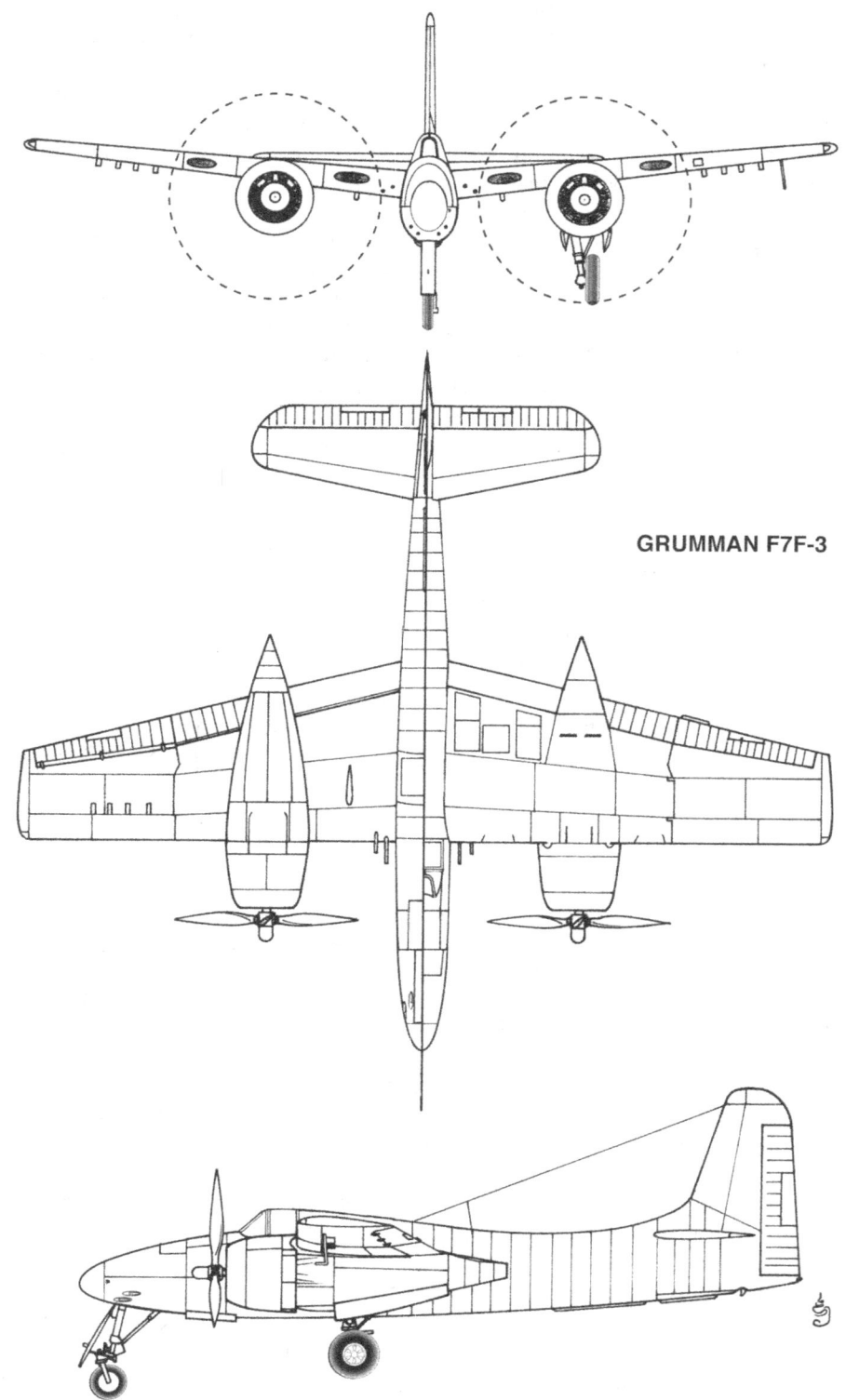

GRUMMAN F7F-3

Top: An F7F-1 single-seat day fighter assigned to VMF-911 at MCAS Cherry Point in 1945. Progress in the war plus continuing carrier qualification problems led to a reassessment of the F7F program. *Bottom:* The sixth F7F-3N as seen in 1946 prior to delivery. Marine F7F-3Ns later serving with VMF(N)-513 and -542 saw extensive combat action as night fighters and intruders during the Korean War.

Grumman built 189 single-seat F7F-3 day fighters followed by 60 two-seat F7F-3N night fighters. The -3s featured a strengthened airframe and enlarged vertical fin, and in -3N, the .50-cal. nose guns were deleted to make room for a bulbous radome housing an SCR-720 radar. A number of single-seat F7F-3 day fighters were subsequently modified for installation of cameras and other photographic equipment and re-designated F7F-3Ps. F7F production ended in November 1946 following delivery of 13 F7F-4Ns, which differed in having more airframe strengthening and a streamlined nose radome that housed an APS-19 radar. The -4Ns were sent to NATC, where, in late 1946, they successfully completed carrier trials aboard *Franklin D. Roosevelt*. Earlier efforts to complete carrier qualifications with F7F-3Ns had not been successful and the -4N was the only F7F version to be certified for carrier operations. In 1948 a number of F7F-2s were converted to F7F-2D target drone controllers, which involved removal of armament and installation of an F8F-type cockpit and canopy behind the pilot.

VMF-911 was the first to receive F7F-1s and served as a transitional training unit. Deliveries of F7F-2Ns to VMF(N)-531 began in January 1945 and the squadron deployed overseas in August. F7F-3s began equipping east and west coast Marine fighter squadrons in mid–1945 but were withdrawn after only two or three years of service. From mid–1945 to mid–1946, F7F-3Ns initially entered service with VMF(N)-533 and -534, but were later transferred to VMF(N)-513 and -542. During 1950–1953, F7F-3Ns saw extensive combat from land bases in Korea, flying night fighter and interdiction missions, and in July 1951, an F7F-3N of VMF(N)-513 accounted for first Marine night "kill" of the war. Marine F7F-3Ps also flew photo-reconnaissance sorties over Korea while serving with the MAG-11 photographic unit. After the Korean War, remaining F7Fs served with Marine reserve units until 1955 and the last Navy F7F-2D drone controllers were retired in late 1957.

Grumman F8F Bearcat 1945–1952

TECHNICAL SPECIFICATIONS (F8F-1)

Type: Single-place fighter-bomber
Manufacturer: Grumman Aircraft Engineering Corp., Bethpage, New York.
Total produced (all models): 1,058
Power plant: One 2,100-hp Pratt & Whitney R-2800-34W (water injection) 18-cylinder radial driving a four-bladed Aeroproducts fully-reversible, constant-speed propeller.
Armament: Four fixed forward-firing .50-cal. machine guns and up to 2,000-lbs. of bombs or four HVAR rockets on wing pylons.
Performance: Max. speed 421-mph at 19,700 ft.; cruise 163-mph; ceiling 38,700 ft.; range 1,105 mi. (internal fuel).
Weights: 7,070-lbs. empty, 12,947-lbs. loaded.
Dimensions: Span 35 ft. 10 in., length 28 ft. 3 in., wing area 244 sq. ft.

The F8F was the ultimate development of the Grumman propeller-driven fighter series that had begun with the FF-1. The Model G-58 was conceived in mid–1943 as the smallest and lightest airframe that could be evolved around an R-2800 engine. Ordered by BUAER in November 1943 as the XF8F-1, it was the first Navy fighter classified as a deck-launched interceptor (DLI). According the DLI concept, a fighter would be launched from the carrier, then directed on an intercept vector to incoming hostile aircraft by another aircraft equipped with airborne early-warning radar (e.g., TBM-3Ws). In addition to its DLI function, the XF8F-1 was intended to fulfill the fighter-bomber role of the F6F-5.

The first prototype flew on August 21, 1944 and in October a contract was placed for 2,023 F8F-1s; in early 1945, General Motors was brought in to produce 1,876 more under license as the F3M-1. Testing revealed a phenomenal 4,570 ft./min. climb rate (compared to the F6F-

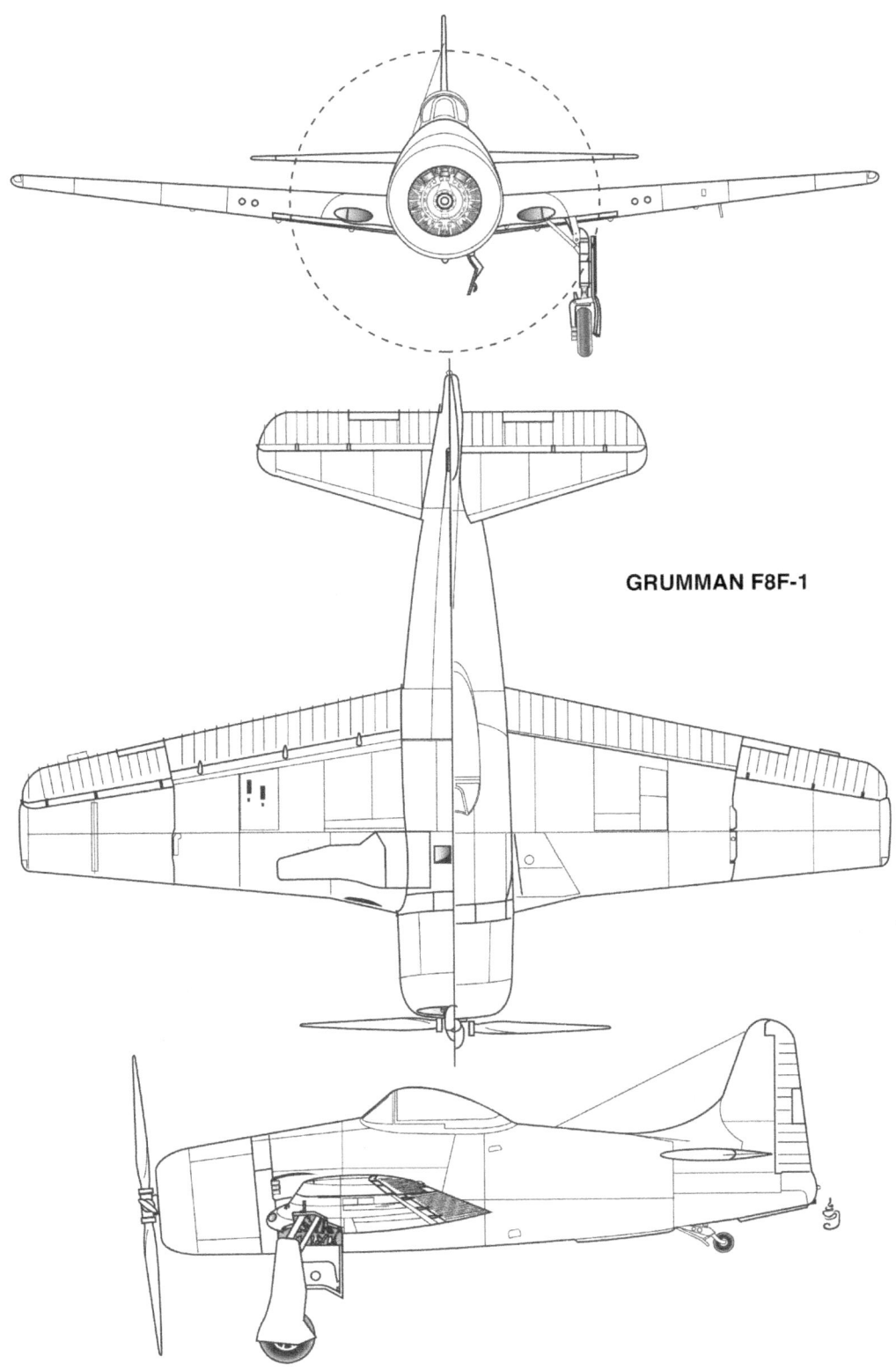

GRUMMAN F8F-1

F8F-1 armed with HVAR rockets seen while serving at the Navy testing range at NAF Inyokern in the early 1950s. The bottoms of wings were painted white so that observers on the range could see the weapons leave the aircraft. French F8Fs were used as fighter-bombers in Indo-China in the mid–1950s.

5's 2,980 ft./min.) and a top speed of 424-mph. Delivery of production aircraft began in February 1945, however, VJ-Day cutbacks caused Grumman's contract to be reduced to 770 aircraft and GM's to be cancelled altogether. The 552 F8F-1s built were followed by 126 F8F-1Bs with four 20-millimeter cannons, and 15 radar-equipped F8F-1Ns. Starting in 1948, Grumman produced 293 F8F-2s featuring a revised engine cowling, taller tail fin, and 20-millimeter armament, plus 60 photographic F8F-2Ps and 12 F8F-2N night fighters.

VF-19 was the first squadron to become operational with F8F-1s in May 1945, and F8F-1s and -2s had become the Navy's standard shipboard fighter by 1948, equipping 24 squadrons. But the arrival of combat-capable jet fighters (e.g., F9F and F2H) in mid–1949 caused the F8F's active career to be very brief, all fighter variants having been withdrawn from frontline units by the end of 1950, with F8F-2Ps remaining active a while longer until 1952. Many were afterward transferred to reserve and training units, where they continued in service until 1954, and the Marine Corps used a small number of F8F-2s for operational training in 1952 and 1953. After Navy service, 250 surplus F8Fs were transferred to the French *Armée de l'Air* and another 129 to the Royal Thai Air Force. The French F8Fs saw extensive combat as fighter-bombers in Indo-China in the mid–1950s and were later absorbed into the independent South Vietnamese Air Force.

Goodyear F2G Super Corsair 1944–1947

TECHNICAL SPECIFICATIONS (F2G-2)
Type: Single-place fighter-bomber
Manufacturer: Goodyear Aircraft Corp., Akron, Ohio.
Total produced (two models): 15

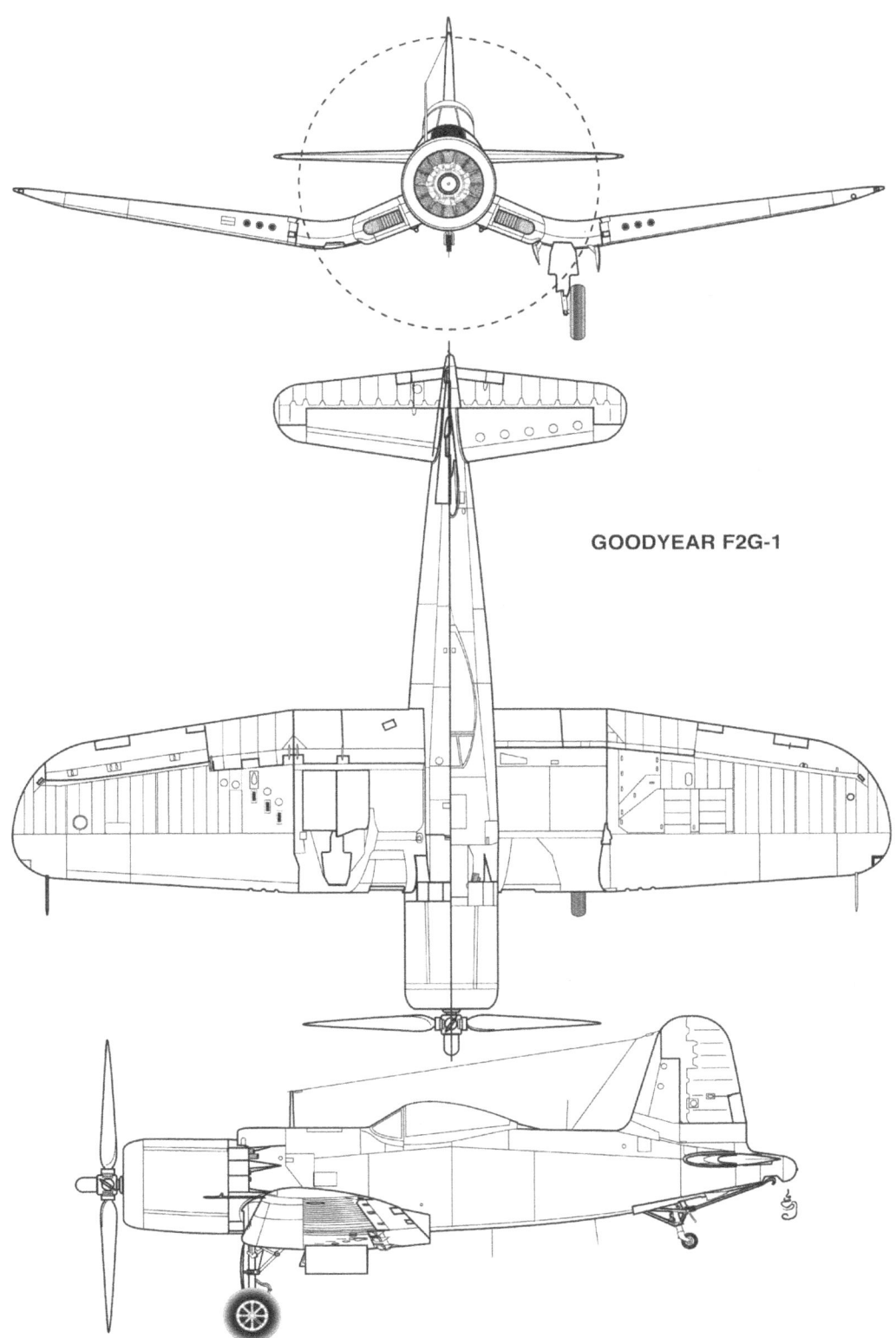

GOODYEAR F2G-1

One of five F2G-1s as it appeared in 1947 while assigned to NATC. Most of the original production ordered (418 aircraft) was earmarked to serve with the Marines from land bases.

Power plant: One 3,000-hp Pratt & Whitney R-4360-4 28-cylinder radial driving a four-bladed Hamilton Standard fully-reversible, constant-speed propeller.
Armament: Four fixed forward-firing .50-cal. machine guns and up to 3,200-lbs. of bombs or eight HVAR rockets on wing pylons.
Performance: Max. speed 431-mph at 16,400 ft.; ceiling 38,800 ft.; range 1,190 mi. (internal fuel).
Weights: 10,249-lbs. empty, 15,422-lbs. loaded.
Dimensions: Span 41 ft., length 33 ft. 9 in., wing area 314 sq. ft.

The F2G was an independent development by Goodyear based upon the F4U/FG airframe. Goodyear had been license-producing F4U-1 variants as the FG-1, -1A, and -1D since 1942, and in early 1944, BUAER initiated a program to adapt installation of the four-row R-4360 engine to the FG airframe. The purpose of the project was to evolve an aircraft for the Marine Corps which was capable of functioning either as low-level interceptor to be used against Japanese *Kamikaze* aircraft or as a fighter-bomber. After completion of initial test flights in March 1944, Goodyear was awarded a contract for 418 land-based F2G-1s plus 10 F2G-2s equipped for carrier operations. In addition to the modifications to the cowling and forward fuselage necessitated by the larger engine, the F2G-1 featured a cut down rear turtledeck with an all-around vision bubble canopy. As testing indicated the need for an increase in vertical tail area to offset increased torque, 15 inches of height was added to the base of the fin and rudder.

Only five F2G-1s and five F2G-2s had been delivered when Goodyear's production contract was cancelled right after V-J Day, and five more almost complete F2G-1s were delivered shortly afterward. Some of these aircraft were tested by NATC until 1947, and then sold as surplus. In the hands of civilian operators, a number of F2Gs went on to achieve fame in the late 1940s air racing circuit.

Berliner-Joyce F2J 1933

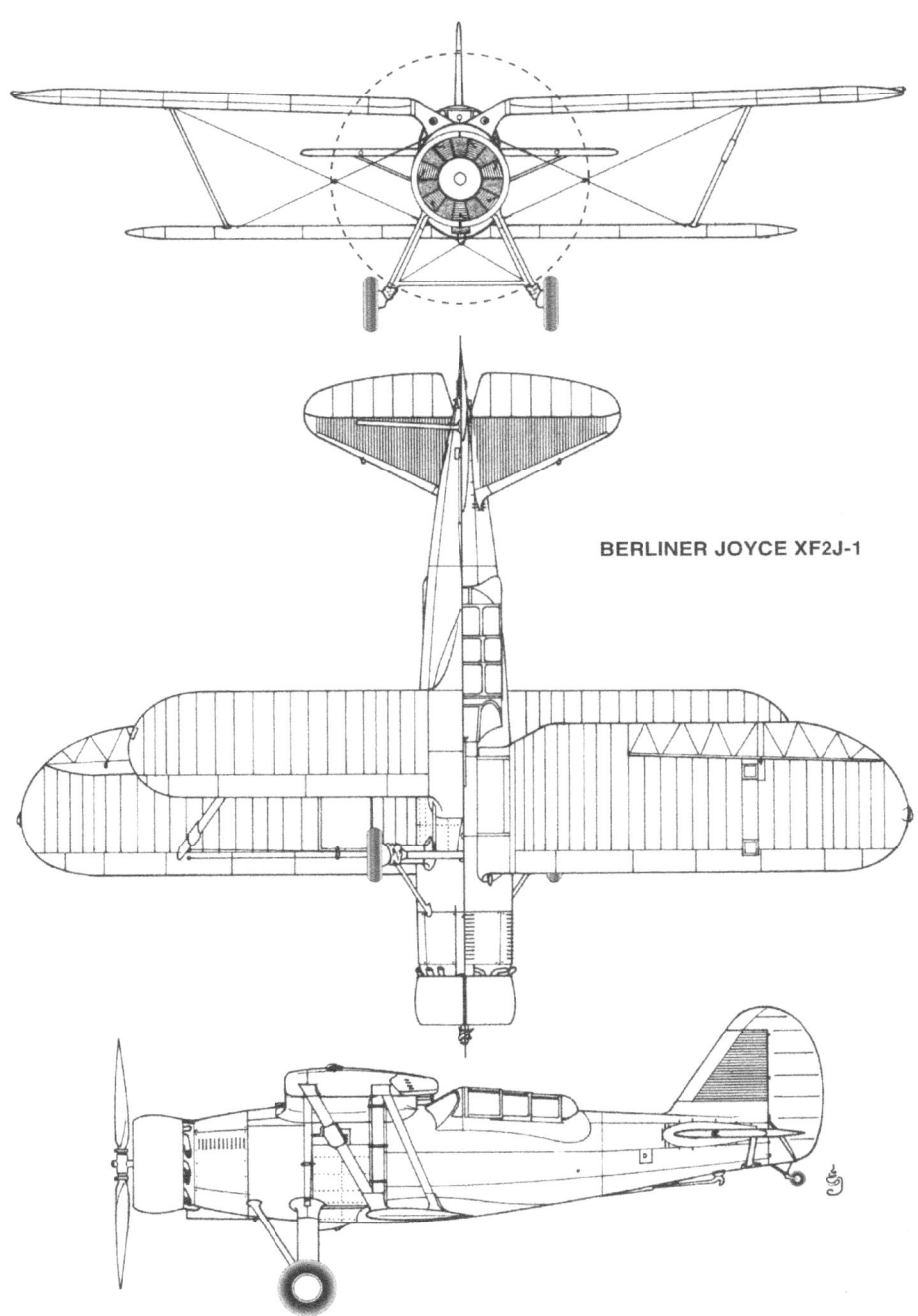

BERLINER JOYCE XF2J-1

TECHNICAL SPECIFICATIONS (XF2J-1)

Type: Two-place fighter
Manufacturer: Berliner-Joyce Aircraft Corp., Baltimore, Maryland
Total produced: 1

The short-lived XF2J-1 while at Anacostia for trials in 1933. The two-seat fighter concept ultimately evolved into the mid–1930s scout-bomber requirement.

Power plant: One 625-hp Wright R-1510-92 14-cylinder radial driving a two-bladed Hamilton Standard fixed-pitch propeller.
Armament: One fixed forward-firing .30-cal. machine gun, one flexible .30-cal. rear machine gun, and up to 500-lbs. of bombs carried externally.
Performance: Max. speed 193-mph at 6,000 ft.; ceiling 21,500 ft.; combat range 522 mi.
Weights: 3,211-lbs. empty, 4,851-lbs. loaded.
Dimensions: Span 36 ft., length 28 ft. 10 in., wing area 304 sq. ft.

One of the final products of the short-lived Berliner-Joyce Aircraft Corporation (1929–1935), the F2J was built to fulfill the same multi-role biplane fighter requirement as the contemporaneous FD and F3U, but, unlike them, was not tied to a specific BUAER design. Following an unsuccessful effort with its single-seat XFJ-1 and -2, Berliner-Joyce received a contract in June 1931 to construct a two-seat fighter prototype under the designation XF2J-1. Much of its general design concept was borrowed from the company's two-seat Army Y1P-16 fighter, whose chief characteristic was upper wings that gulled into the fuselage instead of being supported by conventional cabane struts. Like the rival FD and F3U, the XF2J-1 featured fixed landing gear, a metal-clad fuselage, and fabric-covered wings. Sometime after delivery, a fully enclosed cockpit canopy was also installed.

Completion of the prototype extended over a two-year period and delivery to Anacostia did not occur until mid–1933. Testing subsequently revealed poor visibility (presumably due to the wing configuration) and sub-standard performance compared to other new scout and fighter types, so no further development was undertaken.

General Motors FM Wildcat 1942–1945

TECHNICAL SPECIFICATIONS (FM-2)

Type: single-place fighter-bomber
Manufacturer: Eastern Aircraft Division of General Motors, Detroit, Michigan.
Total produced (all USN models): 5,904

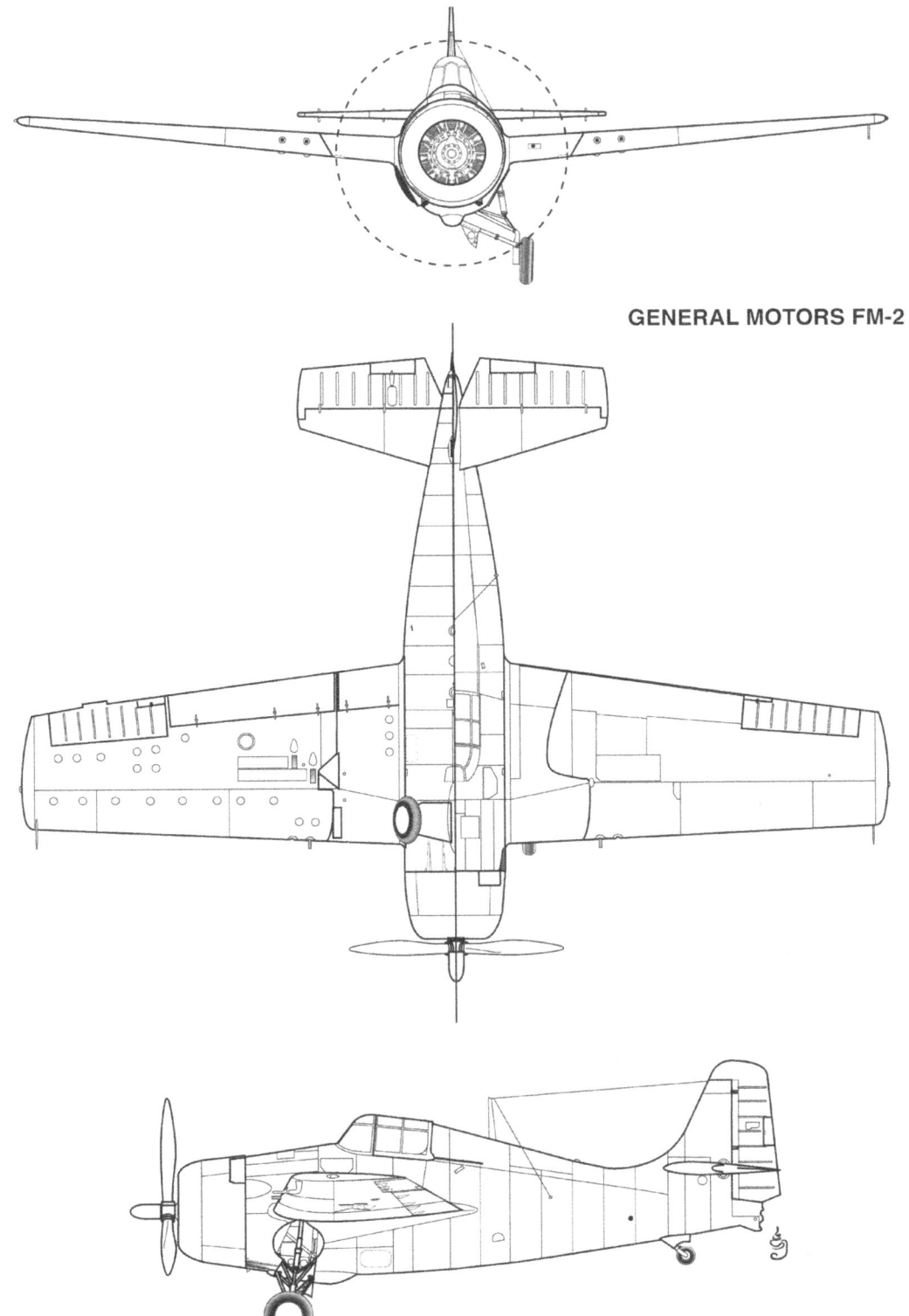

GENERAL MOTORS FM-2

Late-war FM-2s in Pacific dark glossy sea blue paint scheme. Based on the XF4F-8, the FM-2 was the first version of the *Wildcat* to possess significant air-to-ground capability. Almost all served aboard escort carriers.

Power plant: One 1,350-hp Wright R-1820-56 9-cylinder radial driving a three-bladed Curtiss Electric fully-reversible, constant-speed propeller.
Armament: Four fixed forward-firing .50-cal. machine guns and up to 500-lbs. of bombs or six HVAR rockets on wing pylons.
Performance: Max. speed 332-mph at 28,800 ft.; cruise 164-mph; ceiling 34,700 ft.; range 1,310 mi. max., 900 mi. loaded.
Weights: 5,448-lbs. empty, 8,271-lbs. loaded.
Dimensions: Span 38 ft., length 28 ft. 11 in., wing area 260 sq. ft.

The FM was a direct development of Grumman's F4F fighter series. The first General Motors (GM) model, the FM-1, was in fact a license-built duplicate of the F4F-4, and 1,127 FM-1s were delivered to Navy from late 1942, plus an additional 312 to the Royal Navy under Lend-Lease as *Martlet Vs*. In late 1942, GM began a second development based upon the substantially revised Grumman-built XF4F-8. This version, ordered into production as the FM-2, was 500-lbs. lighter than previous F4F variants and featured a new turbo-supercharged R-1820–56 engine and taller tail fin to offset increased torque. Fitted with wing racks for bombs and HVAR rockets, it was also the first *Wildcat* having significant fighter-bomber capabilities. BUAER's decision to manufacture FM-2s alongside larger and faster F6Fs and F4Us was tied to its suitability for operations from smaller escort carriers. (Note: 82 CVEs were completed between 1941–1945.)

Deliveries of FM-2s to active fleet units began in September 1943 and continued through August 1945, at which point 4,777 examples had been built, including 370 supplied to the Royal Navy as *Wildcat VIs*. In Atlantic CVE operations, FM-2s were typically paired with TBMs for anti-submarine patrol; in the Pacific, FM-2s also flew air cover and air-to-ground sorties in support of invasion forces. When the war ended, most of the CVE fleet was decommissioned and their FM-2s were withdrawn and scrapped.

Vought F2U 1929

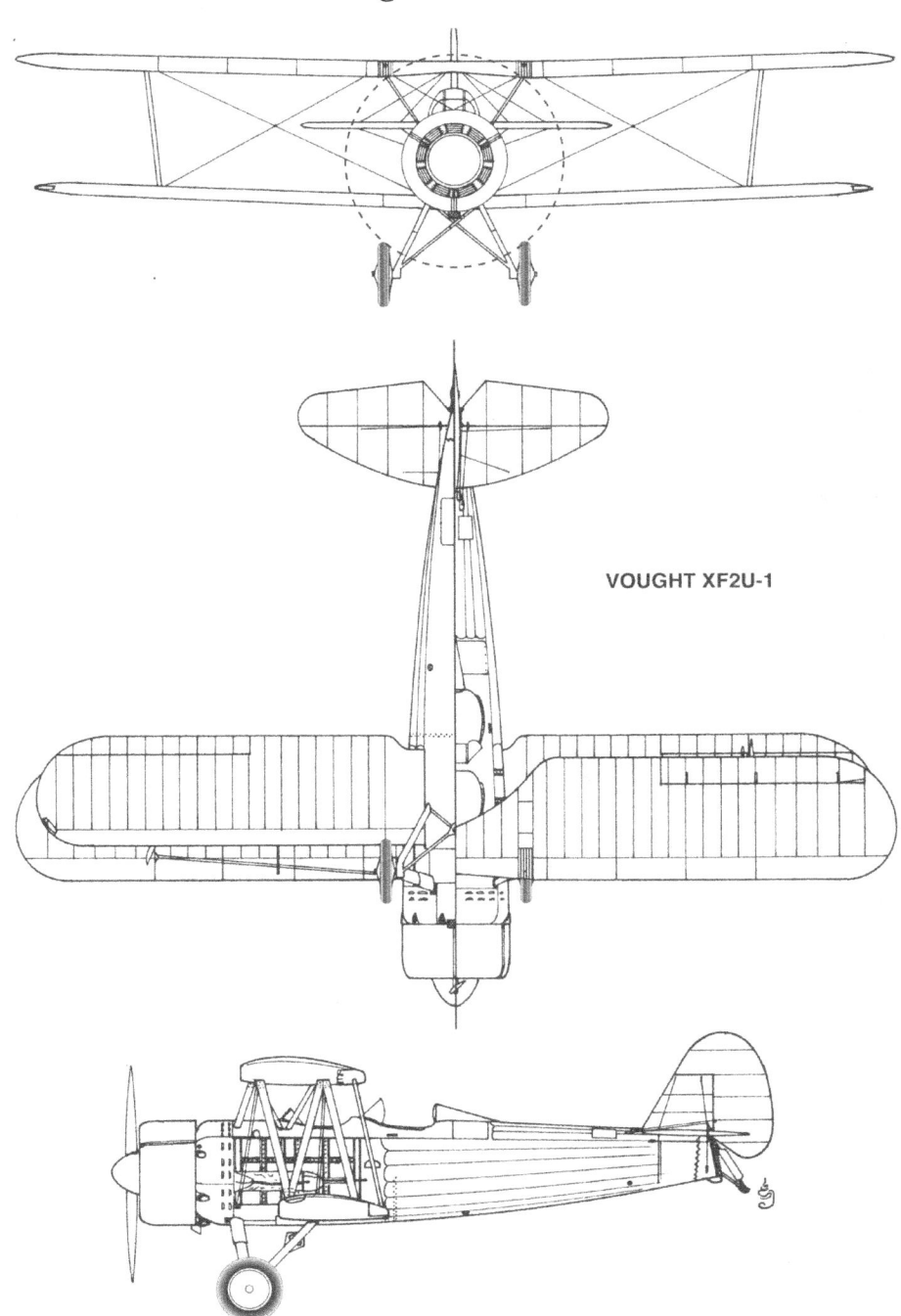

TECHNICAL SPECIFICATIONS (XF2U-1)

Type: Two-place fighter
Manufacturer: Chance Vought Corp., Long Island City, New York.
Total produced (all models): 1

Intended to compete with the Curtiss F8C, the XF2U-1 emerged in 1929 with an innovative NACA cowling. Many of its aerodynamic characteristics were derived from Vought's successful series of O2U float and observation planes.

Power plant: One 450-hp Pratt & Whitney R-1340C 9-cylinder radial driving a two-bladed Hamilton Standard fixed-pitch propeller.
Armament: Two fixed forward-firing .30-caliber machine guns, one flexible .30-caliber machine gun in rear cockpit, and up to 474-lbs. of bombs carried externally.
Performance: Max. speed 146-mph at s.l.; ceiling 18,700 ft.; combat range 495 mi.
Weights: 2,539-lbs. empty, 4,208-lbs. loaded.
Dimensions: Span 36 ft., length 27 ft., wing area 318 sq. ft.

Ordered under a BUAER contract issued in 1928, the XF2U-1 represented an attempt by Vought to offer the Navy a design that would be competitive against Curtiss' F8C-4/-5 two-seat fighter/dive-bomber. Like Curtiss during this period, Vought was a major Navy contractor, having delivered over 400 aircraft (huge volume in those days) since 1918. Sharing many aerodynamic and structural characteristics with Vought's successful O2U series, the XF2U-1 prototype emerged with an NACA-type cowling and slightly larger overall dimensions than the rival F8C. The prototype was delivered to the Navy for trials in June 1929, but BUAER apparently reasoned that its performance offered no advantage over existing F8Cs, and further development was discontinued.

Vought F4U (FG, F3A) and AU Corsair 1940–1955

TECHNICAL SPECIFICATIONS (F4U-4)

Type: Single-place fighter-bomber
Manufacturer: Chance Vought Division of United Aircraft Corp., Stratford, Connecticut.
Total produced (all USN/USMC models): 14,346
Power plant: One 2,450-hp Pratt & Whitney R-2800-18W (water injection) 18-cylinder radial driving a four-bladed Hamilton Standard fully-reversible, constant-speed propeller.
Armament: Six fixed forward-firing .50-cal. machine guns and up to 2,000-lbs. of bombs or two 11.75 in. rockets and six HVAR rockets on wing pylons.

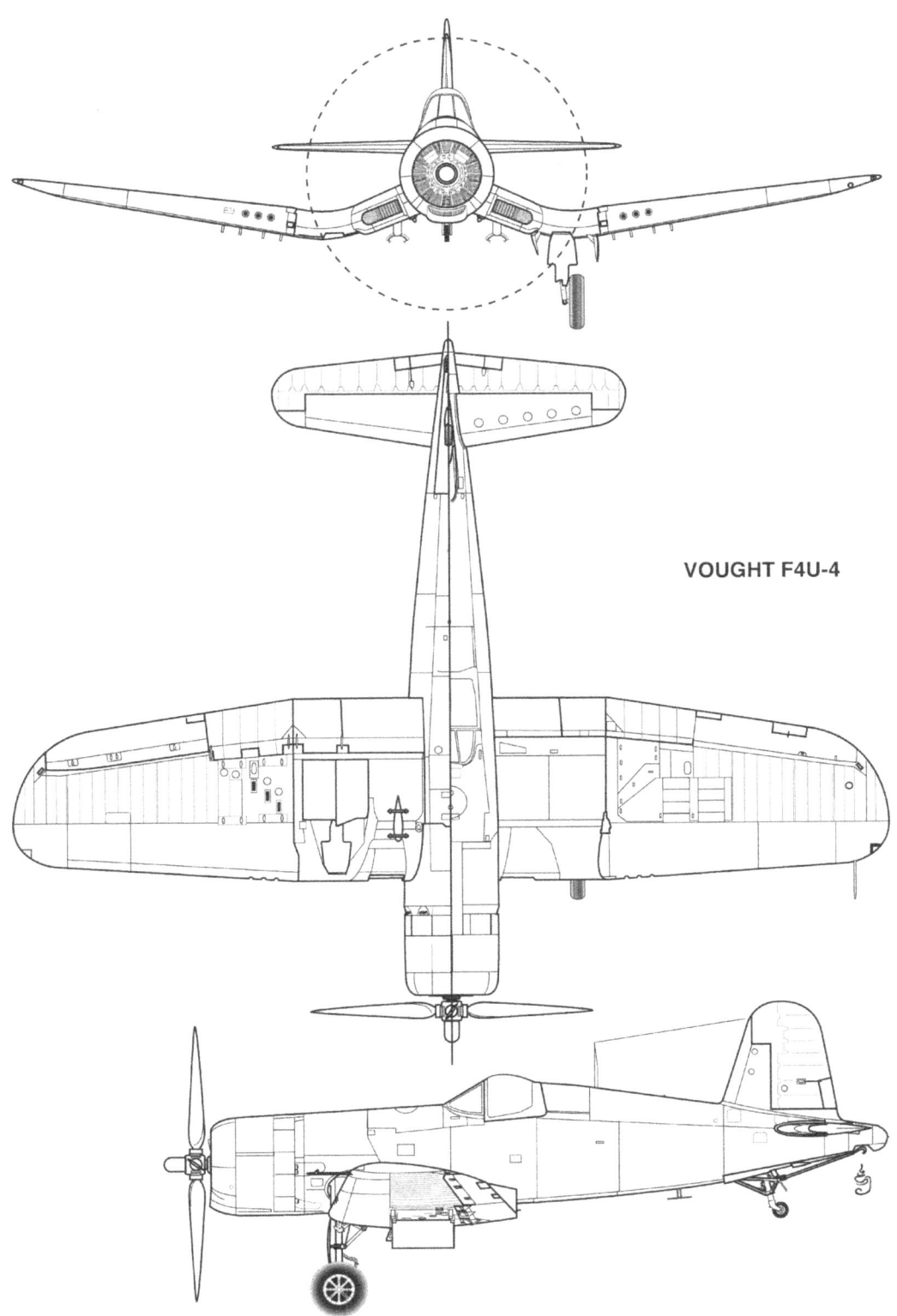

VOUGHT F4U-4

Top: Late block F4U-4, notable by its flat windscreen, seen with eight HVAR rockets. F4U-4 production continued after the war and included 294 F4U-4Bs armed with four 20-mm cannons. Final examples retired from the Navy reserve in 1956. *Bottom:* One of 315 F4U-5Ns built between 1947 and 1951. F4U-5Ns saw extensive service during the Korean War; they were operated from carriers by the Navy and from land bases by the Marines.

Performance: Max. speed 446-mph at 26,200 ft.; cruise 215-mph; ceiling 41,500 ft.; range 1,560 mi. max., 1,005 mi. loaded.
Weights: 9,205-lbs. empty, 14,670-lbs. loaded.
Dimensions: Span 41 ft., length 33 ft. 8 in., wing area 314 sq. ft.

While the F4U is universally regarded as one of the most outstanding air superiority fighters of World War II, its prowess as a ground attack platform kept it in production longer (1942–1952) than any other type of Navy or Marine propeller-driven fighter. Originating from

The AU-1, designed entirely to a Marine Corps requirement, was the slowest *Corsair* variant (238-mph at 9,500 feet) but could lift twice the payload of the F4U-4 and possessed more armor protection.

a 1938 BUAER requirement for a new monoplane shipboard fighter, Vought's Model V-166B was evolved around the experimental 2,000-hp XR-2800-4 engine and characterized by inverted gull wings designed to provide ground clearance for a large-diameter (i.e., 13 ft. 3 in.) three-bladed propeller while keeping the length of the landing gear legs and ground angle to a minimum. BUAER ordered a single prototype in June 1938 as the XF4U-1, and after it flew on May 29, 1940, it became the first U. S. fighter to exceed 400-mph in level flight. But the latest reports on the European air war revealed that to be effective in combat, the XF4U-1 would need heavier gun armament, more armor protection, and self-sealing fuel tanks. Revisions to the basic design necessitated moving fuel tanks from the wings to the fuselage in order to accommodate four more .50-cal. guns plus relocating the cockpit three feet aft to allow for a new fuselage tank positioned over the center-of-gravity.

In June 1941, after approval of design changes, Vought was given a contract for 585 F4U-1s and the first production model flew in June 1942, followed by initial deliveries to the Navy in late July. Carrier trials conducted aboard *Sangamon* in September 1942 proved unsatisfactory; restricted visibility during approach from the aft-located cockpit and poor handling qualities at low airspeeds caused F4U-1s to be rated unsuitable for carrier operations. As a direct consequence, F4U-1s were thereafter issued to Marine land-based units, which, from early 1943, commenced combat operations in the Southwest Pacific theater. To boost *Corsair* production, contacts were placed with Goodyear and Brewster to manufacture license-built versions respectively as the FG-1 and F3A-1. These models were to be strictly land-based, being built without wing-folds. Introduction of a raised canopy and cockpit floor, raised tailwheel leg, wing stall strip, and modified main gear struts on the F4U-1A in mid–1943 remedied the type's chief carrier shortcomings, but land-based units, Marine and Navy, continued to be principal users until the Navy finally cleared the type for carrier operations in mid–1944.

Though not designed to carry external ordnance, F4U-1s/-1As began flying fighter-bomber sorties after being retrofitted with Brewster racks allowing a 1,000-lb. bomb to be carried on the centerline. In August 1943 the F4U-1C with four 20-mm cannon armament went into service but was discontinued after 200 had been delivered. The F4U-1D, the first true fighter-bomber version, built also as the FG-1D and F3A-1D, appeared in April 1944 with wing racks for two 1,000-lb. bombs, pylons for eight HVAR rockets, and a 2,250-hp R-2800-8W engine. By the war's end, total Navy and Marine production of all -1 variants numbered 13,385, plus 2,382 to the Royal Navy and Royal New Zealand Air Force as *Corsair Is* (-1), *IIs* (-1A), and *IIIs* (-1D).

In 1943 thirty-two F4U-1s modified for installation of an autopilot and wing-mounted air-interception radar were re-designated F4U-2s and served initially with Navy and Marine land-based night fighter units. Design work on a high-altitude XF4U-3 equipped with a turbo-supercharger was begun in 1942, but low wartime priority postponed completion of the prototype until 1946, and the project was eventually discontinued after delivery of only two examples (i.e., one XF4U-3 built by Vought and one FG-3 built by Goodyear). The F4U-4, featuring a 2,450-hp R-2800-18W engine driving a four-bladed propeller, more armor protection, and a revised cockpit arrangement, appeared in April 1944 and deliveries to operational units commenced in late October. By V-J Day, 1,912 F4U-4s had been completed, plus 200 built by Goodyear as FG-4s. Goodyear's contract was cancelled but Vought production continued until 1947, including a further 445 F4U-4s, 294 F4U-4Bs armed with four 20-mm cannons, nine F4U-4Ps equipped with cameras, and one F4U-4N with radar.

Development continued post-war, and in 1946 Vought introduced the XF4U-5 with a 2,850-hp R-2800-34W engine having a two-stage supercharger, four 20-mm cannons, a blown canopy, and refinements to the cockpit. A foot was added to the forward fuselage to house the two-stage blower, and the -5 was the first version having completely metalized wings. From 1947 to 1951, Navy and Marine units took delivery of 223 F4U-5 fighter-bombers, 315 F4U-5N/NL night fighters, and 30 camera-equipped F4U-5Ps. Developed in 1949 to a Marine Corps requirement for low-altitude close air support, the XF4U-6, re-designated XAU-1 in 1951, carried 4,000-lbs. of external ordnance and possessed additional armor protection. Marine units accepted delivery of 111 production AU-1s in 1951 and 1952. *Corsair* production finally ended in December 1952 when the last of 94 F4U-7s (essentially F4U-4s with AU-1 refinements) was completed for the French *Aeronavale*.

VMF-124 was first Marine squadron declared combat-ready with F4U-1s in December 1942 and commenced operations from Guadalcanal in February 1943. As deliveries continued into 1943, F4U-1s replaced F4Fs in all principal Marine fighter units. Land-based VF-17 became the first F4U-equipped Navy combat unit in September 1943. Royal Navy *Corsair IIs* deployed from HMS *Victorious* in April 1944 were the first actually utilized in carrier combat. F4U-1Ds and FG-1Ds were not embarked aboard U. S. Navy carriers for combat duty until January 1945 and served primarily in VBF squadrons.

During the post-war downsizing, only F4U-4s were retained in active Navy and Marine units, with many F4U-1Ds and FG-1Ds being transferred to the reserves. As new F4U-4Bs began entering service in 1946–1947, F4U-4s also began the transition to reserve units. F4U-5s began to equip Navy and Marine squadrons in 1947–1948, followed in 1950–1951 by F4U-5Ns and F4U-5Ps. Throughout the Korean War (1950–1953), Navy and Marine *Corsairs* operating from carrier and land bases saw extensive combat in the roles of close air support, night air defense and interdiction, and tactical reconnaissance. During 1953–1954, remaining F4Us and AUs were phased-out of active service, some serving with reserve units until 1956. French *Corsairs* remained active until the early 1960s and a number of ex-Navy and Marine F4Us served with air forces in South and Central America into the 1970s.

Brewster SBA (SBN) 1936–1942

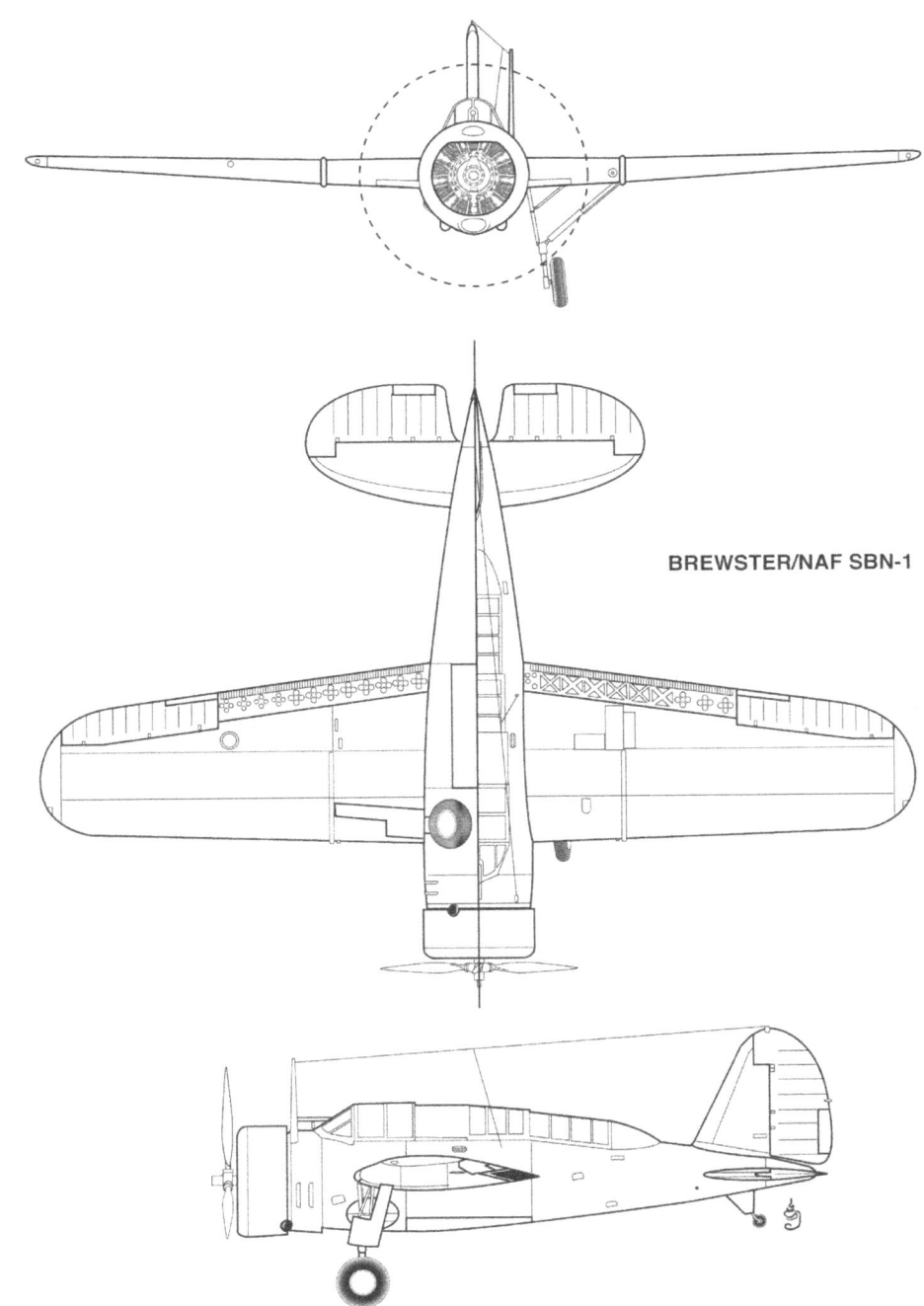

BREWSTER/NAF SBN-1

TECHNICAL SPECIFICATIONS (SBN-1)

Type: Two-place dive-bomer
Manufacturer: Brewster Aeronautical Corp., Long Island City, New York; Naval Aircraft Factory, Philadelphia, Pennsylvania.

One of the thirty SBN-1s built by the Naval Aircraft Factory from 1939 to 1942. Production was so slow that the type was obsolete by the time it reached operational units. They served briefly with VB-3 of the *Saratoga* Air Group.

Total produced: 31
Power plant: One 950-hp Wright R-1820-38 9-cylinder radial driving a three-bladed Hamilton Standard variable-pitch propeller.
Armament: One fixed forward-firing .50-cal. machine gun, one flexible .30-cal. rear machine gun, and one 500-lb. bomb carried in internal bay.
Performance: Max. speed 254-mph at 15,200 ft.; cruise 117-mph; ceiling 28,300 ft.; range 1,110 mi. max., 1,015 mi. loaded.
Weights: 4,503-lbs. empty, 6,759-lbs. loaded.
Dimensions: Span 39 ft., length 27 ft. 8 in., wing area 259 sq. ft.

The SBA was the first original aircraft design of the controversial Brewster Aeronautical Corp. Though Brewster's roots were traceable to a 19th century horse carriage business, the company in truth had been completely restructured in 1932 with the principal aim of obtaining Navy aircraft contracts. Having no business of its own at the time, Brewster commenced operations by performing subcontract work for Vought and Grumman. When BUAER circulated the requirement for a new monoplane scout-bomber (SB) in mid–1934, Brewster was invited to submit a proposal based upon a somewhat revised specification. Unlike Vought's XSB2U-1 and Northrop's XBT-1, Brewster's aircraft, designated the XSBA-1, would be a mid-wing design incorporating an internal bomb bay and use the larger diameter R-1820 powerplant. Brewster received a contact to construct a single prototype in October 1934 and the completed aircraft was delivered to the Navy for tests in April 1936.

Early trials revealed less than expected performance, causing the prototype to be returned to the factory for modifications. When the XSBA-1 reappeared in 1937 with an up-rated engine, revised cowling, three-bladed propeller, and raised canopy, top speed had risen to 263-mph, the fastest of any monoplane SB type thus far tested. BUAER awarded a contract to manufacture 30 airplanes in September 1938, not to Brewster, but to the government-owned Naval Aircraft Factory (NAF) as the SBN-1. Since by that time Brewster was heavily occupied with the F2A-1 fighter project, BUAER reasoned that the company lacked plant capacity to produce the XSBA-1 in quantity. Ironically, NAF's production proceeded at such a lethargic rate that the first SBN-1s were not delivered until late 1940 and the balance of the contract was not completed until early 1942, by which time the type was already obsolete. SBN-1s served briefly with VB-3 of *Saratoga's* air group and were later used as trainers by VT-8 aboard *Hornet*.

Brewster SB2A Buccaneer 1936–1942

TECHNICAL SPECIFICATIONS (SB2A-2)

Type: Two-place dive-bomer
Manufacturer: Brewster Aeronautical Corp., Johnsville Division, Johnsville, Pennsylvania.
Total produced (actually delivered to USN/USMC): 301
Power plant: One 1,700-hp Wright R-2600-8 14-cylinder radial driving a three-bladed Curtiss Electric fully-reversible, constant-speed propeller.
Armament: Two fixed forward-firing .50-cal. machine guns in fuselage, two fixed forward-firing .30-cal. machine guns in wings, two flexible .30-cal. machine guns in rear cockpit, and one 500-lb. bomb in internal bay.
Performance: Max. speed 274-mph at 12,000 ft.; cruise 161-mph; ceiling 24,900 ft.; range 1,675 mi. max., 720 mi. loaded.
Weights: 9,924-lbs. empty, 14,289-lbs. loaded.
Dimensions: Span 47 ft., length 39 ft. 2 in., wing area 379 sq. ft.

Despite having three new types of monoplane scout-bombers in production, BUAER by early 1939 had concluded that larger, more powerful designs would be needed to equip the Navy's emerging carrier force. In April 1939, Brewster was selected to build a prototype of its proposed Model 340 under the designation XSB2A-1. Taking much from the earlier SBA design, the XSB2A-1 was evolved as a mid-wing planform having inward-retracting landing gear, an internal weapons bay, plus a dorsal turret. In December 1940, amid concerns of war, BUAER gave Brewster a production contract for 140 SB2A-1s before the prototype was completed. The company also obtained orders from Great Britain and the Netherlands for 912 export models as the *Bermuda* and Model 340D, respectively. Mass-production of the new type was to take place at Brewster's new plant in Johnsville, Pennsylvania.

The XSB2A-1 flew for the first time on June 17, 1941, appearing with a dummy dorsal turret aft of the cockpit. Testing and combat requirements necessitated lengthening the fuselage one foot two inches, replacing the turret with flexible mounts, revising the canopy, enlarging fin area, and installing armor and self-sealing tanks, which upped empty weight nearly 3,000-lbs. and seriously degraded expected performance. Meanwhile, mismanagement problems led to a Navy takeover (by Presidential order) of all Brewster plants in April 1942. The U.S. government also seized all foreign orders, so that the 80 SB2A-2s delivered to the Navy from mid–1942 were actually British *Bermudas* lacking folding wings or arresting gear. In mid–1943 the Marine Corps received 162 land-based Dutch 340Ds as the SB2A-4. The only carrier-capable variants, the 60 SB2A-3s, appeared in early 1944, but by then Curtiss SB2Cs were re-equipping all fleet VB/VS squadrons. All operational Navy and Marine SB2A variants were used as trainers; and the other 469 examples completed at Johnsville apparently never entered service and were simply junked.

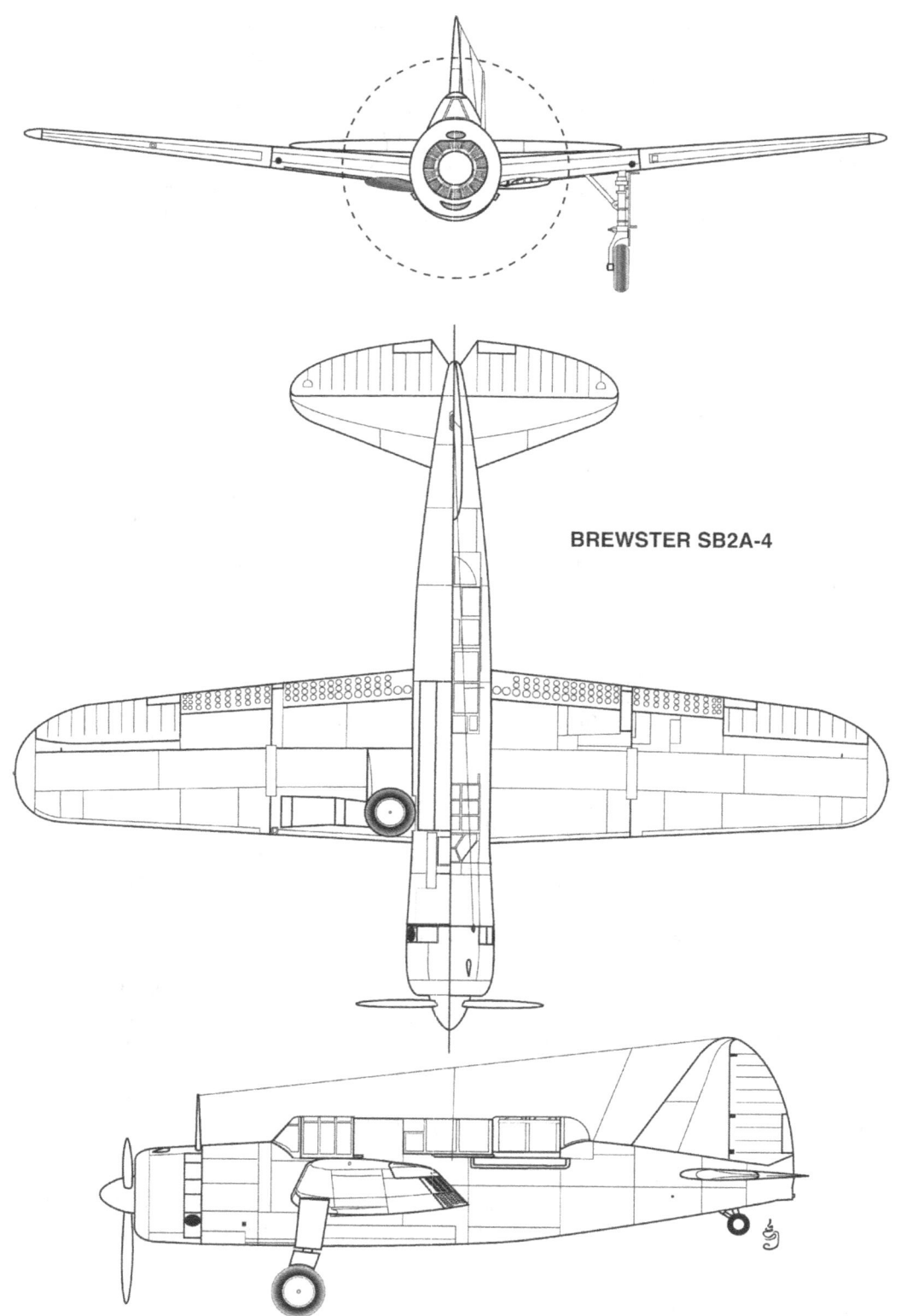
BREWSTER SB2A-4

SB2A-2, as shown, was originally a British *Bermuda* and lacked folding wings and arresting gear. All SB2A variants were used by the Navy and Marines as trainers. The USAAF A-34 was never ordered.

Curtiss SBC (F12C, S4C) Helldiver 1933–1942

TECHNICAL SPECIFICATIONS (SBC-4)

Type: Two-place dive-bomber
Manufacturer: Curtiss-Wright Corp., Curtiss Aeroplane Division, Buffalo, New York.
Total produced: 270
Power plant: One 950-hp Pratt & Whitney R-1820-34 9-cylinder radial driving a three-bladed Hamilton Standard variable-pitch propeller.
Armament: One fixed forward-firing .30-caliber machine gun and one flexible .30-cal. machine gun in rear cockpit and up to 1,000-lbs. of bombs carried externally.
Performance: Max. speed 237-mph at 15,200 ft.; cruise, 127-mph; ceiling 27,300 ft.; combat range 590 mi. (500-lb. bomb)
Weights: 4,841-lbs. empty, 7,141-lbs. loaded.
Dimensions: Span 34 ft., length 28 ft. 4 in., wing area 317 sq. ft.

    The Curtiss SBC not only became the last combat biplane in the active Navy and Marine Corps inventory, but was the last combat biplane of any type to be manufactured in the U. S. Arising from requirements for a retractable-gear, two-seat fighter similar to Grumman's FF/SF series, the Curtiss design was originally completed in late 1933 as a parasol-wing monoplane under the designation XF12C-1. Because of evolving naval requirements, the fighter designation was changed briefly to XS4C-1, and in early 1934, to XSBC-1. During dive-bombing tests conducted in mid–1934, the prototype was destroyed in a crash attributed to failure of the parasol wing.

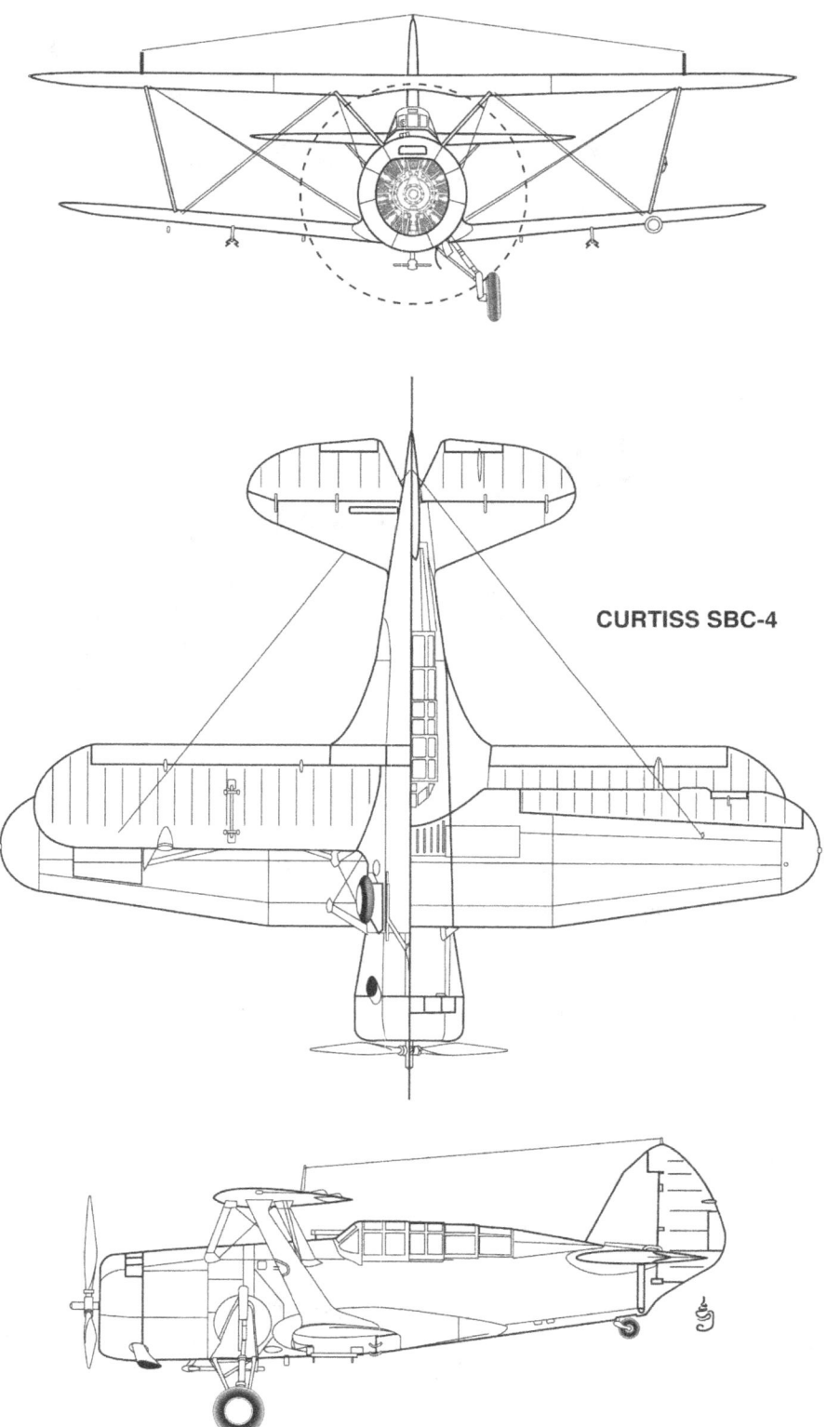

CURTISS SBC-4

The SBC-4 was the last biplane dive-bomber to be operated by the Navy and Marines. Although a small number were still in frontline units when the U. S. entered World War II, none ever saw combat.

In April 1935 BUAER ordered a second prototype built in a biplane configuration as the XSBC-2, and the new aircraft arrived for testing in December of the same year. The XSBC-2 was in effect a complete redesign, with revisions to the cowling, fuselage, and entire tail group. After a change to the 825-hp R-1535 engine and successful competitive trials against the XSBF-1 and XB2G-1, Curtiss was given a contract in August 1936 to produce 83 aircraft as the SBC-3, and deliveries to fleet units commenced in mid–1937. In early 1938 Curtiss introduced the improved SBC-4, which, equipped with a 950-hp R-1820 engine plus other refinements, doubled bomb load to a more lethal 1,000-lbs. Curtiss received a production order for 174 SBC-4s in January 1938, and deliveries commenced in March 1939. When 50 SBC-4s were diverted to France in 1940, production of the Navy and Marine order extended into 1941.

Starting in July 1937 and continuing into 1938, SBC-3s were delivered to VS-5 (*Yorktown*), VS-3 (*Saratoga*), and VS-6 (*Enterprise*). The Marines received only one SBC-3 in 1938. SBC-4s initially equipped VS-2 aboard *Lexington* in 1939 and later VS-8 and VB-8 of the *Hornet* air group in 1941. In 1939–1940, SBC-4s were allocated in threes or fours to eleven different Naval Reserve units. The Marine Corps received its first SBC-4 in 1940, and the type was equipping VMO-151 and VMO-155 by mid–1941. At the time of the Japanese attack on Pear Harbor in December 1941, some 69 SBC-3s and 117 SBC-4s remained in the Navy and Marine active inventories, though none ever saw combat. After active service, a number of SBCs were thereafter used as trainers.

Curtiss SB2C (SBF, SBW) Helldiver 1940–1949

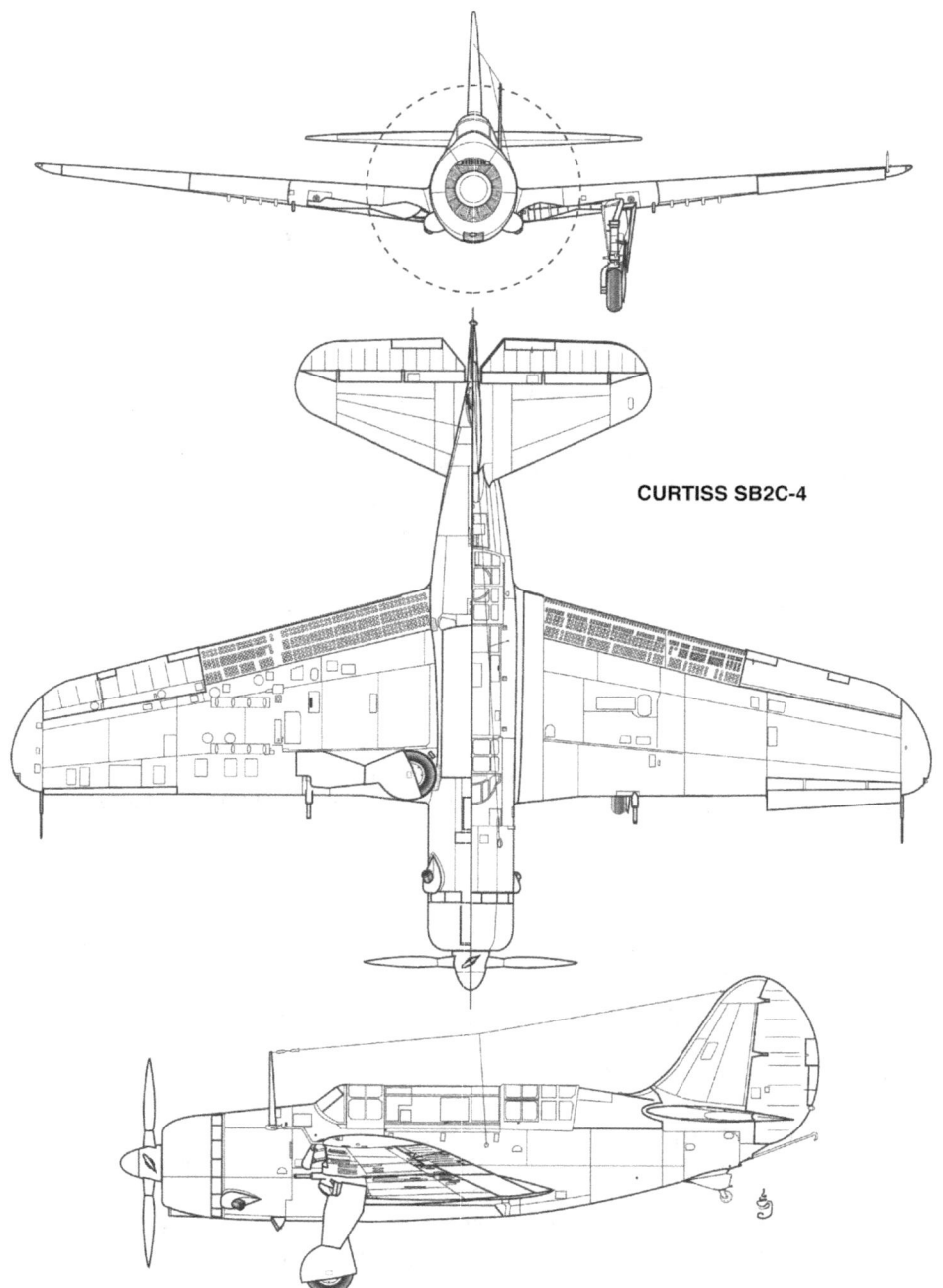

CURTISS SB2C-4

TECHNICAL SPECIFICATIONS (SB2C-4)

Type: Two-place dive-bomer
Manufacturer: Curtiss-Wright Corp., Airplane Division, Columbus, Ohio; Canadian Car & Foundry Co., Montreal, Canada; and Fairchild Aircraft Ltd., Longueuil, Canada.

Top: SB2C-1 shown entering a dive with brakes extended. Lengthy development problems delayed operational deployment until mid–1943. The 778 SB2C-1Cs came with 20-mm cannons as standard fixed armament. *Bottom: The* SB2C-5, as shown here, appeared in early 1945. The chief improvements of the -5 were a frameless pilot's canopy and increased fuel capacity. The type remained in frontline service until replaced by single seat ADs and AMs in the late 1940s.

Total produced (all models): 7,203
Power plant: One 1,900-hp Wright R-2600-20 14-cylinder radial driving a four-bladed Curtiss Electric fully-reversible, constant-speed propeller.
Armament: Two fixed forward-firing 20-millimeter cannon in wings, two flexible .30-cal. machine guns in rear cockpit, and up to 1,000-lbs. carried internal and 1,000-lbs. external.
Performance: Max. speed 295-mph at 16,700 ft.; cruise, 158-mph; ceiling 29,100 ft.; combat range 1,165 mi. (1,000-lb. payload).

Weights: 10,547-lbs. empty, 16,616-lbs. loaded.
Dimensions: Span 49 ft. 9 in., length 36 ft. 8 in., wing area 422 sq. ft.

The Curtiss SB2C was the Navy's chief scout-bomber from late 1943 until the end of World War II, replacing Douglas SBDs in carrier-based combat operations. In May 1939, under requirements comparable to Brewster's XSB2A-1, BUAER ordered an R-2600-powered scout-bomber prototype from Curtiss under the designation XSB2C-1. As part of the general naval expansion triggered by the European war and increasing friction with Japan, the SB2C-1 was ordered into large-scale production in November 1940 before the prototype flew. In order to increase plant capacity, Curtiss established a new factory for SB2C production at Columbus, Ohio.

The program received a severe setback when the XSB2C-1 was destroyed in a crash only days after its first flight on December 18, 1940. Due to extensive revisions to the basic design, which included enlarging the vertical tail surfaces, lengthening the fuselage, and adding armor protection and self-sealing fuel tanks, the first production model did not fly until June 1942. And with more than 800 design changes required, the Columbus plant fell seriously behind on its production schedule, so that deliveries to the Navy did not commence until the following December.

After the 200th SB2C-1, Curtiss produced 778 SB2C-1Cs with wing armament changed to two 20-mmm cannon in place of four .50-cal. guns. The XSB2C-2 was a floatplane prototype that never reached production. The first of 1,112 SB2C-3s appeared in early 1943, equipped with uprated R-2600-20 engines and four-bladed propellers. From early 1944, 2,045 SB2C-4s were produced with wing fittings for eight HVAR rockets or up to 1,000-lbs. of bombs, and the -4E version mounted a yagi fixed antenna radar below each wing. The final production version, the SB2C-5, featured a frameless front canopy and increased fuel capacity, and 970 examples were delivered from February 1945 until production ceased the following October. Two XSB2C-6 prototypes with R-2800 engines and longer fuselages were built but never produced.

Helldiver production was also undertaken by two Canadian companies, Fairchild Ltd. producing 300 as the SBF-1, SBF-3, and SBF-4E and Canadian Car & Foundry 894 as the SBW-1, SBW-3, SBW-4 and -4E, and SBW-5. Twenty-six Canadian-built examples were delivered to the Royal Navy but never used operationally. Of the 900 Helldivers originally built for the USAAF as the A-25A, most were diverted to the Marine Corps in 1943–1944 as the SB2C-1A.

Despite the fact that production SB2C-1s were initially received by VS-9 in December 1942, the type did not become fully operational until nearly a year later, in November 1943, when SB2Cs of VB-17 attacked Rabaul. Over the next seven months, SB2Cs replaced SBDs in all shipboard VS and VB units, from then on participating in every Navy offensive operation up to war's end in August 1945. SB2Cs did not start reequipping Marine squadrons until later in 1944, and at a slower rate. When the war ended in 1945, SB2Cs remained in active fleet service until replaced by single-seat Douglas ADs and Martin AMs from 1947 to 1949.

Douglas SBD Dauntless 1938–1945

TECHNICAL SPECIFICATIONS (SBD-5)

Type: Two-place dive-bomber
Manufacturer: Douglas Aircraft Company, El Segundo Division, El Segundo, California.
Total produced (all USN/USMC models): 4,899
Power plant: One 1,200-hp Wright R-1820-60 9-cylinder radial driving a three-bladed Hamilton Standard fully-reversible, constant-speed propeller.
Armament: Two fixed forward-firing .50-cal. machine guns, two flexible .30-cal. rear machine guns, and up to 2,250-lbs. of bombs carried externally.
Performance: Max. speed 252-mph at 13,800 ft.; cruise 139-mph; ceiling 24,300 ft.; range 1,565 mi. max., 1,115 mi. loaded.

First Series • 1926–1946

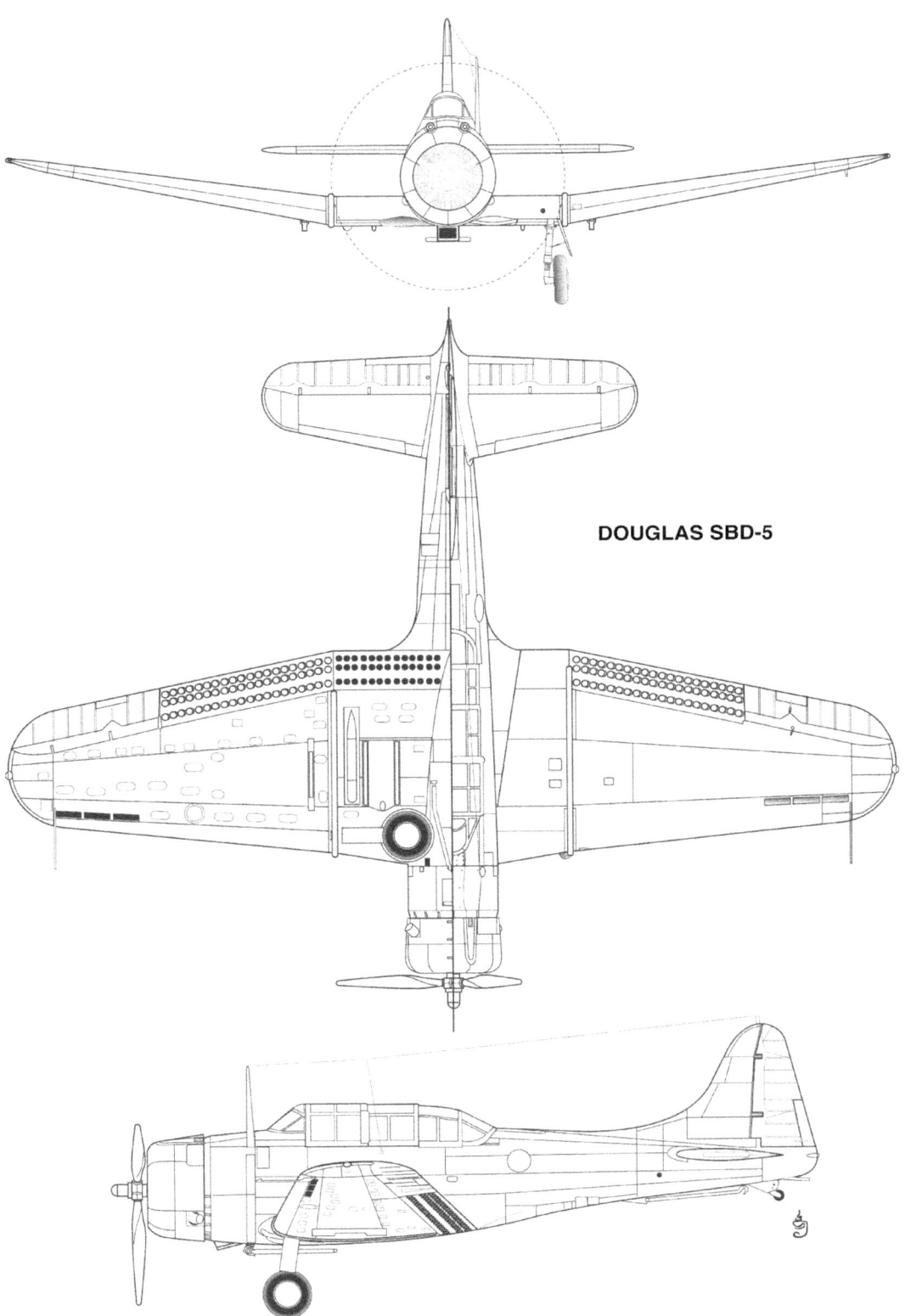

DOUGLAS SBD-5

The SBD-2 shown here has been retrofitted with a constant-speed prop. SBD-2s were initially equipped with VB-6 and VS-6 aboard *Enterprise* in mid–1941 but had been replaced with SBD-3s by the time of the early naval battles of World War II.

Weights: 6,533-lbs. empty, 10,700-lbs. loaded.
Dimensions: Span 41 ft. 6 in., length 33 ft., wing area 325 sq. ft.

Although BUAER viewed the SBD as a stopgap design when it entered service in 1940, it was destined to become, in terms of tactical success, the most important Navy and Marine Corps dive-bomber type of World War II. The origins of the SBD relate back to BUAER's 1934 requirement for a monoplane scout-bomber, which resulted, among other things, in a production contract being given to Northrop in late 1936 for its BT-1. At the time Northrop's name changed to Douglas Aircraft, El Segundo Division, in 1938, the firm was about to complete work on its XBT-2, an improved derivative having a 1,000-hp. R-1820-32 engine and a redesigned landing gear that retracted flush into the wing roots. The plane made its first flight in April 1938, and further refinements such as a reshaped fin/rudder and a new canopy enclosure created a new model that was ordered into production in 1939 as the SBD-1.

BUAER had originally contemplated terminating SBD production in early 1942 at 174 (i.e., 57 SBD-1s, 87 SBD-2s, and 30 SBD-3s) but the intervention of World War II kept the assembly line moving until mid–1944, resulting in a further 470 SBD-3s, 780 SBD-4s, 3,025 SBD-5s, and finally, 450 SBD-6s. Another 953 were completed for the AAF as the A-24 (SBD-3), A-24A (SBD-4), and A-24B (SBD-5). The SBD series was continually improved during its production life: the SBD-2 included hydraulically actuated landing gear; the SBD-3, self-sealing tanks, protective armor, and forward guns increased from .30-calibre to .50-calibre; the SBD-4, a 24-volt electrical system; the SBD-5, 1,200-hp. R-1820-60 engine, reshaped cowling, and reflector-type gun/bombsight; and SBD-6, 1,350-hp. R-1820-66 engine.

All SBD-1s were assigned to the Marine Corps (VMB-2 in 1940 and VMB-1 in 1941) and in 1941, SBD-2s first equipped VB-6 and VS-6 aboard *Enterprise* and VB-2 aboard *Lexington*. SBD-3s began arriving in mid–1941 and by December were equipping air groups aboard *Lexington, Saratoga, Yorktown,* and *Enterprise*. The most noteworthy combat engagement involving SBDs occurred between 4–6 June 1942 when SBD-3s operating from *Yorktown, Enterprise,*

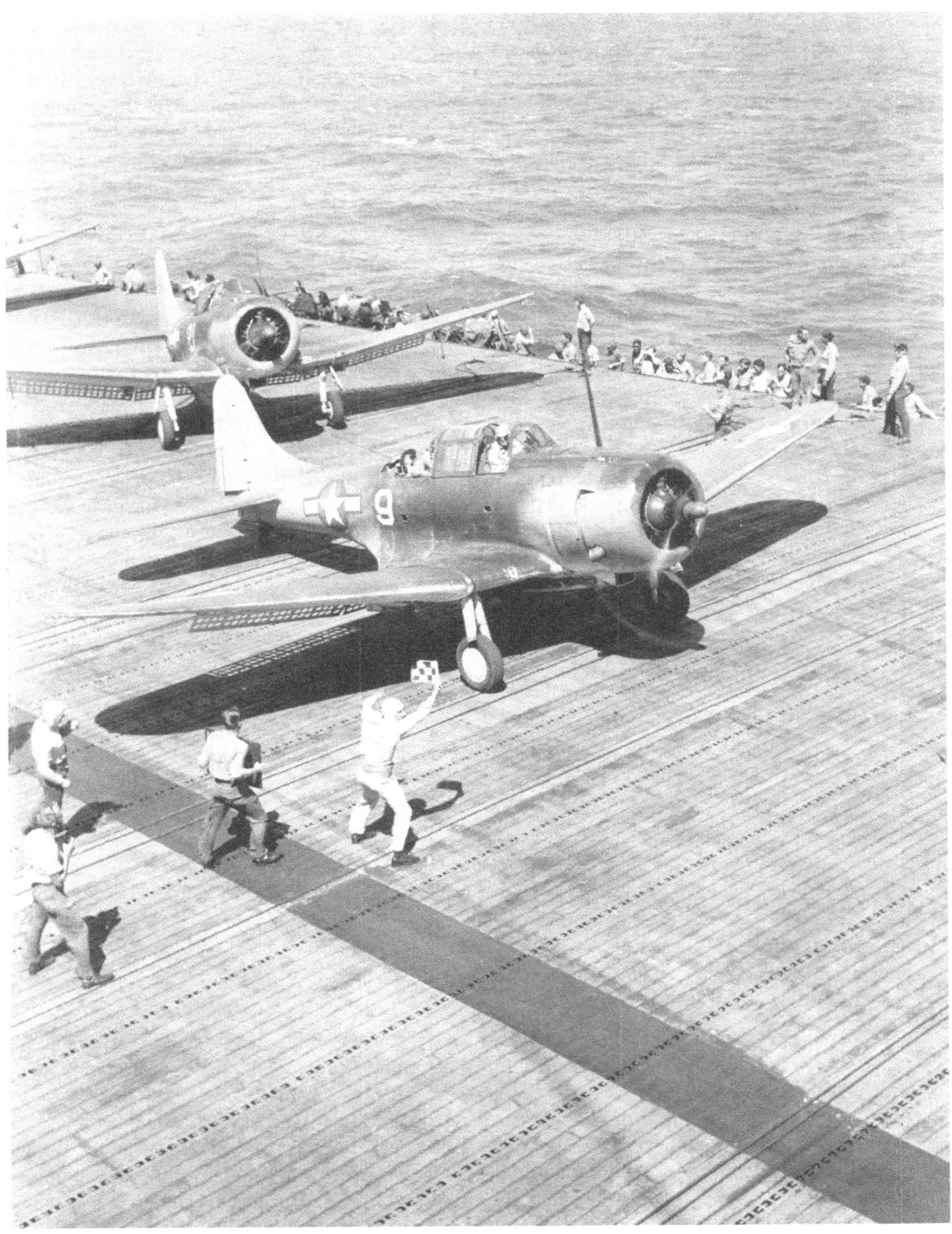

SBD-5s lined up on carrier deck for takeoff, probably in late 1943 or early 1944. All Navy SBDs had been replaced in frontline service by SB2Cs by mid–1944 but continued to operate with Marine units up to the end of the war.

and *Hornet* sunk four Japanese aircraft carriers during the Battle of Midway. Through the course of 1942, SBDs reequipped all fleet VB and VS units until they gradually began to be replaced by Curtiss SB2Cs starting in late 1943. The last combat sorties flown by Navy SBDs occurred in June 1944 during the Battle of the Philippine Sea. Commencing with the invasion of Guadalcanal in August 1942, SBDs formed the backbone of land-based Marine tactical air operations, participating in every major Pacific campaign right up to the end of hostilities in 1945. After the war, small numbers of SBDs were briefly used as utility hacks at shore bases.

After seeing the success of German *Stukas* in *blitzgrieg* tactics, the Army Air Corps (AAC) borrowed several Douglas SBD-1 dive-bombers from the Marine Corps in mid–1940, assigning them to the 24th Bombardment Squadron for evaluation. After a favorable report, the War Department ordered 78 examples as the A-24, which, powered by a 1,000-hp Wright R-1820, was essentially identical to the Navy SBD-3 sans carrier arrestment gear. Production A-24s, not delivered until mid–1941, went on to equip three squadrons of the new 27th Bombardment Group (Light) and one squadron of the 3rd Bombardment Group (Light) of the recently constituted U. S. Army Air Forces (AAF). In April 1942, A-24s of the 27th BG(L) began flying combat sorties from Port Moresby, New Guinea, but were withdrawn in July due to excessive losses. Between July 1942 and December 1943, 90 more A-24s, 120 A-24As (SBD-4s), and 615 A-24Bs (SBD-5s) were delivered to the USAAF. The only other unit taking the type into actual combat was the 58th Bomb Squadron (Dive), which briefly flew its A-24Bs against Japanese installations in the Gilbert Islands during December 1943. Earlier, in August 1943, the A-24B equipped 407th Bomb Group had flown a raid against Kiska in the Aleutian Islands only to discover that the area had already been vacated by the Japanese. Once withdrawn from combat units, AAF A-24s were used as target tugs and utility hacks.

Douglas SB2D (BTD) Destroyer 1943–1945

TECHNICAL SPECIFICATIONS (XSB2D-1)
Type: Two-place dive-bomber; one-place bomber-torpedo
Manufacturer: Douglas Aircraft Company, El Segundo Division, El Segundo, California.
Total produced (all models): 29
Power plant: One 2,300-hp Wright R-3350-14 18-cylinder radial driving a three-bladed Hamilton Standard fully-reversible, constant-speed propeller.
Armament: Two fixed forward-firing 20-millimeter cannon in the wings, one upper and one lower .50-cal. machine gun in remote-controlled barbettes, and up to 2,000-lbs. of bombs carried in an internal bay.
Performance: Max. speed 346-mph at 16,100 ft.; cruise 180-mph; ceiling 24,400 ft.; range 1,480 mi. (1,000-lb. payload).
Weights: 12,458-lbs. empty, 19,140-lbs. max. loaded.
Dimensions: Span 45 ft., length 38 ft. 7 in., wing area 375 sq. ft.

Coming off the same drawing boards as the highly successful A-20 and A-26 USAAF tactical bombers, the Douglas SB2D fell victim to the rapidly changing combat requirements of World War II. Ordered by BUAER in June 1941, the XSB2D-1, though heavier and more complex, was conceived to fulfill the same mission as the SBD and SB2C. Douglas had been testing aircraft with retractable tricycle landing gear since 1938, and the XSB2D-1 was the first carrier-based aircraft to incorporate the feature. The design also introduced an advanced gun system allowing a single gunner to remotely train and fire upper and lower guns housed in power-operated barbettes. Like the Vought F4U, the wings were gulled to minimize the length of the main gear legs. But by the time the XSB2D-1 made its first flight on April 8, 1943, BUAER had already determined that future attack aircraft would be single-seat bomber-torpedo (BT) types with fixed guns. In mid–1943 Douglas removed the gunner's position and

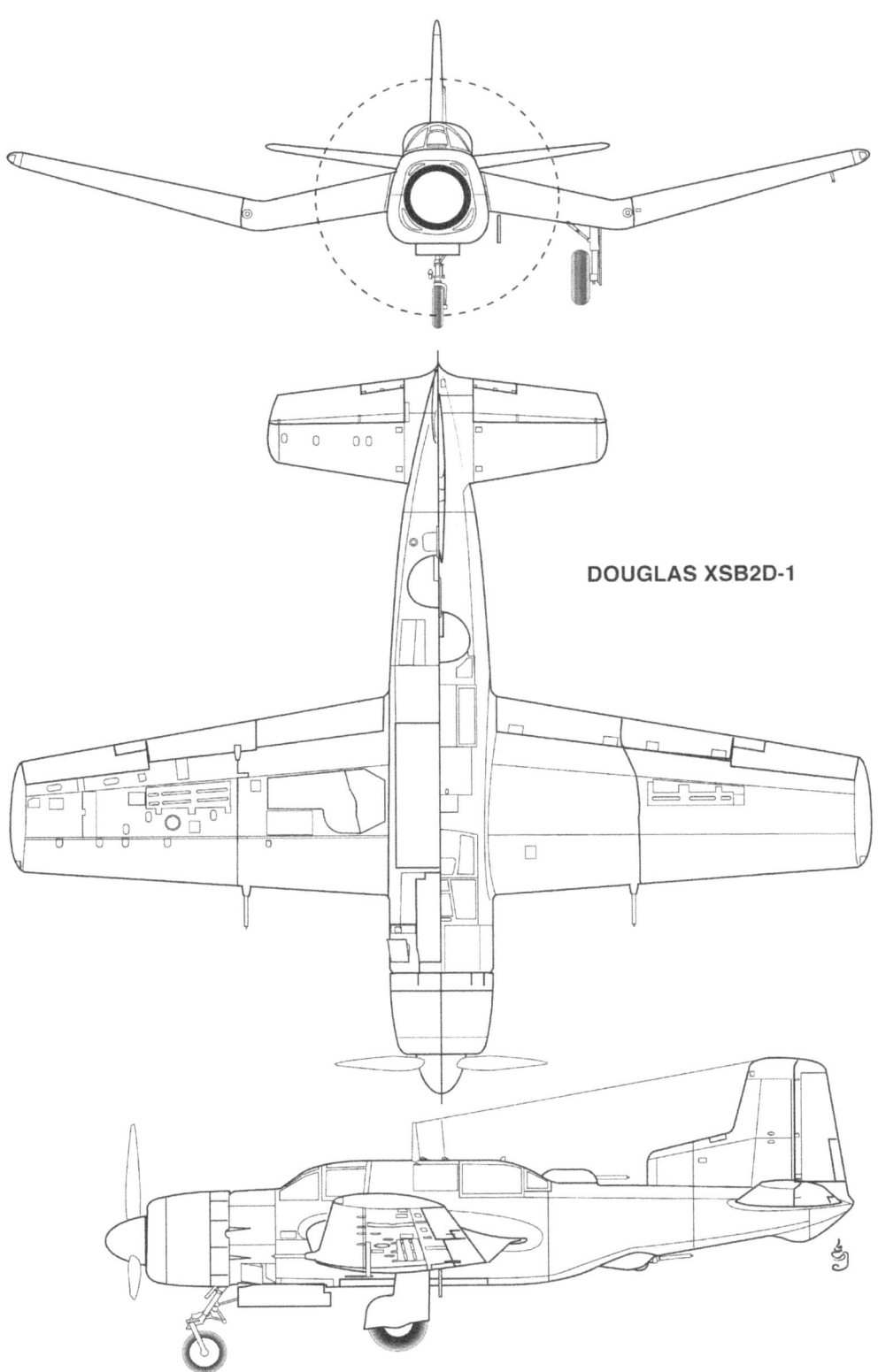

DOUGLAS XSB2D-1

The XSB2D-1 in mid–1943 before the turrets were removed. After the Navy issued the new single-seat BT requirement in the fall of 1943, Douglas removed the gunner's position and resubmitted the design as the XBTD-1.

enlarged the bomb bay to accommodate a torpedo or 1,200-lbs. of additional bombs, then resubmitted the design as the XBTD-1.

As a stopgap measure, Douglas received a contract to produce 358 BTD-1s, but at the same time, BUAER went ahead and solicited new BT proposals from Martin, Curtiss, and Kaiser-Fleetwings. In June 1944, Douglas recommended that the BTD program be cancelled in favor of the XBT2D-1, a simpler design that reverted to a tailwheel layout and externally carried ordnance. BUAER approved Douglas' proposal and BTD production was terminated when 28 examples had been delivered. None of the production models were used in operational service.

Grumman SBF 1936

TECHNICAL SPECIFICATIONS (XSBF-1)

Type: Two-place dive-bomer
Manufacturer: Grumman Aircraft Engineering Corp., Bethpage, New York.
Total produced: 1
Power plant: One 700-hp Pratt & Whitney R-1535-72 14-cylinder radial driving a two-bladed Hamilton Standard variable-pitch propeller.
Armament: One fixed forward-firing .30-cal. machine gun, one flexible .30-cal. machine gun in rear cockpit, and up four 500-lbs. of bombs carried externally.
Performance: Max. speed 215-mph at 15,000 ft.; ceiling 26,000 ft.; combat range 688 mi.

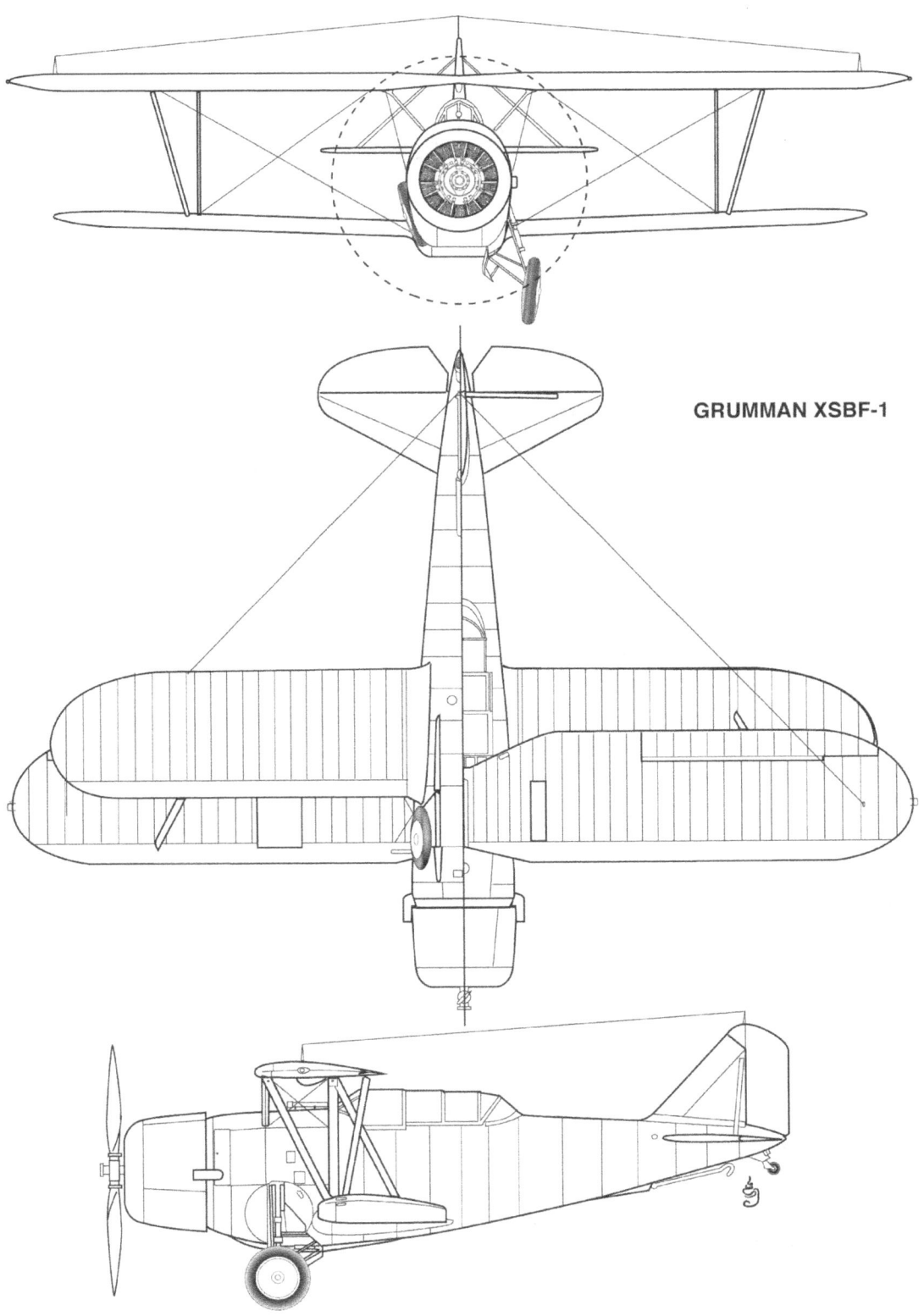

GRUMMAN XSBF-1

The sole XSBF-1 as delivered to Anacostia in early 1936. The aerodynamic configuration was very similar to Grumman's FF/SF series. The Curtiss XSBC-2 was selected for production over the XSBF-1 and the Great Lakes XB2G-1.

Weights: 3,395-lbs. empty, 4,442-lbs. max. loaded.
Dimensions: Span 31 ft. 6 in., length 25 ft. 9 in., wing area 310 sq. ft.

The Grumman SBF was one of three retractable-gear biplane designs built for the newly-created scout-bomber (SB) requirement issued by BUAER in 1934. Ordered from Grumman in March 1935, the XSBF-1 was essentially a re-engined development of the basic SF-1 airframe having a somewhat shorter, broader-chord wing and dive-bombing apparatus. After the XSBF-1 prototype was delivered for testing in February 1936, it was subjected to competitive trials against the Great Lakes XB2G-1 and Curtiss XSBC-2. In August, when the Navy announced that the Curtiss entry had been selected for production, no further development of the XSBF-1 was undertaken.

Vought SBU (F3U) 1933–1941

TECHNICAL SPECIFICATIONS (SBU-1)

Type: Two-place dive-bomber
Manufacturer: Chance Vought Division of United Aircraft Corp., Stratford, Connecticut.
Total produced (all models): 125
Power plant: One 700-hp Pratt & Whitney R-1535-80 14-cylinder radial driving a two-bladed Hamilton Standard variable-pitch propeller.
Armament: One fixed forward-firing .30-cal. machine gun and one flexible .30-cal. machine gun in rear cockpit and up to 500-lbs. of bombs carried externally.
Performance: Max. speed 205-mph at 8,900 ft.; cruise 122-mph; ceiling 23,700 ft.; range 548 mi. loaded.
Weights: 3,645-lbs. empty, 5,618-lbs. max. loaded.
Dimensions: Span 33 ft. 3 in., length 27 ft. 9 in., wing area 327 sq. ft.

The Vought SBU was the first of the new SB-types to enter operational service and the last type of combat aircraft with fixed-gear to be placed in production by the Navy. It began

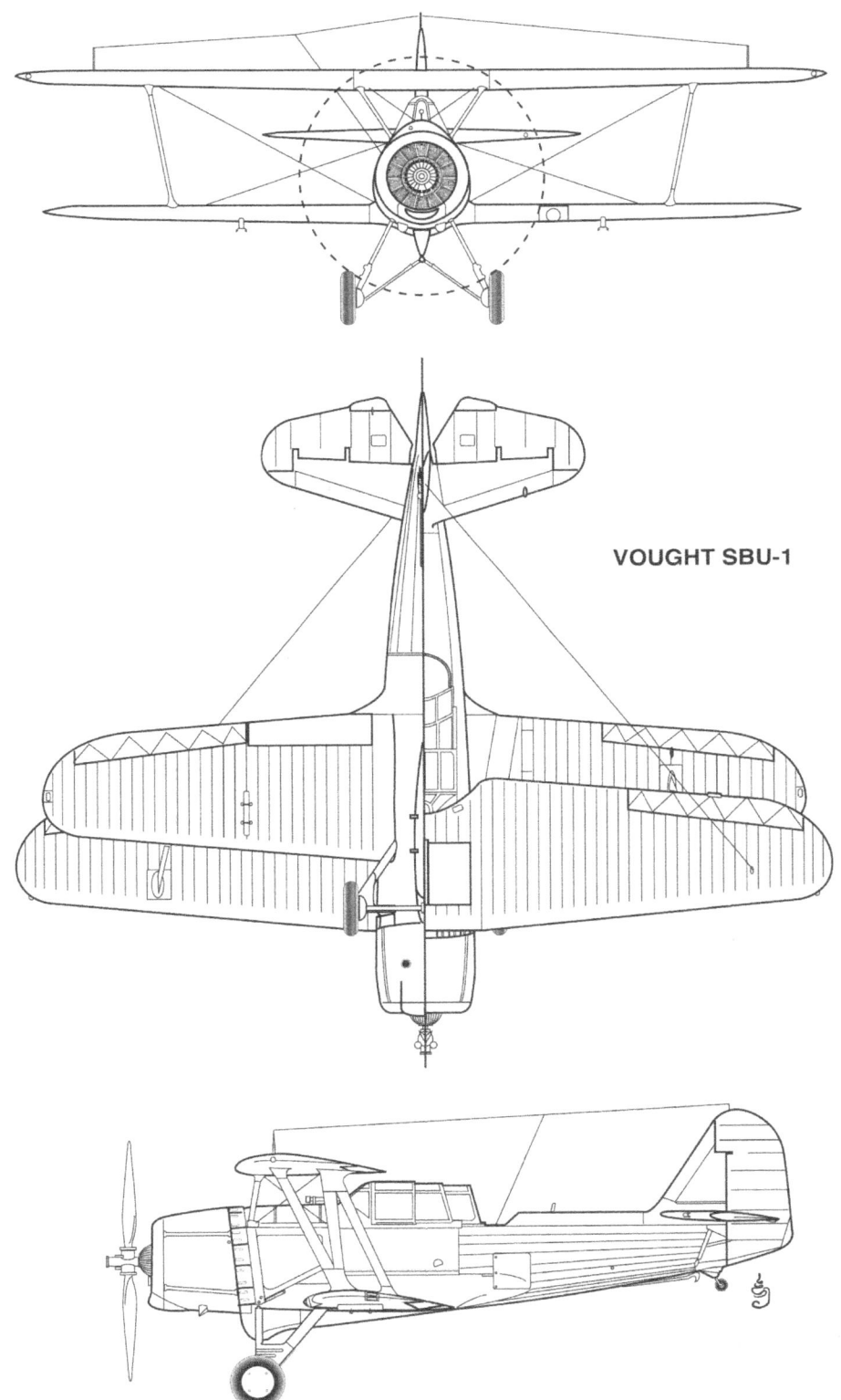

VOUGHT SBU-1

The SBU-1 in June of 1934 after being re-worked as a scout-bomber. SBU-1s served in carrier air groups aboard *Lexington, Saratoga*, and *Ranger* from 1935 until 1940. Most SBU-2s were delivered directly to reserve units.

life in June 1932 under the designation XF3U-1 as a two-seat fighter laid down in accordance with BUAER Design 113. When the XF3U-1 prototype arrived at Anacostia for testing in June 1933, however, the Navy was by that time in the process of abandoning the two-seat fighter concept, and the aircraft was returned to the factory to be reworked as a scout-bomber with the offer that it would most likely be placed in production. Revisions to the basic design included enlarging and strengthening the wings, increasing fuel capacity, and adding dive-bombing apparatus.

Under the new designation XSBU-1, the prototype was returned to the Navy in June 1934, and after changes to the vertical tail surfaces and cowling, Vought received a production order for 84 SBU-1s in January 1935 and deliveries began the following November. A second batch of 40 aircraft was ordered in November 1936 as SBU-2s with R-1535-98 engines and minor detail changes.

VS-3B of *Lexington's* air group received the first production SBU-1s in November 1935, followed by VS-2B aboard *Saratoga* and VS-1B aboard *Ranger*. Most SBU-2s never saw front-line service but were delivered new to Navy and Marine reserve units during 1937. All SBU-1s had been retired from fleet squadrons by the end of 1940, and SBU-2s were withdrawn from reserve units during 1941. Some 83 remaining SBUs finished their career as trainers at NAS Pensacola and NAS Corpus Christi.

Vought SB2U Vindicator 1936–1942

TECHNICAL SPECIFICATIONS (SB2U-1)

Type: Two-place dive-bomber
Manufacturer: Chance Vought Division of United Aircraft Corp., Stratford, Connecticut.

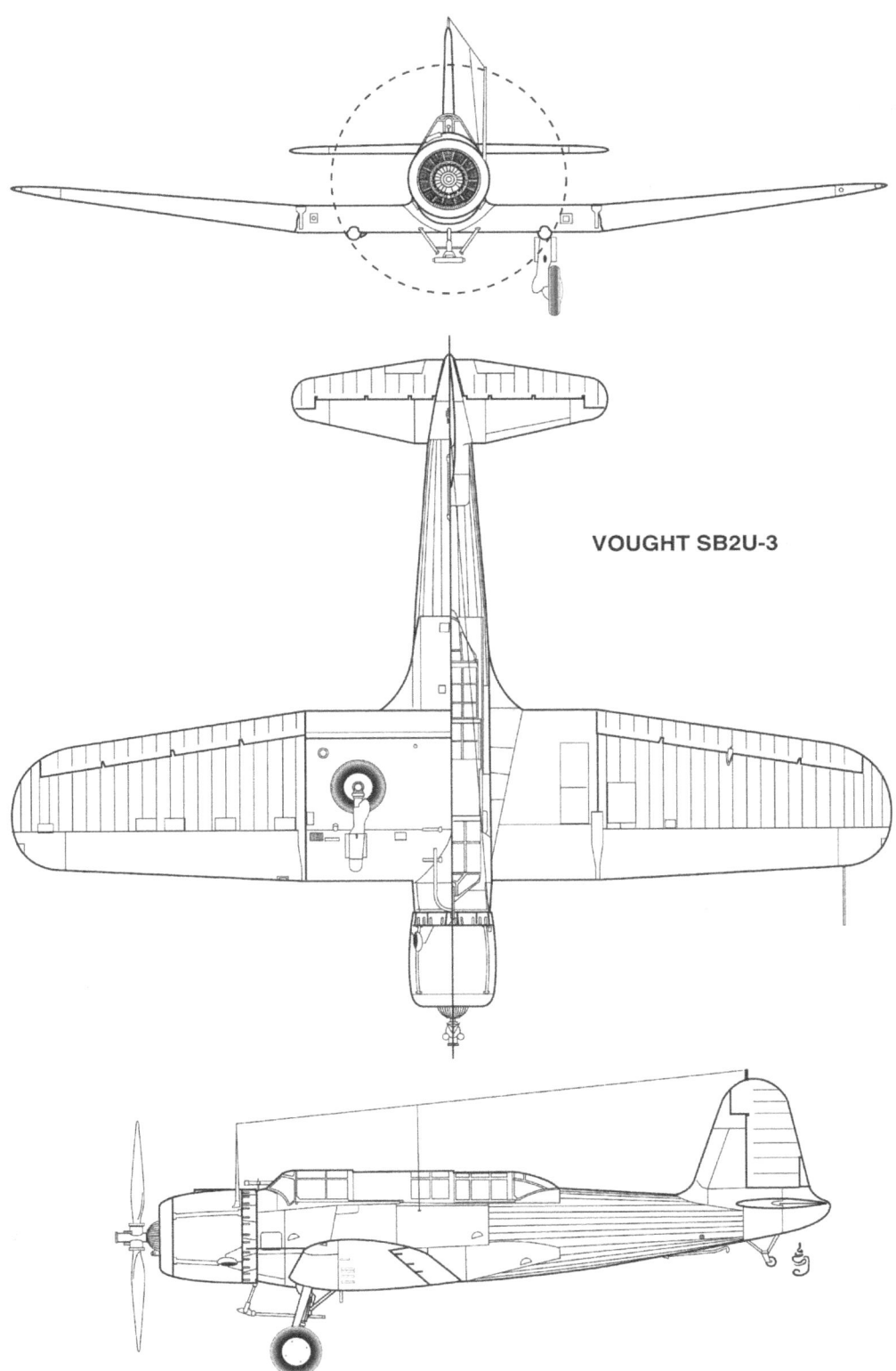

VOUGHT SB2U-3

SB2U-1s of VB-3 in the *Saratoga* Air Group in the late 1930s. Most had been replaced by SBDs by the time the U. S. entered World War II. Midway-based SB2U-3s of VMSB-231 were the only examples of the type to actually see combat.

Total produced (all USN/USMC models): 170
Power plant: One 825-hp Pratt & Whitney R-1535-96 14-cylinder radial driving a two-bladed Hamilton Standard variable-pitch propeller.
Armament: One fixed forward-firing .50-cal. machine gun and one flexible .30-cal. machine gun in rear cockpit and up to 1,000-lbs. of bombs carried externally.
Performance: Max. speed 250-mph at 9,500 ft.; cruise 143-mph; ceiling 27,400 ft.; range 635 mi. (1,000-lb. payload).
Weights: 4,676-lbs. empty, 7,278-lbs. max. loaded.
Dimensions: Span 42 ft., length 34 ft., wing area 305 sq. ft.

Following the Douglas TBD by two months, the Vought SB2U was the first monoplane scout-bomber to join the fleet. Ordered by BUAER in October 1934, the XSB2U-1 was one of *seven* scout-bomber prototypes authorized that year (i.e., the XBT-1 and XSBA-1 monoplane designs, plus the XB2G-1, XSBC-2, XSBF-1, and XSB3U-1 biplane designs). By doing this, BUAER hoped to solve two problems at once: (1) find out whether or not monoplanes could be safely operated from carriers; and (2) regardless of outcome, obtain new airplanes to equip Navy's growing carrier force. The design of the XSB2U-1 mixed newer aerodynamic ideas with older construction methods, appearing with fabric covering on the aft fuselage and on the wings aft of the main spars. The prototype made its first flight on January 4, 1936 and was delivered to Anacostia three months later. In trials conducted through the summer of 1936, the monoplanes clearly outperformed the biplanes in terms of speed (and thus time to target) and climb, while still demonstrating acceptable approach speeds and wave-off characteristics.

In October 1936, Vought received a production order for 54 SB2U-1s, and deliveries to fleet units began in December 1937. A second batch of 58 aircraft was ordered in January 1938 as the SB2U-2, with changes in equipment and a small increase in gross weight, and they started entering service later the same year. The final version, ordered in September 1939 as the SB2U-3, came with an uprated R-1535-102 engine, increased fuel capacity, and a .50-cal. gun in the rear position. Nearly all of the 57 SB2U-3s produced were allocated to the Marine Corps in 1940–1941. One SB2U-1 was modified as a floatplane but no production was undertaken. Vought also built two export versions, 20 to the French in 1939 as the V-156-F3 and 50 to the Royal Navy under Lend-Lease in 1941 as the V-156-B1.

The first production SB2U-1s equipped VB-3 of the *Saratoga* air group, followed by *Lexington's* VB-2. By early 1940, SB2U-1s and -2s were also serving with VB-4 (*Ranger*) and VS-72 (*Wasp*, commissioned April 1940). Although SB2Us were still equipping the *Ranger* and *Wasp* air groups when the war broke out in December 1941, none were ever involved in combat actions. VMSB-231, one of two Marine squadrons operating SB2U-3s, flew combat sorties against the Japanese fleet from Midway Island in June 1942, but the type was soon replaced by SBDs in active units. After active service, a number of SB2Us were used in the Advanced Carrier Training Groups (ACTGs).

Vought SB3U 1936–1938

TECHNICAL SPECIFICATIONS (XSB3U-1)

Type: Two-place dive-bomber
Manufacturer: Chance Vought Division of United Aircraft Corp., Stratford, Connecticut.
Total produced: 1
Power plant: One 750-hp Pratt & Whitney R-1535-82 14-cylinder radial driving a two-bladed Hamilton Standard variable-pitch propeller.
Armament: One fixed forward-firing .50-cal. machine gun and one flexible .30-cal. machine gun in rear cockpit and up to 500-lbs. of bombs carried externally.
Performance: Max. speed 215-mph at 8,900 ft.; ceiling 26,500 ft.; range 590 mi. (500-lb. payload).
Weights: 3,876-lbs. empty, 5,837-lbs. max. loaded.
Dimensions: Span 33 ft. 3 in., length 28 ft. 2 in., wing area 327 sq. ft.

Produced in parallel to the monoplane SB2U, the biplane SB3U was perhaps the most extreme example of BUAER's official ambivalence toward the suitability of monoplanes for carrier operations. In February 1935, four months after authorizing three scout-bomber monoplane prototypes, BUAER ordered a retractable-gear biplane from Vought under the designation XSB3U-1. Utilizing the same basic airframe and engine as the SBU-2, the XSB3U-1 incorporated a rearward-folding landing gear and a somewhat longer chord cowling. It is noteworthy that the XSB2U-1 and XSB3U-1 prototypes were completed and delivered to Anacostia at the same time. Trials held between the two types unquestionably confirmed the superiority of the monoplane's aerodynamics: though 500-lbs. heavier and dimensionally larger than the XSB3U-1, the monoplane XSB2U-1, equipped with an identical power plant, was nonetheless faster by 15-mph, had similar range, and could carry twice the bomb load, while exhibiting the same 66-mph stall speed. The sole XSB3U-1 prototype was thereafter retained at Anacostia for test purposes until 1938.

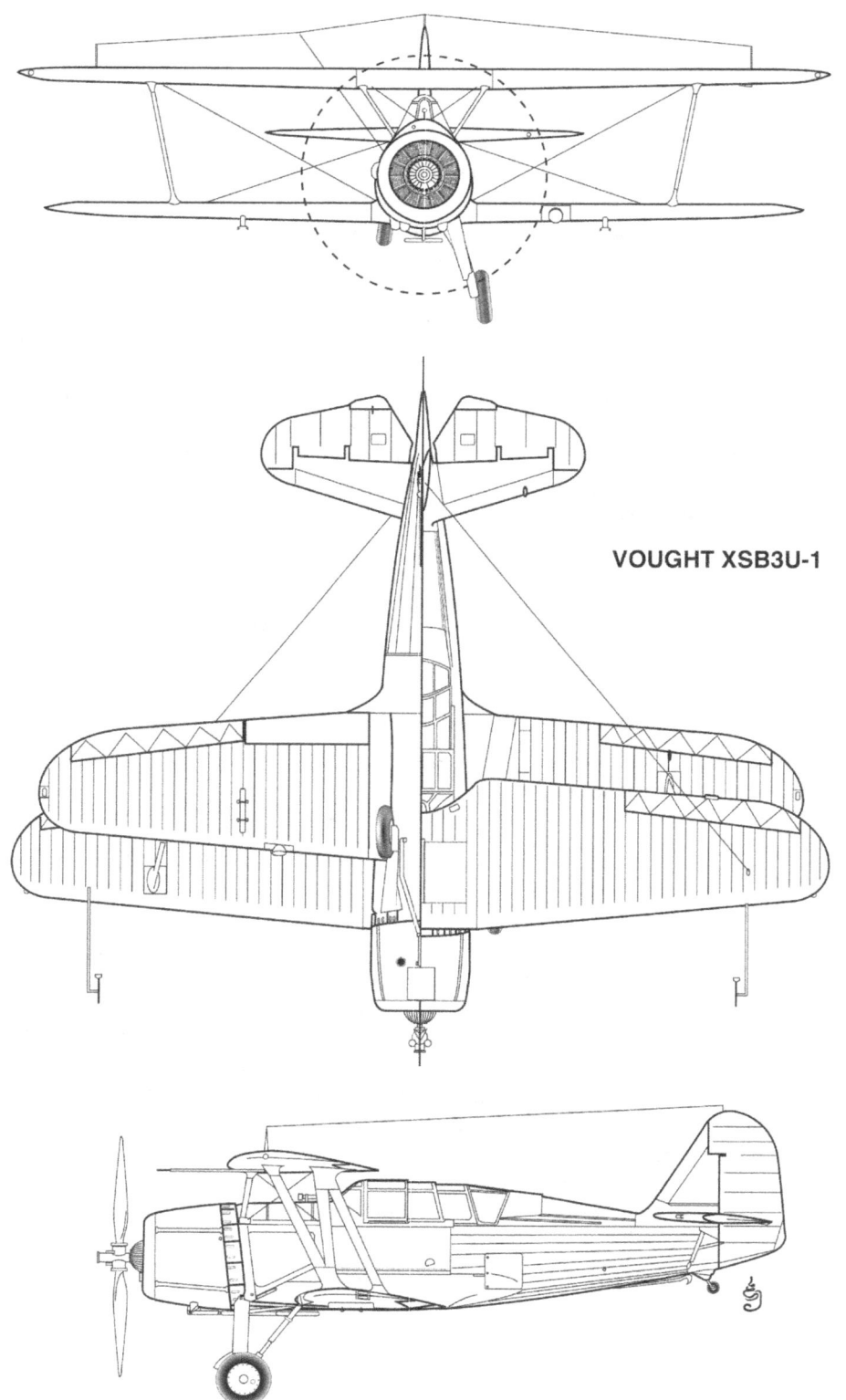

VOUGHT XSB3U-1

The sole XSB3U-1 prototype as seen at Anacostia in 1936. Delivered the same time as the XSB2U-1, this type probably represents the best example of official Navy reluctance to adopt monoplane carrier aircraft.

Douglas T3D 1931–1933

TECHNICAL SPECIFICATIONS (XT3D-2)

Type: Three-place torpedo plane
Manufacturer: Douglas Aircraft Co., Santa Monica, California.
Total produced: 1
Power plant: One 800-hp Pratt & Whitney R-1830-54 14-cylinder radial driving a two-bladed Hamilton Standard fixed-pitch propeller.
Armament: One fixed forward-firing .30-cal. machine gun, one flexible .30-cal. rear machine gun, and up to 1,000-lbs. of bombs or one torpedo carried externally.
Performance: Max. speed 142-mph at s.l.; ceiling 13,800 ft.; combat range 748 mi.
Weights: 4,876-lbs. empty, 8,543-lbs. loaded.
Dimensions: Span 50 ft., length 35 ft. 6 in., wing area 649 sq. ft.

Ordered in June 1930, the Douglas XT3D-1 signified an early attempt by BUAER to find a torpedo plane replacement for the T4M/TG series. When the prototype was delivered to Anacostia for testing in October 1931, it featured such innovations as a metal wing structure covered by fabric and a townsend drag ring around the single-row R-1860 engine; however, because the new type's general performance was only marginally better than the TG-2 (a license-built T4M with an R-1820 engine), it was returned to the factory for modifications. The prototype reappeared in February 1933 as the XT3D-2, with a twin-row R-1830 engine, NACA-type cowling, and wheel spats on the landing gear. Trials revealed an improvement in speed and range, but not enough to justify placing the type in production, and further development was abandoned.

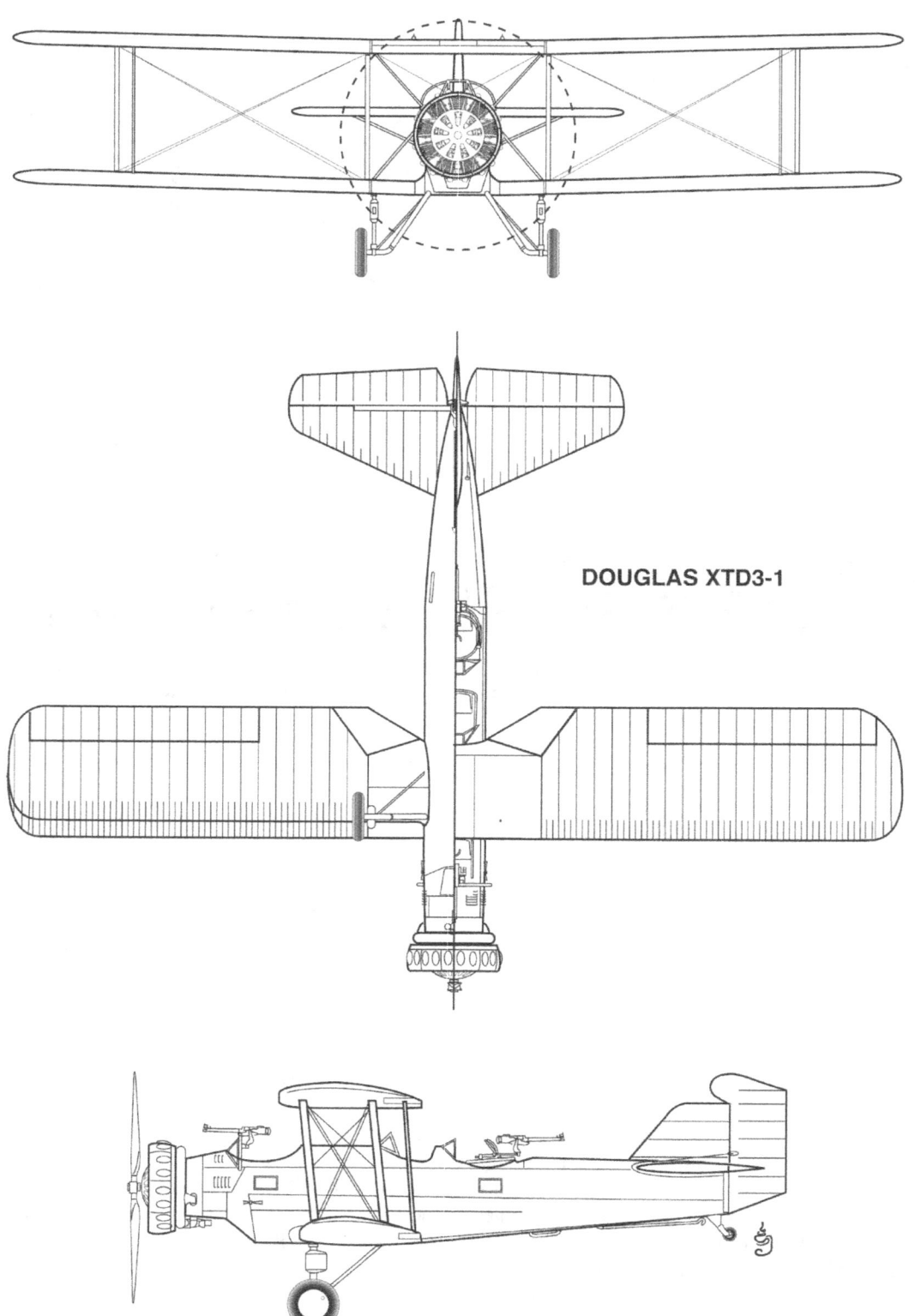

DOUGLAS XTD3-1

XT3D-1 as delivered to Anacostia for trials in fall of 1931. Although this aircraft was returned to the factory and reappeared in early 1933 with a more powerful engine, new cowling, and spatted landing gear, no production was ordered.

Douglas TBD Devastator 1935–1942

SPECIFICATIONS (TBD-1)

Type: Three-place torpedo-bomber
Manufacturer: Douglas Aircraft Co., El Segundo Division, El Segundo, California.
Total produced: 130
Power plant: One 900-hp Pratt & Whitney R-1830-64 14-cylinder radial driving a three-bladed Hamilton Standard variable-pitch propeller.
Armament: One fixed forward-firing .30-cal. machine gun, one flexible .30-cal. rear machine gun, and up to 1,000-lbs. of bombs or one torpedo carried externally.
Performance: Max. speed 206-mph at s.l.; cruise 128-mph; ceiling 19,700 ft.; range 716 mi. (with 1,000-lb. payload).
Weights: 6,182-lbs. empty, 10,194-lbs. max. loaded.

    The TBD was the first type of monoplane combat aircraft to be placed in production and enter service with the Navy. In mid–1934, to keep pace with new carrier construction and also replace its aging fleet of T4M/TG torpedo planes, BUAER issued a completely new requirement for a torpedo-bomber (TB) type and authorized two prototypes: a monoplane from Douglas designated the XTBD-1 and a biplane from Great Lakes designated the XTBG-1. Both aircraft were to be powered by an R-1830 engine, have retractable landing gear, and carry a crew of three. The XTBD-1 prototype was test flown on April 15, 1935 and delivered to Anacostia just nine days later. Flight trials conducted through the balance of 1935 indicated not only superior performance over the rival XTBG-1 biplane, but far better stability and overall handling characteristics. Douglas received a contract in February 1936 for 114 TBD-1 production models, which differed in having an uprated engine, a raised canopy enclosure, more ver-

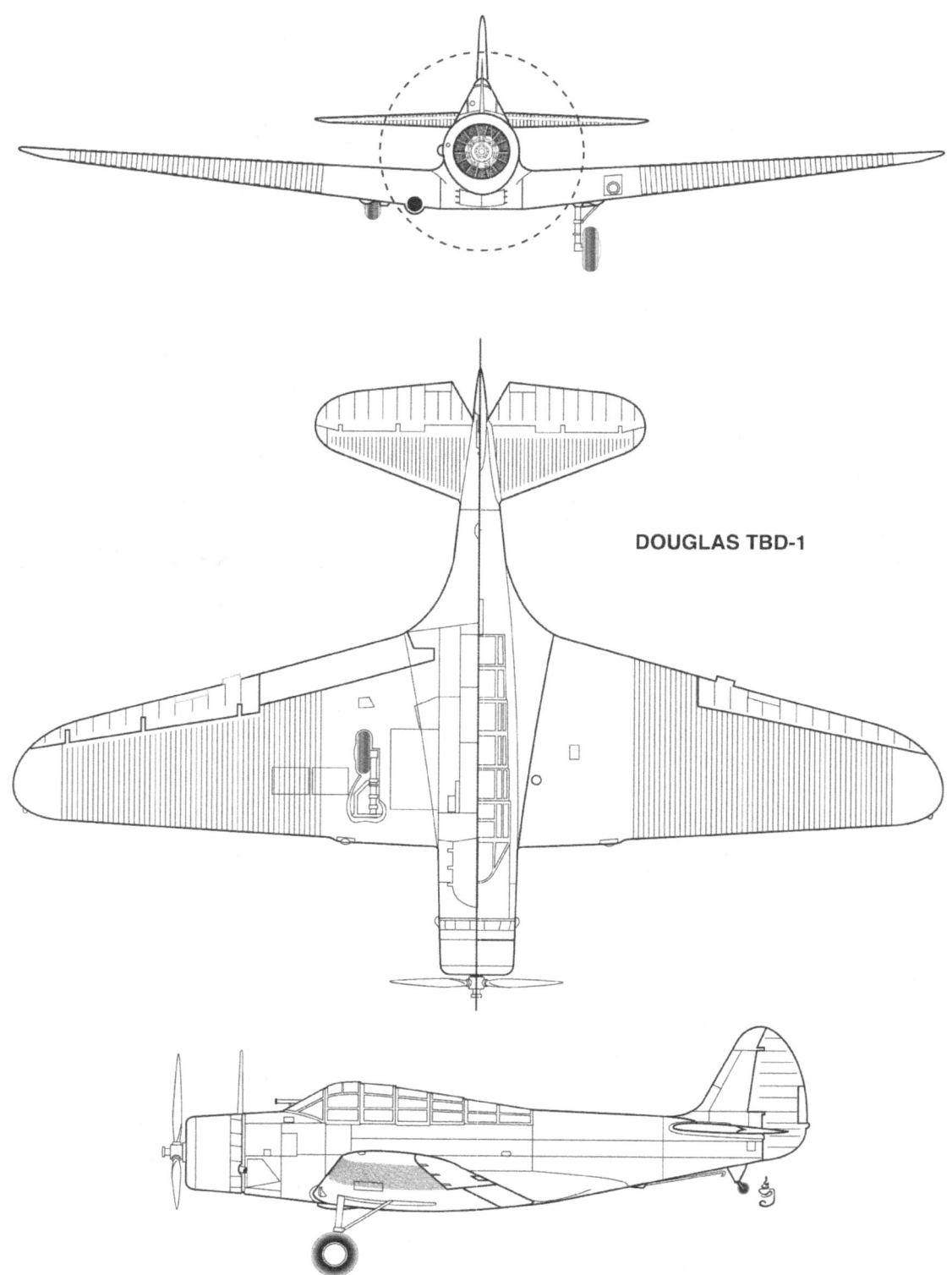

DOUGLAS TBD-1

TBD-1 of VT-2 in the *Lexington* Air Group, circa 1940. The tail color was bright yellow. During 1941, the colorful orange-yellow and silver paint scheme on fleet aircraft was changed to overall light gray.

tical fin area, and a revised cowling. After the type had entered service, 15 more TBD-1s were added to the order in August 1938.

Deliveries of TBD-1s began in early October 1937 and the first squadron to receive the type was VT-3 of *Saratoga's* air group. From mid–1938 onwards, TBD-1s equipped VT-2 of *Lexington*, VT-5 of *Yorktown*, and VT-6 of *Enterprise*, and finally, in late 1941, VT-8 of *Hornet*. TBDs were the Fleet's standard torpedo-bomber when the U.S. entered World War II and were involved in the very earliest carrier actions of 1942 against land-based Japanese targets in the Marshall and Gilbert Islands. However, in the carrier-to-carrier engagements which followed, TBDs proved to be highly vulnerable to both enemy antiaircraft fire and fighters, and during the Battle of Midway in June 4–5, 1942, 41 of 47 TBDs launched were lost. After being replaced by Grumman TBFs in mid–1942, surviving TBDs served a while longer as trainers.

Douglas TB2D Skypirate 1945–1946

TECHNICAL SPECIFICATIONS (XTB2D-1)

Type: Three-place torpedo-bomber
Manufacturer: Douglas Aircraft Co., El Segundo Division, El Segundo, California.
Total produced: 2
Power plant: One 3,000-hp Pratt & Whitney R-4360-8 28-cylinder radial driving an eight-bladed Aeroproducts contra-rotating, constant-speed propeller.
Armament: Two fixed forward-firing 20-millimeter cannons, two .50-cal. machine guns in a power-operated dorsal turret, one flexible .50-cal. machine gun in ventral bay, and up to 4,000-lbs. of bombs or four torpedoes carried on wing racks.
Performance: Max. speed 340-mph at 15,600 ft.; cruise 141-mph; ceiling 24,500 ft.; range 2,880 mi. max., 1,250 mi. loaded.
Weights: 18,405-lbs. empty, 34,760-lbs. max. loaded.
Dimensions: Span 70 ft., length 46 ft., wing area 605 sq. ft.

The Douglas TB2D was the largest and heaviest single-engine, propeller-driven aircraft

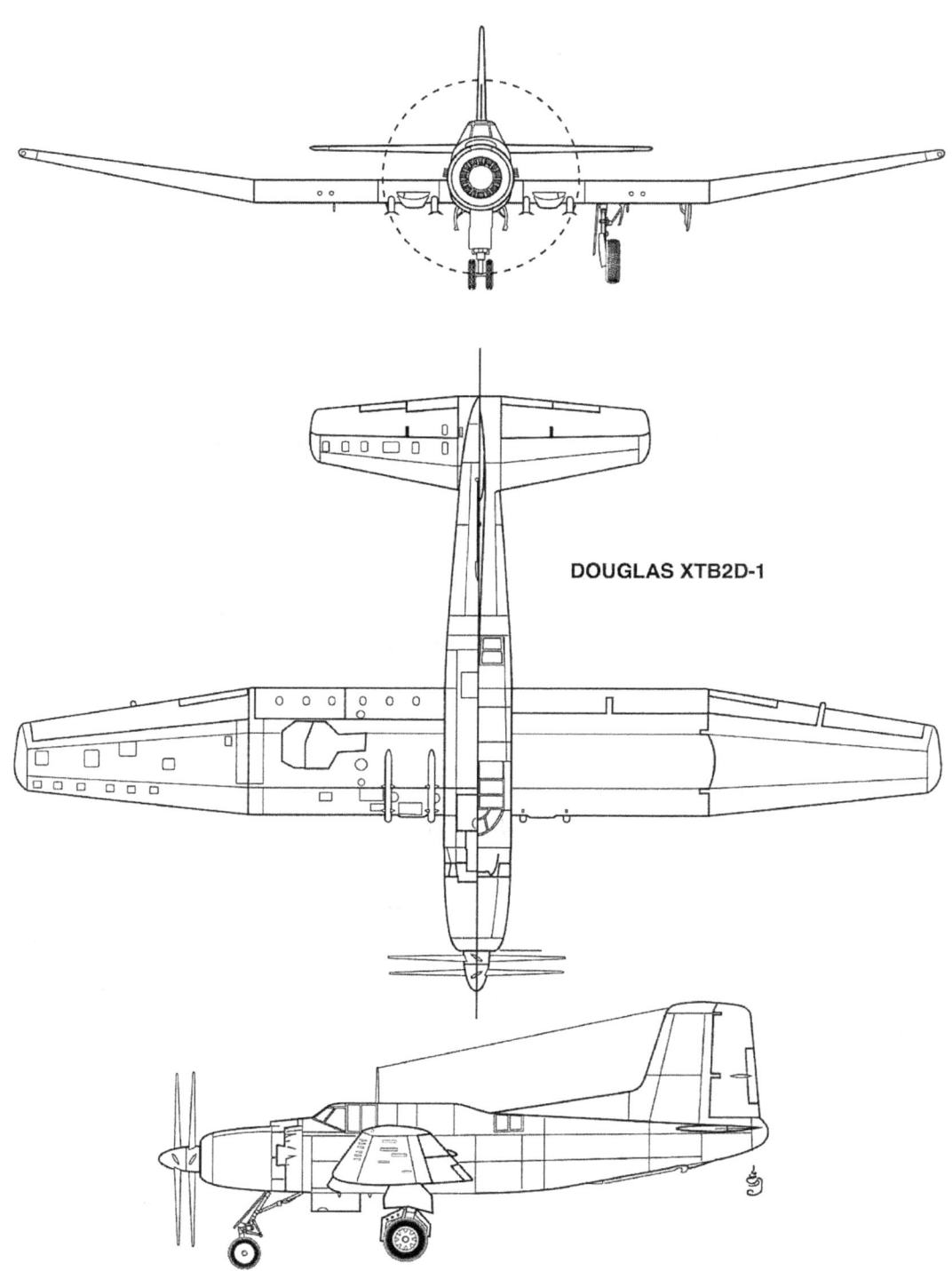

DOUGLAS XTB2D-1

ever designed to operate from an aircraft carrier. In 1942, before the U. S. had secured island bases within striking distance of the Japanese Home Islands, the Navy envisaged the need for a long-range, heavy attack force that would operate from the planned 45,000-ton *Midway* class of carriers. The same year Douglas submitted a design proposal for a torpedo-bomber projected to have fifty percent more range and twice the payload of the Grumman TBF. After

The sole XTB2D-1 prototype moments before touchdown. It was the largest propeller-driven, single-engine aircraft ever designed for carrier operations, but by the time it flew, the Navy's need for a very long range aircraft had disappeared.

reviewing proposals, BUAER awarded Douglas a contract in October 1943 to build two prototypes under the designation XTB2D-1. Because the aircraft was too large to operate from any existing carrier, its development priority was necessarily tied to the pace of the *Midway* construction program, and in late 1943, with Japan in retreat in the southwest and central Pacific, naval planners elected to cancel three of the six ships ordered and delay their completion until early 1945.

Though single-engine, the design dimensions and loaded weight of the XTB2D-1 were comparable to twin-engine USAAF tactical bombers like the B-25 and the A-26, and many of the type's engineering characteristics were in fact derived from Douglas's excellent A-26 design. However, by the time the first prototype flew on March 14, 1945, the need for a long-range carrier force had been forestalled and BUAER was instead focusing its energies on development of smaller and simpler single-seat attack designs that could operate from *Essex* class carriers. Like many other projects, the XTB2D-1 did not survive the post-war scale-backs and was cancelled in 1946.

Grumman TBF (TBM) Avenger 1941–1954

TECHNICAL SPECIFICATIONS (TBF-1C)

Type: Three-place torpedo-bomber
Manufacturer: Grumman Aircraft Engineering Corp., Bethpage, New York; also built by Eastern Aircraft Division, General Motors.
Total produced (all USN/USMC models): 8,810
Power plant: One 1,700-hp Wright R-2600-8 14-cylinder radial driving a three-bladed Hamilton Standard fully-reversible, constant-speed propeller.

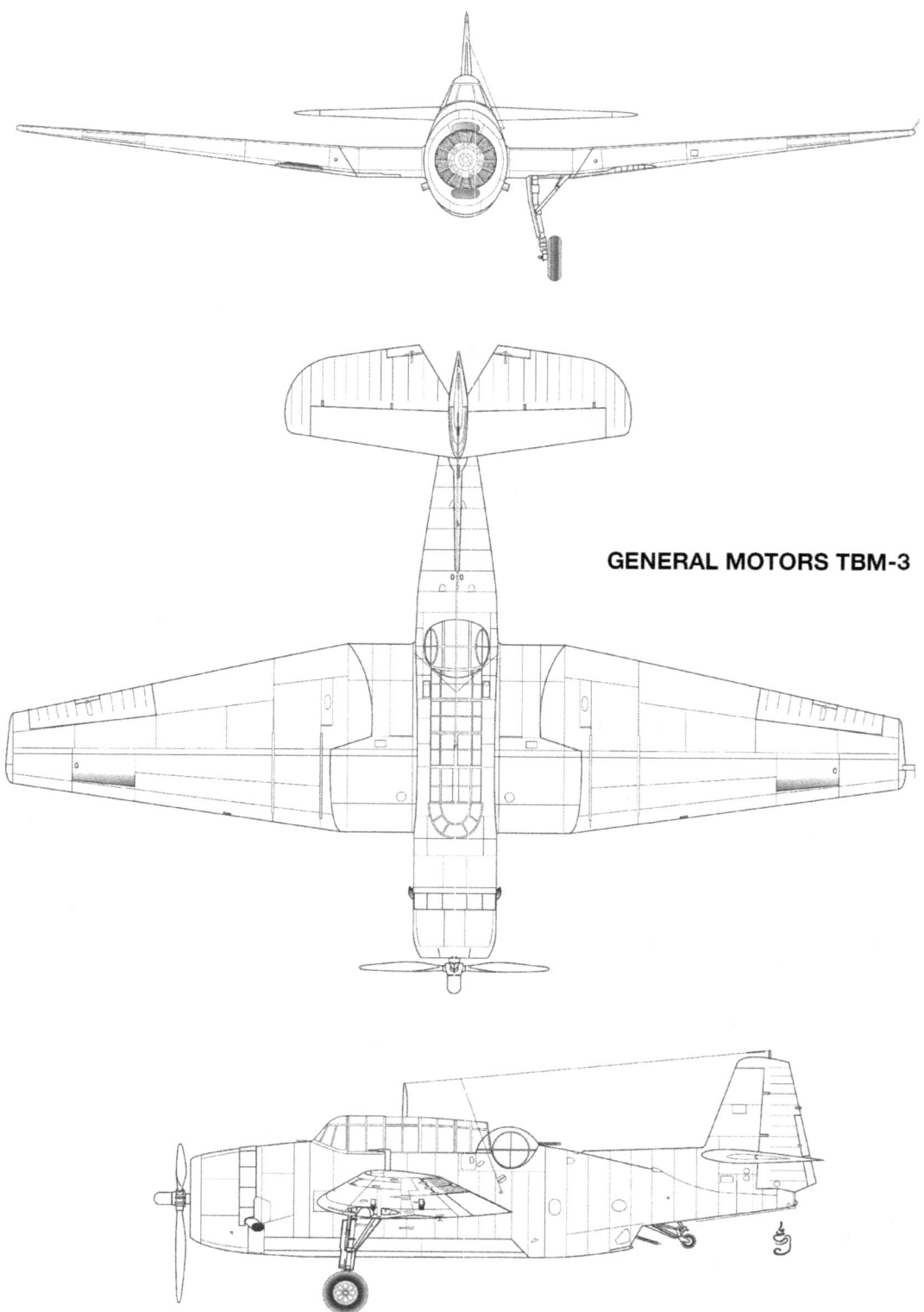

GENERAL MOTORS TBM-3

Top: TBF-1C positioned for catapult-assisted takeoff in early 1944. TBFs carried bombs and rockets on most missions and used a glide-boming tactic for weapons delivery. Grumman had delivered 1,895 to Navy and Marine units by the end of 1943. *Bottom:* A pair of TBM-3Es serving with VS-25 during the late 1940s. While most had been replaced in attack units by 1948, some continued with ASW units until 1952. The last examples converted for COD duties were retired in 1954.

Armament: One fixed forward-firing .30-cal. machine gun in nose, two fixed forward-firing .50-Cal machine guns in wings. one flexible .50-cal. machine gun in dorsal power turret, one flexible .30-cal. machine gun in ventral position, one torpedo or up to 2,000-lbs. of bombs carried in an internal bay. Performance: Max. speed 257-mph at 12,000 ft.; cruise 153-mph; ceiling 21,400 ft.; range 2,335 mi. max., 1,105 mi. loaded.
Weights: 10,555-lbs. empty, 17,364-lbs. loaded.
Dimensions: Span 54 ft. 2 in., length 40 ft., wing area 490 sq. ft.

    The TBF/TBM series is universally regarded as having been the most successful Navy and Marine Corps torpedo-bomber design of the World War II era. Its origins can be traced to a BUAER requirement issued in early 1940 for a TBD replacement having more horsepower, improved speed, range and payload, and much better defensive protection. To eliminate the drag of external stores, particularly torpedoes, BUAER also specified that the new type be designed with an internal bomb bay. Proposals were received from Grumman and Vought, and in April 1940 prototypes for both were ordered as the XTBF-1 and XTBU-1, respectively. The Navy was in such a hurry to obtain new torpedo-bombers that 286 TBF-1s were ordered before the prototype has flown. The XTBF-1 made its first flight on August 1, 1941, and service trials were completed by December. In early January 1942, the war emergency generated an order for an additional 1,600 TBF-1s, and on top of that, a contract was given to the Eastern Aircraft Division of General Motors to build many more under license as the TBM-1. By the end of 1943, Grumman had delivered the last of its 1,895 Navy and Marine TBF-1s and -1Cs, plus 395 more lend-leased to Britain as *Avenger* Is. Eastern Aircraft Division, from November 1942 onwards, produced 6,520 TBM variants for the Navy and Marine Corps plus an additional 526 for the Royal Navy under lend-lease as *Avenger* IIs and IIIs.

    The TBF/TBM series received numerous upgrades and modifications both during and after the war: the TBF/TBM-1C added fixed .50-cal. machine guns to each wing; TBM-3, a 1,900-hp R-2600-20 engine and wings strengthened to carry pylon-mounted rockets; and TBM-3E, a wing-mounted radar pod. Special purpose versions included the TBF-1D and TBM-3H with special radar, the TBF-1CP and TBM-3P with cameras, and the TBF-1L with a bomb bay-mounted searchlight. The TBF-2 was never built; an XTBM-4 prototype with a strengthened airframe was tested, but the production contract for 900 aircraft was cancelled when the war ended. Post-war modifications frequently entailed removal of the turret and addition of new equipment: the TBM-3W ASW "hunter" version had a faired-over turtledeck and a large belly radome in place of the bomb bay; the TBM-3N carried wing-mounted radar for night attack operations; the TBM-3Q was equipped with ECM components; and the TBM-3R was transformed into a 7-seat transport for COD (carrier on-board delivery) duties.

    TBF-1s first entered service in May 1942 with VT-8 of the *Hornet* air group but not in time to embark for sea duty; however, six of these aircraft did arrive at Midway Island on June 1, and four days later, during torpedo attacks launched from the island against the Japanese fleet, four were destroyed. From mid–1942 onwards, TBF-1s reequipped all carrier-based VT units and land-based VMTB units; and in early 1944, new TBMs began replacing war-weary TBFs as well as equipping new units being formed. While torpedo attacks continued against smaller warships, submarines, and merchant vessels, glide-bombing became the most common tactic employed by TBFs/TBMs in combat operations. After the war, TBMs were slowly phased-out of frontline attack duties as single-seat Douglas ADs and Martin AMs took their place; TBMs modified for the ASW, night attack, ECM, and COD roles continued to operate until 1954.

Grumman TB3F Guardian 1945–1947

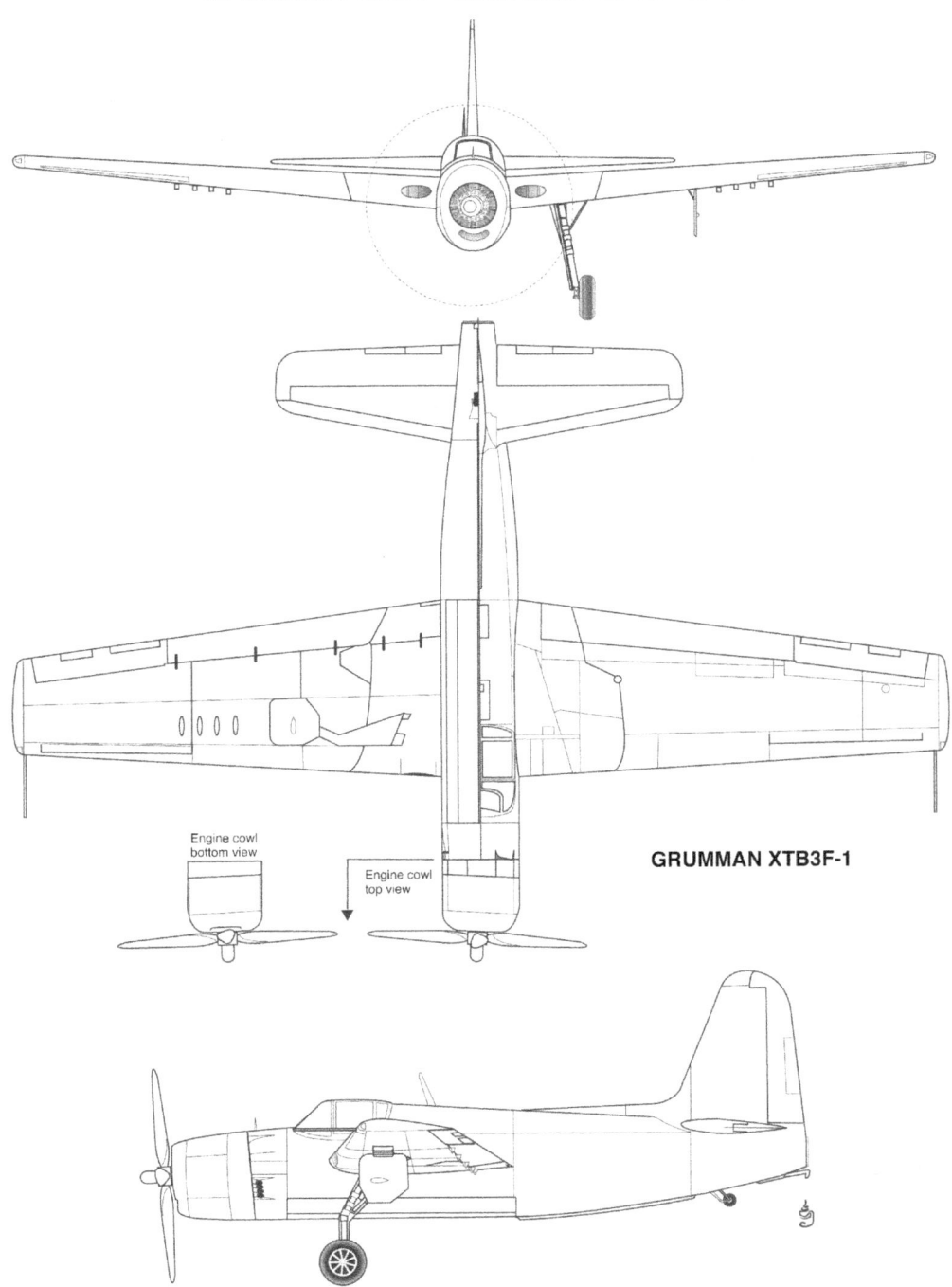

GRUMMAN XTB3F-1

TECHNICAL SPECIFICATIONS (XTB3F-1)

Type: Single-place torpedo-bomber
Manufacturer: Grumman Aircraft Engineering Corp., Bethpage, New York.
Total produced: 2

The XTB3F-1 soon after its first flight in late 1945. The J30 turbojet buried in the fuselage was never tested in flight. After the project was cancelled, it reemerged in 1949 as the AF-2W, -2S, and -3S ASW platform with piston power only.

Power plant: One 2,300-h.p. Pratt & Whitney R-2800-46 18-cylinder radial driving a four-bladed Hamilton Standard constant-speed propeller and one Westinghouse 19XB-2B (J30) turbojet, rated at 1,660-lbs./s.t.
Armament: (No defensive armament) Two torpedoes or up to 5,000-lbs. of bombs carried in an internal bay.
Performance (est.): Max. speed 356-m.p.h. at altitude; cruise 160-m.p.h.; ceiling 23,000 ft.; range 1,500 mi.
Weights (est.): 12,500-lbs. empty, 20,000-lbs. loaded.
Dimensions: Span 60 ft. 8 in., length 43 ft. 4 in., wing area 549 sq. ft.

During the late World War II period, Grumman had hoped to replace its highly successful TBF with a twin-engine aircraft similar in layout to its F7F fighter, however, two projects, the XTB2F-1 and the XTSF-1, were both cancelled in 1944 before prototypes were built. BUAER was simultaneously investigating practical methods for introducing turbojet-powered aircraft to carrier aviation, and in late 1944 queried Grumman about the feasibility of installing an auxiliary turbojet engine in the tail section of a single-seat TBF. Grumman's response, Design 70, shared the mid-wing planform and bomb bay arrangement of the TBF but was otherwise an entirely new airframe; and when built, became the largest single-seat aircraft yet conceived for carrier operations. In February 1945 BUAER approved Grumman's proposal and awarded a contract for two prototypes as the XTB3F-1.

The operational concept behind the TB3F envisaged the turbojet being used only for takeoff and for bursts of speed in combat situations; moreover, with the extra speed, it was believed than gun armament would be unnecessary. During jet operations, the 19XB engine would be fed air via a system of ducts leading from intakes in the wing roots, and exhaust expelled through a tailpipe extending beneath the empennage. The first of two XTB3F-1 prototypes made its first flight on December 19, 1945 on piston-power only. The turbojet installation had been test run on the ground, but persistent problems with the air intake ducting precluded its testing in flight. With a week after the first flight, BUAER abruptly directed Grumman to halt further development.

Although the mixed-power XTB3F-1 came to an very sudden end, the airframes got a reprieve: in January 1946 BUAER ordered Grumman to remove the turbojets and rework both prototypes for the ASW "hunter" and "killer" roles. First flown in 1949, 386 of these aircraft were ultimately produced as the AF-2W, -2S, and -3S and remained in active service until 1955.

Great Lakes TBG 1935–1936

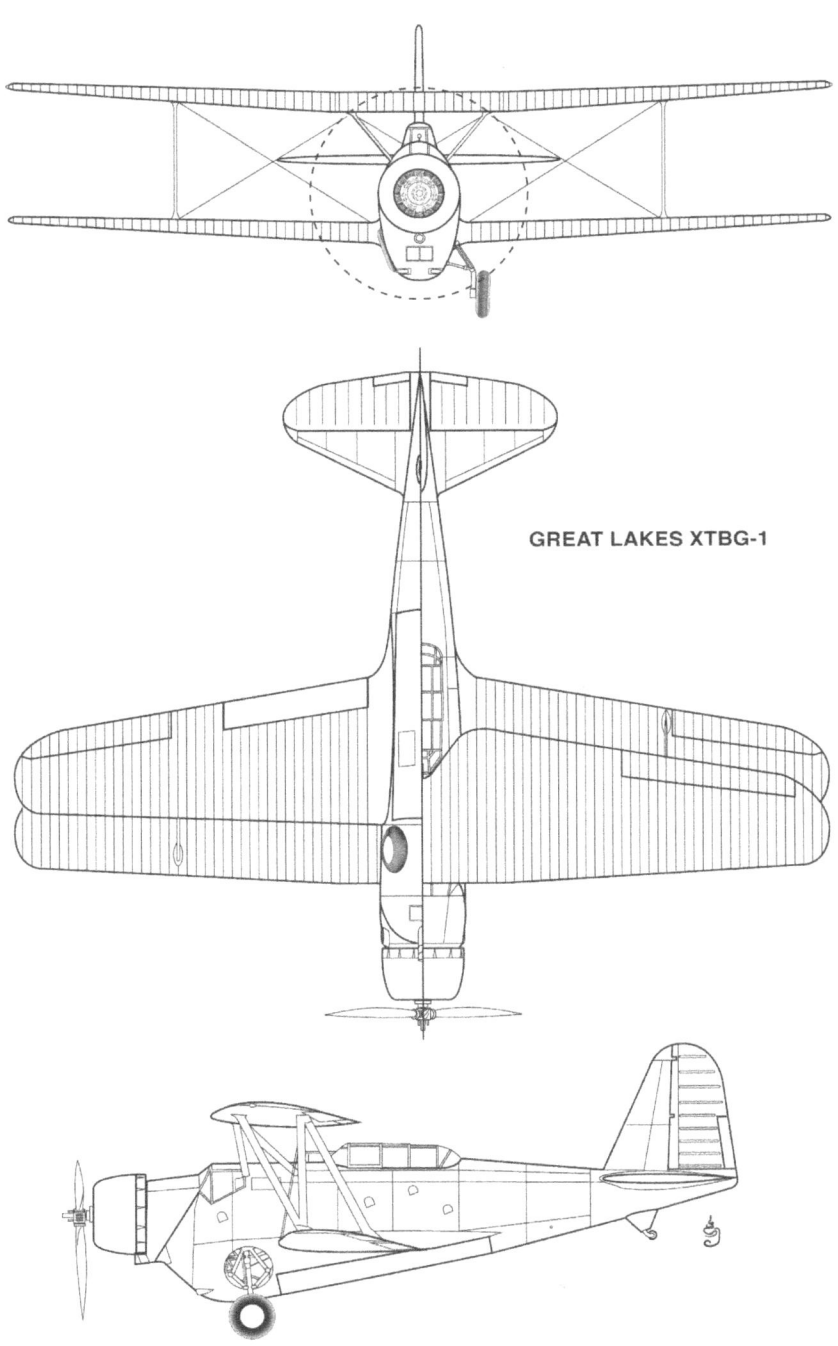

GREAT LAKES XTBG-1

TECHNICAL SPECIFICATIONS (XTBG-1)

Type: three-place torpedo-bomber
Manufacturer: Great Lakes Aircraft Corp., Cleveland, Ohio.
Total produced: 1

XTBG-1 as delivered to Anacostia in mid–1935. BUAER ordered it as a hedge against the possibility that the monoplane Douglas TBD would be too "hot" for carrier operations. Great Lakes folded soon afterward.

Power plant: One 800-hp Pratt & Whitney R-1830-60 14-cylinder radial driving a three-bladed Hamilton Standard variable-pitch propeller.
Armament: One fixed forward-firing .30-cal. machine gun, one flexible .30-cal. rear machine gun, and up to 1,000-lbs. of bombs or one torpedo carried in internal bay.
Performance: Max. speed 185-mph at 7,000 ft.; ceiling 16,400 ft.; combat range 586 mi.
Weights: 5,323-lbs. empty, 9,275-lbs. loaded.
Dimensions: Span 42 ft., length 35 ft. 1 in., wing area 547 sq. ft.

The TBG was the last type of torpedo-carrying biplane considered by the Navy and the final product of Great Lakes before that company ceased operations. In June 1934, BUAER selected Great Lakes to build a retractable-gear biplane torpedo-bomber prototype under the designation XTBG-1 in what was to be a biplane versus monoplane fly-off. The design was essentially a fifteen percent scale-up of the basic BG/B2G blueprint, adding a bombardier's station beneath a low-profile canopy located forward of the cabane struts. Following delivery of the XTBG-1 prototype to Anacostia in August 1935, testing revealed not only poor stability, but levels of performance that were generally inferior to Douglas's rival XTBD-1 monoplane. Development was abandoned in early 1936 and Great Lakes, lacking any production prospects, closed its doors soon afterward.

Martin T3M 1926–1930

TECHNICAL SPECIFICATIONS (T3M-2)
Type: three-place torpedo plane
Manufacturer: Glenn L. Martin Co., Cleveland, Ohio.
Total produced: 100
Power plant: One 710-hp Packard 3A-2500 12-cylinder inline driving a three-bladed Hamilton Standard fixed-pitch propeller.

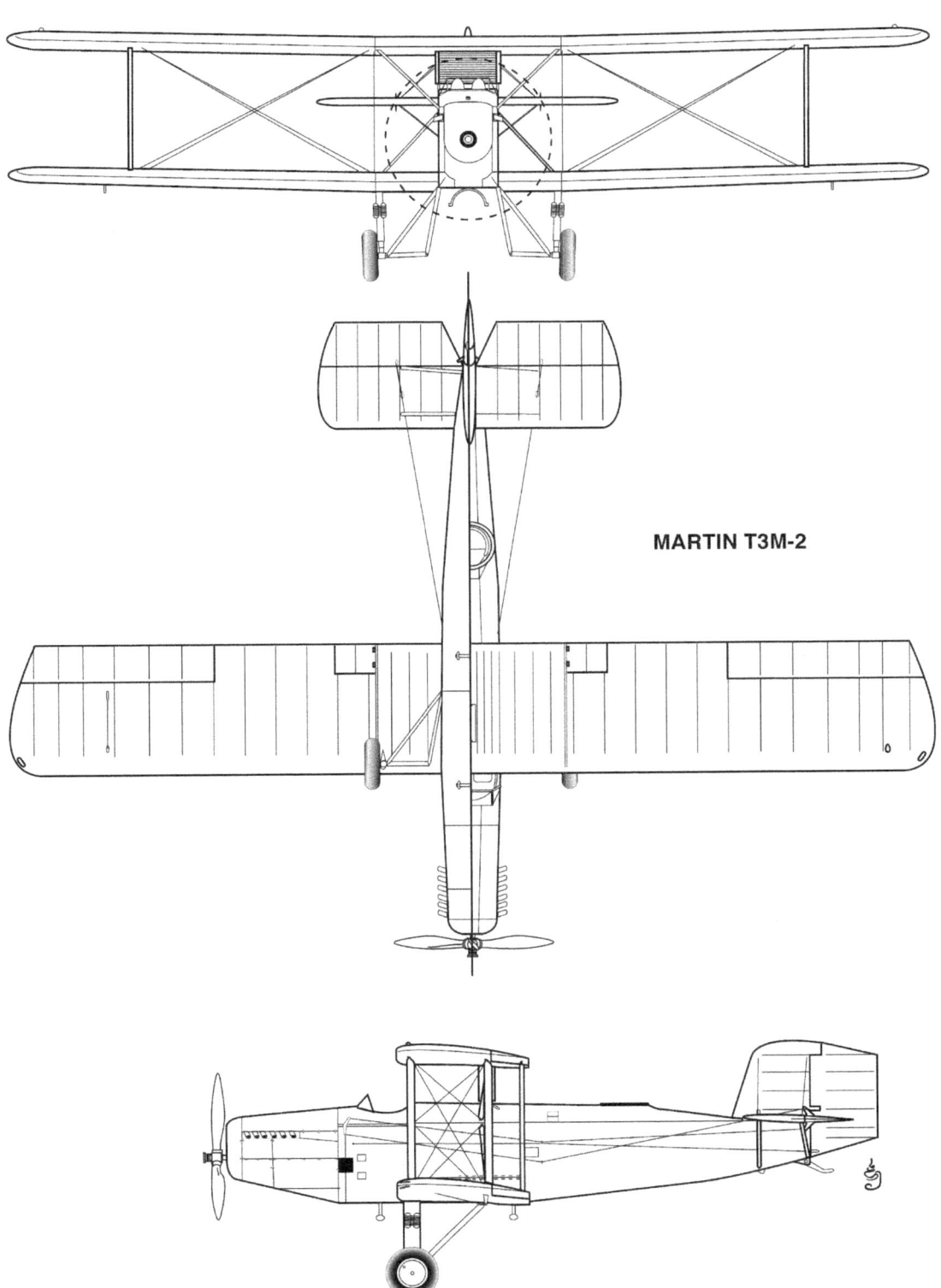

MARTIN T3M-2

T3M-2 seen dropping parachutists. The front cockpit, where a crewmember is seen facing aft, is the bombardier's station. This aircraft was attached to VT-2 of the *Langley* Air Group during the late 1920s.

Armament: One flexible .30-cal.rear machine gun in rear cockpit and one torpedo or up to 1,500-lbs. of bombs carried externally.
Performance: Max. speed 109-mph at sea level.; ceiling 7,900 ft.; combat range 634 mi.
Weights: 5,814-lbs. empty, 9503-lbs. loaded.
Dimensions: Span 56 ft. 7 in, length 41 ft. 4 in., wing area 883 sq. ft.

 The T3M-2 is credited with the distinction of being the first Navy attack aircraft specifically developed for carrier operations. After Martin had delivered 26 examples of its T3M-1 landplane/floatplane design in 1926, BUAER asked for a more powerful derivative having greater wing area, redesigned crew locations, and arresting gear. The carrier mission perceived for the new type not only encompassed torpedo attack, but included bombing and scouting as well. The resulting T3M-2, flown in early 1927, had equal span wings (unlike the short upper wing of the T3M-1), a 135-hp increase in power, three individual cockpits in tandem for the pilot, bombardier, and gunner/observer, plus a tailhook to engage arresting wires. After acceptance, Martin was given a contract to built 100 of the type.

 Deliveries of T3M-2s to active service units began in mid–1927, and by the end of the year they were equipping VT-1S aboard the newly commissioned *Lexington* and VT-2B of *Langley*. T3M-2s also were assigned to shore-based torpedo squadrons, where they served as the Navy's standard single-engine torpedo plane. Like many naval aircraft of this era, however, the T3M-2 was rapidly overtaken by newer types and began to be replaced in frontline service as early as mid–1928 and had been relegated to utility status by 1930.

Martin T4M (TG) 1927–1937

TECHNICAL SPECIFICATIONS (T4M-1)

Type: Three-place torpedo plane
Manufacturer: Glenn L. Martin Co., Cleveland, Ohio; Great Lakes Aircraft Corp., same location.

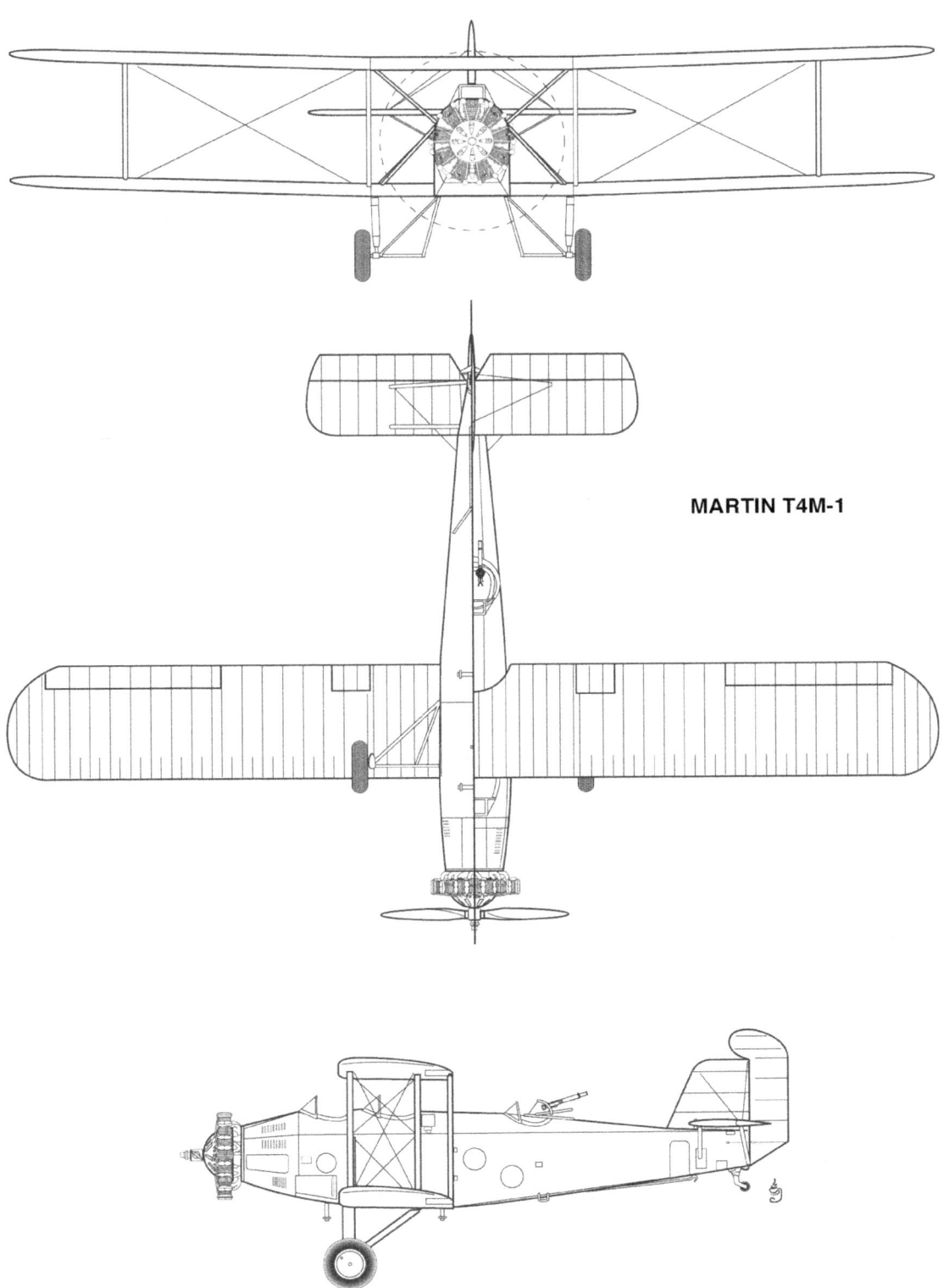

MARTIN T4M-1

The T4M-1, the fleet's standard torpedo plane from 1928 to 1937. The example shown here had been released from active service and assigned to VN-12, a Naval Reserve training unit based at Robertson Field in St. Louis.

Total produced (all models): 153
Power plant: One 525-hp Pratt & Whitney R-1690-24 9-cylinder radial driving a three-bladed Hamilton Standard fixed-pitch propeller.
Armament: One flexible .30-cal. rear machine gun in rear cockpit and one torpedo or up to 1,500-lbs. of bombs carried externally.
Performance: Max. speed 114-mph at sea level.; cruise 98-mph; ceiling 10,150 ft.; combat range 363 mi.
Weights: 3,931-lbs. empty, 8,071-lbs. max. loaded.
Dimensions: Span 53 ft., length 35 ft. 7 in., wing area 656 sq. ft.

The T4M/TG biplane was the Navy's principal carrier-based torpedo aircraft from 1928 until it was replaced during 1937 by Douglas TBD monoplanes. When BUAER began expressing a preference for aircraft equipped with air-cooled engines, Martin, in early 1927, modified the first T3M-2 prototype to accept installation of the R-1690 *Hornet* radial and delivered it for tests as the XT3M-3. Experimental trials were sufficiently encouraging that BUAER ordered an improved *Hornet*-powered prototype from Martin under the designation XT4M-1. When the XT4M-1 arrived for testing in April 1927, it had smaller, narrow-chord wings, a balanced rudder, and many other refinements to the overall fuselage design. Like the T3M-2, it was convertible to floatplane operations. Martin was awarded a production contract for 102 T4M-1s in June 1927 and deliveries to fleet units began in mid–1928. Great Lakes acquired Martin's Cleveland plant and production rights to the T4M in late 1928 and produced a further 18 aircraft delivered in early 1930 as the TG-1. In July 1930 Great Lakes received an order for 32 additional aircraft to be equipped with Wright R-1820-86 *Cyclone* engines under the designation TG-2. Delivered from mid–1931, the TG-2 offered a 10-mph increase in top speed and improved rate-of-climb.

VT-2B of *Saratoga*'s air group received its first T4M-1s in August 1928, followed by VT-1B aboard *Lexington* later in the year, and both units were augmented with deliveries of TG-1s in 1930. When TG-2s began arriving in June 1931, the T4M-1s/TG-1s of VT-2B were transferred to shore-based utility or reserve units; those with VT-1B experienced a similar fate when the unit converted to Martin BM-1 dive-bombers in 1932. BUAER's efforts to find a T4M/TG replacement in the early 1930s were not successful, with the result that TG-2s remained active with VT-2B until the first TBD-1s began arriving in October 1937. Many T4Ms/TGs saw service in Navy and Marine reserve units up through the late 1930s and six were still listed on the naval inventory in December 1941.

Martin T6M 1930–1931

TECHNICAL SPECIFICATIONS (XT6M-1)

Type: Three-place torpedo plane
Manufacturer: Glenn L. Martin Co., Baltimore, Maryland.
Total produced: 1
Power plant: One 575-hp Wright R-1820-58 9-cylinder radial driving a two-bladed Hamilton Standard fixed-pitch propeller.
Armament: Two flexible .30-cal. rear machine guns in rear cockpit and one torpedo or up to 1,500-lbs. of bombs carried externally.
Performance: Max. speed 124-mph at s. l.; ceiling 11,600 ft.; combat range 323 mi.
Weights: 3,500-lbs. empty, 6,841-lbs. max. loaded.
Dimensions: Span 42 ft. 3 in., length 33 ft. 8 in., wing area 502 sq. ft.

Ordered by BUAER in mid–1929, the T6M (note, the T5M became the BM, as reported earlier) represented one of several unsuccessful attempts to generate a replacement for the T4M/TG series of torpedo planes. The XT6M-1 prototype, featuring an all-metal fuselage and tail group, was delivered to Anacostia for official evaluations in December 1930. Since its general performance was no better than, and in some instances inferior to the TG-2, no production was ordered. A similar fait awaited the Douglas XT3D-1/2 a year later.

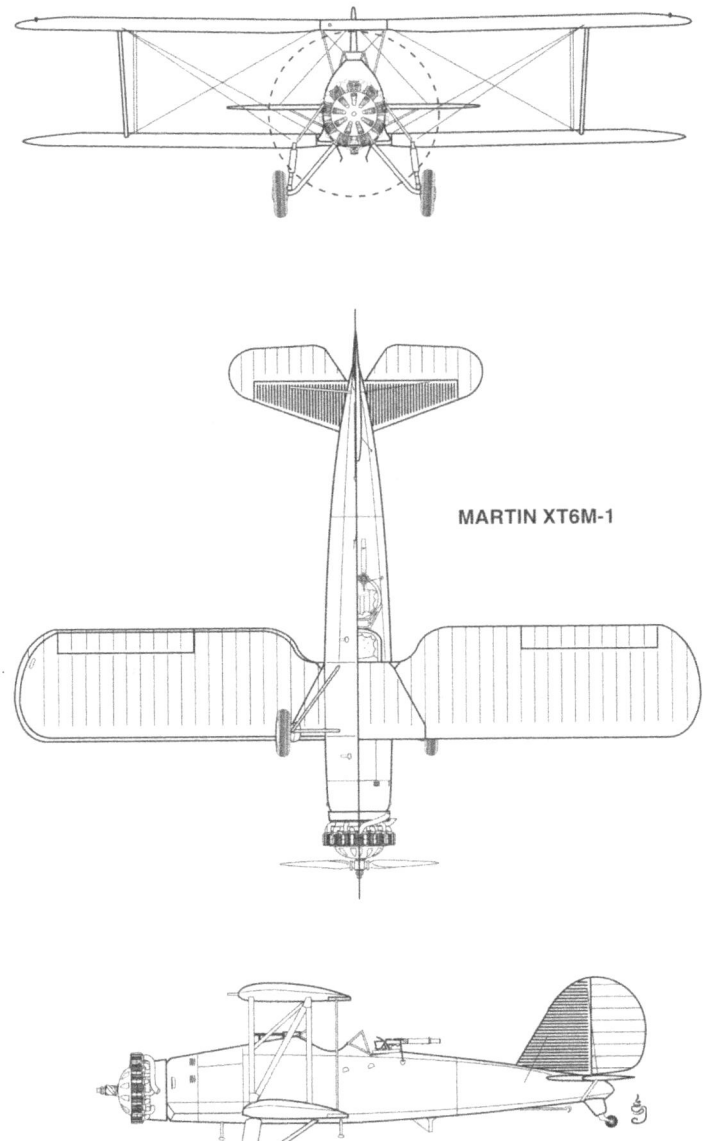

MARTIN XT6M-1

The single XT6M-1 as it appeared in early 1931. BUAER's attempts to replace its obsolescent T4Ms would not be realized until the advent of the TBD monoplane in 1937.

Vought TBU (TBY) Sea Wolf 1941–1945

TECHNICAL SPECIFICATIONS (TBY-2)

Type: Three-place torpedo-bomber
Manufacturer: Chance Vought Division of United Aircraft Corp., Stratford, Connecticut; Consolidated-Vultee Aircraft Corp., San Diego, California.
Total produced (all models): 182
Power plant: One 2,000-hp Pratt & Whitney R-2800-20 18-cylinder radial driving a three-bladed Hamilton Standard fully-reversible, constant-speed propeller.
Armament: Three fixed forward-firing .50-cal. machine guns, one .50-cal machine gun in power-operated dorsal turret, on flexible .30-cal. machine gun in ventral tunnel, and up to 2,000-lbs. of bombs or one torpedo carried in an internal bay .
Performance: Max. speed 306-mph at 13,000 ft.; cruise 168-mph; ceiling 27,200 ft.; range 1,505 (with 1,000-lb. payload).
Weights: 11,022-lbs. empty, 18,488-lbs. max. loaded.
Dimensions: Span 56 ft. 11 in., length 39 ft. 3 in., wing area 440 sq. ft.

But for the aircraft production priorities dictated by America's sudden entry into World War II, the TBU/TBY might have shared billing with Grumman's famous TBF as one of the Navy's top combat aircraft of the wartime period. By 1940 the Navy was planning a massive expansion of its carrier force and needed many aircraft to equip new air groups, plus, its standard torpedo-bomber, the Douglas TBD, was rapidly approaching obsolescence. Early the same year, BUAER had issued a requirement for a new torpedo-bomber having better speed, payload, and defensive armament and, in April, authorized prototypes to be built by both Grumman and Vought as the XTBF-1 and XTBU-1, respectively.

As the design evolved, the XTBU-1 shared the mid-wing over bomb bay layout of the XTBF-1 while possessing a smaller fuselage cross-section and 10 percent less wing area. After the XTBU-1 prototype flew on December 22, 1941 (6 months after the XTBF-1), testing revealed

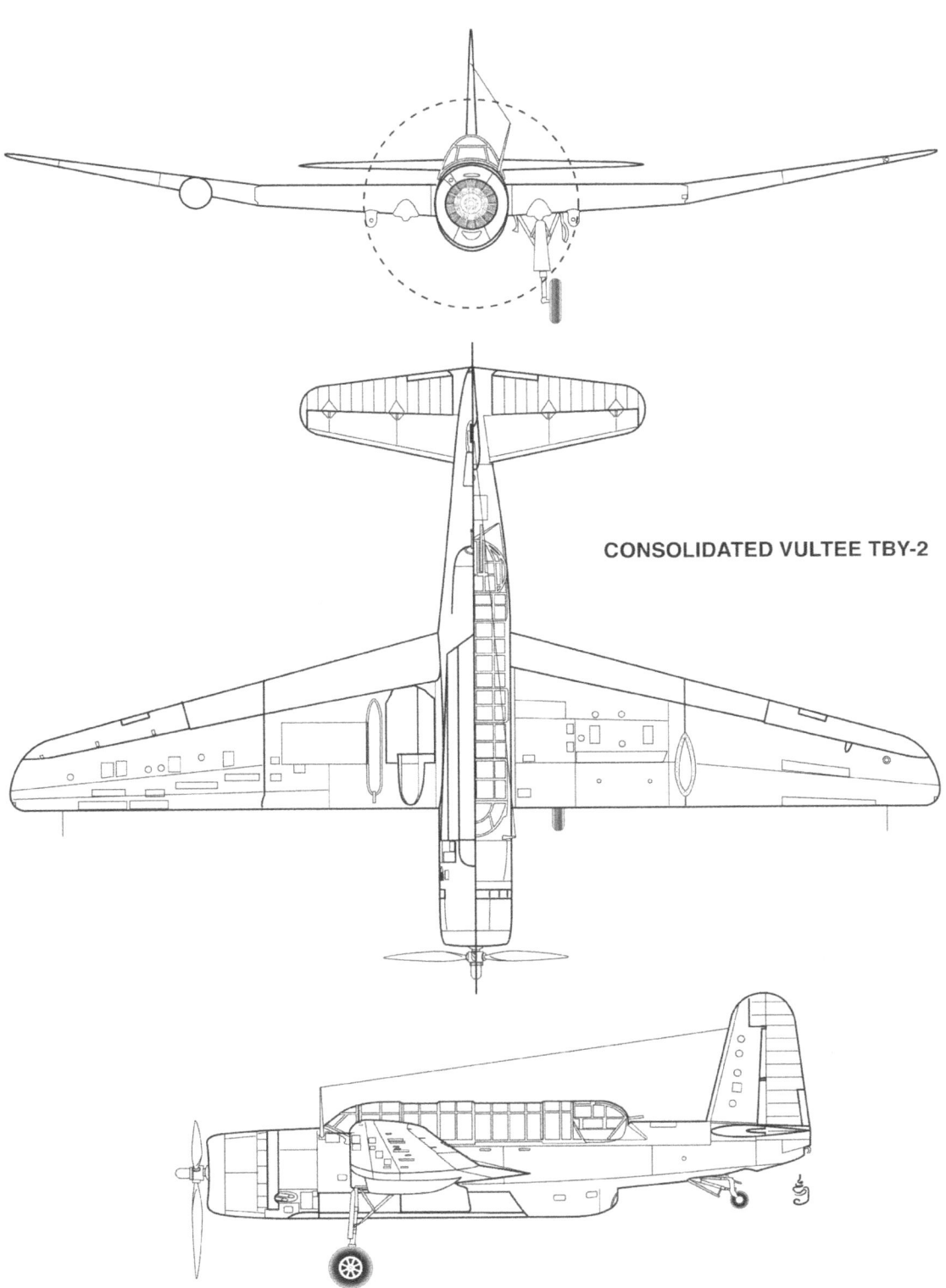

TBY-2 production model as completed in the fall of 1944. Although the XTBU-1 had flown in late 1941, Consolidated was only able to complete 180 license-built TBYs by the time the war ended in 1945.

performance superior to the TBF in terms of speed and rate-of-climb; however, due the priority placed on F4U production, Vought lacked plant capacity to mass-produce another aircraft. In September 1943 production rights were transferred to Consolidated-Vultee, which included a contract to manufacture 1,100 aircraft as the TBY-2. The first production TBY-2 flew in August 1944 and was delivered to the Navy in November, but as a result of production delays, only 180 had been completed by September 1945, and the remainder of the contract, which included 600 improved TBY-3s, was cancelled.

TBY-2s went into squadron service with VT-97 in April 1945 and began equipping other units soon afterward, but continuing operational problems caused the type to be withdrawn and replaced with TBMs. A number of TBY-2s survived as utility hacks at shore bases until the last was stricken from the naval inventory in 1947.

SECOND SERIES • 1946–1962

Designation	Manufacturer	Dates
AD	Douglas Aircraft Co.	1945–1968
A2D	Douglas Aircraft Co.	1950–1953
AJ	North American Aviation, Inc.	1948–1962
A2J	North American Aviation, Inc.	1952–1953
AM	Glenn L. Martin Co.	1944–1950
F4D	Douglas Aircraft Co.	1951–1964
F9F (Straight Wing)	Grumman Aircraft Engr.	1947–1959
F9F (Swept Wing)	Grumman Aircraft Engr.	1951–1959

Designation	Manufacturer	Dates
F2H	McDonnell Aircraft Corp.	1947–1959
F3H	McDonnell Aircraft Corp.	1951–1964
FJ (Swept Wing)	North American Aviation, Inc.	1951–1962
F7U	Chance Vought Aircraft Co.	1951–1957

Douglas AD (BT2D, A-1) Skyraider 1945–1972

TECHNICAL SPECIFICATIONS (AD-4)

Type: Single or multi-place attack
Manufacturer: Douglas Aircraft Co. El Segundo Division, El Segundo, California
Total produced (all models): 3,180
Power plant: One 2,700-hp Wright R-3350-26W (water injection) 18-cylinder radial driving a four-bladed Aeroproducts fully-reversible, constant-speed propeller.
Armament: Two fixed forward-firing 20-millimeter cannons and up to 8,000-lbs. of mixed ordnance carried externally.
Performance: Max. speed 321-mph at 20,000 ft.; cruise 200-mph; ceiling 32,500 ft.; range 3,000 mi. max., 900 mi. loaded.
Weights: 11,712-lbs. empty, 21,483-lbs. loaded.
Dimensions: Span 50 ft. 9 in., length 38 ft. 2 in., wing area 400 sq. ft.

Too late for World War II, the Douglas AD series went on to achieve a stunning combat record in both Korea and Vietnam during a career that stretched over two decades. Its story began in September 1943, when BUAER circulated the new requirement for a single-seat bomber-torpedo (BT) aircraft intended to replace SBDs, SB2Cs, and TBMs. Douglas originally submitted a proposal for the XBTD-1, which was basically a rehash of its less than successful XSB2D design; then in June 1944, the company surprised BUAER by asking for cancellation of the BTD program in favor of a totally new concept. Its proposed XBT2D-1 was much closer to BUAER's bomber-torpedo criteria: a simple design with a tailwheel layout in which weapons were carried on external racks beneath a bottom-mounted wing. For dive-bombing, Douglas introduced a new type of dive brake system consisting of flat panels that extended from the sides and belly of the fuselage. BUAER was sufficiently interested in the new concept to award Douglas a contract for 25 pre-production BT2D-1s, and after the first prototype flew on 15 March 1945, increased the order to 548 production aircraft.

The huge government cutbacks imposed after V-J Day resulted in the BT2D contract being reduced to 277 aircraft, and when the BT designation was changed to A for attack in early 1946, the plane became the AD-1. Service trials were completed in late 1946 and by early 1947, production AD-1s began replacing SB2Cs and TBMs in fleet units. The final 25 aircraft were delivered as AD-1Qs, a specialized ECM sub-variant that featured a separate compartment aft of the pilot for a radar operator. When the AD-1 had been in service less than a year, BUAER selected it as the Fleet's standard single-seat attack type and made plans to acquire improved versions. Deliveries of 152 AD-2s having the more powerful R-3350-26W engine, stronger wings, a new canopy design, and fully enclosed wheel covers began in mid–1948 and were joined by an additional 21 AD-2Qs and one AD-2QU target tug. During 1948–1949 the Navy took delivery of 127 AD-3s possessing even more airframe strengthening, longer stroke landing gear, and a redesigned tailwheel, plus 15 three-seat night attack AD-3Ns, 31 three-seat early-warning AD-3Ws fitted with belly radomes, and 21 two-seat AD-3Qs.

The AD-4, introduced in 1949 with increased takeoff weight, a stronger tailhook, and a P-1 autopilot, also came in night attack, early-warning, and ECM sub-variants.

BUAER originally anticipated AD production would end in 1950 when the last of 180 AD-

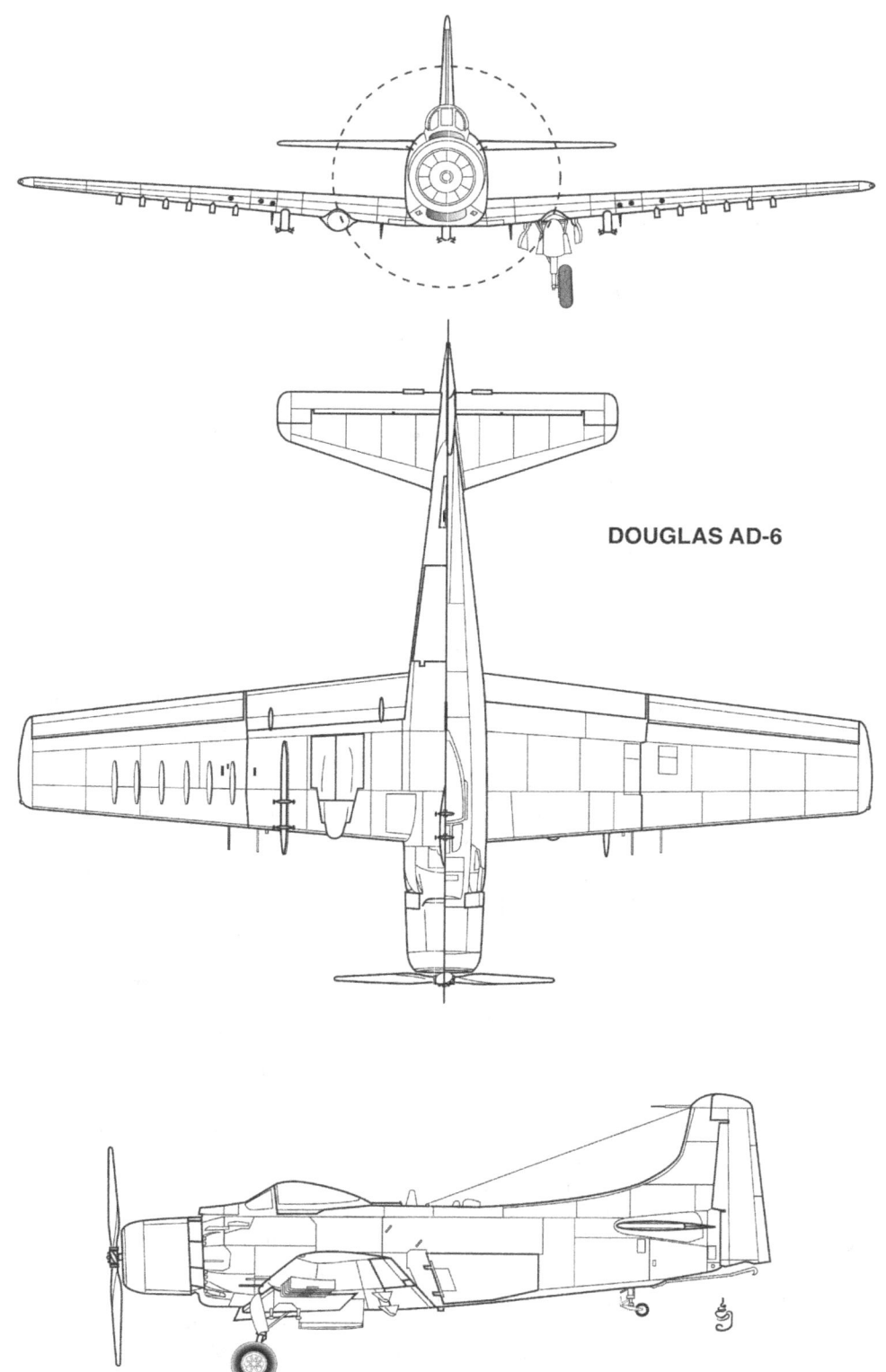

DOUGLAS AD-6

One of the 25 pre-production BT2D-1s loaded with twelve HVARs and two *Tiny Tim* rockets. Effectiveness of board-type speed brakes caused NATC officials to rate the BT2D-1 (later AD-1) as the best dive-bombing platform they had ever tested.

4 variants were delivered, but naval involvement in the Korean War, which began in June 1950, had the unexpected effect of continuing AD production nonstop and led to demand for development of new versions. By the end of 1952, 1,051 AD-4s (all variants) had been delivered, and they were followed by 165 AD-4Bs armed with four 20-mm cannons and also configured to carry a tactical nuclear weapon, the first single-seat naval aircraft to have such capability.

Originally envisaged as a four-seat ASW platform, the AD-5 emerged with a fuselage lengthened by two feet and widened to permit side-by-side seating for a pilot and three crewmembers under an elongated canopy. Fin area was increased and the dive-brakes on the sides of the fuselage were deleted. But even before the first AD-5 flew in August 1951, BUAER changed its mind and earmarked it for production as an attack aircraft. The 212 standard attack

Top: **AD-4B of VA-146 has missed the wires and is about to take the barrier. The -4 was the most numerous *Skyraider* variant produced (1,051 aircraft) and the -4B was the first single-seat carrier aircraft configured to carry a tactical nuclear weapon.** *Bottom:* **The basic versatility of the design is indicated by this AD-4N night attack variant serving with VMC-2 in 1953. Marine VMCs also operated AD-2Q ECM versions and AD-4W AEW versions.**

Late in its career, this ex-Navy AD-5 (A-1E) is shown delivering ordnance in Vietnamese Air Force (VNAF) markings. Most USAF and VNAF A-1E missions in Vietnam were single pilot. VNAF operated them up to the end, in 1975.

versions subsequently built came with conversion kits, which, in addition to its basic attack function, allowed the type to be used either as a transport (12 seats), cargo carrier, ambulance, or target tug. Production AD-5s began entering service in late 1953 and were followed by 218 AD-5W early-warning and 239 AD-5N night/all-weather attack sub-variants, 54 of which were later modified as AD-5Q ECM aircraft.

The refinements of the AD-4B, plus LABS (low-altitude bombing system), new bomb racks, a jettisonable canopy, and a hydraulic tailhook were standardized in the single-seat AD-6, which flew in 1953 and replaced AD-4s during 1954–1956. After delivery of 713 AD-6s, the final model was the single-seat AD-7, which differed in having a more powerful R-3350-26WB engine, stronger landing gear, and stronger outer wing panels. AD production finally ended in February 1957 when the last of 72 AD-7s rolled off El Segundo's assembly line.

ADs were destined to remain in active naval service for 22 years—considerably longer than BUAER expected. In late 1946-early 1947, VA-19A, VA-3B, and VA-4B were the first squadrons to receive ADs, and by the eve of the Korean war, the type was equipping sixteen Navy and two Marine attack squadrons. In Korea, ADs operating from both carriers and land bases earned a reputation as the best all-around attack aircraft in the combat zone. Besides flying day attack, night attack, countermeasures, and early-warning missions, it was the only aircraft in the theater capable of delivering 2,000-lb. bombs against hardened targets (like bridges and dams) with dive-bomber precision. After Korea, AD's carried on as naval aviation's standard single-seat attack type and reached their peak in the mid–1950s when they equipped 29 Navy and 13 Marine squadrons. Even though a gradual phase-out of the type began in 1956 with the arrival of A4Ds, BUAER still planned to keep its ADs in service until the early 1960s. Moving somewhat faster, the Marine Corps retired its last AD-6 at the end of 1959.

When the tri-service system was adopted in September 1962, those ADs remaining in service were re-designated as follows: AD-5=A-1E; AD-5W= EA-1E; AD-5Q=EA-1E; AD-5N=A-1G; AD-6=A-1H; and AD-7=A-1J. In 1964, plans to retire the type were postponed by military developments in Southeast Asia, where A-1s subsequently flew hundreds of combat sorties as part of the ongoing carrier task force stationed off the coast of Vietnam. Owing to their slower speed and excellent loiter range, A-1s were considered the best tactical aircraft available for escorting troop-laden helicopters and ground-fire suppression in rescue combat air patrol (RESCAP) operations. Though never intended for air-to-air confrontations, Navy A-1Hs were in fact credited with the downing of North Vietnamese MiG-17s on two occasions. The type's active naval career ended in 1968 when the last single-seat combat sortie was flown by an A-1H of VA-25 in February and the final ECM mission by an EA-1E of VAQ-33 in December.

In the early 1960s, as U. S. military involvement in Southeast Asia increased, the USAF found itself without any type of attack aircraft that could be adapted to slow, close-in operations like counter-insurgency (i.e., COIN: suppression and interdiction of guerilla troops and supplies) or RESCAP. Several different types of aircraft, all prop-driven, were evaluated at the Special Warfare Center located at Eglin AFB in Florida, including several ex-Navy A-1 *Skyraiders*. Once the tests were concluded, USAF officials immediately made plans to acquire 150 surplus wide-body A-1Es from Navy stocks to be overhauled for expected service in Vietnam. Modifications included addition of dual controls and weapons racks not normally carried on Navy E models. Actual combat operations commenced in early 1964 with the 34th Tactical Group based at Ben Hoa AB in South Vietnam. A-1E sorties were initially flown with a Vietnamese observer in the right seat for the purpose of target identification, but for most of its service the type was flown as a single-pilot attack aircraft. As they became available from Navy stocks in the mid and late 1960s, the USAF also began to operate single-seat A-1Hs and Js which became especially well-known for their "Sandy" operations—RESCAPs escorting the "Jolly Greens" (i.e., Sikorsky HH-53 helicopters) deep into North Vietnamese or Laotian airspace to rescue downed American pilots and aircrew. The USAF operated A-1s on Sandy missions up until November 7, 1972, when American involvement in Vietnam was almost at an end.

Skyraiders were probably the most numerically important aircraft to operate with the Air Force of the Republic of Vietnam (VNAF). In fact, the American government began the transfer of surplus Navy AD-6s (A-1Hs) to the VNAF in 1960, and as they became available, more followed. VNAF *Skyraider* pilots were initially trained by the Navy at NAS Corpus Christi and later by the Air Force at Hurlburt AFB. During the so-called "Vietnamization" of the war between 1969–1972, many Air Force A-1s were simply turned over to the VNAF when U. S. forces left the country. During this time the VNAF reached a peak strength of eight *Skyraider* squadrons, and they were operated in combat all the way up to the fall of Saigon in April 1975. Although a number of VNAF A-1s are known to have fallen into North Vietnamese hands, no apparent effort was made to put them back into service. Beginning in 1951, the British Royal Navy Fleet Air Arm (FAA) began taking delivery of AD-4Ws for use aboard its carriers in the airborne early-warning role. The first 20 aircraft were new, but the remaining 30 of 50 delivered were supplied from U. S. Navy stocks. Known as the *Skyraider* AEW.1, the type remained in frontline service with the FAA until replaced by Fairey *Gannets* in 1962. A number of these aircraft were thereafter converted to target tugs and operated by the Swedish Air Force until the early 1970s. Forty surplus AD-4s were sold to the French Air Force in 1959 and thereafter flew combat in support of French forces in Algeria and Chad (1960) and in French Somaliland and Madagascar (1963). French *Skyraiders* remained in service in small numbers until the early 1970s, and some of these were turned over to the Cambodian Air Force, where they were briefly used against Viet Cong and North Vietnamese troops.

Douglas A2D Skyshark 1950–1954

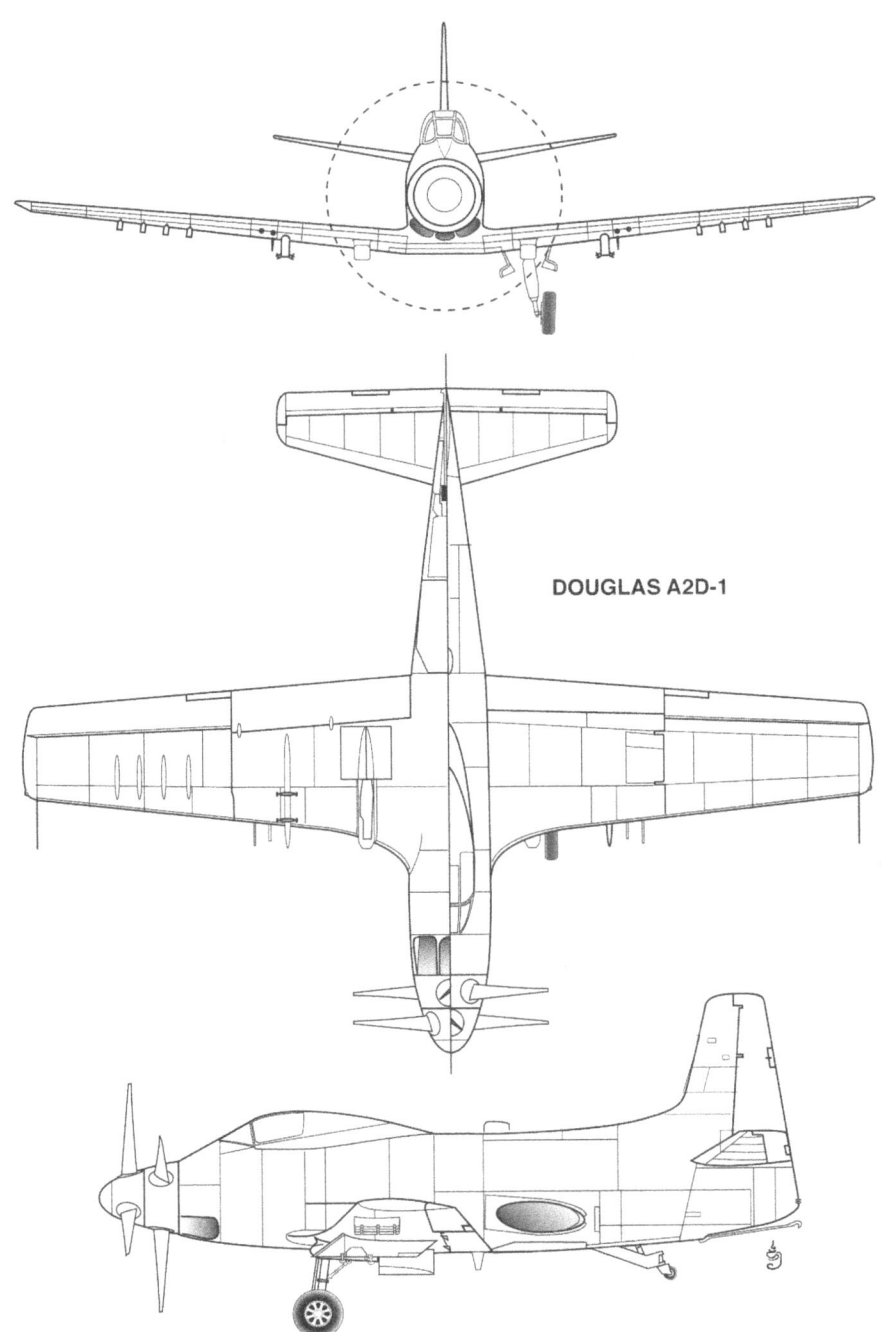

DOUGLAS A2D-1

TECHNICAL SPECIFICATIONS (XA2D-1)

Type: Single-place attack
Manufacturer: Douglas Aircraft Co., El Segundo Division, El Segundo, California
Total produced: 12

One of nine pre-production A2D-1s over southern California in 1953, the only turboprop-powered attack type ever seriously considered by the Navy. Only five of the pre-production aircraft were actually flown.

Power plant: One 5,035-shp Allison XT40-A-2 double turboprop engine driving a six-bladed Aeroproducts contra-rotating, constant-speed propeller.
Armament: Four fixed forward-firing 20-millimeter cannons and up to 5,500-lbs. of mixed ordnance carried externally.
Performance: Max. speed 501-mph at 25,000 ft.; cruise 276-mph; ceiling 48,100 ft.; range 637 mi. loaded.
Weights: 12,944-lbs. empty, 18,720-lbs. loaded.
Dimensions: Span 50 ft., length 41 ft. 3 in., wing area 400 sq. ft.

The A2D was the only type of turboprop-powered attack aircraft to receive serious consideration for production by the Navy. The project was originally begun by BUAER in 1947 as an effort to adapt Douglas's proven AD design to turboprop power, and two prototypes were ordered under the designation XA2D-1. But as development progressed, the design bore little similarity to the AD other than a superficial resemblance. A completely new fuselage was created around the complex XT40 powerplant and drive system, which comprised two T38 engines connected via drive shafts to a common transmission. In the case of a shutdown, each engine could operate independently and drive one or both propellers. The wing was also new, having a thinner-section airfoil and large wing root extensions. On paper, the XA2D-1's projected performance was so promising that BUAER ordered 10 pre-production models, and soon followed with an order for 339 production A2D-1s on three separate contracts.

The first flight of the XA2D-1 was made on May 26, 1950 from Edwards Air Base. Early testing immediately revealed severe problems with the double engine and drive system. And to make matters worse, the prototype crashed in mid–December 1950 due to engine failure, killing the Navy test pilot. When testing resumed after the second XA2D-1 flew in April 1952, problems with the T40 engines and drive system continued, and shortly thereafter, BUAER cancelled the contract on all but 10 pre-production examples. The first pre-production A2D-1 flew in June 1953 and nine more were completed, but the last four were never flown. A Douglas test pilot safely ejected from the second pre-production A2D-1 in August 1954 following a gearbox failure. No further development was undertaken after 1954.

North American AJ (A-2) Savage 1948–1962

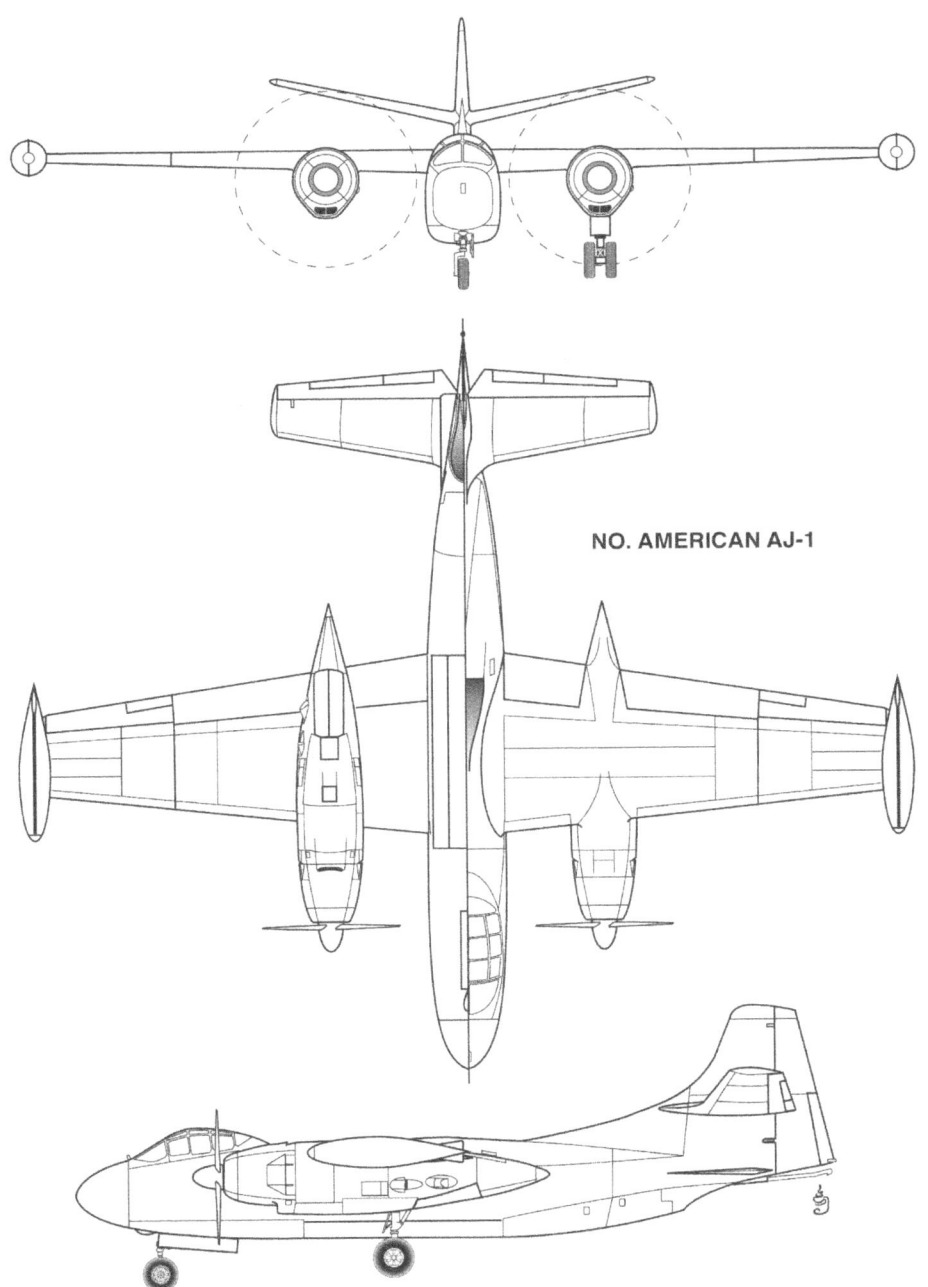

NO. AMERICAN AJ-1

TECHNICAL SPECIFICATIONS (AJ-2)

Type: Three-place heavy attack
Manufacturer: North American Aviation, Inc., Inglewood, California; AJ-2s manufactured at Columbus, Ohio plant.

Top: AJ-1 while attached to NATC, probably in early 1950. The first carrier-based nuclear strike aircraft, AJ-1s became operational with VC-5 in March 1950 and deployed aboard the *Coral Sea* in early 1951. *Bottom:* AJ-2 of VAH-6 taking off from the *Bennington* in 1956 or 1957. As AJs were replaced by newer A3Ds (A-3s) in 1956 and 1957, many were converted as fleet tankers and remained in service a few years longer.

Total produced (all models): 136
Power plant: Two 2,300-hp Pratt & Whitney R-2800-48 18-cylinder radials driving four-bladed Hamilton Standard fully-reversible, constant-speed propellers and one Allison J33-A-10 turbojet, rated at 4,600-lbs./s.t.
Armament: (No defensive armament carried) Up to 10,500-lbs. of bombs carried in an internal bomb bay.
Performance: Max. speed 471-mph at 35,000 ft.; cruise 260-mph; ceiling 45,000 ft.; range 3,056 mi. max., 1,670 mi. loaded.
Dimensions: Span 72 ft. 2 in. (over tanks), length 63 ft. 10 in., wing area 835.5 sq. ft.

Soon after the U. S. produced the first atomic bombs in 1945, Navy officials began to advocate using carriers to launch nuclear-armed aircraft against targets of strategic value. This policy led BUAER, in late 1945, to issue a requirement for a mixed power aircraft capable of operating from *Midway* class CVBs and lifting the payload dictated by early versions of the atomic bomb (e.g., Mk.3 "Fat Man" plutonium bomb weighed 10,300-lbs). North American responded with company model NA-146, proposing a 25-ton aircraft (the heaviest thus far designed for carrier operations) powered by two R-2800 piston engines and a J33 turbojet buried in the fuselage. The jet engine, fed air via a flush inlet on top of the fuselage, would be employed only for takeoff and for dash speed during target ingress-egress. In June 1946 BUAER authorized construction of three prototypes as the XAJ-1, and the first flight was made on 3 July 1948. North American was awarded a production contract following which 55 AJ-1s were manufactured at Inglewood between mid–1949 and early 1952.

Production AJ-1s differed from the prototypes in having structural improvements, framed canopies, 300-gallon tip tanks, a crew increase to three, and folding wings and vertical tail for carrier stowage. The AJ-2, which flew in 1952, featured a revised cockpit arrangement, no dihedral in the horizontal stabilizer, and R-2800-48 engines. Fifty-five AJ-2s were produced in Columbus from early 1953 to early 1954 and 42 AJ-1s were subsequently returned to the factory and converted to AJ-2 standard. North American also manufactured 26 AJ-2P reconnaissance versions which were delivered to heavy photographic squadrons.

AJ-1s became operational with VC-5 in March 1950 and made their first carrier deployment aboard *Coral Sea* early the next year. Following delivery to VC-6, VC-7, and VC-8 in 1951–1952, three-plane detachments of AJ-1s were commonly assigned to *Midway* and improved *Essex* class carriers in rotating deployments, and during 1952–1953, detachments of nuclear-armed AJ-1s were also stationed at South Korean bases as a deterrent against Communist invasion over the 38th parallel. From mid–1951 onwards, AJs were armed with the 7,600-lb. Mk.6 atomic bomb, which could be fused to yield from 8 to 160 kilotons. AJ-2s began reaching squadron service in late 1953, and in mid–1955 VC units assigned the strategic nuclear mission were reclassified as heavy attack (VAH). The entrance of the pure-jet A3D-1 marked the phase-out of the AJ's nuclear mission, and the transition was complete by the end of 1958. After the changeover, many AJs were converted to aerial tankers, which involved installation of extra fuel tanks plus a hose, drogue, and reel unit in the bomb bay, and this development resulted in several new VAH squadrons being formed specifically for the refueling role. The process of replacing AJs with A3D (KA-3) tankers began in 1959, and the very last AJ tanker had been withdrawn from active service by the end of 1962. AJ-1s and -2s still listed on the Navy inventory as of September 1962 were re-designated A-2A and A-2B, respectively, though none appear to have been on flight status; the small number of AJ-2 tankers remaining in service became KA-2Bs.

North American A2J Super Savage 1952–1953

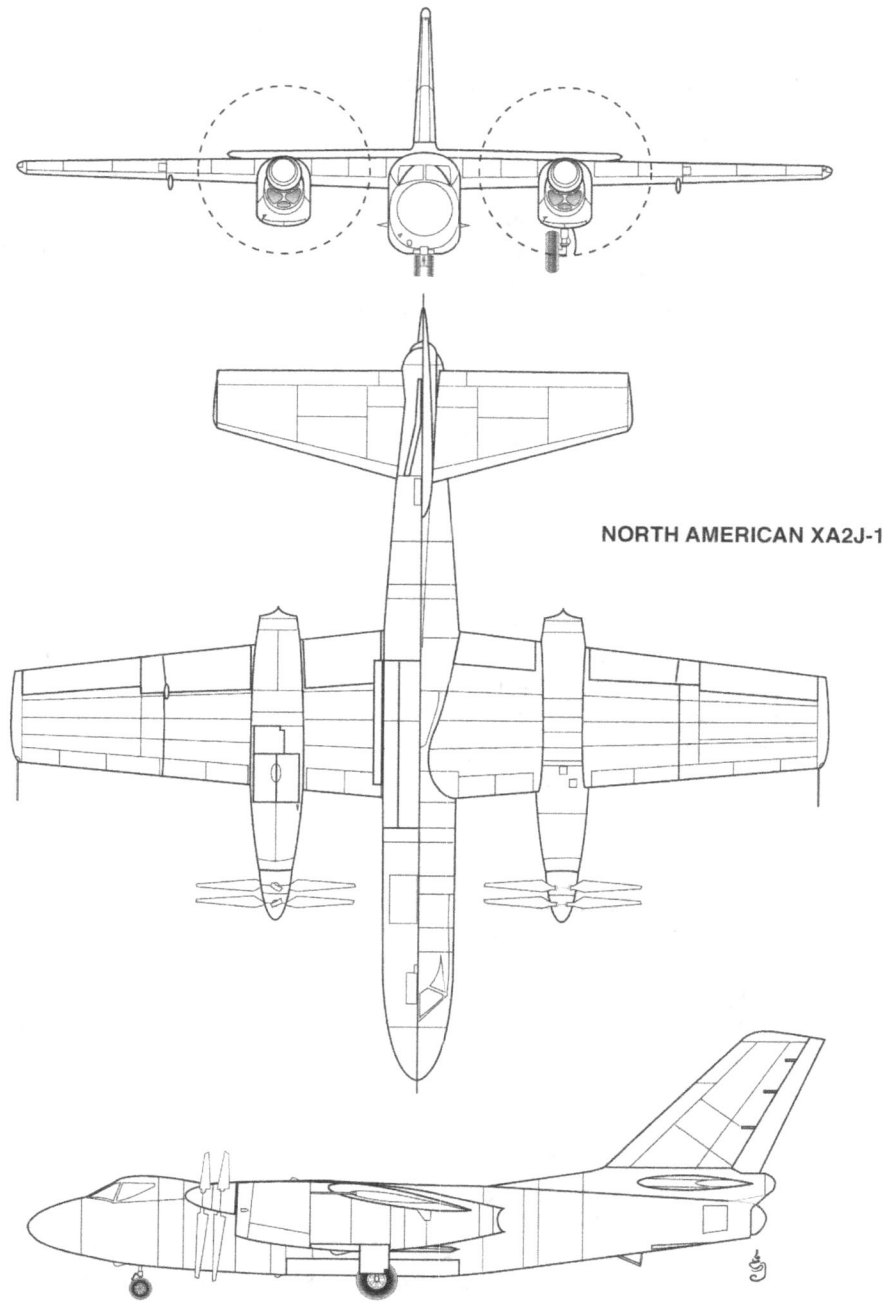

NORTH AMERICAN XA2J-1

TECHNICAL SPECIFICATIONS (XA2J-1)

Type: Three-place heavy attack
Manufacturer: North American Aviation, Inc., Inglewood, California.
Total produced: 1

By the time the short-lived XA2J-1 flew in early 1952, BUAER had already formed serious reservations over the reliability of its T40 powerplants. In any case, performance was similar to the composite-powered AJ.

Power plant: Two 5,035-shp Allison T-40-A-6 turboprop engines driving six-bladed Aeroproducts contra-rotating, constant-speed propellers.
Armament: Two 20-millimeter radar-directed cannon in tail and up to 10,500-lbs. of bombs carried in an internal bay.
Performance: Max. speed 451-mph at 24,000 ft.; cruise 400-mph; ceiling 27,500 ft.; range 2,180 mi. (with 8,000-lb. payload)
Weights: 35,350-lbs. empty, 61,200-lbs. max. loaded.
Dimensions: 71 ft. 6 in., length 70 ft., wing area 835.5 sq. ft.

In company with the Douglas A2D, the A2J represented another attempt by BUAER to achieve better performance from a conventional airframe by means of turboprop power. In October 1948, only a few months after the XAJ-1 prototype had flown, BUAER authorized North American to commence work on a turboprop-powered replacement under the designation XA2J-1. Like the contemporaneous XA2D-1, the XA2J-1 was powered by the experimental T40, which utilized a pair of T31 engines connected to a common gearbox. The shoulder-mounted wing of the AJ was essentially unchanged except for new engine nacelles. The fuselage was lengthened six feet to compensate for the longer nacelles, and with the increased power expected from the T40 engines, the auxiliary turbo jet was deemed unnecessary. The rear fuselage was extensively redesigned to house radar-guided tail guns and the vertical tail surfaces were enlarged and given sweepback.

However, by the time the XA2J-1 prototype made its first flight on January 4, 1952, BUAER had formed serious reservations over the reliability of the T40 engine based on recent experience with the XA2D-1 project. Moreover, the pure-jet Douglas XA3D-1, slated to fly sometime later in the year, appeared to be a much better prospect for the Navy's next generation strategic nuclear bomber. When testing of the XA2J-1 failed to achieve levels of performance better than its AJ predecessor, the program was cancelled before the second prototype had flown.

Martin AM (BTM) Mauler 1944–1950

TECHNICAL SPECIFICATIONS (AM-1)
Type: Single-place attack (two-place on ECM version)
Manufacturer: Glenn L. Martin Co., Baltimore, Maryland.
Total produced: 151
Power plant: One 3,000-hp Pratt & Whitney R-4360-4 28-cylinder radial driving a four-bladed Curtiss Electric fully-reversible, constant-speed propeller.
Armament: Four fixed forward-firing 20-millimeter cannons and up to 8,000-lbs. of mixed ordnance carried externally.
Performance: Max. speed 334-mph at 20,000 ft.; cruise 189-mph; ceiling 30,500 ft.; range 2,350 mi. max., 845 mi. loaded.
Weights: 15,100-lbs. empty, 25,000-lbs. max. loaded.
Dimensions: Span 50 ft., length 40 ft. 8 in., wing area 496 sq. ft.

Martin's AM (BTM) was the frontrunner in the race for the Navy's new single-seat attack aircraft until Douglas's AD (BT2D) entered the competition. It was one of four designs (i.e., XBTD-1, XBTC-1, XBTK-1, and XBTM-1) approved in late 1943 under BUAER's new requirement for a single-seat bomber-torpedo (BT) aircraft. Martin, eager to secure a new Navy contract, completed the XBTM-1 mockup in February 1944 and had the first prototype flying by August. In early testing, the XBTM-1 had achieved an impressive 367-mph top speed and lifted a phenomenal 8,500-lb. payload, however, unsatisfactory flying characteristics suggested that major modifications would be needed before the type could become operational. In January 1945 BUAER nevertheless awarded Martin an order for 750 BTM-1s with the hope that the plane's deficiencies could be remedied before it was tooled for production; then due to the V-J Day cutbacks of late 1945, the contract was subsequently reduced to 149 aircraft.

In February 1946 BUAER dropped the bomber-torpedo designation in favor of "A" for attack, and the BTM-1 became the AM-1. The factory revisions dictated by early testing were prolonged to the extent that NATC was unable to begin carrier trials with AM-1 production models until early 1947, by which time competing Douglas AD-1s were already entering squadron service. After carrier trials revealed the need for additional structural and aerodynamic changes, Martin's contact was further reduced to 99 AM-1s and 29 two-seat AM-1Qs ECM aircraft. While NATC evaluations were still ongoing, VA-17A (later VA-174) became the first squadron to reequip with AM-1s in March 1948, followed by VA-85 in November. With the aim of equipping two more squadrons, BUAER partially reinstated the contract to include 15 more AM-1s, and deliveries to VA-44 and VA-45 began in the spring of 1949. However, a combination of high accident rates during carrier operations and poor maintainability caused AM-1s to be withdrawn from active attack squadrons by the end of 1949. A small number of AM-1Qs remained active in composite squadrons only a year longer. Remaining AM-1s and -1Qs were transferred to reserve units, where they served until the end of 1953.

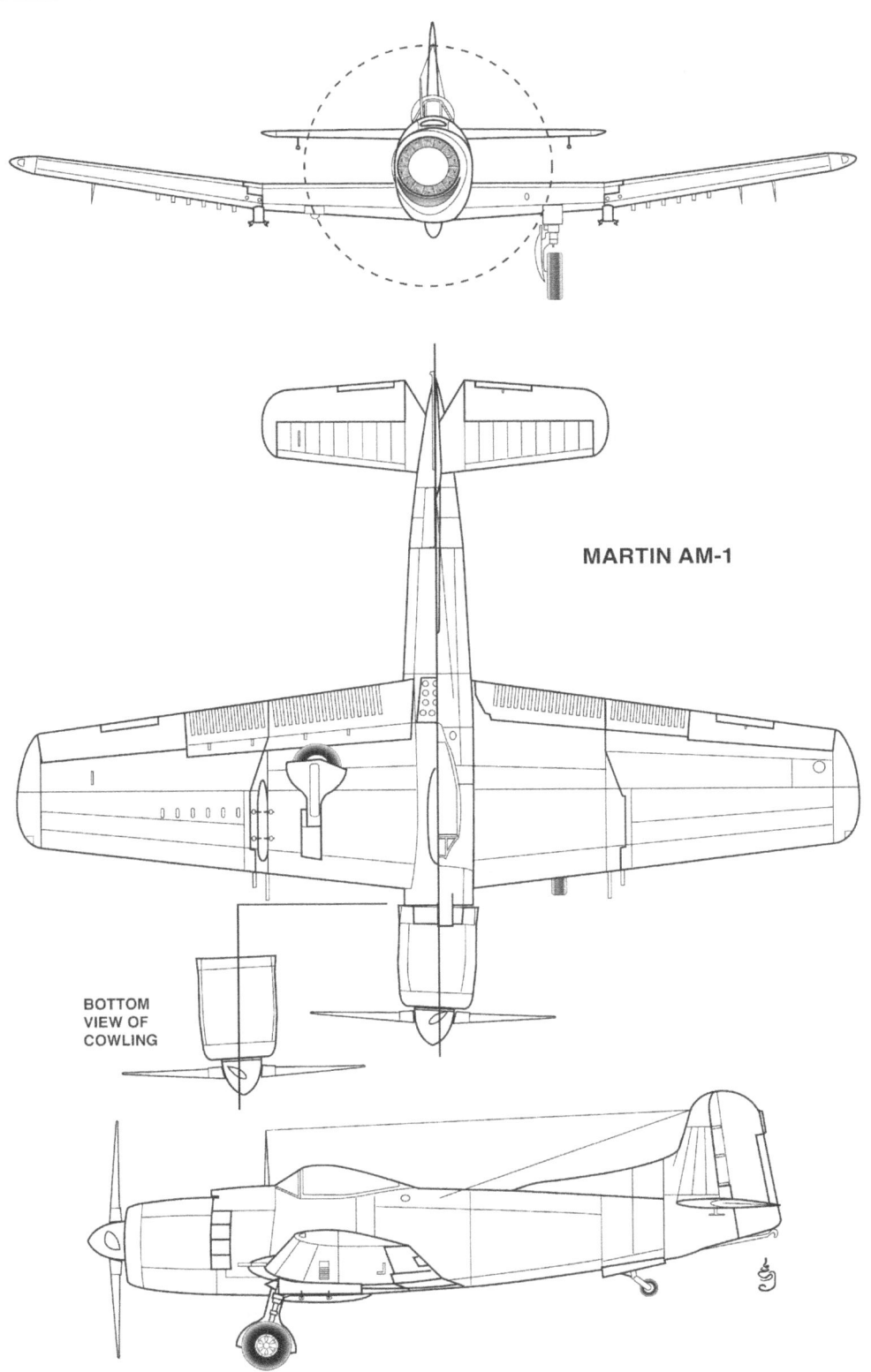

Factory publicity photograph of production AM-1s showing their phenomenal load carrying capabilities to good advantage. Chronic operational problems caused BUAER to limit both production and service life.

Douglas F4D(F-6) Skyray 1951–1964

TECHNICAL SPECIFICATIONS (F4D-1)

Type: Single-place fighter-bomber
Manufacturer: Douglas Aircraft Co., El Segundo Division, El Segundo, California.
Total produced: 422
Power plant: One Pratt & Whitney J57-P-8B turbojet engine, rated at 10,500-lbs./s.t. dry, 16,000-lbs. with afterburning.
Armament: Four fixed forward-firing 20-millimeter cannons and two AIM-9 *Sidewinder* missiles or up to 4,000-lbs. of bombs or rockets on wing pylons.
Performance: Max. speed (clean) 723-mph at s.l.; cruise 587-mph; ceiling 55,000 ft.; range 1,220 mi. max., 593 mi. loaded.
Weights: 16,024-lbs. empty, 27,116-lbs. max. loaded.
Dimensions: Span 33 ft. 6 in., length 45 ft. 8 in., wing area 557 sq. ft.

    The Douglas F4D was the first operational Navy and Marine jet capable of exceeding Mach 1 in level flight. The design originated from a 1947 BUAER requirement for a delta-wing deck launched interceptor (DLI), the delta configuration being seen is a means to optimize both rate-of-climb and level speed. Douglas, however, abandoned the pure delta approach in favor of a tailless design having swept wings of extremely low-aspect ratio, and in December 1948, the company received a contract to build two prototypes under the designation XF4D-1. Like a

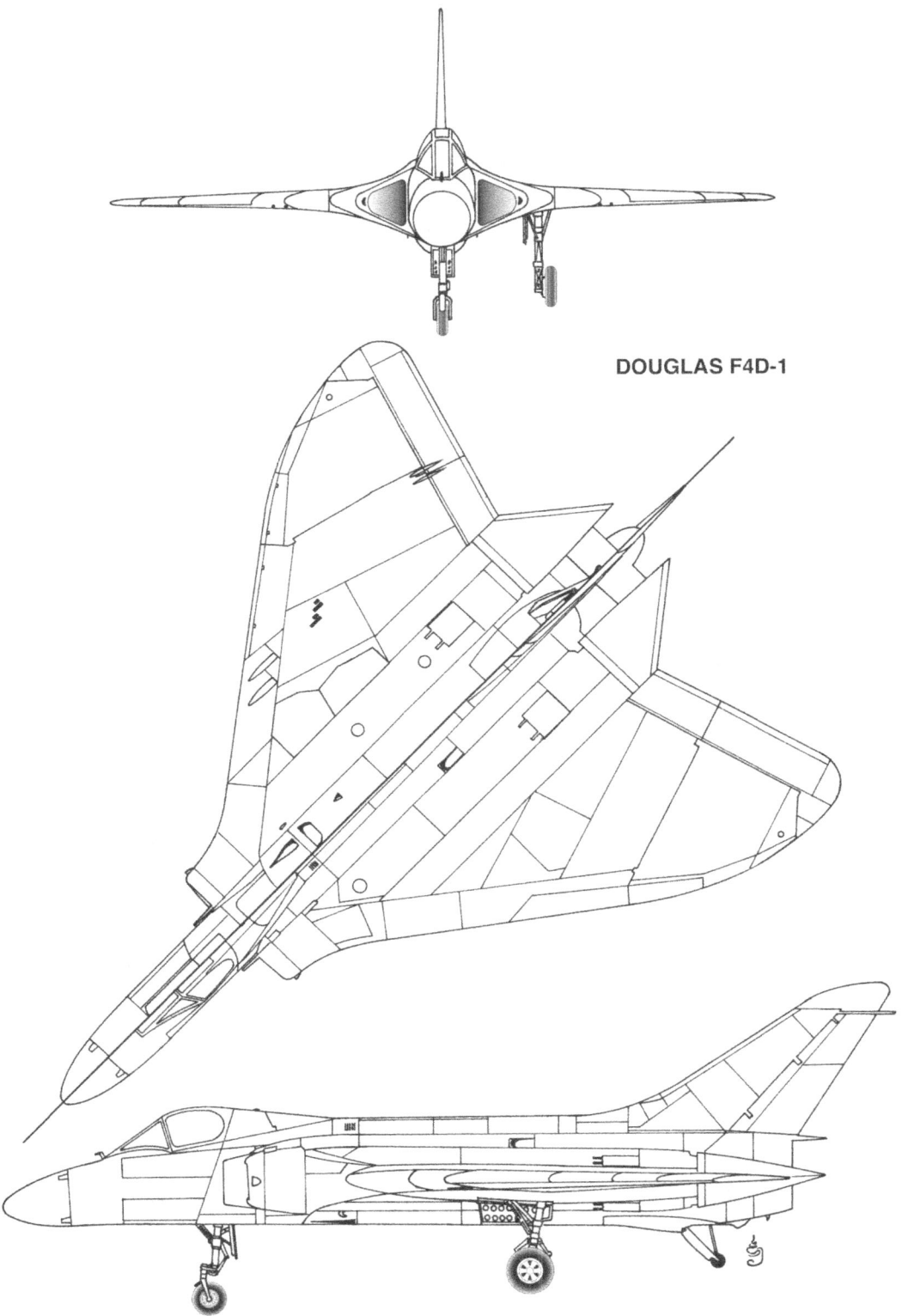

DOUGLAS F4D-1

Production F4D-1 prior to delivery to an operational unit, probably in 1956 or 1957. VC-3 became the first unit to equip with the type in April 1956. Introduction of newer types like the F-8 and F-4 resulted in a relatively short service career.

number of other Navy jet projects of that era, the XF4D-1 was to be powered by an afterburning Westinghouse XJ40 powerplant. When the J40 program ran into serious difficulties, the XF4D-1 prototype made its first flight on January 23, 1951 with an Allison J-35 engine. In the spring of 1952 Douglas received a production order for 230 F4D-1s on the premise that J40 engines would be available in time. Both prototypes subsequently flew with the J40 installed, and achieved supersonic speeds, but continuing problems with the entire J40 program led to a decision in March 1953 to switch to the more reliable Pratt & Whitney J57.

Although the first J57-equipped production F4D-1 flew in June 1954, extended acceptance trials delayed service entry with operational units until early 1956. Delivery of F4D-1s to Navy and Marine Squadrons continued through December 1958, when production terminated after 420 examples had been built. VC-3 (later VFAW-3) was the first Navy unit to receive F4D-1s in April 1956, followed a few months later by VF-74; VMF-115 received its F4D-1s in early 1957, and by the end of 1958, the type was equipping eleven Navy and six Marine squadrons. In September 1962, the F4D-1 was re-designated F-6A under the new tri-service scheme. The phase-out of F4D-1s began as early as 1960 and the final examples were withdrawn from active service in early 1964. Although F4D-1s were deployed to Taiwan in 1958 in response to the Quemoy-Matsu Crisis and to Guantanomo in 1962 during the Cuban Missile Crisis, none saw any combat.

Grumman F9F (straight-wing) Panther 1947–1956

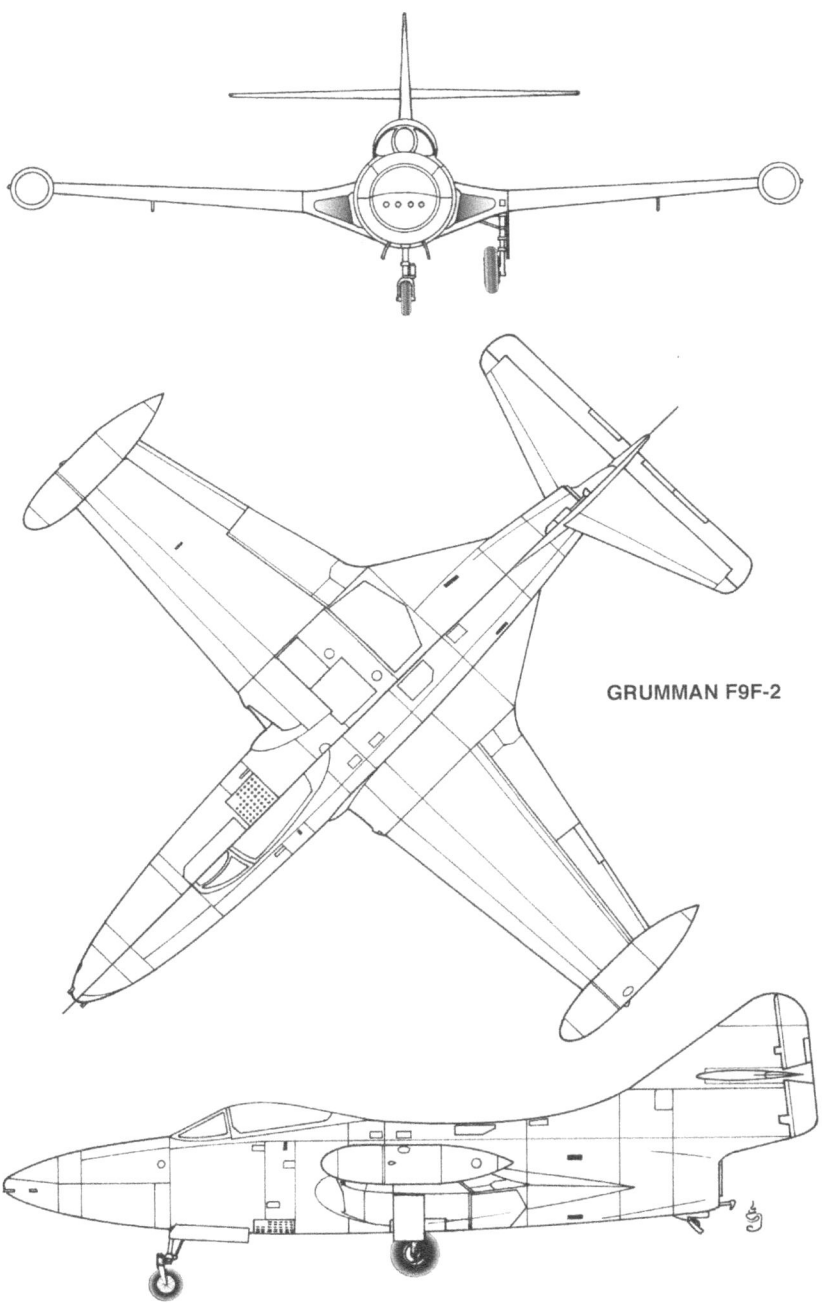

GRUMMAN F9F-2

TECHNICAL SPECIFICATIONS (F9F-5)

Type: Single-place fighter-bomber
Manufacturer: Grumman Aircraft Engineering Corp., Bethpage, New York.
Total produced (all models): 1,388

Top: F9F-2 of VMF-311. When this squadron supported the breakout at the Chosin Reservoir in December 1950, Grumman F9Fs were the first type of jet aircraft to be used by the Marines in combat. *Bottom:* F9F-5 with factory numbering on the nose. The -5 was nine inches longer, had a taller tail fin, and came with a more powerful J48 engine. They served with Navy and Marine fighter and attack squadrons until 1956.

Power plant: One Pratt & Whitney J-48-P-6A turbojet engine, rated at 6,250-lbs./s.t.
Armament: Four fixed forward-firing 20-millimeter cannons and up to 2,000-lbs. of bombs or rockets on wing pylons.
Performance: Max. speed 579-mph at 5,000 ft.; cruise 481-mph; ceiling 42,800 ft.; range 1,300 mi. clean, 886 mi. loaded.
Weights: 10,147-lbs. empty, 18,721-lbs. max. loaded.
Dimensions: Span 38 ft., length 38 ft., wing area 250 sq. ft.

The Grumman F9F-2 holds the distinction of having been the first type of Navy and Marine Corps jet aircraft to be used in combat. Though intended originally for fleet defense and fighter escort, straight-wing F9F variants saw their widest combat employment in the role of fighter-bombers. Grumman's XF9F-2 proposal appeared in 1946 as a late entry in the Navy's ongoing jet fighter competition between North American, Vought, and McDonnell. (Note, as the XF9F-1, it had originally been laid down a twin-jet, two-seat night fighter.) BUAER awarded Grumman a contract for two prototypes in late 1946, and the first example flew on November 24, 1947, powered by a Rolls-Royce *Nene* engine imported from Britain. The XF9F-3 with an Allison J-33-A-8 flew in August 1948. An initial production contract awarded the same year specified 47 F9F-2s with Pratt & Whitney J42s (license-built *Nenes*) and 54 F9F-3s with J33s, but as events transpired, U.S. production of the more powerful J42 proceeded on schedule and most F9F-3s were ultimately completed as -2s. Deliveries to operational units commenced in mid-1949.

The F9F-5, first flown in December 1949, featured a nine-inch fuselage extension for increased fuel capacity, a taller vertical fin, and a J48 engine (license-built Rolls-Royce *Tay*), which increased thrust by 1,250-lbs. The similar F9F-4 was re-engined with the more powerful Allison J33-A-16. Production of 619 F9F-5s, 39 F9F-5Ps (photo-recon), and 109 F9F-4s began in 1951, and deliveries were completed by the end of 1952. In service, most F9F-4s were converted to J48s, becoming indistinguishable from -5s.

The first operational unit to receive F9F-2s/3s was VF-51 in May 1949, followed within months by VMF-115 and VF-11. On June 25, 1950, operating from *Valley Forge* off the Korean coast, F9F-2s of VF-51 became the first Navy jets to see combat action, and on July 3, 1950, two F9F-2s of VF-51 shot down a North Korean Yak-9, scoring the first air-to-air kill by a Navy jet. Marine F9F-2s with VMF-311 began flying close air support and interdiction sorties in December 1950. F9F-4/5s began replacing -2s in 1952–1953 and served in frontline Navy and Marine units until 1956; many F9F-5s were used in training units and reserve squadrons until 1958. A number of these were thereafter converted to F9F-5K drone or F9F-5KD drone directors, the last example being stricken from the inventory in the mid-1960s.

Grumman F9F(F-9) (swept-wing) Cougar 1951–1959

TECHNICAL SPECIFICATIONS (F9F-8)
Type: Single-place fighter-bomber (two-place TF-9J trainer/FAC)
Manufacturer: Grumman Aircraft Engineering Corp., Bethpage, New York.
Total produced (all models): 1,876
Power plant: One Pratt & Whitney J-48-P-8A turbojet engine, rated at 7,250-lbs./s.t.
Armament: Four fixed forward-firing 20-millimeter cannons and two AIM-9 *Sidewinder* missiles or up to 4,000-lbs. of bombs or rockets on wing pylons.
Performance: Max. speed 647-mph at 2,000 ft.; cruise 516-mph; ceiling 42,000 ft.; combat range 1,058 mi.
Weights: 11,866-lbs. empty, 24,763-lbs. max. loaded.
Dimensions: Span 34 ft. 6 in., length 42 ft. 2 in., wing area 337 sq. ft.

In late 1950, the appearance of the MiG-15 in Korea combined with delays in existing Navy

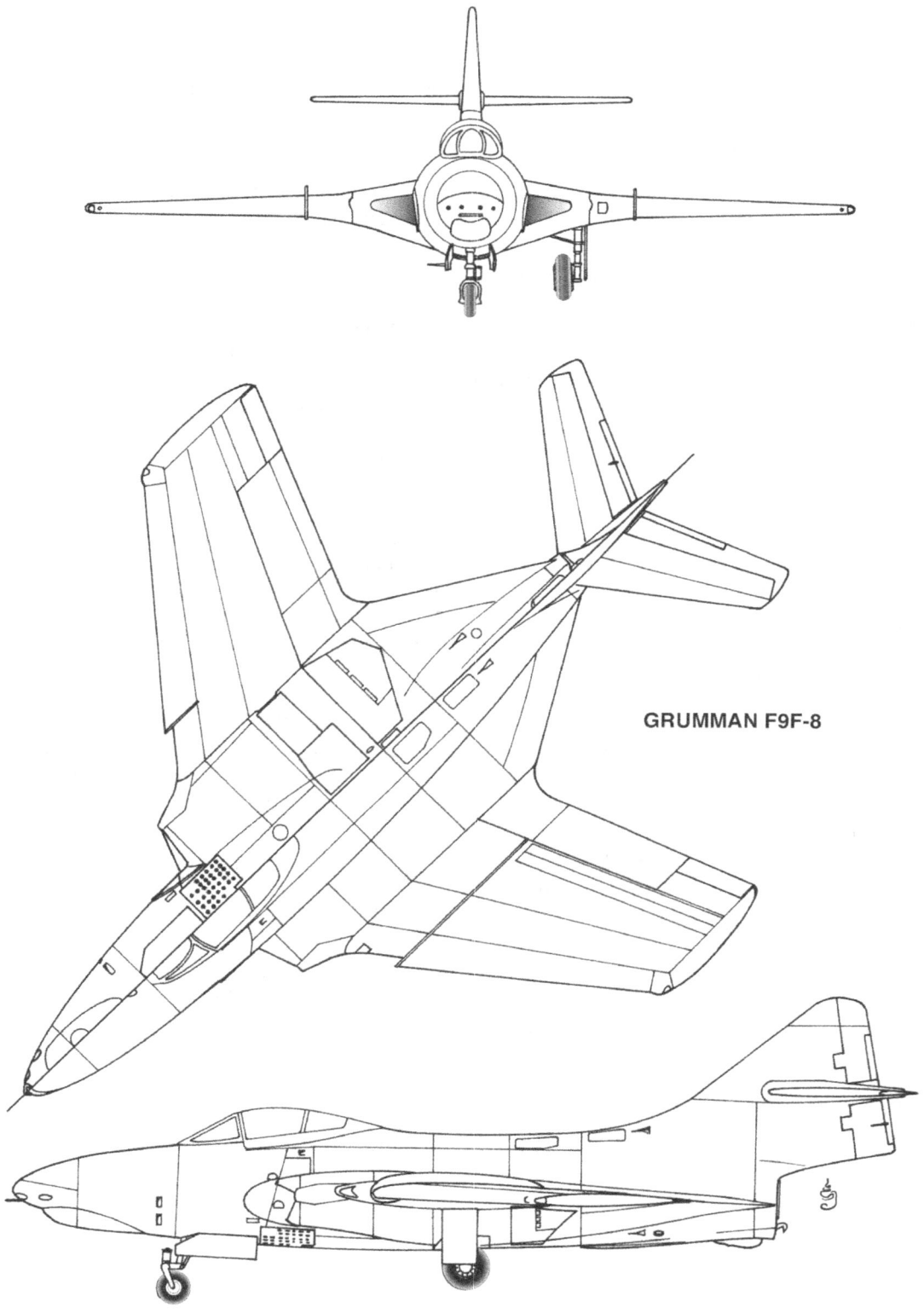

GRUMMAN F9F-8

Top: F9F-6 fitted with test probe shown here carrying two tactical nuclear "shapes." The introduction of the swept wing on the -6 made it 100-mph faster than the F9F-5. Increased fuel capacity due to a lengthening of the fuselage offset the loss of tip tanks. *Bottom:* Two-seat F9F-8T (TF-9J) shown in training colors. The -8T was fully mission capable and used in Vietnam by the Marines as a FAC aircraft, the only *Cougar* variant to actually see combat.

fighter programs (i.e., F7U, F4D, F3H) prompted BUAER to press Grumman for a swept-wing derivative of the F9F-2/5 *Panther*. The resulting XF9F-6 was essentially an F9F-5 fuselage adapted to wings and tail surfaces swept to 35-degrees. The fuselage was lengthened two feet to permit greater internal fuel (in lieu of tip tanks) and a J48-P-8 was installed, boosting thrust by 1,000-lbs. Work proceeded rapidly and the first prototype flew on September 20, 1951. In testing, the XF9F-6 proved to be 100-mph faster than the F9F-5, and once stability problems were solved by the addition of an all-flying stab and spoilers, it showed above-average carrier handling characteristics.

F9F-6s were ordered into production in early 1952 and began entering squadron service later the same year. The order for 649 F9F-6s included 60 F9F-6Ps and was supplemented by 118 virtually identical F9F-7s having J33-A-16 engines. The F9F-8, flown in December 1953, had a fuselage stretch of eight inches for more fuel and a fifteen square foot addition to the wings that produced a noticeable saw tooth leading edge. F9F-8s were later retrofitted with UHF homing antennas in a fairing beneath the nose, nose-mounted refueling probes, plus hardware to carry two *Sidewinder* missiles. In service, a number of F9F-8s fitted with LABs computers became F9F-8Bs with tactical nuclear capability. Delivery of 601 F9F-8s and 110 F9F-8Ps was completed in mid 1957. The first dual-control F9F-8T, lengthened 34 inches for a second cockpit, flew in April 1956, and 399 examples were delivered from 1956 to 1960. F9F-8Ts came with two less 20-mm cannons but were otherwise fully mission capable. An all-weather, radar-equipped version of the F9F-8T was proposed in 1955 but never built.

F9F-6/7s first went service with VF-32 in November 1952 and were equipping 20 Navy squadrons in 1955. None went to active Marine units. The first F9F-8s began replacing F9F-6s in April 1954 and eventually served with eight Navy and five Marine squadrons. All F9F-8s had been phased out of active Navy and Marine units by the end of 1959, the last F9F-8Ps in 1960. F9F-6s served in both Navy and Marine reserve squadrons until the late 1950s and F9F-8s saw use in both reserve and training units until the mid–1960s. In September, all *Cougars* remaining in the naval inventory were re-designated: F9F-6 to F-9F, F9F-7 to F-9H, F9F-8 to F-9J, F9F-8B to AF-9J, and F9F-8T to TF-9J. The First F9F-8Ts were delivered to Naval Training Command in 1957 and remained in service until early 1974. Four T-9Js assigned to the Marine Corps were used in South Vietnam during 1966–1967 to direct air strikes against Viet Cong positions, the only *Cougar* variant to have seen combat.

McDonnell F2H Banshee 1947–1959

TECHNICAL SPECIFICATIONS (F2H-2)

Type: Single-place fighter-bomber
Manufacturer: McDonnell Aircraft Corp., St. Louis, Missouri.
Total produced (all models): 892
Power plant: Two Westinghouse J34-WE-34 turbojet engines, rated at 3,250-lbs./s.t. each.
Armament: Four fixed forward-firing 20-millimeter cannons and up to 1,000-lbs. of bombs or rockets on wing pylons.
Performance: Max. speed 575-mph at s.l.; ceiling 48,500 ft.; range 1,475 mi. max., 620 mi. loaded.
Weights: 11,146-lbs. empty, 22,312-lbs. max. loaded.
Dimensions: Span 41 ft. 9 in. (without tip tanks), length 40 ft. 2 in., wing area 294 sq. ft.

Though originally intended for fleet defense, McDonnell's F2H *Banshee* became one of naval aviation's most versatile carrier jets of the 1950s. The F2H was a direct development of the XFD-1 (produced as the FH-1 *Phantom*), one of three jet designs ordered by BUAER in late 1943. Soon after the XFD-1 flew in January 1945, BUAER authorized McDonnell to build three prototypes of an enlarged, more powerful version under the designation XF2D-1. The first prototype XF2D-1 was flown on January 11, 1947, and flight trials indicated a significant

Second Series • 1946–1962

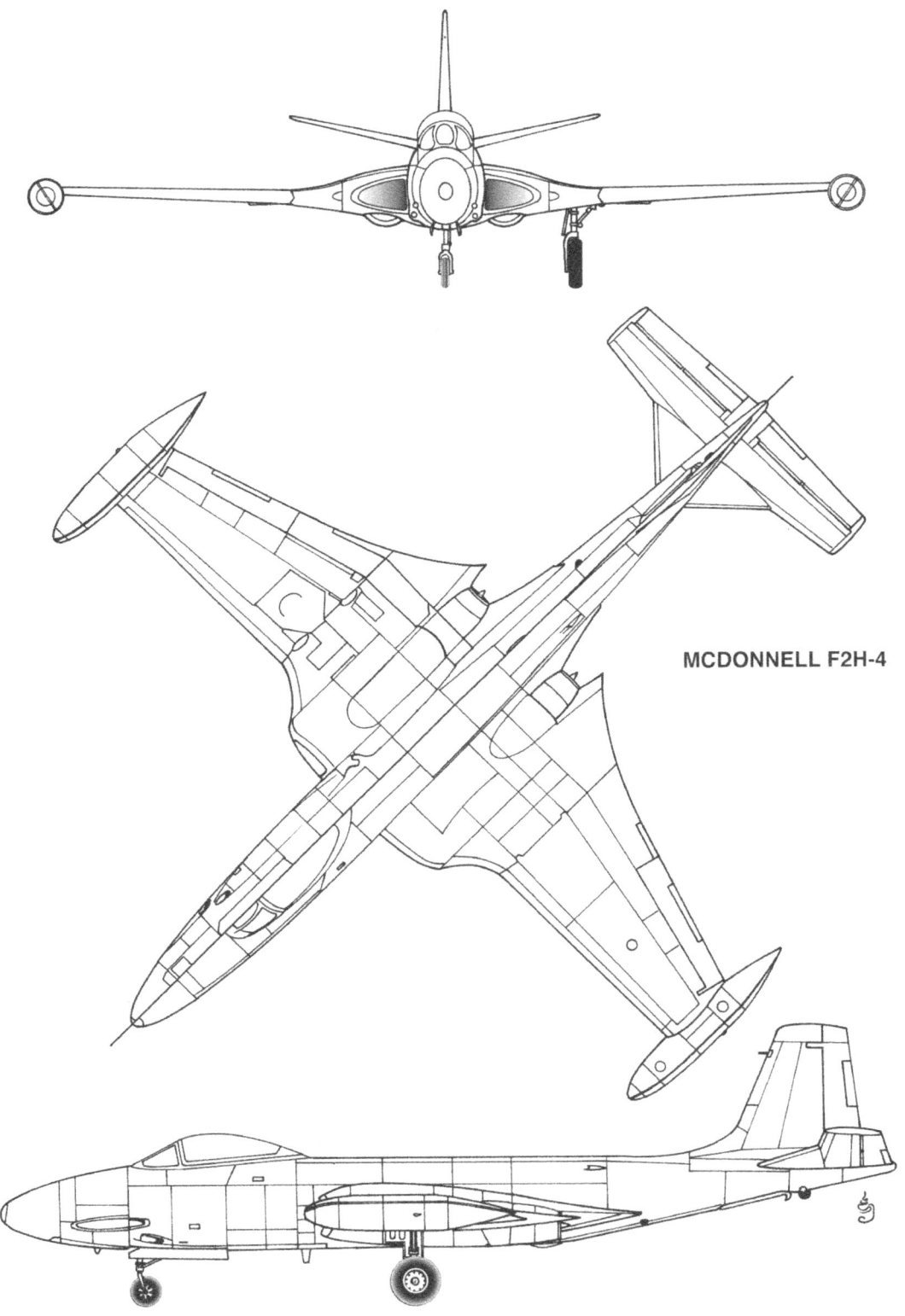

MCDONNELL F2H-4

Top: F2H-2 day fighter version shown with factory numbers prior to service delivery. The F2H-2B was the first carrier jet equipped to carry a tactical nuclear weapon. By the end of 1952, F2H-2s and -2Bs were serving in eight Navy and three Marine squadrons. *Bottom:* F2H-3 of VF-41 serving aboard *Randolph* in 1956 and 1957. Although designated a fighter, the stretched *Banshee* was developed as a stopgap to give the fleet all-weather tactical nuclear strike capability.

increase in performance over not only the FD-1 but also over two other competing jet designs (i.e., North American FJ-1 and Vought F6U-1). In May 1947, after McDonnell's letter designator had been changed to "H," the company received a contract to build 56 production models as the F2H-1. Service trials began in the summer of 1948 and the type was declared operational later the same year.

The F2H-2, introduced in early 1948, featured a fuselage lengthened one foot to house more internal fuel, 200-gallon tip tanks, hardpoints on the wings for bombs and rockets, and a more powerful version of the J34. The new type was also offered as a F2H-2N night fighter having an elongated nose section that housed an APS-19 search radar. McDonnell received orders for 174 F2H-2s and 12 F2H-2Ns in May 1948, and soon after initial deliveries began in late 1949, a further 172 F2H-2s were added to the contract. The F2H-2B was externally identical to the F2H-2 except for a strengthened wing that could carry one Mk.7 or Mk.8 tactical nuclear weapon. In early 1950, BUAER directed McDonnell to develop an unarmed photo-reconnaissance version as the F2H-2P, which appeared in October with a camera-equipped nose section lengthened two feet three inches. A total of 23 F2H-2Bs and 58 F2H-2Ps were delivered by May 1952.

In 1951 BUAER assigned McDonnell a project to develop a longer-range, all-weather variant of the *Banshee*. Modifications included: fuselage lengthened eight feet to increase internal fuel by 30 percent; increased wing area at the root chord; enlarged vertical tail surfaces; horizontal stab moved to the tail cone and given 10-degrees dihedral; nose section redesigned to accept a an APQ-41 radar set; four 20-mm cannons repositioned; and new weapons racks for bombs, rockets, or a tactical nuclear weapon. The all-weather F2H-3 flew in early 1952, followed by production orders for 250 aircraft, and began equipping Navy and Marine squadrons in mid 1952. In 1953 McDonnell introduced a follow-on F2H-4 with J34-WE-38 engines, rated at 3,600-lbs./s.t., and an improved Hughes APG-37 radar. *Banshee* production ended in late 1953 when the last of 150 F2H-4s was delivered.

The only active unit operational with F2H-1s was VF-171 in from late 1948 to late 1949, until they were replaced with F2H-2s. From then until early 1952, F2H-2 day fighters entered service with eight Navy and three Marine squadrons, and F2H-2Ns were allocated to three Navy composite squadrons. From mid 1952, F2H-2Ps began joining Navy composite squadrons and equipped two Marine photographic squadrons. *Banshees* made their combat debut over Korea in August 1951 and served throughout the conflict as fighter-bombers, night fighters, and tactical reconnaissance platforms. During 1953–1954, most -2 variants were phased out of active service and transferred to Navy and Marine reserve units. From late 1952, F2H-3s and -4s formed much of the Naval aviation's all-weather fighter and strike capability, reaching a peak of thirteen Navy and two Marine squadrons by the middle of the 1950s. The last F2H-3/4s were withdrawn from active squadrons in 1959 and continued to serve with reserve units until 1961.

McDonnell F3H(F-3) Demon 1951–1964

TECHNICAL SPECIFICATIONS (F3H-2)

Type: Single-place fighter-bomber
Manufacturer: McDonnell Aircraft Corp., St. Louis, Missouri.
Total produced (all models): 519
Power plant: One Allison J71-A-2 turbojet engine, rated at 9,700-lbs./s.t. dry, 14,400-lbs. with afterburning.
Armament: Four fixed forward-firing 20-millimeter cannons and four AIM-7 *Sparrow* missiles or four
    AIM-9 *Sidewinder* missiles or up to 6,000-lbs. of bombs or rockets on fuselage and wing stations.
Performance: Max. speed 716-mph at s.l.; ceiling 42,650 ft.; range 1,370 mi. max., 1,180 mi. loaded.
Weights: 21,287-lbs. empty, 39,000-lbs. max. loaded.
Dimensions: Span 35 ft. 4 in., length 58 ft. 11 in., wing area 519 sq. ft.

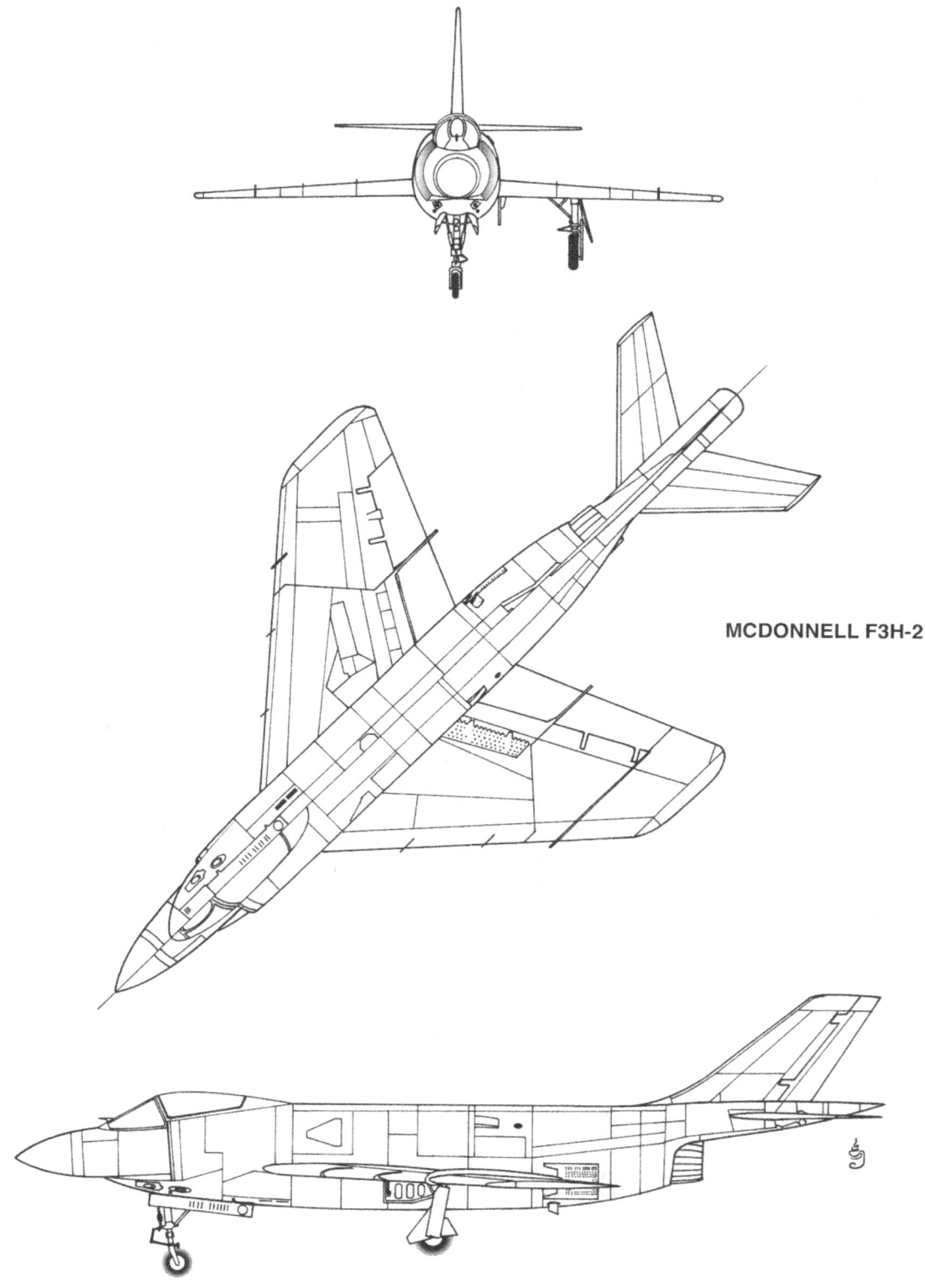

MCDONNELL F3H-2

F3H-2 of VF-41 on cruise aboard the *Independence* in 1959. The F3H was one of the victims of the ill-fated J40 engine program, and by the time the type entered service with J71 engines in 1956, BUAER had newer and better designs in the pipeline.

The F3H was originally conceived in response to a mid–1948 BUAER requirement for a carrier-based day fighter that would possess overall performance at least comparable to the newest swept-wing USAF fighters (e.g., the North American F-86). After being selected over eleven competing proposals, McDonnell received a contract in September 1949 to build two prototypes under the designation XF3H-1. The design utilized a conventional layout with wing and tail surfaces swept to 45-degrees, and like the F4D-1, was to be powered by the ill-fated Westinghouse J40. Even before the XF3H-1 flew on August 7, 1951, BUAER inserted a requirement for all-weather capability and issued an order for 150 production models as the F3H-1N. In what proved to be a costly mistake, testing soon revealed that F3H-1Ns, for their size and weight, were seriously underpowered, and the J40 engine was so prone to malfunctions that all 56 aircraft completed at that time were grounded. Rather than cancel the entire program, however, a decision was made in 1953 to substitute the Allison J71 engine.

The first J71-powered F3H-2N flew in April 1955 and deliveries to squadrons began in early 1956. To compensate for weight added by the new engine installation, wing area of the F3H-2N was enlarged 77 square feet by increasing chord from the root along the trailing edge. The first two production batches, 140 F3H-2Ns (armed with guns and *Sidewinders*) and 80 F3H-2Ms (armed with guns and *Sidewinders* or *Sparrows*), were intended primarily as deck-launched interceptors, whereas the 239 F3H-2s were optimized for the air-to-ground role. *Demon* production was completed in April 1960.

Initially entering service with VF-14 in March 1956, F3H-2 variants ultimately equipped 22 Navy Squadrons; none were issued to the Marine Corps. When tri-service designations were adopted in 1962, the F3H-2 became the F-3B, F3H-2N the F-3C, and F3H-2M the MF-3B. The type began to be replaced by F-8s and F-4s in the early 1960s and VF-161 retired its last F-3B in September 1964.

North American FJ (AF/F-1) (swept-wing) Fury 1954–1962

TECHNICAL SPECIFICATIONS (FJ-3)

Type: Single-place fighter-bomber/attack
Manufacturer: North American Aviation, Inc., Columbus, Ohio.
Total produced (all swept wing models): 1,112
Power plant: One Wright J65-W-4B turbojet engine, rated at 7,650-lbs./s.t.
Armament: Four fixed forward-firing 20-millimeter cannons and up to 2,000-lbs. of bombs or rockets on wing pylons.
Performance: Max. speed 681-mph at s.l.; cruise 400-mph; ceiling 46,800 ft.; range 1,784 mi. max., 990 mi. loaded.
Weights: 12,205-lbs. empty, 21,024-lbs. max. loaded.
Dimensions: Span 37 ft. 1 in., length 37 ft. 7 in., wing area 302 sq. ft.

In early 1951, developments in the Korean War led BUAER to seek a navalized derivative of North American's highly successful F-86 *Sabre,* and three prototypes were ordered under the designation XFJ-2. (Note, the straight-wing FJ-1, which had been manufactured in 1947–1948, was a completely different airframe.) A contract for 300 aircraft was awarded to North American on the basis of a design proposal even before the first prototype flew on December 27, 1951. While the first XFJ-2 was essentially a J47-powered F-86E with catapult points and a V-frame arrestor hook, production FJ-2s came with folding wings, a lengthened nose wheel strut, four 20-mm cannon armament, raised cockpit and canopy, no dihedral in the horizontal stabilizer, and stronger landing gear. As a result of the USAF production priority on F-86Fs, only 25 FJ-2s had been delivered when the Korean War ended, and the contract was cut to 200 aircraft. Additionally, FJ-2s had demonstrated marginal (if not completely unsatisfactory) handling traits during carrier trials, with the consequence that all production was allocated to land-based Marine units.

Work on the follow-on FJ-3 began in March 1952 and the first example flew the following August. The FJ-3 featured a more powerful J65 engine with an enlarged nose intake, plus revisions to the wing that markedly improved carrier handling qualities. FJ-3s began entering operational service in the fall of 1954, and 538 had been delivered when production ceased in August 1956. The last 80 aircraft were completed as FJ-3Ms capable of carrying two AIM-9 *Sidewinder* missiles.

The FJ-4, though technically in the same series, was actually an all-new airframe. A redesigned fuselage held 50 per cent more internal fuel and new thin-section wings (similar to the F-100) incorporated leading edge droops which improved slow speed control. Armament consisted of four 20-mm cannons and four *Sidewinder* missiles. The first FJ-4 flew in October 1954 and 130 production models were delivered from February 1955 to March 1957. The final *Fury*, the FJ-4B, was a dedicated ground attack version that flew in December 1956. The FJ-4B possessed stronger wings, LABS for tactical nuclear weapons, air refueling capability, plus provisions to carry up to five *Bullpup* AGM-12 air-to-ground missiles. Delivery of the 352 FJ-4Bs began in mid–1957 and was completed in May 1958.

The FJ-2 entered operational service with VMF-122 in January 1954 and equipped five more Marine squadrons during 1954–1955. All were withdrawn in 1957–1958. VF-173 accepted delivery of the first FJ-3s in September 1954, and FJ-3/3Ms ultimately equipped eleven Navy

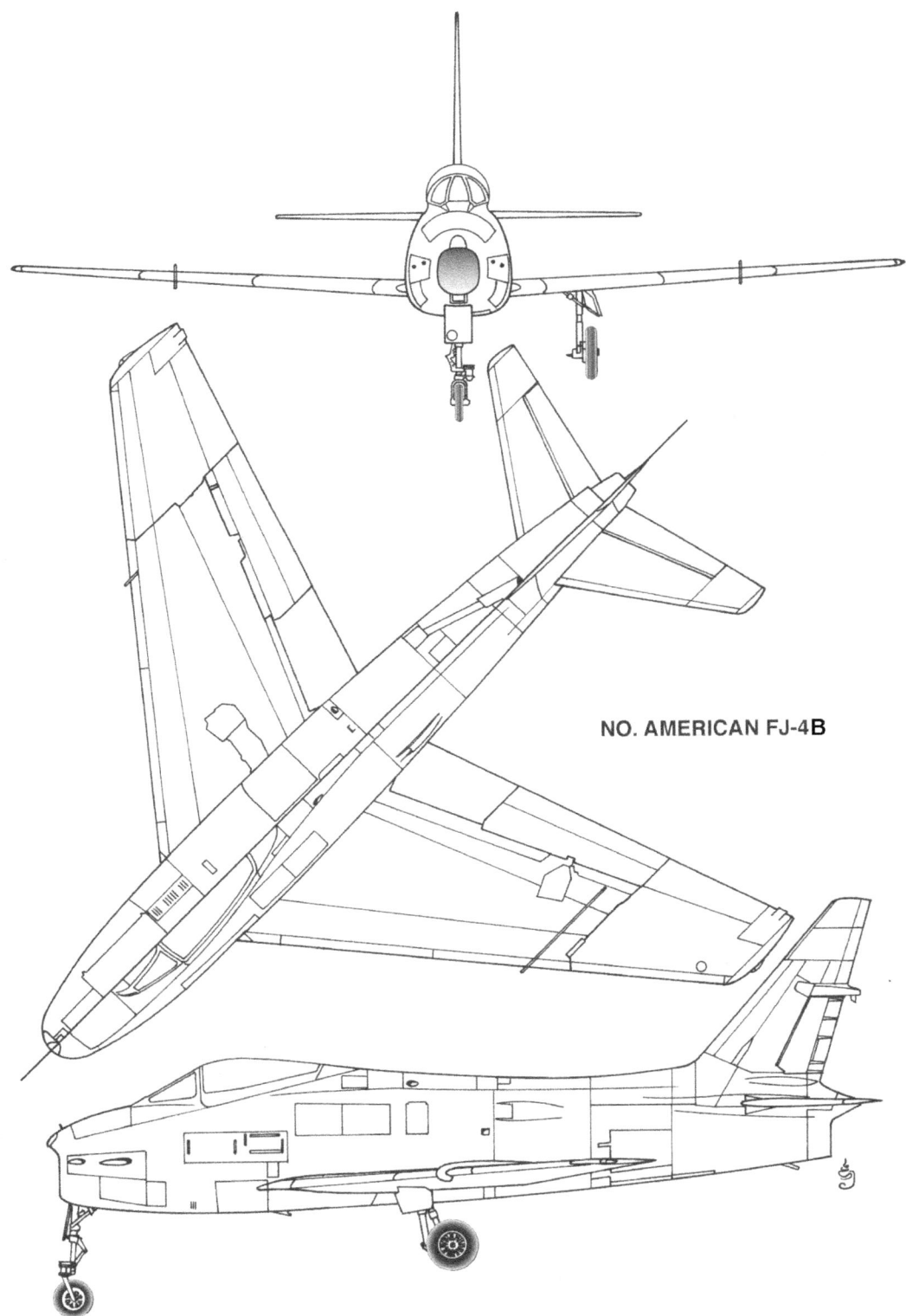

NO. AMERICAN FJ-4B

Top: FJ-3 of VF-21 aboard the newly commissioned *Forrestal* in 1956. While the new paint scheme of gull gray over white was authorized in February 1955, it was accomplished over a period of years as aircraft went into overhaul. *Bottom:* Virtually a complete re-design, the FJ-4B appeared in late 1956 as a dedicated ground attack version. The -4B equipped ten Navy and three Marine squadrons from 1958, but had been completely withdrawn from active service by the end of 1962.

and four Marine squadrons until the type was retired from active service in 1960. From 1955, all FJ-4 day fighters were delivered to Marine Squadrons VMF-232, -235, and -451, and remained in service until 1959. FJ-4Bs equipped ten Navy and three Marine squadrons, making their first operation deployment in early 1958 with VA-214 aboard *Hornet*. All FJ-4Bs had been withdrawn from active units by the end of 1962. After active service, many FJ-3s, -4s, and -4Bs continued with reserve units until the mid–1960s. In 1962, under the new tri-service designations, FJ-3 was changed to F-1C, FJ-4 to F-1E, and FJ-4B to AF-1E.

Vought F7U Cutlass 1951–1957

TECHNICAL SPECIFICATIONS (F7U-3)
Type: Single-place fighter-bomber
Manufacturer: Chance Vought Division of United Aircraft Corp., Dallas, Texas.
Total produced (all F7U-3 variants): 290
Power plant: Two Westinghouse J46-WE-8A turbojet engines, each rated at 4,600-lbs./s.t. each dry, 6,000-lbs. with afterburning.
Armament: Four fixed forward-firing 20-millimeter cannons and up to 5,500-lbs. of bombs or rockets on wing pylons.
Performance: Max. speed 696-mph at s.l.; cruise 518-mph; ceiling 46,500 ft.; range 817 mi. max., 696 mi. loaded.
Weights: 18,262-lbs. empty, 31,642-lbs. max. loaded.
Dimensions: Span 39 ft. 9 in., length 44 ft. 3 in., wing area 535 sq. ft.

The Vought F7U is generally regarded as one of the most unorthodox aircraft to have achieved operational service with the Navy. Originating from a 1945 BUAER requirement for a 600-mph deck-launched interceptor, Vought's V-346A design proposal owed much of its unique configuration to research data on tailless aircraft acquired from the Germans after World War II. The data indicated that elimination of horizontal tail surfaces would avoid the extreme nose down forces experienced by conventional airframes at speeds above Mach 0.75. Three prototypes were ordered under the designation XF7U-1 and the first was flown on September 29, 1948. Powered by two J34 engines, the XF7U-1 featured a low-aspect ratio wing swept to 38-degrees with the vertical tail surfaces mounted on the wings at mid span. Roll and pitch control was accomplished by interconnected "ailevators" (elevons) located on the wings' trailing edges. For slow flight, the wings included moveable, full-span leading edge slats, but no flaps. Fourteen F7U-1 production aircraft were delivered in 1950, but after lengthy trials, they were rated unsatisfactory for carrier operations due to poor pilot visibility (caused by the very high angle of attack required at approach speeds), unacceptable wave-off characteristics, and arrestment problems.

The similar F7U-2 was cancelled, but the significantly modified F7U-3 appeared in December 1951 with more powerful J46 engines, enlarged wings, totally redesigned nose which housed an all-weather radar and fire-control system, wing pylons for external tanks or air-to-ground ordnance, and a belly pack for thirty-two 2.75-inch FFARs. Although ordered in mid–1950, prolonged service acceptance delayed deliveries of the first of 180 F7U-3s to fleet units until early 1954. This was followed in 1955 by 98 F7U-3Ms, which could carry four *Sparrow* AIM-7 beam-riding missiles. Twelve unarmed F7U-3P photo-recon aircraft were also built but never became operational. Starting with VF-81 in May 1954, F7U-3/3Ms eventually equipped a total of ten Navy fighter and attack squadrons by 1955, but because of new types coming into service (e.g., A4D-1s, FJ-4Bs) their active career was very brief, the last examples being retired from VA-166 in September 1957. Two F7U-3s were briefly evaluated by the Marine Corps in 1955 but never used operationally.

II—USN and USMC Attack Aircraft

VOUGHT F7U-3

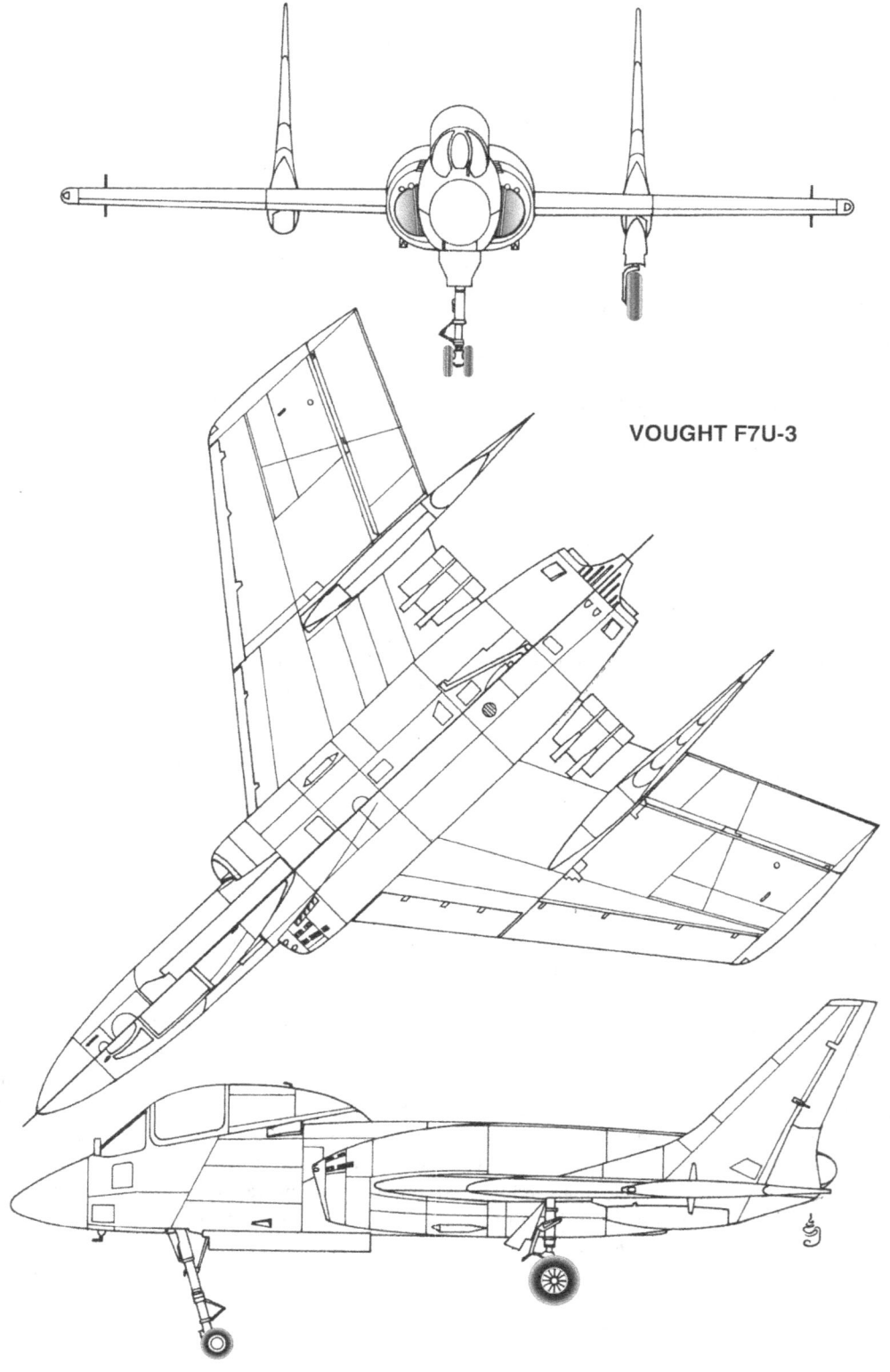

F7U-3M (missile-armed) of VF-212 serving aboard the *Bon Homme Richard* in 1956 and 1957. The 98 -3Ms built in 1955 were configured to carry AIM-7 *Sparrow* beam-riding missiles. All had been withdrawn from the fleet by the fall 1957.

THIRD SERIES • 1962–PRESENT

Designation	Manufacturer	Dates
A-3	Douglas Aircraft Corp.	1952–1991
A-4	Douglas Aircraft Corp.	1954–1990
A-5	North American Aviation, Inc.	1958–1979
A-6	Grumman Aerospace Corp.	1960–1996
A-7	Ling-Temco–Vought Corp.	1965–1991
AV-8	McDonnell-Douglas Corp.	1970–Present
F-4	McDonnell Aircraft Corp.	1958–1992
F-8	Chance Vought Aircraft Co.	1955–1976
F-111	(see, F-111 in Part I)	
F-14	Grumman Aerospace Corp.	1970–Present
F/A-18	McDonnell-Douglas Corp.	1978–Present
F-35	(see, F-35 in Part I)	
X-47	Northrop-Grumman Corp.	2003–Present

Douglas A-3 (A3D) Skywarrior 1952–1991

TECHNICAL SPECIFICATIONS (A-3B)

Type: Three-place heavy attack
Manufacturer: Douglas Aircraft Co., El Segundo, California.
Total produced (all models): 283
Power plant: Two Pratt & Whitney J57-P-10 turbojet engines, rated at 10,500-lbs./s.t. each.
Armament: Two radar-controlled 20-millimeter cannons in tail turret and up to 12,000-lbs. of bombs or mines carried in an internal bay.

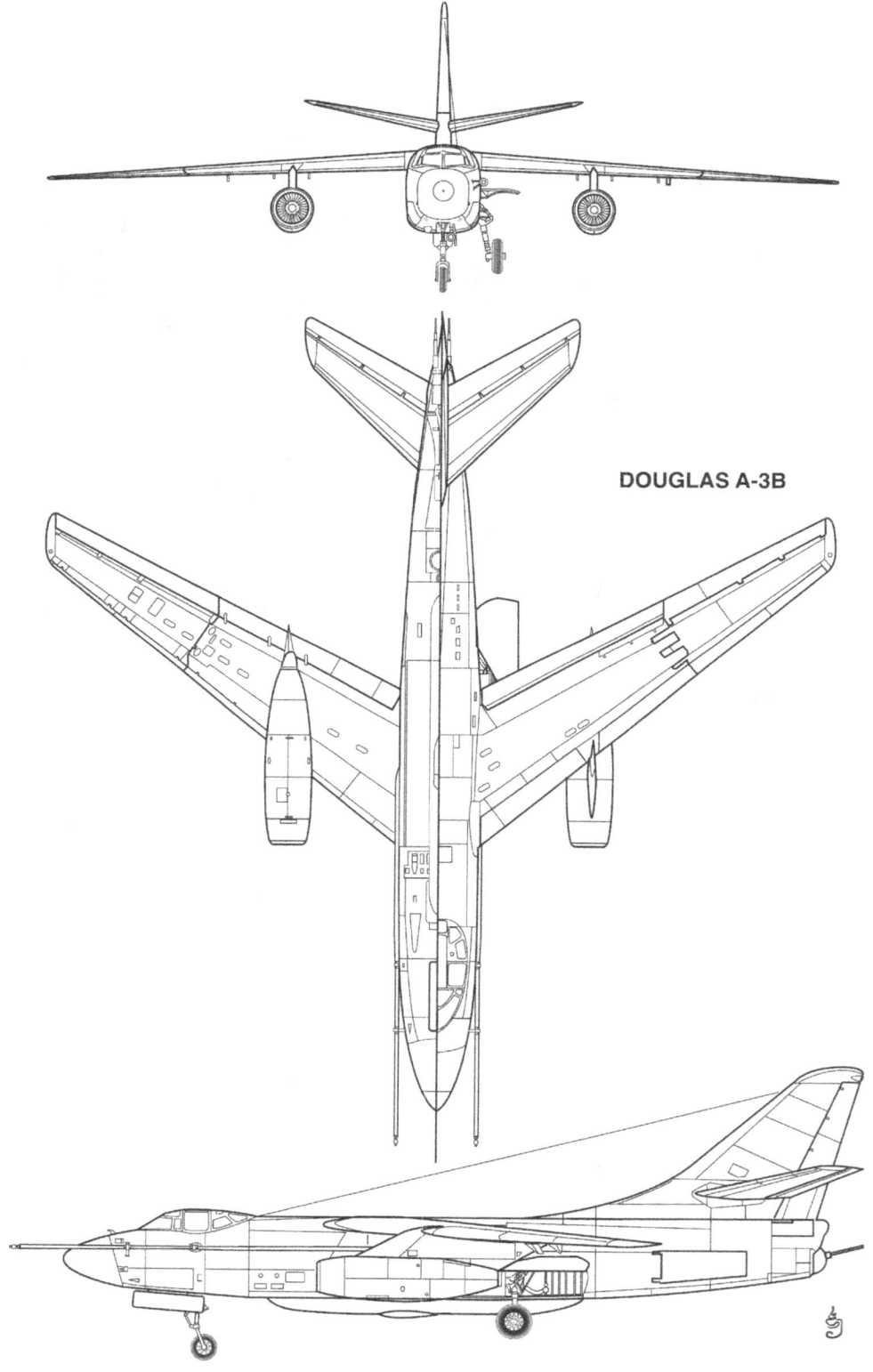

DOUGLAS A-3B

Top: A-3B (A3D-2) of VAH-1 seen making JATO assisted takeoff in 1961. This unit deployed for a cruise aboard the *Independence* the same year. The phase-out of A-3s as nuclear strike bombers began in the early 1960s. *Bottom:* EKA-3B TACOS (tanker aircraft/countermeasures or strike) seen later in its career serving with VAQ-131 while attached to the *John F. Kennedy*. The last land-based ERA-3Bs were retired in the fall of 1991.

Performance: Max. speed 640-mph at s.l.; cruise 502-mph; ceiling 42,300 ft.; range 2,650 mi. (with 4,100-lb. load).
Weights: 39,620-lbs. empty, 78,000-lbs. max. loaded.
Dimensions: Span 76 ft. 6 in., length 74 ft. 9 in., wing area 812 sq. ft

Beginning life as a strategic nuclear bomber, the active career of the Douglas A-3 spanned over 35 years in a variety of tactical roles. Its origins can be traced to a 1947 BUAER requirement for a carrier-based jet-propelled bomber that could carry a 10,000-lb. atomic bomb but would gross no more than 100,000-lbs. loaded. Douglas submitted a proposal in mid-1948 for a swept-wing, twin jet design having a projected loaded weight of 68,000-lbs., and in March 1949, was given the go-ahead to build two prototypes plus a static test airframe under the designation XA3D-1. Like a number of other Navy jet projects of that era, it was to be powered by the experimental Westinghouse J40 engine. After three years of design effort, the XA3D-1 emerged as a conventional planform having a thin, shoulder-mounted wing of 36-degrees sweepback and engine nacelles slung below the wings on pylons. The wing was kept very clean by designing the main landing gear to retract into flush fuselage wells, and both the wings and the tail fin could be folded for carrier stowage. The three-man crew was grouped in a pressurized cockpit, and instead of ejection seats, bailouts would be effected via an escape chute located at the rear of the cockpit. The first prototype was completed and flown on October 28, 1952, but immediate problems with the J40 engines led Douglas to propose a change to Pratt & Whitney J57s, and the first re-engined example was flown in September 1953.

The 50 A3D-1s ordered in 1952 were intended to evaluate the concept of a carrier-based strategic nuclear deterrent plus the feasibility of operating such large and complex aircraft at sea. All were delivered to the Navy during 1956. The A3D-2, the definitive operational type, began appearing in early 1957 and differed in having a stronger airframe, uprated J57-P-10 engines, and a redesigned weapons bay. Other changes introduced over the -2's production life included installation an in-flight refueling probe on the port side, removable tanker package in the weapons bay, revised nose radome housing a new radar/bomb-director system, and replacement the tail turret with a dovetail fairing that contained new ECM equipment. The 164 A3D-2s, serving in eight heavy attack squadrons (VAH), formed the Navy's primary carrier-based strategic nuclear force up until the early 1960s, when defense policy began shifting in favor of submarine-launched ballistic missiles.

The Navy also used a number of specialized *Skywarrior* versions. Eleven A3D-2Qs, built in 1958, were electronic warfare platforms, which, in addition to electronic equipment, had a pressurized compartment in place of the bomb bay to accommodate four radar/ECM-operators. Douglas delivered 30 photographic A3D-2Ps in 1958–1959, which housed up to 12 cameras in the forward bay and flash bombs in the rear bay. The last models produced were 12 A3D-2T bombardier-navigator trainers having a pressurized cabin that held an instructor and four trainees. In 1962 all *Skywarrior* variants were re-designated as follows: A3D-1 to A-3A, A3D-2 to A-3B, A3D-2Q to EA-3B, A3D-2P to RA-3B, and A3D-2T to TA-3B; later, 85 A-3Bs converted to permanent tankers without bombing equipment became KA-3Bs, and later still, 34 of these retrofitted with ECM equipment became EKA-3B TACOS (tanker aircraft/ countermeasures or strike). Five TA-3Bs were subsequently modified as high-speed VIP transports, accommodating up to nine passengers, and eight RA-3Bs, fitted with special electronic equipment and chaff dispensers, became ERA-3B 'electronic aggressor' aircraft.

In 1965–1966, as U.S. involvement in the Vietnam War escalated, A-3Bs of VAH-2, -4, and -8 were initially used in combat as conventional bombers and aerial mine layers against lightly defended targets; after 1966, however, VAH operations were limited to tanker and TACOS sorties. During the same time period, RA-3Bs flew nighttime reconnaissance missions over North Vietnam while EA-3Bs were used to gather vital electronic intelligence on enemy radar systems. In 1969–1971, Grumman KA-6Ds and EA-6Bs replaced KA-3Bs and EKA-3Bs in the tanker and TACOS roles, though two Naval Reserve squadrons, VAK-108 and -208, operated its KA-3Bs tankers until 1988–1989. EA-3Bs were finally withdrawn from active carrier duty in late 1987 but were retained in service by shore bases. In early 1991 EA-3Bs of VQ-2 flew their final missions in support of Operation *Desert Storm*. Land-based ERA-3Bs also continued to provide electronic threat simulation training until the last example was retired from VAQ-33 in September 1991.

Douglas A-4 (A4D) Skyhawk 1954–1990

TECHNICAL SPECIFICATIONS (A-4E)
Type: Single-place attack
Manufacturer: Douglas Aircraft Co., El Segundo, California; later moved to McDonnell-Douglas Corp., Long Beach, California.
Total produced (all USN/USMC models): 2,617
Power plant: One Pratt & Whitney J52-P-6A turbojet engine, rated at 8,500-lbs./s.t.
Armament: Two 20-millimeter cannons and underwing pylons for up to 8,200-lbs. of mixed ordnance.
Performance: Max. speed (clean) 685-mph at s.l.; cruise 496-mph; ceiling 49,000 ft.; range 2,055 mi. max., 920 mi. loaded.
Weights: 9,284-lbs. empty, 24,500-lbs. max. loaded.
Dimensions: Span 27 ft. 6 in., length 40 ft. 1 in., wing area 260 sq. ft.

Until very recently, the Douglas/McDonnell-Douglas A-4 series held the record for having the longest production life (1954–1979) of any naval strike aircraft. The A-4 was originally evolved to meet a 1950 BUAER requirement for a carrier-based attack aircraft capable of delivering tactical nuclear weapons and performing conventional interdiction missions as well. Although the specification listed a permissible loaded weight of 30,000-lbs., the design which emerged signified an exceptional effort by Douglas to reverse the trend toward increasing weight and complexity by placing strict emphasis on structural simplicity and weight control. The resulting XA4D-1 offered an aircraft that not only weighed-in at half the permissible limit (loaded) but also fulfilled or exceeded requirements in all other categories. A very compact tailed delta planform and tall landing gear stance (to allow weapons clearance) were the design's most noticeable characteristics. Propulsion would be derived from a Wright J65-W-2 turbojet, rated at 7,200-lbs./s.t. (license-built Armstrong-Siddeley *Sapphire*). Mockup inspection took place in March 1952 and in June a contract was placed for two prototypes and a pre-production batch of aircraft. The first prototype was flown on 22 June 1954 and the first pre-production A4D-1 followed in August. Deliveries to operational units began in late 1956.

The A4D, re-designated A-4 in September 1962, was ultimately manufactured in nine major variants for the Navy and Marine Corps: the 165 A-4As (A4D-1) produced from 1954 to 1957 differed from the prototypes in having a framed windscreen, cannon armament, LABS for toss-bombing, and a complete avionics package; the 542 A-4Bs (A4D-2), which began entering service in 1957, featured a 7,770-lbs./s.t. J65-W-16A engine, a single-skin, powered rudder, single-point pressure fueling system, new gun sight, changes to the cockpit layout, and later included in-flight refueling probes; the 639 A-4Cs (A4D-2N), introduced in 1960, had a nose lengthened 9 inches to house terrain-avoidance radar for all-weather operations; the 500 A-4Es (A4D-5), which started reaching fleet squadrons in late 1962, came with a 8,500-lbs./s.t. Pratt & Whitney J52-P-6A engine, two extra weapons stations on the wings, a low-level ejection seat (Escapac), and a nose lengthened a further 5 inches for additional avionics and navigational equipment; the 241 TA-4Fs, first delivered in 1966, were fully mission-capable dual control versions having a second cockpit with a raised seat plus a 9,300-lbs./s.t. J-52-P-8A engine, nosewheel steering, and wing lift spoilers installed above the flaps; and the 147 A-4Fs,

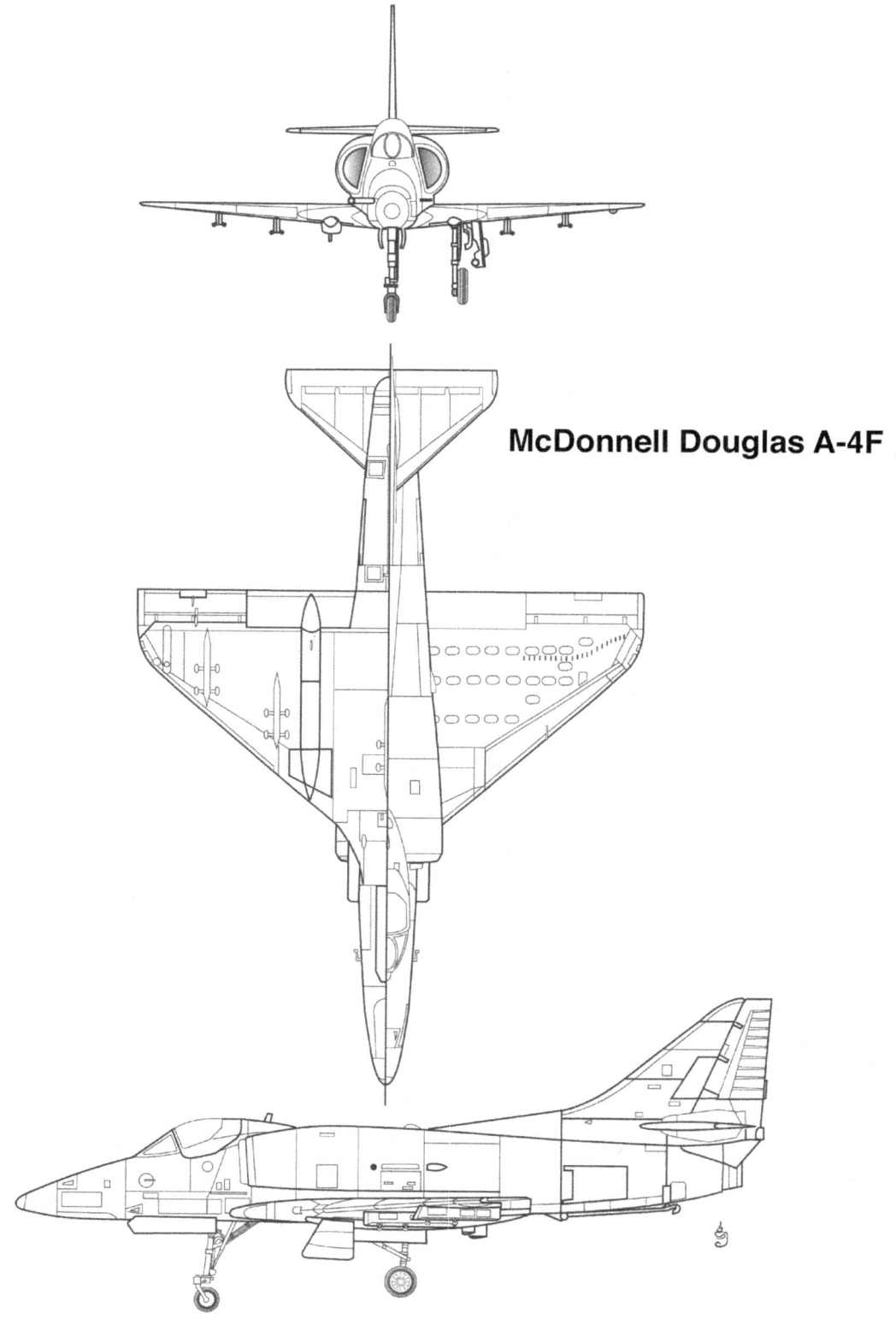

McDonnell Douglas A-4F

One of the earliest A4D-1s (A-4A) serving with VMA-211, probably in 1957 or 1958. The type was operational with four Navy squadrons by the end of 1956. Marines replaced their last prop-driven AD-6s with A4Ds in 1959.

delivered in 1967–1968, were single-seat attack variants with TA-4F upgrades, built for the purpose of replacing A-4 combat losses in Vietnam. During service, A-4Fs (and some A-4Es) were retrofitted with a humped fairing behind the cockpit that housed additional avionics.

In the late 1950s, proposals for an A4D-3 (engine change) and A4D-4 (new wing planform) never progressed beyond the designs stages. Starting in mid–1969, after A-4E production terminated, Naval Training Command took delivery of 226 two-seat TA-4Js lacking full tactical equipment to replace its aging TF-9J (F9F-8T) advanced trainer fleet. Also in 1969, 100 A-4Cs were re-designated A-4Ls after receiving the 8,400-lbs./s.t. J65-W-20 engine, dorsal avionics pod, and lift spoilers. All A-4Ls were assigned to the Naval Air Reserve. A Marine Corps requirement issued in 1969 for a close air support light attack aircraft led to development and, ultimately, production of 160 A-4Ms. Dubbed *Skyhawk II*, the A-4M was powered by the J52-P-408A, rated at 11,200-lbs./s.t., and featured a new windscreen and wider canopy, a squared-off fin to house an IFF antenna, and a drogue chute. During their eight years of production, A-4Ms were upgraded to receive HUDs, bomb directors with television and laser tracking systems, and state-of-the-art defensive components. In 1978 twenty-three two-seat TA-4Fs having the electronic upgrades of the A-4M (less bomb directors) were re-designated OA-4Ms and delivered to the Marine Corps as fast forward air controllers. A-4 production finally ended in February 1979 when the last A-4M rolled off the assembly line at Long Beach. In addition to Navy and Marine production, McDonnell-Douglas manufactured 277 A-4s in five variants for foreign users (i.e., A-4G/TA-4G, A-4H/TA-4H, A-4K/TA-4K, A-4KU/TA-

Top: Two Vietnam-era A-4Es of VMA-223 pictured in the Grand Canyon. With the change to the J52 engine, the E picked a 10 percent increase in power. Unlike the Marine Corps, the Navy began the process of replacing A-4s with A-7s as early as mid–1967. *Bottom:* A-4M of VMA-324 shown in 1971 firing *Zuni* FFAR. The M was much improved over previous *Skyhawk* variants and remained in active service with the Marines until 1990, and continued with Marine reserve units until 1994.

4KU, and A-4N) and many other A-4s were sold to Argentina, Malaysia, Singapore, Brazil, and Indonesia from Navy and Marine stocks.

A-4As (A4D-1s) became operational with VA-34, VA-72, VA-83, and VA-93 in late 1956, and by the end of 1957 had joined five more Navy attack squadrons. As improved A-4Bs (A4D-2s) began reaching Navy and Marine units in 1957, most A-4As were withdrawn from active service and sent to reserves units. The all-weather A-4C (A4D-2N), the most numerous version produced, reached service in 1960 and at one time, served with twenty-three Navy and nine Marine squadrons, the last examples being withdrawn from active units in 1970. Navy and Marine squadrons operating A-4Bs began reequipping with A-4Es in late 1962, though some A-4Bs stayed in frontline units as late as 1967. Deliveries of A-4Fs, the last tactical version built for the Navy, commenced in late 1967 to augment units already equipped with A-4Bs and -Es. Starting with the Tonkin Gulf incident of August 1964, A-4s became one of the key naval combat aircraft of the Vietnam War. Throughout the conflict, carrier-based Navy A-4s operating from *Yankee Station* carried out strikes against the North and those from *Dixie Station*, together with land-based Marine A-4s, flew combat sorties against targets in South Vietnam and Cambodia. From 1973 to 1986, A-4Fs served as the standard aircraft for the Navy's Blue Angels flight demonstration team.

The last A-4Fs were retired from active Navy squadrons in late 1975 and remained in naval reserve units until 1978; a smaller number remained in use as aggressor aircraft with the Navy's "Top Gun" school until the mid-1980s. The last TA-4Js were withdrawn from Naval Training Command in late 1999, however, several are reportedly still flying with VC-8 as adversary trainers and target tugs. VMA-324 was the first Marine unit to receive A-4Ms, and by the end of 1976 five light attack squadrons had equipped with the type. The two-seat OA-4Ms entered service in 1978. OA/A-4Ms were finally retired from active Marine service in February 1990 and continued to serve with reserve units until 1994.

North American A-5 (A3J) Vigilante 1958–1979

TECHNICAL SPECIFICATIONS (RA-5C)
Type: Two-place heavy attack/reconnaissance
Manufacturer: North American Aviation, Inc., Columbus, Ohio.
Total produced (all models): 115
Power plant: Two General Electric J79-GE-10 turbojet engines, each rated at 10,900-lbs./s.t. dry, 17,900-lbs. in afterburning.
Armament: None (Note: A-5A/Bs carried one 2,350-lb. Mk.28 thermonuclear bomb in a linear bay between the engines plus 4,000-lbs of conventional bombs or AGM-12 *Bullpup* missiles on underwing pylons.)
Performance: Max. speed 1,385-mph (Mach 2.1) at 40,000 ft.; max. cruise 1,254-mph (Mach 1.9); ceiling 67,000 ft.; range 2,050 mi. max. (subsonic), 1,094 mi. (combat).
Weights: 37,498-lbs. empty, 79,588-lbs. max. loaded.
Dimensions: Span 53 ft., length 75 ft. 10 in., wing area 754 sq. ft.

Though manufactured only in modest numbers, the A-5 probably introduced more technological innovations than any other single type of aircraft in the history of naval aviation. Work on its design began in late 1953 as a company-funded project called the North American General Purpose Attack Weapon (NAGPAW), then in 1954, it was presented to BUAER as an unsolicited proposal. The mission and design requirements (i.e., a carrier-based nuclear bomber with Mach 2 dash capability at altitude) were finalized in a June 1956 contract authorizing two prototypes under the designation XA3J-1 (later changed to YA3J-1).

The general aerodynamic configuration of the YA3J-1 introduced trends still seen today: shoulder-mounted, low-aspect ratio wings; all-moving slab-type horizontal stabilizers; slender

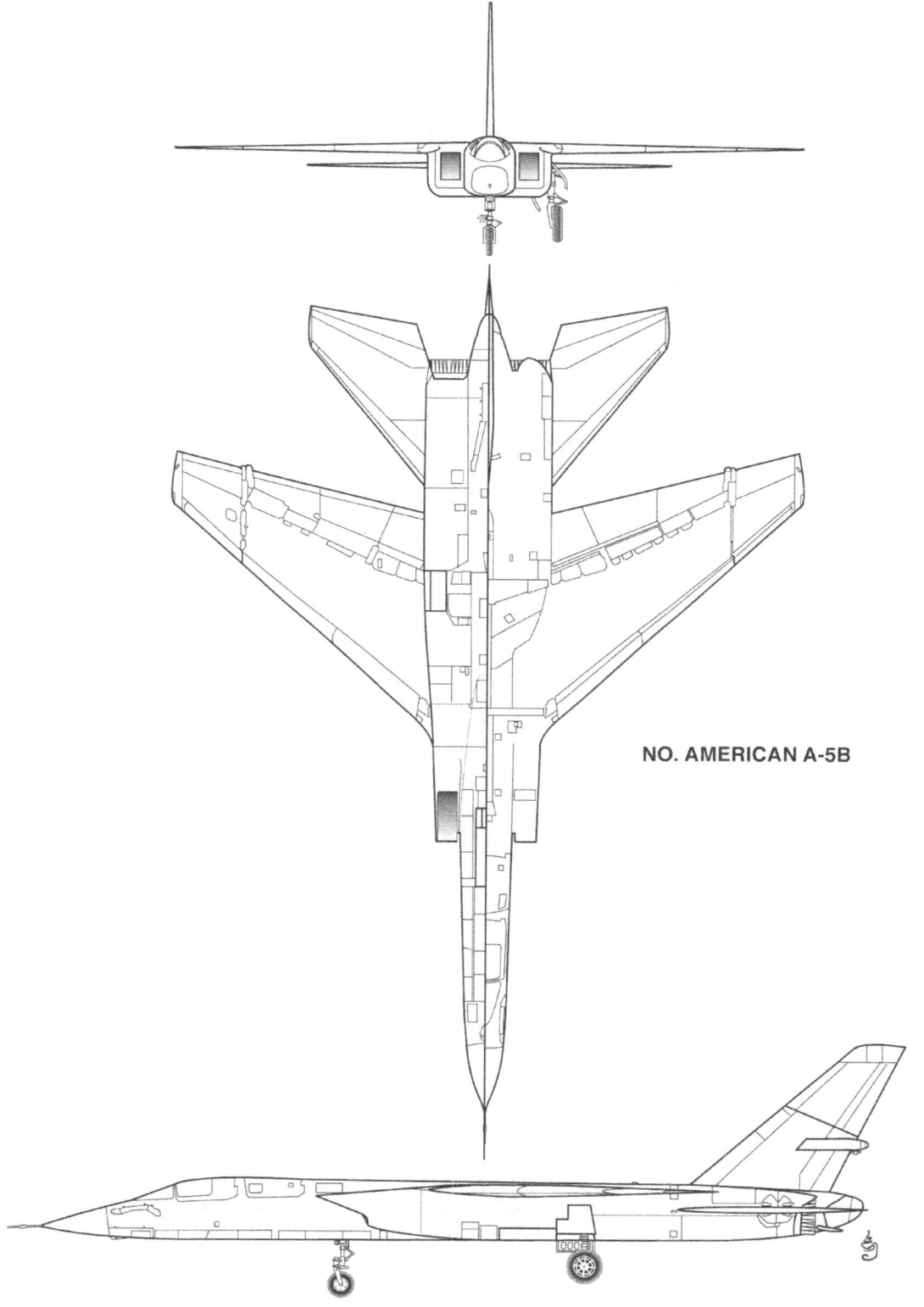

NO. AMERICAN A-5B

Top: By the time the A-5B (A3J-2), as shown here, began entering operational service in mid–1962, the Navy was already moving away from a carrier-based strategic nuclear mission in favor of ICBMs launched from submarines. *Bottom:* RA-5C of RVAH-6 recovering aboard *Ranger* in mid–1960s. Sixty-one RA-5Cs were converted from A-5As and Bs, and the remaining 36 were new build. Last examples were withdrawn from fleet service in 1979.

forward fuselage flanked by long, box-like engine bays extending to the tail; variable engine intakes and exhaust nozzles; and landing gear retracting flush into the fuselage sides. The wings had no ailerons, using for roll control a combination of hinged leading edge spoilers and trailing edge deflectors. The wings were also fitted with 'blown' flaps, a system that bled high-pressure air over the flaps when they were lowered, increasing lift and reducing angle of attack required during the approach. The maiden flight of first YA3J-2 took place on August 31, 1958, and it went supersonic on September 5.

In January 1959 BUAER awarded North American a contract for 59 production A3J-1s. The first 14 were to be used for development and testing, but the remainder, once operational, would begin replacing A3Ds as the Navy's primary carrier-based strategic nuclear deterrent. Deliveries of A3J-1s to VAH-3, a transitional training unit, began in June 1961, and the type became fully operational with VAH-7 in August 1962, followed in early 1963 by VAH-1. The A3J-1 was to be followed by the A3J-2 with more powerful engines, a humped upper fuselage contour that increased internal fuel, and leading edge droops on the wings to improve slow speed control; and plans were also made to develop an A3J-3P high-speed reconnaissance version. In September 1962, when the tri-service system went into effect, the designation of the A3J-1 was changed to A-5A, the A3J-2 to A-5B, and the A3J-3P to RA-5C.

During 1964, as the result of a major policy shift to submarine-launched ballistic missiles, the Navy began a rapid phase-out its carrier-based strategic nuclear bombers, both A-5As and A-3Bs. The 18 A-5Bs then under construction were completed as RA-5Cs, and 43 A-5As were subsequently returned to the factory and remanufactured to RA-5C standards. During the Vietnam War, the RA-5C assembly line was reopened and 36 more were delivered. Squadrons operating A-5As began transitioning to RA-5Cs in mid–1964 and were re-designated Reconnaissance Heavy Attack (RVAH). By 1966, nine RVAH squadrons were operating RA-5Cs and a tenth was established in 1968. During the Vietnam War (1964–1972), RA-5Cs were the Navy's most important tactical reconnaissance asset, completing a total 32 combat cruises while assigned to eight different RVAH units. Eighteen RA-5Cs were lost to enemy action, the highest loss rate of any Navy aircraft during the war. The phase-out of the RA-5C began in 1974 and the last examples were withdrawn in late 1979.

Grumman A-6 (A2F) Intruder 1960–1997

TECHNICAL SPECIFICATIONS (A-6E)
Type: Two-place attack bomber.
Manufacturer: Grumman Aerospace Corp., Bethpage, New York.
Total produced (all attack models): 693
Power plant: Two Pratt & Whitney J-52-P-8A/B turbojet engines, rated at 9,300-lbs./s.t. each.
Armament: (No defensive armament) Up to 17,280-lbs. of bombs, rockets, or AGM missiles on fuselage centerline and four wing pylons.
Performance: Max. speed 653-mph at s.l.; cruise 474-mph; ceiling 42,400 ft.; max. range 3,300 mi., 1,010 mi. loaded.
Weights: 27,892-lbs. empty, 60,400-lbs. max. loaded.
Dimensions: Span 53 ft., length 54 ft. 9 in., wing area 529 sq. ft.

During an active naval career spanning over three decades (1963–1996), Grumman's A-6 established itself as one of naval aviation's truly outstanding aircraft, and as a carrier-based tactical bomber, its offensive payload and range remain unequalled by any type of aircraft in service today (or planned for the foreseeable future). The design originated in response to a 1957 BUAER requirement for a 575-mph, two-seat attack aircraft that could operate at low-level in any type of weather. In early 1958, after considering eight different proposals, BUAER selected Grumman's G-128 design as the winner and authorized construction of a full-scale

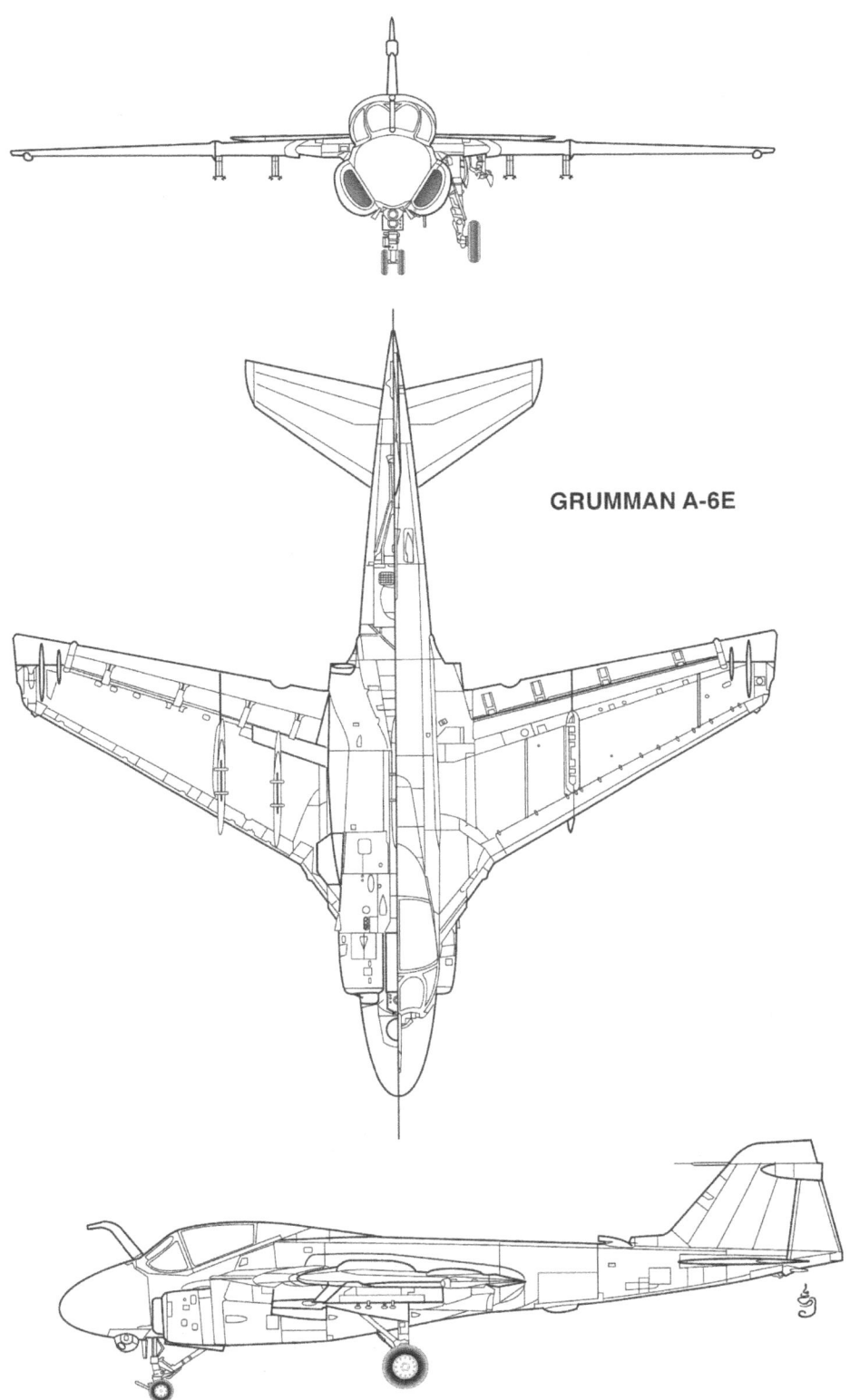

GRUMMAN A-6E

Top: **Publicity photograph of A2F-1 (A-6A) showing the array of weaponry the type was equipped to carry. The digital integrated attack navigation system (DIANE) of the A-6A gave the Navy and Marines unprecedented all-weather attack capabilities.** *Bottom:* **A-6E of VA-65 based at NAS Oceana in low-visibility paint scheme adopted by the Navy in 1982. Like so many A-6 squadrons after Operation Desert Storm, VA-65 was disestablished in 1993.**

mockup. Four development aircraft were ordered in March 1959 under the designation YA2F-1 and the first example flew on April 19, 1960. The type subsequently entered production as the A2F-1 and began entering service in early 1962. Its designation changed to A-6A in September 1962.

Since supersonic performance was unnecessary, the A2F-1/A-6A appeared with non-afterburning engines, long-span wings of 23-degrees sweepback, and a bulbous nose section to accommodate a large radar array. The cockpit with side-by-side seating was positioned well forward under a large canopy. Mid-mounted wings featured leading edge slats and full span flaps, with roll control provided by differential flap movement (i.e., flaperons) at slow speeds and spoilers hinged to the upper wing surfaces at high speeds. Early models had speed brakes extending from the aft fuselage but during development these were replaced by split brakes on the wingtips. The most advanced feature of the design was its digital integrated attack navigation system (DIANE) in which the data from the two radars (search and track), navigation, and bombing systems were fed into a high-speed digital computer that displayed information on two cockpit screens, one for the ground below and the other for the airspace ahead. With this information, the aircraft could identify and attack targets in zero visibility.

Production of the A-6A was completed in late 1970 after 488 examples had been delivered to the Navy and the Marine Corps. Between 1967–1970, a number of specialized variants were converted from existing A-6A airframes: 19 became A-6B SAM suppression aircraft, wired for anti-radiation missiles and having their DIANE systems replaced by missile detection and tracking equipment; another 12 became A-6C special night operations aircraft equipped with pod-mounted forward-looking infra-red (FLIR) sensors and low-light television cameras (LLLTV); and a total of 90 became KA-6D tankers, thereafter replacing KA-3Bs as the fleet's primary carrier-based tanker. The tanker conversion necessitated removal of all tactical systems, plus installation of an internal hose and reel system and new fuel tanks.

From 1970, Grumman switched to production of the A-6E. Though outwardly identical to -A models, A-6Es came with an entirely new electronics suite, including radar, computer, and weapons delivery system. Production ultimately involved conversion of 240 existing A-6As plus the manufacture of 95 new airframes. In an improvement program started in 1978, 228 A-6Es were retrofitted with target recognition attack multi-sensor (TRAM) packages, a gyro-stabilized chin turret containing a FLIR and laser tracking/targeting system that interconnected to the radar. In the early 1980s, as A-6 airframes began to show evidence of age, the A-6F program was initiated with the aim of remanufacturing the existing A-6 fleet with all new electronics, GE F404 turbofan engines, new epoxy/composite wings, and additional weapons stations; however, due to the scheduled replacement of the A-6 by the General Dynamics A-12, the program was cancelled in 1988 after only five development aircraft had been completed. As a stop-gap measure, the Navy did institute a program in 1988 to replace the metal wings of A-6Es with new composite wing units similar to those designed for the A-6F, and the conversion process was 85 percent complete at the time the type was withdrawn from service.

Initial deliveries of production A-6As to VA-42 for transitional training began in February 1962 and the type became fully operational with VA-75 in October 1963, followed shortly by VA-65 and VA-85; VMA(AW)-242 became the first operational Marine A-6A unit in October 1964. From mid–1965 onwards, the A-6A established itself as one of the key naval strike aircraft deployed in the Southeast Asia combat theater, especially in night and marginal weather operations. Carrier-based Navy A-6A units were typically assigned missions over North Vietnam while land-based Marine *Intruders* operated primarily in the South. In addition, A-6Bs, serving alongside A-6As, flew SAM suppression missions; A-6Cs engaged in night interdiction sorties over the Ho Chi Minh Trail in Laos; and from late 1970, KA-6Ds undertook fleet tanker duties from *Yankee* and *Dixie Stations*.

After Vietnam, A-6s were used again in 1983 to support U.S. involvement in Lebanon and also during the invasion of Granada. In 1984 A-6Es operating from *America* and *Coral Sea* participated in retaliatory air strikes flown against Libya. A-6Es of VA-95 operating from *Enterprise* sunk an Iranian frigate in April 1988 during the so-called Tanker War. In late 1990, six carrier battle groups equipped with seven A-6E squadrons arrived on station in the Persian Gulf and on January 17, 1991, began flying combat missions in support of Operation *Desert Storm*. Navy A-6Es carried out precision air strikes against military targets within Iraq, combined with attacks on Iraqi naval vessels operating in the Gulf. During the campaign, A-6Es made the first combat use of an AGM-84E SLAM missile. After *Desert Storm*, Navy and Marine units began a general phase-out of the A-6E. And because of military downsizing, many of these units were not reequipped with new aircraft but completely disestablished. VA-75, the last operational A-6E unit, was deactivated in February 1997.

Ling-Temco–Vought A-7 Corsair II 1965–1993

TECHNICAL SPECIFICATIONS (A-7E)

Type: One or two-place attack.
Manufacturer: Ling-Temco-Vought Corp., Dallas, Texas.
Total produced (all versions): 1,641
Power plant: One Allison TF41-A-1 turbofan engine (license-built Rolls-Royce *Spey*), rated at 14,500-lbs./s.t.
Armament: One 20-millimeter M61 rotary cannon and up to 15,000-lbs. of bombs, rockets, or AGMs on two fuselage and six wing stations.
Performance: Max. speed 698-mph at s.l. (clean); cruise 507-mph; ceiling 38,800 ft.; range 2,800 mi. max., 1,400 mi. loaded.
Weights: 19,940-lbs. empty, 42,000-lbs. max. loaded.
Dimensions: Span 38 ft. 9 in., length 46 ft. 2 in., wing area 375 sq. ft.

In early 1963 the Navy initiated a design competition known as VAL (light attack aircraft) with the aim of finding a successor to the Douglas A-4. Whereas the A-4 had been designed with the primary mission of delivering a single tactical nuclear weapon, the VAL was specifically intended to carry a variety of conventional ordnance. In order to minimize development costs, all VAL proposals were to be based upon existing designs; supersonic performance was not required. In February 1964, after considering proposals from Douglas, Grumman, North American, and Ling-Temco-Vought (LTV), the Navy selected LTV's V-463 as the winning design under the designation YA-7A. The design of the YA-7A was evolved from an F-8 *Crusader* airframe in which the fuselage was shortened eight and a half feet to accommodate a non-afterburning Pratt & Whitney TF30 turbofan. The airframe (projected to handle three times the typical weapons load of the F-8NE) received major structural strengthening. By redesigning the wings with 21-inch tip extensions and reduced sweepback, the need for the variable-incidence feature of the F-8 was eliminated.

LTV received a contract for seven pre-production YA-7As in March 1964, followed in November by an order for 35 production aircraft. After first prototype flew on September 17, 1965, 140 A-7As were added to the order with the understanding that the type would enter service in 1967. As it turned out, A-7As were initially delivered to fleet readiness squadrons (VA-174 and VA-122) in September-October 1966, were declared combat-ready in mid-1967, and were flying their first combat missions over Vietnam by December. Operational experience revealed that, compared to the A-4E/F, the A-7A not only carried twice the combat load, but was easier to maintain, less vulnerable to combat damage, and possessed far better range. A-7A was succeeded in production in 1968–1969 by 196 A-7Bs, which came with TF30 engines of 850-lbs. more thrust and improvements to the flaps. The 69 A-7Cs produced in 1969 were

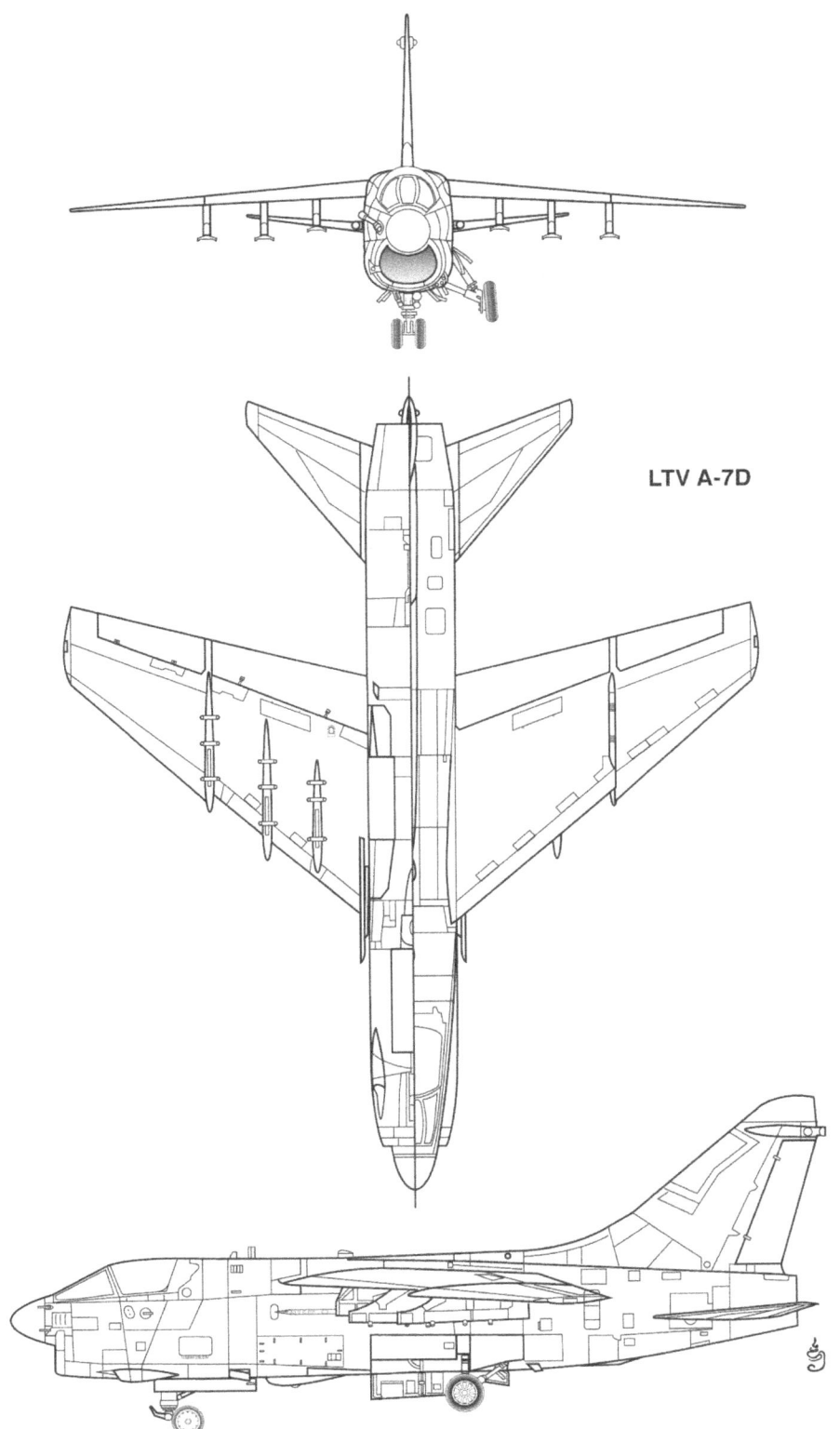

LTV A-7D

Top: A-7Es of VA-81 over NAS Cecil Field in 1970s. By the time of Operation Desert Storm in early 1991, only two A-7 units, VA-46 and VA-72, remained active, but managed to complete over 800 combat sorties before the conflict ended. *Bottom:* USAF A-7D in Vietnam-era camouflage. The type deployed for combat duty in TAC units during late 1972. A-7s were retired from active USAF service in 1981 but continued with ANG units until 1993.

interim versions that included new avionics, HUDs, and an M61 rotary cannon in place of the two fixed 20-mm guns.

In 1970, production switched to the A-7E (essentially a naval version of the USAF A-7D), which incorporated all of the improvements of the -C plus a 20 per cent power increase derived from installation of the Allison TF41 turbofan engine (a license-built Rolls-Royce *Spey*). The last of the 535 A-7Es built was delivered to the Navy in 1983. In 1976–1977, LTV reworked 60 A-7Bs and -Cs into two-seat, dual-control trainers by adding a 34-inch fuselage plug ahead of the wing, and they were redelivered as TA-7Cs. Though having slightly less range, these two-seaters were otherwise fully mission capable. Eight TA-7Cs equipped with special electronic pods in 1982 were subsequently re-designated EA-7L electronic aggressor aircraft. In 1984 forty-one TA-7Cs and eight EA-7Ls were upgraded with TF41 engines but their designations remained unchanged. In addition to Navy production, LTV built 459 A-7Ds and 30 two-seat A-7Ks for the USAF and Air National Guard; 60 new A-7Hs and five TA-7Hs (similar to A-7Ds/A-7Ks) were sold to Greece; and 68 rebuilt A-7s were transferred to Portugal and Thailand. The advanced YA-7F (i.e., A-7 "plus") was never considered by the Navy and was ultimately cancelled by the USAF in 1990.

VA-86 was the first squadron to become operational with A-7As in June 1967; VA-147 took them into combat for the first time from *Ranger* in December the same year. During 1967–1969, 20 fleet squadrons reequipped with A-7A/Bs, with nine more transitioning to A-7Es in 1970–1971. In the interval, A-7s replaced A-4s as the Navy's chief single-seat attack aircraft in Southeast Asia, and as more A-7Es arrived, they replaced A-7A/Bs in frontline units. After Vietnam, the combat career of Navy A-7s continued in 1983, flying air strikes against Syrian missile sites during the U. S. intervention in Lebanon then close air support sorties during the invasion of Granada. In 1986, A-7s launched from *America* and *Coral Sea* participated in attacks on Libyan military positions as part of Operation *El Dorado Canyon*, and in 1988, during the Tanker War, A-7s from *Enterprise* flew strikes in the Persian Gulf against Iranian oil platforms and patrol boats. By the time of Operation *Desert Storm* in January 1991, only two active A-7E squadrons remained, VA-46 and VA-72 aboard *Kennedy*, however, by the end of the conflict, these two units had accomplished 817 combat sorties at a mission completion rate of 99.7 percent, with no losses to themselves. VA-46 and VA-72 both were formally disestablished in May 1991 and the last operational EA-7Ls were withdrawn from VAQ-33 and VAQ-34 in early 1992.

In late 1965, after bending to Army pressure to acquire a subsonic close air support (CAS) aircraft, the USAF contracted with LTV to develop the A-7D. The first YA-7D, flown in April 1968, was powered by the same TF30 engine as the A-7A/C, but definitive production models came with more powerful Allison TF41s and included other enhancements such as a HUD, a computerized navigation and fire-control system, as well as a 20-mm M61 rotary cannon in place of the single-barreled units. The first production A-7D flew in September 1968, and the USAF had accepted 459 examples when production ended in late 1976. During 1979, after being modified for installation of a second cockpit, one A-7D was re-designated TA-7D, and 30 more aircraft were subsequently produced from 1981 to 1984 as the A-7K. All A-7Ks were delivered directly to Air National Guard units.

A-7Ds first entered operational USAF service in September 1970 with the 354th Tactical Fighter Wing at Myrtle Beach AFB in South Carolina and were deployed to the combat theater in Southeast Asia in late 1972. Operating out of Korat RTAFB in Thailand from October 1972 to August 1973, the A-7Ds of the 354th flew 12,928 ground attack sorties against target in Cambodia, Laos, and North Vietnam for a loss of only four aircraft to enemy action, the lowest loss ratio of any USAF tactical aircraft in the combat zone. After Vietnam, A-7Ds equipped three TAC wings and two ANG squadrons, but were retired from active USAF service during 1981 as they were replaced by A-10As. Most ex-USAF A-7Ds were thereafter transferred to ANG squadrons, and together with two-place A-7Ks, eventually equipped a total of 14 ANG squadrons. The last ANG A-7s were retired by units in Ohio, Iowa, and Oklahoma in 1993. The A-7s acquired by Greece and Thailand are reportedly still in service.

McDonnell-Douglas AV-8 Harrier 1970–Present

TECHNICAL SPECIFICATIONS (AV-8B)

Type: One or two-place V/STOL attack.
Manufacturer: McDonnell-Douglas Corp., St. Louis, Missouri and British Aerospace, United Kingdom.
Total produced (all models): 310
Power plant: One Rolls-Royce *Pegasus* F402-406 vectored thrust turbofan, rated at 21,180-lbs./s.t.
Armament: One fuselage-mounted 25-millimeter GAU-12 rotary gun system, up to 9,000-lbs. of ordnance on seven external stations, or four AIM-9L/M *Sidewinders* (air-to-air load).
Performance: Max. speed (clean) 629-mph at s.l.; ceiling 50,000 ft.; range 2,441 mi. max., 104 mi. (max. load with VTO), 683 mi. (combat load, STO), and 721 mi. (deck-launched air-to-air).
Weights: 13,086-lbs. empty, 19,185 max. loaded (VTO), 31,000-lb. max. loaded (STO).
Dimensions: Span 30 ft. 4 in., length 46 ft. 4 in., wing area 230 sq. ft.

The AV-8 *Harrier* currently holds the distinction of being the only attack aircraft capable of vertical takeoff and landing (VTOL) to have entered operational service with the U. S. armed forces. The events leading up to acquisition of the AV-8 began in early 1965 when the NATO Tripartite Evaluation Squadron (TES) was formed to conduct trials with a number of Hawker P.1127 *Kestrel* VTOL development aircraft. The *Kestral* differed from other VTOL experiments in having vectored thrust, i.e., rotable engine exhaust nozzles that enabled the aircraft to transition from vertical to level flight without radical changes in pitch. When the TES program terminated in 1966 after Germany withdrew support, the British government independently pursued development of its own military variant of the *Kestral,* the *Harrier* G.R.Mk.1, the first example of which flew in late 1966. Around the same time, one of the six TES *Kestrels* allotted to the U.S. was turned over to the Naval Air Test Center, where Marine Corps pilots were given the opportunity to carry out trials which included VTOL operations from the assault ship *Raleigh.*

Continuing interest in the *Harrier* led to a group of Marine pilots being sent to the U.K. in early 1969 to conduct formal flight evaluations, and soon afterward, the Marine Corps officially requested procurement of 114 aircraft. In order to bypass the U.S. government policy that forbade purchases of foreign-made military aircraft, an agreement was concluded between Hawker-Siddeley (later British Aerospace) and McDonnell-Douglas authorizing the latter to license-build an American version, the AV-8A, in the U.S. Since it was highly impractical for McDonnell-Douglas to establish an assembly line on so small a scale, completed AV-8As were in fact crated-up in the U.K. then shipped to McDonnell-Douglas for eventual delivery to the Marine Corps. Congressional authorization was ultimately granted to purchase 102 AV-8A single-seat attack variants plus 8 TAV-8A two-seat trainers. The American versions were essentially identical to their British counterparts (i.e., G.R.Mk.1 and T.Mk.4), except for avionics, US-made ejection seats (Stencel SIIIS-3), and certain weapons components. The first 12 AV-8As were delivered to the Marine Corps in 1970 direct from Hawker-Siddeley, and the remainder came from McDonnell-Douglas over the next three years. VMA-513 was the first Marine unit to become operational with the AV-8A in April 1971, followed by VMA-542 in January 1972, and VMA-231 in May 1973. While the AV-8A's capabilities represented an enormous improvement in tactical air mobility and responsiveness, the first ten years of operational experience was plagued by an unusually high mishap rate involving 55 (peacetime) aircraft losses.

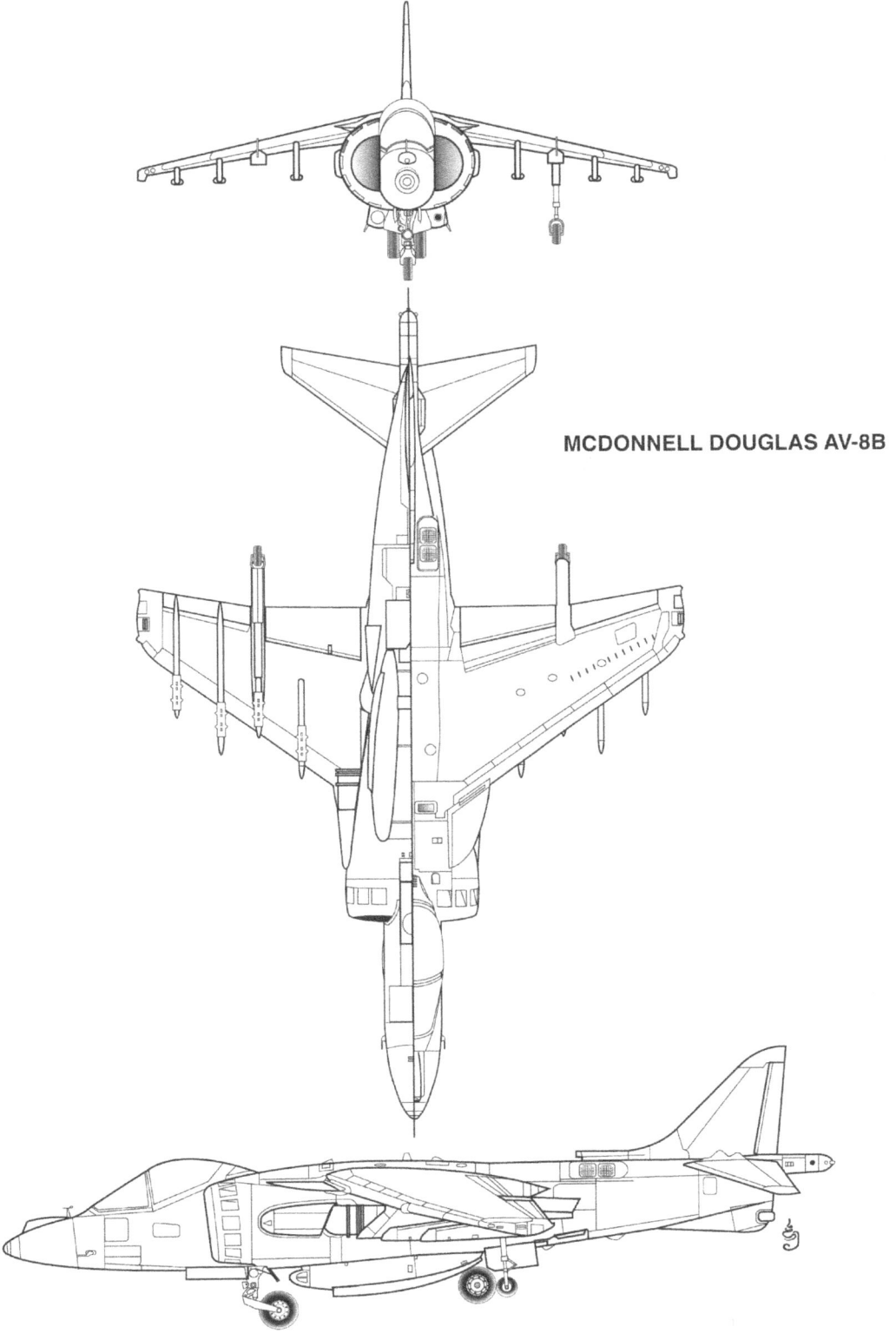

MCDONNELL DOUGLAS AV-8B

Top: Marine AV-8A of VMA-513 seen making a vertical landing aboard an LPH. It was the first V/STOL attack aircraft of any type to operate in the U. S. armed forces. Most of the surviving As were upgraded as AV-8Cs between 1979 and 1984. *Bottom:* AV-8B shown prior to delivery. The type was placed in slow-rate production, re-equipping Marine squadrons from 1983 until 1990. A total of 182 aircraft were delivered, including 20 two-seat TAV-8Bs.

As early as 1973, the deficiencies of the AV-8A and British *Harrier* variants led to joint effort between McDonnell-Douglas and British Aerospace to develop a second generation VTOL replacement. Initial conceptual studies generated the AV-16A, an enlarged airframe that would require development of a larger *Pegasus*-type engine; however, the project collapsed in 1975 after British Aerospace withdrew due to financial constraints. At this juncture, McDonnell-Douglas elected to separately pursue a more modest approach in the shape of an improved AV-8 variant that retained the existing *Pegasus* powerplant. The outcome of this effort, the AV-8B, featured an entirely new, bigger wing, which, combined with extensive use of lighter composite materials, effectively doubled the aircraft's useful combat load. Stores pylons were increased from four to seven and a new, raised canopy was installed to improve all-around visibility. The cockpit received state-of-the-art digital systems (similar to the F/A-18), which included a large HUD and HOTAS (hands-on-throttle-and-stick) controls. The first flight of an AV-8A fitted with the new wing was made in late 1978, but the first true AV-8B prototype did not fly until November 1981.

Between 1979 and 1984, while the AV-8B was still under development, 47 of the surviving AV-8As were upgraded as AV-8Cs, receiving in the process an airframe overhaul, belly lift devices (designed for the AV-8B) that increased weapons load, updated ECM suite, improved radios, onboard oxygen generation system (OBOGS), and strip formation lights. When the first batch of AV-8Bs arrived in late 1983, VMAT-203 was given the task of training pilots and maintenance personnel. During 1985–1988 the three original AV-8A/C units (VMA-231, VMA-513, and VMA-542) began converting to the AV-8B and retiring their AV-8Cs. Then in line with Marine Corps plans to retire A-4Ms in light attack units, four more squadrons (VMA-211, VMA-214, VMA-223, and VMA-311) reequipped with AV-8Bs between 1988 and 1990, bringing total AV-8B production to 162 attack variants and 20 TAV-8B two-seat trainers.

In 1990 sixty-six AV-8Bs were upgraded to night attack capability [i.e., AV-8B(NA)] by receiving forward-looking infrared sensors (NAVFLIR), a moving map, and night-vision equipment. All AV/TAV-8Bs began a 10-year retrofit program in 1993 to replace their F402-406 engines with the 23,800-lb./s.t. F404-408, which incorporates a digital control system. The first radar-equipped AV-8B+ was test flown in 1993, and 27 examples were delivered to Marine squadrons starting in 1997. The B+ has all the improvements of the AV-8B(NA) plus a tactical airborne radar that provides multiple target tracking with the ability to perform air-to-air or air-to-surface weapons delivery in conditions of marginal visibility, day or night. A side-by-side program to remanufacture 72 older AV-8Bs to the B+ standard was completed in late 2003, bringing the AV-8B+ total to 100 aircraft. In 1991, operating from relatively unprepared sites, Marine AV-8B squadrons were the most forward-deployed aviation units during *Operation Desert Storm*. Eighty-six AV-8Bs attached to VMA-513, VMA-542, and VMA-231 flew 3,657 combat sorties against targets in Kuwait and Iraq, with four losses. More recently, Marine AV-8B(NA)/B+s deployed aboard the amphibious assault ships *Bataan* and *Bonhomme Richard* participated in the invasion of Iraq in the spring of 2003. Under current plans, existing Marine AV-8B variants are scheduled remain in service until replaced by Lockheed-Martin F-35Bs in 2018.

McDonnell F-4 (F4H) Phantom II 1958–1996

TECHNICAL SPECIFICATIONS (F-4B)

Type: Two-place fighter-bomber
Manufacturer: McDonnell Aircraft Corp. (later McDonnell-Douglas Corp.), St. Louis, Missouri.
Total produced (all versions): 5,057
Power plant: Two General Electric J79-GE-8B turbojet engines, each rated at 10,900-lbs./s.t. dry, 17,000-lbs. with afterburning.

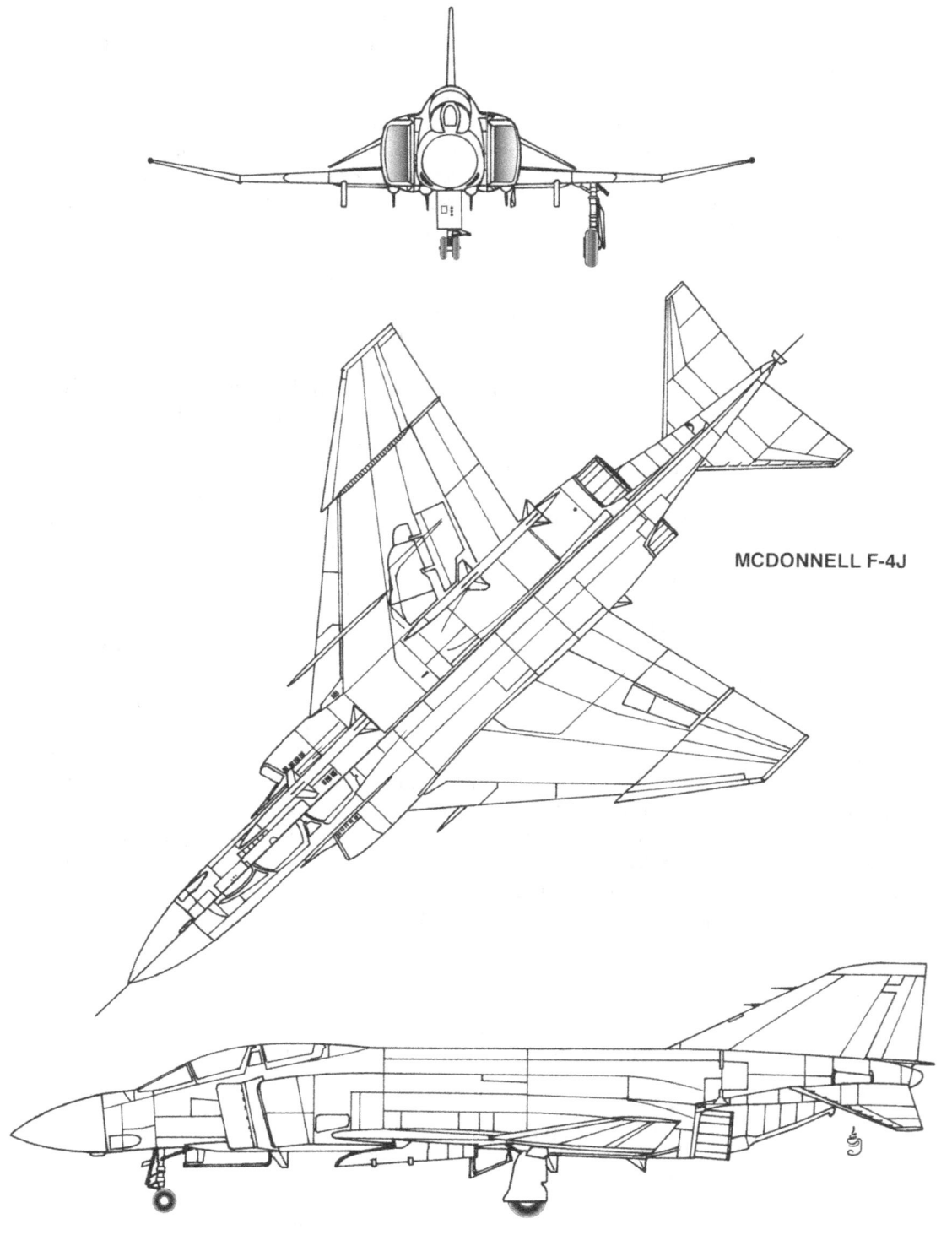

MCDONNELL F-4J

Top: F-4Bs of VF-84 "Jolly Rogers" during cruise aboard the *Independence* in 1965. The last of 649 B models was delivered in early 1967, by which time they were serving in 29 different Navy and Marine squadrons. *Bottom:* VF-33 traded its F-4Bs for F-4Js in 1967, then a year later deployed aboard the *America* for combat duty off the coast of North Vietnam. In July 1968, an F-4J of this unit downed a VPAF MiG-21, the first east coast Navy fighter squadron to do so.

F-4S (foreground) and F-4N attached to VX-4. Abrupt cancellation of the VFAX program in 1974 led to the remanufacture of 476 F-4B and Js as F-4Ns and Ss, respectively. Last examples were retired from the Marine reserves in 1992.

Armament: Six AIM-7 *Sparrow* missiles or four AIM-7 and four AIM-9 *Sidewinder* missiles, or up to 16,000-lbs. of bombs or rockets on one fuselage and four wing stations.
Performance: Max. speed 1,485-mph (Mach 2.2) at 48,000 ft.; ceiling 62,000 ft.; range 2,300 mi. max., 900 mi. loaded.
Weights: 28,000-lbs. empty, 54,600-lbs. max. loaded.
Dimensions: Span 38 ft. 5 in., length 58 ft. 4 in., wing area 530 sq. ft.

Besides having been naval aviation's first Mach 2 fighter-bomber, the McDonnell F-4 serves as the best example of the post-war naval trend toward a multi-role aircraft whose tactical mission is defined primarily by its weapons load rather than its airframe. The origins of the design go back to 1953, when McDonnell unsuccessfully tried to interest BUAER in a twin-engine variant of the F3H *Demon*. After McDonnell's bid lost out to Vought's XF8U-1 proposal, BUAER encouraged the company to re-work the design into an all-weather attack aircraft, i.e., the XAH-1. However, when McDonnell resubmitted its attack proposal in mid–1954, BUAER responded with a substantially revised requirement, this time for a two-seat, all-weather deck-launched interceptor (DLI) armed only with missiles.

McDonnell's persistence was finally rewarded in May 1955 when BUAER awarded a contract to build two prototypes of its proposed interceptor (Project 98-Q) under the designation YF4H-1. Following mockup completion in late 1955, a decision was made to use the

Top: Pair of USAF F-4Es from the 469th Tactical Fighter Squadron, 388th TFW, based at Korat RTAFB in Thailand. Firing of the new M61 20-mm internal cannon initially caused problems with gas ingestion in engines, leading to flameouts. *Bottom:* F-4G "Wild Weasel" with AGM-78 Standard ARMS. All 116 Gs were derived from F-4Es specially modified for the SEAD role. F-4Gs were the USAF's primary SEAD platform when Operation Desert Strom commenced in January 1991.

larger J79 engines in place of the original J65s, with the expectation that the added power would give the plane Mach 2 performance. Before the prototype was completed, wind tunnel tests revealed that the YF4H-1's planned aerodynamic configuration would be unstable at high speeds and thus Mach limited. To correct the problem, the horizontal stabilizer received 23-degrees of anhedral and the outer wing panels were cranked to 12-degrees diheral with sawtooth leading edges, producing the type's characteristic appearance. The YF4H-1 also featured other innovations such as 'blown' flaps and slats, which used engine bleed air to keep the airflow attached to the wings at high angles of attack, and combination flaperons/spoilers for roll control.

The first YF4H-1 flew on May 27, 1958, and after initial flight trials were completed later that year, it was selected for production over Vought's competing XF8U-3. Forty-five development aircraft were delivered as the F4H-1F and definitive production models were manufactured as the F4H-1. With the nineteenth F4H-1F, the cockpit was elevated and the canopy enlarged and a larger, more bulbous radome was added to the nose. Carrier suitability tests commenced in early 1960 and the type began reaching transitional training units (VF-101 and VF-121) in early 1961, followed by deliveries to operational units in mid–1961. When the tri-service designation system was adopted in the fall of 1962, the F4H-1F became the F-4A and the F4H-1 the F-4B. The last of 649 F-4Bs was delivered in March 1967, by which time the type was serving in 29 Navy and Marine Corps squadrons. The RF-4B photo-recon variant made its first flight in March 1965, and all 46 examples were delivered to the Marine Corps between 1965–1970. Twelve F-4Bs were re-designated F-4Gs in 1964 (not to be confused with the later USAF F-4G) when they were modified to test and evaluate a two-way tactical communications and datalink system; they were later remanufactured as F-4Ns.

The F-4B was succeeded in production by the F-4J, which flew for the first in June 1965. The F-4J introduced a number of upgrades, including an AJB-7 bombing system that improved its air-to-ground capabilities, AWG-10 pulse-Doppler radar fire control, the F-4G datalink system, J79-GE-10 engines with 17,900-lbs./s.t., strengthened landing gear with larger main wheels and bulged gear doors, and slotted stabilators that reduced approach speed from 157-mph to 144-mph. F-4Js began entering service in late 1966 and 522 had been delivered when production ceased in January 1972.

In a program to extend service life, 228 F-4Bs were rebuilt and modernized during 1972–1973 as F-4Ns, receiving structural improvements, new electrical systems, F-4J-type slotted stabilators, ECM equipment, and new fire-control systems. Deliveries of F-4Ns to operational units began in early 1973. In an analogous program conducted in 1977–1979, 248 F-4Js were upgraded as the F-4S, which involved a structural and electrical rebuild as well as a new weapons control system, and, after the forty-fourth aircraft, two-position leading edge slats that markedly improved turning ability. Besides Navy and Marine production, McDonnell built 2,640 *Phantom IIs* in five USAF variants (see below) plus another 1,155 sold to foreign users (F-4E, RF-4E, F-4EJ, F-4F, F-4K, and F-4M).

F-4Bs entered operational service with VF-74 and VF-114 in mid–1961 and started their first carrier cruise with VF-102 aboard *Enterprise* in August 1962. The first Marine squadron to equip with F-4Bs was VMF(AW)-314 in June 1962. F-4Bs of VF-142 and VF-143 began flying combat in the Tonkin Gulf in August 1964 while serving aboard *Constellation*; Marine F-4Bs of VMFA-531 commenced land-based operations from Da Nang in April 1965. From 1964–1973, Navy F-4s completed 84 combat cruises from 12 different carriers on *Yankee* and *Dixie* stations, and in air-to-air actions, accounted for 38 kills against seven losses. Marine F-4s were most often operated from land bases in the close air support and interdiction roles, though one MiG-21 kill was recorded by VMFA-333 operating from *America* in 1972. Ten Navy and eight Marine squadrons reequipped with F-4Ns in 1972–1973, but from 1974 onwards, many Navy units began to replace their F-4s with the newer Grumman F-14As, though a number continued in the reserves until the early 1980s; F-4Ns remained in active Marine service until 1985.

Seven navy and thirteen Marine squadrons reequipped with the F-4S during 1978–1979. Active Navy F-4Ss initially served in air wings aboard the smaller *Midway* class carriers until 1986, and F-4Ss operating with the naval Reserve were finally retired in May 1987. In the late 1980s, frontline Marine units began to phase-out their F-4Ss in favor of F/A-18A/Bs. The last Marine Reserve F-4S was retired from VMFA-112 in January 1992.

Ironically, the USAF was destined to become the largest and longest user of the *Phantom* series. In early 1962, by order of the Department of Defense (DOD), two Navy F4H-1s were delivered to Langley AFB in Virginia in USAF markings under the designation F-110A, and in March, following official evaluations, DOD announced that F-110As and RF-110As reconnaissance versions would be ordered in quantity for the USAF. When the tri-service designation scheme went into effect in September 1962, the F-110A became the F-4C and the RF-110A the RF-4C. The main differences from F/RF-4B were dual controls for two-pilot operations, bulged wheel doors for larger tires, and a boom-type aerial refueling system. The USAF accepted delivery of 583 F-4Cs from November 1963 to May 1966. The 505 RF-4Cs received between 1964 and 1974 were also configured to carry a tactical nuclear weapon. The F-4D, which appeared in early 1966, featured new avionics and weapons system, and the last of 793 examples joined the USAF inventory in February 1968. Equipped with a 20-mm M61 rotary cannon, the F-4E was flown for the first time in June 1967, but development problems delayed delivery of operational models until late 1968. Eight hundred thirty-one F-4Es had been received by the end of 1976, at which point all USAF production ended. Starting in mid–1978, 116 F-4Es became F-4Gs when they were modified with electronic and weapons components to specialize them for SEAD (suppression of enemy air defense) mission, most commonly referred to as "Wild Weasels."

The 12th Tactical Fighter Wing became the first frontline USAF unit to be equipped with the F-4C in January 1964. F-4Cs saw their first combat action in April 1965 with the 15th TFW out of Ubon RTAFB in Thailand. In addition to becoming the USAF's primary air-to-air fighter in Southeast Asia, F-4s loaded with bombs regularly attacked targets in North Vietnam. F-4Ds began entering USAF service in March 1966 and began replacing F-4Cs in TFWs based in Southeast Asia during 1967. The first F-4Es arrived in Thailand to join the 388th TFW in December 1968, and though problems with the internal cannon, particularly the ingestion of gun gases by the engines, hampered their effectiveness in combat for the next two years, they did account for the downing of 21 MiGs in the latter part of the war, five completely with gunfire. Following Vietnam, the USAF began replacing F-4s in the air superiority role with new F-15A/Bs as soon as 1975, but the process of replacing F-4Es in TAC fighter-bomber units extended far longer, not being fully completed until late 1990, when the 4th TFW was reequipped with F-15E *Strike Eagles*. But at the time Operation Desert Storm began in January 1991, RF-4Cs remained active and F-4Gs were the only SEAD aircraft in the USAF inventory.

The last active RF-4C was retired and transferred to the ANG in the spring of 1991, however, F-4Gs of the 52nd FW remained active until late 1995, at which time they were replaced by F-16CJs. RF/F-4s enjoyed a 25-year career with ANG units: F-4Cs served from 1972 to 1989 with 16 different squadrons; RF-4Cs from 1971 to 1996 with 10 squadrons; F-4Ds from 1977 to 1992 with 14 squadrons (replaced F-4Cs in three); F-4Es from 1985 to 1991 (replaced RF/F-4Cs and F-4Ds); and F-4Gs from 1991 to 1996 with two squadrons (replaced RF-4Cs). Over 700 F-4s are thought to still be active with air forces of the following nations: Egypt, Germany, Greece, Israel, Japan, South Korea, Spain, and Turkey.

Vought F-8 (F8U) Crusader 1955–1976

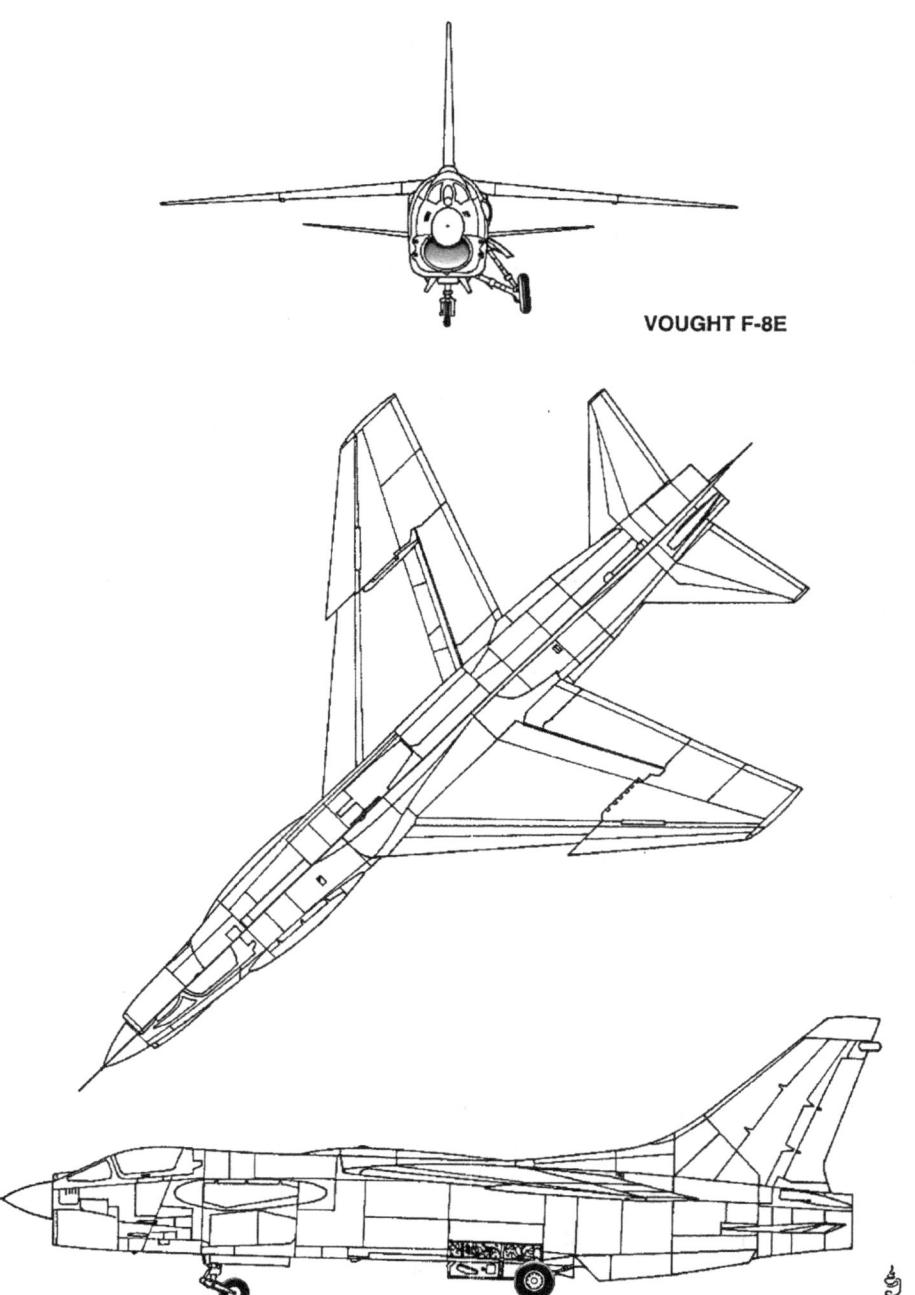

VOUGHT F-8E

TECHNICAL SPECIFICATIONS (F-8E)

Type: One-place fighter-bomber
Manufacturer: Chance Vought Division of United Aircraft Corp. (later Ling-Temco-Vought Corp.), Dallas, Texas.

Top: F8U-1 (later F-8A) serving with VMF-312 in the late 1950s. Fourteen Navy and ten Marine squadrons were equipped with F8Us by 1962. Later, F-8s operating off the Vietnam coast established the highest kill rate (6 to 1) of any Navy fighter in the conflict. *Bottom:* F-8J of VF-191 seen ashore. This unit deployed its aircraft for a cruise aboard the *Oriskany* in 1969, then again in 1976 for what would be the last active Navy assignment of the F-8. The last French F-8E(FN)s were not retired until 1999.

Total produced (all USN/USMC models): 1,117
Power plant: One Pratt & Whitney J57-P-20 turbojet engine, rated at 10,700-lbs./s.t. dry, 18,000-lbs. with afterburning.
Armament: Four fixed forward-firing 20-millimeter cannons, four AIM-9 Sidewinder missiles or up to 5,000-lbs. of bombs, rockets, or two ASM-12 *Bullpup* missiles on wing pylons.
Performance: Max. speed 1,133-mph (Mach 1.7) at 35,000 ft.; cruise 570-mph; ceiling 59,000 ft.; range 1,425 mi. max., 1,100 mi. loaded.
Weights: 17,836-lbs. empty, 34,100-lbs. max. loaded.
Dimensions: Span 35 ft. 8 in., length 54 ft. 6 in., wing area 350 sq. ft.

The Vought F-8 was first Navy and Marine aircraft to break the 1,000-mph mark, and more than any other aircraft up to that time, ushered naval aviation into the Supersonic Age. Its origins can be traced to a 1952 BUAER requirement calling for a deck-launched interceptor (DLI) that could climb to 25,000 feet in one minute and accelerate to an intercept speed of Mach 1.2. In May 1953, after considering twenty-one proposals from eight different manufacturers, BUAER selected Vought's V-383 design under the designation XF8U-1. The design's most outstanding feature was a variable-incidence wing in which the entire center-section could be raised in flight to increase angle of incidence by seven degrees during takeoffs and landings. Moreover, while in the raised position, wing camber was increased by full span leading edge droops, plus flaps and ailerons that automatically lowered to 25-degrees. The long fuselage was area-ruled and the cockpit placed well forward behind a nose with a chin-type engine intake below a radome that housed a fire-control radar. Armament consisted of four 20-mm cannons, two *Sidewinder* missiles, and thirty-two 2.75-inch FFARs in a retractable belly pack. BUAER ordered three prototypes in mid–1953, and the first XF8U-1 flew on March 25, 1955. Testing subsequently revealed the need for very few changes.

Production F8U-1s were delivered for naval evaluations in December 1956 and began to equip operational squadrons in March 1957. A total of 218 F8U-1s were built in 1955–1958, followed by 130 F8U-1Es, which differed in having an improved ranging radar. The first photo-recon F8U-1P flew in December 1956 and 144 examples were delivered by early 1960. The 187 F8U-2s received by Navy and Marine units in 1959–1960 featured uprated J57 engines, ventral strakes on the tail for improved high-speed stability, and the ability to carry four *Sidewinder* missiles. These were followed by 152 F8U-2Ns delivered in 1960–1962 with improved radar and avionics and approach power compensators (i.e., a computer stabilization system that controlled airspeeds during carrier approaches). First flown in 1961, the F8U-2NE was the final production model and the first variant having substantial air-to-ground capabilities. Improvements included an extended radome containing an all-new search and fire-control radar, a new housing for an infra-red scanner, and a humped fairing in the wing center-section that enclosed an avionics package for *Bullpup* air-to-ground missiles. Two external wing racks could carry *Zuni* rocket pods, two *Bullpups*, or up to 5,000-lbs of bombs. The last of 286 F8U-2NEs built came off the assembly lines in mid–1964. When the tri-service system went into effect in September 1962, the F8U series was re-designated as follows: F8U-1 to F-8A, F8U-1E to F-8B, F8U-1P to RF-8A, F8U-2 to F-8C, F8U-2N to F-8D, and F8U-2NE to F-8E.

Besides Navy and Marine production, Vought built 42 *Crusaders* for the French *Aeronavale,* which were delivered in late 1964 under the designation F-8E(FN). After production ceased, several upgrade programs were initiated during the mid and late 1960s to improve weapons capability and extend service life: 89 F-8Ds were remanufactured as F-8Hs with more powerful J57-P-20A engines, F-8E-type underwing pylons, and *Bullpup* fire-control systems; 136 F-8Es were rebuilt as F-8Js with J57-P-20A engines and slow-speed boundary-layer control [i.e., a bleed air system over the trailing edge flaps introduced on F-8E(FN)]; 87 F-8Cs and 61 F-8Bs were re-designated as F-8Ks and F-8Ls, respectively, when they received F-8E-type underwing wing pylons and new cockpit lighting; and, finally, 73 RF-8As were remanufactured as RF-8Gs with J-57-P-20A engines, ventral strakes on the tail, and radar warning receivers.

Following three months of trials with VX-3, F8U-1s entered operational service with VF-32 in March 1957, and before the end of the year, were equipping five Navy squadrons plus Marine squadron VMF-122. As deliveries of the type continued, fourteen Navy and ten Marine squadrons were operating F-8As, -Bs, -Cs, and -Ds by the end of 1962. During the same timeframe, a number of frontline reconnaissance units also reequipped with the F8U-1P/RF-8A, and during the Cuban Missile Crisis in October 1962, two of these units, Navy squadron VFP-62 and Marine squadron VMCJ-3, flew the low-level photo sorties that provided key evidence of the presence of missiles in Cuba. As F-8Es began entering service in 1963–1964, they replaced older F-8As, -Bs, and -Cs, and many of the latter were transferred to reserve units. *Zuni*-armed F-8Es of VF-51 and VF-53 flying from *Ticonderoga* in May 1964 made the first retaliatory strike against North Vietnamese torpedo boats in the Gulf of Tonkin. From mid–1964 Navy F-8s formed the principal fighter-bomber component aboard *Essex* and *Midway* class carriers serving off the coast of Vietnam and established the best air-to-air kill ratio (i.e., 6 to 1) of any U.S. fighter during the conflict. McDonnell F-4s began to replace F-8s in the late 1960s, so that by 1972, only four active Navy squadrons remained. F-8s saw combat with five Marine squadrons in Vietnam, serving mostly from shore bases at Da Nang and Chu Lai in close air support and interdiction roles. F-8Js of VF-191 and VF-194 made their final cruise aboard *Oriskany* in 1976, by which time there were no F-8s left flying in either the Navy or Marine reserves. Photo-recon RF-8Gs enjoyed the longest Navy career, remaining active with the fleet until March 1982. Thirty-five ex-Navy F-8Hs were transferred to the Philippine Air Force in 1977 and remained in service until 1988; and the very last *Aeronavale* F-8E(FN) was withdrawn in 1999.

In 1956, as a competitor in BUAER's Mach 2 fighter contest, Vought began work on the Pratt & Whitney J75-powered XF8U-3 *Crusader II*. While having an external resemblance to the F8U-1, the XF8U-3 was virtually a new airframe. The first prototype flew in mid–1958, followed by two more prototypes; however, despite impressive performance (Mach 2.21, combat ceiling 60,000 feet), it was cancelled in late 1958 in favor of the two-place F4H-1.

Grumman F-14A/D Tomcat 1970–2006

TECHNICAL SPECIFICATIONS (F-14D)

Type: Two-place fighter-bomber
Manufacturer: Grumman Aerospace Corp., Bethpage, New York.
Total produced (all USN models): 632
Power plant: Two General Electric F110-GE-400 turbofan engines, each rated at 16,090-lbs./s.t. dry, 26,795-lbs. in afterburning.
Armament: One 20-millimeter Vulcan M61A1 rotary cannon; six AIM-7 *Sparrow* missiles and two AIM-9 *Sidewinder* missiles; or six AIM-54 *Phoenix* missiles and two AIM-9 *Sidewinder* missiles; or four AIM-54 *Phoenix,* two AIM-7 *Sparrow* missiles, and two AIM-9 *Sidewinder* missiles; or four AGM-88 *HARM* missiles; or up to 14,000-lbs. of bombs carried on fuselage and wing stations.
Performance: Max. speed, 1,544-mph (Mach 2.34) at 40,000 ft., 914-mph at s.l.; ceiling, 58,000 ft.; range, 2,400-mi. max., 640-mi. loaded.
Dimensions: Span, 64 ft. 1in. (extended), 38 ft. 2 in. (swept); length 62 ft. 8 in; wing area, 565 sq. ft.
Weights: 42,000-lbs. empty, 75,000-lbs fully loaded.

In terms of dash speed and BVR (beyond visual range) kill capability, the Grumman F-14 had no peer as a carrier-based fighter, and when the last examples left service in 2006, they were not succeeded by any type of aircraft having comparable performance. The process of bringing the F-14 to life began over forty-one years ago, in early 1966, when, amid official doubts

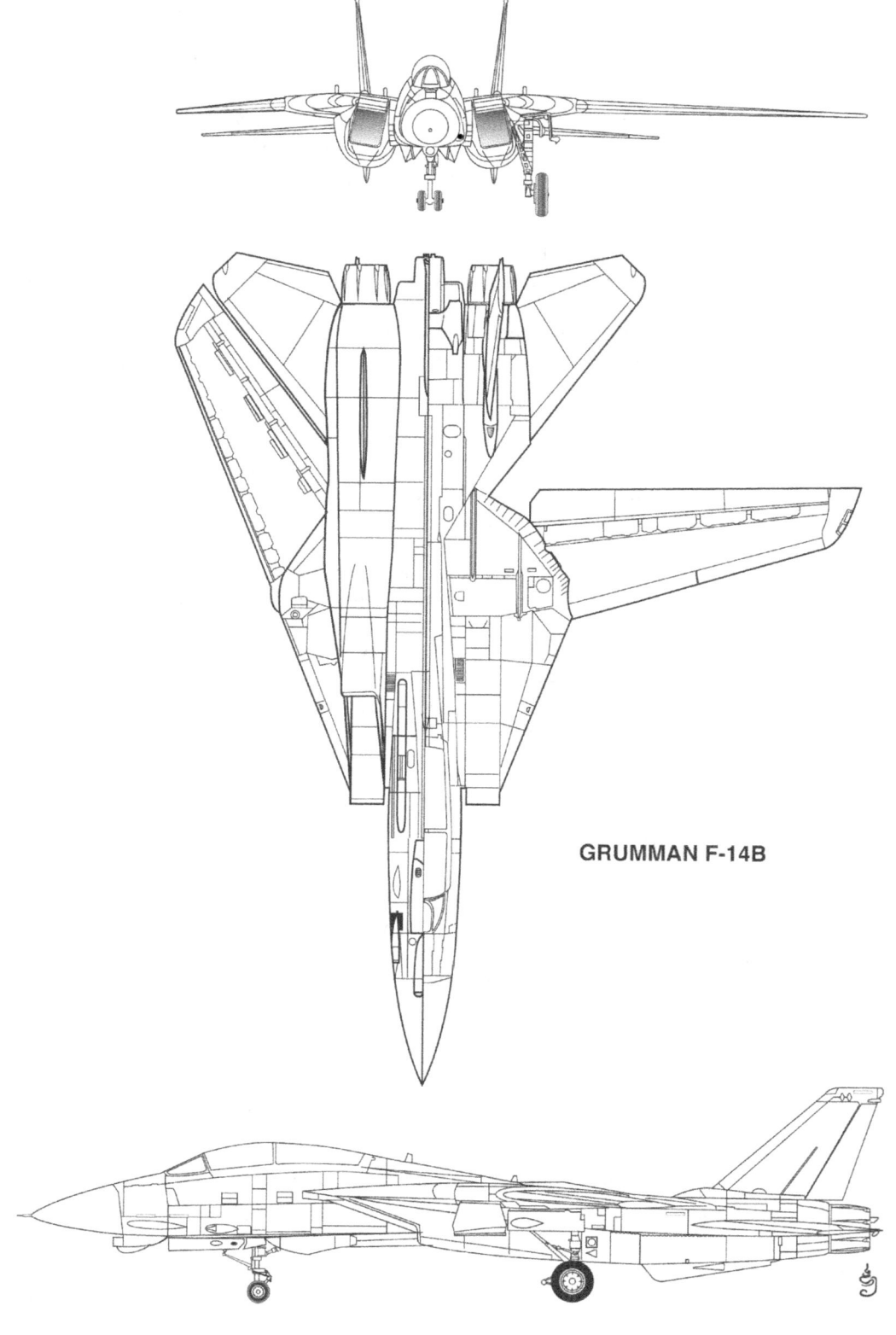

GRUMMAN F-14B

F-14A of VF-1, wings fully swept, going into the vertical. Flying from the *Enterprise*, F-14As of VF-1 made their combat debut in April 1975 when they flew patrols over Saigon during the evacuation of American personnel.

F-14B of VF-74 in the late 1980s. This unit was the first to take delivery of the improved F-14A+ that was later re-designated F-14B. The squadron was disestablished in April 1994 after 50 years of Navy service.

over the future of the F-111B project, the Navy authorized Grumman (itself a major F-111 subcontractor) to proceed with a design study for an entirely new interceptor. In mid–1968, as soon as the F-111B had officially been cancelled, the Navy asked contractors for bids on a project headed VFX (fighter experimental), a Mach 2+, two-seat deck-launched interceptor (DLI) that would replace the McDonnell F-4. The VFX requirement also specified that the aircraft be able to carry up to 14,500-lbs. of air-to-ground munitions on external racks. Grumman, with a major head start, submitted its G-303 design against four other competing proposals, and in January 1969, was picked as the winning VFX bid and given a development contract under the designation F-14A.

While borrowing the variable-geometry layout and Pratt & Whitney TF30 turbofans of the F-111B, the F-14A presented a substantially altered aerodynamic configuration which was approximately 10 per cent smaller overall. The cockpit was arranged in tandem, with the radar intercept officer seated behind the pilot. The engines, widely spaced in pod-like bays, were fed air by large, adjustable ramp intakes whose operation was controlled by a computer that monitored engine speed, air temperature, air pressure, and angle-of-attack. The aft fuselage was essentially an aerodynamic fairing between the engines that added to lift and reduced supersonic trim drag. The wings could be swept from a minimum of 20-degrees to a 68-degree maximum, with the angle being automatically controlled in flight by a Mach sweep programmer (i.e., air data computer). Full-span leading slats and trailing edge flaps were used in the slow flight regime, and the slats could also partially extend for combat maneuvering. Roll control was provided by wing-mounted spoilers up to 57-degrees of sweep, then by differential movement of the horizontal stabilizers. The F-14, then and now, carries the most the potent air-to-air armament of any interceptor in any air arm. Much of its weapons suite was derived from the F-111B, which included an AWG-9 radar and AWG-15 fire-control computer having the ability to track multiple targets at ranges of over 100 miles. The Hughes AIM-54 *Phoenix* missiles, also an F-111B by-product, can be launched from distances up to 125 miles and achieve target lock-on in the terminal attack phase via a fully-active seeker head (i.e., "fire and forget"). At medium ranges, targets may be engaged with AIM-7 *Sparrows,* and at shorter ranges, with heat-seeking AIM-9 *Sidewinders* and a 20-mm rotary cannon.

The F-14A prototype made its first flight on December 21, 1970, but was destroyed nine days later as a result of an in-flight hydraulic failure. After the second prototype flew in May 1971, the program moved swiftly, with the first production models being delivered in October 1972; service evaluations and carrier qualifications were completed by mid–1974. Total F-14A production between 1972 and 1978 numbered 557, with 80 also being built in 1974–1975 for the Iranian Air Force as the F-14AGR. Starting in 1979, fifty F-14As received full reconnaissance capabilities when modified to carry the tactical air reconnaissance pod system (TARPS), a 17-foot-long, fuselage-mounted pod that housed two cameras and an infra-red scanner. In 1973 one F-14A was given the interim designation F-14B after being re-engined with Pratt & Whitney F401-P-400 turbofans, but development was discontinued due to troubles with the engine and budgetary restrictions placed on the overall F-14 program. A second engine program begun in 1981 resulted in the development of the General Electric F110-GE-400 turbofan, following which, in mid–1984, Grumman was awarded a contract to build 38 new airframes plus convert 32 existing F-14As to the new GE engines under the designation F-14A(Plus). Deliveries were completed by mid–1990, and in May 1991 the F-14A(Plus) was re-designated F-14B.

While F-14B development was still in progress, the Navy initiated another program to produce a yet more advanced *Tomcat* derivative, which, in addition to F110 engines, would receive a state-of-the-art electronics suite, and a contract was given to Grumman in 1985 to develop a new version as the F-14D. Testing of electronic components was carried out with four F-14A development prototypes during 1986–1990, and the first definitive F-14D was flown in February 1990. The fully digital electronics suite of the F-14D centers around a multi-mode APG-71 radar which can be used for both ground mapping (air-to-ground) and air-search (air-to-air). Although the Navy had originally hoped for a production run of 127 aircraft, only 55 F-14Ds were completed, 18 of which were converted from existing F-14A airframes, and the last examples were delivered to the Navy in early 1993.

The cancellation of the A-12 in 1991 caused the Navy to seriously consider a new role for F-14s in air-to-ground operations. During the mid–1990s, all F-14Ds and F-14Bs, plus a number of F-14As, underwent a series of conversions which brought about the knick-name "Bombcat." The Bombcats were equipped with software systems enabling them to deliver precision munitions (i.e., smart bombs and AGMs) and were also retrofitted to carry low-altitude navigation and targeting infra-red for night (LANTIRN) pods which greatly enhanced the type's all-weather and night capabilities. During the 1990s, other programs to extend the *Tomcat's* service life were proposed: the *Quickstrike* F-14 envisaged a long-range strike-fighter variant with capabilities comparable to the USAF's F-15E *Strike Eagle*; the *Super Tomcat 21* offered an enhanced air superiority fighter version with twice the combat radius of the F-14D; and the Attack *Super Tomcat 21* would have been a long-range version optimized for strike. But as a consequence of the military downsizing that followed the end of the Cold War, none of these projects ever reached fruition.

The operational deployment of F-14As commenced with VF-1 and VF-2 aboard *Enterprise* in September 1974, followed within months by VF-14 (*Kitty Hawk*) and VF-32 (*John F. Kennedy*). And over the next eleven years, all frontline Navy fighter units exchanged their F-4s for F-14s. In the two decades following, F-14s saw extensive employment in their air superiority role: flying top cover over Saigon in 1975 during the American withdrawal from Vietnam;

recording the first *Tomcat* air victories in 1981 against two Libyan Su-22 *Fitters* in the Gulf of Sidra; supporting U.S. military campaigns in Lebanon and Grenada in 1983; escorting retaliatory strikes in Libya in 1986; in another Gulf of Sidra incident in 1989, shooting-down a pair of Libyan MiG-23 *Floggers*; and providing high cover over the Persian Gulf in 1988–1989 during the so-called 'tanker war.' All through the course of Operation *Desert Storm* in 1991, F-14s maintained air superiority near the carriers and escorted Navy strike packages, but encountered little opposition from Iraqi fighters during the campaign. The phase-out of F-14As began soon after the Gulf War, with ten squadrons having been disestablished by the end of 1996.

F-14s were used for the first time in air-to-ground operations in Bosnia in 1995, and LANTIRN-equipped Bombcats made their combat debut in December 1998, flying air strikes against Iraqi targets during Operation *Desert Fox*. After September 1, 2001, as part of Operation *Enduring Freedom* in Afghanistan, Bombcats flew close-support strikes and marked targets with LANTIRN for F/A-18s. F-14s may have participated in the American invasion of Iraq in the spring of 2003, but details are not known at the time of this writing. The departure of the *Tomcat* from the fleet in of 2006 marked the end of a long line of Grumman "cats" going back 76 years.

McDonnell-Douglas F/A-18 Hornet 1978–Present

TECHNICAL SPECIFICATIONS (F/A-18C)
Type: Single or two-place fighter/attack
Manufacturer: McDonnell-Douglas Corp. (now Boeing Aerospace), St. Louis, Missouri.
Total produced (USN/USMC models): 1,048 A/Ds, 548 E/Fs planned.
Power plant: Two General Electric F404-GE-400 turbofans, each rated at 10,600-lbs./s.t.dry, 15,800-lbs. in afterburning.
Armament: One 20-millimeter Vulcan M61A1 rotary cannon; two AIM-120 AMRAAM missiles and two AIM-9 *Sidewinder* missiles, or two AIM-7 *Sparrow* missiles and two AIM-9 *Sidewinders*, or six AIM-9 *Sidewinders* (air-to-air load); or up to 13,700-lbs. of ordnance on nine external stations (air-to-ground load).
Performance: Max. speed 1,196-mph (Mach 1.8) at 36,000 ft.; ceiling 50,000 ft.; range 1,800+ mi. max., 580 mi. loaded.
Weights: 23,831-lbs. empty, 56,000-lbs. max.
Dimensions: Span 37 ft. 6 in., length 56 ft., wing area 400 sq. ft.

The F/A-18 *Hornet*, which currently serves as Navy and Marine aviation's principal air superiority and strike aircraft, has been produced (1978–2007) longer than any other type of naval combat plane, and if predictions hold true, will remain in production another seven years. The origins of the F/A-18 can be traced to the late 1960s, when, following cancellation of the ill-fated F-111B, the Navy began to actively seek a multi-role aircraft that would not only accomplish the missions of the Douglas A-4, Grumman A-6, and LTV A-7, but possess the air-to-air capabilities of the McDonnell F-4 as well. During the early 1970s, a number of ideas were generated under the heading VFAX (carrier fighter-attack experimental) but none were approved. In late 1974, as an alternative to VFAX, the U.S. Congress directed the Navy to investigate development of the General Dynamics YF-16 and the Northrop YF-17, the two USAF candidates in the LWF/ACF (light-weight fighter/air combat fighter) competition. After considering both types, Navy officials concluded that the airframe design and twin-engine layout of the YF-17 came closer to meeting naval requirements. Since Northrop had no recent experience with carrier-based aircraft, McDonnell-Douglas was brought in to collaborate on a naval adaptation of the YF-17. Originally, the design proposal called for distinct fighter and attack versions, but subsequent advancements in the development of the avionics and weapons systems made it practical to merge both functions into a single airframe. In January 1976, after

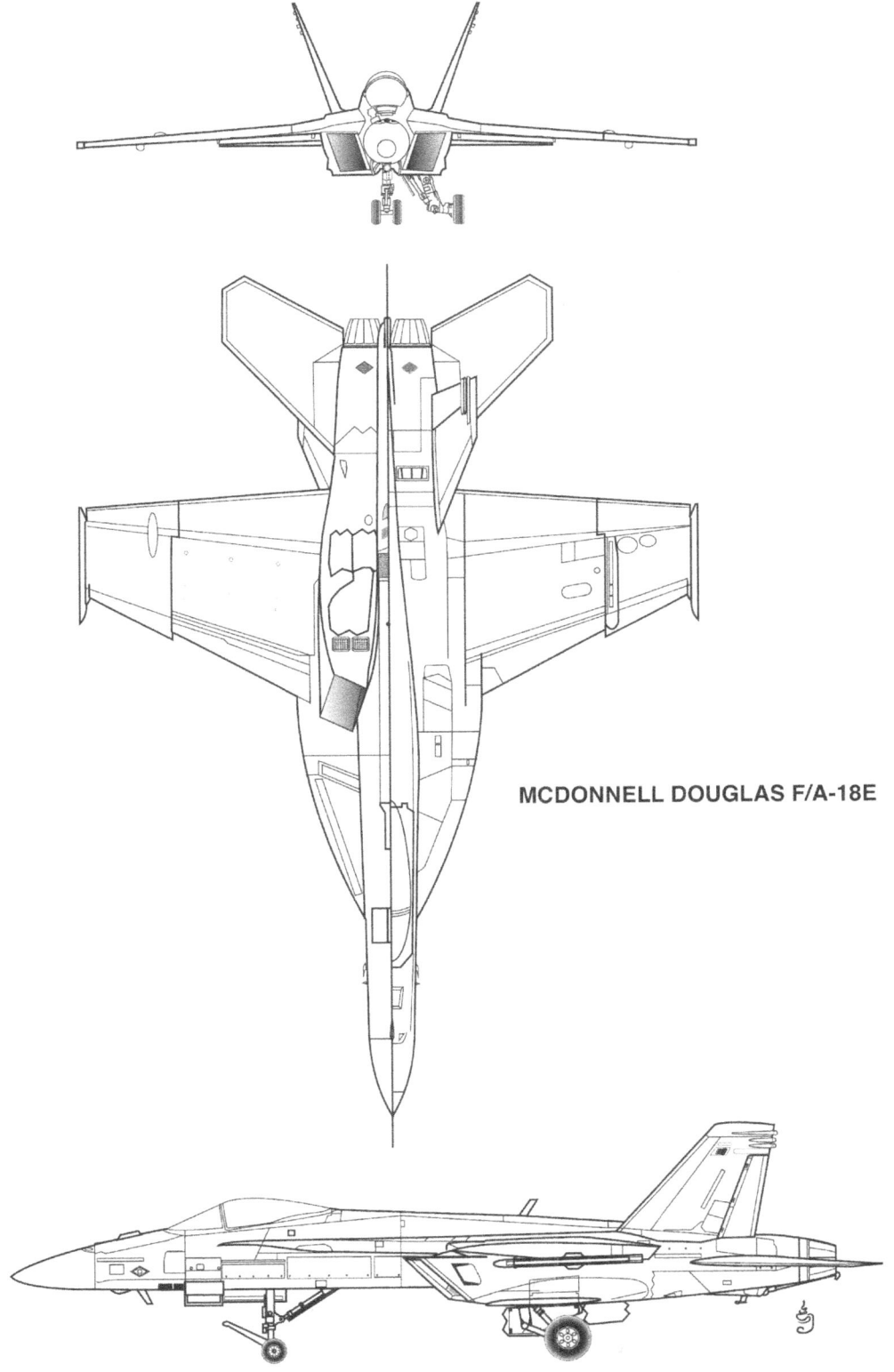

MCDONNELL DOUGLAS F/A-18E

Top: One of the eleven pre-production F-18As delivered to the Navy for evaluation during 1979 and 1980. Deliveries of production started in mid–1980 and the type's official designation was changed to F/A-18A in April 1984. *Bottom:* A block 24 F/A-18C serving with VFA-82 "Marauders" while deployed aboard the *America*. The "300" side number indicates the squadron commander's aircraft. Note AIM-120 AMRAAMs carried inboard.

Two-seat F/A-18F of VFA-106. The Es and Fs are easily identifiable by their larger, more squared-off intakes. The Navy plans to acquire a minimum of 548 F/A-18E/Fs by the end of 2010. None have been ordered by the Marine Corps.

the design work had been approved, McDonnell-Douglas/ Northrop received a contract for nine single-seat development aircraft as the F-18A and two two-seat trainers as the TF-18A.

While following the general aerodynamic configuration of the YF-17, the F-18 was in fact an entirely new design. To save weight, graphite/epoxy composite materials were used in the structures of the fuselage, wings, and tail surfaces. Integration of air superiority and strike functions was made possible by extensive use of digital computer technology in the control and weapons systems. It was the first production naval aircraft to employ 'fly-by-wire,' a control system in which the aircraft was literally flown through a computer. Control inputs from the pilot were transmitted to a digital processor, which simultaneously analyzed the signal against flight data (i.e., airspeed, altitude, angle-of-attack, etc.) and moved the control surfaces accordingly. All flight and tactical information was depicted on a heads-up-display (HUD) and two multi-function display screens on the instrument panel. The systems were primarily managed via hands-on-throttle-and stick (HOTAS) controls that placed all important switches at the pilot's fingertips. Avionics included an automatic carrier landing system (ACLS), which permitted arrested landings in zero visibility conditions. The Hughes APG-65 radar could be configured to track targets in either air-to-air or air-to-ground modes, permitting the aircraft to perform *both* missions on the same sortie.

The first F-18A flew on November 18, 1978, and all eleven development aircraft were flying by March 1980. The original production order specified 780 aircraft and was later raised to 1366. Deliveries of production F/TF-18As began in May 1980, and the type became fully operational in early 1983. In April 1984, the official designations of the F-18A and TF-18A were changed to F/A-18A and F/A-18B, respectively. The two-seat F/A-18B retained full mission capability with only six percent less internal fuel. After delivery of 371 of F/A-18As and 39 F/A-18Bs, production switched to the F/A-18C/D, which flew for the first time in September 1987. The differences between A/B models and the F/A-18C/D were entirely internal, i.e., an improved mission computer and countermeasures systems plus compatibility with AIM-120 *AMRAMM* air-to-air missiles and AGM-65 *Maverick* and AGM-64 *Harpoon* air-to-ground missiles. Since 1988, F/A-18C/Ds have been equipped to full night-attack standard with a thermal imaging navigation system, forward looking infra-red (FLIR) targeting pod, and night vision equipment. Starting with 1991 production blocks, F/A-18C/Ds came with F-404-GE-402 powerplants raising available thrust by 1,800-lbs. per engine. In the mid–1990s the F/A-18's APG-65 radar was replaced by the APG-73 system providing faster processing speed and enlarged memory. *Hornet* production continued unabated when Boeing acquired McDonnell-Douglas in August 1997, and the final example of the C/D series, an F/A-18D, was delivered in August 2000.

The Navy had originally hoped to replace the F/A-18 with a navalized version of the USAF's advanced tactical fighter (ATF), but as events turned out, the winning entry, the Lockheed YF-22, proved to be too costly to supply the numbers of aircraft that would be needed after the year 2000. Because of the risks associated with ATF, the Navy simultaneously investigated the feasibility of procuring an improved derivative of the F/A-18 under a plan known as *Hornet 2000*, which eventually led, in early 1992, to a contract for the development of the F/A-18E (single-seat) and F (two-seat) *Super Hornet*. Though sharing 90 percent of the F/A-18C/D's avionics and software, the F/A-18E/F has been redesigned to include state-of-the-art cockpit displays, a 34-inch fuselage extension, two additional multi-mission weapons stations, a 25 percent increase in wing area, a 35 percent increase in engine power (General Electric F414-GE-400 engines with 22,000-lbs./s.t. each), and a 33 percent increase in internal fuel capacity. At a slight cost in top speed (Mach 1.6), the *Super Hornet* possesses a 40 percent improvement in combat range (800 miles) and can carry a 30 percent greater external load (17,750-lbs.) The first F/A-18E flew in November 1995, delivery of production models began in late 1998, and the type entered operational service in late 1999. Under current contracts, the Navy intends to buy a minimum of 548 *Super Hornets* through 2010, with tentative plans to keep the type in production until 2014.

In 2002 Boeing received the go-ahead to develop the EA-18G *Growler*, a two-seat electronic countermeasures version of the F/A-18F that will over time replace the Grumman EA-6B *Prowler*. Because of advances in computerization, the EF-18G will not only undertake the electronic warfare mission of the four-seat EA-6B, but will also keep much of the F/A-18F's offensive capability. Production of least 90 EA-18Gs is planned according to current estimates.

In late 1980 and early 1981, after completing operational evaluations with VX-4 and VX-5, F/A-18A/Bs were initially issued to VFA-125 and VFA-106 and VMFAT-101 for training purposes, and in early 1983, Marine squadrons VMFA-314 and VMFA-323 were the first to become fully operational with the type. As deliveries continued over the next five years, F-18A/Bs supplanted A-7s and F-4s in most fleet squadrons and A-4s and F-4s in Marine squadrons. When deliveries of F/A-18C/Ds started in the late 1980s, some F/A-18A/Bs were transferred to Navy and Marine reserve units. In March 1986, *Hornets* saw their first combat action in the Gulf of Sidra during Operation *Prairie Fire*, making the first operational use of AGM-88A *HARM* missiles against shore-based Libyan SAM sites. During Operation *Desert Storm* in 1991, Navy and Marine F/A-18s, operating from carriers and shores bases, flew a diversity of missions including fleet air defense, SEAD (suppression of enemy air defenses), interdiction, close air support, and counter air support, and F/A-18Cs of VFA-81 scored the first *Hornet* air-to-air kills when they shot down two Iraqi F-7As (Chinese-built MiG-21s). Since *Desert Storm*, the F/A-18 has become naval aviation's principal strike aircraft, equipping thirty-four Navy and twenty

Marine frontline squadrons by the mid–1990s. By the end of 2002, the combined *Hornet* fleet had achieved its five-millionth flight hour.

VFA-115 became the first Navy squadron to be declared combat-ready with F/A-18E *Super Hornets* in June 2001, and the type is equipping four more active squadrons as of mid–2004. After September 11, 2001, *Super Hornets* of VFA-115 flew missions off Afghanistan in support of Operation *Enduring Freedom* and more recently, saw action in Operation *Iraqi Freedom*, where they flew air defense sorties and expended more than 380,000-lbs. of munitions. In addition to Navy and Marine production, the F/A-18 has been one of the most widely exported American military aircraft over the past 20 years: Canada, 98 CF-18A and 40 CF-18B; Australia, 57 F/A-18A and 18 F/A-18B (upgraded to C/D status); Spain, 60 EF-18A and 12 EF-18B (E = Espana; upgraded to C/D status); Finland, 57 F/A-18C and 7 F/A-18D; Malaysia, 8 F/A-18D; Kuwait, 21 F/A-18C and 8 F/A-18D; and Switzerland, 26 F/A-18C and 8 F/A-18D.

Northrop-Grumman X-47 Pegasus UCAV-N 2003–Present

TECHNICAL SPECIFICATIONS X-47A [X-47B]
Type: Unmanned attack system
Manufacturer: Northrop-Grumman Aerospace Corp., El Segundo, California.
Total produced: 1 X-47A; 2 X-47Bs ordered.
Power plant: One Pratt & Whitney JT15D-5C non-afterburning, high-bypass turbofan rated at 3,190-lbs. /s.t. dry (same engine as used in the Beech T-1A *Jayhawk* and several business jets). [The engine to be used on the X-47B has not been revealed].
Armament: None. [X-47B projected 4,500-lb. munitions payload to include bombs, GBUs, anti-radiation missiles, JDAMs, and other as yet unspecified air-to-ground weapons.]
Performance (estimated): Cruise speed subsonic [Mach 0.85], combat ceiling 35,000 ft. [40,000 ft.]; range 1,000 mi. [X-47B expected to have unrefueled range of 3,000 mi. with combat load.]
Weights: 3,836-lbs. empty, 5,905-lbs. max. loaded. [Weights of the X-47B have yet to be determined.]
Dimensions: Span 27 ft. 8 in., length 27 ft. 11 in., wing area 389 sq. ft. [Dimensions of the X-47B have yet to be finalized.]

Currently being developed under the acronym UCAV-N (unmanned combat air vehicle—naval), the Northrop-Grumman X-47 is the first carrier-borne attack aircraft designed from the outset to be a pilotless system. Unmanned air vehicles (UAVs) in various forms (e.g., target drones, glide bombs, cruise missiles, etc.) have been used since World War II, but the level of technology that enables them to perform more complex, two-way missions is a fairly recent development. Just within the past twenty years, reconnaissance UAVs capable of transmitting 'real time' information have evolved from miniature aircraft powered by snowmobile or motorcycle engines (e.g., the AAI Corp./Israel Aircraft Industries *Pioneer*, operational in 1986 and deployed by the Army, Navy, and Marine Corps during the Gulf War in 1991) to larger, more versatile systems like the General Atomics Aeronautical Systems, Inc. RQ-1 *Predator*, which became fully operational in 1999 during the Kosovo campaign. The *Predator*, nominally a full-size aircraft (span 41 ft. 8 in., gross weight 2,250-lbs.) carrying an array of electro-optical, infra-red, and radar sensor equipment, can be controlled beyond line-of-sight range via a satellite downlink, then loiter on station for up to 24 hours. The even newer, jet-powered Northrop-Grumman RQ-4A *Global Hawk* is larger yet (span 116 ft., gross weight 25,600-lbs.) and can range almost 14,000 miles at speeds up to 400-mph and altitudes up to 65,000 ft. *Global Hawks* began entering service with the USAF in late 2001; a definitive naval version specially equipped for maritime operations, made its first flight in November 2004.

In the mid–1990s, the Defense Advanced Research Projects Agency (DARPA) began seriously considering the possibility of developing a UAV with offensive capabilities, i.e., an unmanned combat air vehicle (UCAV). Since that time, two major programs have materialized

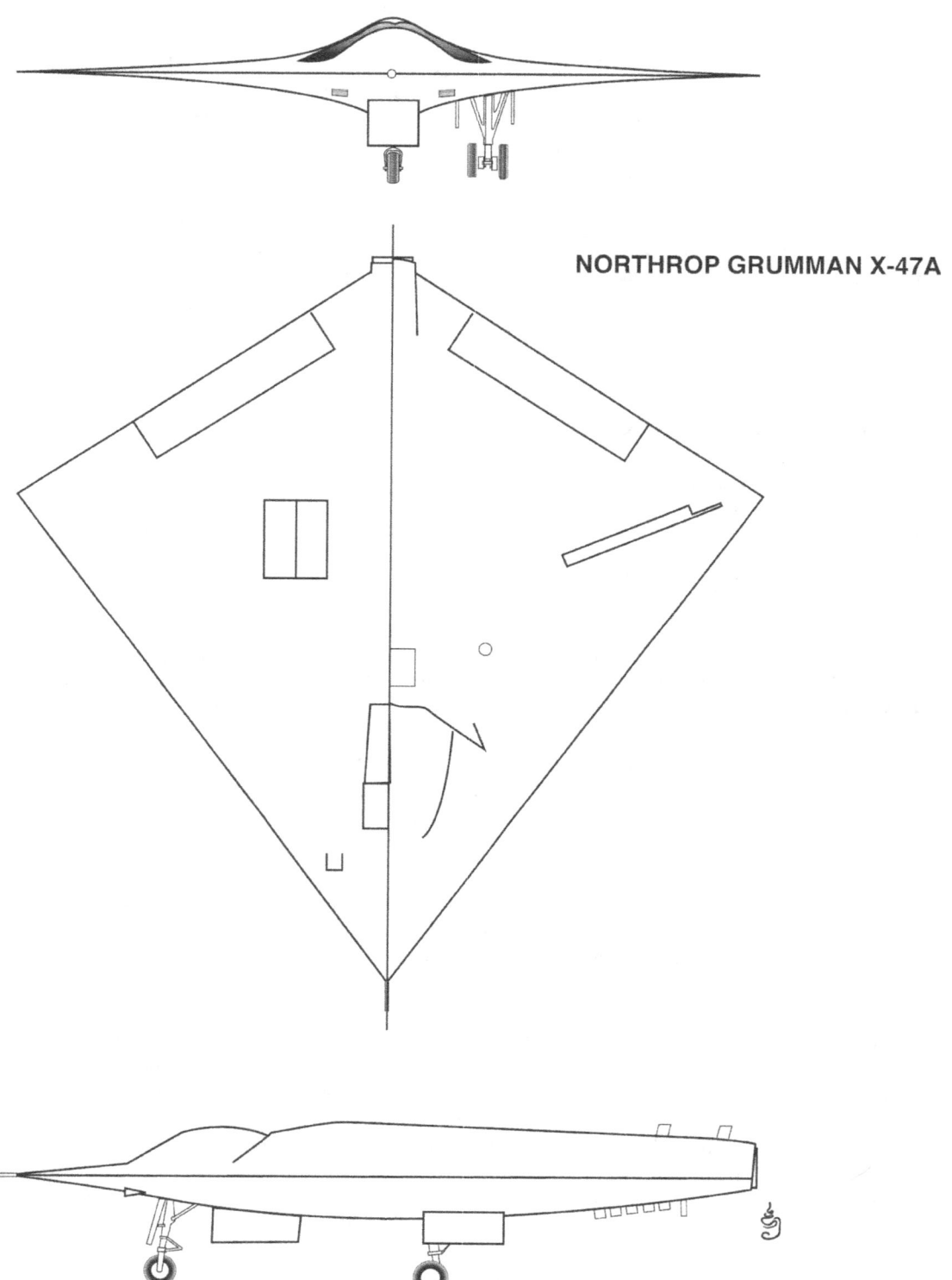

NORTHROP GRUMMAN X-47A

Mockup of X-47B showing detail of wing fold. Its aerodynamic similarity to the B-2 is apparent. Initially, UCAVs are envisaged as operating cooperatively with manned aircraft to undertake more dangerous missions like SEAD and armed reconnaissance.

under DARPA supervision: the USAF's Boeing X-45 land-based UCAV in 1999 and the Navy's Northrop-Grumman X-47 carrier-based UCAV-N in 2000. The X-45A demonstrator made its first flight in May 2002 and the X-47A was flown in February 2003; and at the time of this writing, both aircraft are reportedly in the concept demonstration phase of flight testing. In the foreseeable future, DARPA envisages fully operational UCAVs as working cooperatively with manned systems such as F-15s, F-16s, F/A-18s, F-35s, and AV-8s, undertaking inherently dangerous missions such as suppression of enemy air defenses (SEAD); over a longer term, however, UCAVs are seen as possibly being developed to the level where they can completely supplant manned aircraft in the tactical role!

In a move that bears a strong resemblance to the earlier JSF contest, the UCAV program underwent a major shift in June 2003 when DARPA announced that the X-45 and X-47 programs were to be merged under the title Joint Unmanned Combat Air Systems (J-UCAS). Like JSF, the goal of J-UCAS will be to eventually select a single prime contractor to manufacture the definitive UCAV production model. Current plans are to obtain two X-45Cs and two X-47Bs for the purpose of comparative evaluations, at the conclusion of which (possibly 2010) a winner will be selected. The J-UCAS requirements for UCAV/UCAV-N are still evolving but at present include: (1) low-observable [stealth] airframe; (2) cruise speed Mach 0.85 [e.g., 564-mph at 35,000 ft.]; (3) ceiling 40,000 ft. [12,200m]; (4) combat range 1,495 mi. [2,400km]; (5) munitions payload 4,500-lbs. [2,040kg]; (6) internal weapons bays plus wing pylons for external stores; (7) mid-air refueling capability; (8) a synthetic aperture radar/moving target indicator [SAR/MTI] system; and finally, (9) a unit cost in the range of $10 to $15 Million per aircraft. (Note, SAR employs a relatively small antenna to produce a broad beam by utilizing the Doppler shift of the signal moving across a target to create the azimuth [i.e., horizontal direction] resolution of a vary narrow beam; MTI processes the radar signal to show only targets that are in motion.)

On the Navy side of the project, the Northrop-Grumman X-47A demonstrator appeared in early 2003 as an arrowhead-shaped flying wing planform. Its low-observable shape arises from a leading edge sweep of 55-degrees, a trailing edge taper of 35-degress, and the absence of any vertical tail surfaces. The avionics, engine, and accessories are buried in a bulged wing center-section. Three-axis control is maintained by a combination of elevons and "inlaids," which are spoiler-type devices hinged to the top and bottom wings forward of the wingtips that can induce yaw or act as speed brakes. Fabrication of the X-47A's largely all-carbon composite airframe was sub-contacted to Burt Rutan's Scaled Composites, Inc. Although designed to withstand the stress of carrier landings, the X-47A demonstrator was completed without arresting gear. The aircraft's nerve center is a fully-integrated vehicle management computer (VMC) that simultaneously processes all data for flight and engine control, mission command and control, and navigation. The VMC hardware also incorporates "brick wall" memory and processor partitions that enable the system to perform multiple tasks without degrading performance.

The follow-on X-47B is scheduled to make its first flight sometime in 2007 and thereafter commence a two to three-year operational assessment phase. Drawings and mockups of the X-47B indicate the addition of constant chord wing extensions that will presumably improve maneuverability and the low-speed stability needed for carrier operations. Planners within J-UCAS hope that UCAVs will be ready to be introduced into actual military operations sometime after 2010. Are we on the verge of a paradigm shift in military aviation? If UCAVs can be successfully developed into reliable tactical weapons platforms, some defense analysts predict that the current F-35 JSF program will be seriously cut back. In March 2006, the Department of Defense announced that USAF participation in J-UCAS had been cancelled and only the UCAV-N portion of the program (i.e., X-47) would be continued.

APPENDIX 1

Attack Aircraft Designations and Nomenclature

USAAC, USAAF, AND USAF ATTACK AIRCRAFT

A standardized alpha-numeric system for designating different types of Army aircraft first appeared in 1919, and with variations, a comparable system remains in effect today. In 1948, the USAF officially dropped the "A" for attack designation, so that the A-26, the only designated attack type then active, became the B-26; and similarly, pursuit (P) was changed to fighter (F), so that the P-51 became the F-51, and so on. When the tri-service system for all U.S. military aircraft was adopted in September 1962, it terminated the numeric sequence of preexisting USAF aircraft types and started over. Except in the case of the F-110A, which was re-designated F-4C, the old attack, bomber, and fighter designations ended with A-45, B-87, and F-111, respectively. The anomalous application of F-117 to the first stealth fighter in the early 1980s is explained in the text. With occasional caveats, the alpha-numeric system is normally expressed in the following order: SUB-VERSION—TYPE—TYPE NUMBER—VERSION. For example, OA-10A translates to: O = Forward Air Control Sub-Version, A = Attack, -10 = Tenth Type, and A = First Version. When improvements or changes are made to a major version, it is generally expressed as a production block suffix number, e.g., F-86F-30 (denotes 30th production block) or F-16C-50 (denotes 50th production block). An "X" preceding the designation generally reflects experimental status and a "Y" or "Y1" indicates a pre-production service test model. While not covering all possible USAAC, USAAF, and USAF designations, the following will provide a key to the letters and numbers applicable to the specific aircraft types covered in Part I of this book:

Type Designations		*Dates Used*
A =	Attack/Light Bombardment	1924–1948
A =	Attack	1964–Present
B =	Bomber, Medium and Heavy	1924–1948
B =	Bomber, Tactical and Strategic	1948–Present
C =	Cargo and Transport	1924–Present
F =	Fighter	1948–Present
OV =	Armed Reconnaissance	1965–1995
P =	Pursuit	1924–1948
T =	Trainer	1948–Present

Sub-Version	Dates Used
A = Attack	1948–Present
E = Electronic Warfare and ECM	1948–Present
J = Suppression of Enemy Air Defenses	1992–Present
N = Night Attack	1967–1970
O = Forward Air Control	1990–Present
R = Tactical Reconnaissance	1948–Present
T = Trainer	1948–Present
X = Experimental	1924–Present
Y = Pre-Production Service Test Model	1940–Present
Y1 = Service Test Production Batch	1924–1940

USN AND USMC ATTACK AIRCRAFT

A standardized system for designating different types of naval aircraft first appeared in 1922 and remained in effect with minor variations until September 1962, after which a common tri-service designation system was adopted for all aircraft serving within U.S. military branches. The pre–1962 system used a combination of letters and numbers to identify particular aircraft, in the following order: TYPE—MODEL—MANUFACTURER—VERSION—SUB-VERSION. For example, SB2C-4E translates to: SB = Scout Bomber, 2 = Second Model, C = Curtiss-Wright Corporation, -4 = Fourth Version, and E = Radar-Equipped Sub-Version. The tri-service system uses the following order: SUB-VERSION—TYPE—TYPE NUMBER—VERSION. For example, OA-4M translates to: O = Forward Air Control Sub-Version, A = Attack, -4 = Fourth Type, and M = Eleventh Version (note, "I" is never used and "D," in this example, was skipped to avoid confusion with the pre–1962 designation). An "X" preceding the designation generally denotes experimental status and a "Y" indicates a pre-production service test model. The following does not list all possible naval aircraft designations but will nonetheless provide a key to the letters and numbers applicable to the specific aircraft types covered in Part II of this book:

Type Designations	Dates Used
A = Attack	1946–Present
AV = Attack V/STOL	1971–Present
B = Bomber	1929–1940
BF = Bomber-Fighter	1934–1937
BT = Bomber-Torpedo	1943–1946
F = Fighter	1925–Present
O = Observation	1925–1935
S = Scout	1925–1935
SB = Scout Bomber	1934–1946
T = Torpedo	1925–1934
TB = Torpedo-Bomber	1934–1946
TS = Torpedo-Scout	1943–1946

Sub-Versions	Dates Used
B = Special Armament	1942–1950
B = Nuclear Capable	1951–1962
C = Special Armament	1942–1946
E = Radar Equipped	1942–1946
E = Early-Warning/Countermeasures (ECM)	1962–Present
F = Night/All-Weather Operations	1962–1968
M = Missile-Carrying	1953–1962

Sub-Versions   *Dates Used*
N = Night/All-Weather Operations   1942–1962
NA = Reconfigured to Day Attack   1953–1962
NE = All-Weather fighter-bomber   1955–1962
NL = Night/Cold Weather Operations   1950–1962
O = Forward Air Control   1978–1994
Q = Countermeasures (ECM)   1945–1962
W = Early-Warning   1945–1962
X = Experimental   1925–Present
Y = Service Test Model   1946–Present

Manufacturer Identifier   *Dates Used*
A = Brewster   1935–1945
B = Boeing   1925–1946
C = Curtiss-Wright   1925–1946
D = Douglas   1925–1962
D = McDonnell   1944–1947
F = Grumman   1931–1962
F = Canadian-Fairchild   1942–1947
G = Great lakes   1928–1940
G = Goodyear   1942–1953
H = McDonnell   1947–1962
J = Berliner-Joyce   1930–1934
J = North American   1936–1962
K = Kaiser-Fleetwings   1943–1946
M = Martin   1925–1962
M = General Motors   1942–1945
N = Naval Aircraft Factory   1925–1960
T = Northrop   1935–1946
U = Chance Vought   1926–1962
W = Canadian Car & Foundry   1942–1947
Y = Consolidated (later Convair)   1931–1962

APPENDIX 2

Attack Aircraft Unit Organization

USAAC, USAAF, AND USAF ATTACK UNITS

Since World War I, the U.S. Army Air Service, and after it, the U.S. Army Air Corps (USAAC), U.S. Army Air Forces (USAAF), and U.S. Air Force (USAF) have all used a simple system of numbers followed by acronyms to abbreviate air combat and support units (e.g., 3rd TFW = Third Tactical Fighter Wing). The following lists the acronyms that appear in Part I of this book:

Acronym	Description	Acronym	Description
ACS	Air Commando Squadron	FTW	Flying Training Wing
ACW	Air Commando Wing	FW	Fighter Wing
AG	Attack Group	OTU	Operational Training Unit
AS	Attack Squadron	PG	Pursuit Group
BG	Bombardment/Bomb Group	PS	Pursuit Squadron
BG(L)	Bombardment Group (Light)	SAS	Strategic Aerospace Squadron
BG(M)	Bombardment Group (Medium)	SAW	Strategic Aerospace Wing
BG(T)	Bomb Group (Tactical)	SOS	Special Operations Squadron
BS	Bombardment/Bomb Squadron	SOW	Special Operations Wing
BW	Bomb Wing	SRS	Strategic Reconnaissance Squadron
BW(L)	Bomb Wing (Light)	SRW	Strategic Reconnaissance Wing
BW(T)	Bomb Wing (Tactical)	TASS	Tactical Air Support Squadron
CCTW	Combat Crew Training Wing	TBS	Tactical Bomb Squadron
CCTS	Combat Crew Training Squadron	TBW	Tactical Bomb Wing
CTS	Combat Training Squadron	TFS	Tactical Fighter Squadron
DET	Detachment	TFW	Tactical Fighter Wing
ECS	Electronic Combat Squadron	TFTS	Tactical Fighter Training Squadron
FBG	Fighter-Bomber Group	TFTW	Tactical Fighter Training Wing
FBS	Fighter-Bomber Squadron	TRS	Tactical Reconnaissance Squadron
FBW	Fighter-Bomber Wing	TRW	Tactical Reconnaissance Wing
FIS	Fighter Interceptor Squadron	TTS	Tactical Training Squadron
FIW	Fighter Interceptor Wing	TTW	Tactical Training Wing
FS	Fighter Squadron		

Groups and squadrons formed the basic organizational element of USAAC and USAAF air combat units until 1947, when the newly established USAF began creating operational wings. However, many of the preexisting air groups continued their unit identity within the new wing structure. Unlike the divisions and wings seen during World War II, which were variegated organizations controlling a mixture of operational and administrative functions, the postwar operational air wings are typically self-supporting entities which have a specified mission activity at an assigned base. The 388th Fighter Wing, presently operating three F-16C squadrons and their seven support units out of Hill AFB in Utah, stands as a good example. It was activated in 1953 as a fighter-bomber wing (FBW) and deactivated in 1957; reactivated in 1962 as a tactical fighter wing (TFW) and deactivated for a second time in 1964; reactivated again in 1966 as a TFW, with its named being shortened to fighter wing (FW) in the mid–1990s, when the USAF ceased to recognize the distinction between tactical fighter and fighter interceptor units.

USN and USMC Attack Units

Squadrons have formed the basic organizational component for both Navy and Marine aviation units since the post–World War I era. Standard nomenclature for aviation squadrons was first adopted by the Navy Department in 1920, and with variations, the same system is still in use today. Using a scheme analogous to aircraft, squadrons have been identified by a combination of letters and a number, i.e.: AIRCRAFT CATEGORY—MISSION—SECONDARY OR SPECIAL MISSION (when applicable)—SQUADRON NUMBER. For example, VAH-2 translates to: V = Heavier-Than-Air, Fixed-Wing, A = Attack, H = Heavy, and -2 = Squadron Number Two. The secondary or special mission letter has sometimes been expressed parenthetically, as in VA(H). Since 1924, Marine Corps squadrons have been distinguished by the letter "M," initially as a suffix (e.g., VB-6M), but after 1937, as part of the prefix (e.g., VMB-1). With respect to the aircraft covered in Part II of this book, their squadron and mission assignments may be identified by the following acronyms:

Acronym	Description	Acronym	Description
VA	Attack	VFA	Fighter-Attack/Strike-Fighter
VA(AW)	All-Weather Attack	VF(AW)	Fighter All-Weather
VAH or VA(H)	Heavy Attack	VFC	Composite Fighter
VA(HM)	Attack Mining	VFN or VF(N)	Night Fighter
VAK	Tactical Aerial Refueling	VO	Observation
VAL or VA(L)	Light Attack	VS	Scouting
VAQ	Tactical Countermeasures	VS	Anti-Submarine (ASW)
VB	Bombing	VMSB	Marine Scout Bombing
VBF	Bombing-Fighter	VT	Torpedo and Bombing
VC	Composite Squadrons	VMTB	Marine Torpedo and Bombing
VCN	Night Composite Squadron	VTN	Night Torpedo
VF	Fighter	VX	Experimental

As carriers began entering the fleet in the 1920s, the aviation squadrons assigned to them were organized into carrier air groups (CVGs) and initially identified by their carrier (e.g., *Saratoga* Air Group) but after 1942 were identified by number (e.g., beginning with CVG-9). In 1944, CVGs were reorganized according to carrier affiliation—CVBG (large), CVG (medium), CVLG (light), and CVEG (escort)—and in 1946, reorganized again—CVBG (battle), CVG (attack), CVLG (light), and CVEG (escort). Then in 1948 all carrier air groups reverted back to CVG irrespective of carrier affiliation. Starting in 1958, replacement air groups were identified as RAGs and combat readiness air groups as CRAGs, and in 1960, antisubmarine carrier air groups as CVSGs. In 1963, all groups were renamed wings and became, respectively, CVWs, RAWs, CRAWs, and CVSWs. In 1968, the Naval Air Reserve was reorganized into wings known as CVWRs.

APPENDIX 3

Attack Aircraft Designs That Never Flew

Illustrated and described below are attack aircraft proposals, which, despite receiving official military designations, never progressed beyond the detailed design or mockup stages of development or were ultimately flown under different designations.

USAAC, USAAF, AND USAF ATTACK DESIGNS

Designation	Manufacturer	Dates
A-15	Glenn L. Martin Co.	1934–1935
A-39	Kaiser-Fleetwings Corp.	1942–1943
A-40	See, SB3C under Paragraph B, below	
A-42	See, B-42 in Part I, above	
A-43 (F-87)	Curtiss-Wright Corp.	1944–1948
A-44	See, B-53 under Paragraph A, below	
A-45	See, B-51 in Part I, above	
B-53	Convair Aircraft Corp.	1944–1948
B-68	Glenn L. Martin Co.	1952–1957
D-188A (F-109)	Bell Aircraft Corp.	1959–1961

Martin A-15 (1934–1935)

The limited speed, range, and payload of single-engine attack types (e.g., A-8/12, A-17) developed in the early and mid–1930s gave some Army officials serious doubts about their adequacy in combat, while, at the same time, Depression Era budget restraints had the effect of placing development of more complex aircraft on hold. In 1934, out of a desire to make use of an existing design, the USAAC's Material Division studied the feasibility of converting a Martin B-10 bomber to an attack configuration. By reducing bomb load and associated equipment, the XA-15 would be a ton lighter than the bomber version and reach an estimated top speed of 215-mph. But before any progress could be made, the private venture Curtiss XA-14 (see, Part I, above) flew in mid–1935, and its performance (i.e., 254-mph top speed) surpassed the XA-15 by such a margin that the project was abandoned.

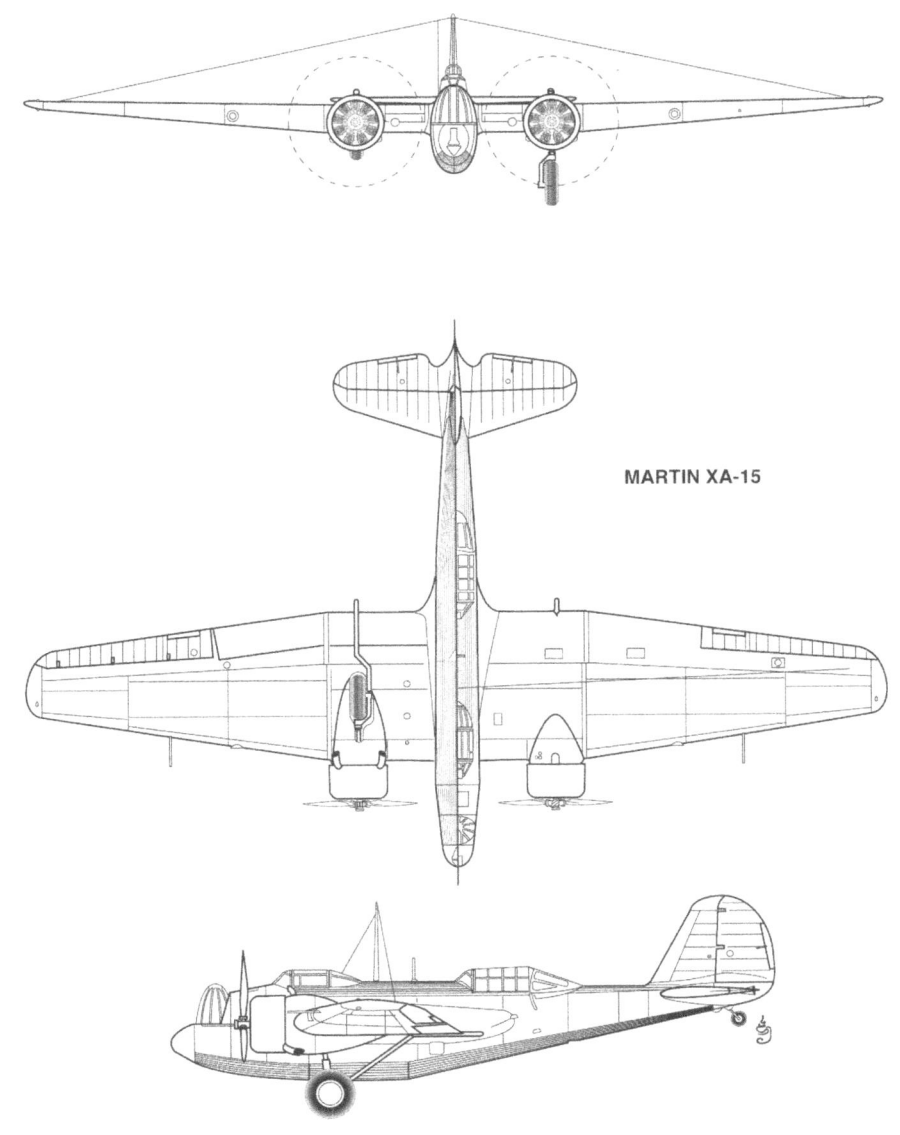

Kaiser-Fleetwings A-39 (1942–1943)

Little is known about the XA-39 other than it was apparently an early attempt by Kaiser-Fleetwings (a pseudonym for the aviation division of Henry J. Kaiser's mammoth industrial concern) to interest the USAAF in an in-house aircraft design. Some sources list the XA-39 as a twin-engine proposal, however, available drawings indicate that it was a single-engine ground attack type to be powered by a Pratt & Whitney R-2800, which is more consistent with the single-engine aircraft that Kaiser-Fleetwings actually built for the Navy in 1944-1945 (see, BTK in part II, above). Conceived in either 1942 or 1943, the XA-39 had a projected wingspan of 55 feet 9 inches, a length of 42 feet 9 inches, and a maximum takeoff weight of 20,500-lbs. Armament was to have been four .50-caliber machine guns, two 37-mm cannons, and up to 3,000-lbs of bombs carried externally, which is suggestive of the ground attack mission.

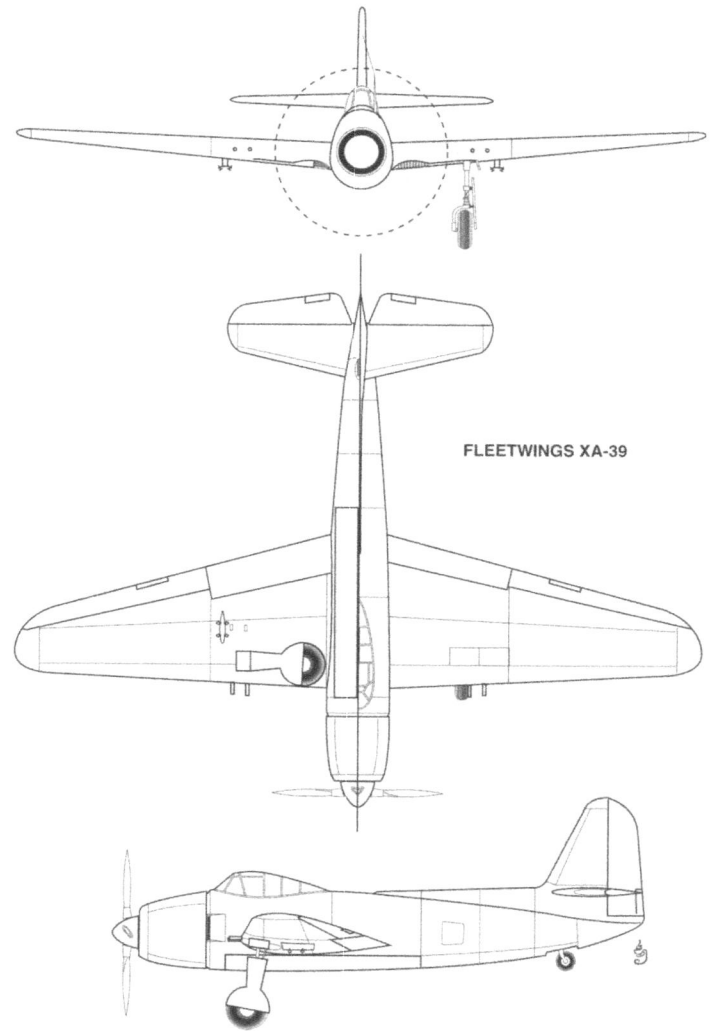

Although the USAAF assigned a designation and may have ordered prototypes, the project was cancelled before it proceeded past the study phase.

Curtiss A-43 (F-87) (1944–1948)

In 1944, after soliciting proposals for a jet-propelled tactical bomber, the USAAF assigned project designations to Curtiss (XA-43), Convair (XA-44), and Martin (XA-45). The smallest of the three designs, the XA-43 was envisaged to have ten fixed .50-caliber machine guns for strafing, two remotely-controlled .50-caliber guns in a tail barbette, plus two internal bomb bays in the belly of the fuselage. But in March 1945, before any construction of a prototype had taken place, the design was re-worked as the XP-87 night fighter to be considered along with Northrop's proposed XP-89. The re-designated XF-87, which made its first flight in March 1948, became the last aircraft completed by the Curtiss-Wright Airplane Division before it shut its doors.

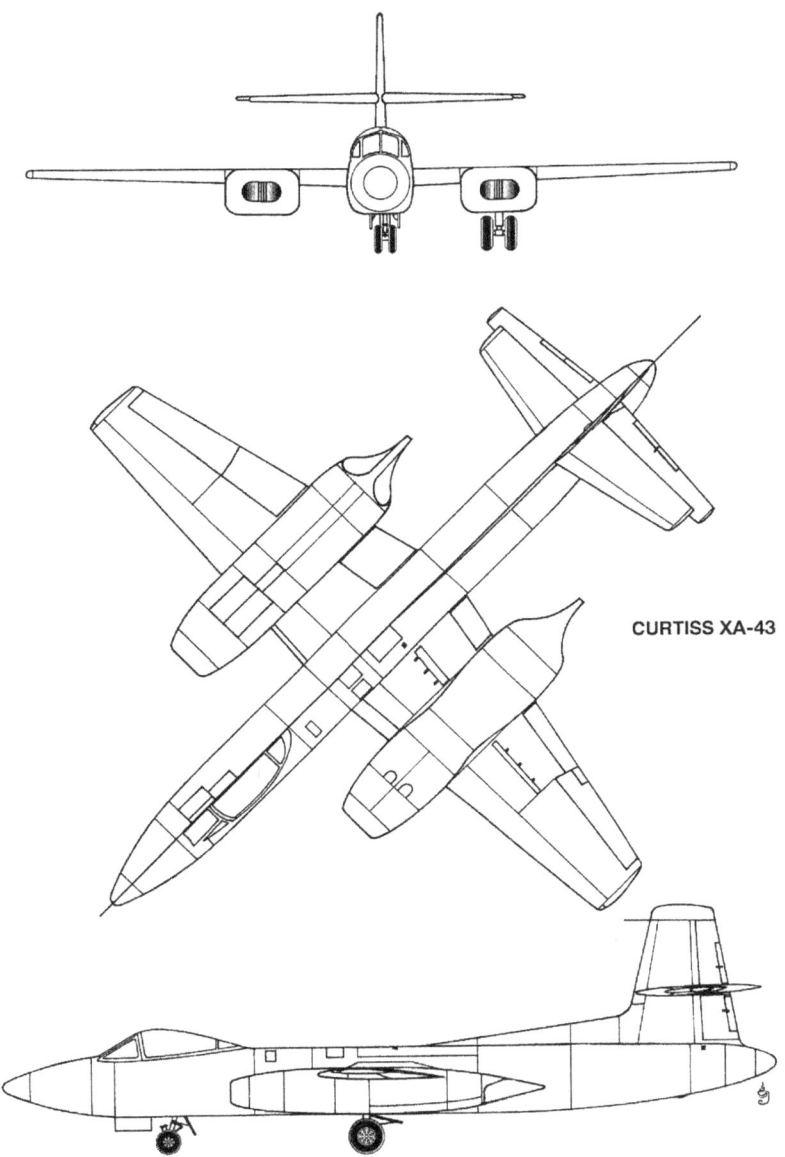

CURTISS XA-43

Convair (Consolidated-Vultee) B-53 (1944–1948)

The A-44 was the second of three design proposals made in response to the USAAF's 1944 tactical bomber requirement. While still in the preliminary design stages, Convair's design staff was strongly influenced by captured German research (i.e., the Junkers Ju 287V-1), which suggested that a tailless layout with the wings swept forward at a 30-degree angle would increase the critical Mach number while simultaneously avoiding the problem of wingtip stalling attributed to sweptback wings. As the design of the XA-44 emerged, the wings also incorporated variable-incidence tip panels that could be defected upward in order to increase angle-of-attack on takeoff and landings. Proposed power was three General Electric J-35 turbojet engines of

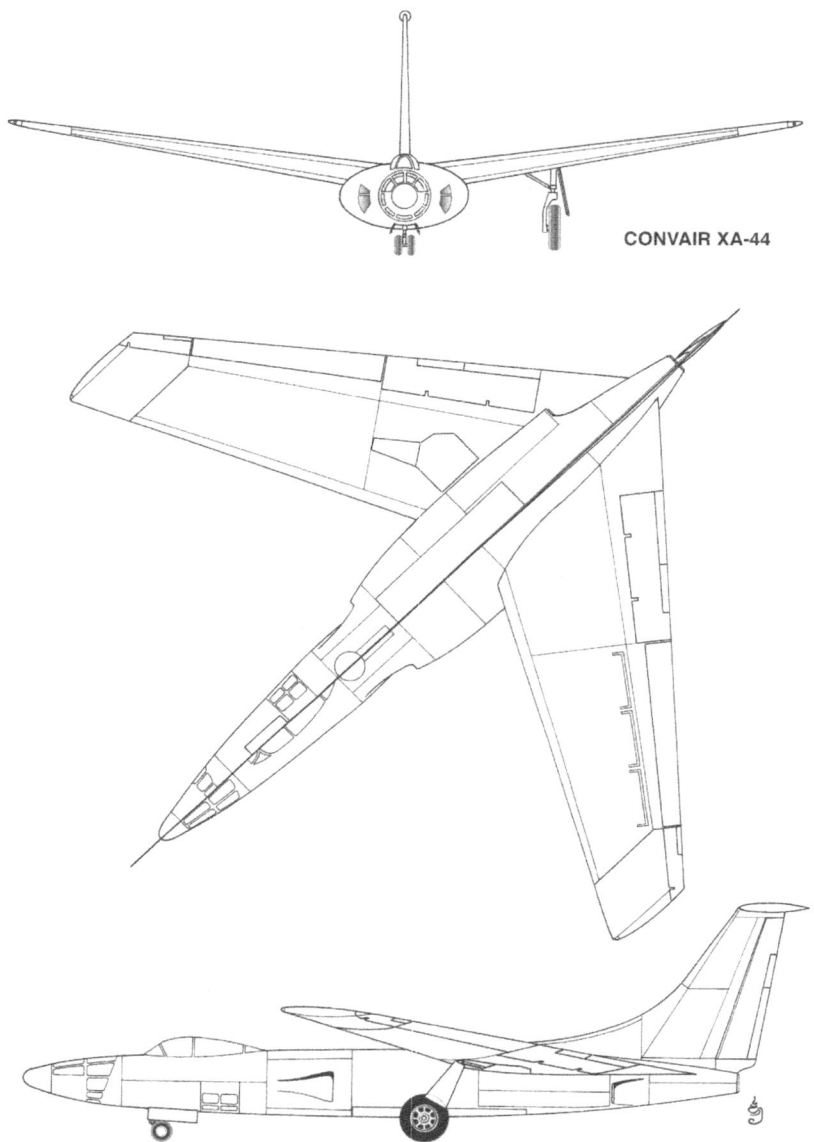

CONVAIR XA-44

4,000-lbs./s.t. each, to be arranged abreast in a broad oval-section fuselage. The aircraft was projected to have a wingspan of 80 feet 7 inches, a length of 79 feet 6 inches, with an estimated takeoff weight of 60,000-lbs. Planned armament consisted of 12,000-lbs of bombs in an internal bay, 40 HVAR rockets on wing stubs, four moveable .50-caliber machine guns in two retractable turrets, and, in the solid-nose ground attack version, twenty fixed .50-caliber machine guns. Estimated performance was a top speed of 580-mph, a ceiling of 44,000 feet, and a maximum range of 2,000 miles. Two aircraft were ordered in 1946 and their official designation was changed to XB-53 in 1948; however, later the same year, the USAF limited prototype construction to Martin's entry (see, B-51 in Part I, above) and cancelled the XB-53 before the two airframes could be completed.

Martin B-68 (1952–1957)

In 1952, soon after the XB-51 had been cancelled and the B-57 *Canberra* placed in production as a stopgap choice, the USAF renewed its quest to find a high-performance tactical bomber by inviting Douglas and Martin to submit proposals under a fresh requirement known as Weapons System 302A. Douglas's more conservative XB-66 proposal (see, B-66 in Part I, above), based on its Navy XA3D-1 design, was selected after brief consideration because it was thought to have less development risk than Martin's XB-68, a more far-reaching delta concept. However, in 1954, when development of the XB-66 became protracted, Martin was invited to re-submit the XB-68 proposal along with competing bids from North American and Boeing. Martin was thereafter selected to proceed to the detailed design and mockup stages, and as the project evolved between 1954 and 1956, the original delta concept was abandoned in favor of a slender fuselage with very thin, low-aspect ratio wings and a T-tail arrangement.

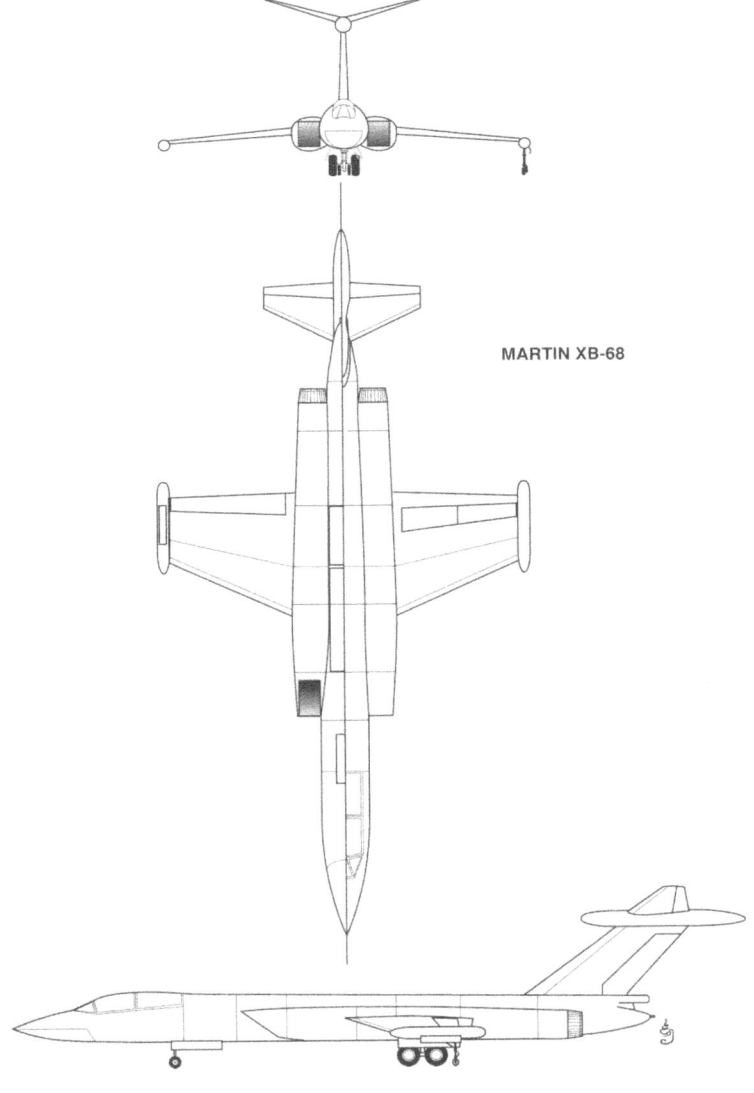

MARTIN XB-68

The final design depicts a larger and heavier aircraft than the XB-66, with a wingspan of 53 feet, a length 109 feet 8 inches, and a takeoff weight of over 102,000-lbs. The two side-mounted J-75 engines were expected to produce a top speed in excess of Mach 2. But the XB-68 came to an abrupt end in early 1957, when, citing stringent budget limitations and higher priority of other weapons systems, the USAF cancelled the project.

Bell D-188A V/STOL (F-109) (1959–1961)

Whether or not this aircraft actually received the XF-109 designation is not clear, but it does present a good example of the USAF's 1950s-era "speed at all costs" mindset as it applied

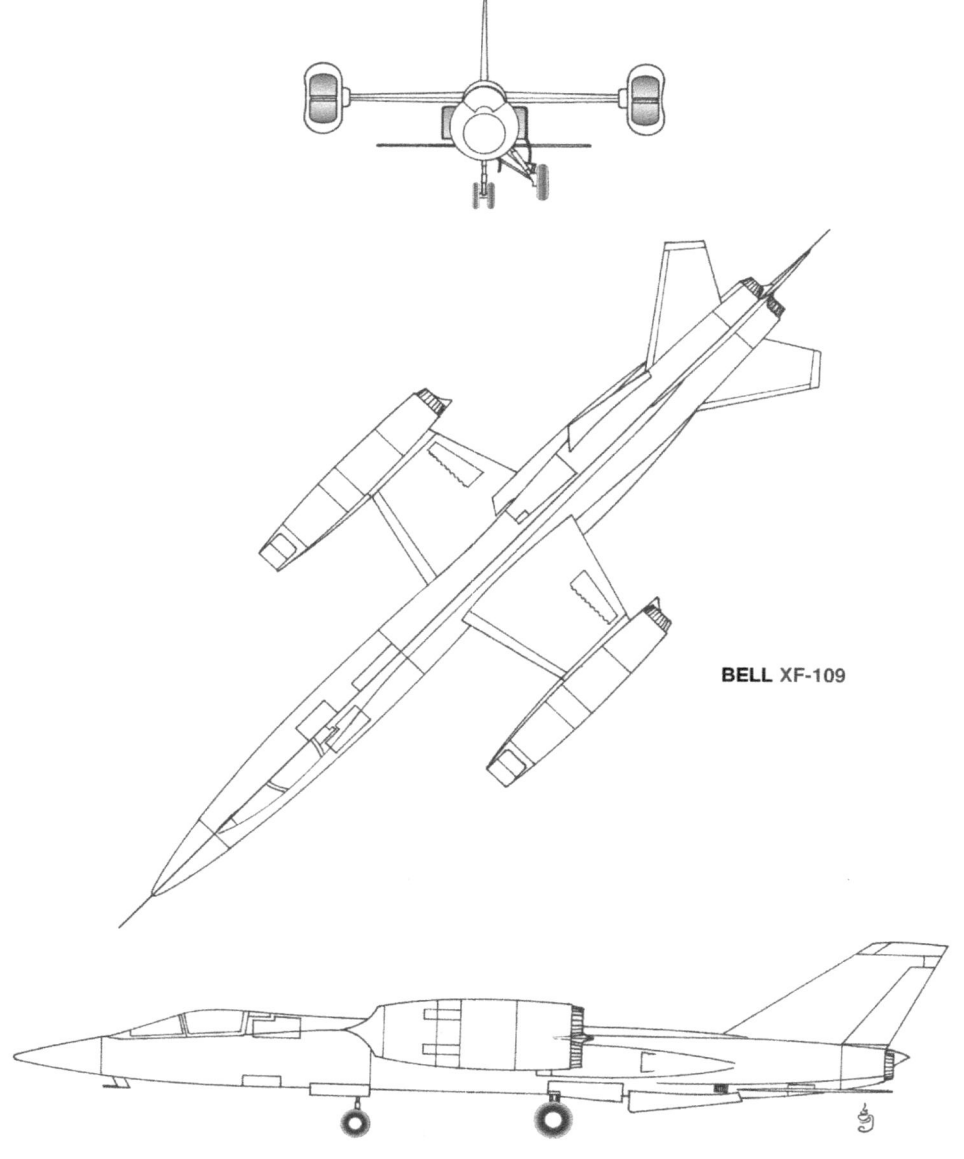

BELL XF-109

to an unusual V/STOL tactical fighter concept. Bell Aircraft, by this time primarily a manufacturer of helicopters, tendered its V/STOL Model D-188A design as an unsolicited proposal. Although the USAF had participated in a couple of V/STOL projects during the mid-1950s (i.e., McDonnell XV-1 and Bell XV-3), it had never shown any interest in the development of a V/STOL fighter. But in 1959, when Bell offered the D-188A with the magic word "supersonic," in fact, a projected performance of Mach 2 or better, the USAF was sufficiently impressed to join with the Navy in awarding Bell a contract to proceed with detailed design and mockup work. The mockup was completed and ready for inspection by the spring of 1961. With the possible exception of rotating engine nacelles located on the wingtips, the design of the D-188A presented a fairly straightforward aerodynamic configuration. Its most unusual feature was arrangement of its eight General Electric J-85 turbojet engines: four in the fuselage, consisting of two on the centerline for rearward thrust and two vertically at the c.g. for downward thrust, plus two on each wingtip in nacelles that could be rotated within an arc of 100-degrees, thus permitting the aircraft to move rearward in hover. The two centerline and four wingtip engines were to be equipped with afterburners for high-speed flight. The mockup dimensions indicated a wingspan of 23 feet 9 inches and a length of 62 feet; according to USAF data, estimated maximum takeoff weight was 23,917-lbs. (which, with eight engines and the fuel needed to run them, seems unrealistic). Planned armament was four 20-mm cannons, 108 2.75-inch FFARs, and up to 4,000-lbs. of bombs on external stations. Following mockup inspections, neither the USAF nor the Navy elected to pursue Bell's unusual V/STOL project any further.

USN AND USMC ATTACK DESIGNS

Designation	Manufacturer	Dates
SB3C	Curtiss-Wright Corp.	1942–1943
TB2F	Grumman Aircraft Engr. Corp.	1942–1944
TSF	Grumman Aircraft Engr. Corp.	1944
A2U	Chance Vought Co.	1951–1954
AH	McDonnell Aircraft Corp.	1953–1954
F12F	Grumman Aircraft Engr. Corp.	1954–1956
AV-16	McDonnell-Douglas Corp.	1973–1975
A-12	General Dynamics Corp.	1988–1991

Curtiss SB3C (1941–1943)

In late 1941, BUAER assigned the designation XSB3C-1 to the Curtiss Model 93 and authorized the company to proceed with the construction of two prototypes. The Army indicated sufficient interest in the project to assign the designation XA-40, but no orders for an aircraft were ever placed. The new aircraft was ordered to fulfill substantially the same Navy scout-bomber requirement as the competing Douglas XSB2D-1. The prototypes were initially designed to be powered by the 2,500-hp. Wright R-3350, with the provision of later upgrading to the 3,000-hp Pratt & Whitney R-4360. Though dimensionally similar to the SB2C, the XSB3C-1 (span 48 ft., length 35 ft. 5 in.) was projected to carry twice the bomb load (2,000-lbs.) at higher airspeeds (max. speed 348-mph, cruise 230-mph). Details of its defensive armament are not known, but the SB specification would have called for a gunner/observer. In late 1943, after BUAER issued the new requirement for a single-seat bomber-torpedo aircraft, the XSB3C-1 was cancelled while the prototypes were still under construction.

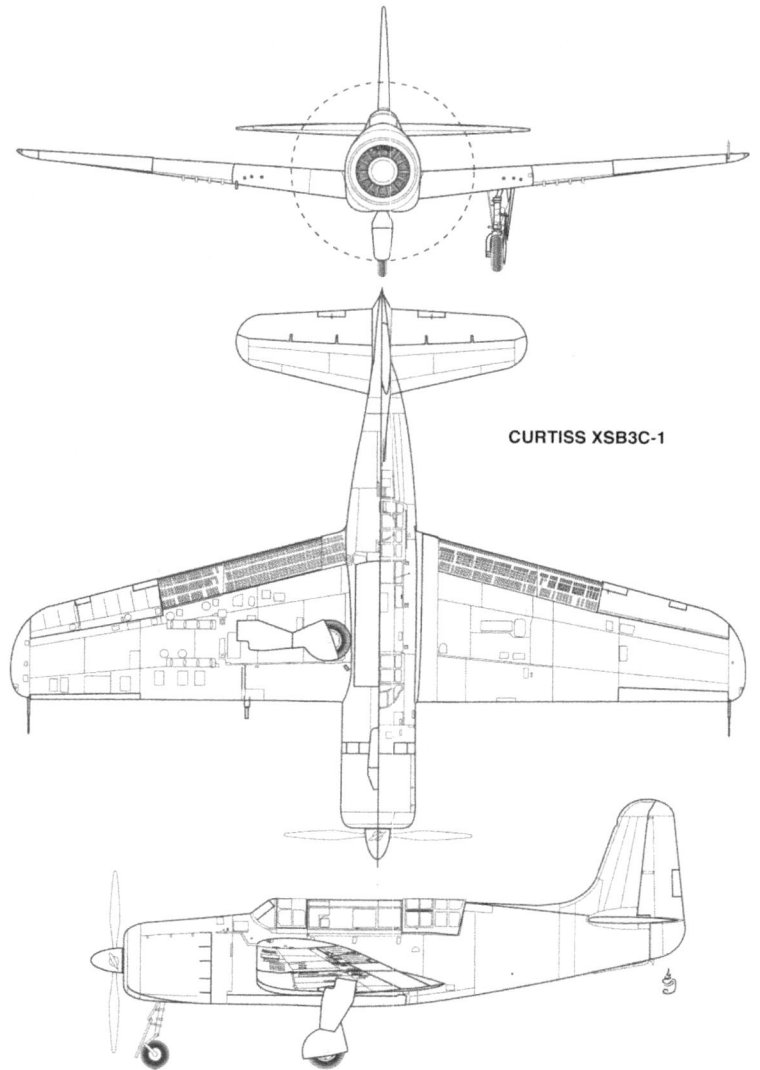

Grumman TB2F (1942–1944)

In late 1942, after BUAER had authorized construction of the twin-engine XF7F-1 fighter, Grumman sought to interest the Navy in a similar design for a torpedo-bomber. Grumman's design G-55, receiving the designation XTB2F-1, proposed a three-place aircraft somewhat larger than the F7F that would be powered by the same Pratt & Whitney R-2800 engines. Defensive armament consisted of two powered fuselage turrets each mounting two guns plus four fixed forward-firing guns in the wings. Up to 8,000 pounds of ordnance, bombs or torpedoes, would be housed in an internal bomb bay. Estimated top speed was 300-mph and with bomb bay and external fuel tanks, a patrol range of 2,280 miles. When BUAER officials inspected the XTB2F-1 mockup in early 1944, however, they concluded that at a projected take-off weight of 45,000-lbs., the aircraft would be far too heavy to operate from even the largest carriers then under construction. Soon afterward, the project was cancelled.

APPENDIX 3—*Attack Aircraft Designs That Never Flew* 427

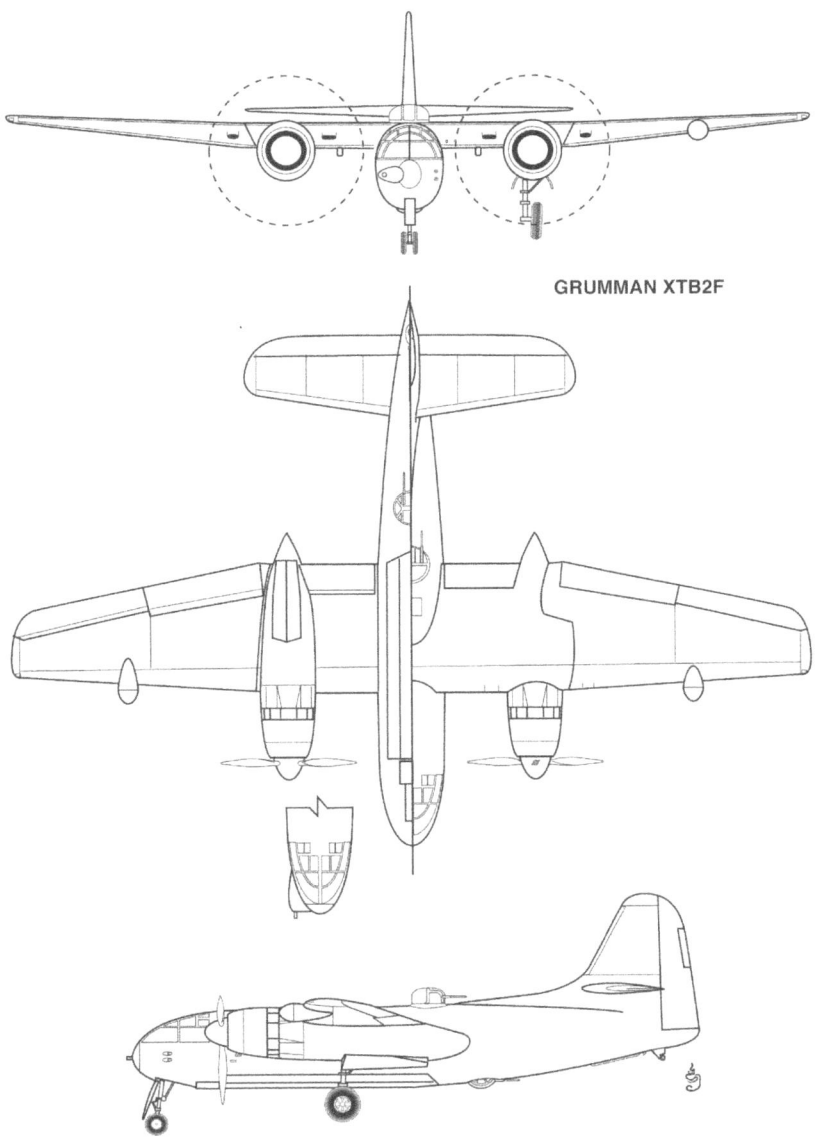

Grumman TSF (1944)

In early 1944, as Design G-66, BUAER authorized Grumman to develop a carrier-based, torpedo-carrying aircraft based upon the F7F-1 airframe, designated XTSF-1. It was the only naval aircraft that ever received the torpedo-scout (TS) designation. Planned modifications to the general F7F layout included the addition of a TBF-type bomb bay and a separate compartment for a radio operator. Two prototypes were ordered, and BUAER inspected a partial fuselage mockup in October 1944. However, unsatisfactory F7F carrier trials demonstrated that the proposed TSF would most likely be unsuited for operations from CVEs, and the project was terminated in December 1944.

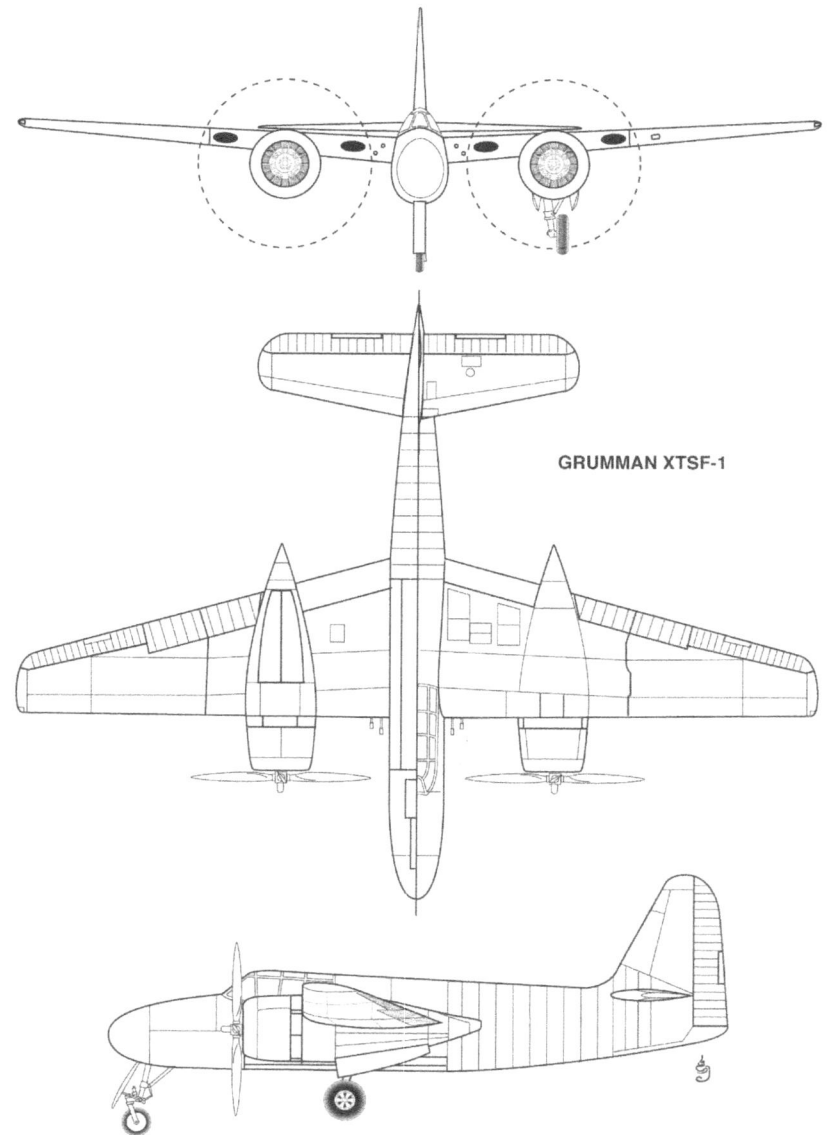

McDonnell AH (1953–1954)

In late 1953, after McDonnell's proposal for a twin-J65 powered F3H (Model 98B [F3H-G] project) lost out to Vought's XF8U-1, BUAER encouraged the company to re-work the basic design into an all-weather dedicated attack aircraft, designated the XAH-1, issuing in mid–1954 a letter of intent for two prototypes and one static test aircraft. The proposed AH-1, to be powered by two afterburning General Electric J79 engines, would carry, on eleven external stations, more than twice the weapons load of the F3H-2. Then only two months later, in December 1954, before the XAH-1 could proceed past the mockup stage, the Navy changed directions again and requested McDonnell to modify the proposal, this time for a missile-armed, two-seat interceptor. The end result became the record-setting YF4H-1 (F-4A).

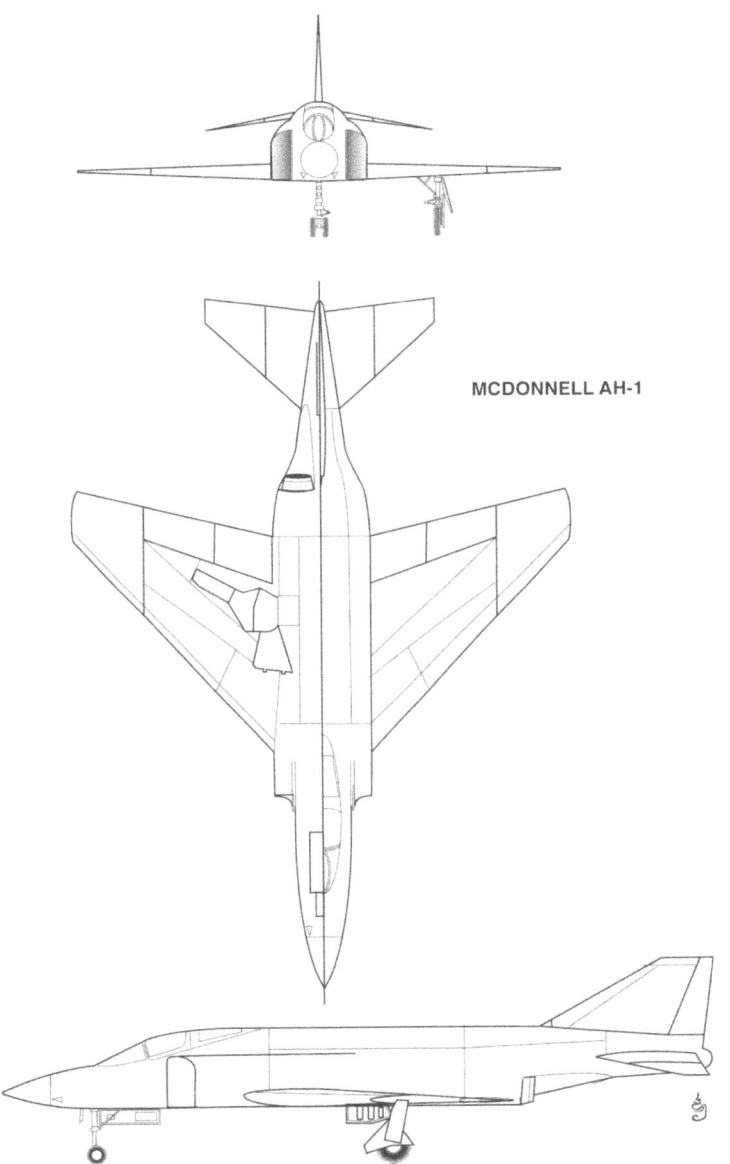

MCDONNELL AH-1

Grumman F12F (1954–1956)

In late 1954, in parallel to McDonnell's YF4H-1 project, BUAER authorized Grumman to proceed with the preliminary design phase of its proposed Model 118 twin-engine, two-seat all-weather interceptor, assigning two bureau numbers to the project for future prototypes under the designation XF12F-1. Like the YF4H-1, the XF12F-1 was to be powered by a pair of General Electric J79-GE-3 afterburning turbojets, armed only with missiles, and equipped with a Raytheon APQ-50 all-weather fire-control/radar system. Aerodynamic features included a wide-oval, area-ruled fuselage flanked by ramp-type intakes, broad, thin-section wings swept 80-degrees from the root to 25 percent chord then 55-degrees to the tips, and an all-flying horizontal stabilizer mounted high up on the vertical tailplane. The completed XF12F-1 would have been a large airplane: a wingspan of 43 feet 11 inches, a length of 58 feet 6 inches, with a maximum takeoff weight of 46,510-lbs. Estimated performance was a top speed in excess of Mach 2 and an operational ceiling above 60,000 feet. In 1956, after deciding to pursue McDonnell's YF4H-1 proposal, BUAER ordered Grumman to discontinue development.

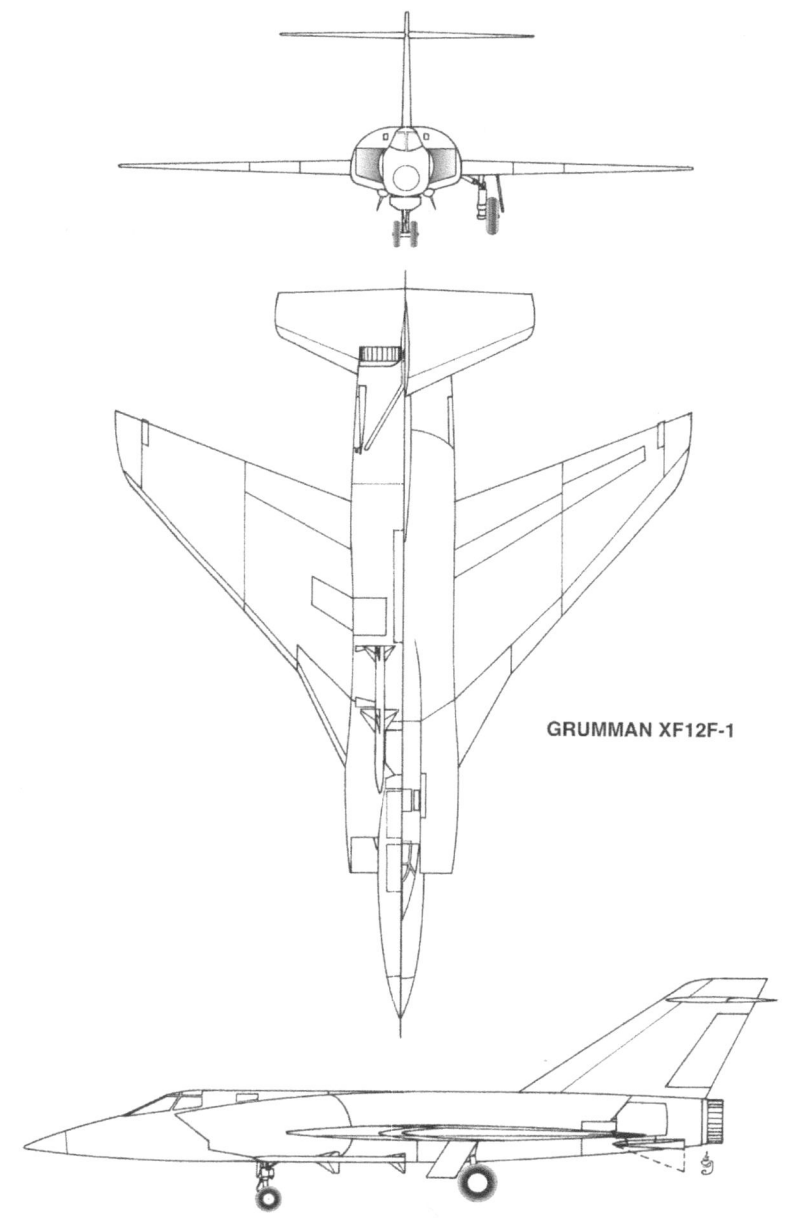

GRUMMAN XF12F-1

McDonnell-Douglas/British Aerospace AV-16 (1973–1975)

While the McDonnell-Douglas/British Aerospace AV-8A *Harrier* represented a quantum leap in tactical air mobility when it entered service with the Marine Corps in 1970, its limited

APPENDIX 3—*Attack Aircraft Designs That Never Flew*   431

weapons load (5,000-lb.) did not favorably compare to other light attack jets of the time (e.g., A-4E, 8,200-lbs.; A-7E, 15,000-lbs.); and the RAF's almost identical GR. 1 version suffered from the same problem. In 1973 these deficiencies led McDonnell-Douglas and British Aerospace to enter into a joint venture to develop a *Harrier* replacement. The resulting AV-16B *Super Harrier* envisaged an enlarged but aerodynamically similar airframe to be powered by a larger and more powerful derivative of the Roll-Royce *Pegasus* vectored-thrust engine. In 1975, British Aerospace withdrew for financial reasons, and the project collapsed. Afterward, McDonnell-Douglas chose to pursue a more modest approach that in time produced the AV-8B.

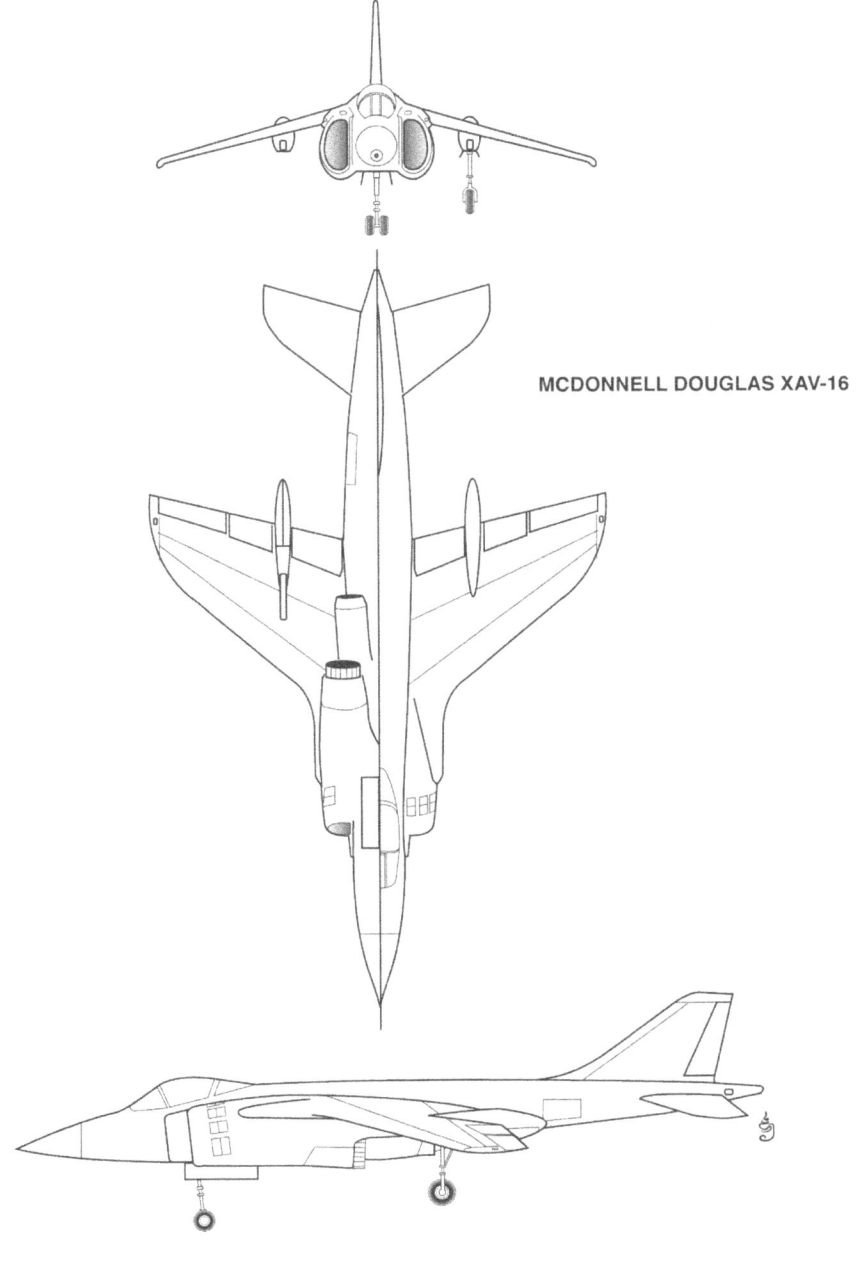

MCDONNELL DOUGLAS XAV-16

General Dynamics A-12 Avenger II (1988–1991)

The Navy initiated the ATA (advanced technology aircraft) project in the early 1980s with the aim of producing a stealth strike aircraft that would replace the Grumman A-6E. In early 1988 the team of General Dynamics/McDonnell-Douglas was selected as prime contractor under the designation XA-12. The design evolved as a triangular shaped, flying wing planform utilizing low-observable (stealth) technology and was to have been powered by two General Electric F412-400 non-afterburning turbofans. Design specifications were: length 37 feet 3 inches, wingspan 70 feet 3 inches; weights, 39,999-lbs. empty, 80,000-lbs. maximum takeoff; a top speed of 580-mph at s.l.; and a combat range of 1,840 miles. Originally, the Navy had planned to procure 620 A-12s and the Marine Corps another 238. But a couple of years after the project started, it ran into troubles: significant engineering problems with the composite materials used in the structure had upped the aircraft's design weight by a factor of 30 percent; and development of the highly advanced radar and electronics suite was seriously behind schedule. Development costs rose to such an extent that, by 1990, it had become apparent the contract was going to exceed its ceiling by $1 billion or more and the A-12's service entry was going to be delayed beyond the planned phase-out of the A-6Es in the mid–1990s. Following an official inquiry, the Navy terminated the contract in January 1991.

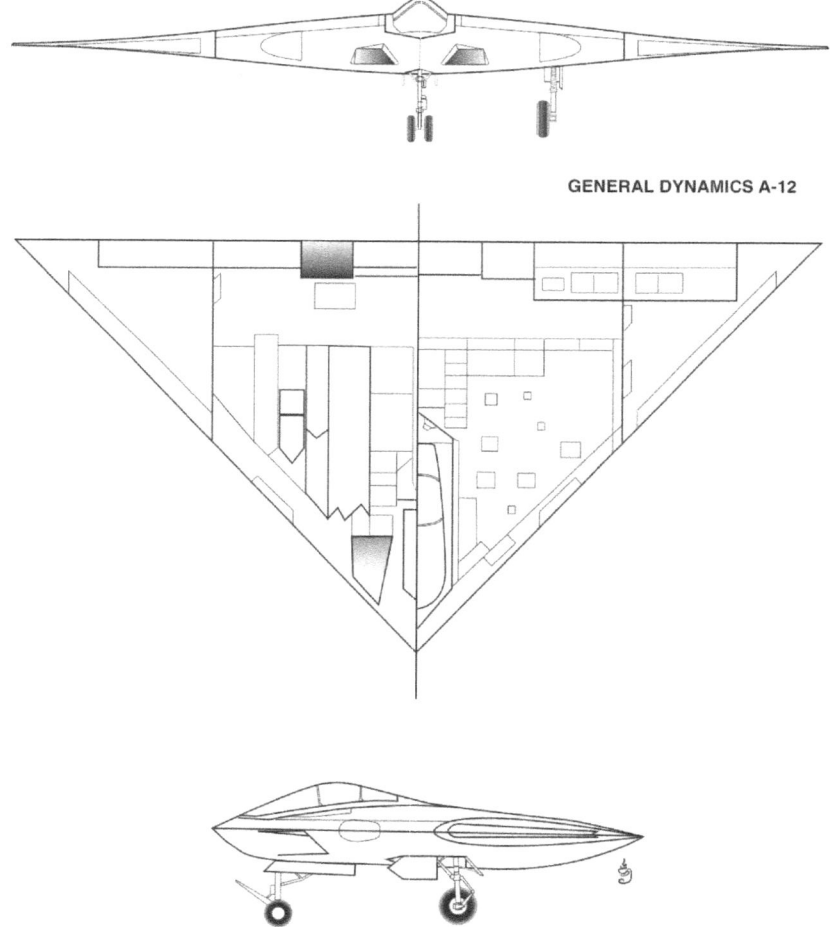

GENERAL DYNAMICS A-12

APPENDIX 4

Evolution of Weapons and Tactics

Twentieth century experience in land and sea warfare has plainly demonstrated that aircraft are the most versatile weapons platforms yet devised by man. The only real limitations weapons place upon an aircraft are takeoff weight and the airframe stress during delivery maneuvers. Otherwise, an aircraft can rapidly change its mission—air-to-air, air-to-ground, or a combination of both—by simply altering its weapons load. With certain exceptions like torpedo attack and specialized gunships, both land-based and naval attack aircraft have utilized similar types of weapons—guns, bombs, rockets, and missiles—to carry out their mission.

GUNFIRE

During World War I, strafing with fixed, forward-firing guns was the earliest method of ground attack to be used by an airplane. Accepted tactics contemplated a very low approach to the target in which the guns were fired from a shallow dive at nearly point-blank range. Small-caliber machine guns were standard armament, and most American attack aircraft were still equipped with relatively light .30-caliber guns until the late 1930s. Combat reports from Europe, especially after 1939, caused both the number and caliber of fixed guns to increase dramatically. Heavier guns not only caused more destruction but permitted strafing attacks to be made from higher altitudes (e.g., 500–1,000 feet) and longer distances from the target. During World War II, .50-caliber machine guns became the standard strafing weapon for all services, though some aircraft augmented their machine guns with one or more 20-mm cannons (the P-38 and late-production F6F-5) while a few types were actually produced with 20-mm cannon main armament (early P-51, F4U-1C, and most SB2Cs). P-39s equipped with a 37-mm cannon firing through the propeller hub were briefly used in a ground attack role by the USAAF but saw far more action with the Soviet Air Force. The largest guns used operationally during the wartime era were the nose-mounted 75-mm cannons of the B-25G and H, which had been developed specifically for low-level shipping strikes. Other ground attack aircraft were tested with various combinations of 37-mm and 75-mm guns, but none were used operationally except very early versions of the A-26B.

In the late 1940s, Navy and Marine aircraft standardized 20-mm cannon armament on their fighter-bombers and attack types, and the USAF followed suit during the early and mid–1950s. The F-104C of 1958 was the first tactical aircraft to be armed with the 20-mm M61*Vul-*

can rotary cannon, and variations and improvements of this gun have since equipped the F-105, F-4E/G, F-14, F-15, F-16, F/A-18, and F-22. Some aircraft, especially those lacking internal guns like the F-4C/D, have been configured to carry a pod-mounted variation of the M61 known as the SUU-16A, and the AV-8A utilized the Swedish-made 30-mm Aden pod. General Electric's 30-mm GAU-8 *Avenger* rotary cannon, the most powerful aircraft gun in existence, was developed specifically for the AX program (i.e., A-10A) in the early 1970s. The slightly smaller GAU-12 *Equalizer,* firing high-power NATO 25-mm ammunition, presently arms the AV-8B and will equip all versions of the F-35. After modest beginnings with comparatively light 7.62-mm rotary miniguns in the AC-47, specialized gunships such as the AC-130H have moved up to truly awesome levels of firepower with guns like the 20-mm M61, 40-mm Bofors, and 105-mm howitzer. According to recent defense reports, directed energy (DE) weapons such as lasers and microwave beams, some of which can be non-lethal, are in the pipeline for application to both attack aircraft and gunships.

BOMBING

As a ground attack weapon, bombs, mostly light fragmentation types, came into common use during the last two years of World War I, and since that time, have become the most widely employed type of ordnance in air attack. Free-fall (i.e., "dumb") bombs have been produced in a wide variety of weights (4 to 4,000-lbs.) and categories (general purpose, light case, semi-armor piercing, armor-piercing, fragmentation [including cluster types], incendiary, and chemical). From World War II well into the Vietnam era, the M-series (e.g., 250-lb. M57, 500-lb. M64, and 1,000-lb. M65 general purpose bombs) were the most common types, followed in the mid–1960s by low-drag bombs specifically developed as external stores for fast-moving jets (e.g., 250-lb. Mk. 81, 500-lb. Mk. 82, and 1,000-lb. Mk. 83, etc.). Over the history of military aviation, the objective of placing free-fall bombs on their targets generated a diversity of tactics together with a wide assortment of aircraft and equipment designed to employ those tactics, to wit:

Level Bombing

Dropping bombs from a level flight attitude was the earliest method used, and to achieve any degree of accuracy, tactics called for a treetop-level approach in which bombs were released practically over the target, thereby subjecting the aircraft to intense ground fire. As technology in sighting mechanisms improved, bombing altitudes progressively increased. In 1931, a ten-year effort by the Naval Bureau of Ordnance resulted in the introduction of the world's first gyro-stabilized, fully-synchronous bombsight, the Norden Mk. 15, permitting accurate level bombing from altitudes over 10,000 feet. During World War II, derivatives of the famed Norden bombsight equipped USAAF light, medium, and heavy bombers as well as Navy and Marine torpedo-bombers. Because optical systems like the Norden sight were practically useless at night or during poor visibility, "look-down" bombing radars, initially developed during World War II for heavy bombers, began equipping many smaller tactical aircraft during the post-war era. SHORAN (short-range navigation), a system that homed-in on intersecting radar beacons up to a distance of 300 miles, was installed on tactical bombers like the B-26, B-45, and B-57. Ironically, as high and medium altitude bombing techniques improved during the 1950s, simultaneous developments in air defense weapons, especially radar-controlled antiaircraft guns, surface-to-air missiles, and interceptor aircraft, forced a return to low-level bomb delivery tactics and generated a host of new technologies such as SEAD, EW, AWACS, and stealth.

Dive and Glide-Bombing

Although the Navy began dive-bombing tests in the mid–1920s, the Marine Corps is generally credited with developing the first combat-tested techniques during its Nicaraguan campaign of 1927. The idea was simple: the airplane itself was aimed at the target, diving at so high an angle (i.e., 70 to 80 degrees) that the bombs followed its path to the point of impact. The Navy's first purpose-built dive-bomber appeared in 1930, and successive types remained in Navy and Marine service until replaced by single-seat attack aircraft in the late 1940s. Although the USAAC did finally adopt the tactic in 1940, it discarded specialized dive-bombers in favor of single-seat fighter-bombers during the course of World War II.

Another Navy development, glide-bombing was conceived in the late 1930s due to the inherent difficulties of hitting a moving target (like a ship) from a level bombing attitude. Since Navy torpedo-bombers were not stressed for high-G pullouts, they were unable to duplicate the steep bomb release angles of dive-bombers, but tests did reveal that they could safely deliver bombs at 40 to 50 degrees and achieve acceptable levels of accuracy. During World War II, glide-bombing became the principal bomb-delivery tactic of single-seat fighter-bombers not equipped with dive-brakes (e.g., F6F, F4U, P-47, and P-51) and was adopted in the post-war era by jet fighter-bombers (e.g., F9F, F2H, F-80, F-84, etc.). As more and more jet aircraft assumed the attack role, traditional naval dive-bombing tactics (i.e., release angles in excess of 50-degrees) ceased to be used. Today, the term "dive-bombing" is used generically to describe any bomb delivery made from a dive (i.e., 10 to 50 degrees).

Skip-Bombing

The invention of this tactic in 1943 is generally credited to the Southwest Pacific theater-based 5th Air Force USAAF as a means of attacking Japanese shipping. Identical to the principle of skipping a smooth stone across a pond, the bomb was released about 200 feet over the water at 200–230-mph, approximately 300 yards before reaching the target. Set to detonate 11 to 12 seconds after impact, the bomb would "skip" across the water in a horizontal trajectory and penetrate the side of the ship. The tactic was initially combat-tested with B-17Fs but saw its most extensive application with A-20s and B-25s that had been reconfigured as gunships. The tactic was subsequently adopted by Marine PBJ (B-25) units operating in the Pacific and reportedly used in other theaters.

Toss-Bombing

Developed during World War II as an alternative to dive and glide-bombing, toss-bombing is a tactic in which the aircraft enters a dive and the bomb is released during the pull-up, normally at higher altitudes than in a dive or glide-bombing delivery. The pull-out maneuver gives the bomb additional forward velocity so that it is tossed above the original line-of-sight to the target, then falls in a trajectory which intersects the target. Post-war developments saw the introduction of bomb directors (i.e., computers that calculate airspeed, altitude, and dive angle), enabling a bomb to be released automatically at the optimal moment of pull-out. Toss-bombing techniques are still valid today for delivery of unguided (i.e., "dumb") bombs.

Loft-Bombing

Also called "over the shoulder" bombing, loft-bombing was developed during the 1950s to enable aircraft delivering nuclear weapons to escape the effects of the blast. Using this tactic, the bomb is released during a half-loop maneuver, placing it in an upward trajectory *away* from the aircraft, after which the aircraft continues over the top, rolls-upright (i.e., the first half of a Cuban-8 maneuver), and accelerates in the opposite direction at maximum speed. The bomb maintains an upward arc that delays its fall and detonation until the aircraft can distance itself from the blast. In order to execute the maneuver accurately, nuclear-capable aircraft were equipped with a gyro-stabilized analog computer known as LABS (low-altitude bombing system), which automated bomb release at the optimal point of the maneuver. Although LABS has since been superceded by more modern systems, loft-bombing remains an accepted tactic for delivering nuclear weapons.

Modern Bombing Systems

The advent of smart weapons and systems driven by state-of-the-art computers has totally revolutionized tactical bombing. The technology available today not only offers pilots more latitude in the tactics to be used, but also allows them to deliver their weapons at progressively greater stand-off distances, thus avoiding the most heavily defended areas. Contemporary attack aircraft like the F-16C and F/A-18E are fitted with a stunning array of laser, infrared, and radar tracking components plus inertial and satellite (GPS) guidance systems, which are all integrated into the bombing system via digital computer technology. Once the pilot designates a target, the bombing system will automatically follow through with an attack solution. One notable innovation in modern systems is a heads-up display (HUD) that projects all relevant tactical information onto a combining glass directly in front of the pilot. Using HUD data, a pilot may designate multiple targets and continue to refine the target solution all the way to the point of weapons release, and with precision munitions, the point of impact. HUDs are in currently being replaced by the even newer helmet-mounted display (HMD), which not only projects similar tactical information onto the pilot's helmet visor, but also enables him to designate a target by simply looking at it.

Guided Bombs

Research and development into guided bomb units (GBUs), popularly called "smart bombs," actually predates World War II, but deployment of the first operational examples dates from the late 1960s during the Vietnam War period. The earliest GBUs were guided by low-light television cameras and controlled by an operator aboard the aircraft who transmitted steering signals to the bomb. The next generation used laser guidance wherein the target was "illuminated" by a target designator situated either on the ground or aboard an aircraft. Both guidance methods were limited to weather conditions that permitted the target to be seen or illuminated. Contemporary systems, like the joint direct attack munition (JDAM), now rely upon satellite (GPS) and/or inertial (INS) navigation systems capable of operating in all weather conditions.

TORPEDO ATTACK

Developed by the Naval Bureau of Ordnance during the mid–1920s, the first American-made aerial torpedoes were at first perceived as naval aviation's primary anti-ship weapon, and as a result, the very first carrier-based attack aircraft were torpedo planes. Although eclipsed to some extent by dive-bombers during the 1930s, torpedo attack was still an important naval tactic when the U.S. entered World War II. The release parameters of the Mk. 13, the type of torpedo in use at the time, were exceedingly narrow: an altitude of 50 feet or lower and airspeed of 132-mph or slower within 2,000 yards of the target. Combat experience, in particular the Battle of Midway in June 1942, revealed that this approach profile left torpedo-bombers perilously vulnerable to both antiaircraft fire and fighter attack. The USAAF's short-lived interest in torpedo attack ended when two of four torpedo-laden Martin B-26s were destroyed while attempting to attack the Japanese fleet from Midway Island. Improvements made to torpedoes during the war restored the viability of the tactic by increasing release limits to 2,400 feet and 400-mph. Although post-war naval attack aircraft like the AD and AM were equipped to carry torpedoes, the weapon was never again used in combat. The advent of high-speed jets and guided anti-ship missiles since the 1950s has essentially left the aerial torpedo with little tactical utility other than as an ASW weapon, where it is still in use today.

UNGUIDED ROCKETS

While the exact origins of unguided aerial rockets are not entirely clear, they became a standard attack weapon of the American arsenal during World War II. The M-8 "bazooka tube," a tube-launched 4.5-inch diameter folding-fin rocket mounted on wing pylons in clusters of three, was initially introduced into combat on USAAF P-38s and P-47s during 1943 and was later mounted on P-51s. After dissatisfaction with the 3-inch British RP rocket, the Navy developed the 5-inch high-velocity air rocket (HVAR), a fixed-fin projectile having a 143-lb. warhead, and began deploying them in combat during 1944. The HVAR was also adopted by the USAAF, and later versions featured a RAM armor-piercing warhead for use against tanks. The weapon was used extensively by all services in Korea and remained in the military inventory until the late 1950s. Also developed by the Navy in 1944, the 11.75-inch *Tiny Tim* carried a warhead equivalent to a 500-lb. armor-piecing bomb and designed to be used against ships and hardened ground targets. *Tiny Tims* carried by F6Fs and TBMs were deployed in combat during the last year of the war and were used again in Korea on F4Us and ADs.

Placed in production for the USAF in 1950, the 2.75-inch *Mighty Mouse* folding-fin aircraft rocket (FFAR) was housed either in multiple (e.g., 14+) trays that retracted into the belly of an aircraft or in wing-mounted expendable pods. Though originally designed as an air-to-air bomber killer, FFARs were later adapted for ground attack and used by the USAF, Navy, and Marines during the Vietnam War. Still in service, the current version is known as the *Hydra 70* (i.e., 70-mm) and may be fitted with ten different special purpose warheads. The 5-inch pod-mounted, folding-fin *Zuni*, a naval development, appeared in 1957 as a replacement for the HVAR and subsequently saw extensive combat use in Southeast Asia from 1965 to 1972. Modern versions are carried in a four-round LAU-10 launcher and may be fitted with specialized warheads like the *Hydra*. Out of safety concerns, the Navy withdrew the *Zuni* from carrier operations in the late 1980s, but the weapon is still used from land bases. Since the Navy currently maintains a considerable stockpile of the *Zuni,* there has been some interest in fitting it with a precision guidance seeker (i.e., a "smart" rocket).

AIR-TO-GROUND GUIDED MISSILES

Ground Attack Missiles

Losses sustained in attacking heavily defended ground targets during the Korean War prompted Navy officials to initiate development of an air-to-ground guided missile (AGM) compact enough to be carried by a single-seat attack aircraft. The earliest type, the Martin AGM-12 *Bullpup,* was basically a short-range (9.2–11.5 miles) optically guided bomb within a rocket-assisted airframe. The AGM-12A entered service with the Navy in 1959 and the improved AGM-12B with the USAF in 1965. Combat experience in Vietnam revealed serious shortcomings in the *Bullpup's* guidance system and led to introduction of the TV-guided Martin AGM-62 *Walleye,* which was in USAF, Navy, and Marine service from 1967 until the early 1990s. In reality, the *Walleye* was not a missile but an un-powered glide-bomb. The next major development, the USAF-sponsored Hughes AGM-65 *Maverick,* appeared in 1972 as a small (463-lb.), TV-guided missile having a 14-mile range. Improved variants, the laser-guided AGM-65E went into service with the Marine Corps in 1985 and the imaging-infrared-guided (IIR) AGM-65F began reaching Navy units in 1989. Raytheon, the current prime contractor on *Maverick,* is now promoting an enhanced version with a data-linked GPS-INS guidance system and improved stand-off range.

Efforts to produce a truly long-range AGM were not realized until introduction of the McDonnell-Douglas (now Boeing) AGM-84E *Harpoon*/SLAM (stand-off land attack missile) in the 1990s. The *Harpoon* was originally conceived in the early 1970s as an all-weather, over-the-horizon anti-ship missile capable of being launched either from ships, submarines, or aircraft. The SLAM version comes with a GPS-INS navigation system and uses infrared terminal guidance. Launched from F/A-18s or B-52s, the missile can carry its 488-lb. warhead a distance of 75+ miles at over 500-mph. During 1997–2001, the Navy initiated a major retrofit known as SLAM-ER (expanded response), which will double the range, increase target penetration, and come with a software package that allows the pilot to retarget the missile's impact point during the terminal phase of the attack. SLAM-ER will equip F/A-18s and the F-15K being developed for export to Korea. New versions of SLAM are reportedly under development and expected to become operational in the future. The Navy's AGM-123 *Skipper,* carried only by the A-6E and phased-out in the mid–1990s, was essentially a 1,000-lb. Mk. 83 bomb retrofitted with a rocket booster and a laser-guidance system. Similarly, the USAF's AGM-130 is rocket-powered 3,640-lb. GBU-15 smart bomb designed to provide greater standoff ranges from low altitudes. While the AGM-130 is only carried by the F-15E at present, a lightweight version (i.e., AGM-130LW) is being developed for the F-16C. The AGM-154 Joint Standoff Weapon (JSOW) is a 1,000-lb. GPS/INS-guided glide bomb offered in three variants—AGM-154A sub-munitions (bomblets) type, AGM-154B anti-armor type, and AGM-154C general purpose type—which began entering Navy and Marine service in 1999. The USAF withdrew from the program in 2005.

Antiradar Missiles

During and since Vietnam, suppression of enemy air defenses (SEAD) has become vital to both the tactical success and survivability of the attack mission. The AGM-45 *Shrike,* an anti-radiation (ARM) missile derived from the AIM-7 *Sparrow,* was originally developed by the Navy in the late 1950s to home-in on ship-based fire-control radars. Carried initially by A-4s and A-6s, the Mach 2 missile could deliver its 149-lb. warhead against targets 25 miles away. It later equipped USAF F-100F and F-105F/G "Wild Weasels" in Southeast Asia, where it was employed against land-based surface-to-air missile (SAM) radars. However, the *Shrike* was limited by its overhead (lofted) launch trajectory, a fixed frequency seeker, and the fact once the enemy radar was turned off, the missile was "blind." Developed by the Navy but also extensively used by the USAF, the AGM-78 *Standard* ARM, introduced in 1968, overcame many of the *Shrike's* limitations by offering a wider launch envelope, more powerful warhead, greater range (56 miles), plus, via computer circuits, the ability to "remember" the location of the target after its radar had been shut down. The AGM-88 HARM (H = high-speed), featuring improved seeker sensitivity and a 92-mile launch range, began entering service in the 1980s and currently equips the USAF, Navy, and Marines. An improved version, the AGM-88E Advanced Anti-Radiation Guided Missile (AARGM), is in the development stages.

DEFENSIVE COUNTERMEASURES

Another significant factor contributing to the survivability of attack mission since the 1960s has been the addition of components like radar warning receivers (RHAW/RWR), countermeasures pods (ECM), and chaff and flare dispensers, all of which enable the pilot to detect, jam, decoy, and/or possibly evade hostile defenses. In modern strike aircraft like the F-15E, F-16C, or F/A-18E, all such components run off a fully integrated defense and countermeasures suite that includes an enhanced RWR, ECM pod, towed fiber-optic jammer, and chaff/flare dispensers containing over 100 units. Today, the ultimate aircraft defense scheme is stealth (i.e., low-observable technology), which is actually a combination of design characteristics, airframe materials, and systems that all work together to reduce an aircraft's radar cross-section (RCS) and infrared signature to such low levels that it cannot be detected by normal electronic means. The success of the *Have Blue* project, followed by the operational deployment of the F-117A in the early 1980s, has more than vindicated the idea, and contemporary programs like ATF (F-22) and JSF (F-35) has given the U.S. a technological edge in tactical air power that no other nation is likely to duplicate in the foreseeable future.

Bibliography

Books and Journals

Appel, Bernard. "Bombing Accuracy in a Combat Environment." *Air University Review,* July-August 1975.

Axe, David. "Clouds on the Horizon for Pilot-Less Bombers." *National Defense,* August 2006.

Berger, Carl, ed. *The United States Air Force in Southeast Asia 1961–1973.* Washington, D.C.: Office of Air Force History, 1977.

Bowers, Peter M. "Scout Bomber." *Wings,* vol. 15, no. 2, April 1985.

Bowman, Martin W. *USAAF Handbook 1939–1945.* Mechanicsburg, Pennsylvania: Stackpole Books, 1997.

Chesneau, Roger. *Aircraft Carriers of the World, 1914 to the Present.* Annapolis, Maryland: Naval Institute Press, 1984.

Condon, John P. *Corsairs to Panthers: U.S. Marine Aviation in Korea.* Washington, D.C.: Diane Publishing Co., 2002.

Cox, Gary C. "Beyond the Battle Line: U.S. Air Attack Theory and Doctrine 1919–1941." Thesis, School of Advanced Air Power Studies, Maxwell AFB, Alabama, 1995.

Dean, Jack. "Dive Bomber." *Wings,* vol. 15, no. 2, April 1985.

_____. "Pacific War." *Airpower,* vol. 31, no. 4, July 2001.

Dorr, Robert F. "Hornet." *World Airpower Journal,* Spring 1998.

_____, and David Donald, *Fighters of the United States Air Force.* New York: The Military Press, 1990.

Fahey, James C., ed. *USAF Aircraft 1947–1956.* Wright-Patteron AFB, Ohio: Air Force Museum Foundation, Inc., 1978.

_____, ed. *U.S. Army Aircraft 1908–1946.* New York: Ships and Aircraft, 1946.

Friedman, Norman. *U.S. Naval Weapons.* Annapolis, Maryland: Naval Institute Press, 1985.

Futrell, Robert F. *The United States Air Force in Korea.* Rev. ed. Washington, D.C.: Office of Air Force History, 1983.

Green, William. *War Planes of the Second World War. Fighters, Vol. 4.* Garden City, New York: Hanover House, 1961.

_____. *The World's Fighting Planes.* Garden City, New York: Doubleday, 1964.

_____, and Roy Cross. *The Jet Aircraft of the World.* Garden City, New York: Hanover House, 1957.

Grossnick, Roy A. *United States Naval Aviation 1910–1995.* Washington, D.C.: Naval Aviation History Branch, U.S. Government Printing Office, 1996. (Available online in PDF format at www.history.navy.mil.)

Gunston, Bill. *American Warplanes.* New York: Crescent Books, 1986.

_____. *The Illustrated Encyclopedia of Aircraft Armament.* New York: Crown, 1988.

Hallion, Richard P. "Battlefield Air Support, A Retrospective Assessment." *Air University Review,* Spring 1990.

_____. *The Naval Air War in Korea.* Mt. Pleasant, South Carolina: The Nautical & Aviation Publishing Company, 1986.

Harding, Stephen. *U.S. Army Aircraft since 1947.* Stillwater, Minnesota: Specialty Press, Inc., 1990.

Jones, Lloyd S. *U.S. Bombers B1–B70.* Los Angeles: Aero, 1962.

_____. *U.S. Fighters 1925 to 1980s.* Fallbrook, California: Aero, 1975.

Kasulka, Duane. *USN Aircraft Carrier Air Units. Vol. 1 1946–1956.* Carrollton, Texas: Squadron/Signal Publications, 1985.

_____. *USN Aircraft Carrier Air Units. Vol. 2 1957–1963.* Carrollton, Texas: Squadron/Signal Publications, 1985.

Knaack, Marcelle S. *Encyclopedia of U.S. Air Force Aircraft and Missile Systems, Vol. I: Post World War II Bombers 1945–1973.* Washington, D.C.: Office of Air Force History, 1986.

_____. *Encyclopedia of U.S. Air Force Aircraft and Missile Systems, Vol. II: Post World War II*

Bombers 1945–1973. Washington, D.C.: Office of Air Force History, 1988.

Larkins, William T. *U.S. Navy Aircraft 1921–1941.* Concord, California: Aviation History Publications, 1961.

———. *USMC Aircraft 1914–1959.* Concord, California: Aviation History Publications, 1959.

Lawson, Robert L., ed. *The History of U.S. Naval Airpower.* New York: Crown, 1985.

Margiotta, Franklin D., ed. "History of Airpower." *Brassey's Encyclopedia of Military History and Biography.* Washington, D.C.: Brassey's, 1994.

Matt, Paul R., and Bruce Robertson. *United States Navy and Marine Corps Fighters 1918–1962.* Los Angeles: Aero, 1962.

Miska, Kurt H. "Grumman Attack Aircraft Since 1945." *A.A.H.S. Journal,* vol. 14, no. 4, Winter 1969.

Morrison, Samuel Eliot. *The Two-Ocean War.* Boston: Little, Brown & Company, 1963.

Nichols, John B., and Barrett Tillman. *On Yankee Station: The Vietnam Naval Air War.* Annapolis, Maryland: Naval Institute Press, 1987.

Preston, Anthony, and Louis S. Casey. *Sea Power: A Modern Illustrated Military History.* New York: Exeter Books, 1979.

Smith, Peter C. *History of Dive Bombing.* Annapolis, Maryland: The Nautical & Aviation Publishing Company, 1981.

Swanborough, Gordon, and Peter M. Bowers. *United States Navy Aircraft Since 1911.* 2d ed. Annapolis, Maryland: Naval Institute Press, 1976.

Taylor, Michael J. H. *Warplanes of the World 1918–1939.* New York: Charles Scribner's Sons, 1981.

Terzibaschitsch, Stefan. *Aircraft Carriers of the U.S. Navy.* Annapolis, Maryland: Naval Institute Press, 1989.

Tirpak, John A. "The Three Fighters." *Air Force Magazine,* vol. 84, no. 7, July 2001. (Reference to F/A-18, F-22, and F-35).

Trimble, William F. *Wings for the Navy: A History of the Naval Aircraft Factory, 1917–1956.* Annapolis, Maryland: Naval Institute Press, 1996.

Wagner, Ray. *American Combat Planes.* 3d ed. Garden City, New York: Doubleday, 1982.

Winton, John. *Air Power at Sea: 1945 to Today.* New York: Carroll & Graff, 1987.

WEBSITES

"ATA Concept Formulation." A-12 Avenger site, www.invisible-defenders.org.

"AV-8 Harrier Variants." Military Resources Global Security site, www.globalsecurity.org/military/systems/aircraft/av-8-variants.htm.

Baugher, Joseph. American Military Aircraft site, http://home.att.net/~jbaugher/uscombataircraft.html.

Condon, John P. "History of Marine Corps Aviation." Marine Corps Historical Center site, www.navy.history.mil/download/mca-m1.pdf.

"F/A-18 Background Info." Boeing Aerospace site, www.boeing.com/defense-space/military/fa18/fa18_4back.htm.

"F-35 Joint Strike Fighter." FAS Military Analysis Network site, www.fas.org/man/dod-101/sys/ac/f-35.htm.

"Fact Sheet." Fact sheets on various aircraft and weapons. Air Force Website, www.af.mil/factsheets.

Goebel, Greg. "The Lockheed Martin F-35 Joint Strike Fighter." In the Public Domain site, www.vectorsite.net/avf35.html.

Parsch, Andreas. Directory of U.S. Military Missiles and Rockets site, www.designation-systems.net.

"Records of the Bureau of Aeronautics 1911–1972" (Record Group 72), National Archives Site (NARA), www.archives.gov/research_room.html.

"United States Marine Corps Organization." Marine Corps site, www.tecom.usmc.mil.

U.S. Military Aircraft Designations 1911–1999 site, www.driko.org/usdes.html.

Various topics on naval weapons. The Ordnance Shop site, www.ordnance.org.

Index

A-1E 337–338
A-1G 337
A-1H 337–338
A-1J 337–338
A-2 11–14
A-2A 343
A-2B 343
A2D-1 339–340
A2F-1 380–381
A-3 14–16
A-3A 16, 370
A-3B 16, 367–370
A3D-1 370
A3D-2 370
A3D-2P 370
A3D-2Q 370
A3D-2T 370
A3J-1 375, 378
A3J-2 377–378
A3J-3P 378
A-4 16
A-4A 371, 373, 375
A-4B 371, 375
A-4C 371, 373, 375
A4D-1 371, 373, 375
A4D-2 371, 375
A4D-2N 371, 375
A4D-3 373
A4D-4 373
A4D-5 371
A4-E 371, 374–375
A-4F 371–373, 375
A-4G 373
A-4H 373
A-4K 373
A-4KU 373, 375
A-4L 373
A-4M 373, 375
A-4N 375
A-5A 378
A-5B 376–378
A-6A 380–381
A-6B 381
A-6C 381

A-6E 378–382
A-6F 381
A-7 16–18
A-7A 382, 385
A-7B 382
A-7C 382, 385
A-7D 383–386
A-7E 384–386
A-7F 385
A-7H 385
A-7K 385–386
A-8 18–21
A-9 21
A-9A 161–164
A-10 21
A-10A 164–168
A-10C 167–168
A-10N/AW 167
A-11 21–23
A-11A 23
A-12 19–21, 432
A-13 23–25
A-14 25–27
A-15 418–419
A-16 25, 183
A-17 27–30
A-17A 27–30
A-18 23–25
A-19 30–32
A-19A 32
A-19B 32
A-20 33–35
A-20A 33–37
A-20B 36–37
A-20C 36
A-20D 36,
A-20E 36
A-20F 36
A-20G 33–37
A-20H 37
A-20J 36–37
A-20K 37
A-21 37–40
A-22 40–42

A-23 56
A-24 298, 300
A-24A 298, 300
A-24B 298, 300
A-25 see SB2C
A-26 46
A-26A 50
A-26B 44–50
A-26C 48–49
A-26D 48
A-26E 48
A-26G 48
A-26H 48
A-27 50–52
A-28 52–45
A-28A 52–54
A-29 52–54
A-29A 52–54
A-29B 52–54
A-30 54–56
A-30A 56
A-31 56–59
A-31A 59
A-31C 59
A-32 59–61
A-32A 60–61
A-33 30
A-34 7, 291
A-35A 57–59
A-35B 56–59
A-36A 62–64
A-37 64–66, 218
A-37A 213
A-37B 213–214
A-37D 213
A-38 67–69
A-39 419–420
A-40 425
A-41 69–71
A-42 91
A-43 420–421
A-44 421–422
A-45 117
AC-47D 206–208

AC-119G 208–209
AC-119K 208–209
AC-123K 210–211
AC-130A 211–212
AC-130E 211
AC-130H 211–213
AC-130U 213
AD-1 333
AD-1Q 333
AD-2 333
AD-2Q 333
AD-2QU 333
AD-3 333
AD-3N 333
AD-3Q 333
AD-3W 333
AD-4 333, 335, 337–338
AD-4B 335–337
AD-4N 333, 336
AD-4W 333, 338
AD-5 335, 337
AD-5N 337
AD-5Q 337
AD-5W 337
AD-6 334, 337
AD-7 337
AF-1E 365
AF-2S 322
AF-2W 322
AF-3S 322
AF-9J 356
AGM-12 438
AGM-12A 438
AGM-12B 438
AGM-45 438
AGM-62 438
AGM-65 438
AGM-65E 438
AGM-65F 438
AGM-78 438
AGM-84E 438
AGM-88 439
AGM-88E 439

AGM-123 438
AGM-130 438
AGM-130LW 438
AGM-154 438
AGM-154A 438
AGM-154B 438
AGM-154C 438
AH 392, 428–429
AJ-1 341–343
AJ-2 342–343
AM-1 346–348
AM-1Q 346
AT-18 54
AT-18A 54
AT-23A 82
AT-23B 82
AT-28D 213–215
AT-28E 215
AT-33A 215–216
AT-37D 218
AT-38B 219–221
AU-1 229n, 285–286
AV-8A 386, 388–389
AV-8B 386–389
AV-8B+ 389
AV-8B(NA) 389
AV-8C 389
AV-16A 389, 430–431
Aardvark 171–175
Aden 30-mm gun pod 434
Advanced Anti-Radiation Guided Missile (AARGM) 439
Advanced Manned Strategic Aircraft program (AMSA) 174
Advanced Tactical Aircraft (ATA) program 233, 431–432
Advanced Tactical Fighter (ATF) program 10, 233, 439
Air attack doctrine 3–6, 227–228
Air attack terminology 1–2
Air Combat Fighter (ACF) program 9, 232
Air Corps Act (1926) 3
Air Corps Tactical School 3, 3n
Air Interdiction (AI) 1, 3–5, 8
Air/Land Battle Doctrine 5
Air Liaison Officer (ALO) 4

Air Service Field Officer's School 3n
Airacobra 94–96
Aircraft guns 433–434
Air-to-Ground Guided Missiles (AGM) 437–439
Antisubmarine warfare wings 417
Apache 62
"Area Rule" principle 155, 398
Arnold, Gen. Henry H. 3, 7, 8n, 64, 83
Attack aircraft designations and nomenclature: USAAC, USAAF, and USAF 413–414; USN and USMC 414–415
Attack aircraft designs that never flew: USAAC, USAAF, and USAF 418–425; USN and USMC 425–432
Attack aircraft procurement: USAAC, USAAF, USAF 6–10; USN, USMC 228–234
Attack aircraft unit organization: USAAC, USAAF, and USAF 416–417; USN and USMC 417
Attack/Fighter Experimental (AF-X) program 233
Attack Experimental (AX) program 9, 161–167
Atomic bombs 231, 231n 343
Atwood, Lee 42, 76
Automatic Carrier Landing System (ACLS) 407
Avenger 317–320
Avenger II 432
Avenger 30-mm rotary cannon 163–164, 167, 434

B-1A 174
B-1B 175
B-2 10n, 196
B2G-1 237–238
B2Y-1 245–247
B-10 6, 418–419
B-17 3n
B-18 71

B-21 42
B-22 71
B-23 71–73
B-25 76–78
B-25A 77–78
B-25B 75–78
B-25C 77–78
B-25D 77–78
B-25E 77
B-25F 77
B-25G 77–78
B-25H 74–78
B-25J 73–78
B-26 79–83
B-26A 82–84
B-26B 48–50, 79–84
B-26C 48–50, 82–84
B-26D 82
B-26E 82
B-26F 82–84
B-26G 82–84
B-26K 48–50
B-27 84
B-28 84–86
B-28A 86
B-34 86–89
B-34A 86–88
B-37 88–89
B-42 89–92
B-42A 90–92
B-43 109–112
B-45 112–113
B-45A 112–115
B-45C 113–115
B-46 115–117
B-47 112
B-48 112
B-51 117–120
B-53 421–422
B-57A 120
B-57B 120–123
B-57C 121–123
B-57E 123
B-57G 123
B-66B 124–127
B-68 423–424
BFB-1 247–249
BFC-2 249, 251–252
BF2C-1 249–252
BG-1 235–236
BM-1 239–241
BM-2 239–241
BT-1 241–243
BT-2 243
BT2C-1 254–256
BT2D-1 333, 335
BTC-1 254
BTC-2 252–254
BTD-1 301–302, 333
BTK-1 256–258
BTM-1 346
BY-1 243–245

Baltimore 54–56
Banshee 356–359
Battlefield air interdiction (BAI) 1, 4–5, 4n, 9
Bearcat 272–274
Beech airplanes: A-38 67–69
Beisel, Rex 16
Bell airplanes: D-188A (F-109) 424–425; P-39 94–96; P-63 106–109
Berliner-Joyce airplanes: F2J 277–278
Bermuda 289
"Black Spot" 210–211
Blown flaps 378, 394
Boeing airplanes: BFB (F6B) 247–249; EF-18G 408; F8B 258–260; F/A-18E/F 408–409; X(F)-32 197–200; X-45 203–205
Boeing-Stearman airplanes: A-21 (X-100) 38–40
Bombing 434–436
Boston 33–37
Boundary-layer control 398
Brewster airplanes: A-32 59–61; F3A (F4U) 285–286; SBA (SBN) 287–289; SB2A (A-34) 289–291
Brewster rack 286
Bronco 223–226
Buccaneer 289–291
Bullpup missile 438

C-47D 206
C-119G 208
C-123K 210
C-130A 211
C-131 206
Canadian Car & Foundry airplanes: SBW (SB2C) 294–296
Canberra 120–123
Carrier Fighter-Attack Experimental (VFAX) program 232
Cessna airplanes: A-37 216–219
Charger 221–223
Close Air Support

INDEX

(CAS) 1, 3–5, 8–9, 228
Cluster Bomb Unit (CBU) 210
Cobra 184–187
Cold War (1945–1991) 4–5, 8–10, 231
Combat Lancer program 175
Consolidated airplanes: A-11 21–23; BY 243–244; B2Y 245–247
Consolidated-Vultee airplanes: A-31, A-35 56–59; A-41 69–71; TBY 330–332
Convair airplanes: B-46 115–117; Model 48 221–223
Cook-Craigie production plan 8, 8n
Corsair 282–286
Corsair II 382–386
Cougar 353–356
Counter-Insurgency (COIN) operations 5, 9
Crusader 396–399
Curtiss airplanes: A-3, A-4 14–16; A-8, A-10, A-12 18–21; A-14, A-18 25–27; A-43 (F-87) 420–421; BFC (F11C), BF2C 249–252; BTC 252–254; BT2C 254–256; F8C 260–262; SBC 291–293; SB2C 294–296; SB3C 425–426
Cutlass 365–367

D-2 64–66
D-2A 64
D-3 64
D-188A 424–425
DB-1 6n
DB-7 33, 37
DC-3 206
DH-4 6, 13
Do 17 6n
DX-2 64
Dauntless 296–300
Deck Launched Interceptor (DLI) 274, 348, 361, 365, 392, 398, 402
Defense Advanced Research Projects Agency (DARPA) 9–10, 233
Defensive Countermeasures 439
Demon 359–362
Department of Defense (DOD) 8, 232
Destroyer 124–127, 300–302
Devastator 313–315
Digital Attack Navigation system (DIANE) 381
Direct Air Attack 1
Directed Energy (DE) weapons 434
Dive-Bombing 4, 7, 229, 435
Doolittle, James H. 78, 83
Douglas airplanes: A-2 11–13; A-3 (A3D) 367–371; A-4 (A4D) 371–375; A-20 33–37; A-26 (B-26) 44–50; A-33 (8A) 30; AC-47 206–208; AD (BT2D, A-1) 333–338; A2D 339–340; B-42 89–92; B-43 109–112; B-66 124–127; FD 262–264; F4D (F-6) 348–350; SBD (A-24) 296–300; SB2D (BTD) 300–302; T3D 311–313; TBD 313–315; TB2D 315–317
Downward-Looking Infra-Red (DLIR) system 189
Dragon 71–73, 84–86

EA-1E 337
EA-1F 337–338
EA-3B 370–371
EA-6B 408
EA-7L 385
EB-57E 123
EB-66B 124, 126–127
EB-66C 127
EB-66E 127
EF-18G 408–409
EF-35 203
EF-111A 175
EKA-3B 369–371
ERA-3B 370–371
Electronic Countermeasures (ECM) 439
Electronic Warfare (EW) 1, 5, 9
Enforcer 106
Enhanced Tactical Fighter (ETF) program 9, 176, 183
Equalizer 25-mm rotary cannon 200, 386, 434

F-1C 365
F-1E 365
F-2 183
F2A-1 230n, 289
F2D-1 356
F2G-1 275–276
F2G-2 274–276
F2H-1 356, 359
F2H-2 356, 358–359
F2H-2B 358–359
F2H-2N 359
F2H-2P 359
F2H-3 358–359
F2H-4 357, 359
F2J-1 277–278
F2U-1 281–282
F3A-1 285
F3A-1D 286
F-3B 362
F-3C 362
F3H-1 361
F3H-1N 361
F3H-2 359–362
F3H-2M 361–362
F3H-2N 362–362
F3H-G 428
F3M-1 272
F3U-1 306
F-4A 394
F-4B 389, 391, 394
F4B-3 247
F4B-4 247
F5B-1 247
F-4C 395
F-4D 395
F4D-1 348–350
F-4E 393, 395
F-4F 394
F4F-4 280
F4F-8 280
F-4G 393, 394–395
F4H-1 392, 394, 428
F4H-1F 394
F-4J 391, 394
F-4K 394
F-4M 394
F-4N 392, 394
F-4S 392, 394–395
F4U-1 285–286
F4U-1A 285–286
F4U-1C 286
F4U-1D 286
F4U-2 286
F4U-3 286
F4U-4 282–284, 286
F4U-4B 286
F4U-4N 286
F4U-4P 286
F4U-5 286
F4U-5N 286
F4U-5NL 286
F4U-6 286
F4U-7 286
F-5 168
F-5A 168–171
F-5B 168
F-5C 171
F-5D 171
F-5E 168, 170–171
F5F-1 269
F-5G 171
F-6A 350
F6B-1 247
F6F-3 268
F6F-3E 268
F6F-3N 268
F6F-4 268
F6F-5 267–269
F6F-5K 269
F6F-5N 269
F6F-5P 269
F6F-6 269
F7F-1 269, 271
F7F-2D 272
F7F-2N 269
F7F-3 269–270, 272
F7F-3N 271–272
F7F-3P 272
F7F-4N 272
F7U-1 365
F7U-2 365
F7U-3 365–366
F7U-3M 365, 367
F7U-3P 365
F-8A 397–398
F-8B 398–399
F8B-1 258–260
F-8C 398–399
F8C-1 229n, 260, 262
F8C-2 262
F8C-3 262
F8C-4 261–262
F8C-5 260, 262
F8C-6 262
F8C-7 262
F-8D 398–399
F-8E 398–399
F-8E (FN) 398–399
F8F-1 272–274
F8F-1B 274
F8F-1N 274
F8F-2 274
F8F-2N 274
F8F-2P 274

F-8H 398–399
F-8J 398–399
F-8K 398
F-8L 398
F8U-1 397–399
F8U-1E 398
F8U-1P 398–399
F8U-2 398
F8U-2N 398
F8U-2NE 398
F8U-3 399
F-9F 356
F9F-1 353
F9F-2 351–353
F9F-3 351–353
F9F-4 353
F9F-5 351–353
F9F-5K 353
F9F-5KD 353
F9F-5P 353
F9F-6 355–356
F9F-6P 356
F9F-7 356
F9F-8 353–356
F9F-8B 356
F9F-8T 356
F-9H 356
F-9J 356
F11C-1 249
F11C-2 249
F11C-3 249
F12C-1 291
F12F 429–430
F-14A 401–403
F-14AGR 403
F-14A (Plus) 403
F-14B 400, 403
F-14D 403
F-14X 232
F-15A 176
F-15B 176
F-15C 176
F-15D 176, 178
F-15E 176–179
F-15I 178
F-15K 178
F-15S 178
F-16 179, 182
F-16/79 183
F-16A 181–184
F-16B 182–184
F-16C 179–184
F-16CJ 183–184
F-16D 183–184
F-16DJ 183–184
F-16N 183–184
F-16XL 182–183
F-17A 184–187
F-18A 406–407
F-19 187
F-20A 171
F-22A 190–194

F-22B 194
F-23A 194–197
F-32A 197–200
F-32B 197–200
F-35A 200–203
F-35B 200, 202–203
F-35C 200, 202–203
F-47D 102
F-47N 101–102
F-51D 104–106
F-51H 104–106
F-51K 105–106
F-80 127, 129
F-80A 129
F-80B 129–130
F-80C 127–130
F-82E 130–132
F-82F 131–132
F-82G 131–132
F-82H 131–132
F-84A 135
F-84B 135–136
F-84C 135–136
F-84D 134–136
F-84E 135–136
F-84F 136–139
F-84G 132–136
F-86A 140, 143
F-86D 140
F-86E 140, 143
F-86F 140–143
F-86H 140, 142–143
F-87 420–421
F-88A 147
F-96A 136
F-100 143
F-100A 143, 146
F-100B 143, 160
F-100B1 160
F-100C 143, 145–146
F-100D 143–147
F-100F 146–147
F-101A 147–150
F-101B 8n, 150
F-101C 147, 150
F-102A 8n
F-103 8n
F-104 151
F-104A 151, 153–154
F-104B 151, 153–154
F-104C 151–154
F-104D 151, 154
F-104DJ 151
F-104F 151
F-104G 151, 154
F-104J 151
F-104S 151, 154
F-105A 154–155
F-105B 154–155, 157–158
F-105C 157
F-105D 154–158

F-105E 157
F-105F 157–158
F-105G 157–158
F-106 151
F-106A 8n
F-107A 158–161
F-109 424–425
F-110A 395
F-111A 171, 173–175
F-111B 173–174
F-111C 174–175
F-111D 174–175
F-111E 172, 174–175
F-111F 173–175
F-111G 175
F-117A 187–190
F/A-18A 407–409
F/A-18B 407–409
F/A-18C 408–409
F/A-18D 408–409
F/A-18E 408–409
F/A-18F 407–409
F/A-22A 194
FB-111A 174–175
FC-47D 206
FD-1 262–264, 356
FF-1 264–266
FG-1 285
FG-1D 286
FG-3 286
FG-4 286
FH-1 356
FJ-1 278, 359, 362
FJ-2 278, 362
FJ-3 362, 364–365
FJ-3M 362
FJ-4 362, 365
FJ-4B 362–365
FM-1 280
FM-2 278–280
Falcon 14–16, 260
Fairchild airplanes: AC-119 208–209; NC(AC)-123 210–211
Fairchild of Canada airplanes: SBF 294–296
Fairchild-Republic airplanes: A-10 164–168
Fat Man atomic bomb 343
Fennec 213
Fighter-bomber 4, 8, 229, 232–233
Fighting Falcon 179–184
Fleet Ballistic Missile (FBM) 231, 370
Fleet Marine Force (FMF) 228
Fly-By-Wire (FBW)

control system 160, 182, 186–187, 189, 193, 196
Flying Box Car 208
Fokker (General Aviation) airplanes: A-7 16–18
Folding-Fin Aircraft Rocket (FFAR) 437
Forrestal class carriers 231, 231n
Forward Air Control (FAC) 1, 4–5, 9, 225
Forward-Looking Infra-Red System (FLIR) 167, 176, 210
Fury 362–365

G-23 266
G-51 269
G-55 426–427
G-58 272
G-66 427–428
G-70 322
G-118 429
G-128 378
G-303 402
Gamma 2C 23
Gamma 2E 23
Gamma 2F 24, 30
GAU-2/A rotary cannon 218
GAU-8 *Avenger* rotary cannon 163–164, 167, 434
GAU-12 *Equalizer* rotary cannon 200, 386, 434
General Aviation (Fokker) airplanes: A-7 16–17
General Dynamics airplanes: F-111 171–175; F-16 179–184; A-12 432
General Motors (Eastern Aircraft Division) aircraft: FM 278–280; TBM 318–320
Germany 3–4, 6–7
Glide-Bombing 435
Global Hawk 203, 409
Global Positioning Systems (GPS) 436
Goodyear airplanes: F2G 274–276; FG 285–286
Great Lakes airplanes:

B2G 237–238; BG 235–236; TBG 323–324; TG 328–329
Grizzly 67–69
Growler 408
Grumman airplanes: A-6 (A2F) 378–382; F6F 267–269; F7F 269–272; F8F 272–274; F9F (Straight Wing) 351–353; F9F (Swept Wing) 353–356; F12F 429–430; F-14 399–404; FF (SF) 264–266; SBF 302–304; TBF 317–320; TB2F 322, 426–427; TB3F 321–322; TSF 322, 428
Guardian 321–322
Guided Bomb Units (GBU) 436
Gulf War 5
Gunship-Transport Experimental [AC(X)] program 213
Gunships 8–9, 37, 77–78, 82, 206–213

H87A 62
Hands-On-Throttle-and-Stick (HOTAS) controls 202, 389, 407
Harpoon missile 438
Harrier 386–389
Have Blue project 9, 187, 189, 439
Havoc 33–37
Hawk II 249
He 111 6n
Heads-up display (HUD) system 436
Hellcat 267–269
Helldiver 260–262, 291–296
Helmet Mounted Display (HMD) system 202, 436
Hercules 211
High-Speed Anti-Radiation Missile (HARM) Appendix IV
High-Velocity Air Rocket (HVAR) 437
Hornet 404–409

Hornet 2000 233, 408
Hudson 52, 54
Hughes, Howard 64, 66
Hughes aircraft: A-37 64–66
Hydra 70-mm rocket 437

Indirect Air Attack 1
Inertial Navigation Systems (INS) 436, 438
Interceptors 8, 8n
Intruder 203, 378–382
Invader 44–50, 62

JD-1 49
JD-1D 49
JM-2 84
Ju 86 6n
Joint Advanced Fighter Engine (JAFE) 10, 193
Joint Advanced Strike Technologies (JAST) 10, 197
Joint Direct Attack Munition (JDAM) 436
Joint Standoff Weapon (JSOW) 438
Joint Strike Fighter (JSF) 10, 197–203, 233, 439
Joint Unmanned Combat Air System (J-UCAS) 10, 233

KA-2B 343
KA-3B 370–371
KA-6D 381
Kaiser-Fleetwings airplanes: A-39 419–420; BTK 256–258
Kartveli, Alexander 135, 154
Key West Agreement of 1948 4
Kindleberger, J. H. "Dutch" 62
King, Adm. Ernest J. 227
Kingcobra 106–109
Kittyhawk 98
Korean War 4, 8, 232

LAU-10 rocket pod 437
Lead-in-Fighter (LIFT) program 219
Leading edge root extensions (LREX) 186

Level Bombing 434
Light Armed Reconnaissance Aircraft (LARA) 221, 223, 225
Light Attack Aircraft (VAL) program 382
Lightning 92–94
Lightning II 200–203
Light-Weight Fighter (LWF) program 232
Ling-Temco-Vought (LTV) airplanes: A-7 382–386
Lockheed airplanes: A-28 52–64; A-29 52–54; AC-130 211–213; B-34 86–89; B-37 88–89; F-80 (P-80) 127–130; F-104 151–154; F-117 187–190; P-38 92–94
Lockheed-Detroit airplanes: A-9 21
Lockheed-Martin airplanes: F-22 190–194; F-35 200–203
Lodestar 88
Loft-Bombing 435
Low Altitude Bombing System (LABS) 436
Low-Altitude Navigation and Targeting for Night (LANTIRN) 5, 176, 179, 404
Low-Level-Light Television (LLLTV) camera 5n, 123, 210, 213, 381, Appendix IV
Low-Observable Technology (stealth) 187, 439

MF-3B 362
M-8 "bazooka tube" 437
M61 *Vulcan* rotary cannon 151, 433–434
Magruder, Peyton 79
Marauder 79–84
Marine Air Ground Task Force (MAGTF) 228
Marine aircraft procurement 228–229
Marine Forces Atlantic (MARFORLANT) 228n
Marine Forces Pacific

(MARFORPAC) 228n
Mark 3 nuclear bomb 343
Mark 6 nuclear bomb 343
Mark 7 nuclear bomb 4n, 231n
Mark 8 nuclear bomb 231n
Mark 13 aerial torpedo 435–436
Mark 20 gunsight 206
Martin airplanes: A-22 40–42; A-30 (A-23) 54–56; AM (BTM) 346–348; B-26 79–84; B-51 117–120; B-57 120–123; B-68 423–424; BM (T5M) 239–241; T3M 324–326; T4M 326–329; T6M 329–330
Martlet 280
Maryland 40–42
Mauler 346–348
Maverick missile 438
McDonnell, James S. 40
McDonnell airplanes: AH 428–429; F2H 356–359; F3H (F-3) 359–362; F-4 (F4H) 389–395; F-101 147–150
McDonnell-Douglas airplanes: AV-8 386–389; AV-16 430–431; F-15 176–179; F/A-18 404–409
Midway, Battle of 298, 300
Midway class carriers 231, 231n
Mighty Mouse folding-fin aircraft rocket (FFAR) 437
Mitchell 73–79
Mitchell, Brig. Gen. Billy 227
Mixmaster 89–92
Model 8A 30
Model 14 52
Model 37 88
Model 48 221–223
Model 93 425
Model 98B 428
Model 340 289
Model 400 258
Modern Bombing Systems 436

Moffett, R. Adm. William 227
Multi-Role Fighter (MRF) 10, 233
Mustang 64, 102–106

N-156 168
NA-26 50
NA-40 42, 74
NA-40B 42–44
NA-44 50
NA-62 76
NA-69 50, 52
NA-72 50, 52
NA-73 62, 105
NA-98X 78
NA-130 112
NA-146 343
NC-123K 210–211
Naval Aircraft Factory airplanes: SBN 287–289
Naval Bureau of Aeronautics (BUAER) 227–228, 229–232
Naval Bureau of Weapons (BUWEPS) 232
Navigation Forward-Looking Infra-Red (NAVFLIR) sensor 389
Navy Air Combat Fighter (NACF) program 232
Navy Unmanned Combat Air Systems (N-UCAS) 205, 409, 411–412
Nighthawk 187–190
North American airplanes: AJ 341–343; A2J 344–345; A-5 (A3J) 375–378; A-27 50–52; A-36 62–64; AT-28 213–215; B-25 73–79; B-28 84–86; B-45 112–115; F-82 (P-82) 130–132; F-86 140–143; F-100 143–147; F-107 158–161; FJ (F-1) 362–365; OV-10 223–226; P-51 (F-51) 102–106
North American General Purpose Attack Weapon (NAGPAW) 375
Northrop airplanes: A-13 (A-16) 23–25; A-17 (A-33) 27–30; BT 241–243; F-5 (F-20) 168–171
Northrop-Grumman airplanes: X-47 409–412

O-1 5, 9, 16
O-1B 16
O-1E 16
O-2 5, 9, 13
O2C-1 262
O2U 282
OA-4M 373, 375
OA-10A 167–168
OC-1 262
OC-2 262
OV-9 223
OV-10A 223–226
OV-10B 226
OV-10C 226
OV-10D 226
OV-10D+ 226
OV-10E 226
OV-10F 226
OV-10G 226
Observation aircraft 6, 229
Orenco IL-2 6n

P-6E 249
P-24 21
P-25 21
P-38 92
P-38J 92–93
P-38L 92–94
P-39 94
P-39Q 94–96
P-40 96, 98
P-40B 98
P-40C 98
P-40D 98
P-40F/L 98
P-40K/M 98
P-40N 96–98
P-47 99, 102
P-47B 99
P-47D 99–102
P-47F 99
P-47G 99
P-47H 99
P-47J 99
P-47N 99, 101–102
P-50 269
P-51 62, 64, 105
P-51D 102–106
P-51F 105
P-51G 105
P-51H 104–105
P-51J 105
P-51K 105
P-59 7n
P-63 108

P-63A 107–108
P-63B 108
P-63C 108
P-63D 108–109
P-63E 109
P-70 35–36
P-80 129
P-80A 129
P-80B 129
P-82 130
P-82B 130
P-82E 130
P-84A 135
P-84B 135
PA-48 106
PB-2A 23
PBJ-1C 78
PBJ-1D 78
PBJ-1G 78
PBJ-1H 78
PBJ-1J 78
PBO-1 54
PV-1 88–89
PV-2 88
PV-3 88
Panther 351–353
Pave Coin program 106
Pave Nail laser designation system 226
Pave Spectre program 211
Pegasus 409–412
Phantom 356
Phantom II 389–395
Pioneer 203, 409
Predator 203, 409
Provider 210
Prowler 203

RA-3B 370
RA-5C 375, 377–378
RAM armor-piercing warhead 437
RB-26C 48
RB-45C 114–115
RB-57A 120, 123
RB-57 121
RB-57E 123
RB-57F 123
RB-66A 124
RB-66B 127
RB-66C 127
RF-4B 394–395
RF-4C 395
RF-4E 395
RF-5A 168
RF-5E 171
RF-8A 398–399
RF-8G 399
RF-80A 130
RF-84F 136, 139
RF-101A 147, 149–150

RF-101G 150
RF-101H 150
RF-105B 154, 157
RP rocket 437
RQ-1 203, 409
RQ-4A 203, 409
Radar Absorbing Materials (RAM) 187, 189, 193
Radar Cross-Section (RCS) 187, 193, 200, 439
Radar Warning and Homing Receivers (RHAW/RWR) 439
Raptor 190–194
Reeves, Capt. Joseph M. 227
Republic airplanes: F-84 (P-84) (Straight Wing) 132–136; F-84 (Swept Wing) 136–139; F-105 154–158; P-47 (F-47) 99–102
Republic (Fairchild) airplanes: A-10 164–168
Rescue Combat Air Patrol (RESCAP) 338
Research and Development Board 8, 8n
Roosevelt, Pres. Franklin D. 7

S4C-1 291
SB2A-1 289
SB2A-2 289, 291
SB2A-3 289
SB2A-4 289–290
SB2C-1 295–296
SB2C-1A 296
SB2C-1C 295–296
SB2C-2 296
SB2C-3 296
SB2C-4 294–296
SB2C-4E 296
SB2C-6 296
SB2D-1 300–302
SB2U-1 306–309
SB2U-2 309
SB2U-3 309
SB3C-1 425–426
SB3U-1 309–311
SBA-1 287–289
SBC-1 291
SBC-2 293
SBC-3 293
SBC-4 291–293
SBD-1 4n, 243, 298
SBD-2 298
SBD-3 298, 300

INDEX 449

SBD-4 298, 300
SBD-5 296–300
SBD-6 298
SBF-1 296, 302–304
SBF-3 296
SBF-4E 296
SBN-1 287–289
SBU-1 304–306
SBU-2 306
SBW-1 296
SBW-3 296
SBW-4 296
SBW-4E 296
SBW-5 296
SF-1 266
SUU-11A gun pod 206
SUU-16A gun pod 434
Sabre 140–143
Savage 341–343
Scout aircraft 229
Sea Wolf 330–332
"Shadow" 208–209
Shooting Star 127–130
Short-Range Navigation (SHORAN) system 7n
Shrike 18–21
Shrike II 25–27
Skip-Bombing 435
Skyhawk 371–375
Skyhawk II 375
Skypirate 315–317
Skyraider 333–338
Skyray 348–350
Skyshark 339–340
Skywarrior 367–371
SLAM-ER (expanded response) 438
Soviet Union 4, 8,
Spanish Civil War 3, 6
Special Operations Squadrons (SOS) 206–207
"Spectre" 211–213
"Spooky" 206
"Spooky II" 211–213
Stand-Off Land Attack Missile (SLAM) 438
Starfighter 151–154
Stealth (Low-Observable Technology) 187, 439
"Stinger" 208–109
Super Carrier program 231
Super Corsair 274–276

Super Hornet 408–409
Super Sabre 143–147
Super Savage 344–345
Super Tomcat 21 403
Suppression of Enemy Air Defense (SEAD) 1, 9

T3D-1 311–313
T3D-2 311
T3M-1 326
T3M-2 324–326
T3M-3 328
T4M-1 326–329
T5M-1 240
T6M-1 329–330
T-28 213
T-28D 215
T-33A 216
T-37B 218
T-38 168
T-38B 219
T-38C 219
TA-3B 370
TA-4F 371, 373
TA-4G 373
TA-4H 373
TA-4J 373, 375
TA-4K 373
TA-4KU 373, 375
TA-7C 385
TA-7D 385
TA-7H 385
TAV-8A 386
TAV-8B 388–389
TB2D-1 315–317
TB2F-1 322, 426–427
TB3F-1 321–322
TBD-1 313–315
TBF-1 320
TBF-1C 317, 319–320
TBF-1CP 320
TBF-1D 320
TBF-1L 320
TBF-1P 320
TBF-2 320
TBG-1 323–324
TBM-3 318, 320
TBM-3E 319–320
TBM-3H 320
TBM-3N 320
TBM-3Q 320
TBM-3R 320
TBM-3W 320
TBU-1 330, 332

TBY-2 330–332
TBY-3 332
TF-9J 355–356
TF-18A 407
TF-104G 151
TG-1 328–329
TG-2 328–329
TSF-1 322, 428
Tactical Air Command (TAC) 4–5, 9
Tactical air power 3–6,
Tactical Fighter Experimental (TFX) 8, 171, 173, 232
Tactical nuclear doctrine 4–5, 231
Tactical nuclear weapons 4–5, 4n, 231, 231n, 436
Thunderchief 154–158
Thunderflash 136, 138–139
Thunderjet 132–135
Thunderstreak 136–139
Tiger 168–171
Tigercat 269–272
Tigershark 171
Tiny Tim aircraft rocket 437
Tomahawk 98
Tomcat 399–404
Torpedo Attack 436–437
Torpedoes 436–437
Toss-Bombing 435–436

UB-26J 49
UC-67 73
Unguided Rockets 437
Unmanned Air Vehicle (UAV) 203, 409
Unmanned Combat Air Vehicle (UCAV) 203, 205, 409, 411–412

V-11 32
V-72 59
V-90 69
V-156-B1/F3 309
V-166B 285
V-346A 365
V-383 398
V-463 382

VB-26B 50
VE-7 229
Vengeance 56–59
Ventura 86–89
Vertical/Short Takeoff and Landing (V/STOL) 386, 424–425
Vietnam War 5, 8–9, 228, 232
Vigilante 375–378
Vindicator 306–309
von Karmen, Doctor Theodore 8n
Voodoo 147–150
Vought airplanes: F2U 281–282; F4U 282–286; F7U 365–367; F-8 (F8U) 396–399; SBU (F3U) 304–306; SB2U 306–309; SB3U 309–311; TBU 330–332
Vultee airplanes: A-19 30–32; A-31 35, 56–59; A-41 69–71

WB-57F 123
WB-66D 127
Warhawk 96–98
Whitcomb, Richard T. 155
Wild Weasels 146, 156–158, 395
Wildcat 278–280
Woods, Robert 21
World War I 3, 6,
World War II 4, 7–8, 228, 230

X-32A 197–200
X-32B 197–200
X-35 202
X-45A 203–205, 411
X-45C 203, 205, 411
X-47A 409–412
X-47B 409, 412
X-100 38–40
XV-1 425
XV-3 425

Y, service test designations 18, 21, 414

Zuni aircraft rocket 437

www.ingramcontent.com/pod-product-compliance
Lightning Source LLC
Chambersburg PA
CBHW080935020526
44116CB00034B/2602